BIOGRAPHICAL DICTIONARY OF AMERICAN BUSINESS LEADERS

BIOGRAPHICAL DICTIONARY OF AMERICAN BUSINESS LEADERS

A–G

JOHN N. INGHAM

GREENWOOD PRESS
WESTPORT, CONNECTICUT • LONDON, ENGLAND

Library of Congress Cataloging in Publication Data

Ingham, John N.
  Biographical dictionary of American business
leaders.

  Includes bibliographies and index.
  1. Businessmen—United States—Biography. I. Title.
HC102.5.A2I53   1983   338.092'2 [B]   82-6113
ISBN 0-313-21362-3 (lib. bdg. : set)
ISBN 0-313-23907-X (lib. bdg. : v. 1)
ISBN 0-313-23908-8 (lib. bdg. : v. 2)
ISBN 0-313-23909-6 (lib. bdg. : v. 3)
ISBN 0-313-23910-X (lib. bdg. : v. 4)   AACR2

Library of Congress Catalog Card Number: 82-6113
ISBN: 0-313-21362-3 (set)
ISBN: 0-313-23907-X (v. 1)
ISBN: 0-313-23908-8 (v. 2)
ISBN: 0-313-23909-6 (v. 3)
ISBN: 0-313-23910-X (v. 4)

First published in 1983

Greenwood Press
A division of Congressional Information Service, Inc.
88 Post Road West, Westport, Connecticut 06881

Printed in the United States of America

10 9 8 7 6 5 4 3 2 1

FOR MY PARENTS

CONTENTS

PREFACE

This dictionary is composed of 835 biographical entries. Because a number of these are multiple-entry biographies, the total number of individuals on which biographical information is supplied is 1,159. The goal of the dictionary is to provide information on the "historically most significant business leaders" from colonial times to the present. Unlike most works of this nature, all research and writing of these biographies was done by the author. There were no massive research grants, no armies of researchers and writers to aid in the project. The greatest advantage of this approach is in the uniformity of standards in research, writing, and information presented. The disadvantages are legion, perhaps, but the major problem was that it precluded doing any research in primary sources, or the general presentation of information that was not at least somewhat available in previously published materials.

The goal was to make the dictionary as comprehensive and definitive as possible within the constraints of the present researcher's time and the space allotted to him for publication. Within each entry the basic biographical information is presented, along with a summary of the business activities of the individual and the significance of that person in the history of American business. A bibliography of the most relevant literature is appended to each biography. The entries average about 750 words in length, although several of those on business leaders of rare significance may run well over 3,000 words. A special effort was also made to include a representative sample of black and women business leaders in the collection. Each represents about three percent of the total.

The dictionary is designed so that the reader has several means of access to the biographies. The entries are arranged in alphabetical form, so that those with the name or names of individual business leaders can find them easily in that fashion. An asterisk (*) after the name of a person mentioned within an entry indicates that there is a separate sketch of that person in this work. At the end of the biographies are eight appendices which allow the reader to generate relevant biographies in other ways. In these appendices, business leaders are arranged according to: the principal industries in which they were engaged; the major company or companies in which they had involvement; their place of birth; their place of principal business activity; their birth date; their ethnicity; their religion; and the final appendix is a list of women business leaders. These appendices allow the reader a great series of options in gaining access to the biographies. In this way one can easily look up biographies of those involved in, say, rubber manufacturing or motion pictures. Similarly, if the reader wanted a list of those business leaders active in a particular area, they could be easily generated from the relevant appendix. By cross-referencing, however, the reader can develop much more highly specialized listings.

If, for example, the reader wished to generate a list of merchants in Boston in the early nineteenth century, he or she could first turn to the Boston list in the appendix of Principal Area of Business Activity. Having generated that basic list, the reader would then proceed to the category of merchants under the appendix listing business leaders by industry. Finally, the reader would turn to the appendix listing business leaders by birth date, finding those Boston merchants born between about 1750 and 1790. If the reader wanted a still more specialized list, say Boston merchants of the early nineteenth century who were members of the Congregational Church, he or she would then turn to the appendix listing business leaders by religion. The possibilities are almost endless.

One of the most difficult tasks in putting together this dictionary, and certainly its final result will engender some controversy, was in deciding which business leaders should be considered the "historically most significant." This is obviously an interpretive, not an objective, classification, nor is it easy to give a definitive set of criteria for inclusion or exclusion in the collection. The reader deserves, however, to know something about how the basic list of 835 entries was compiled. First of all, "historically most significant" does not necessarily imply that these business leaders were always the most financially successful. Most were, but a few were ultimate failures. Nor does inclusion on the list indicate that the business leader was a nice person, or that he or she somehow fits into my conception of what a good business leader should be. Some, in fact, are included because they were out and out scoundrels, but in that role they have been accorded prominence by historians and other chroniclers of the American past. There are others whose names have never appeared in the major accounts of business, but were chosen by either myself or the board of consulting editors because they seemed to represent important trends or manifestations in the American business community. That is, they were chosen not because they were unique, but because they were typical.

The basic process for inclusion in the collection was as follows. First, I went through several of the major recent works in American business history, and from them compiled a list of some 450 business leaders who were mentioned in all or most of these. This list was then sent out to twenty prominent historians of various phases of American business activity. I asked these historians, first, if they would agree to comment on the appropriateness of these business leaders for inclusion, to excise those whom they did not feel warranted it, and to suggest additional names, along with reasons why they should be included. Second, I asked if they would be willing to review completed biographies and serve as consulting editors for the dictionary. Of the twenty historians contacted, nine did not wish to participate in the collection in any way, two indicated that they would assist in the selection of biographies for inclusion but would not be able to review biographies, and nine were willing to both help choose business leaders for inclusion and to review completed biographies. The latter nine then became the members of the editorial board.

The results of the responses of the eleven historians who agreed to help choose business leaders for inclusion resulted in some twenty-five to thirty names being deleted from the original list, along with the inclusion of about 125 to 150 others. In addition, general comments as to criteria for inclusion led me to do a great deal of additional research in more specialized materials, generating some 300 or so additional entries in these more specialized fields. Every attempt was made to make the list as comprehensive and definitive as possible, and in the end the final decision for inclusion rested with myself. I did not always agree to their suggestions for inclusion, so final responsibility for those names included must rest on my shoulders. I am sure everyone will not be wholly satisfied with the final list (in fact, it may be that no one is satisfied with the final list), but, as one of the consulting editors said to me at one point, it is virtually impossible to include "everyone's favorite entrepreneur." I can only hope that the final collection represents a good and fair cross-section of American business leaders over time.

In any project of this magnitude, the author incurs a long series of debts which must be acknowledged. First of all, I can't say enough about the marvelous work done by the board of consulting editors. They not only reviewed the lists and made suggestions, but also did an enormous amount of work in reading the completed biographies on business leaders in their field. Their suggestions at every point made a major difference in the quality of the dictionary, and the degree to which the collection and the individual biographies are a success is largely due to their contribution. At the same time I must stress that no one of the editors read all of the biographies, nor did I always take their advice, so that those imperfections which still remain are solely my own responsibility, not theirs.

I must also acknowledge my debt to Professor Louis Galambos of Johns Hopkins University and George Green of the University of Minnesota. Although time constraints precluded them from reviewing the finished biographies, both of them read over my original list of business leaders and made helpful suggestions for inclusion and deletion. In addition, Professor Don Davis of the University of Ottawa provided me with some hard-to-find information on Joseph Boyer of Burroughs Adding Machine, and Professor Stephen Reiss suggested the inclusion of Albert G. Spalding. I would also like to thank my friend and colleague at the University of Toronto, R. Craig Brown, who encouraged me in the early phases of the project, and asked many penetrating questions which helped determine the directions it would take.

I have also been fortunate to have had the help and support of some truly fine editors at Greenwood Press. The collection was first suggested to me by Arthur H. Stickney at Greenwood, and he helped it through its formative stages. For the last two years or so, I have worked most closely with Cynthia Harris on the project, and she has provided a great deal of help in the form of useful suggestions and has given much encouragement. At various critical points, James T. Sabin has also provided me with much needed support and encouragement. Overall, I have received the kind of help and sustenance from Greenwood Press that most authors only dream about, and I can't express my thanks adequately.

I would like to thank the Humanities and Social Sciences Committee of the Research Board of the Office of Research Administration of the University of Toronto for a grant which enabled me to defray a portion of the typing expenses of this undertaking. I would also like to thank my typists, Cheryl Swartz Kessel and Robin Chelin, for their expert typing and unfailing good humor in dealing with this massive project. Finally, I would like to thank my family for the support, encouragement and tolerance they have shown me during the years I have been struggling with this enormous enterprise. My wife, Gwynne, helped me research biographies during the early months of the project until the demands of finishing her advanced degree and obtaining full-time work precluded direct participation. Her love and support in succeeding months have done much to ease my task. I would also like to thank my children for tolerating me walking around for some three years with my mind absorbed with American business leaders rather than their interests and concerns. During this time my eldest son, John, has grown from a teenager to a fine young adult of whom I am very proud. My second son, Jim, has grown from a child to a teenager of great charm and ability. Finally, my youngest child, Susan, has tolerated my absorption with the project with maturity far beyond her seven years, adjusting her time with daddy to fit the demands of the collection. Without the love and support of all of them during the past several years, I never would have had the emotional strength to continue.

INTRODUCTION

It will be impossible in the short space available to give the reader anything resembling a comprehensive history of American business from colonial times to the present. To provide those insights the author urges that the reader consult one or more of a number of excellent books on American business history which have appeared in recent years.[1] It is also hoped that simply reading the biographies in some fairly organized fashion will provide significant insights for the reader in a number of areas not available elsewhere. What I would like to do here is to provide the reader with some sense of the themes and patterns which guided the selection of subjects and the writing of the biographies.

Business in the colonial period primarily revolved around commerce and land. The two most important categories of business leaders were the seaport merchants and the large planters in the South. Another important business activity revolved around land speculations and developments of various kinds. In addition, a significant number of women achieved prominence as printers and publishers in the colonial period, to the extent that publishing has remained one of the very few large scale business enterprises largely open to women to the present day.

In the late eighteenth and early nineteenth centuries these traditional activities of business leaders began to undergo vast expansion in scale. The seacoast merchant increasingly found himself engaged in far-flung international endeavors, which although they did not change the fundamental form of business enterprise, did greatly expand their influence and the profits which could be made from these activities. At the same time, the opening of western areas within the United States also expanded the activities of merchants, planters and land speculators on the domestic scene. Great fortunes were made in these activities, important mercantile financial institutions were founded, and the basis was laid for a group of indigenous capitalists who would do much to fuel greater expansion and change in the economy in the later nineteenth century.

At about the same time these more traditional business enterprises were experiencing their "golden age," new business enterprises of great significance were also making their appearance. One of the most important of these lay in manufacturing. During the first twenty-five years of the nineteenth century the textile industry was inaugurated and put on a solid footing in the United States, providing the inspiration for further expansion and development in manufacturing. At about the same time came important developments in transportation, with instigation of important packetship enterprises in oceanic travel, along with steamboats for river transportation. These formed the basis for a revolution in transportation and communications during the mid and late nineteenth century.

This revolution in transportation and communication was fueled most importantly by the development of America's vast railway network between 1840 and 1890. Some of the country's most important business leaders were those who financed, built, or managed these huge railway enterprises, and many of the modern theories of business organization were developed by them. The great communications breakthroughs began at about the same time, with the development of the telegraph, with the transoceanic cable coming somewhat later. The final development along this line in the nineteenth century was the telephone. In the twentieth century the revolution continued, with the automobile and aircraft replacing the railroad in many of its passenger functions, and the telegraph being supplemented by radio, television and the computer.

These revolutionary developments in transportation and communication made possible a number of important changes in the American economic system in the late nineteenth century. One of the most important of these in the early period lay in great new opportunities to exploit the natural resources of the continent. These ranged from the cattle industry and farming to lumbering and mining, all of which fueled a great expansion of activity in many formerly unsettled parts of the continent. The changes in transportation and communications also helped bring about veritable revolutions in distribution and production in the United States. In distribution what was most remarkable was the transformation in the size and speed of these business activities. As late as the 1840s the traditional mercantile firm still dominated distribution, operating much as it had for generations. Then, within a relatively short period of time, it was replaced by the modern mass marketeer who "purchased directly from the growers, manufacturers, and processors of commodities and goods and sold directly to retailers or final consumers."[2] At a somewhat later period the railroad and telegraph gave rise to mass production by encouraging the concentration within a single establishment of all or nearly all the processes involved in making a product. Here the changes came more slowly because of the need for technological breakthroughs.

With the integration of mass production with mass distribution by the late nineteenth century through the process of vertical integration, there soon came a demand for horizontal integration in the interests of stabilizing prices and rationalizing business activity. This trend first evolved among the railroads, but soon spread to the industrial sector, setting off a great merger wave in the late nineteenth and early twentieth centuries. This development brought the emergence of finance capitalism. In an earlier age, most types of business, with the exception of transportation enterprises, could be started without a huge outlay of capital. Under these circumstances initial funds could be raised locally and expansion financed by internal investment. But as industrial technologies became more intricate and expensive, and they saw the necessity to bring a large number of firms under the umbrella of one organization, the capital needs could only be met by investment bankers.

As business enterprises became larger they increasingly came to the attention of the government, especially at the federal level. The first movements towards government intervention in business developments of a regulatory nature came from demands by smaller businesses or other elements of the business community or general public who complained of the threat of these large-scale organizations to the American ethic. As government became more involved, however, particularly in the period just before, during, and after World War I, businessmen themselves began to advocate government regulation of their industries as a means of rationalizing the marketplace. One of the significant stories of the twentieth century is the increasingly closer ties (not always amicable, to be sure) between government and business.

The twentieth century, particularly the period after 1920, saw the general maturing of business in the United States. One of the principal features of the maturation process involved the rise of multinational enterprise. Many of the large integrated corporations of the early twentieth century became the nation's first multinationals. They first created extensive foreign marketing organizations, then later built factories abroad. Another feature of this maturation process was the culmination of the managerial revolution in American business, whereby hired managers increasingly took command of the central sectors of the American economy. At the same time, the twentieth century, particularly the period after World War II, has seen the decline and stagnation of several of the key industries that fueled American expansion in the nineteenth century, most particularly railroads and iron and steel. In their place, a whole panoply of new business organizations has appeared.

One of the most important of these lies in the area of business "services"— advertising, public relations, corporate law, managerial consulting, and the like. In addition, there is a whole new range of service industries, ranging from the great explosion in restaurants and drive-ins to a whole host of leisure-time activities. Along with these developments are new industries created by technology, such as computers, photo-copiers, electronic business machines, instant photography, and a number of others which have created massive companies and great fortunes in the generation since World War II. Finally, there have been important changes in corporate form since 1945, the most important of which has been the emergence of the conglomerate—the stringing together of a series of unrelated companies under one masthead for the single purpose of the profitability of combination.

This dictionary is not an act of glorification of American business leaders nor of the American business system. Nor is it designed to "muckrake" the careers of business leaders over time. Instead, it is hoped that these biographies give a fair and balanced approach to business leaders and the business system. No moral judgements are made, but if a business leader used repressive labor policies, or was caught with his hand in some sort of financial "cookie jar," that fact is made known. At the same time, an attempt is made to understand the variety of pressures and exigencies under which business leaders at any given time operated, so that even some of the seemingly most reprehensible practices are at least viewed in context.

NOTES

1. The two books I have found most helpful for a general understanding of American business are: Elisha P. Douglass, *The Coming of Age of American Business*, 1971; and Alfred D. Chandler Jr., *The Visible Hand: The Managerial Revolution in American Business*, 1977. I would recommend that anyone start with those two works before progressing to others. Other general works of value include: John Chamberlain, *Enterprising Americans*, 1963; Thomas C. Cochran, *The American Business System*, 1955; and *Business in American Life*, 1972; Robert Sobel, *The Age of Giant Corporations*, 1972; Ben B. Seligman, *The Potentates*, 1971; Glenn Porter, *The Rise of Big Business, 1860-1910*, 1973; Chandler's *Strategy and Structure*, 1962; and two books by Mira Wilkins, *The Emergence of Multinational Enterprise*, 1970; and the *Maturing of Multinational Enterprise*, 1974. Mention might also be made of a few other general books: Matthew Josephson has written two scintillating though largely wrong-headed books on American business—*The Robber Barons*, 1934, and *The Money Lords*, 1972. In a similar vein are: *The Age of the Moguls*, 1953, by Stewart Holbrook and *The Lords of Creation*, 1935, by Frederick Lewis Allen. All read very well, but must be used with care. For more specialized works, I draw your attention to bibliographies appended to the individual biographies contained within.

2. Chandler, *Visible Hand*, p. 207.

GUIDE TO BIBLIOGRAPHIES AND ABBREVIATIONS

The bibliographies appended to each of the biographies are not intended to be exhaustive or definitive. Instead, they indicate to the reader those sources used by the author in preparing the biography, and/or those sources which will be most useful in understanding the evolution of the particular industry or time with which the biography was involved. Most bibliographies are divided into two parts. Part **A** indicates those sources containing direct biographical information on the subject. Part **B** indicates those sources valuable for background information. The entries in Part A are organized in such a manner that the sources most likely to be in the reader's own library are presented first (such as *Dictionary of American Biography, Encyclopedia of American Biography*, and *Who Was Who*), followed by booklength biographies of the individual. The entries in Part B are organized in strict alphabetical order, without reference to the importance of their insights on the subject.

Following are the abbreviations most commonly used in the bibliographical entries:

DAB	Dumas Malone ed., *Dictionary of American Biography*, 1928–Present.
EAB	John Garraty ed., *Encyclopedia of American Biography.*
NCAB	*National Cyclopedia of American Biography*, 1892–Present.

BIOGRAPHICAL DICTIONARY OF AMERICAN BUSINESS LEADERS

A

ABBOTT, ROBERT (November 28, 1868–February 29, 1940). Publisher, *Chicago Defender*. Born Frederica, St. Simon's Island, Georgia, son of slave parents, Thomas Abbott and Flora Butler. His father died shortly after he was born, and five years later his mother married John R. Songstakke, owner of a general store. Later, his stepfather became a school teacher and Congregational clergyman. Robert Abbott was educated at Beech Institute in Savannah, Georgia, and after a brief stay at Claflin University in Orangeburg, South Carolina, he went to Hampton Institute in Virginia where he graduated in 1896. While at Hampton, he came under the influence of the ideas of Booker T. Washington. After graduation he entered Kent College of Law in Chicago where he received an LL.B. in 1899, but did not practice law afterwards.

Instead, Mr. Abbott turned toward publishing. As a youth he had worked as a printer for his father's paper, the *Woodville* (Georgia) *Times*. Thus, he got several jobs as a printer in Chicago, and in 1905 established the four page, handbill sized *Chicago Defender* with a total capitalization of twenty-five cents.

The *Defender* became the most spectacular business success during the migration era in black Chicago. It played a major role in encouraging Southern readers to come north, and by 1918 its circulation was estimated at 125,000. During these years the *Defender* became a national newspaper and was circulated in over 71 towns. Abbott sought representatives throughout the country and often employed railroad porters and waiters to distribute the paper in the South. As its readership broadened, the paper began to attract national advertisers, carrying advertisements not only for Chicago stores, but also for nationally distributed products. Despite this, however, the *Defender* was forced to depend primarily upon circulation for its revenue.

By the 1920s Abbott was well on his way towards becoming Chicago's first black millionaire. His next goal was to acquire his own printing plant. During the Chicago riots of 1919, the white printing firm which had been printing the paper refused to print it out of fear of retaliation from white rioters. This incident prompted Abbott to purchase a cylinder press and install it in a building on Indiana Avenue. The new facilities were opened in 1921. With 68 employees and a plant valued at nearly a half million dollars, the *Defender* was by far the largest Negro business in Chicago and one of the largest in the country. Abbott served as president and treasurer of the Robert S. Abbott Publishing Company until his death. He was also a member of the Race Relations Commission of Chicago in 1919.

In 1918, at age 50, he married Helen (Thornton) Morrison, a widow from Athens, Georgia. They were divorced in 1933, and a year later he married Edna Rose (Brown) Denison, a widowed mother of four children. In 1932 he was stricken with tuberculosis, which led to his death in Chicago eight years later. (**A.** *DAB*, Supplement 2; Roi Ottley, *The Lonely Warrior*, 1955; Metz P. T. Lochard, "Robert S. Abbott: Race Leader," *Phylon*, 1947. **B.** Allen Spear, *Black Chicago*, 1967.)

ADAMS, ALVIN (June 16, 1804–September 1, 1877). Expressman, Adams Express. Born in Braintree, Massachusetts, son of Jonas Adams and Phebe Hoar. He was left an orphan at an early age, the youngest of nine children, and was cared for by a guardian and older brothers in Andover, Vermont. At age sixteen he left school and worked for several years for a stage and hotel proprietor in Woodstock, Vermont.

He then engaged in the produce business but went bankrupt in the depression of 1837. After that he went to New York City where he engaged in business, again meeting failure. In 1840, with Ephraim Farnsworth, he established Adams and Company by purchasing two season tickets from New York City to Boston and return. He and his partner then contracted to carry valuables, securities, and bundles for delivery. His service was used by banks, merchants, and individuals making valuable shipments. After a time Farnsworth left the business and was replaced by William B. Dinsmore and his son, William B. Jr., who married Adams' daughter. In 1841 they bought the Norwich route to Boston from William F. Harnden,* and four years later all his routes between Boston and New York. In 1842 they extended their agencies to Philadelphia and later to Baltimore, Washington, Pittsburgh, Cincinnati, Louisville, and St. Louis. It was there that Adams came into competition with Wells, Fargo, and Company. In 1849 Adams entered the California field, where he established thirty-five offices in towns and mining camps. Three years later he established branch offices and banking houses in Australia, but this venture was not successful.

The Adams Express Company was incorporated in 1854 with $10,000,000 in capital, with Adams as president and Dinsmore as secretary-treasurer. They absorbed several smaller companies, including Harnden and Company, which had developed a lucrative business with immigrants destined for the United States in the transfer of parcels and sale of money orders and railway and steamship tickets. During this period, Adams was able to compete on equal terms with American Express. Before long, however, the firm succumbed to the speculative excesses of the times and failed in 1855, losing its dominant position to Wells, Fargo. The reorganized Adams firm continued on a smaller scale during and after the Civil War but never regained its former preeminence.

In the years before the advent of the railroads as prime carriers of passengers and freight, the stagecoach and express companies were the dominant force in this enterprise. Adams Express was one of four companies which dominated the field, the others being American Express, Wells Fargo, and National. Although its heyday was relatively shortlived, Alexander Adams' express company stands as one of the most significant business ventures of the antebellum period.

In 1831 he married Ann Rebecca Bridge of Boston, and they lived in Watertown, Massachusetts, in relative seclusion, until he died. (**A.** *DAB; Appleton's Cyclopedia of American History*; **B.** Alvin F. Harlow, *Old Way Bills: The Romance of the Express Companies*, 1934.)

ADAMS, CHARLES FRANCIS JR. (May 27, 1835–March 20, 1915). Financier and business critic, Union Pacific Railroad. Born in Boston, Massachusetts. Son of Charles Francis Adams and Abigail Brooks, and grandson and great-grandson of presidents John Quincy Adams and John Adams. He graduated from Harvard in 1856 and studied law for two years in the office of Richard H. Dana Jr., being admitted to the bar in 1858. He saw military service in the Civil War from 1861 to 1865, entering as a first lieutenant, leaving as a colonel, and later breveted a brigadier general. After the war Adams joined with various railroad enterprises in the north and became noted as a railroad commissioner and arbitrator. In 1869 he was appointed a member of the board of railroad commissioners of the state of Massachusetts, serving until 1879, with seven years as chairman. In the latter year he was elected a member of the board of arbitration of the Trunk Line Railroad Organization, serving as either chairman of the board or sole arbitrator until 1884, when he was made president of the Union Pacific Railroad, succeeding Jay Gould,* and held that position until 1890.

When Adams assumed the presidency of the Union Pacific and examined the books and records of the company he discovered that the assets had been juggled and the accounts rigged. He declared the company's financial statements a fraud. This created a severe panic among the stockholders and caused the government to question Gould as to his tactics. In the end Adams could not salvage the company and resigned his position. He and his brother Henry, in 1886, recorded the antics of Jay Gould, Jim Fisk,* and other railroad moguls in *The Chapters of Erie*, one of the earliest pieces of anti-business "muckraking," which set the tone for many works to follow.

Despairing of the business world, Adams then turned to public service work and writing. He served as chairman of the Massachusetts Park Commission from 1892 to 1895, and during the same period was appointed to the Board of Overseers of Harvard College. He also turned to historical investigations of New England history and published a biography of Richard Henry Dana. He was married in 1865 to Mary Hone Ogden of Newport, Rhode Island.

Mr. Adams' significance in the history of American business lies more in his skill and influence as a critic, especially of railroad practices of the time, than it does in his skill and success as an entrepreneur and financier. His *Chapters of Erie* helped to pave the way for the passage of the Interstate Commerce Act by Congress in 1887. (*NCAB*, 8:353; *DAB; EAB; New York Times*, March 21, 1915.)

ADAMS, KENNETH STANLEY (August 31, 1899–March 30, 1975). Oilman, Phillips Petroleum. Born in Horton, Kansas. Son of John Valentine Adams and Lavella Stanley. His father was a railway engineer. Young Adams was educated at public schools in Kansas City, Kansas, and at the University of Kansas (1917–1920). In his final year he left college and joined the Phillips Petroleum Company in Bartlesville, Oklahoma. Beginning as a clerk in the warehouse division, he advanced to district operation manager in the production department in 1922. Adams' advancement continued to be rapid, and in 1932 he was named assistant to the president. Three years later he was named treasurer, director and member of the executive committee, and in 1938 became executive vice-president and, a few months later, president of the company. He served in that capacity until 1951, when he became chairman of the board.

The company had been founded in 1917 by Frank Phillips* and Lee E. Phillips, and in the year in which Adams became president had a gross income of $77,519,908, with 7,948 employees. When he retired from that office there were 18,381 employees and a gross income of $522,957,618. As president, he made the company into the world's largest owner of natural gas reserves. He arranged for the complete vertical integration of the production stages from crude oil at the well head to the assortment of finished products the company marketed. This involved the establishment of refining plants in the Midwest, leasing huge acreages of oil producing properties, and the laying of over 3,000 miles of pipe lines to the refining centers.

In 1950, the company's crude oil production reached 35,526,634 barrels, and it had 10,932 producing oil and gas wells on properties totaling 841,451 developed acres. Gas sales were 1,381,657,000 cubic feet daily, and the sale of all finished liquid products was 3,317,979,022 gallons. The company maintained 15,656 retail marketing outlets. Adams also directed the expansion of the company into Venezuela, Mexico, Colombia and Canada, and the acquisition of numerous subsidiary companies. By 1979 Phillips Petroleum was the twelfth largest petroleum company in the United States, with sales of $9.5 billion. It had 30,000 employees in that year, and was producing oil in seven countries and looking for more in 21 others.

A Presbyterian and a Democrat, Adams served as a director of the American Petroleum Institute and as president of the Chamber of Commerce of Bartlesville. In 1924 he married Barbara Blanche Keeler of

Bartlesville, the daughter of a cattleman. They were divorced in 1945, and the following year he married Dorothy Glynn Stephens of Medira, Texas. He had five children. His eldest son, Kenneth S. Jr. (b. 1923) became president and chairman of the board of Ada Oil Company (later Ada Resources) of Houston, Texas, and owner of the Houston Oilers football team, among other enterprises. (*NCAB*, H:85; *Who Was Who in America*, vol. 6; *Who's Who in America*, 1978-79.)

ADAMS, THOMAS JR. (April 11, 1846–August 4, 1926). Manufacturer, American Chicle Company. Born in Brooklyn, New York, son of Thomas Adams and Martha Dunbar. In 1866, at age 20, young Adams went to Mexico, where he experimented with chicle (a gum substance from the Mexican Sapodilla tree). After unsuccessful attempts to convert it into commercial rubber, he decided to utilize it in the manufacture of a chewing gum, a use to which it was sometimes put by the native Indians. In association with his father, Adams started a small factory in Jersey City, New Jersey, with capital of $35,000. At first, the Adams had little success in finding a market for their new and unique product. To develop public acceptance they at first supplied it to shopkeepers to be given away with each purchase of candy. Later, when they began to add sugar and flavoring to the chicle, it began to develop its own popularity. In 1869, Adams and Sons was organized with Thomas Adams Sr. as president to manufacture chewing gum on a large scale. A large factory was built in Brooklyn in 1888, and upon the retirement of his father in 1898, Thomas Jr. became president of the company.

It was at this point that the firm began a vigorous expansion. In 1899, Adams and Sons, in association with the Beeman Chemical Company, W. J. White and Son of Cleveland, S. T. Britton of Toronto, Ontario, Kisme Gum of Louisville, and J. P. Primley of Chicago, formed the American Chicle Company. In 1900 this company acquired a controlling interest, and in 1914 purchased outright, the Sen-Sen Chiclet Company, which had been organized in 1900. Adams served as president of the company from its foundation until he retired from active business in 1922. He remained a large stockholder of the concern until his death in New York City. During his years as president he continued to expand and absorb other companies. In 1916 he purchased the Sterling Gum Company with a plant in Long Island City, New York, and established subsidiary companies in London, England, Mexico, and Toronto, Ontario, and had a large interest in the Chicle Development Company, which through concessions controlled over 5,000,000 acres of chicle producing land in Guatemala, Mexico, and British Honduras. The main factory of the American Chicle Company was established at Newark, New Jersey, in 1903, and in 1920 construction was begun on a new plant in Long Island City, with a floor area of 550,000 square feet. In the 1950s American Chicle was sold to Warner-Lambert

Pharmaceutical Company, and by 1979 was the largest chewing gum manufacturer in the United States.

Adams was a Republican and married Emma Mills of Jersey City, New Jersey, in 1871, and Elizabeth Flood of New York City in 1925. He had three children. A classic American entrepreneur, he discovered a potential use for a substance which up to that time had little commercial value. Recognizing an innate physiological need for most humans to chew on something, he broke down market resistance to the product and helped make it into an American and world habit. (*NCAB*, 21:191.)

AINSWORTH, JOHN COMMIGERS (June 6, 1822–December 30, 1893) and **Ainsworth, John Churchill** (January 4, 1870–May 27, 1943). Bankers, U.S. National Bank of Oregon. The elder **John C. Ainsworth** was born in Springboro, Warren County, Ohio, the son of George Ainsworth and Anchor Death. Both parents died when he was young and he was reared by his grandfather, who was a schoolmaster. At age thirteen he entered the employ of his uncle, James F. Death, a merchant. Ainsworth removed with him to Farmington, Iowa, in 1839, where he became proprietor of the mercantile establishment at the age of eighteen. He then moved to Keokuck, Iowa, where he purchased a steamboat and operated on the Mississippi River for a number of years. Samuel Clemens (Mark Twain) was his pilot for a time. The discovery of gold in California lured him to Sacramento. After one year there he moved to Oregon where he built and operated the first steamboat on the Columbia River. When gold was discovered on the Frazier River in British Columbia in 1858, Ainsworth navigated steamboats to the mining districts. He developed a financial interest in the Union Transportation Company and was captain of its freight steamer running between Portland and the Dalles on the Columbia River. This firm was succeeded by the Oregon Steam Navigation Company, capitalized at $172,000, with Ainsworth as president. The company had full control of river transportation in the area by 1862, when it was acquired by the Northern Pacific Railroad, and he served as its managing director until 1873. He and several associates then purchased the stock of the navigation company and operated it independently until 1880 when it was sold to Henry Villard* for $5,000,000.

For his next venture, in partnership with R. R. Thompson, Ainsworth developed Redondo Beach in Santa Monica, California, building docks for seagoing vessels and making all harbor improvements, including eighteen miles of railway to Los Angeles. In 1893 he organized the Ainsworth National Bank of Portland and the Central National Bank of Oakland, California, serving as president of both.

He was married three times. His first wife was Augusta Kendall of Boston. Then, in 1851, he married Nancy Jane White of Oregon City, and in 1864, Mrs. Fannie Babbitt Barber. He had six children, including **John Churchill Ainsworth**, the eldest.

The younger Ainsworth was born in Portland, Oregon, an offspring of his father's third marriage. He received a bachelor of science degree at the University of California in 1891, and an M.S. in electrical engineering in 1892. He then joined the Central Bank of Oakland. A year later, after his father's death, he went to Portland as head of the Ainsworth National Bank. In 1902 he consolidated it with the U.S. National Bank of Portland under the latter name and remained as president. The Wells, Fargo and Company's bank was added in 1905 and later combinations were made with the Lumberman's National Bank (1917) and the Ladd and Tilton Bank in 1925. He served as president of the bank until 1931 when he became chairman of the board, which he remained until his death. Under his direction the U.S. National Bank of Portland became one of the leading financial institutions in the Pacific Northwest, with resources in 1942 of $307,742,000, and deposits of $294,702,000. The bank operated twenty-six branches throughout the state and was affiliated with the Clark County National Bank of Vancouver, Washington.

In addition to his banking activities, Ainsworth was president of the States Steamship Company and organized the Portland Railway Company and the Portland Hotel Company. He was one of the leading factors in the construction of the Oregon Coast Highway, and in 1932 became chairman of the Oregon State Highway Commission. He also served as president of the City Planning Commission of Portland and commissioner of the port of Portland. He was a Presbyterian and Republican and married Alice Heitchu of Portland in 1901. (*NCAB*, 25:204; D:361; 33:277.)

ALDRICH, NELSON W. (November 6, 1841–April 16, 1915). Banker, entrepreneur, and U.S. Senator. Born at Foster, Rhode Island, son of Anon E. Aldrich and Abby Ann Burgess. His ancestors had come to Providence in 1631. Nelson Aldrich was educated for one year at East Greenwich, Rhode Island Academy, followed by employment with the wholesale grocery firm of Waldron and Weightman of Providence. Two years later he enlisted in the Civil War, serving a few months until he contracted typhoid fever. He was discharged and returned to Waldron and Weightman, becoming a partner in 1865. In 1872 he was elected a director of the Roger Williams Bank, and in 1877 president of the First National Bank, both of Providence. He was also president of the Providence Board of Trade. In addition, he became one of the incorporators of the Providence, Hartford and Fishkill Railroad and an organizer of the United Traction and Electric Company, incorporated in 1893 to acquire and operate street railways and electric light and power companies. He served as its president from 1893 to 1902. Aldrich's traction holdings in New England were sold to the New York, New Haven and Hartford RR in 1906.

Mr. Aldrich was also deeply involved in Republican politics at an early stage. In 1869 he was elected as an independent Republican in a Democratic ward to the Providence Common Council, of which he was president from 1871 to 1873. He was also selected as a delegate to the Republican National Convention in 1872, and as chairman of the Republican State Convention in 1876. His service on the common council was followed by two terms in the state legislature, where he was speaker in 1876. Two years later he was elected to the U.S. House of Representatives, and reelected in 1880. Before the close of his second term he was selected as U.S. senator to fill a vacancy. He remained in the Senate for nearly thirty years, compiling an outstanding record as a statesman.

Being assigned to the finance committee, Aldrich assisted in framing the tariff bill of 1883, and in 1888 drafted a substitute for the Mills tariff bill which became the basis for the McKinley tariff Act of 1890. He served as a powerful and intimate advisor to three presidents: William McKinley, Theodore Roosevelt, and William Howard Taft. Becoming chairman of the finance committee of the Senate in 1899, thenceforth his major interest was in the field of governmental finance. He wrote the Gold Standard Act of 1900; wrote into the Aldrich-Vreeland Act a provision for the appointment of a national monetary commission to reform the currency system, and was appointed chairman of this commission. He drew up what was called the Aldrich plan, but it failed. His last important piece of legislation was the Payne-Aldrich Tariff of 1909, which led to a tariff revolt and helped defeat the Republican party in 1910 and 1912.

Aldrich decided not to stand for re-election in 1910, and retired at the end of his term in 1911. But he remained chairman of the monetary commission until its work was completed. He married Abby P. Chapman of Providence in 1866, and they had eleven children. His daughter, Abby Greene Aldrich, married John D. Rockefeller Jr.* (A. *DAB; NCAB*, 25:20; *New York Times*, April 17, 1915; *EAB; Who Was Who*, vol. 1; N. W. Stephenson, *Nelson W. Aldrich*, 1930; B. Matthew Josepson, *The Politicos*, 1938.)

ALEXANDER, ARCHIE ALFONSO (1888–1958). Black contractor, Alexander and Repass. Born in Ottumwa, Iowa, son of a janitor who later moved to a farm near Des Moines. Archie Alexander was educated in the public schools of Des Moines and then attended the University of Iowa, where he was an outstanding tackle on the football team. He graduated in 1912 with a degree in civil engineering. His first job was as a design engineer for the Marsh Bridge engineering firm in Des Moines. In 1914 he formed his own firm, Alexander and Higbee, in partnership with a white fellow employee. The firm secured contracts to build bridges, sewer systems, viaducts, and also built a conduit for the University of Iowa. His partner met with an accident and the firm continued as A. A. Alexander Incorporated for 4 years. Then, in 1929, Mr. Alexander joined with a white ex-classmate in organizing the engineering firm of Alexander and Repass. They built a million dollar sewage disposal plant at Grand Rapids, Michigan, a civilian air field at Tuskegee, Alabama, the million dollar Tidal Basin Bridge in Washington, D.C., a power plant in Nebraska, the K. Street Freeway in Washington, D.C., and railway bridges in Iowa and Missouri.

In 1954, President Eisenhower appointed Alexander governer of the Virgin Islands, only the second black territorial governor. Ill health forced him to resign in 1955.

A remarkably gifted and successful black businessman, Alexander was one of the few who was able to transcend the economic bounds of the black ghetto with his business activities. Engaged in direct competition with white construction and engineering companies, his firm had remarkable success. (*NCAB*, 49:252; E. A. Toppin, *Biographical History of Blacks* (1971) 246–47.)

ALEXANDER, HENRY CLAY (1902–1969). Banker, Morgan Guaranty Trust. Born on a farm near Murfreesboro, Tennessee, the son of Ellis Dewitt Alexander, who ran a feed store. Young Alexander was educated at Vanderbilt University and Yale Law School, receiving his law degree in 1925. Upon graduation he joined the New York law firm of Davis, Polk, Wardell, Gardiner and Reed, and at age 32 was made a partner. During the Nye congressional investigations of the munitions industry he acted as counsel to J. P. Morgan* the younger. Making a favorable impression, he was afterward invited by Morgan to join the banking firm as a partner.

Alexander became a protegé of the then Morgan president, George Whitney, and during World War II was put in charge of the trust department as a vice-president. In this capacity he profoundly changed the way in which the Morgan bank did business. For years the bank had operated as a wholesale bank, serving only the top echelon of the business, financial, and government community. The bank did not solicit business, but rather waited for business to come to it. Alexander changed all that. He trained a whole new generation of employees, known as "bird dogs," because they were deployed across the country to pursue business that had formerly come in by itself.

In 1959, when Morgan bank merged with Guaranty Trust Company, Alexander was made chairman of the board and chief executive officer. He served in that capacity until he retired in 1967. As was true of most Morgan executives, he served on the board of directors of a large number of corporations. In 1956 he organized the Downtown Lower Manhattan Association to promote the redevelopment of the area. He was married to Janet Hutchinson and had four children.

Mr. Alexander was a leading representative of the "new breed" of banker who emerged after World War II. As such he took the lead among bankers in using greater aggressiveness in the development of new business. (*New York Times*, December 15, 1969.)

ALEXANDER, MARY SPRATT PROVOOST (April 17, 1693–April 18, 1760). Colonial merchant. Born in New York City, daughter of John Spratt and Maria (DePeyster) Shrick. Her father had been born near Glasgow, Scotland, and became a merchant in New York and a speaker for the irregular assembly during the Leisler Rebellion in 1689. Her mother was from a respected Dutch family of goldsmiths, and had first married Paulus Schrick, and then John Spratt in 1687. After Spratt's death in 1697 she married David Provoost, a merchant of Huguenot-Dutch ancestry. After Maria DePeyster died in 1700, the Spratt children went to live with their maternal grandmother.

In 1711 Mary Spratt Provoost married Samuel Provoost, a younger brother of her mother's third husband. He was also a merchant and she invested her inheritance in his trading ventures. She had three children by this marriage before her husband's death in about 1720. In 1721 she married James Alexander, who had immigrated to America in 1715, and became one of the leading lawyers in the city. During the next thirty-nine years Mary Alexander's life was divided between caring for her growing family, continuing the Provoost mercantile enterprises, and supporting her husband's political career.

Under her leadership the business grew extensively. She imported goods on such a large scale that it was said that hardly a ship docked in New York City without a consignment of goods for her. She sold these goods in her own store and, during the French and Indian War, supplied General Shirley's Fort Niagara expedition with food, tools, cannon, and boats. In 1743 her and her husband's fortune was estimated at 100,000 pounds, and they had a magnificent mansion on Broad Street.

She had seven children by her second husband, of whom five reached maturity. Of these, William became his mother's business partner. He was an aide to General Shirley during the French and Indian War and served under General Washington during the American Revolution. A daughter, Mary, married Peter Van Brugh Livingston, a merchant who was also prominent in New York's revolutionary politics. The elder Mary's second husband died in 1756 and she administered his estate until her own death four years later. She had originally belonged to the Dutch Reformed Church, but later became an Anglican. (*NAW.*)

ALLEN, WILLIAM MCPHERSON (September 1, 1900–   ). Aircraft manufacturer, Boeing Company. Born in Lolo, Montana, son of Charles Maurice Allen, a mining engineer, and Gertrude Maud Hughes. William Allen graduated from Montana State University in 1922 and received his law degree from Harvard in 1925. At that time he joined the Seattle law firm of Donworth, Todd and Higgins, which acted as counsel for the

Boeing Airplane Company. Allen helped set up Boeing Air Transport in 1926, was named a director of the company in 1931, and several years later took charge of contracts and financing. At the beginning of World War II he drew up the first "cost plus fixed fee" contract for war production.

Upon the death of Boeing president Philip G. Johnson, in 1945, Allen took over as president of the company, just as wartime demand for aircraft virtually ceased. The company was forced to close temporarily and 25,000 employees were dismissed. Allen soon announced that Boeing was prepared to start construction on 50 Strato-cruisers for commercial aviation use, though he had no orders for the planes. One year later 55 of the huge planes had been ordered by commercial airlines. Although Boeing lost $13.5 million on these planes, Allen had succeeded in holding together his engineering staff and in providing continuity of operations. Under his leadership, Boeing's engineering staff designed the B-47 Stratojet medium bomber.

Allen's next challenge came in 1948 when some 15,000 machinists went on strike demanding a union shop and a strict seniority clause. Allen termed the strike illegal and was upheld by the U.S. Court of Appeals. After three months the strikers returned to work under a contract without a union shop or seniority provisions. Allen then reorganized the management system, providing a rating system for every employee and an incentive program for 7,000 of the workers.

By 1951 Boeing had a backlog of 1.25 billion dollars in orders, employed 50,000 workers, and was engaged in filling government orders for B-47's, B-50's, and C-97's (Stratofreighters). Much of the work was sub-contracted by Boeing to avoid over-expanding the company. Under Allen's leadership Boeing developed guided missiles which could be used for peacetime purposes, a jet transport, an analog computer, and a gas turbine engine. In 1952 Boeing's B-52 was chosen by the Air Force as its intercontinental bomber, and the company was given a contract for 70 of the planes. In 1959 the Boeing 707 Jetliner inaugurated the jet age in commercial aviation, and twenty years later Boeing had built 60 percent of the jets then in airline service.

In the later years of Allen's tenure as president (1945–1970) and chairman of the board (1970–1972), Boeing's nearly unbroken record of success and prosperity began to falter. In the 1960s Allen had committed Boeing to making the 747 jumbo jet, but when the planes were ready, the airline industry had no great need for them. From 1969 to 1972 Boeing didn't receive a single order for a 747. Congress then halted Boeing's work on the controversial SST (Supersonic Transport). To help itself through this period Boeing secured a government-guaranteed loan from the Nixon administration. Allen served as chairman emeritus of Boeing after 1972. By 1980 Boeing had regained its position as the leader in the field of commercial aviation and was the seventh largest defense contractor in the nation. It was also the nation's largest exporter, with sales of planes and spare parts outside the United States totalling some $4 billion (4 percent of all U.S. manufactured exports).

A Protestant and a Republican, Allen was married twice. In 1927 he married Dorothy Dixon, and in 1948 Mary Ellen Agen. (**A.** *Current Biography*, 1953; *Who's Who in America, 1978-79*; **B.** Milton Moskowitz et al., *Everybody's Business*, 1980.)

ALLIS, EDWARD PHELPS (May 12, 1824–April 1, 1889) and **William Watson Allis** (November 14, 1849–October 10, 1918). Machinery manufacturers, Allis-Chalmers Company. **Edward P. Allis** was born in Cazenovia, New York, the son of Jere Allis and Mary White. He was raised in relative comfort and prosperity on his father's farm in upstate New York, and educated at Union College in Schenectady, New York, from which he graduated in 1845. He went to Milwaukee two years after the admission of Wisconsin as a state (1850) and engaged in the leather business. He built extensive tanneries at Two Rivers, Wisconsin, but in 1854 disposed of his holdings and confined his operations to banking and real estate. During the first year of the Civil War, Allis bought a small iron foundry in Milwaukee and established the Reliance Iron Works, which he built into one of the largest industrial plants in the city.

In 1869, when the city of Milwaukee was installing a water system, the E. P. Allis Company underbid competitors and obtained the contract, even though it had no machinery for making pipe. Nevertheless, Allis installed the necessary pumps and engines for the Milwaukee job and within a few years became known as one of the largest machine shops in the country. When the roller process was adopted by American flour millers, the Allis works made the new machinery required in hundreds of mills throughout the country. Saw mill, mining machinery and heavy pumps were made at the Milwaukee plant, and the famous Corliss engines were also built there. Before E. P. Allis's death in 1889, sales amounted to three million dollars per year, with 1,200 employees. He was the Greenback party's candidate for governor of the state in 1877. In 1848 he married Margaret Watson of Geneva, New York, by whom he had twelve children.

His son, **William W. Allis**, was born in Milwaukee, and educated at the Delaware Literary Institute in Franklin, New York, and at Antioch College in Yellow Springs, Ohio, taking special engineering and scientific courses. He then entered his father's machinery works. In 1891 the company was made into a corporation under the name of Edward P. Allis Company, which it retained until 1901. During this period the works were greatly expanded, employing 4,000 men and achieving recognition as the leading manufacturing works of its kind in the world. William W. Allis was president of the company during this period, and in 1901 merged it into the Allis-Chalmers Corporation, with a paid-in capital of $36 million. He served as chairman of the board of the new corporation until his death. He was a Republican and Unitarian, and in 1877 married Mary Simmons Phillips of Milwaukee. They had one daughter. His brother, Charles Allis (May 4, 1853–July 22, 1918), was also a major factor in the company. Beginning with the firm in 1868, he served as its secretary-treasurer, and was president of Allis-Chalmers from 1901 to 1905. (*DAB; NCAB*, 7:546; 18:54.)

AMES, OAKES (June 10, 1804–May 8, 1873) and **Oliver Ames** (November 5, 1807–March 9, 1877). Financiers, Union Pacific Railroad. **Oakes** was born at Easton, Massachusetts, and **Oliver** at Plymouth. Both boys were educated in district schools and then entered their father's Easton shovel factory at an early age at menial positions. In 1844 their father retired and the two boys took over the business. They rapidly expanded the firm, sending large consignments of shovels to California in 1848 on a credit basis. They took a huge loss on this venture, but recouped it in the Australian gold rush and the agricultural development of the Northwest. At the beginning of the Civil War the business was valued at four million dollars, and war orders doubled its value to eight million.

In 1865 Oakes and Oliver Ames became involved in the Credit Mobilier, a company formed to carry on the construction of the Union Pacific Railway. Credit Mobilier had been promoted by George Francis Train and Thomas C. Durant,* a vice-president of Union Pacific, to keep the profits from the building of the railway in the hands of a small group of people. By 1865 it had a capital of $2,500,000 and Credit Mobilier proved to be an enormous financial success for its stockholders. As the tracks of the Union Pacific were pushed across the Great Plains, the Credit Mobilier collected the funds from the U.S. government and the public domain, which were then declared as dividends for the stockholders of Credit Mobilier.

In order to forestall any congressional investigations of their activities, Oakes Ames (a member of Congress from Massachusetts) and other officers of Credit Mobilier began distributing free stock in the House and Senate and to members of the executive branch, especially vice-president Colfax Schuyler. This was soon followed by a falling-out among the officers of Credit Mobilier, and an associate, Col. H. S. McComb, filed suit in Pennsylvania courts alleging misuse of the stock by the Ames brothers. After much pressure a congressional commission of inquiry was established in 1872 to investigate the matter and Congress passed a resolution condemning Ames, Schuyler, and several others. During this same time (1868–1871), Oliver Ames served as president of Union Pacific, continuing as director of the concern until his death.

Both of the Ames brothers were prominently involved in politics. Oakes Ames was a Free Soiler and one of the earliest adherents to the Republican party when it was organized in the state. In 1860 he was a member of the Executive Council of Massachusetts and in 1862 was elected to the U.S.

Senate. He was reelected four times, serving until he died. Oliver Ames was a Whig and then a Republican, and in 1852 and 1857 was elected to the state senate. He was also vice-president of the Massachusetts Total Abstinence Society. They were Unitarians.

Oakes Ames married Eveline O. Gelman of Easton, Massachusetts, in 1827 and had five children. His eldest, Oakes Angier Ames, became a partner in the shovel factory in 1856, and in 1877 became president of the company. Another son, Oliver Ames II, was a partner in the shovel works and president of the Union Pacific. A Republican, he was elected governor of Massachusetts in 1887 and reelected in 1888. Oliver Ames married Sarah Lothrop of Easton and had two children. His son, Frederick L. Ames, was a partner in the shovel firm until he died in 1893. He was also associated with Henry L. Higginson* and T. Jefferson Coolidge* in the financing of railroads, the telegraph, and the telephone, and became one of the major backers of General Electric Company. (**A.** *DAB; NCAB*, 2:200; 14:201; 28:466; *New York Times*, May 9, 1873; March 10, 1877; October 25, 1895; *Who Was Who in America*, vol. H. **B.** Jay B. Crawford, *The Credit Mobilier of America*, 1880; Robert Fogel, *Union Pacific: A Case in Premature Enterprise*, 1960.)

AMORY, THOMAS (May, 1682–June 20, 1728). Colonial merchant. Born in Limerick, Ireland, son of Jonathan Amory, a merchant in Dublin. Thomas was taken as an infant to the West Indies, and in 1686 to Charleston, South Carolina, where his father became a landowner, speaker of the colonial assembly, and advocate general. In 1694 Thomas was sent to London to be educated and five years later became an apprentice to Nicolas Oursel, a French merchant in London. In 1706 Oursel sent him as his factor to Terceira in the Azores. There he established himself as a merchant, trading with Portugal, England, Holland, and America. In 1712 he purchased a French prize ship and went to Europe to dispose of her, but lost part of the cargo and had to recoup his losses.

In 1719 Amory sailed for Boston, and then traveled to South Carolina, Rhode Island, Pennsylvania, and New York during the next two years in search of an opening for trade. He finally decided to settle in Boston, where he purchased land and built a wharf and still house. He rapidly extended his business to the other English colonies, the West Indies, the Azores, England, Ireland, and Europe, developing an international trade. He also became a ship builder and distilled rum and turpentine.

In 1721 he married Rebecca Holmes, daughter of a tavern owner in Boston. After his death seven years later, Mrs. Amory carried on the importing business and supervised the management of the distillery until 1743. Mr. Amory was typical of the many successful merchants who founded their mercantile fortunes in Massachusetts in the seventeenth century. His wife, Rebecca Holmes Amory, was also typical of a less well known phenomenon—the colonial wife who assumed management of her husband's affairs after his death with great success. (**A.** *DAB*; Gertrude E. Meredith, *The Descendents of Hugh Amory*, 1901. **B.** W. B. Weedon, *Economic and Social History of New England*, 1898.)

ANDERSON, JOSEPH REID (February 6, 1813–September 7, 1892). Iron manufacturer, Tredegar Iron Works. Born at his father's home, Walnut Hill in Virginia. Son of William Anderson and Anna Thomas. His grandfather, Robert Anderson, came from the North of Ireland to Philadelphia in 1756, and his mother was the daughter of a Maryland planter. In 1832, Joseph Anderson entered West Point military academy, and was graduated a second lieutenant in 1836. He joined the Army Corps of Engineers at Ft. Pulaski, Georgia, until he resigned in 1837. After serving for a short time as assistant engineer for the state of Virginia, in 1838 he became chief engineer of the Valley Turnpike Company, which built the highway between Staunton and Winchester, Virginia. He left its employ in 1841, when he became an agent of the Tredegar Iron Company at Richmond.

In 1843 Anderson leased the Tredegar Works and became owner in 1848. He developed the company into one of the leading iron manufacturing works in the country, building over 40 locomotives for southern railroads and supplying cannon for the U.S. government, among other products. At the outbreak of the Civil War, the Confederate Capital was moved to Richmond to protect the iron works, which was vital to the Confederate economy and war effort. Anderson himself was a secessionist and entered into agreements to supply several southern states with cannon and ammunition after secession. He also entered the Confederate army as a brigadier general in 1861; he was wounded in 1862 and resigned his commission.

Thereupon he returned to his iron works, which became the sole source of heavy guns and other materials for the Confederacy during the war. There were some 900 workers at the plant during the war, most of whom were black slaves, making it the South's largest single industrial concern. The plant was confiscated by the Federal government in 1865 and given back in 1867. At that point it was reorganized with Anderson as president, which he remained until his death.

In addition to his ironmaking activities, he was a member of the Virginia House of Delegates from 1852 to 1856, chairman of the Common Council of Richmond in the 1870s, and president of the Chamber of Commerce of Richmond in 1874 and 1875. He was married twice: in 1837 to Sally Grahen and later to Mary Pegram. (*DAB; NCAB*, 12:423; Charles B. Dew, *Ironmaker to the Confederacy: Joseph R. Anderson and the Tredegar Iron Works*, 1966.)

ANNENBERG, MOSES LOUIS (February 11, 1875–July 24, 1942) and **Walter H. Annenberg** (1908–   ). Publishers and race track wire services, *Daily Racing Form*. **Moses** was born in Kalwischen, East Prussia, son of

Jewish parents, Tobias Annenberg and Sarah Greenberg. In 1882 his father, a farmer and storekeeper, emigrated to the United States, followed by the rest of the family in 1885. They settled in Chicago. The family was very poor. Moses only had a scant amount of schooling and went into his father's junk business. He later worked as a Western Union messenger, a starter for a livery stable, and a bartender.

When William Randolph Hearst* arrived in Chicago, he hired Moses' brother, Max, as circulation manager. Max then hired Moses to solicit subscriptions for the *Evening American* in 1900. By 1904, when Hearst started a morning paper, the *Examiner*, Moses Annenberg became circulation manager. The appearance of the *Examiner* sparked a ferocious competitive war between the Hearst papers and their older rivals. In the battle for street position to sell papers, Annenberg resorted to virtual gang warfare to win his battle. Although he and his brother were successful in this fight, their methods were to tarnish Moses' reputation for the rest of his life.

In 1907, however, Moses quarreled with Max and moved to Milwaukee. He pawned his wife's jewelry in order to start an agency to distribute all the Chicago newspapers in the city. The business expanded rapidly, and he established similar agencies in twenty other cities. His first substantial profits, however, came from a promotion scheme suggested to him by his wife—a newspaper coupon offering teaspoons decorated with state seals. With the profits on this he was able to invest in Milwaukee real estate ventures, automobile garages, and apartment buildings.

In 1917 Moses joined Arthur Brisbane in the publication of the *Wisconsin News* and tripled the circulation to 80,000. Brisbane then sold out to Hearst, and Annenberg remained as publisher for one year. Hearst brought him to New York to become circulation manager for all Hearst newspapers and magazines and a member of the executive council. In 1924 he became president and publisher of Hearst's newly acquired *New York Mirror*.

In 1926 he resigned from the Hearst organization to devote his time to his own interests, especially the *Daily Racing Form*, which he had purchased in 1922. Later, he added other horse racing papers, such as the *New York Morning Telegram*. In 1927 he worked his way into the racing wire services, which supplied instant information on racing results to subscribers, mostly bookmakers. Annenberg bought a one-half interest in the General News Bureau in Chicago in partnership with John L. Lynch and devoted the next seven years to driving out his competitors. After 1930 he absorbed the three major compiling services and established a near monopoly supplying the information from twenty-nine race tracks to about 15,000 bookmakers. To get rid of his partner, Lynch, he started a rival business called Nationwide News Service. By manipulating the prices and services of both businesses, Annenberg forced Lynch out, General News Bureau was discontinued, and Nationwide took over. Using similar tactics, Annenberg drove his partners out of the *Daily Racing Form*. In this way he established his control over racing newspapers and other publications used by bettors, such as scratch sheets.

Annenberg prospered greatly even during the depression, and he was worth $19,500,000 in 1938. In 1939, however, he was faced with two separate indictments from grand juries, one dealing with income tax evasion, and the other with his race track information monopoly. His indictment for income tax evasion charged him with owing $5,500,000 in taxes, penalties, and interest from 1932 to 1936. At the same time, federal pressure on his race track information business brought about the collapse of the system. A.T. & T., Western Union, and Illinois Bell Telephone all agreed to end services to leased facilities, and Annenberg dissolved Nationwide.

He pleaded guilty to the charge of income tax evasion in 1940 and agreed to pay ten million dollars to the government for income taxes dating back to 1923. He was also sent to the federal penitentiary at Lewisburg. The other charges against him and his son were then dropped or reversed. While in prison his health deteriorated, and he was released in 1942. A month later he died of a brain tumor at Mayo Clinic.

Earlier Moses had re-entered the general newspaper publishing business with the founding of the *Miami Tribune* in 1934. Then, in 1936, he purchased the 107 year old *Philadelphia Inquirer* for about $6,750,000. It had been declining in circulation, but he revived it through the use of more comic strips and sensationalist picture magazines. The circulation of the daily paper rose 23 percent in two years, and the Sunday paper rose 55 percent. He used the paper to get into state politics on the side of the Republican organization of Joseph N. Pew Jr.* Annenberg had supported Roosevelt in 1932 and 1936, but broke with him after that. His political emergence in Pennsylvania came at the same time that both the state and federal governments were investigating him.

In 1899 he married Sadie Cecelia Friedman, daughter of a Chicago merchant. They had nine children. **Walter H. Annenberg**, one of their children, was to continue and expand his father's publication empire.

Walter reorganized his father's businesses into Triangle Publications, with a net worth of $8,000,000. By 1969, when he sold the *Philadelphia Inquirer*, Triangle was worth $136,000,000. Walter had joined his father's business in 1922. After his father's death, he founded *Seventeen Magazine* in 1944, which was edited by his sister, Mrs. Enid Haupt. He also acquired a radio and television station in Philadelphia, WFIL, along with stations in Alliance and Lebanon, Pennsylvania, Binghamton, New York, New Haven, Connecticut, and Fresno, California. His greatest publishing success, however, came with the publication of *T.V. Guide* in 1953, by consolidating several local television magazines he had acquired into one national magazine with local inserts. It grew rapidly to have the largest circulation of any magazine in the U.S., with a circulation in 1968 of 14,000,000. In 1957 he acquired the *Philadelphia Daily News*. He and his sister owned about

85 percent of Triangle Publications, and were major shareholders in Girard Trust and Campbell Soup. In 1969 he was appointed Ambassador to Great Britain by President Nixon. (*DAB*, Supplement 3; *New York Times*, July 21, 1942; *Current Biography*, January, 1970; *Washington Post*, February 24, 1969; Gaeton Fonzi, *Annenberg*, 1970.)

APPLETON, NATHAN (October 6, 1779–July 14, 1861). Textile manufacturer, Lowell Mills. Born in New Ipswich, New Hampshire, son of Isaac Appleton and Mary Adams. He was educated at a local academy and then entered into trade with his brother Samuel. They established a partnership in 1794 which continued until 1809. He then established another partnership with his brother Eben, which was dissolved during the War of 1812. He made a sizable fortune in overseas trade, and in 1813 invested $5,000 in Francis C. Lowell's* power mill for making cloth at Waltham, Massachusetts. Two years later his firm became the sales agent for the factory. He helped establish the principles of management of the early American textile industry—power machinery with cheap female labor and a separate selling organization. Appleton and Lowell also founded the city of Lowell, Massachusetts, and by 1840 had mills in operation worth $12,000,000. They set up other centers in Manchester, New Hampshire, and Lawrence, Massachusetts.

Appleton also established the Suffolk System in which a group of Boston banks checked bank notes (which passed for money) of rural banks. Appleton was part of a group of fifteen Boston families known as the "Boston Associates", which by 1850 controlled 20 percent of the nation's cotton spindleage, 30 percent of Massachusetts railroad milage, 39 percent of Massachusetts insurance capital, and 40 percent of Boston banking resources. A very tightly knit group, their power extended even beyond these simple figures. They controlled water power on the Connecticut and Merrimack rivers and levied water rates on their textile manufacturing competitors who depended upon these waters. They held patents on many important machines, and collected royalties on their use. Builders of canals and railroads, they owned important transportation facilities in their state and section. They financed their activities through their own banks, insured them through their own insurance companies, and influenced state, local, and national politics.

Appleton was elected to Congress in 1830 over Henry Lee. While in Congress he helped frame the protective tariff of 1832, opposed Henry Clay's compromise tariff of 1833, and strongly supported President Jackson in the Nullification Controversy. Later, he fought Jackson on the National Bank issue, but broke with Nicholas Biddle* over his contraction of loans. In 1841 he wrote a pamphlet, *Currency and Banking*, supporting the establishment of a national bank. He felt slavery was essentially a local institution and refused to support William Lloyd Garrison and other antislavery groups, causing Charles Sumner to refer to him as one of the "Lords of the Loom." He opposed secession, however, and supported the Union in 1861. He lived in a luxurious mansion on Beacon Street in Boston and was one of the organizers of the Boston Athenaeum, serving as its treasurer from 1816 to 1827. He was twice married, first in 1806 to Maria Theresa Gold of Pittsfield, who died in 1833. In 1839 he married Harriet Coffin Sumner of Boston. He had seven children, one of whom married Henry Wadsworth Longfellow. (**A.** *DAB; NCAB*, 11:110. **B.** Nathan Appleton, *Introduction of the Power Loom and the Origin of Lowell*, 1858; Vera Shlakman, *Economic History of a Factory Town*, 1935; Caroline Ware, *The Early New England Cotton Manufacture*, 1931.)

ARCHBOLD, JOHN DUSTIN (July 26, 1848–December 5, 1916). Oil refiner, Standard Oil Company. Born in Leesburg, Ohio, son of Rev. Israel Archbold and Frances Dana. His father was a Methodist minister of Irish descent and his mother was a member of the prominent Dana family of Massachusetts. When he was eleven years old his father died, so he was able to obtain only a few years of formal education. At an early age Archbold went to work in a country store at Salem, only a few miles from the Pennsylvania oil districts. At age eighteen he entered the oil fields, seeking a fortune in the new frenzy of speculation which erupted after the Civil War. Going to work in the office of W. H. Abbott, he became a partner in 1867. They were very successful in their dealings until they found themselves blocked by John D. Rockefeller's* Standard Oil Company, which was getting rebates from the railroads. But Archbold united the leading oil men of the Titusville region against this outside force. The move was successful, at least in the short run, as Standard Oil backed off, and then took Archbold into their own company.

Archbold continued under his own corporate identity as the Acme Oil Company, but the firm was actually part of Standard Oil. In January, 1882, Acme Oil was legally as well as administratively incorporated into Standard Oil with the formation of the Trust, of which Archbold became a trustee. Later, when the firm was incorporated, he became a director until his death. Nor was he just a figurehead in the larger concerns of the huge oil company. It was he who conducted many of the delicate and secret negotiations of the company over the years. He was also generally regarded as John D. Rockefeller's closest associate in the firm. Archbold usually acted as the principal spokesman for the company in government investigations and the like. After 1896, although Rockefeller retained the title of president, and Archbold was vice-president, the latter was the dominant force in the concern. His goal was stabilization, and he put his energies toward the creation of an efficient system of distribution, including control of pipelines, location of refineries at points convenient to markets, perfection of plant operation, and the economical utilization of oil by-products.

As a result of the Supreme Court decision of 1911, Archbold became president of Standard Oil of New Jersey, holding that office until his death. Only Rockefeller himself had greater influence in the development of Standard Oil and the oil industry generally in his time. In 1870 Archbold married Annie Mills of Titusville. They had four children. (**A.** *DAB; NCAB*, 21:114; *New York Times*, December 16, 1916. **B.** Ralph W. and Muriel E. Hidy, *Pioneering in Big Business*, 1955.)

ARDEN, ELIZABETH (Elizabeth Nightingale Graham) (December 31, 1884–October 18, 1966). Cosmetic manufacturer, Elizabeth Arden Company. Born in Woolbridge, Ontario, Canada, daughter of William Graham and Susan Pierce Todd. She was educated in Canadian schools and by tutors. At age seventeen she became an apprentice nurse, then worked in a bank, a truss manufacturing company, a real estate office, and a dentist's office where her promotional idea doubled the business.

In 1909 she went to New York City where she took a job as a secretary for Eleanor Adair, a London cosmetic firm. There she learned the basic facial massage technique. In the same year she opened a salon in partnership with Elizabeth Hubbard. The venture failed. Undaunted, she opened her own salon and created a new name, Elizabeth Arden, for the enterprise. She borrowed $6,000 from a relative for expensive interior decoration, and the business was so successful that she was able to repay the loan in a few months.

The business grew rapidly. In 1914 she opened a branch in Washington, D.C., and in 1922 branches in Boston and Paris. By 1929 she had become wealthy and world famous. In time she owned 150 salons throughout the world and her products were sold in twenty-two countries. Her product line listed over 1,000 different items. For fourteen years she worked to create a light and fluffy cleansing cream, and finally a young chemist, A. F. Swanson, developed one for her, called Omoretta. The second product in her line was Ardera Skin Tonic. This was followed by rouges and eye shadow. In 1934 she opened a deluxe health resort at her horse farm in Maine, and later opened a winter resort in Phoenix.

A Republican and Episcopalian, she married Thomas Jenkins Lewis, a silk manufacturer, in 1915. They were divorced in 1935. In 1942 she married the Russian born Prince Michael Evlanoff. They were divorced in 1944. She remained sole owner of Elizabeth Arden Cosmetics until her death. (*New York Times*, October 18, 1966; *Current Biography*, July, 1957; December, 1966; *Saturday Evening Post*, April 24, 1948; *Time*, May 6, 1946; *Fortune*, October, 1938; *Cosmopolitan*, June, 1956; *Who Was Who*, vol. 4.)

ARMOUR, PHILIP DANFORTH (May 16, 1832–January 6, 1901) and **Jonathan Ogden Armour** (November 11, 1863–August 16, 1927). Meat packers, Armour & Company. **Philip Armour** was born in Stockbridge, New York, the son of Danforth Armour and Julia Ann Brooks. His Scotch-Irish grandfather had come to the U.S. in 1720. He was educated in district schools and Cazenovia Academy, working after school on his father's farm. In 1852, with 30 other men, Armour started overland to California. On arrival, he worked as a miner and later constructed sluices. After earning several thousands of dollars, he returned home in 1856. He was lured west again in a short time, going to Cincinnati and then to Milwaukee. There he formed a partnership with a friend, Frederick B. Miles, in the wholesale grocery and commission business.

The partnership with Miles was dissolved in 1863, and he joined with John Plankington in the firm of Plankington, Armour and Company, grain dealers and meat packers. They made their first big financial killing in the pork futures market at the end of the Civil War. They had promised to deliver pork at $40 a barrel, but when the Confederacy began to collapse, prices fell to $18, netting them two million dollars. Afterward Philip allied with his brother, Herman O. Armour (1837-1901) in his commission house of H. O. Armour and Company. They added a pork packing plant in 1868, and in 1870 the firm became Armour and Company. In 1875 the company was moved to Chicago, with Philip taking charge.

Armour was one of the first packers to bring live hogs to the city and to supervise his own slaughtering. He was also the first to begin utilization of formerly waste products. He was a great systematizer and innovator in methods which resulted in significant economies for the plant and industry. But it was the development of a sure method of refrigeration by Gustavus Swift* that opened up significant expansion for Armour and the rest of the industry. Armour bought his own refrigeration cars and set up district plants in eastern cities. He next turned his attention to the export trade, and sent refrigerated beef and pork to England, France, and Germany.

In 1879 he established the Armour Brothers Bank in Kansas City, Missouri, with another brother, Andrew Watson Armour (1829-1892), as president. Armour was also a spectacular speculator on the exchange. He executed a bear raid on pork in 1879, a wheat deal in 1882, and in 1897 broke a "corner" in wheat attempted by Joseph Leiter. By the end of the century his wealth was estimated at some fifty million dollars and his plants employed 15,000 workers.

The prestige of the firm was diminished, however, by the "embalmed beef" scandals of 1898-1899, when the government accused packers of treating meat with chemicals. The matter was rapidly hushed up, but Armour's health began to fail, and he withdrew from active plant management after 1899.

He founded Armour Mission in Chicago, built the Armour Flats for working class families, and founded Armour Institute of Technology. In 1862 he married Malvina Belle Ogden of Cincinnati. One of his sons was **J. Ogden Armour.**

The younger Armour was born in Milwaukee and entered Yale in 1881, but didn't finish. He then entered Armour & Company, and was soon made a partner. Upon the death of his father in 1901, he took over direction of the firm. Under his management, sales increased from two hundred million dollars in 1900 to one billion dollars in 1920. He set up additional plants throughout the U.S. and when he retired in 1923, the firm employed over 40,000 persons. Like his father, he was a large operator on the Chicago Board of Trade and a director of many corporations. But he lost financial control of the company in 1923, and in 1926 faced charges of fraud against his wheat company. He died in London, England. In 1891 he married Lolita Sheldon of Suffield, Connecticut, and had one daughter. (*DAB; NCAB*, 7:248; 23:57; *New York Times*, January 7, 1901; August 17, 1929; *Who Was Who*, vol. 1; H. Leech and J. C. Carroll, *Armour and his Times*, 1938.)

ASH, ROY LAWRENCE (October 20, 1918–   ). Manufacturer and financier, Litton Industries. Born in Los Angeles, California, the son of Charles K. Ash, a hay and grain broker, and Fay E. Dickson. Mr. Ash was educated in the public schools of Los Angeles. After graduation from high school in 1935, he went to work in the city cash collection department of the Bank of America National Trust until he entered the army in 1942. Ash went to Officers Candidate School and then elected the Army Air Force's Statistical Control Service, headed by Tex Thornton.* Its function was to adapt modern management controls and techniques to the needs of the Army Air Force. When the war was over, Ash did not follow Thornton and another fellow officer, Robert McNamara,* to Ford Motor Company. Instead, he went to Harvard Graduate School of Business, where he earned his M.B.A. in 1947.

Afterward he went to Bank of America as chief statistical control analyst in San Francisco. In 1949, Thornton, now operating head of Hughes Aircraft, brought Ash into that firm as controller. In 1953 Thornton and Ash left Hughes to found their own company, known as Electro-Dynamics Corporation, partly financed by Lehman Brothers banking house, and bought Litton Industries, a small West Coast producer of microwave tubes. Litton then embarked on one of the most daring and successful courses of acquisition attempted in the U.S. Astutely swapping shares of its electronics stock, it bought interests in larger companies. By 1961 it had completed twenty-five mergers and operated 48 plants in nine countries. Litton sales amounted to $245 million, about 53 percent of which was military, and the rest industrial and commercial.

Ash was the financial and technical wizard of Litton, with Thornton the promoter and visionary. Ash was successively vice-president, vice-president and treasurer, and executive vice-president until 1961, when he became president. By 1965 the firm had sales of over nine hundred million dollars and produced 5,000 different items, including credit cards, trading stamps, microwave ovens, submarines, automated cargo ships, NASA's space suits, and the world's largest oil rig. The company's sales exceeded one billion dollars for the first time in 1966, but suffered hard times in the economic downturn of 1968. Each of Litton's divisions operates autonomously, controlled by top management only in financing and major policy.

Litton Industries was the first modern conglomerate, a collection of wildly disparate parts selected solely on the basis of whether they could make money for the parent company. By the end of the 1970s more than 100 different businesses operated under the Litton umbrella. Thornton and Ash always purchased going concerns and let them keep operating without a lot of interference. As Thornton once explained, "We had to grow fast. There wasn't time to learn a business, train people, develop markets. . . . We bought time, a market, a product line, plant, research team, sales force. It would have taken years to duplicate this from scratch."

Ash was president of Litton until 1972, when he became an assistant to President Nixon and director of the Office of Management and Budget in Washington, D.C. He served in that office until 1975 when he became chairman of the board and chief executive officer of Addressograph-Multigraph Corporation. A Roman Catholic and Republican, he married Lila M. Hornbeck in 1943. They have five children. (*Current Biography*, 1968; *Who's Who in America*, 1978–79; *New York Times*, September 10, 1961; *Time*, September 15, 1961.)

ASHLEY, WILLIAM H. (c. 1778–March 26, 1838). Western fur trader. Born in Powhatan County, Virginia. He received a fair amount of schooling for the time and at an early age acquired business interests in Virginia. Sometime between 1803 and 1805 he settled in Missouri and engaged in the extraction of saltpeter at Ashley's Cave and in the manufacture of gunpowder with Andrew Henry. He also undertook several lead mining ventures.

In the early 1820s he abandoned lead mining for fur trading in St. Louis, in which Henry already had a considerable interest. In 1822 and 1823 he sent an expedition up the Missouri River to Yellowstone, where he established a post. Ashley and Henry also set up another post named Ft. Kiowa in southwest South Dakota in 1823. Their chief contribution to fur trading, however, came in 1824, when they developed the rendezvous system of operations. This vastly extended their range of operations and established a more transient, flexible, and in many ways more complex organization than existed under the old practice of building durable trading posts. Each year Ashley and Henry named the place for the rendezvous, which could now be moved around yearly, with the changing fortunes of the fur trade. There was no year-round expense, no standing defiance of the Indians. It was far cheaper to operate this way, but it required more organizational skill, a constant attention to detail, and the ability to shift operations. They conducted their last annual rendezvous near the Great Salt Lake in 1826. It took them seventy days to travel from the Salt Lake to St. Louis, and after the journey they retired from active business.

Ashley was also intimately involved in Missouri politics. He became a general in the territorial militia in 1822 and in 1820 had been elected lieutenant governor of the newly formed territory. He ran for governor in 1824 and the U.S. Senate in 1829, but was defeated. In 1831 he was elected to Congress on an anti-Jackson ticket, and served there until 1837. While in Congress he was an active champion of western causes and sat on the House committee on Indian Affairs. In 1836 he again ran for governor of Missouri, but was defeated.

He was married three times: first, to Mary Able, who died in 1821; then to Eliza Christy in 1825. She died in 1830. His third marriage was to Mrs. Elizabeth (Mass) Wilcox in 1832. (**A.** *DAB*. **B.** Harrison Clifford Dale, *Ashley-Smith Expedition . . .* , 1918; Daniel Boorstin, *The Americans: The National Experience*, 1965; Hiram M. Chittenden, *The American Fur Trade of the Far West*, 3 vols., 1902.)

ASTOR, JOHN JACOB (July 17, 1763–March 29, 1848) and **William B. Astor** (September 19, 1792–November 24, 1875). Fur trader and financier, American Fur Company, and real estate investor. **John J. Astor** was born in Waldorf, Duchy of Baden, Germany, son of John Ashdoer, a butcher. Ashdoer was not a particularly industrious person and his family was in need most of the time. Jacob was educated in local schools and at age seventeen left home. He built a raft to sail up the Rhine and earned enough to pay for his passage to England. When he arrived in London he worked for his brother, George, who had set up a musical instrument store. He remained there about three years, studying the language. At the end of the Revolutionary War in 1783, Astor set sail for America. He had about $25, seven flutes, and a steerage berth. On board he met a man who had traded furs with the Indians, so he chose that as his future occupation.

He arrived in New York City in the spring of 1784 and by 1786 had set up his own shop, where he operated as a fur factor and also sold musical instruments. About that time he married Sarah Todd, who not only brought a dowry of some $300, but had a good business head and was especially good at the valuation of furs. Astor made many trips to the nearby frontier for furs. He was particularly aided by the Jay Treaty, which modified trade restrictions between Canada and the U.S. He was now able to import directly from Montreal, which increased his business greatly. By 1800 he had amassed $250,000 and was a leading factor in the fur trade. At about the same time he began to make large purchases of city real estate, which later would form the bulk of his fortune. In 1801 he built a lavish new home at Broadway and Vesey, which was later the location of the Astor House hotel.

Astor entered the second phase of his career in 1808 when, with several partners, he formed the American Fur Company, designed to give him a monopoly in the western fur trade. The Louisiana Purchase had opened limitless opportunities for the expansion of the fur trade, and the company established posts from the Great Lakes to the Rockies staffed by small traders who traded with the Indians and sent out their own expeditions. In the beginning most of the trappers who traded with the company were independent, being advanced money by Astor. They soon fell into debt with him, however, and in return for Astor's financing were forced to deal exclusively with the American Fur Company. All of the operations of the company were exploitive, at least to some degree, and it was bitterly hated by the traders who were caught up in it.

In an attempt to capture the trade of the West Coast and its connections with the Far East, Astor and others formed the Pacific Fur Company in 1810 and established Fort Astoria on the Columbia River as a headquarters for the trade. The subordinate posts in the interior would ship furs to Astoria, which would in turn ship them to China, where they would be sold, and the ships reloaded and sailed to New York. Although this became Astor's most famous venture, it was also his least successful business operation. Portents of trouble emerged when the first shipload of pioneers to the fort were lost to an Indian massacre and explosion. Then Astor's very heavy investments were lost when the War of 1812 broke out; he surrendered the fort to the British in 1813 for only $58,000.

During the war, Astor lent vast sums of money to the government, in concert with Stephen Girard.* In 1816 he persuaded Congress to pass a law forbidding aliens (except by executive permit) to engage in the fur trade, except as employees. This effectively shut the British out of fur trade in the area. By 1817 all of the Mississippi Valley posts of the Northwest Company as well as those of the Southwest Company were taken over by Astor. In 1821–1822 he got Congress to abolish government trading posts, and in the latter year established the western department of the American Fur Company at St. Louis. He absorbed his chief competitor, the Columbia Fur Company, in 1827, and reorganized the territory.

Astor was not particularly successful in the far west, and in 1854 sold out all his fur interests. After that time, he devoted himself almost exclusively to his real estate interests and banking. By the time of his death he left an estate of some $20,000,000, making him the richest man in America. The sole beneficiary was his son, **William B. Astor**.

William was born in New York and educated in public schools until age sixteen. He was then sent to Heidelberg, and after two years to Goettingen. In 1815 young Astor returned to America and became a partner in his father's fur business. His position in the fur company was always subordinate to that of his father; he functioned primarily as a faithful and industrious clerk. After the death of his father, he continued to buy New York real estate, and became known as the "landlord of New York." Many of the buildings he owned were converted into crowded tenements. Despite public furor over these buildings, he refused for years to make any improvements. Finally, in 1861, he demolished many of the old rookeries and erected simple but substantial buildings in their place.

In 1818 he married Margaret Armstrong, daughter of General John Armstrong, Secretary of War under President Madison. He had two sons: John J. III and William B. Jr. His eldest son, John (1822–1890), became head of the entire Astor estate upon his father's death in 1875. He continued the policy of buying urban real estate and developed few interests outside that field. The younger son, William (1829–1892), was involved in the real estate ventures, but also built railroads in Florida and erected houses in Jacksonville. (**A.** *DAB; NCAB*, 8:102; 104; *Who Was Who*, vol. H; *New York Times*, November 25, 1875; Harvey O'Connor, *The Astors*, 1941; Kenneth W. Porter, *John Jacob Astor: Businessman*, 2 vols., 1931. **B.** Grace L. Nute, "The Papers of the American Fur Company," *American Historical Review*, 1927, 519–38.)

AUSTIN, MOSES (October 4, 1761–June 10, 1821) and **Stephen Fuller Austin** (November 3, 1793–December 27, 1836). Manufacturer, financier, and Texas land speculators. **Moses Austin** was born in Durham, Connecticut, the son of Elias and Eunice Austin. He was educated there and at Middletown, Connecticut, which was a lead mining center during the Revolution. In 1783 he joined the Manning, Merrill & Company importing firm in Philadelphia. The business was reorganized in 1784 and Moses established a branch at Richmond, Virginia—Moses Austin and Company. By 1789 he had acquired the Chiswell Lead Mines in southwest Virginia, and moved to the mines while continuing the Richmond business. The mines were worked with slave labor and had a very large output. Austin also cultivated the adjacent farms to provide food for the slaves and animals.

In 1796–1797 Moses Austin went to Missouri to look over lead mines in the area. He got a land grant and established the town of Potos. For the next twenty years he carried on a lead mine and mill, saw mill, flour mill, store, and so forth. By 1812 he was worth $160,000, but was finding himself hard pressed by debts. In 1816 he helped organize the Bank of St. Louis, but the venture failed and wiped out his entire estate. So, in 1820 he went to San Antonio, Texas, and applied to establish 300 families in Texas. The permit was granted in 1821, but he died before concluding his arrangements for the move. In 1784 he married Maria Brown, a Philadelphia Quaker. They had one daughter and two sons.

His son, **Stephen**, was born at the lead mines in Wythe County, Virginia, but grew up in Missouri. Between ages 11 and 14 he was educated at Colchester, Connecticut, and then spent two years at Transylvania University in Lexington, Kentucky. Afterward he joined his father's ill-fated Bank of St. Louis venture as a director, while also working as a storekeeper and manager of the lead mines.

In 1820 he went to Arkansas, where he was appointed a judge on the judicial circuit. Upon arrival, however, he decided against taking the position, and went to New Orleans, where he studied law and worked at the *Louisiana Advertiser*. In 1821 he yielded to his father's plans about moving families to Texas. After his father's death, he took over the project, and in 1822 planted the first legal settlement of Anglo-Americans in Texas. He was given extraordinary powers in the area, until 1828 acting as executive, law maker, supreme judge, and military commandant. He also had absolute authority to admit immigrants. By 1825 he had settled 300 families.

He fixed the land system, pushed back the Indians, mapped the province, charted the bays and rivers, promoted commerce with the U.S., and kept a steady stream of immigrants flowing into the area. He encouraged the erection of gins and saw mills and the establishment of schools. He was a masterful promoter of Texas interests in the U.S.; by 1835 there were 20,000 Americans in Texas. He led the Texans in their revolt against the Mexican Republic before he died. He never married. **A.** (*DAB; NCAB*, 5:157; 6:70; Eugene C. Barker, *Life of Stephen F. Austin*, 1925. **B.** Mattie A. Hatcher, *The Opening of Texas to Foreign Settlements*, 1927.)

AUTRY, ORVON GENE (September 29, 1908–   ). Entertainer, radio and television station entrepreneur, and baseball club owner. Born in Tioga, Texas, the son of Delbert Autry and Elnora Ozment. He graduated from high school in 1925 and got his first job as a railway telegraph operator in Supulpa, Oklahoma. Autry wanted to be a professional baseball player and played on semi-pro teams in the area, but also earned money singing in local clubs, and toured for a couple of months with the Fields Brothers Marvelous Medicine Show. After a time, he went to New York City to seek work as a singer. He was not successful and went back to Oklahoma, where he got a salaried singing and story-telling program as "Oklahoma's Yodeling Cowboy" at station KVOO in Tulsa. (He had worked as a cowhand at times while in high school, but always got fired from his jobs because his singing distracted the other workers.) He continued to work for the railroad, and he and his fellow train despatcher, Jimmy Long, wrote "That Silver Haired Daddy of Mine," which brought Autry his first success. It sold 30,000 copies in the first month, and four million by 1940.

In 1930 Autry went to Chicago to sing at the Sears owned station WLS for $35 a week. He appeared on "National Barn Dance" and the "National Farm and Home Hour," becoming a nation-wide radio performer. He soon went to Hollywood to appear as the lead in the serial, *The Phantom Empire*, but his first major picture was *Tumbling Tumbleweeds*, a musical, relatively non-violent western dubbed a "horse opera." He appeared in eight low-budget "quickies" in a year, which played mostly in small towns of the west and southwest. By 1937 and 1938 he was making "big-time" guest appearances on major radio programs. He also made substantial royalties from 48 to 50 commercial products, from cap pistols to shaving cream, which bore his name. Autry was one of the first of a new breed of entertainers who prospered because they were able to identify their personalities with a large number of business enterprises, many of which they also ran. This was perhaps his greatest significance on the American business scene.

In 1942 he went into the army and was assigned to the entertainment section. But he pushed for active duty and became a pilot, flying air transport in Europe, to the China-Burma theater and the South Pacific. After his discharge in 1945, he did USO shows. In 1947 he formed Gene Autry Productions to make films on a profit-sharing basis with Columbia Studios. Within a short time he owned a chain of Texas movie theaters, a flying school, three western radio stations, five ranches, and two cowboy music publishing houses.

In 1961 he purchased and became chairman of the board of the California Angels American League baseball club, and also was president of Flying A Productions. He owned station KOOL-TV in Phoenix, Arizona, and radio stations KMPC in Hollywood, California; KSFO in San Francisco; KVI in Seattle, Washington; and KEX in Portland, Oregon. He has received enormous royalties over the years from some 250 songs he has written. He married Ina Mae Spivey in 1932. (*Current Biography*, December, 1957; *Who's Who in America*, 1977–78; *New York Times*, October 27, 1940; *Saturday Evening Post*, September 2, 1930.)

AVERY, SEWELL LEE (November 4, 1873–October 31, 1960). Manufacturer and retailer, U.S. Gypsum Company and Montgomery, Ward and Company. Born in Saginaw, Michigan, son of Waldo Allerd Avery, a wealthy lumberman, and Ellen Lee. Avery was educated at Michigan Military Academy and received a law degree from the University of Michigan in 1894. He began his career with his father's gypsum firm, Albaster Company, in 1894. In 1901 he formed the United States Gypsum Company. He was president of the firm until 1936 and chairman of the board until 1951. It started as a modest sized company with limited cash resources, but Avery built it into one of the largest firms of its kind in the world. The firm produced sheetrock, wallboard, rocklath, and Red Top Plaster. Avery showed himself to be a very shrewd organizer, and he hired chemists and engineers to find new uses for gypsum. He was so successful that when he retired as president in 1936, the firm was capitalized at $61,000,000, had mines or factories at 47 locations in North America, and manufactured more than 75 commodities.

In 1931 J. P. Morgan Jr.* asked him to become a director for U.S. Steel. Eight months later Avery was made chairman of the board of Montgomery,

Ward and Company. When he took over, the firm was in severe financial difficulties. In 1936 he became a full time executive of the company and directed the organization as chairman of the board until he retired in 1955. At Montgomery Ward he hired top merchandising men from other fields and instituted numerous reforms. The business improved greatly, but before long there was dissension in the ranks of management. By 1940 several key men had resigned, including the president. Most of the problems resulted from Avery's insistence on running a one man show.

He was a great foe of the New Deal, and in 1935 Ward's was deprived of the use of the NRA Blue Eagle. Then, during the war, a great conflict arose between Avery and the War Labor Board over the power of the board to regulate labor relations. In 1942 the WLB ordered Ward's to sign a long contested contract with the CIO's United Mail Order, Warehouse and Retail Employees Union, with a maintenance of membership provision (a compromise between an open and closed shop). Avery protested that decision, but finally signed, after spending $400,000 in advertising opposing it. When the contract expired a year later and the NLRB held a new election, the dispute was referred to the president. When the union called a strike, the president set a deadline for Ward's compliance with the WLB and a cessation of the strike with an immediate NLRB election. The strikers returned the next day, but Avery refused to grant maintenance of membership. The government then bodily removed Avery from his office and seized the company.

Although Montgomery Ward had been very successful under Avery's management, doing an annual mail order business of $700 million, along with 575 retail stores, at the time of his retirement in 1955, it remained a highly centralized organization. Avery ruled the company with an autocratic hand until his retirement, and only then did the firm set up a new, decentralized administrative structure closely modeled on that of their competitor, Sears, Roebuck and Company. Avery was a Republican and married Hortence Lenore Wisner in 1899. He had four children, one of whom died young. In 1926–1927 he served as vice-president of the Chicago Crime Commission and was a vice-president of Hull House in Chicago. (**A.** *NCAB*, 49:356; *Current Biography*, June, 1944; *New York Times*, November 1, 1960; *Who Was Who*, vol. 4; *Fortune*, January, 1935; February, 1936; *Time*, May 8, 1944. **B.** Alfred D. Chandler Jr., *Strategy and Structure*, 1962.)

AYER, FRANCIS WAYLAND (February 4, 1848–March 5, 1923). Pioneer advertising executive, N. W. Ayer & Son. Born in Lee, Massachusetts, son of Nathaniel Wheeler Ayer and Joanna B. Wheeler, and member of a family which had come to America in 1636. His father had trained as a lawyer, but became a school teacher. Francis Ayer grew up in western New York, taught in district schools, and attended the University of Rochester for one year. He came to Philadelphia, where his father had opened a girl's school, and found employment as an advertising solicitor for a religious newspaper. In 1867 he founded N. W. Ayer & Son, with the company consisting of himself, his father, a bookkeeper, and $25 in cash. Francis Ayer became senior partner upon his father's death in 1873.

Francis Ayer developed the "open contract" plan of operating in 1875, by which he made himself the responsible agent of the advertiser, which was a new innovation in the profession. He also developed trademarks, slogans, pictorial displays and all the other paraphernalia of the business as it developed in the twentieth century. This, in turn, made possible the development of the modern newspaper and popular magazine. During his first year of operation the firm did $15,000 worth of business and in ten years had unchallenged leadership among advertising agencies in the U.S. Branch offices were established in New York, Boston, Chicago, and San Francisco.

In 1880 Ayer began to publish *The American Newspaper Annual* and in 1909 bought the *Newspaper Directory*, a standard reference work for newspaper publishers and advertisers. One of his firm's major successes was the development of "Uneeda Biscuit" for the National Biscuit Company. Other clients included: American Telephone and Telegraph, American Sugar Refining, R. J. Reynolds Tobacco, Steinway and Sons, Charles E. Hires, International Correspondence Schools, Kellogg Company, E. R. Squibb and Sons, Aetna Life Insurance, Phoenix Mutual Life Insurance, National Carbon Company, and the Encyclopedia Britannica.

Ayer also had a variety of other interests. He was president of Merchants National Bank of Philadelphia from 1895 to 1910, when it merged with the First National Bank. He developed a 2,000 acre farm at Meredith, New York, and went into butter, milk powder and stock raising business on a large scale. He was also president of the Camden and Suburban Railway Company and the Camden Horse Railway. A fervent Baptist, he was superintendent of the Sunday School of North Baptist Church of Camden, New Jersey, and president of the New Jersey State Convention of Baptists for 25 years. He was married twice: in 1875 to Rhandera Gilman, who died in 1914, and in 1919 to Martha K. Lawson. (**A.** *DAB; NCAB*, 20:154; *New York Times*, March 6, 1923. **B.** Ralph M. Hower, *The History of an Advertising Agency: N. W. Ayer & Son*, 1949; John W. Jordan, ed., *Encyclopedia of Pennsylvania Biography*, vol. 13; N. S. B. Gras and H. Larson, eds., *Casebook in American Business History*, 1939, p. 460 ff.)

AYER, FREDERICK (December 8, 1822–March 14, 1918). Financier, American Woolen Mills. Born at Ledyard, Connecticut, son of Frederick Ayer, a saw and grist mill owner, and Persis Cook. He was educated in the public schools of Ledyard and a private academy in Baldwinsville, New York. Ayer found his first employment in a general store, after which he went to Syracuse, New York, to manage another store. In 1844 he formed a partnership with Dennis McCarthy in a store—McCarthy and Ayer. The venture lasted for eleven years when, in 1855, he joined his brother, Dr. James C. Ayer,* at Lowell, Massachusetts, in the manufacture of proprietary medicines. Frederick was treasurer of the J. C. Ayer firm until 1893, when he retired.

In 1871 he and his brother purchased a controlling interest in the stock of the Tremont Mills and Suffolk Manufacturing Company of Lowell, effecting a consolidation under the name of Tremont and Suffolk Mills. In 1885 they purchased the entire property of the Washington Mills at Lawrence, Massachusetts. In 1899 Frederick Ayer was one of the organizers of American Woolen Mills, of which he served as president until succeeded by his son-in-law, William M. Wood.* He was also organizer of the New England Telephone and Telegraph Company and the Lake Superior Ship Canal Railway and Iron Company, and was a director of many other concerns.

Although less well known than many other financiers of his time, Ayer's influence was broadly felt in regional and national economic affairs. His woolen mill at Lawrence was one of the largest in the world, and the scene of a dramatic strike in 1912. He was also an important financial factor in the early telephone and telegraph industry. He was married twice. His first wife was Cornelia Wheeler, whom he married in 1852. She died in 1878. He then married Ellen B. Banning of St. Paul, Minnesota. He had seven children. (*NCAB*, 15:320; *New York Times*, March 15, 1918; *Who Was Who*, vol. 1.)

AYER, HARRIET HUBBARD (June 27, 1849–November 23, 1903). Cosmetic manufacturer, Recamier Manufacturing Company. Born at Chicago, Illinois, daughter of Henry George Hubbard, a land owner and real estate dealer, and Juliet Elvira Smith. Harriet Hubbard was educated at Sacred Heart Academy in Chicago, and at age sixteen married Herbert C. Ayer, son of a prominent iron manufacturer in the city. For several years she devoted herself to being a homemaker and caring for her children, but found her life devasted when one of her children died of smoke inhalation in the Chicago Fire of 1871. While in Paris recovering from the mental depression produced by this traumatic event, she became interested in the latest clothing fashions. Upon her return to Chicago, her marriage began to deteriorate, while at the same time her husband's iron mill failed. In 1883 she left her husband, placed her daughters in boarding school, and went to New York City to find some means of support.

Upon being hired by an antique furniture firm in the city, Harriet Ayer proved to be a successful saleswoman, and soon opened a shop in her own home. After being commissioned by James Seymour to decorate and furnish his yacht, he promised to give her financial backing in a business endeavor. She went to Paris where she was able to convince a chemist to make up some jars of skin cream, and in 1886 she decided to manufacture the cream in New York, calling her firm Recamier Manufacturing Company. Ayer became president of the firm and commenced writing her own advertising campaign, bragging that her skin cream was used by the most beautiful women in Europe. To provide substantiation for this, she was able to secure endorsements from the Princess of Wales, along with a well known singer, actresses, and society women.

Although her product and firm were immediately successful, serious family troubles and legal suits began to undermine this success. In 1889 she brought suit against James Seymour (whose son had married her eldest daughter in 1888), charging that he was conspiring against her and trying to defraud her of her interests in Recamier. This highly publicized case was decided in her favor. At the same time, however, Ayer was sued by a French woman who charged her with having stolen the beauty cream formula. Again, the court decision was in Ayer's favor. By 1893, however, her finances were depleted and she felt unable to trust anyone. That same year her ex-husband signed an order committing her to an insane asylum without her knowledge or consent. After being detained for a year in an asylum in Bronxville, New York, she was unable to reclaim her business upon her release.

Ayer then began a lecture tour called "Fourteen Months in a Madhouse," which was very successful. She toured the nation until 1897, when she went to work for the *New York World* and wrote the first beauty column for the newspaper. This was very successful, and her newspaper work led her to investigate the conditions of working girls and got her involved in suffragette activities. Soon she was doing feature stories for the paper, which she continued for the rest of her life. She also wrote a book, *Harriet Hubbard Ayer's Book of Health and Beauty*, in 1902. Her youngest daughter, Margaret, succeeded her on the *World* and married its editor, Frank Cobb. Mrs. Ayer was an Episcopalian.

Although Recamier Manufacturing only had a shortlived success, Harriet Ayer's significance lies in her early recognition that standards of beauty could by the late 19th century be established over large geographic areas— even nationally—as her New York *World* column on beauty signified. She was also one of the earliest to move into one of the few areas—cosmetics— that was open to women, when so many other occupations and product lines were not. (Willard & Livermore, *American Women*, I, p. 40; *NCAB*, 43:452; *NAW; Who Was Who*, vol. 4; Margaret H. Ayer and Isabella Taves, *The Three Lives of Harriet Hubbard Ayer*, 1957; *New York Times*, November 26, 1903.)

AYER, JAMES COOK, DR. (May 18, 1818–July 3, 1878). Manufacturer, proprietary medicines. Born in Ledyard, Connecticut, son of Frederick Ayer Sr. and Persis Cook, and brother of Frederick Ayer,* the financier.

His father died when he was seven years old. His mother's father owned a small flannel mill, and James got his first mechanical training there. He attended school at Preston and Norwich, and was sent to live with his uncle, James Cook, in the new city of Lowell, Massachusetts. There he attended Lowell High School, after which he entered the apothecary shop of Jacob Robbins, while studying medicine at the same time. He received his medical degree from the University of Pennsylvania.

In 1841 Ayer purchased Robbin's drug store with money borrowed from his uncle. While running the store, he devised a remedy for pulmonary problems called "Ayer's Cherry Pectoral," a pioneer among patent medicines. He used extensive advertising and added sugar coated pills in 1854, extract of sarsaparilla in 1855, an ague cure in 1857, and "Ayer's Hair Vigor" in 1869. His brother, Frederick, joined him in the business in 1855. They bought a large property for manufacturing the products in Lowell in 1857, and James Ayer was the master of every process in the shop.

Ayer's patent medicine business grew to be one of the largest in the industry during the nineteenth century. By the end of the century the firm was grossing some $120,000 a year in an industry dominated by pygmies rather than giants. Along with Brandreth, the Hostetters, and, of course, Lydia Pinkham,* Ayer ran one of the most extensive medicine businesses of the time. Of even greater significance was the range of his advertising and promotion methods. In the early 1850s Ayer began publishing an almanac to extol the virtues of his Cherry Pectoral, and his *American Almanac* had a greater circulation than any other. By the end of the nineteenth century the firm was printing an average of sixteen million copies a year, reaching a peak of twenty-five million in 1889. In that year the firm's own publishing plant printed, folded, and sent to binding 100,000 almanacs a day, which were issued in 21 languages around the world. To promote his product, he also made up specially prepared boxes of Cherry Pectoral which he sent to foreign dignitaries, including the Emperor of Japan, the Sultan of Turkey, the Queen of Spain, the King of Siam, the Emperor of China, the President of Peru, and the Czar of Russia. He also sent bushels of cathartic pills for the Czar's armies.

When pressure began building for passage of the Pure Food and Drug Act (1906), Ayer's company decided (in 1905) to print on the labels of all its remedies the complete formulas in plain English, giving exact quantities. They pleaded with other proprietary drug manufacturers to follow suit, but few did. In the 1870s Ayer began investing the profits from his drug business in textile enterprises with his brother. He also built the Lowell and Andover Railroad in 1874 and was interested in mining. He bought into the Lake Superior Ship Canal and Iron Company, and acquired timber lands in Florida, where he erected saw mills. He married Josephine Miller Southwick in 1850. (**A.** *DAB.* **B.** F. W. Colbur, *History of Lowell and its Peoples*, 1920; James Harvey Young, *The Toadstool Millionaires*, 1961.)

B

BABBITT, BENJAMIN TALBOT (1809–October 20, 1889). Soap manufacturer. Born in Westmoreland, Oneida County, New York, son of Nathaniel Babbitt, a farmer and blacksmith, and Betsy Holman, who had migrated there from Connecticut. The area was a raw frontier when Benjamin Babbitt grew up, so he had little opportunity for formal education. As a youth he worked on the farm and in the blacksmith shop. At age eighteen he left the farm, agreeing to pay his father $500 annually for five years as a payment for loss of his services. He hired out in the winters as a lumberman and in the summers as a mechanic, quickly proving himself to be a mechanical genius, becoming an expert wheelwright, steamfitter, file maker, blacksmith, and general mechanic.

At age 25 he established a small machine shop in Little Falls, New York, where he worked for twelve years, making pumps, engines, farm machines, and manufacturing one of the first workable mowing machines in the country. But the mill was twice destroyed by floods, so he came to New York City in 1843. At this point he turned his hand to chemistry. He developed an original and cheaper method of making saleratus (a component of potash, much used as an ingredient in baking powders), which he put on the market, becoming a dominant figure in the manufacture of the product. He soon added a yeast, a baking powder, a soap powder, and various kinds of soap. "Babbitts Best Soap" became a household word in the mid-nineteenth century and his soap business brought him an immense fortune for the time.

He invented nearly all the machines used in his own soap factory and improved methods of putting up caustic alkali, extracting glycerin, and boiling soap. His early factory was in New York City, but was later moved to New Jersey. From 1842 to 1889 a total of 108 patents were issued to him, covering almost every conceivable field, including ordnance and armor during the Civil War. After the war he became absorbed with the steam engine and had several patents in the field.

A close friend of P. T. Barnum,* he shared his flair for advertising and promotion and was one of the first to advertise his products by giving them away during special promotions and by using theater stage curtains for advertising. He had branch houses in Philadelphia, Cincinnati, and other cities. Married to Rebecca McDuffie, he had two daughters. (**A.** *DAB;* *NCAB*, 8:12; W. B. Brown, *The Babbitt Family History*, 1912; *New York Times*, October 21, 1889. **B.** Samuel Colgate, "American Soap Industry," in Chauncey M. Depew, *One Hundred Years of American Commerce*, 1895.)

BABST, EARL D. (July 6, 1870–April 23, 1967). Corporate lawyer and executive, National Biscuit Company and American Sugar Refining. Born in Crestline, Ohio, son of Jacob Babst and Mathilde Stall. His grandfather had come to America from France in 1823. Earl Babst was educated in the schools of Crestline, Kenyon Military Academy in Gambier, Ohio, and Kenyon College. He received a Ph.B. from the University of Michigan in 1893 and a law degree there in 1894.

He began his law practice with Otto Kirchiner in Detroit, where he remained until 1902. Moving to Chicago, he became a partner of the firm of Green, Peters and Babst until 1906. The firm acted as counsel for American Radiator, American Can, and National Biscuit, among others, and Babst became involved in extensive litigation over trademarks and patents. In 1906 he went to New York City as general counsel for the National Biscuit Company and was made first vice-president of the firm. He remained there until 1915, being much involved in the development of trademark packaging, which was replacing the old bulk methods.

In 1915 he went to American Sugar Refining as president. He remained in that position until 1923, and was chief executive officer until 1937. From 1925 until his retirement in 1951, he was also chairman of the board. He continued as a director until 1955. The firm had been founded in 1887 as an amalgamation of numerous sugar refineries. When Babst took over, he began a program of rehabilitation of equipment and initiated the construction of a modern refinery at Baltimore, Maryland, which was completed in 1922. In 1919 he purchased a raw sugar plantation at Cunagua, Cuba, and also built a mill at that location. He then bought an adjoining plantation and mill in 1922. The entire complex covered 525 square miles and had 180 miles of railroad.

Just as he had been involved in trademarks and brandnames in his earlier activities, he also brought strong new identities for his sugar products. He developed the brand names Domino and Franklin, promoted advertising, uniform laws in packaging, and pushed for the expansion of the packaged food industry. He formed the Sugar Institute, serving as its first president, and during World War I represented the United States on the International Sugar Commission.

An Episcopalian, he married Alice Edwina Uhl in 1903 and had two daughters. (*NCAB*, 54:471; *New York Times*, April 25, 1967; *Who Was Who*, vol. 4.)

BACHE, JULES SEMON (November 9, 1861–March 24, 1944). Stock brokerage, Bache and Company. Born in New York City, son of Semon Bache and Elizabeth van Praag. His father was a native of Bavaria who had immigrated to the U.S. in the 1840s. Semon Bache became one of the country's leading manufacturers of quality mirrors and glass fabricators. Jules Bache was educated at Charles Institute in New York and in Frankfort,

Germany. He also engaged in extensive travel in Europe. Upon his return to the U.S. he joined his father as a sub-manager, but left in 1880 to become cashier of his uncle's New York brokerage house, Leopold Cohn and Company. He was made treasurer in 1881, a partner in 1886, and head of the firm in 1892, when it became J. S. Bache and Company.

In 1893 J. S. Bache and Company was accused of malpractice by the New York Stock Exchange, but the charge was not proven. Nevertheless, Bache sold out on the Exchange. The firm continued to prosper, however, and financed numerous large enterprises, handling the reorganization of the American Spirits Manufacturing Company in 1895, the Glucose Sugar Refining Company in 1897, the Distilling and Cattle Feeding Company (known as the "whiskey trust") in 1905, and the Cosmopolitan Fire Insurance Company in 1906. At the same time, Bache rapidly expanded into the branch brokerage business. This was done to tap the growing middle class market for stocks. By 1905 he had branch offices in Albany, Troy, Philadelphia, Rochester, Newark, Montreal, and Liverpool, England. To service these branches, he had one of the most extensive private wire systems in the U.S. By 1945 he had 37 branch houses and 800 employees.

Bache was also vice-president of the Chrysler Corporation from 1929 to 1943, president of Dome Mines from 1918 to 1943, and chairman of the board there from 1943 to his death. He foresaw and survived the 1929 crash by reducing brokers loans of some two hundred million dollars prior to the panic. When the banks closed in 1933, Bache extended currency to customers, and during World War II maintained evening office hours as an accommodation to war workers. In 1947 Bache and Company sponsored the first financial news program on television. By the 1960s, Bache and Company was the second largest stock brokerage firm in the U.S., and the largest Wall Street firm operating continually under one management. Mr. Bache was a Republican and, although of Jewish descent, became an Episcopalian. He married Florence Rosalie Scheflet in 1892 and had two daughters.

In 1945 the firm was taken over by Mr. Bache's nephew, Harold L. Bache. He had been born in New York City in 1894, the son of Leopold S. Bache, Jules Bache's brother. Harold Bache joined Bache and Company in 1914 and became a partner in 1926. (*DAB*, Supplement 3; *NCAB*, 34:349; *Current Biography*, May, 1944; *New York Times*, March 25, 1944.)

BACON, ROBERT (July 5, 1860–May 27, 1917). Banker, J. P. Morgan and Company. Born in Boston, son of William B. Bacon and Emily C. Low. His father was a merchant and shipper in the city. Robert was educated in private schools in the city and received an A.B. from Harvard in 1880. Upon graduation, he entered the banking house of Lee, Higginson and Company until 1883, when he joined E. Rollins, Morse and Brothers. He began as a clerk, and became a partner. In 1894 Bacon was made a junior partner at J. P. Morgan* and Company and Drexel and Company in Philadelphia. As a Morgan partner he was involved in three major developments: the relief of the government in the depression of 1895; the formation of U.S. Steel in 1901; and the creation of Northern Securities Company in 1903.

He was also in charge of Morgan and Company during the great Morgan-Hill* battle with Harriman* over the Northern Pacific, engineering the "corner" of Northern Pacific stock in 1901 which brought on the panic of that year. In 1902 he helped negotiate the creation of International Mercantile Marine, into which several English, German, and American transatlantic steamship lines were merged. He retired in 1903, but in 1905 was made Secretary of State by his ex-classmate, Theodore Roosevelt. He served until 1909, becoming Ambassador to France from 1909 to 1912. In 1917 he was commissioned a major in the quartermaster corps of the army, but died soon after his appointment. He was a Republican, and an Episcopalian.

He married Martha Waldron Cawdin and had four children. His eldest son, Robert Low Bacon, was a member of Congress from New York from 1923 to 1935. (**A.** *DAB; NCAB*, 14:16; *Who Was Who*, vol. 1; James Brown Scott, *Robert Bacon: Life and Letters*, 1923. **B.** Frederick Lewis Allen, *The Great Pierpont Morgan*, 1948.)

BAER, GEORGE FREDERICK (September 26, 1842–April 26, 1914). Coal operator, Reading Company and Philadelphia and Reading Railroad. Born in Somerset County, Pennsylvania, son of Major Soloman Baer and Ann Baker, both of German ancestry. He was educated at Somerset Institute and Somerset Academy, and at age thirteen became a "printer's devil" at the *Somerset Democrat* for two years. He then entered Franklin and Marshall College at Lancaster, Pennsylvania.

In 1861, he and his brother became owners of the *Somerset Democrat*, where their political policy aroused much resentment, and a mob tried to wreck their plant. In 1862 Baer organized a militia company, was elected its captain, and served for one year before returning to Somerset to study law. He was admitted to the bar in 1864. In 1868 he moved to Reading, Pennsylvania, where he set up a lucrative practice. He particularly gained wealth and notoriety by instituting several suits against the Philadelphia and Reading Railroad. He was so successful that the company hired him as their counsel.

This began an entirely new phase in Baer's life. He became a director of the company and soon formed an association with J. P. Morgan* as the latter's local representative. He helped Morgan set up his plan to unite all coal carrying railroads with terminals in New York City, and when Morgan gained control of the Reading Company in 1901, Baer was made president. Then in 1902 came the great strike, declared by the United Mine Workers, in which 147,000 workers laid down their tools. Baer refused to deal with the strikers.

Although George Baer was certainly not the first capitalist to take an uncompromising stance with striking workers, he gained nationwide notoriety with his position. He not only refused any arbitration or mediation of the dispute, but indicated he would brook no interference by any outside party, including the government. He was particularly castigated for his statement, "The rights and interests of the laboring man will be protected and cared for—not by the labor agitators, but by Christian men to whom God in his infinite wisdom has given the control of the property interests of the country and upon the successful management of which so much depends." This unleashed a storm of protest on his head, and symbolized for many at the turn of the century the very essence of the Robber Baron. But Baer refused to budge until President Theodore Roosevelt brought the two sides together and personally forced the coal companies to arbitrate.

He was president of the Reading Company, the Philadelphia and Reading Railroad, the Philadelphia and Reading Coal and Iron Company, and the Central Railroad of New Jersey. He was also a director of Bethlehem Steel, Carbon Steel, and Pennsylvania Steel companies. He was a member of the Reformed Church, and left a fortune of some $15,000,000. He married Emily Kimmel in 1866. (**A.** *DAB; NCAB*, 14:37. **B.** Matthew Josephson, *The Robber Barons*, 1934; George E. Mowry, *The Era of Theodore Roosevelt*, 1958.)

BAILEY, JAMES ANTHONY (1847–April 11, 1906). Circus operator, Barnum and Bailey Circus. Born in Detroit, Michigan, his family name was McGuinness, but he was left an orphan at age 10 and sent to live with a guardian on a farm. He was mistreated there and ran away, securing employment on a farm near Pontiac, Michigan. When the Robinson and Lake Circus visited the area, he joined up and his industry and ability allowed him to advance rapidly within the organization. In 1863 he enlisted in the army to fight in the Civil War, and at the close of hostilities re-entered the circus business.

He worked as an advance agent and became a partner of James Cooper in the firm of Cooper and Bailey. In 1876 he took the circus to Australia and then to South America. Shortly after that, he bought the Great London Circus and combined it with the Cooper Circus, making it the leader of the circus world, even larger than P. T. Barnum's.* In 1881 Barnum and Bailey combined their interests, and it became the world reknowned Barnum and Bailey Circus. After Barnum's death in 1891, James Bailey was sole proprietor, and in the same year purchased the Adam Forepaugh Circus. After that he took his circus on a tour of England, Europe, and then the entire world, remaining on tour for some eight years.

He was also co-owner with William F. Cody of the Buffalo Bill Wild West

Exhibition. Bailey had an extraordinary talent for advertising and sound business sense. He created the "Ethnological Congress" and the spectacle "Nero," and brought over Jumbo the Elephant from the Royal Zoological Society in London. In 1868 he married Ruth Louisa McCaddon of Zanesville, Ohio. They had no children. After his death the circus was sold to the Ringling* family. (*DAB; NCAB*, 24:87; *New York Times*, April 12, 1906; *Who Was Who*, vol. 1.)

BAKER, GEORGE FISHER (March 27, 1840–May 2, 1931). Banker and financier, First National Bank of New York. Born in Troy, New York, son of George Ellis Baker and Eveline Stevens. His father was a shoe merchant, state legislator, and private secretary to William H. Seward. George F. Baker was educated at Williamsburg School in Dedham, Massachusetts, and Seward University in Florida, New York. At age sixteen he became a clerk in the state banking department at Albany, New York. In 1863, in conjunction with stockbrokers in New York City, he organized the First National Bank of New York. The bank did a lucrative business in the sale of government bonds during the war, and, with the approval of national banking authorities, soon became the nation's largest underwriter of government and (to a lesser degree) corporate bonds.

George Baker was elected president of the bank in 1877, retaining that office until 1901, when he became chairman of the board. During his presidency he was involved in a large number of major corporate transactions. In 1885 he purchased the Richmond and Danville Railroad and in 1897 the Central Railroad of New Jersey. In the process he became closely allied with J. P. Morgan* and was named to the finance committee of U.S. Steel when it was organized in 1901. In addition, he served on the board of directors of some 43 banks and corporations during his career, including positions of influence in Mutual Life and New York Life Insurance. In banking he helped control the Guaranty Trust and Bankers Trust companies with the aid of Morgan interests, and also helped organize the New York Chamber of Commerce.

A Unitarian and Republican, he married Florence Tucker Baker of Louisville, Kentucky, in 1869. They had three children, one of whom, George F. Jr., succeeded him at First National Bank. George Jr. was born in New York City in 1878 and after graduating from Harvard in 1899, joined J. P. Morgan and Company. After one year there, he became assistant cashier at First National Bank of New York. He was made vice-president and director in 1906, vice-chairman of the board in 1923, and chairman from the death of his father in 1931 until his own death in 1937. He was also president of First Security Company, and the largest stockholder and director in several corporations, including U.S. Steel and A. T. & T. In 1911 he married Edith Brevoort Kane and had four children, one of whom married the banker John M. Schiff. (*DAB*, Supplement 1; *NCAB*, 23:75;

43:487; *New York Times*, May 31, 1937; *Who Was Who*, vol. 1.)

BALDWIN, MATTHEW (November 10, 1795–September 7, 1866). Locomotive manufacturer, Baldwin Locomotive. Born at Elizabethtown, New Jersey, son of William Baldwin, a carriage maker. His father died when he was four years old and his fortune was lost, so the family was raised in poverty. Matthew Baldwin did manage to receive a fair amount of education and then was apprenticed to Woolworth Brothers, jewelry manufacturers in Philadelphia. At age 24 he set up his own shop, but six years later abandoned the business, when he went into partnership with David Mason, first engaged in making engraving and bookkeeper's tools, then hydraulic presses. This was followed by the manufacture of copper rolls for printing calico from a steel matrix. Then, in 1827, he constructed a six horsepower noiseless stationary engine and began engine building.

In 1831 he exhibited a dummy locomotive and two cars, then constructed one of the first American locomotives actually used in transportation for the Philadelphia Germantown Railroad—"Old Ironsides". It was made of iron and wood, weighing six tons. Able to travel at speeds up to 28 miles per hour and draw up to 30 tons, it could run only in fair weather, and horses had to be used to pull the train on bad days. The business expanded steadily from that point on and successfully weathered several panics. In 1854, Matthew Baird became a partner until the death of Baldwin. They sold many engines to the government during the Civil War, and by 1866 had sold over 1,500 locomotives.

Baldwin Locomotive Works became the giant of the locomotive industry, and by 1870 was turning out one locomotive per day. Matthew Baldwin himself was the principal developer of locomotive technology in the 1830s, and his locomotives were sold in Britain and Europe, as well as America. The chief early figure in the development of railway locomotives, his great contribution was to lighten and stabilize engines so that they could take curves on light track.

In 1824 he helped found the Franklin Institute for the betterment of labor, and in 1826 underwent a religious conversion, becoming a sunday school superintendent, conducting a bible class for thirty-five years. In 1835 he founded a school for black children and helped support the black evangelist, Pompey Hunt. He was a member of the state constitutional convention in 1837 and served in the state legislature in 1854. A temperance man and abolitionist, he married Sarah C. Baldwin (a distant relation) in 1827 and they had one son and two daughters. (*DAB; NCAB*, 9:476; Appleton, *Cyclopedia of American Biography; Who Was Who*, vol. H.)

BALL, FRANK CLAYTON (November 24, 1857–March 19, 1943). Jar and lid manufacturer, Ball Brothers Company. Born in Greensburg, Trumbull County, Ohio, son of Lucius Styles Ball, a farmer, and Maria Polly Bingham.

At age six, his family moved to Grand Island on the Niagara River. Two years later they moved to Tonawanda, New York, and in 1868 to a small farm near Canandaigua, New York. Frank was educated in public school and Canandaigua Academy. His father died in 1878, and an uncle in Buffalo, New York, undertook to launch Frank and his older brother, Edmund Burke Ball, on a business career. In 1880, after several false starts, they began a small business manufacturing wood jacketed tin cans in which oils and varnish were shipped. The firm was called Ball Brothers Company, with Frank Ball as president.

The firm prospered through constant improvements in manufacturing, aggressive salesmanship, and an alertness in meeting demands for new products. They developed a pump for dispensing kerosene in grocery stores when it became a popular product. They then manufactured a one gallon kerosene can for family use which was replaced by the more popular glass oil jar. In 1882 Ball Brothers began producing its own glass containers and in 1885, on finding that the patent on the "Mason Improved Fruit Jar" had expired, began making glass fruit jars and caps.

In 1887 they built a new factory in Muncie, Indiana, being lured there by a free natural gas well and the offer of $5,000 in relocation expenses from the town. They converted the company into a corporation at that time, with Frank Ball as president, Edmund as vice-president and general manager, and George Ball as treasurer. The company enjoyed phenomenal growth and by the mid-1920s its output had grown to one million gross jars per year with an annual income of over ten million dollars. They also built several factories elsewhere and began making their own zinc jar caps and cardboard shipping cartons and rubber jar rings.

Even during the depression of the 1930s the firm did well, with sales and profits increasing as people turned more and more to home canning to cope with the hard times. In 1938 Ball Brothers and several others were convicted of conspiring to restrict trade in the glass container industry and steps were taken to end such operations. Frank Ball was president until his death in 1943. The family gave over seven million dollars in benefactions to Muncie and the state of Indiana, most notably two million to Indiana State Normal School, which became Ball State Teachers College in 1929.

He married Elizabeth Wolfe Brady of Muncie in 1893 and had five children. He was a Republican and a Universalist and then a Presbyterian. His business interests outside the glass jar industry included a large interest in a steamship company operating on the Great Lakes, presidency of Inter-state Automobile Company of Muncie, which manufactured a six cylinder car until taken over by General Motors in 1919, and presidency of Muncie and Western Railroad and of New Castle and Muncie Traction, and treasurer of the Muncie and Portland Traction Company. (**A.** *DAB*, Supplement 3; *NCAB*, A:202. **B.** Robert and Helen Lynd, *Middletown in Transition*, 1937, pp. 75-76.)

BARBER, OHIO COLUMBUS (April 20, 1841–February 4, 1920). Match manufacturer, Diamond Match Company. Born in Middlebury (later Akron), Ohio, one of nine children of George Barber and Eliza Smith. The elder Barber was a native of Connecticut and a cooper who started a match manufacturing plant in Akron in 1847. Young Barber was educated in area schools until age sixteen, when he joined his father as a match salesman. Traveling by wagon throughout Indiana, Michigan and Pennsylvania, he proved a natural salesman, and the business prospered. In 1862 he took over entire control of the firm from his father, and two years later organized the Barber Match Company.

After the Civil War, the match industry began to replace the old hand production methods with machines. Along with three other firms, Barber Match was at the forefront of this technological revolution in the industry. For a number of years these companies had each served their own regional market, but in the late 1870s began competing with one another for the national market. After a brief period of this competition, the four combined in 1881 to form the Diamond Match Company, controlling about 85 percent of the trade in the industry. Barber, along with E. B. Beecher and William Swift, combined the best attributes of the various machines they had independently developed to produce the first modern, continuous, automatic match machine, revolutionizing the industry. Barber was vice-president of the consolidation from 1881 to 1885 and president from 1888 to 1913. He then served as chairman of the board until his death six years later.

Barber and his partners also moved rapidly to develop a vertically integrated manufacturing and sales organization. They organized straw-board and paperboard plants to make packing boxes for their matches, and began consolidating production in large plants. In 1891 Barber laid out and developed the city of Barberton, Ohio, near Akron, and the production of some thirty match plants was soon concentrated in one large plant at this location. They also built a sales organization which was responsible for establishing and maintaining contact with wholesalers, for handling local advertising, and for coordinating the flow of products to jobbers and retailers. They established a buying organization to purchase wood paper and chlorate of potash directly from producers, and soon had their own sawing and woodworking mills in Wisconsin and New England. In the 1890s they began construction of the largest match factory in the world in Liverpool, England, which was soon followed by plants in Peru, Switzerland, Chile, and Germany.

O. C. Barber also had a variety of other business interests. He established the Diamond Rubber Company, which was later absorbed by B. F. Goodrich; was one of the founders and president of the First National Bank of Akron; and constructed the Akron and Barberton Belt Line Railway. He was married twice, in 1866 to Laura C. Brown of Akron, who died in 1894, and in 1915 to Mary F. Orr of Akron. He had one daughter. (**A.** *DAB; NCAB*, 24:169; 34:488. **B.** Alfred D. Chandler Jr., *The Visible Hand*, 1977; Herbert Manchester, *Diamond Match Company*, 1935; O. C. Barber, "The Match Industry," in C. M. Depew, *One Hundred Years of American Commerce*, 1895.)

BARD, THOMAS ROBERT (December 8, 1841–March 6, 1915). California oil producer, land developer, and politician, Union Oil Company. Born in Chambersburg, Pennsylvania, son of Robert McFarland Bard, a lawyer, and Elizabeth Little. The Bard family came to Pennsylvania in 1741 from Northern Ireland, and Thomas' father was Whig candidate for Congress from the area in 1850. The elder Bard died in 1850, when Thomas was but nine years old, leaving the family in strained but still relatively comfortable circumstances. He was educated at Chambersburg Academy, and at age seventeen began reading law in the offices of Judge George Chambers, descendent of the town's founder. His family's fortunes worsened in 1859, so Thomas took a job with a surveying party of the Huntington and Broad Top Railroad for a few months, when he became a bookkeeper in the firm of a relative (David Zeller) in Hagerstown, Maryland. The company was a freight forwarding business and by age twenty young Bard became a partner in the enterprise.

Some years later, in 1864, his boyhood friend, Frank Thomson (then superintendent of the Pennsylvania Railroad's Eastern Division and later president of the line), intervened with Col. Thomas A. Scott,* president of the line, to have Bard appointed Scott's personal representative in California. Scott had reaped enormous profits from the Pennsylvania oil boom during the Civil War, and had recently invested in oil-bearing lands in the West. Bard's general duties were to protect Scott's interests in the development of these lands, which had been purchased in association with Levi Parsons. They established the California Petroleum Company, capitalized at ten million dollars, and also set up the Philadelphia and California Petroleum Company, capitalized at one million dollars. Prospects looked very good for the new concern, but in 1865, just as Bard arrived in California, Benjamin Silliman's geologic reports were challenged by the scientific community. Nonetheless, Bard began drilling for oil in tar beds, at first having little success. Against the advice of the firm's geologists he advocated deep drilling, finally hitting a 20 barrel a day "gusher" at 550 feet in 1866. The strike was made, however, just as the bottom fell out of the oil market and eastern refineries were dumping oil on the California market. Bard had spent $200,000 of the company's money to bring in the well and now there as no market for the crude. Scott ordered him to cease all drilling and the first California oil bubble burst.

Bard and Scott then turned their attention to agricultural land development, which absorbed Bard's attention for the next twenty years and made both men very wealthy. Bard and Scott began acquiring large Spanish colonial land grants (using highly questionable tactics), subdivided the land, and sold or leased it to new settlers. Bard used a variety of promotional techniques to attract settlers from the East, aiming at the Americanization of the region. As a portent of the future, they sold the land, reserving to themselves, the oil and hydrocarbon rights, which would later be exploited by Bard's Union Oil Company. During this same period Bard began investing in land in his own right, laying the basis for his own private fortune. During the 1870s and 80s a tremendous land boom came to California which greatly boosted the two men's profits in their land ventures, and in the late 1880s Bard began to sever his connections with the Scott estate, in order to proceed unimpeded with his own business and political interests.

As he developed his land interests, Bard also began branching into a series of related ventures in Southern California. In 1871 he built a wharf in the Santa Barbara channel, then the only wharf on the California coast between Santa Cruz and San Pedro. This opened a doorway to the world for the lands and peoples of the region it served and for many years kept the area free of domination by the Southern Pacific Railroad. It figured directly in the inauguration of the sheep and swine raising industries in the area, and Bard built a large warehouse adjoining the wharf for the storage of grain. This made Bard a grain broker and speculator, and since he had a great deal more liquid capital than his competitors, he was able to make loans at lower rates of interest, thus assuring him dominance in the field. He also became a shipowner and started the sugar beet industry on his lands at La Colonia, with a processing factory at Oxnard. He subsequently became a large-scale sheep raiser in his own right.

In the early 1880s Bard began moving back into the oil business with a small concern known as Mission Transfer Company, which owned several thousand acres of land in the Ventura area, with tanks, pipelines, and a small refinery. In 1886 he organized the Sespe Oil Company to drill for oil in the Sespe Canyon, and at the same time Mission Transfer was purchased by Lyman Stewart* and Wallace Hardison, with Bard remaining as president. A short time later the Hardison and Stewart Oil Company was organized, capitalized at one million dollars, with Stewart as president. It erected a new kerosene refining plant with a capacity of 14,000 barrels a year, but the company remained in precarious financial condition. To alleviate this problem, they built a wooden oil tanker with a capacity for 6,500 barrels of oil in steel tanks, the first tanker ever built. The ship was completed in 1889, and it forced a reduction in rail rates from one dollar to thirty cents a barrel. Later that year the three men decided to consolidate Hardison and Stewart Oil, Mission Transfer, and Sespe Oil into the Union Oil Company of California. The new firm was organized in 1890, capitalized at five million dollars, with Bard as president.

Almost from the beginning Bard and Stewart (who was vice-president) were at loggerheads over company policy. From Stewart's point of view, Bard was a shortsighted profit-taker who viewed the oil business as essentially a mining operation. In Bard's view, the goal of Union Oil was to extract as much crude as possible, sell it to others to refine, and invest the profits in other operations. Bard, on the other hand, viewed Stewart as a reckless plunger and a poor manager of operations. Whatever the basis of the dispute, it was to dominate the affairs of Union Oil until Bard left the board in 1900. The new company started life with 26 producing wells that yielded over 84,000 barrels of crude in 1890, one-quarter of California's production. In the following year they engaged in more drilling, bringing in wells on Bard's land in Torrey Canyon that produced 70,000 barrels annually. In 1892 they purchased the Los Angeles Oil Company, which held 800 acres of promising oil land in the Los Angeles basin, and in the same year brought in Adams Number 28, California's biggest gusher to that date, which produced 15,000 barrels in the first year of operation. This touched off a great new oil stampede to Southern California in which thousands of shallow pits were dug, flooding the market with oil. In 1893 prices fell to twenty-five cents a barrel and the company was forced to retrench drastically.

In 1894 Bard resigned as president of Union, with Stewart taking his place after a few months of wrangling. Bard continued to play an important role in the company during the next five years, however, and continually challenged Stewart for control of the firm. The whole dispute finally came to a head in 1899. Bard had organized the United Stockholders Association in an attempt to take control of the company, but was defeated and resigned from the board in 1900. In that same year he was elected United States Senator and soon sold off his interests in Union Oil.

Bard had become intimately involved in Republican party politics in California almost from the moment of his arrival, and his land deals particularly, whether for oil or agriculture, benefited from his political involvement. He had been elected to the board of supervisors of the county in 1866, and was elected state senator in 1877. Beyond that, he played a powerful role in local and state Republican party politics, always as a member of the anti-Southern Pacific faction within the party. He was elected in 1900 to fill an unexpired term in the U.S. Senate, but proved himself a poor politician and failed at re-election in 1904. After that time he remained a power in the state central committee of the Republican party and allied himself with Hiram Johnson, who became the reform governor of California in 1910. Bard was a strong anti-temperance man and member of the Anti-Saloon League of California. A Presbyterian, he married Mary B. Gerberding, daughter of one of the founders of the San Francisco *Evening Bulletin*. They had three sons and four daughters. (**A.** *NCAB*, 12:57; *New York Times*, March 6, 1915; *Who Was Who*, vol. 1; William H. Hutchinson, *Oil, Land and Politics, the California Career of Thomas Robert Bard*, 2 vols., 1965. **B.** Frank J. Taylor and Earl M. Welty, *Black Bonanza*,

1950; H. F. Williamson and A. R. Daum, *The American Petroleum Industry*, 1959.)

BARKSDALE, HAMILTON MACFARLAND (June 30, 1861–October 18, 1918). Business executive, duPont Company. Born in Richmond, Virginia, the son of Dr. Randolph Barksdale and Elizabeth Beirre MacFarland. The family was very distinguished in the city, having been in Virginia for over a century prior to his birth. He was educated at McGuire's School in Richmond and received a degree in civil engineering from the University of Virginia in 1882. His first jobs took him to undeveloped areas in the state of Mississippi and later to Columbia, South Carolina. In 1885 he joined the engineering corps of the Baltimore and Ohio Railroad, and while engaged in railroad building near Wilmington, Delaware, Barksdale became acquainted with members of the duPont family who, under Lammot duPont* Sr., had broken away from the main company. They were working on the development of the new explosive dynamite, which the parent company at that time was obstructing. Barksdale then joined their firm, the Repauno Chemical Company, becoming secretary and then treasurer in 1893. (He had, in 1890, married Ethel duPont, the daughter of Victor duPont.*) When Repauno was taken over by Eastern Dynamite in 1893, and then absorbed by the duPont interests, Barksdale was made its general manager.

It was Barksdale who was responsible for the development of the ideas of systematic management started by Lammot duPont. He first was given the responsibility for building a new sales organization to increase the sales of dynamite, and then worked out a larger "system of management" for the entire administrative system of the company, forming a manufacturing, an engineering, and a purchasing department. In 1902 Barksdale joined the parent duPont Company, working with the three duPont cousins (Alfred,* Pierre* and, Coleman*), along with Amory Haskell, to create the same kind of administrative organization for that firm. Their first step was to consolidate manufacturing, concentrating production in a few of the larger plants. They next set up three administrative departments to coordinate, appraise, and plan the work of the plants. Following that a nationwide marketing organization was established, along with a development department for improving product and high explosives. In 1911 he became general manager of the company, but remained too involved in the day-to-day work of the firm, so he was made acting president in 1913 for one year, when he went into virtual retirement. During World War I, however, he organized the American Nitrogen Company, acting as its vice-president and president, to manufacture nitric acid for explosives. He was also a director of Empire Trust Company of New York, Washington Trust Company, Chevrolet Motors, and of General Motors for a short time.

Much of Barksdale's work as head of the high explosives department was codified in the duPont "Bible" or "how-to" manual, and he is generally recognized as one of the "fathers" of scientific management. He and his wife had four children, one of whom married F. Donaldson Brown,* a duPont and General Motors executive. (**A.** *NCAB*, 22:49. **B.** Alfred D. Chandler Jr., *Strategy and Structure*, 1962; Chandler and Stephen Salsbury, *Pierre S. duPont and the Making of the Modern Corporation*, 1971; Ernest Dale and Charles Meloy, "Hamilton MacFarland Barksdale and the duPont Contributions to Scientific Management," *Business History Review*, Summer, 1962, 127–152.)

BARNES, JULIUS HOWLAND (February 2, 1873–April 17, 1959). Grain dealer, business executive, government official, and president of the United States Chamber of Commerce. Born in Little Rock, Arkansas, son of Lucien Jerome Barnes, a banker, and Julia M. Hill. He was educated at public schools in Washington, D.C., and Duluth, Minnesota, then got a job as an office boy in the wheat brokerage house of Wardell Ames. In 1894 he became a member of the firm, and in 1910 was made president of the company. In 1914 the firm became Barnes-Ames Company, and a year later was the largest exporter of grain in the world. It operated grain elevators and grain ships, with main offices in Duluth and New York City. Barnes continued as president until 1930, and also organized Barnes-Duluth Shipbuilding during World War I. He operated the Erie and St. Lawrence Corporation, McDougall-Duluth (shipbuilding) Company, Great Lakes Grain Company, and the General Bronze Corporation. In addition, he was chairman of the Kleanflax Linen Rug Company and Pitney-Bowes Postage Meter Corporation, and publisher of the *Washington Herald*, which he owned.

During World War I he became U.S. wheat director for the federal government and president of the U.S. Food Administration Grain Corporation from 1917 to 1919. Then he was president of its successor, the U.S. Grain Corporation, until it was dissolved in 1920. From 1921 to 1924 he was president of the Chamber of Commerce of the United States, and served as its chairman of the board from 1929 to 1931. A close friend of Herbert Hoover,* Barnes during the 1920s helped spearhead much of the latter's drives for "associational activity." In 1929 he was head of the National Business Survey Conference, and in 1931 chairman of the National Business Corporation. His major disagreements with the Hoover administration were over farm and antitrust policy. After World War II he was instrumental, as president of the St. Lawrence Seaway Association, in reviving interest in the St. Lawrence Seaway Project, living to see its completion in 1959. He was also the author of some forty pamphlets on business and industry.

A member of the Congregational Church and a Republican, Barnes married Harriet Carey of Duluth in 1896. His daughter, Gertrude, married Charles O. Dinley. (**A.** *NCAB*, 53:134; *New York Times*, April 18, 1959; *Who Was Who*, vol. 3. **B.** Ellis W. Hawley, "Herbert Hoover, the Commerce

Secretariat and the Vision of the Associative State, 1921-1928," *The Journal of American History*, June, 1974, 116-140; Joan Hoff Wilson, *Herbert Hoover*, 1975.)

BARNUM, PHINEAS TAYLOR (July 5, 1810-April 7, 1891). Showman, promoter and circus owner, Barnum and Bailey Circus. Born in Bethel, Connecticut, son of Philo F. Barnum and Irena Taylor. His father was a farmer and a general store owner. P. T. Barnum had a variety of occupations until age twenty-five. He kept a store, tended bar, ran an abolitionist newspaper, did odd jobs, and sold tickets for a theater. His first break came when, in 1835, he discovered Joyce Heth, an elderly black woman reputed to be the 161 year old nurse of George Washington. He had documents to prove her sale by Washington's father in 1727 and exhibited her around the country until she died. An autopsy showed she was actually about eighty years old. Barnum then staunchly defended his good faith and received much notoriety and fame from the incident.

Barnum continued to dabble in show business with acrobatic troupes and a few wild animals. Then, in 1841, he bought both Scudder's and Peals' museums in New York City, re-opened a year later as the American Museum. The museum was filled with all sorts of ingenious hoaxes, for example, a Fiji mermaid and a bearded lady. The star attraction of the museum, however, was General Tom Thumb (Charles Sherwood Straten), a five year old dwarf who was less than two feet high and weighed sixteen pounds. He was first displayed in 1842 and attracted over one hundred thousand people in the first year. In 1844 Barnum took him on a highly publicized tour of Europe.

Barnum's greatest triumph came in 1850 when he brought Jenny Lind, the "Swedish Nightingale," to America for a concert tour. She was advertised as being paid a thousand dollars a concert, all of which she supposedly gave to charity. In 1871 Barnum opened his "Greatest Show on Earth" in Brooklyn, where he displayed countless freaks and curiosities, also taking them on tour. One of the greatest attractions was "Jumbo the Elephant," which had been purchased from the London Zoological Society. The large, gentle African elephant remained a star attraction of the show until run over by a locomotive in 1885. The first decade of the existence of Barnum's circus saw the transition from a wagon show to a railroad show. This made it possible to greatly extend the coverage of the circus to a truly national tour for the first time. In 1881 Barnum combined with James A. Bailey* to form the Barnum and Bailey Circus, which became the dominant circus organization in America.

In all his ventures Barnum was a genius in the use of advertising and promotion, and he is regarded as the first large-scale practitioner of many modern publicity techniques. He turned everything to his own fame and advantage, oftentimes even "exposing" his own hoaxes. His great discovery was not that people were easy to fool ("There's a sucker born every minute"), but that much of the public actually enjoyed being deceived. They were flattered that he would use so much ingenuity to try to trick them, and gratified when they were able to see through his hoaxes. It was Barnum who first referred to himself as the "prince of humbug." In many respects, his ability to take advantage of others was in part a product of nineteenth century laissez-faire, and in part traceable to the agrarian population he so often dealt with. His tactics were adopted by a large number of others, including not only patent medicine and lightning rod salesmen, but also many "respectable" firms. A huckster and a charlatan, Barnum touched deep-seated needs in nineteenth century American society, and the public responded by flocking to his "pseudo-events."

In the early 1860s Barnum became involved in politics, sitting in the Connecticut legislature, and later running for Congress. A major benefactor of Tufts College, he was twice married. His first marriage was in 1829 to Charity Hallett, who died in 1873. A year later he married Nancy Fish. He had no children. (**A.** *DAB; NCAB*, 3:258; *New York Times*, April 8, 1891; P. T. Barnum, *The Life of P. T. Barnum*; Charles J. Finger, *Life of Barnum*, 1924; Harvey W. Root, *The Unknown Barnum*, 1928. **B.** Daniel J. Boorstin, *The Image*, 1961.)

BARTON, BRUCE (August 5, 1886–July 5, 1967). Advertising executive, Batten, Barton, Durstine and Osborn. Born Robbins, Tennessee, son of William Eleazar Barton, a Congregational minister, and Esther Treat Bushnell. Bruce Barton grew up in Oak Park, Illinois, and was educated there. Upon graduation from Amherst College in 1907, he became editor of the *Home Herald* in Chicago and managing editor of *Housekeeper*. From 1912 to 1914 he was assistant sales manager of P. F. Collier and Son publishing house, and from 1914 to 1918 was editor of *Everyweek* magazine, published by Crowell Publications. At the end of World War I he took charge of the national publishing operations of the United War Work Campaign, which had been organized by leading welfare organizations.

In 1919, with Alexander F. Osborn and Roy F. Durstine, Barton organized the advertising agency of Barton, Durstine and Osborn, acting as president. In 1928 the firm merged with George Batten Company, becoming Batten, Barton, Durstine and Osborn, with Barton as chairman of the board. At the agency, Barton was a skilled copy writer and a prime mover in many successful advertising campaigns. He was not only responsible for helping to develop a more favorable public image for United States Steel after the Steel Strike of 1919, but also created Betty Crocker for General Mills. His agency was one of those which believed that consumers should be conditioned to fit into the consumption habits the advertising agencies had established for their clients, and they very aggressively pursued this end result.

In addition to his advertising work, Barton was renowned as an author and contributor to magazines. He wrote many articles for *Colliers, Woman's Home Companion*, and others. His most well-known and controversial work was the book, *The Man Nobody Knows* (1925), which protrayed Christ as the "World's Greatest Salesman," and a top-notch businessman who "picked up twelve men from the bottom ranks of business and forged them into an organization that conquered the world." He regarded Jesus' parables as the "most powerful advertisements of all time," and felt that the "principles of modern salesmanship on which businessmen so pride themselves, are brilliantly exemplified in Jesus' talk and work." This became the classic statement of the secularization of religion and the religiosity of business in the 1920s. In the 1930s Barton became involved in politics as a bitter opponent of the New Deal. While serving in Congress from 1937 to 1941, Franklin Roosevelt coined the term "Martin, Barton and Fish" to refer to the most strident critics of his policies. (The other two were Joseph Martin of Massachusetts and Hamilton Fish of New York.)

A Republican and member of the Congregational Church, Barton married Esther M. Randall of Oak Park in 1913. They had three children, and both of his sons entered the publishing field. (**A.** *NCAB*, C:326; *Current Biography*, February, 1961; October, 1967; *New York Times*, July 6, 1967; *Who Was Who*, vol. 4. **B.** Martin Mayer, *Madison Avenue, U.S.A.*, 1965; Joseph J. Seldin, *The Golden Fleece*, 1963; James P. Wood, *The Story of Advertising*, 1958.)

BARTON, ENOS MELANCTON (December 2, 1842–May 3, 1916). Manufacturer, Western Electric Company. Born Lorraine, New York, son of Sidney William Barton and Fannie Bliss. His father was superintendent of schools in the area. Enos Barton was educated in public and private schools, but owing to father's death, was thrown onto his own resources at an early age. He found various kinds of employment: as a telegraph messenger in Watertown, New York, as a clerk in the Watertown post office, and as a school teacher at age sixteen. In 1859 he became a telegraph operator for the New York Central Railroad at Syracuse, New York. Shortly thereafter, he was transferred to Rochester, New York, as a night operator. This enabled him to attend the University of Rochester during the day.

With the outbreak of the Civil War, Barton left the New York Central and obtained a position with Western Union Telegraph in New York City as a night operator, attending New York University during the daytime. Returning to Rochester in 1863 as a day operator, he continued there until 1868, becoming chief operator. In that year he went to Cleveland, Ohio, and with George W. Shawk, organized the firm of Shawk and Barton, manufacturers of telegraph instruments. Within one year Shawk sold out to Elisha Gray, and the firm became Gray and Barton. About the same time

General Anson Stager also became a general partner. The next year they moved the plant to Chicago, where in 1872 the three men founded the Western Electric Manufacturing Company, with a capitalization of $150,000. Stager was chosen president and Barton secretary. While Gray worked on telephone experiments, the other two devoted their attention to the manufacture and sale of telegraph apparatus.

In 1881 the company was reorganized as the Western Electric Company and licensed under the Bell patents to manufacture instruments for AT & T, which controlled the company through ownership of nine million of its fifteen million dollar capitalization. Barton was made vice-president of Western Electric in 1882 and president in 1886, remaining until 1908, when he was named chairman of the board. He retained the latter position until his death. The Western Electric Company is the oldest concern in the United States given to the manufacture of electrical materials and appliances. In addition to the Bell materials, the company also manufactured electric light apparatus for railways and various kinds of electrical appliances.

Barton was a leading spirit in the expansion of company operations. He founded additional plants in New York City, London, Paris, Berlin, and Antwerp, and arranged for the sale of Western Electric products in Canada, Japan, and Australia, as well as throughout the U.S. and Europe. He personally advocated the purchase of the great Hawthorne plant of Western Electric at Cicero, Illinois, and was the guide and teacher of many men, such as Gerard Swope* and Walter S. Gifford,* who later rose to prominence in the electric and telephone industries. When he retired as president in 1908, company sales were $52,724,000.

In 1926, when the manufacture of non-telephone equipment was separated from Western Electric Company, the new firm was named Graybar Electric Company, in honor of the old Gray and Barton partnership. He was married to Katherine Sayle Richardson, who died in 1898, and to Mary Converse Rust, whom he married in 1899. He had eight children. (**A.** *NCAB*, 30:383. **B.** Harold C. Passer, *The Electrical Manufacturers, 1875-1900*, 1957.)

BARUCH, BERNARD MANNES (August 19, 1870–June 20, 1963). Stock market operator and government official. Born in Camden, South Carolina, the son of Simon Baruch and Belle Wolfe. His father had immigrated from Prussia in 1855, and graduated seven years later from the medical college of Virginia. During the Civil War, he served three years as a field surgeon for the Confederate Army. His mother's family were Spanish-Portuguese Jews who had come to America in the 17th century and owned a large plantation in South Carolina. The Baruch family moved to New York City in 1881, where the elder Baruch became a general practitioner and professor at the college of physicians and surgeons of Columbia University.

Bernard Baruch was educated in public schools and entered the City College of New York in 1884, where he was a star athlete. He received his

B.A. in 1889, and got his first job with a firm dealing in druggists glassware. He then worked for a short time for a small banking concern until he joined the brokerage firm of A. A. Hausman and Company. He began as an office boy, in the evenings studying bookkeeping, contract law, and science.

In 1896 he was made a partner in the Hausman firm, and the following year speculated in the sugar market, earning $40,000 on a $200 speculation. With those earnings he bought himself a seat on the stock exchange. By age 30 he was a millionaire, with his principal trading in tobacco, railroads, and copper. In 1903 he left Hausman, setting up his own office in the field of industrial development. He invested in Texas Gulf sulphur, Utah copper, Intercontinental Rubber Company, and the Alaska Juneau Gold Mining Company. His first effort gave the United States continued control of the world sulphur market, the second doubled the world output of copper, the third meant that rubber could be made from the grayule plant, and the fourth, that gold could profitably be extracted from low-grade ore.

Increasingly, however, he found himself being drawn toward government and politics. He was a Democrat, a liberal contributor to party coffers, and a major supporter of Woodrow Wilson in 1916. He then became a member of the advisory commission to the Council of Defense and sold all his various holdings. In 1918 he was made chairman of the War Industries Board, where he drew up the master plan for the industrial mobilization of materials on a priorities system. Then, in 1919, he went to Versailles as a member of the Supreme Economic Council and of the Conference for Capital and Labor.

After the war he occupied himself with the problems of American agriculture, and in 1922 was appointed a member of President Harding's Agricultural Conference, also serving as advisor to the American Farm Bureau Federation and the U.S. Grain Growers Corporation. Although Baruch was a proponent of disarmament after World War I, supporting the League of Nations and a number of disarmament conferences and proposals, the War Industries Board was to come under attack from a number of quarters for "war profiteering." The first investigation was launched in 1918 by the Federal Trade Commission, which published a brief report entitled "Profiteering," containing evidence of "inordinate greed and barefaced fraud," deceptive accounting practices, artificial price inflation, and huge profits taken by basic industries such as steel, oil, and gas. One phenomenon exposed was the practice of paying large salaries and bonuses to corporate officers of war suppliers. This instilled a strong nation-wide sentiment against "war profiteering," which found its way into both the Democratic and Republican party platforms in 1924 and the War Policies Commission Hearings of 1931. This criticism reached its peak in 1934 with the establishment of the Nye Committee in the United States Senate, which lasted about three years. It provided the first systematic study of the structure of the munitions industry and its relation to the military and the international sale of arms. Investigating World War I contracts, it showed that profiteering, especially in Navy contracts, was much more extensive than was generally known. Although Baruch personally escaped censure by the committee, it did cast a cloud over the activities of the War Industries Board.

During the 1930s Baruch became a member of President Roosevelt's "Brains Trust," generally representing the views of conservative, business-oriented Democrats to the president. In the early years he pushed hard for a balanced budget and drastic cuts in spending and opposed Roosevelt's renunciation of the gold standard. In later years he also campaigned against the undistributed profits tax. With the outbreak of World War II, Baruch's experience during the First World War was put to good use. He became a key adviser to the administration, and to Donald Nelson,* head of the War Production Board, and in 1943 was nearly appointed head of the board himself. In 1942 Roosevelt appointed him to head the Rubber Committee to investigate the rubber shortage. His committee proposed the expansion of synthetic rubber output largely on the basis of petroleum, and called for nation-wide gasoline rationing. Baruch also participated in the planning for reconversion at the end of the war, calling for rapid conversion to a peacetime economy.

In 1946 President Truman appointed Baruch as United States representative to the United Nations Atomic Energy Commission, with instructions to implement the Acheson-Lilienthal* report on atomic energy. This report had proposed an ingenious plan for the control of atomic energy which minimized international inspection and did not depend upon sanctions or punishment for violation, and would have barred the Soviets from working on the atomic bomb. The report proposed an international Atomic Development Authority, under the United Nations, that would take over ownership or lease of raw materials needed for atomic energy, operate plants that processed materials for weapons, direct research, and license nuclear activities. Baruch, however, made two critical changes in the report when he presented it to the United Nations. First, he favored appropriate punishment for any nation that violated the control agreement, and, second, proposed that no member nation could veto such punishment. This guaranteed the enmity of the Soviet Union to the proposal, and a hopeless impasse was created.

Jewish and a Democrat, Baruch married Annie Griffen in 1897, and they had two children. (**A.** *NCAB*, A:57; *Current Biography*, August, 1941; July, 1950; September, 1965; *Biographical Encyclopedia of American Jews; New York Times*, June 21, 1965; *Who Was Who*, vol. 4; Bernard Baruch, *Bernard Baruch: The Public Years*, 1960; Hordan Schwartz, *The Speculator*, 1981. **B.** Robert D. Cuff, *The War Industries Board*, 1973; Robert J. Donavan, *Conflict and Crisis*, 1977; Richard E. Kaufman, *The War Profiteers*, 1970; William E. Leuchtenberg, *Franklin Roosevelt and the*

New Deal, 1963; Richard Polenberg, *War and Society*, 1972.)

BATTERSON, JAMES GOODWIN (February 23, 1823–September 18, 1901). Granite manufacturer and insurance executive, Travelers Insurance Company. Born in Wintonbury (later Bloomfield), Connecticut, son of Simon Seeley Batterson and Melissa Roberts. He spent his early years in New Preston, Connecticut, and was educated at a country school and for a short time at an academy. He then went to Ithaca, New York, where he served a three year apprenticeship in a printing shop. Subsequently he was associated in business with his father, who was a tombstone cutter in Litchfield, Connecticut. After reading law for a year, he moved the business to Hartford, Connecticut, and widened the scope of operations to include contract work for residences, office buildings, and public structures. By 1875 the business had grown so large that it was reorganized as a joint-stock company—The New England Granite Works. He introduced many labor saving apparatus and invented a turning lathe for cutting and polishing stone columns. His firm supplied the marble for the Soldiers Memorial at Gettysburg, Pennsylvania, the State Capitol in Connecticut, and the granite for the Library of Congress.

In 1863 he founded the Travelers Insurance Company, becoming a pioneer of accident insurance in the United States. Deriving his basic ideas for the firm's operation by studying English methods for insurance against railroad accidents, his venture was at first opposed and ridiculed by the establishment in the insurance industry. But within two years seventy other companies had arisen to compete with him. All of these failed, and the Travelers charter was soon amended to permit it to do business in general accident and life insurance, and subsequently to take on liability insurance also.

The firm succeeded largely because of Batterson's incessant labors and his stringent insistence on the severest economies from the time of its founding in an upstairs room furnished solely with an old table, a pine desk, and a few chairs. He remained the creative and controlling force behind the company until his death. (*DAB; NCAB*, 6:10.)

BAUSCH, EDWARD (September 26, 1854–July 30, 1944). Optical manufacturer, Bausch and Lomb Company. Born in Rochester, New York, the son of John Jacob Bausch and Barbara Zimmerman. His father had immigrated from Wurtenberg, Germany, in 1849 and founded an optical shop in Rochester in 1853. In 1866, with Henry Lomb as a partner, he formed the Vulcanite Optical Instrument Company, acquiring an exclusive franchise to make optical instruments from hard rubber. Edward Bausch was educated at Rochester Realschule and Rochester High School. After school he worked in his father's shop. He studied engineering at Cornell University from 1871 to 1874, when he returned to assist in the layout of the new factory of Bausch and Lomb Optical Company.

He focused his attention on the design and production of the company's first microscopes, pushing hard to produce quality products at moderate prices. He was able to get the enthusiatic endorsement of Dr. Oliver Wendell Holmes for his microscopes and secured a franchise to manufacture optical instruments designed by Robert B. Tolles and Alvan A. Clark, the leading lens makers in the country. He then struck a similar deal with Charles A. Spencer, America's pioneer microscopist, whose son joined the company. In 1882 Bausch secured his first patent on a Trichnoscope, a microscope designed for use in detecting contaminated meat.

Later his interests began to branch into photography, and he assumed charge of the production of photographic lenses, working in collaboration with George Eastman.* He supplied the lens for the first Kodak in 1888, and in 1891 he patented the iris diaphragm shutter. Until 1912 his firm was the chief supplier for Kodak. In 1888 Bausch obtained a working agreement with the Zeiss Optical Company in Europe, giving him an exclusive franchise on their American markets.

The other Bausch brothers, Henry, Jack, and William, were also with the firm from the early stages, with William handling labor relations and directing the optical glass plant which began operation in 1915. For more than one-half century Edward Bausch was the firm's responsible head, beginning as vice-president in 1899, becoming president upon the death of his father in 1926, then chairman of the board from 1935 until his death. Although he explored new fields of development and took out several patents, Edward Baush's main contribution was in industrial management rather than technological expertise. He married Matilda G. Morrell of Syracuse in 1878. They had no children. (*DAB*, Supplement 3; *NCAB*, 23:343; *Current Biography*, September, 1944; *New York Times*, July 31, 1944; *Who Was Who*, vols. 1 and 2.)

BAYARD, WILLIAM (1761–September 18, 1826). Early merchant and land speculator. Born in Greenwich Village, which at that time lay outside the city of New York, son of Col. William Bayard and Catharine McEvans, of Huguenot ancestry. His father was a leading colonial merchant in New York and an extensive landowner who owned all of the land in the city of Hoboken, New Jersey. An outspoken Tory during the Revolutionary War, he raised a loyalist regiment, and at the end of the war lost his property to confiscation. In 1783 he took his family to England, except for young William, who had just married Elizabeth Cornell, daughter of Samuel Cornell.

In 1786 Bayard formed a partnership with Herman LeRoy in a mercantile firm. For over forty years they were the leading commercial firm in New York City. A cousin, James McEvans, was also later taken into partnership. During the War of 1812, they owned a number of successful privateers, and at end of the war began trading extensively with Europe and the East and West Indies. By 1822, they had several ships trading along the South American coast, taking advantage of the revolutions in the area. They also engaged in extensive land speculation in Genesee County, New York, founding the town of LeRoy.

Bayard was president of the Bank of America, of the Chamber of Commerce of the State of New York, and of Morris Coal Company. He was also chairman of a group of merchants in Philadelphia in 1824 who met to protest tariff increases. (*DAB; NCAB*, 1:498.)

BEATY, AMOS LEONIDAS (September 1, 1870–April 27, 1939). Oil company executive and trade association official; Texaco, Phillips Petroleum, and the American Petroleum Institute. Born in Red River County, Texas, son of William Alexander Beaty, a farmer, and Annie Eleanor Rogers. Amos Beaty was educated at a rural school in Coleman Springs, Texas, and at an academy in Fannin County, Texas. Then he read law in the office of Chambers and Doak in Clarksville, Texas, and at age twenty-one was admitted to the bar. He became a junior partner in Wilkins and Beaty in Sherman, Texas, where he handled several important cases in the oil industry (including the important *Higgins Oil and Fuel Company et al. v. Snow et al.*) which marked his rapid rise. By 1906 he was president of the Texas Bar Association. A year after he became the attorney for the Texas Company (Texaco), headed by Joseph S. Cullinan.* Continuing his rapid ascendence, he was elected general counsel, director, and member of the executive committee in 1913, and moved to the general headquarters in New York City. He was able to secure new laws in 1915 and 1917 which broadened the company's scope of operation and smoothed the way for their entry into the Oklahoma oil fields.

In 1920 he was elected president of the parent company, where he served for six years. During this period he concentrated on the expansion of gasoline production and marketing outlets. He successfully defended his company in a federal suit for unlawful combination in restraint of trade growing out of the pooling of certain oil patents. Named chairman of the board in 1926, he resigned over a disagreement about a year later. He then returned to the practice of law until 1929 when he was made chairman of the board of Transcontinental Oil Company. Then, in 1931, he was named a member of the executive committee of Phillips Petroleum, where he remained for a few years.

Increasingly, however, his interests began to shift towards trade association activities. He had been active in the American Petroleum Institute since its organization, and in 1925 headed a committee to cooperate with the Oil Conservation Board to eliminate waste. While with the association he developed the idea that the only desirable legislation would be to regulate drilling and storage practices and permit agreements between operators to suspend competitive drilling for given periods. He became treasurer of the organization for five years and then was chosen president on a full-time salary. As such he became the unofficial czar of the industry. His major problem during this period was massive overproduction of oil. He tried to cut output to fit demand, but became convinced that voluntary action was insufficient and came out in favor of limited government control. He advocated this policy fearlessly, to the consternation of many oilmen, so he was not re-elected as president.

He also played an active role in formulating the NRA code for the industry, and in 1933 was appointed to the petroleum planning and coordinating committee. He was named chairman of the main committee in 1934. He developed the "Quotas of Commerce" theory which held that government should limit production by denying admission of petroleum or its products in excess of need into the channels of interstate commerce. He resigned at the end of that year to spend full-time as counsel for Phillips Petroleum. Later, he organized the Amos L. Beaty Oil Company, of which he was president until he died. He was a Methodist and Democrat and was married twice. He married Swan Donoho in 1893, and after she died in 1930, he married Martha Wilhelmina McNamara. He had no children. (**A.** *DAB*, Supplement 3. **B.** Harold Williamson et al., *The American Petroleum Industry: The Age of Energy, 1899–1959*, 1963.)

BECHTEL, STEPHEN DAVISON (September 24, 1900–   ). Engineering and construction, Bechtel Corporation. Born in Aurora, Indiana, son of William A. Bechtel and Clara West. He was raised and educated in Oakland, California. During World War I he was with the Army Corps of Engineers in France and after the war enrolled at the University of California, Berkeley, to study engineering. But he left in 1919 to join his father's construction company, W. A. Bechtel Corporation, which was one of the largest firms in the West (worth $20,000,000). He was made vice-president of the company in 1925 and president in 1936.

In 1931 the company had helped to build Hoover Dam, and in 1934–1935 built the San Francisco–Oakland Bay Bridge. In 1937 Stephen, with a school friend, John A. McCone, also formed the Bechtel-McCone Corporation, which was engaged in designing petroleum refineries and chemical plants. During World War II the company geared up to meet wartime needs. They went into the shipbuilding industry, with a shipyard at Sausalito, where they built thirty-four Liberty Ships and twenty-two tankers. They also helped form the California Shipbuilding Corporation and the Marineship Corporation. These companies built 960 freighters and 90 tankers. In 1943 McCone-Bechtel built the Birmingham (Alabama) Aircraft Modification Center and operated it on behalf of the U.S. Army Air Force, modifying 5,710 planes, and manufacturing 600 sets of B-24 wings, along with 5,600 quarter-ton Army trucks.

After the war, they formed Bechtel Brothers, McCone, but Bechtel was not intimately involved in the management of that concern. In 1946 he formed the Bechtel Corporation to consolidate his domestic activities in engineering design and construction. He has been president of the firm ever since. In the 1950s they built the oil pipeline across the Canadian Rockies, and since 1944 the company has been very active in the Middle East. They constructed the Saudi Arabian portion of the pipeline and built one of the world's largest oil refineries at Aden in 1952.

They also began to move increasingly into the field of conventional and nuclear power plants. They built a huge electric power plant at Joppa, Illinois, along with other plants in Korea in the late 1950s. In the 1960s and 70s they dominated the construction of nuclear power plants in the United States, and were a member of the Nuclear Power Group formed to build nuclear reactors. Stephen Bechtel has been a member of the advisory commission to the U.S. Department of Commerce, and a director of Continental Can, U.S. Lines Company, J. P. Morgan and Company, and Industrial Indemnity Company. A Methodist, he married Laura Adaline Piant in 1923. They had two children, and his son, Stephen Jr., became a vice-president of Bechtel Corporation. (*NCAB*, H:114; *Current Biography*, April, 1957; *Who's Who in America*, 1978–79.)

BEDFORD, EDWARD THOMAS (February 19, 1849–May 21, 1931). Oil refiner and corn products refiner, Standard Oil Company and Corn Products Refining Company. Born in Brooklyn, New York, son of Frederick Thomas Bedford and Mary Ann Elizabeth Pace. His father had immigrated from England in 1848 and settled in Brooklyn, becoming an artist and designer. Edward was educated in the public schools of Brooklyn and Westport, Connecticut, after the family moved there. He began his business career as a salesman for Charles Pratt and Company, New York oil merchants. He then became manager of Chesebrough's* vaseline factory for a time until he joined the firm of Boyd and Thompson. In 1872 he became a junior partner with R. J. Thompson, Charles Pratt* and Henry H. Rogers* in an oil firm. In 1880 it was incorporated as Thompson and Bedford Company, becoming the eastern selling agents for Standard Oil Company.

In 1890 he sold his holdings to Standard Oil, becoming a divisional president and later director of the company. He continued as a director and member of the executive committee of Standard Oil until he resigned in 1906. At the same time, he began to develop other business interests. During the 1890s in Europe, he formed Bedford Petroleum Company in Paris, Thompson and Bedford Company in London as a department of the Anglo-American Oil Company, and the Colonial Oil Company in South Africa and South America.

In 1901, with William H. Nichols, president of General Chemical Company, he organized the New York Glucose Company, serving as its president, with a factory at Edgewater, New Jersey. In 1902 Corn Products Company was formed as a consolidation of several competing firms, and in 1906 was joined with New York Glucose as Corn Products Refining Company. Bedford became president of the new consolidation and resigned his position at Standard Oil to devote full time to the new venture. He erected a large new plant at Argo, Illinois. The highly modernized plant maximized usage of corn. From the germ of the kernel they manufactured several forms of oil, including "Mazola." The hulls produced starch, and the remainder became cattle feed. From the starches they produced cornstarch for cooking, laundry starch, and crystal starch for finishing cloth and paper. They also manufactured several forms of sugar, including dextrose and cerelose, and a grain syrup called "Karo."

Bedford was responsible for instituting the packaging era in the industry, and inaugurated intricate machinery for packing and wrapping the ingredients for delivery to the retail consumer. The firm was immensely successful, reaping profits of six million dollars ten years after its founding. He was married in 1871 to Mary Ann Dingee of Bronxville, New York. They had five children. (**A.** *NCAB*, 22:67. **B.** R. W. Hidy and M. E. Hidy, *A History of Standard Oil Company (New Jersey)*, 1955.)

BEECH, OLIVE ANN MELLOR (September 25, 1903–   ). Aircraft manufacturer, Beech Aircraft Corporation. Born in Waverly, Kansas, daughter of Frank B. Mellor and Suzannah Miller. She grew up in a farming community and was educated in the public schools of Paola, Kansas. She then went to business college in Wichita where she studied stenography and bookkeeping. Her first job was as general office assistant in charge of bookkeeping for the Stanley Electric Company in Augusta, Kansas. Then in 1925 she became secretary and bookkeeper for Travel Air Manufacturing Company in Wichita. After a time she was promoted to office manager and secretary to the president, Walter G. Beech, who had founded the firm in 1925.

She and Beech were married in 1930, and in the same year Travel Air merged with Curtiss-Wright Corporation. Travel Air's manufacturing facilities were moved to St. Louis, Missouri, with the head office in New York City. Dissatisfied with these arrangements, Walter Beech resigned from Curtiss-Wright and returned to Wichita. With his wife's assistance, he formed the Beech Aircraft Corporation in 1932. Mrs. Beech was named secretary-treasurer, and in 1936 became a member of the board of directors. Within a short time the company prospered and dominated the market of privately owned and commercial small planes.

During World War II the company manufactured trainers and other airships for the government, also building parts for bombers and other materials. Because of her husband's lengthy illness, Mrs. Beech took over management of the firm during the war. After his death in 1950 she became president of the concern. Upon taking full control, Mrs. Beech turned increasingly to diversified manufacturing—producing corn harvesters, cotton pickers, washing machines, and so forth. During the Korean Conflict, the company again furnished planes to the government and also had large sales abroad for the first time. They continued to manufacture parts for jet aircraft, including window canopies, rudders and stabilizers, and external fuel tanks.

Mrs. Beech is very prominent in the affairs of her home city, serving as director of the Union National Bank, member of the local Chamber of Commerce, and in other activities. She is a Methodist and has two daughters. (**A.** *Current Biography*, June, 1956; *NCAB*, 39:462; G:484. **B.** John B. Rae, *Climb to Greatness: The American Aircraft Industry, 1920-1960*, 1968; G. R. Simonson, *The History of the American Aircraft Industry*, 1968.)

BEHN, SOSTHENES (January 30, 1882–June 6, 1957) and **Hernand Behn** (February 19, 1880–October 7, 1933). Communications executives, International Telephone and Telegraph. They were born at St. Thomas, Virgin Islands, sons of William Behn and Louise Monsanto. Their father was in the import-export business and they were educated in the Virgin Islands, in Corsica, and at St. Barbe College in Paris, France.

After finishing school, Hernand worked for the French Cable Company for a short time and in 1900 went to Puerto Rico to join his uncle in the operation of a sugar plantation. In 1906, he and his brother Sosthenes became partners in Behn Brothers, a brokerage enterprise in Puerto Rico. Prior to this, Sosthenes had gone to the United States in 1898, settling in New York City. He worked for International Express Company until the company's office was closed after the Spanish American War, when he joined Morton Trust Company in New York as a clerk. He was later promoted to foreign exchange manager, before leaving in 1906 to join his brother in Puerto Rico.

In its early years, Behn Brothers dealt largely in extending credit on the sugar crops. As a consequence of a crop failure in 1914, Behn Brothers acquired control of the Puerto Rican Telephone Company, which had been put up as security for a loan on crops. The two brothers decided to make an attempt to maintain the severely crippled telephone company, and after a few years of careful management, the telephone system was markedly improved. The record of this work allowed them to approach the operators of the Cuban Telephone Company in Havana, proposing a merger. This was coupled with the desire to ultimately link the two island telephone companies, not only with each other, but by cable to the U.S. mainland. At the same time they opened negotiations with AT & T for a joint project in laying the cable from Key West, Florida, to Havana, Cuba. The project was held up by the war, but in 1919 they began laying cable. In 1920 the Behns organized the International Telephone and Telegraph Company in order to raise the capital needed for their share in the expense of laying the cable and for further expansion in the field of communications. At that time their holdings included Puerto Rican Telephone, a one-half interest in Cuban Telephone, and a separate enterprise, Cuban-American Telephone and Telegraph Company.

Hernand Behn was named president and Sosthenes Behn chairman of the firm. During the 1920s the company's assets grew from $38,000,000 to $535,000,000 and included a network of cable and local telephone systems around the world, in more than thirty countries. As early as 1922, ITT entered the radio industry through the acquisition of radio companies in Cuba and Puerto Rico. In 1925, International Western Electric, a subsidiary of AT & T, was purchased to form the nucleus of their construction and maintenance operations. Then, in 1928, the firm's operations in international cables were strengthened by the acquisition of control of the Mackey Company, which included the Postal Telegraph System. This provided a system of cable and radio communications among countries in North and South America, Europe, and Asia. One of the most important projects undertaken by the Behns during the 1920s was the creation and operation of a general telephone service in Spain.

The economic and political crises of the 1930s threatened ITT with substantial losses. The National Telephone Company of Spain was under attack during the Spanish Civil War, and was sold at the end of World War II to the government of Spain for $88,000,000. Meanwhile, another telephone system, that of Romania, was sold to the National Bank of that country just a few days prior to its occupation by the Germans in 1940. Contributing to ITT's difficulties during those years was the death of Hernand Behn in 1933. Besides serving as president of ITT, he was also chairman of the board of International Marine Company, president of the Radio Corporation of Cuba, the South American branch of ITT, the Cuban Telephone Company, and the Cuban-American Telephone Company. He had also been vice-president of the Spanish National Telephone Company, vice-chairman of International Standard Electric, Mexican Telephone and Telegraph, Puerto Rican Telephone Company, International Communications Laboratory, and International Telephone and Telegraph Laboratories Incorporated. In 1930 he had set up the Vatican City Telephone system.

After that time, Sosthenes Behn continued to run ITT by himself. It was he who brought the far-flung holdings of the firm closer to the United States during the 1930s and he saw to it that more than one-half of its business was being conducted in North and South America by 1940. Most of the balance was in the British Empire. This was accomplished by the expansion of manufacturing and research facilities in the U.S. and England. He also devised a financial formula by which ITT was able to weather the severe losses of the depression. Since the credit rating of the parent company was low, it was refinanced through the credit of its foreign subsidiaries. The foreign company paid its indebtedness to ITT by floating a local bond issue. In 1930, after many debts had been cleared by various security and title transfers, the Export-Import Bank underwrote $10,000,000 of a $15,000,000 loan, and ITT was able to pay off all its bank loans. After the war, Behn forestalled another threat of confiscation by disposing of the corporation's telephone interests in Argentina to Juan Peron for $95,000,000.

Behn's management of ITT was challenged in 1947 by a group of stockholders headed by C. J. Ryan, who charged him and his board of directors with having received nearly four million dollars in salaries and fees over nine years while the stockholders had received nothing. But Behn prevailed and Ryan and his associates became members of the board. At the time of his retirement a few years later, ITT employed, through one hundred subsidiaries around the world, some 40,000 persons and was doing an annual business in excess of $500,000,000. Behn also served as president of the Havana Docks Corporation and Port of Havana Docks Company and was a director of National City Bank of New York and Capehart-Farnsworth Corporation.

Both the Behn brothers were Roman Catholics, and Sosthenes was a Republican, having become a citizen of the U.S. in 1927. Hernand married Helen Rae of Jersey City, New Jersey, in 1908, and had four children. Sosthenes married Margaret Dunlop of Philadelphia and had three children. (**A.** *DAB, NCAB*, 53:7; *Current Biography*, 1947. **B.** Anthony Sampson, *The Sovereign State of I. T.T.*, 1973.)

BELL, JAMES STROUD (June 30, 1847–April 5, 1915). Merchant miller, Washburn, Crosby Milling Company. Born in Philadelphia, son of Samuel Bell and Elizabeth Faust. His father owned a milling and flour brokerage establishment in the city, and his family had been millers in England and the United States for five generations. He was educated in public schools of Philadelphia, joining his father's business at age sixteen. Five years later he became a partner in the firm, where he remained for twenty years. The company acted as a sales agent for Washburn, Crosby and Company flour mills in Minneapolis.

In 1888 the milling industry went through critical times. Speculation had forced up the price of flour beyond an export basis and millers faced the necessity of making an intensive cultivation of domestic markets. At this juncture Bell was asked to become head of Washburn and Crosby, which was reorganized as Washburn, Martin and Company. He became president a year later, becoming a "merchant miller." He proved to be a great innovator in the milling business. Like National Biscuit Company, he turned to packaging, brandnames, and advertising of his products on a national basis. He helped develop the name Gold Medal for the company's flour, and during the 1890s created selling and buying networks as part of a vigorous program of vertical integration. In 1899 the mills formerly leased by the company were purchased and a branch mill was established in Buffalo, New York, in 1903. Later other branches were established at Louisville, Kentucky, Great Falls, Montana, and Kalispill, Montana. When he took over the concern, it was producing 8,000 barrels per day. At the time of his death, it was producing 27,700 barrels. He was also vice-president of Minneapolis Trust Company.

He was married twice: in 1873 to Sallie Montgomery Ford of Philadelphia, and in 1912 to Mabel Sargent of Boston. He had one child, James Ford Bell of Philadelphia. He was a Presbyterian and a Republican. (**A.** *DAB; NCAB*, 15:41; *New York Times*, April 8, 1915; *Who Was Who*, vol. 1. **B.** Alfred D. Chandler Jr., *The Visible Hand*, 1977; James Gray, *The Story of General Mills*; John Stork and Walter D. Teague, *Flour for Man's Bread*, 1952.)

BELL, WILLIAM BROWN (February 16, 1879–December 20, 1950). Manufacturing chemist, American Cyanamid Company. Born Stroudsburg, Pennsylvania, son of Thomas Alsop Bell, manufacturer of china, and Elizabeth Dunn. William Bell was educated in public schools, received a B.A. from Haverford in 1900, an M.A. in 1901, and a law degree from Columbia University in 1903. After being admitted to the New York bar, he joined the New York City firm of Guthrie, Cravath, Henderson and de Gersdorff, but practiced only a brief time. From 1905 to 1915 he was in newspaper work in Atlantic City, New Jersey, and then managed Pocono Lake Preserve in Pennsylvania. In 1917 he became associated with Air Nitrates Corporation of New York, and during World War I helped construct a hydroelectric nitrogen plant at Muscle Shoals, Alabama.

In 1922 he was elected president of American Cyanamid Company, to succeed Frank S. Washburn, who had been its founder in 1907. Bell remained president and chairman of the board until he died. During his tenure he developed the company into one of the nation's largest chemical companies, manufacturing over 5,000 products and becoming the fifth largest producer of chemicals in the U.S.

American Cyanamid had been formed originally to produce fertilizer from atmospheric nitrogen. When Bell took over, he began a six year program of diversification. During this time he developed new processes for the commercial production of prussiate of soda, dycyandiamide, guanidine rubber accelerators, and Alklyd type coating resins. With the completion of this phase, he began to acquire new companies in 1929. By 1936 he had achieved this purpose and turned to the intensification of research. He established central laboratories in Stamford, Connecticut, where they developed processes for the commercial production of melamine resins, which were used in making work surfaces impervious to scratches and stains. They also developed Plastic Laminate in 1942. During the 1940s and 50s Bell also expanded American Cyanamid's activities in drug research and production.

He was president of the Manufacturing Chemists Association and of the Chemical Alliance, and a director of the National Association of Manufacturers. A Quaker and a Republican, he was chairman of the Republican National Finance Committee in 1936. He was married twice: in 1903 to Susan K. Alsop of Pennsylvania, and in 1950 to Marion Walters. He had one daughter. (**A.** *NCAB*, 46:45; E. L. Fisch, *Lawyers in Industry*. **B.** William Haynes, *American Chemical Industry—A History*, 5 vols., 1954.)

BELMONT, AUGUST (December 2, 1816–November 24, 1890). Financier, August Belmont and Company. Born in Prussia, son of a wealthy Jewish landed proprietor, Simon Belmont, and Fredericka Elsoos. He was educated in the local schools in Prussia and at age fourteen got his start in the Frankfort banking house of Rothschild Brothers by sweeping floors. After three years he was sent to the branch office at Naples as a supervisor, where he carried on a series of successful negotiations with the Papal Court. He then went to Havana, Cuba, and while there, decided to go into business on his own account in New York City in 1837. He rented a small office on Wall Street and established August Belmont and Company, the U.S. agency for the Rothschilds. Within four years he was one of the leading bankers in the country.

During the 1840s he joined the Democratic party and became intimately involved in politics. In 1844 he was appointed counsel general for Austria, serving until 1850, when he resigned over the treatment of Louis Kossuth. Then, in 1853, he was appointed minister to the Netherlands, serving until 1857. Although he had opposed Lincoln in 1860, he supported the Union during the Civil War, and helped persuade England not to back the Confederacy. He retired from active political life in 1872. His political involvements were not unconnected with his banking interests, since he had channeled great amounts of Rothschild funds into the United States Treasury, in return for government securities. Increasingly, however, his sons became the active business heads of the firm in the late nineteenth century.

August Belmont was married in 1849 to Caroline Slidell Perry, the daughter of Commodore Matthew C. Perry. He had three sons and one daughter. His eldest son, Perry, graduated from Harvard in 1872 and then studied law. In 1881 he was elected as a Democrat to Congress, serving four terms. The second son, August Jr., also graduated from Harvard in 1875, but entered his father's banking house, taking full control of the firm in 1890. He died in 1924. He helped to develop transit facilities in New York and was a director or trustee of some thirty companies. He created the Rapid Transit Subway Construction Company in 1900 to build the subway, which became Interborough Rapid Transit in 1902. He also financed the Cape Cod Canal in 1914. He was a Democrat. His son, August III, was also a banker. August Belmont IV, great-grandson of August Belmont, was elected president of Dillon, Read and Company in 1962, and was an innovator in developing new financing methods and techniques. He became particularly noted as an innovator in revenue bonds for financing highway and hydroelectric projects. Unlike his forebears, he was a Republican and an Episcopalian. (*DAB; NCAB*, 11:499; 37:25; K:168; *New York Times*, November 25, 1890; March 30, 1919; *Who Was Who*, vol. 1; Irving Katz, *August Belmont: A Political Biography*, 1968.)

BENEDICT, HENRY H. (October 9, 1844–June 12, 1935). Typewriter manufacturer, Remington Typewriter. Born in German Flats, Herkimer County, New York, son of Micaiah Benedict and Catharine Harper. He graduated from Hamilton College in 1869 and began his business career with Remington Arms Company in Ilion, New York. Soon after joining the firm he urged Philo Remington* to begin the manufacture of typewriters. In 1882 Benedict and Clarence W. Seamans* invited William O. Wychoff to join them and the firm of Wychoff, Seamans and Benedict was organized. They established their headquarters in New York City to sell the new machine known as the Remington Typewriter. Four years later the selling firm purchased the entire Remington typewriter plant at Ilion, and thereafter manufactured as well as sold the typewriter.

Benedict served as supervisor of the foreign department of the firm, establishing agencies in all parts of the civilized world. Upon incorporation of the company in 1895, Benedict became president, also serving as first president of the firm's successor, the Remington Typewriter Company, from 1902 to 1913. At that time he retired from the business to devote himself to collecting art.

He was a Presbyterian and president of the Herkimer County Bible Society. He was married twice: to Marie Nellis of Ft. Plain, New York, who died in 1915; and to Josephine Katharine Magill Geddes of Hamilton, Ontario, Canada. He had two children. (**A.** *NCAB*, A:146; *Who Was Who*, vol. 1. **B.** Bruce Bliven, *The Wonderful Writing Machine*, 1965; Richard N. Current, *The Typewriter and the Men Who Made It*, 1954; Alden Hatch, *Remington Arms*, 1956.)

BENNETT, JAMES GORDON (1785–June 1, 1872). Newspaper publisher, *New York Herald*. Born Keith, Banffshire, Scotland. He was educated there in a Catholic seminary where he trained for the priesthood. In 1819 he left Scotland and emigrated to Halifax, Nova Scotia, where he worked as a teacher for a time before leaving for Portland, Maine, and then Boston, Massachusetts. There he joined Henry W. Dutton Company, printers, working as a clerk in their bookstore.

In 1882 Bennett went to New York City where he wrote for newspapers. A year later he left for Charleston, South Carolina, where he worked for the *Charleston Courier*. This experience made him sympathetic to the

Southern point of view and to slavery. That same year he returned to New York, opening a commercial school. But he was still attracted to the newspaper world, and in 1825 took a post with the *New York Courier*, purchased the paper, and then gave it up. At this point he affiliated himself with Tammany Hall and Martin Van Buren. In 1827 he was made associate editor of the *New York Inquirer*, spending part of his time as its Washington correspondent. Then, in 1829, he was made associate editor of the new *Courier and Enquirer* in New York. This was a staunch Jacksonian paper, and he acted as its active director for three years. When it became a Whig organ in 1832, he resigned. He then started the *New York Globe*, a two-cent newspaper which lasted for one month. After that he purchased a share in a paper called the *Pennsylvanian*, but his old political allies would not give him financial support.

In 1833 the *New York Sun* appeared, the first one-cent paper. A year later Bennett applied for a position on the paper, but was rejected. So, in 1835, he started his own paper, the *New York Tribune*, with four pages at one cent a copy. He had only $500 in capital and no party support, but it became very popular and successful. He stressed coverage of local news and strong editorials, along with a strong disclaimer of political bias. In 1836 he was able to close a lucrative advertising contract with Dr. Benjamin Brandreth, the pill maker, and raised his price to two cents a copy. The *Tribune* had a circulation of 30,000 to 40,000 daily, but he was viciously attacked by his rivals for the flippancy, impudence, and sensationalism of his columns.

The paper became most successful in the 1840s, with a circulation of 50,000 to 60,000 daily. Because of a series of quarrels with Bishop John Hughes of New York and Daniel O'Connell in Ireland, Bennett became a supporter of the Know-Nothing Party. He set up a large corps of domestic and European correspondents and his was the first paper to make lavish use of the telegraph. In the 1860s it was a solidly Democratic paper, and supported Douglas against Lincoln in that year. During the secession crisis, he was in favor of letting the seceding states go peacefully. But he became a moderate unionist after the war broke out and supported Lincoln in 1864. By the time he retired in 1867 the paper's circulation was 90,000 per day. He was succeeded by his son, James G. Bennett Jr. He had been married to Henrietta Agnes Crear, who had come to America from Ireland in 1838. James Jr. joined the *Herald* in the early 1860s and became managing editor in 1866. After 1867 he was chief executive officer. He assembled an unusually able staff, but spent most of his own time in Paris after 1877. (*DAB; NCAB*, 7:241; *New York Times*, June 2, 1872; *Who Was Who*, vol. H.; Oliver Carlson, *The Man Who Made News: James Gordon Bennett*, 1942; Don C. Seitz, *The James Gordon Bennetts, Father and Son*, 1928.)

BERNAYS, EDWARD L. (November 22, 1891–   ). Public relations counselor, E. L. Bernays Company. Born in Vienna, Austria, son of Ely Bernays and Anna Freud. He was brought to the United States in 1892 by his father, who became a successful grain merchant in New York City, and mother, who was a sister of Sigmund Freud. Educated in the public schools of New York City, he graduated from the college of agriculture at Cornell University in 1912. Journalism beckoned, and he became editor of *Dietetic and Hygenic Gazette* in 1912 and the *Medical Review of Reviews.*

From 1913 to 1917 Bernays worked as a publicist for theatrical producers and for the Metropolitan Opera, and in 1918 became a member of the staff of the United States Committee for Public Information, headed by George Creel. After the war he and his future wife, Doris Fleishman, opened their own public relations office. Their first client was the United States War Department, for whom they conducted a campaign to urge the reemployment of ex-servicemen. They also worked for the Lithuanian government to encourage its recognition by the United States.

Although the idea of public relations had been around for some time, and was particularly advanced by the Creel Committee, it was Bernays, more than anyone else, who pioneered in applying it in a private agency. The public relations counselor is one who studies the social sciences to understand, motivate, and direct the responses of large groups of people, and during the 1920s Bernays directed promotional campaigns for hair nets (he convinced some states to pass laws requiring women workers to wear hair nets), Ivory soap, and electric lights. His promotion of the fiftieth anniversary of the electric light in 1939 brought him international recognition. After 1929 he worked for leading firms in autos, banking, construction, food, entertainment, oil, tobacco, real estate, public utilities, and transportation, in addition to handling the promotional affairs of the NAACP.

Bernays also held many state and federal governmental positions, serving during 1930–1931 on President Hoover's* Emergency Task Force on employment, and on a New York State commission on employment in 1942. He was co-chairman of the Victory Bond campaigns in 1943 and in 1953 assisted the State Department in the establishment of the psychological warfare office. He became the first instructor in public relations in the United States when he lectured at New York University, and wrote several books, including *Crystallizing Public Opinion,* in 1923; *Propaganda,* in 1928; and *Biography of An Idea: Memoirs of Public Relations Counselor Edward L. Bernays,* in 1965. He and his wife had two daughters. (*Who's Who in America,* 1978–79; *Biographical Encyclopedia of American Jews; Current Biography,* February, 1942; September, 1960.)

BERWIND, EDWARD JULIUS (June 17, 1848–August 18, 1936). Coal operator and transportation entrepreneur. Born in Philadelphia, son of John E. Berwind and Augusta Guldenferring, Prussian immigrants. His father was a cabinet maker in a Philadelphia piano factory, and Edward

Berwind was educated at the U.S. Naval Academy, graduating in 1869. He served as a naval aide in Washington, D.C., during the Grant administration, until he was discharged in 1872 for a service-related disability.

Berwind joined the Pennsylvania Railroad until the 1880s when he entered the bituminous coal business, forming Berwind, White and Company with his brother Charles and Judge Allison White. This firm was succeeded in 1886 by Berwind-White Coal Mining Company, with which four of the five Berwind brothers were associated. Edward was president of the company from 1886 to 1930, when he became chairman of the board. During these years he was closely associated with J. P. Morgan* in the consolidation, reorganization, integration, and expansion of his coal operations.

Reputed to be the world's largest individual owner of coal mining properties, Berwind was president of six coal companies and director of four others. To integrate his operations from mine to market, he became heavily involved in businesses complementary to the coal industry, such as railroads, steamships, docks, and lumber. He also had controlling interests in two banks in the coal fields and was director of three large insurance companies. Altogether he was a director of over fifty corporations.

His other major business activity was with New York City Rapid Transit, which was one of the largest consumers of Berwind-White coal. Early in his career he was associated with Thomas Fortune Ryan* and P. A. B. Widener* in the Metropolitan Securities Company, which owned New York City's surface transit. He was also treasurer of Rapid Transit Construction Company, which built the Interborough Rapid Transit system, and for many years was chief executive officer of the I.R.T. In 1930 he resigned, shortly before it went into receivership.

He was considered an unsentimental, ruthless, and hard-driving business-man who was quite cavalier in labor relations. He refused to bargain with employees, and his mines were the last bastion of the open shop in the coal fields. In 1886 he married Sarah Vesta Herminie Torrey, daughter of a U.S. consular agent for the State Department. She died without issue in 1922. Several of his nephews, however, became executives with Berwind-White Coal. (*DAB*, Supplement 2.)

BESSE, ARTHUR LYMAN (April 13, 1887–November 24, 1951). Trade association executive. Born in Bridgeport, Connecticut, son of Lyman Waterman Besse and Henrietta Segee. He was educated at Springfield High School in Massachusetts and Lawrenceville Academy and graduated *cum laude* from Harvard in 1907. He then entered into business with his father, who was a partner in a chain of retail clothing stores. Except for a period from 1918 to 1920, he worked for the firm (which had become incorporated as Besse System Company in 1923) until 1926. During this time he served as assistant manager of stores in Springfield, Massachusetts, Kansas City, Missouri, and Syracuse, New York, and was also involved in the firm's management during part of this period. In 1920 he became treasurer of the Sherman Wilton Company, a clothing manufacturer in Boston, remaining there for two years. After the incorporation of his father's firm, he served as its treasurer until 1926. In that year he became president of the National Association of Wool Manufacturers, holding the position until his death. He took over the association at a time when, as the oldest trade association in continuous existence in the United States, it was entering a new phase of its history. The National Industrial Recovery Act of 1933 allowed various industries to propose codes of fair competition. To qualify as the code maker and administrator for the wool manufacturers, the association had to increase its membership. It represented about 50 percent of the industry, as determined by number of workers, payroll, and machinery, when the act was passed. Within eight months it had been expanded to include more than 90 percent. At the beginning of 1934, Besse was elected chairman of the code authority for the industry. During his first twenty months in office, much of his work was related to the industry's code and to the sub-codes of its branches. When the NIRA was declared unconstitutional in 1935, his efforts were directed at securing voluntary compliance with the code. Membership in the association was well maintained.

From its inception, the association had sought "insurance against legislation hostile to the wool manufacture of the country." During Besse's presidency, federal activities bearing on wool manufacture required more attention than ever before. The association considered FDR's program of reciprocal trade agreements (which would have resulted in a lowering of tariff duties on goods) a major threat to the domestic manufacture of wool. Repeatedly Besse objected to the theory and practice of reciprocity. He also directed his attention to legislation that involved fair labor standards, the organization of labor, raw materials, and labelling of goods.

During World War II, the wool industry was confronted with new challenges. In 1939 Besse was a member of a commission appointed to negotiate with Great Britain for the release of Australian wool for the use of American wool manufacturers. He served during and after the war on committees advising the government on defense problems related to the wool textile industry. After the war, competition from abroad became a more serious problem to the industry, especially because of the government's continuing interest in international cooperation in the removal of trade barriers. In 1951 the association filed a brief in opposition to the adherence by the U.S. to the proposed International Trade Organization. Besse argued the case before Congress and wrote several articles detailing his position in trade journals.

He married Eleanor Pass of Syracuse, New York, in 1919, and they had three sons. He was a member of the Congregational Church and a Republican. (*DAB*, Supplement 5; *NCAB*, 41:284; 39:509; *New York Times*, November 25, 1951.)

BIDDLE, NICHOLAS (January 8, 1786–February 27, 1844). Banker. Born in Philadelphia, Pennsylvania, son of Charles Biddle and Hannah Shepard. His father was vice-president of Pennsylvania under the constitution of 1776, and young Biddle was educated in his native city and entered the University of Pennsylvania at age 10. He graduated at age thirteen and went to the College of New Jersey at Princeton where he took advanced work until 1801. He then studied law under his elder brother, William, in Philadelphia.

In 1804 he was appointed secretary to General John Armstrong, minister to France. During 1805–1906 he traveled widely in Europe, and in the latter year became secretary to the legation at London for one year. At that point he returned to Philadelphia, resuming his legal studies and becoming a member of the "Tuesday Club" to write articles on the arts. Turning to politics, he served in the state house of representatives in 1810–1811, and in the state senate from 1814 to 1818. In 1819 he wrote a digest on international exchange, and at the urging of President Monroe, was named one of the five government directors of the Bank of the United States. In 1822 he became president of the bank. Under his direction the business of the bank was centered in the major cities rather than in the frontier areas of the South and West, which created much hostility against him in these areas. But he was generally considered to be a wise and competent manager. When President Andrew Jackson threatened the re-charter of the bank in 1832, Biddle marshalled friends and associates, especially Albert Gallatin, who wrote a powerful article in the *American Quarterly Review* in 1830. Jackson was successful, however, and after the failure of re-charter, Biddle retired in 1839 to his country estate on the Delaware River. Despite the defeat of the bank, it is now recognized by most historians that it served a useful and constructive purpose during the early years of the nineteenth century. And much of the credit for its success must be laid to Biddle's competence as an administrator. On the other hand, the reasons for its defeat were due at least partially to Biddle's singular ineptitude as a politician. Nonetheless, by 1830 the Second Bank of the United States was not only providing high quality local banking services but was operating on a national and international scale. For a brief period it competed most successfully with merchant bankers in financing the flow of domestic and international trade. It was able to do so because it was the only commercial institution to have a number of branches—twenty-two—located in all parts of the country by 1830. No other financial institution operated on this scale.

A member of an old Quaker family, Nicholas Biddle married Jane Craig in 1811. In addition to his other activities, he also wrote the *History of the Expedition of Lewis and Clark* in 1814. (**A.** *DAB; NCAB*, 6:163; *Who Was Who*, vol. H; Thomas P. Govan, *Nicholas Biddle*, 1959. **B.** Ralph C. H. Catterall, *Second Bank of the United States*, 1903; Arthur M. Schlesinger

Jr., *The Age of Jackson*, 1945; Peter Temin, *The Jacksonian Economy*, 1969; J. A. Wilburn, *Biddle's Bank*, 1967.)

BINGA, JESSE (April 10, 1865–June 13, 1950). Black banker, Chicago. Born in Detroit, Michigan, son of William W. Binga and Adelphia Powers. His father was a barber who had come to Detroit in the 1840s. The elder Binga was also interested in real estate and housing. Jesse Binga was educated in the public schools of Detroit and had two years of high school. He then learned the barbering trade from his father and also helped collect rents and maintain his father's properties. After leaving school, he worked for a young black attorney and in 1885 embarked upon an eight year journey as an itinerant barber and transient entrepreneur. He traveled to Chicago, worked as a barber in Kansas City, Missouri, then stopped in St. Paul, Minnesota, and Helena and Missoula, Montana, where his uncle owned a restaurant and some real estate. While in Tacoma, Washington, he opened a barber shop. After a time he moved on to Seattle where he also set up shop. That lasted only a short time before he went to Oakland, California, where he worked as a barber until he entered the service of the Southern Pacific Railway as a porter. He then went to Ogden, Utah, where he worked as a Pullman porter. While in this occupation, he invested in land on a former Indian reservation near Pocatello, Idaho, and by the time he arrived in Chicago in 1893, he had accumulated some capital from his profitable land deals.

His subsequent career paralleled the rise and fall of the dream of developing a black metropolis on Chicago's south side. His rise to prominence as a businessman for over twenty years before the collapse of his financial empire at the start of the depression demonstrates a common pattern for black businesses and businessmen. In 1898 he opened a real estate office on South State Street and prospered by seeking rental property throughout the south side, regardless of discriminatory traditions, helping to open up better quality housing for blacks in the city. In 1905 he leased a seven story building on State Street and opened it to black tenants. In the same year he opened the Binga Bank in a newly constructed office building next door. It was the first bank owned, managed, directed, or controlled by blacks in the north.

With the great migration of blacks to Chicago during and after World War I, Binga grew very wealthy and successful. At one time he owned 1,200 apartment leaseholds, and by 1926 owned more property on State Street than any other person. In 1921 his bank was chartered by the state with a capital and surplus of $120,000. Binga was the leading stockholder and ran it as a privately owned fiefdom. His realty company also expanded. In addition he organized the Binga Safe Deposit Company and promoted a black insurance company. In 1926 he constructed the Binga Arcade as his banking headquarters and as a central office building in the black area of

Chicago. During this time the Binga name became synonymous with black business and success.

Although he was not an active civil rights advocate, his business success, which depended upon enlarging opportunities for blacks in the city, placed him in the center of the racial turmoil that followed World War I. His activities brought him into direct confrontation with the traditional color line in Chicago. He leased apartments and funded mortgages in south side areas previously barred to blacks. White home owners and renters fought to maintain restrictions, but Binga was not intimidated by their threats or actions. In 1919 his office was bombed and in 1919–1920 five attempts were made to bomb his home. But the collapse of the economy after 1929 undermined his business and in 1930 the state auditor ordered his bank closed because liabilities exceeded assets by over $500,000. The major cause of his problems was the deflation of real estate values on the south side, along with the decline of deposits and a large number of unsecured loans and excessive investments in the bank building and site. Binga lost his personal fortune of some $400,000 along with the savings of thousands of average white collar blacks.

Binga then was indicted for embezzlement, but the first trial ended in a hung jury. In 1933, however, he was convicted on five counts of embezzlement and served three years in jail before he was paroled in 1938. After that he worked as a handyman at St. Anselm's Catholic Church. In 1912 he married Eudora Johnson, sister of a Chicago gambling lord, who inherited her brother's $200,000 estate. She died without issue in 1933. (**A.** *DAB*, Supplement 4; Carl Osthous, "The Rise and Fall of Jesse Binga," *Journal of Negro History*, January, 1973; *Dictionary of Black Culture*. **B.** Allen Spear, *Black Chicago*, 1967.)

BINGHAM, WILLIAM (April 8, 1752–February 6, 1804). Merchant and banker, Philadelphia. Born in Philadelphia, son of William Bingham and Mary Stauper. His family had long been prominent in both England and Philadelphia. William graduated from the University of Pennsylvania in 1768, and in 1770 was appointed British counsel at Martinique, serving until 1776. He then spent four years as Continental Agent in the West Indies. Returning to Philadelphia in 1880, he became a founder and director of the Pennsylvania Bank headed by his father-in-law, Thomas Willing.* In 1781 it became the Bank of North America, the first chartered bank in the country. During 1784–1786 he was in Europe, and from 1786 to 1789 served in the Continental Congress. The following year he was elected to the Pennsylvania Assembly, serving until 1795. He was then appointed to the U.S. Senate for one term, 1795–1801.

His widespread real estate investments made him an ardent advocate of internal improvements, and he founded Binghamton, New York, and owned considerable oil lands in Pennsylvania. He served as first president of the Philadelphia and Lancaster Turnpike Corporation. In addition, he owned two million acres of timberland in New England and was an important factor in U.S. shipping. One of Philadelphia's wealthiest and most powerful businessmen, his success lay as much with his social connections as with his business acumen. Bingham added to the prestige of his own family through his marriage in 1780 to Anne Willing, daughter of the wealthy banker, Thomas Willing, and a leader of Philadelphia society. He had two daughters, both of whom married into the Baring family of British bankers, further solidifying his banking and social prestige. (**A.** *DAB; Who Was Who*, H; T. A. Bingham, *Genealogy of the Bingham Family in the United States*, 1898. **B.** E. D. Baltzell, *An American Business Aristocracy*, 1958.)

BIRCH, STEPHEN (March 24, 1872–December 29, 1940). Mining entrepreneur, Kennecott Copper. Born in New York City, son of Stephen Birch and Emily Marshall. He was educated at Trinity School and New York University, but withdrew before receiving his degree. He then became a survey engineer on the projected New York subway routes under William B. Parsons. Subsequently he entered the School of Mines at Columbia University, receiving his M.E. in 1898. After graduation he made a tour of mining properties in the West and was commissioned by Henry O. Havemeyer* to examine mining lands in Alaska. This was a key to the subsequent rapid development of the area. In 1900 he acquired the Bonanza Copper Mine in Alaska for the Alaska Copper Company, and in 1906 a syndicate was formed by J. P. Morgan and Company and Guggenheim Exploration to acquire the mining claims of Alaska Copper Company and to build necessary railway facilities. The Kennecott Copper Company was formed later in the same year and Birch was made managing director of all Morgan*–Guggenheim* interests in Alaska. He built the 196 mile Copper River and Northwestern railway from 1906 to 1911, and in 1912 built the first copper converting plant in Alaska, in one year shipping $20,000,000 worth of ore to the seaboard. To transport metal from Cordova, Alaska, to Seattle and Tacoma, Washington, Birch organized the Alaska Steamship Company in 1907. He also developed the Beatson Copper Company, La Touche Island, Alaska, and was president and general manager of the Alaska Development and Mineral Company, an exploration firm later taken over by Kennecott mines.

In 1915 the Kennecott Copper Corporation was organized to operate all the foregoing enterprises, with Birch as president from its inception until 1933, when he became chairman of the board. He served in the latter position until his death. The Alaskan operations were ceased in 1938, so Birch began acquiring stock in several mining companies—Utah Copper Company, Nevada Consolidated Copper Company, and a company in Chile. Under his direction, the growth of Kennecott Copper was impressive. In

1915 the firm had 450 employees and $10,656,848 in sales. By 1940, when he died, it had 28,872 employees and sales of $177,250,036. Kennecott became the largest copper producer in America and the second largest fabricator of the metal. The firm held an estimated 14 percent of the world's copper and could produce 1,000,000,000 pounds of copper annually.

An Episcopalian and a Republican, he married Mary Celine Rand of Minneapolis in 1916. They had two children. (**A.** *NCAB*, 41:96. **B.** Harold Barger and Samuel H. Schurr, *The Mining Industries, 1899-1939*, 1944; Edwin P. Hoyt, *The Guggenheims and the American Dream*, 1967.)

BIRDSEYE, CLARENCE (December 9, 1886-October 7, 1956). Frozen food producer, Birdseye Frosted Foods. Born Brooklyn, New York, son of Clarence Frank Birdseye, a lawyer, and Ada Underwood. He was educated in Montclair, New York, and entered Amherst College in 1908, but quit two years later. While in college, he worked for the U.S. Biological Survey as a field naturalist, and continued in that position from 1910 to 1912. During the latter two years he also worked as an office boy in a New York insurance agency and as a snow checker for the New York Street Cleaner Department.

In 1912 he left for Labrador, where he engaged in fur trading for four years, traveling by small boat and dog sled for thousands of miles. During another trip to Labrador in 1916 he became interested in the idea of frozen foods, and "quick froze" a winter's supply of rabbit, ducks, and caribou meat. When the U.S. entered World War I, Birdseye became an assistant in the purchasing department of the Washington office of Stone and Webster (1917-1918) and the purchasing agent of the U.S. Housing Corporation. Then, until 1922, he served as assistant to the president of the U.S. Fisheries Association. The next eight years were spent in experiments with the quick freezing method, for which he could afford only seven dollars for tools. In 1924 he borrowed on his life insurance, secured three partners, and formed General Seafoods Company in Gloucester, Massachusetts. There he quick froze fish and rabbits and packed them in old candy boxes.

Although he did not invent the process of quick freezing, his contribution was a system of freezing perishable foods of all kinds in packages by pressing them between refrigerated metal plates. This was extremely rapid and produced hard square bricks which were easy to store and to handle and which retained a high degree of nutrients. By 1925 he had perfected his process and was turning out fresh haddock in frozen packages, but still suffered from financial problems. These were partially alleviated when Wetmore Hodges, son of Charles H. Hodges of American Radiator Company, persuaded J. P. Morgan and Company to provide money for re-financing. In 1929, the company was sold to Postum Company and Goldman Sachs. Postum paid $10,750,000 for 51 percent and Goldman Sachs put up $12,750,000 for 49 percent and sold its interest to the former Postum

Company. The company then became General Foods, to produce Birds Eye Frosted Foods, marketing quick frozen vegetables, fruits, seafoods, and meats.

Birdseye then turned his attention to other fields. He invented reflector and infrared heat lamps and was president of Birdseye Electric Company from 1932 to 1936. He subsequently became president of Dehydrator Incorporated and Process Incorporated, which developed a new quick drying method. It could extract water in ninety minutes, whereas older methods took 18 hours. The process removed virtually all of the water, semi-cooked the product, and greatly cut preparation time. He began producing these foods in in 1946. He married Eleanor Gannett of Washington, D.C., and they had five children. (**A.** *NCAB*, 53:240; *New York Times*, October 9, 1956; *Who Was Who*, vol. 3; *Current Biography*, March, 1946; December, 1956. **B.** Daniel J. Boorstin, *The Americans: The Democratic Experience*, pp. 330–31; Alex Groner, *History of American Business and Technology*, 1972.)

BISSELL, GEORGE HENRY (November 8, 1821–November 19, 1884). Oil refiner, Pennsylvania Rock Oil Company. Born Hanover, New Hampshire, son of Isaac Bissell and Nina Wempe. He was educated at military school in Norwich and at the Kimball Union Academy at Meridian, New Hampshire, and graduated from Dartmouth College in 1845. He was a professor of languages at Norwich University for a time until he went to Washington, D.C., as a correspondent for the Richmond *Whig*. After living in Cuba for a short time, he went to New Orleans where he worked for the New Orleans *Delta*. In 1846 he was elected principal of a new high school and later superintendent of the New Orleans schools. During this time he also studied law and got his law degree from Jefferson College. He then went to New York City and was admitted to the bar in 1853.

A few years later, while on a visit to Dartmouth, Bissell noticed a sample of petroleum from Oil City, Pennsylvania. He decided to send out his partner, J. C. Eveleth, to investigate the source. Finding a ready demand for petroleum for medicinal purposes, Bissell and Eveleth bought and leased some 200 acres of oil lands for $5,000 and in 1854 organized the Pennsylvania Rock Oil Company, the first oil company in the United States. It was capitalized at $500,000 and proceeded to develop the land by digging wells and trenching to collect surface oil; but the returns were meager. As a result, he sent a sample to Professor Silliman of Yale University to see if there could be other uses for the product. Silliman felt there was a potential for many products through distilling, so the company was reorganized with Silliman as president. They continued their digging and trenching until 1858, when they employed Edwin L. Drake to bore for oil in the manner of artesian wells. They struck a rich vein near Titusville which yielded nearly 40 barrels per day. In short order Bissell and the other partners made other land purchases totaling $300,000.

Bissell returned to New York in 1863 and devoted the rest of his life to the promotion of the oil industry in the U.S. and Latin America. He was president of Peruvian Petroleum and Peruvian Refining, which refined most of the petroleum used on the west coast of South America. He was also engaged in banking in New York and in 1864 began to deal in real estate, becoming one of the largest realty holders in the city. In 1855 he married Ophie Griffen of New York City. They had a daughter and a son. (**A.** *DAB; NCAB*, 25:379; *Who Was Who*, vol. H; **B.** Paul H. Giddens, *The Birth of the Oil Industry*, 1938; Ida M. Tarbell, *History of Standard Oil Company*, 2 vols., 1904; H. F. Williamson and A. R. Daum, *The American Petroleum Industry*, 1959.)

BLOOMFIELD, MEYER (February 11, 1878–March 12, 1938). Founder of science of industrial relations. Born in Bucharest, Roumania, the son of Maurice Bloomfield and Bertha Pastmanten. When he was four years old his family emigrated to the United States, settling in New York City's Lower East Side where his father taught English to immigrants. Meyer Bloomfield was educated in the public schools and went to the City College of New York where he got an A.B. in 1899. He earned a second A.B. at Harvard in 1901. As a youth he participated in activities at the neighborhood guild and the University Settlement, which gave him an interest in social work and civic affairs.

Following his graduation from Harvard he became the first director of the Civic Service House in Boston's North End, which worked with recent immigrants in the area, and remained there until 1910. In the meantime he obtained a law degree from Boston University Law School, was admitted to the bar, and worked with lawyer and social activist Frank Parsons, who had organized the Civic Service House in 1905. In 1908 they added a vocational guidance office—the Vocational Bureau of Boston. Two years later Bloomfield became director of the latter organization, remaining there for eight years. During this time he helped to institute counseling in the Boston public schools, helped organize the National Vocational Guidance Association, and wrote two books on vocational guidance, *The Vocational Guidance of Youth* (1911), and *Youth, School and Vocation* (1915).

Bloomfield had early felt the need of tying in his vocational work with the employment departments of business and industrial concerns. In 1910 he had helped to settle a garment strike in New York City, and two years later assisted in the organization of a local Employment Manager's Association in the Boston area to discuss such matters as the education, training, efficiency, and advancement of employees. He did much over the next several years to publicize "the new profession of handling men," becoming a pioneer in what was then known as the personnel management movement.

In 1917 Bloomfield joined the Emergency Fleet Corporation of the U.S. government, becoming chief of its industrial service department. In this position he organized the work of building up the manpower needed in rapidly expanding wartime shipyards. At the end of the war he and his brother, Daniel, organized the firm of Bloomfield and Bloomfield in Boston to deal in industrial relations. The partnership ended in 1923 and Meyer Bloomfield moved to New York, where he specialized in immigration law and served as a consultant in labor relations. He and his brother had earlier established the journal, *Industrial Relations: Bloomfield's Labor Digest*, and Bloomfield was the author of several books, including *Finding One's Place in Life* (1917); *Labor and Compensation* (1917); *Management and Men* (1919); *The New British Labor Movement* (1920); and *Preventive Management* (1930). Bloomfield's career demonstrates the close relationship between welfare and settlement work and industrial relations. Each, perhaps, was a form of control, one focusing on immigration, the other on the workplace.

Bloomfield married Sylvia Palmer, an opera singer, in 1902. They had three children: Catharine Pauline, Joyce Therese and Lincoln Palmer. (**A.** *DAB*, Supplement 3; *New York Times*, March 15, 1938; *Who Was Who*, vol. 1. **B.** John M. Brewer, *Vocational Guidance Management*, 1918.)

BLUHDORN, CHARLES G. (September 20, 1926–February 19, 1983). Conglomerate entrepreneur, Gulf and Western. Born in Vienna, Austria, son of Paul and Rose Bluhdorn. As a youth he was educated in England and came to the United States in 1942. Upon arrival he worked for a cotton brokerage firm in New York City while attending the City College of New York at night. In 1945 he entered the U.S. Army Air Force. After serving in the military he secured a job with an import-export firm in Manhattan and continued his studies at Columbia University in the evenings. In 1949 he started his own import-export business, specializing in commodities. Eight years later he purchased a controlling interest in a small bumper concern, Michigan Bumper Company of Grand Rapids, Michigan. The next year he acquired an auto replacement parts distributing firm, Beard and Stone Electric Company of Houston, Texas. The two companies were merged to form the Gulf and Western Corporation, which began to build an auto parts distribution network in the southwestern states.

In 1960 the firm was renamed Gulf and Western Industries and Bluhdorn was chosen as chief executive officer. By 1970 the company had become the 64th largest industrial corporation in America, with annual sales of $1.6 billion, assets of over $4 billion and some 85,000 employees in all fifty states, Puerto Rico, the Dominican Republic, and forty-six other foreign countries. From 1960 to 1965 its growth was largely through expansion of the auto parts distribution business and the manufacture of parts and assemblies for both the auto parts replacement market and for the auto industry itself. After 1965, Bluhdorn began to move toward diversification. The first significant non-auto parts acquisition was the New Jersey Zinc Company of New York City, purchased in 1965. Next he acquired Paramount Pictures Incorporated, South Puerto Rico Sugar Company, W. E. Bliss Company, Universal-American Corporation, Consolidated Cigar Corporation, and The Brown Company and Associates, among others. The manufacturing division of Gulf and Western is divided into four parts: industrial products, systems, precision engineering, and metals forming.

The industrial products group makes bumpers, grills, and other trim items as well as heavy stamping and chrome plated plastics. It has steel rolling mills and stamping presses and manufactures metal forgings for the aircraft industry and vessels. The systems group ranges from publishing to cable television, traffic control systems, and public safety equipment. The precision engineering group produces marine hardware, prototype jet engine parts, precision cutting tools, and missile components. The metals forming group makes refrigeration and air conditioning equipment, pistons, and self-propelled tractors. The distribution of auto parts is centered in Houston through the American Parts System, which by 1970 had 800 affiliated small jobber outlets. In the area of leisure time activities, Gulf and Western owns Paramount Pictures, with motion picture and television production activities and film distribution operations in the United States and overseas. It is also involved in recordings and sheet music. The firm also owns Famous Players Canadian Corporation, the largest theater chain in North America, with 368 theaters in Canada. Its natural resources business is headed by New Jersey Zinc Company, with zinc mines and smelters, especially in Canada. The food products division entails the South Puerto Rico Sugar Company. Associates Corporation of North America is Gulf and Western's center of financial operations, with a network of 800 offices in the United States, Canada, and Puerto Rico. The Consolidated Cigar Corporation is the world's largest cigar manufacturer, making Dutch Master, El Producto, Muriel, and Tiparillo cigars. Brown Company, in the forest products and paper group, manufactures specialty papers, towels, tissues, paper plates and cups, and plywood. It holds one million acres of farm, timberland, and industrial plants in the U.S., Canada, Europe, and the Caribbean. Mr. Bluhdorn was married and had two children. (**A.** *NCAB*, L:197; *Who's Who in America*, 1978–79. **B.** Robert Sobel, *The Age of Giant Corporations*, 1972, pp. 210, 228.)

BOEING, WILLIAM EDWARD (October 1, 1881–September 20, 1956). Aircraft manufacturer, Boeing Company. Born in Detroit, Michigan, son of Wilhelm Boeing and Marie Ortman. He attended Sheffield Scientific School at Yale University from 1899 to 1902, but did not graduate. Becoming interested in flying, he took instructions from Glenn L. Martin.* Shortly thereafter he founded the Pacific Aero Products Company in 1916. He remained with the firm until 1934, five years after its name had been changed to Boeing Airplane Company. After that time he had no financial interest in the firm, which went on to become one of the leading aircraft producers during World War II and after, manufacturing B-52 jet bombers and the famous 700 series of Boeing aircraft for commercial purposes.

During World War I Boeing had served as a lieutenant in the Navy and after the war teamed up with Glenn Martin to try to persuade the federal government not to release surplus airplanes. When this failed, they turned from aircraft production to the more lucrative field of air transport. With the passage of the Kelly Act in 1925, however, which established the airmail, Boeing returned to production. The first airmail carriers had used World War I planes, but they proved inadequate for the purpose. So Boeing designed and constructed a fleet of bi-planes to be used in the mail service. These new B-40's were bigger than the World War I planes, and powered with a new engine, produced by Pratt and Whitney. With the success of this collaboration, Boeing's firm merged with Pratt and Whitney to form United Aircraft Transport Corporation, of which Frederick Rentschler* of Pratt and Whitney became president, with Boeing as chairman of the board. To this firm was added Hamilton and Standard, the nation's leading producers of propellers and Sikorsky Aircraft Company, a major factor in flying boats and amphibians. With the passage of the new airmail act of 1934, which mandated the separation of aircraft production companies from air transport firms, Boeing took command of the reformed Boeing Aircraft, while Rentschler retained control of United Aircraft Corporation. Boeing was awarded the Guggenheim medal in 1934 for his activities in the aircraft industry. He married Bertha Patten Paschall in 1921, and had a son, William E. Boeing Jr. He made his home in Seattle, Washington, where he died. (**A.** *NCAB*, 36:236; D:120; *New York Times*, September 29, 1956; *Who Was Who*, vol. 3. **B.** H. Mansfield, *Vision: The Story of Boeing*, 1966; Robert Sobel, *The Age of Giant Corporations*, 1972.)

BOIT, ELIZABETH EATON (July 9, 1849–November 14, 1932). Textile manufacturer, Winship, Boit and Company. Born in Newton, Massachusetts, daughter of James Henry Boit and Amanda Church (Berry). Her father was a stationary engineer and later janitor of a school building. She was educated in Newton public schools and Lasell Seminary. At age eighteen she went to work as a timekeeper in the Dudley Hosiery Knitting Mill in Newton Lower Falls. By 1872 she had advanced to the position of forewoman at the finishing or sewing department. In 1883 she became superintendent of the Allston Mills, established by H. B. Schudder, who had been an agent of the Dudley mill. Another employee of the Dudley mill, Charles N. Winship, also went to work for Schudder. Winship was a man with a great deal of inventive and mechanical ability. In 1888 Winship and Boit decided to go into business on their own, with Winship looking after the production end and Boit managing the office and financial matters.

The new concern was called Winship, Boit and Company and founded the Harvard Knitting Mill, specializing in women's underwear, in Cambridge, Massachusetts. They began with three knitting machines, five finishing machines, and a workforce of twenty-five, and were able to produce about twenty dozen garments per day. In one year they moved to Wakefield, Massachusetts, to take advantage of a surplus of women available to work in the factory there. By 1896 the firm employed 160 persons in the mill and 200 doing outside finishing work. They produced 300 dozen garments a day, by now including men's and children's underwear. Enlargements of the plant were made in 1901, 1903, 1907, and 1911, so that at its peak it had a floor space of eight and one-half acres, 850 employees, 500 knitting and 500 sewing machines, and produced 2,000 dozen garments daily. It was the fifth largest (by number of employees) knitting mill in Massachusetts in 1909–1910. In 1920 a profit-sharing plan was instituted with employees, which was continued until 1927. In the late 1920s Miss Boit turned the business over to Charles Winship, and the firm continued to be run under the direction of the Winship family until 1956.

Miss Boit, a Baptist, never married, but lived with a companion, Emma May Bartlett, in her large home in the town of Wakefield. (*NAW*.)

BOOTT, KIRK (October 20, 1790–April 11, 1837). Pioneer textile and machinery manufacturer, Merrimack Manufacturing Company and Locks and Canals Company. Born in Boston, Massachusetts, son of Kirk Boott, an English merchant who settled in Boston shortly after the American Revolution, and Mary Love. Young Boott was educated in England at Rugby Academy and then attended Harvard without graduating. His father secured a commission for him in the British army and he served in England until 1813, when his regiment was ordered to New Orleans and he returned home.

When his father died in 1817 young Kirk took over the family mercantile firm, Boott and Company, expecting to gain a good living from it. He soon found, however, that although the company had a great deal of capital, mercantile prospects were rather dim. He then set about to find an outlet for his family's capital and for his own entrepreneurial energies. In 1821 he and Patrick Tracy Jackson,* another young scion of a wealthy mercantile family, applied for a position as manager of an enterprise projected by several Boston capitalists. Boott was appointed agent and treasurer of the new Merrimack Manufacturing Company, which was given financial backing by Boott and Company. The Merrimack Company was formed to secure and develop the Pawtucket Falls area of East Chelmsford, Massachusetts, which would later be renamed Lowell. It was also to establish a machine shop to supply textile machinery both for its own needs and for those factories to be built in the future, and to engage in the manufacture of cloth. For the next sixteen years Boott played an extremely important part in the affairs of the machine shop and the general development of Lowell.

The water rights of the East Chelmsford area were largely vested in the Proprietors of the Locks and Canals on the Merrimack River (a company which had been formed in 1792 to operate a canal around the Pawtucket Falls), but by 1821 the stock of the company was not selling at a high price and Jackson and Boott were able to acquire a majority of the stock with little difficulty. The Merrimack Company then proceeded to build a dam across the Merrimack River, widened the old Pawtucket Canal, installed new locks, and started two additional canals. All of this was a massive undertaking for the time, with the Pawtucket Canal alone costing $120,000. These tasks were completed in 1823, machinery was moved in, and later that year the Merrimack mills began their operations.

A year later the directors decided to separate the functions of cotton textile manufacture and machinery building, with the latter function being combined with the regulation of water power and real estate. They revived the charter of the Locks and Canals Company, transferring it to the machine shop with all land and water rights. Boott was made agent and treasurer of the new company, with Paul Moody* as plant superintendent. The machine shop was completed in 1825 and began producing machinery for Merrimack and other mills in that year. By the early 1830s it employed nearly 300 men, boasting that it could turn out the complete machinery for a mill of 5,000 spindles in four months.

During the years of Boott's management the machine shop did little innovating in textile machinery, instead building machines under lease from inventors outside of Lowell. Its great innovations, however, came in the generation and transmission of water power. Its skill in practical hydraulics was probably the most potent single factor in the American Industrial Revolution, and made outstanding contributions to its progress. The machine shop developed an exceedingly diverse range of functions. It built or supervised the building of canals, locks, dwelling houses, mill buildings, streets, bridges, and a hotel, besides making innovations in the development of water power. It also made noteworthy improvements in the fields of fire protection, mill heating, lighting, and sanitation, and after 1834 began the manufacture of locomotives.

Boott as agent and treasurer of both Merrimack Manufacturing Company and the Locks and Canal Company dominated the affairs of the companies and of Lowell itself. His British army training had made him a strict disciplinarian and he had a powerful and dominating personality, soon coming to control not only the business affairs of the town, but also the religious, political, and social affairs as well. Under his direction brick boarding houses were built for the largely female operatives, and elaborate rules and regulations for conduct were established for both the mills and boarding houses. He ordered the building of the local Episcopal church, taxing all inhabitants of the town for its support, and tried to control all other aspects of the town's life. He lost a fight with the town's minister, however, over control of the public education system. Boott was a pioneer in the semi-benevolent type of industrial feudalism that would find its antecedents in many corporate towns and plans of the late nineteenth and twentieth centuries, but in practical fact most textile and manufacturing centers followed the Rhode Island rather than the Lowell systems of labor-management relations. An Episcopalian, he married Ann Haden of Derby, England. (**A.** *DAB.* **B.** George S. Gibb, *The Saco-Lowell Shops: Textile Machinery Building in New England, 1813–1949,* 1950; Caroline F. Ware, *Early New England Manufacture,* 1931.)

BORDEN, GAIL (November 9, 1801–January 11, 1874). Pioneer food processor, Borden Milk Company. Born in Norwich, New York, son of Gail Borden and Philadelphia Wheeler. His father was a farmer and descendent of a family which had come to America in 1638. Gail Borden spent his youth on the farm, where he also learned surveying. When he was fourteen years old, his family moved to Covington, Kentucky, and one year later moved on to the Indiana Territory. Here, Borden obtained his only formal schooling during a span of one and one-half years. During the same time he farmed, surveyed, became an expert rifleman, and captained a company of militiamen. From age nineteen to twenty-one he taught in a backwoods school. Because of his health he left home in 1822, going south to settle in Amite County, Mississippi. He taught school there and was county and deputy U.S. surveyor for six or seven years. After his marriage he left with his bride to join his parents in the new Stephen Austin* colony in Texas. While there he did farming and stock raising, and was appointed by Austin to superintend the official surveys of the colony. He represented his district at a convention at San Felipe in 1833 to seek separation from Mexico, and during the war published the only newspaper in the territory.

When the Texas Republic was founded, he completed the first topographical map and laid out the city of Galveston, becoming collector of customs there. From 1839 to 1851 he was agent for the Galveston City Company, a corporation owning large acreages of land upon which the city was built. It was during this period of time that he became acquainted with the hardships of pioneers, one of the greatest of which was that of securing and carrying sufficient food for their migration. Borden set to work at age fifty with the fixed idea of preparing food in a concentrated form, and developed the concept of the meat biscuit.

He then invested all the money he had in a plant to manufacture the meat biscuit. Its value was instantly recognized, but he had great trouble competing with Army food contractors, and Borden lost his entire fortune in the project. While on his way to London in 1851 to receive a medal for his meat biscuit, he was impressed by the plight of immigrant children who lacked a supply of wholesome milk. He then turned his attention to the idea of concentrating milk. He left Texas and went to New Lebanon, New York, where he had friends in the Shaker Colony. He began experimenting in the laboratory to condense milk, using especially a vacuum pan of the type used in making sugar. He got a patent for the process in 1856, when he proved he could keep milk clean while it was being condensed. He wished to begin production immediately, but he lacked the financial resources. This problem was solved when he met Jeremiah Milbank, who gave him money in 1858. The first plant was opened in Wassaic, New York, in 1861. The outbreak of the Civil War in that year was a godsend to the new company, since soldiers needed a way to carry milk. When it worked well with the army it convinced a skeptical public that the new product was safe for consumption, and greatly increased their business.

Borden then returned to Texas, and the town of Borden was created. Here he turned his attention to the concentration of other foods, including fruit juices, tea, coffee, and cocoa. He received a patent in 1862 for concentrated fruit juice. He built plants in Brewster, New York, in 1863 and Elgin, Illinois, in 1865, and several others in New York State and Illinois in succeeding years. He married Penelope Mercer of Amite County, Mississippi, in 1828, and she died in 1844. He next married Mrs. A. F. Stearns and, in 1860, Mrs. Emeline Eunice (Eno) Church. (**A.** *DAB; NCAB*, 7:306; *Who Was Who*, vol. H; Gail Borden, *The Meat Biscuit*, 1850–51; H. W. Comfort, *Gail Borden and His Heritage Since 1857*, 1933; J. B. Frantz, *Gail Borden: Dairyman to a Nation*, 1951; C. R. Wharton, *Gail Borden: Pioneer*, 1941; **B.** Daniel J. Boorstin, The Americans: *The Democratic Experience*, 1973.)

BORDEN, RICHARD (April 12, 1795–February 25, 1874). Pioneer New England manufacturer. Born in Freetown, Massachusetts, son of Thomas Borden and Mary Holloway. He was educated during the winter terms at the district school, while working in his father's farm and grist and saw mills. From ages eighteen to twenty-five, he was manager of his father's grist mill and sailed downriver to collect grain to be milled. He and a shipbuilder, Major Bradford Durfee, had an idea to enlarge operations and constructed boats for the river trade. Then, to make nails and other metal products for the ships, they established in 1821 the Fall River Iron Works. It was originally capitalized at $18,000 but by 1845 its capitalization was $960,000. Borden took an active part in the formation of the company and served as its treasurer and agent for over fifty years.

His connection with the cotton milling industry originated from his position at Fall River Iron. The success of the company had led it to develop schemes for the development of water power for cotton milling. He became part-owner of the Watuppe Reservoir Company, the Troy

Cotton and Woolen Manufacturing Company, and the Fall River Manufacturing Company. He built the American Print Works in 1834 and also engaged in several transportation enterprises. These included the establishment of a line of steamers between Fall River and Providence in 1827, and in 1846, a railway line from Fall River to connect with the New Bedford and Taunton Railroad. He also projected the Cape Cod Railway Company and served as its president. He and his brother, Jefferson Borden, organized a steamship line between Fall River and New York in 1847.

During his career, he was president of the American Print Works, American Linen Company, Troy Cotton and Woolen Manufacturing, Richard Borden Mill Company, and Mt. Hope Mill Company, and served as director of the Annawar and Metacoment Mill companies, and president of the Fall River National Bank. He married Abbey Walker Durfee, daughter of James Durfee, in 1828, and they had seven children. One of his sons, Matthew Chaloner Durfee Borden (1842–1912), took over the American Printing Company in the 1880s and erected several cotton mills at Fall River. Then, in 1892, he built and equipped three large mills for spinning yarn and weaving it into cloth for printing. (*DAB; NCAB*, 10:441; *New York Times*, May 28, 1912; *Who Was Who*, vol. H.)

BOYER, JOSEPH (1848–October 24, 1930). Manufacturer and financier, Burroughs Adding Machine Company, Boyer Machines Company, Chicago Pneumatic Tool Company. Born on a farm near Toronto, Ontario, Canada, the son of a farmer, he was apprenticed as a machinist in 1866. He went to California for a time in 1869 and then established a machine shop in St. Louis, Missouri. He spent a total of thirty-one years in St. Louis with his machine shop, and while there helped William S. Burroughs* develop the adding machine and was the inventor of the first successful pneumatic hammer. He organized the Boyer Machine Company to produce the pneumatic hammer and in 1901 merged it with the Chicago Pneumatic Tool Company. In 1900 he moved the Burroughs Adding Machine Company to Detroit, on the recommendation of Henry Leland, because of supposedly superior labor conditions in the Michigan city. In 1904 he also moved Chicago Pneumatic Tool to Detroit. In 1905 Boyer became president of Burroughs Adding Machine, serving until 1920, when he became chairman of the board, being succeeded as president by his son-in-law, Standish Backus. By 1930 Burroughs Adding Machine was doing a business of $30 million a year, producing 150,000 units annually. Its factory in Detroit had nearly one million feet of floor space and employed close to 10,000 workers.

Boyer was also involved in providing financing to a number of concerns in the early years of the auto industry. He loaned $40,000 to Henry Leland and his two partners to organize a machine shop in 1890 which pioneered in auto parts, especially Olds engines, and he was an important factor in the founding of Cadillac Motor Car Company. When the capital stock of the

Ohio Automobile Company was increased and its name changed to Packard Motor Car Company in 1902, Boyer bought 10 percent of the 2,500 shares at a cost of one hundred dollars a share, becoming part of a small controlling group of Detroit families in the firm. He sold out his interest in 1904, however, when the company's Model "K" lost $200,000. He was also on the board of directors of General Motors Corporation for a few years, until 1915, when he was purged from the board by William C. Durant.* His son-in-law, Backus, was counsel for General Motors from 1909 to 1920, and secretary of the corporation from 1910 to 1916. When Lincoln Motor Company was organized in 1917 to build Liberty engines, Boyer put up $50,000 and became a member of the board of directors. The Leland family owned 57 percent of the stock in the firm, and later Backus also became a board member. The company went into receivership in 1921 because of start-up costs and government lawsuits concerning war profits. Boyer then took part of the mortgage on the company.

Boyer was treasurer of the Detroit Municipal League in 1905 and 1908, and was one of the founders of the Detroit Athletic Club, organized by the new automobile elite in the city. He was a Republican and married Clara A. Libby of St. Louis. One of his daughters married Standish Backus and another married F. K. Stearns Jr., son of the owner of Frederick Stearns and Company, drug manufacturer. (**A.** *Detroit News*, January 17, 1909; *Who Was Who*, vol. 1. **B.** Clarence M. Burton, *The City of Detroit, Michigan*, 1922; Mrs. Wilfred Leland, *Master of Precision: Henry Leland*, 1966; Arthur Pound, *The Turning Wheel: The Story of General Motors Through Twenty-Five Years*, 1934; A. M. Smith, *Industrial Detroit*, 1930; Henry Taylor and Co., *Compendium of the History and Biography of the City of Detroit*, 1909.)

BRADLEY, MILTON (November 8, 1836–May 30, 1911). Parlor game manufacturer and inventor. Born Vienna, Maine, son of Lewis Bradley and Fannie Lyford. His father operated the first starch mill in Maine, located at Mercer, which helped to inaugurate the potato industry in that state. In 1847 the family moved to Lowell, Massachusetts, where Milton graduated from high school in 1854. He then entered the office of Oliver F. Cushing, a draftsman and pattern-maker, peddling stationery to female mill operatives in his spare time. Having saved nearly $300, he entered Lawrence Scientific School at Cambridge, attending during the evening. In 1856 his family moved to Hartford, Connecticut, and Milton went with them. Job prospects were not good for him in the area, however, and he ended up in Springfield, Massachusetts, as a draftsman in the locomotive works of Blanchard and Kimball, which went out of business in 1858. He then set himself up as a mechanical draftsman and securer of patents.

He helped make up the drawings and supervised the construction of a private railroad for the Khedive of Egypt during this time. He also became interested in lithography in 1859 and went to Providence, Rhode Island, to learn the process. In 1860 he brought a press to Springfield and inaugurated the lithography business in western Massachusetts. His most important job was a lithograph of Abraham Lincoln, made from a photograph he had taken at the Republican convention. Business during the Civil War was poor, however, so Bradley came up with the idea of printing parlor games. He created "The Checkered Game of Life," which he peddled personally throughout New York State, where sales were brisk. In 1864 he organized Milton Bradley and Company with J. F. Tapley and Charles W. Bryan. It proved so successful that in 1870 he set up a separate building for the games concern. Tapley and Bryan retired in 1878 and the firm was reorganized as Milton Bradley Company.

Bradley was the pioneer in the American game business, and in the process did much to revolutionize the way in which Americans spent their leisure time. Besides the "Game of Life," he also developed "The Wheel of Life," a scientific toy which was the original moving picture machine. During this same time Bradley also became interested in the development of kindergarten materials. In 1869 he came under the spell of the Froehlian philosophy through Elizabeth Peabody and Edward Wiebe. In that year he published *Paradise of Childhood*, which did much to promote the idea of kindergartens in the U.S. In 1893 Milton Bradley Company purchased the *Kindergarten News* and published it as the *Kindergarten Review*. This magazine was the organ of the international kindergarten movement. He also wrote and published several books on children's play. By 1901, Milton Bradley Company had three departments: lithography; home amusement; and educational materials. Bradley married Villona Eaton in 1860 and Ellen Thayer in 1864. (*DAB; NCAB*, 11:472.)

BRADWELL, MYRA (COLBY) (February 12, 1831–February 14, 1894). Lawyer and publisher, *Chicago Legal News*. Born in Manchester, Vermont, daughter of Eben Colby and Abigail Willey, both members of old New England families. While she was still quite young, her family moved to Portage, New York, where her early education was obtained. Then, in 1843, they went to Chicago, Illinois, and she went to school in Kenosha, Wisconsin, and Elgin, Illinois. She wanted to attend college, but women were not admitted, so she became a school teacher instead. In 1852 she married James B. Bradwell, a native of England, who became a lawyer in the U.S. They first went to Memphis, Tennessee, for two years, and then back to Chicago, where Mr. Bradwell was admitted to the bar in 1855. He later became judge of the Cook County court.

In the meantime, Mrs. Bradwell took up the study of law, but in 1868, after she was not allowed to practice, she set up the *Chicago Legal News*, the pioneer legal weekly of the West. She was editor and business manager of the concern and made it into a highly successful venture. When the plant of the *News* was destroyed by the Great Chicago Fire in 1871, she switched publication to Milwaukee until her plant could be rebuilt. In 1879 she passed the examination for admission to the bar but was refused admittance on the grounds that she was a married woman. She took her case to the Supreme Court of the United States, but was defeated in 1873 on grounds that states had the power to set up qualifications for admission to the bar and that the Supreme Court could not interfere.

In 1882 she secured passage of an act by the Illinois legislature granting all persons, regardless of sex, freedom in selecting a profession. She never renewed her application for admission to the bar, but in 1885 the Illinois Supreme Court issued her a license to practice. In 1892 she was admitted to practice before the Supreme Court of the United States. She was a member of the Illinois State Bar Association and the Illinois Press Association, the first woman in either body. She also summoned the first woman's suffrage convention at Chicago in 1869 and for many years was an executive in the Illinois Woman Suffrage Association and helped form the American Woman Suffrage Association in Cleveland. She was one of the leaders of the World's Fair at Chicago in 1893 and founded the Illinois Industrial School for Girls.

She and her husband had four children, two of whom died in infancy. The two surviving children both became lawyers, and her daughter married a Mr. Helmer, who continued publishing the *Chicago Legal News* until 1925. (*DAB; NAW; NCAB*, 2:137; *Who Was Who*, vol. H.)

BRADY, JAMES BUCHANAN "DIAMOND JIM" (August 12, 1856–April 13, 1917). Salesman. Born in New York City, New York, and educated in its public schools. He first worked as a messenger boy for a firm of lawyers, but after a short time entered the service of the New York Central Railroad, remaining with the firm for seventeen years. He was, successively, messenger, telegraph operator, station agent, train dispatcher, and mechanic. He subsequently entered the railroad equipment field as a traveling salesman, obtaining a position with Manning, Maxwell and Moore, manufacturers of railway machinery. He retained a lifelong connection with that firm, becoming a large stockholder and director. He also went into the manufacture and marketing of a metal-cutting saw on his own account; it was widely adapted by steel plants in the U.S.

His greatest glory came, however, from his connection with the steel car industry. He was first with Fox Pressed Steel Car Company, then Pressed Steel Car Company, and in 1902, with the Standard Car Company. It was with these firms that he made a country-wide reputation as a salesman without peer. He wrote single contracts which ran into the millions of dollars and amassed a considerable fortune from these transactions on his own account. Equally tantalizing to the people of that time was his flamboyant and lavish lifestyle. He had a collection of costly jewels and he lavishly displayed them, earning him the sobriquet, "Diamond Jim." He was also a popular figure on Broadway and owned a racing stable. Since that time, probably every salesman or "drummer" who has hit the road to drum up business has at some time envisioned himself as a "Diamond Jim," even while recognizing the possibility of ending up a "Willy Loman." Mr. Brady died, unmarried, in Atlantic City, New Jersey. (*NCAB*, 19:412; *New York Times*, April 14, 1917; *Who Was Who*, vol. H.)

BRANIFF, THOMAS ELMER (December 6, 1883–January 10, 1954). Airline executive, Braniff Airways. Born in Salina, Kansas, son of J. A. Braniff and Mary C. Baker. The family soon moved to Kansas City, Missouri, where Tom attended the public schools. When the Oklahoma Territory opened up for settlement, the Braniffs moved there in 1901, settling in Oklahoma City. At that time Tom Braniff joined his father's insurance agency. He drove a buckboard through the Kiowa and Commanche Indian territory of western Oklahoma, selling tornado and fire insurance to new settlers. By 1902, Tom had opened up his own office in Oklahoma City, in partnership with Frank Merrill. When Merrill retired in 1919, Braniff purchased his interest. During this time he was also founder and president of T. E. Braniff Investment Company of Oklahoma City. In 1923 he built the Braniff Building, then the tallest building in the city. He had 265 agents for his insurance company, selling more than $1.5 million in premiums per year.

In 1928 he helped finance and later took control of an airline that flew oilmen the 116 miles between Oklahoma City and Tulsa. The "airline" had one single-engine, five passenger plane and a staff of three, one of whom was his brother, Paul, the plane's pilot. Before long, Braniff expanded both northward and southward and established a route between Houston and Chicago. The venture was not initially a success, however, and in 1929 was sold to Universal Aviation Corporation, which was ultimately absorbed by AVCO. In 1930, however, Braniff returned to the business under the name of Braniff Airways, operating between Chicago, Kansas City, Tulsa, Oklahoma City, and Wichita Falls, Texas. The initial capital was $10,000, which was increased to $100,000 in 1931. The airline continued to lose money, however, and Braniff was rebuffed in his attempt to secure an airmail contract from the federal government, since the postmaster general would not give contracts to firms which were not regarded as financially sound.

His response was to organize the Independent Air Transport Operator's Association, which became an important influence in President Franklin Roosevelt's decision to cancel all mail contracts in 1934. This resulted in a revised system of awarding mail contracts, and also required the separation of manufacturing and transportation companies. Under the new system, Braniff received his first mail contract in 1934, being awarded the Chicago-Dallas route. In 1935 Braniff acquired Long and Harmon Incorporated, a

Texas airline with mail routes extending from Amarillo, through to Dallas, to Houston, Brownsville, and Corpus Christi. This also enabled him to provide the first air service between Chicago and the Gulf of Mexico. Braniff prospered with steadily increasing traffic and a consistently higher load factor than other airlines.

Meanwhile, Braniff ventured into international transportation and formed a Mexican company, Aerovics Braniff, S.A. By 1947, however, he was forced out by Pan American Airways, since they refused to allow him to use their airport facilities in South America. His last acquisition was Mid-Continent Airlines in 1952, which extended his operation as far north as Minneapolis–St. Paul. The merger made Braniff the sixth largest airline in the U.S. and the twelfth largest in the world. The firm had assets of $35,000,000 and served 31 cities in nine states. It was the only major airline named for an individual. He was a Roman Catholic, a Democrat, and a staunch supporter of FDR. He married Bess Thurman in 1912, and had two children; both died at an early age. (*DAB*, Supplement 3; *Current Biography*, April, 1952, March, 1954; *New York Times*, January 11, 1954; Charles E. Beard, *Thomas E. Braniff, 1883–1954*.)

BRENT, MARGARET (c. 1601–c. 1671). Colonial land proprietor. Born in Gloucester, England, daughter of Richard Brent and Elizabeth Reid. Her father was Lord of Admington and Lark Stache in England. Margaret was raised a Roman Catholic and had some education in her native country. In 1638 she came to Maryland, with her father, sister Mary, and brother Giles. Her father returned to England a few months later. Lord Calvert gave them a letter recommending that they be granted land on the same terms as the first settlers. Margaret and Mary took up 70 acres, called "Sister Freehold," in St. Mary's City, the capital of the young colony. In 1642 Margaret acquired 1,000 acres from her brother Giles, in payment for debts he owed her and members of the Reid family. The parcel included a mill and a house and she raised livestock there.

The Brent family was very influential during the early years of the Maryland settlement—Leonard Calvert may have married Annie Brent, another sister. Giles was at various times a member of Council, acting governor, and commander of Kent Island. Margaret occasionally appeared before Provincial Court to plead for herself and others. In 1647, Governor Calvert, on his death bed, made Margaret executor of his estate. This was a time of severe crisis in Maryland's affairs, with Calvert having just regained control after the two year Inglis Rebellion of Protestants against the Catholic government of the colony. To put down the insurrection, Calvert brought soldiers from Virginia and pledged his own estate and that of his brother, the proprietor, as security for their pay. This was the difficult situation Margaret Brent inherited on his death.

It was necessary to keep the soldiers quiet until they could be paid, and to accomplish this, they had to be fed. But there was a severe corn shortage, so she had to import corn from Virginia to feed them. She found Leonard Calvert's personal estate inadequate to cover the costs, so she got power of attorney to act for the proprietor, selling his cattle to pay for the corn and to pay off the soldiers. On being paid, the soldiers dispersed, some of them becoming settlers in the colony. In 1647-1648 Miss Brent demanded two votes in the assembly, but was denied even one.

In the meantime, Lord Baltimore suspected the Brents of acting in bad faith with his estate, although the colonial assembly supported her actions. Not long after the Brents left Maryland for Virginia. Margaret and Mary took up lands there in the northern neck in 1651, imported large numbers of settlers, and contributed substantially to the development of that part of Virginia. She never married. (**A.** *NAW*; Julia Cherry Spruill, "Mistress Margaret Brent . . . " *Maryland History Magazine*, 1934. **B.** *Women's Life and Work in the Southern Colonies*, 1938.)

BRICE, CALVIN STEWART (September 17, 1845–December 15, 1898). Railway speculator, Nickle Plate Railway. Born in Denmark, Morrow County, Ohio, son of William K. Brice, a Presbyterian minister, and Elizabeth Stewart. Calvin was educated in the common schools, and entered the prep school at Miami University in Ohio. In 1861, at fifteen years of age, he enlisted to serve in the Civil War, but was rejected because of his youth. He enlisted a year later and served three months before returning to finish his education. He graduated in June 1863, and after teaching for three months, recruited a volunteer infantry company, became its captain, and served until 1865. He then took up the study of law at the University of Michigan and in 1866 was admitted to the bar in Cincinnati.

He soon gained fame as a corporation lawyer, but gave up his practice in 1870 to embark upon his railway enterprises. He became involved with General Ewing and other capitalists in a railroad from Toledo to the Ohio coal fields. In the winter of 1870-1871 he went to Europe to secure a loan for the purpose of completing the line of the Lake Erie and Louisville Railway as far as Lima, Ohio. This became the Lake Erie and Western Railroad, and Brice became its president in 1887. He also assisted in construction of a division of the Erie Railroad, known as the Chicago and Atlanta, and was responsible for the location of the machine shops of the Lake Erie and Western and the Dayton and Michigan Railroads in his home town of Lima.

Brice was responsible for the conception, building, and profitable sale of the New York, Chicago and St. Louis Railway (known as the "Nickle Plate Railroad"). He was connected with ten other railroads all over the United States as an investor and an official. His greatest project was a railway in China under concession from the Imperial government. This was launched under the name of the China-American Development Company, also known as "Brice Chinese Syndicate," which had exclusive rights of way between Canton and Hankow, with adjacent mining rights. He died before he was able to get it under way. He was never paid a dollar of salary in his railway ventures, making all of his money in investments and speculation. He was also a promoter of many local interests in Lima and one of the leading figures in the Southern Trust Company. Among the railroads in which he had a financial interest were: Chicago and Alliance; Ohio Central; Richmond and Danville; Richmond and West Point Terminal; Memphis and Charleston; Kentucky Central; and Marquette, Houghton and Ontanagan. He was also president of the Cleveland, Akron and Columbus, and vice-president of the Duluth, South Shore and Atlantic and others. Brice helped to reorganize the East Tennessee, Virginia and Georgia Railroad; the Knoxville and Ohio; the Mobile and Birmingham; and the Memphis and Charleston railways. In 1893 he formed a syndicate to construct a railroad in Jamaica, which was taken over in 1896 by the government.

He was also quite active in politics as a Democrat. He was an elector for Tilden in 1876 and Cleveland in 1884, also serving in the latter year as a delegate to the Democratic Convention and as a member of the National Committee. In 1889 he was elected chairman of the Democratic National Committee, and in 1890 was elected to the U.S. Senate to succeed Henry B. Payne. He was a firm opponent of Bryan and the silverites in 1896. He married Catharine Olivia Neily of Lima in 1870 and they had four sons and two daughters. (**A.** *DAB; NCAB*, 27:75; *New York Times*, December 16, 1898. **B.** Alvin Harlow, *Road of the Century*, 1947.)

BRIDGES, ROBERT (d. 1656). Colonial iron manufacturer. Robert Bridges emigrated from England to Massachusetts in 1641, becoming a freeman in that year. He immediately took a prominent part in the community, serving as a captain of the militia, and in 1644 was elected to the General Court. In 1646 he was elected speaker in the House of Representatives and the following year became an assistant, continuing in that position until his death. For many years he was the only magistrate in Lynn.

His greatest importance derives from his connection with the first iron works established in America. Bog iron had been discovered at an early date, but it wasn't until 1642 that a serious effort was made to take advantage of the discovery. Bridges took specimens from the Saugus River and took them to London to secure capital. A company was formed, "The Company of Undertakers for the Iron Works," with a capital of 1,000 pounds. Skilled workmen were brought over and an industry was established in 1643 at Hammarsmith (near Lynn) on the Saugus River. The firm had a monopoly for twenty-one years, and the colonial authorities gave it liberal funds and religious immunities to aid its growth. But the works met with only indifferent success and Bridges soon lost interest in it. Nevertheless, the works supplied most of the iron used in the colony for many years.

Bridges was also interested in the Braintree Iron Works. He was a stern and unyielding Puritan and married Mary Woodcock of London. (*DAB; NCAB*, 24:365; C. H. Pope, *Pioneers of Massachusetts*, 1900, p. 68.)

BROOKER, CHARLES FREDERICK (March 4, 1847–December 20, 1926). Metals manufacturer, American Brass Company. Born in Litchfield, Connecticut, son of Martin Cook Brooker and Sarah Maria Seymour. His family had come to Connecticut in 1695 and his father was a farmer. As a youth Charles worked on his father's farm and attended Litchfield and Torrington district schools. At age twelve he became a clerk in a general store in Torrington and then in Waterbury. His manufacturing career was started in 1864, when, at age seventeen, he was employed by Lyman W. Coe in the Wolcottville Brass Company. He became a topnotch salesman for the firm and was soon made an executive. Upon the death of Coe, he was named president of the concern.

Brooker was identified with the development of the brass industry of Connecticut for sixty-five years, and as a business organizer his most important work was the formation of the American Brass Company in 1899. This was a holding company into which were amalgamated four of the leading brass manufacturing units of the Naugatuck Valley. Thirteen years later the subsidiary companies were dissolved and American Brass became an operating company. His original business connection, Wolcottville Brass Company, had been started in 1829 by Israel Coe, father of Lyman W. Coe. This was the first firm in America to manufacture sheet brass and brass kettles in quantity, and was a pioneer in making rolled brass for other manufacturers. It was later renamed Coe Brass Manufacturing Company. In 1899, this firm was amalgamated with Ansonia Brass and Copper Company, Holmes, Booth and Haydens, and the Benedict-Burnham Manufacturing Company to form American Brass. In later years, the Chicago Brass Company and Birmingham Brass Company were added to the concern.

In 1921 Anaconda Copper Mining Company approached Brooker with a plan for consolidation. He approved the proposal and American Brass was purchased by Anaconda Copper Mining. Brooker served as president of American Brass from 1900 to 1920 and later as chairman of the board. He acted as a chief figure in its reorganization in 1921 and served as a director of the Anaconda Company. He was also president of Torrington Savings Bank. An active Republican, he was elected to the Connecticut House of Representatives in 1875 and to the state senate in 1893. He was also a member of the Republican state committee, and a key member of the Republican National Committee from 1900 to 1908. He served as a delegate to Republican national conventions from 1900 to 1920.

An Episcopalian, he married Julia F. Clarke Farrel of Ansonia in 1894. She died in 1917. (**A.** *DAB; NCAB*, 18:42. **B.** Clive Day, *The Rise of Manufac-*

turing in Connecticut, 1935; Grace P. Fuller, *An Introduction to the History of Connecticut as a Manufacturing State*, 1915; William G. Lothrop, *The Development of the Brass Industry in Connecticut*, 1936.)

BROOKINGS, ROBERT SOMERS (January 22, 1850–November 15, 1932). Businessman, government official, and foundation executive. Cupples Company, War Industries Board, and Brookings Institution. Born in Cecil County, Maryland, son of Dr. Richard Brookings and Mary Carter. His ancestors were among the early settlers of northeastern Maryland. Brookings' father died when he was two years old and his mother was remarried, to Henry Reynolds, a Baltimore carpenter. Brookings had little formal education, with one year at West Nottingham Academy and a few months at a business school in Baltimore. His life falls into three distinct phases: in the first phase, between seventeen and forty-six, he concentrated on his successful business activities; in the second phase, from forty-six to sixty-five, he was concerned with the development of higher education; and in the third phase, after sixty-five, he was involved in the articulation of governmental research and policies as a government official and foundation officer.

At age seventeen Brookings became a clerk in Samuel Cupples Woodenware Company in St. Louis, Missouri, where his brother, Henry, worked. He soon proved himself successful as a salesman and became virtual head of the company by age twenty-two. Within a decade Cupples Company stood at the head of its field and Brookings was recognized as one of the outstanding businessmen of the Middle West. His success broadened into real estate, lumbering, and transportation, and his crowning achievement was the construction, in 1895, of the Cupples Station, which occupied twelve blocks in the industrial section of St. Louis, serving as a private railway terminal for many of the largest manufacturing and mercantile concerns of the city. The terminal did much to revolutionize the distribution of goods in St. Louis and served as a model for other cities.

In 1896, with his net worth at several millions of dollars, Brookings decided to retire from active business to devote his fortune and his time to the cause of higher education. He became president of the University Corporation of Washington University in St. Louis, gave Cupples Station to the university as a basic endowment, and persuaded others to contribute funds for buildings and endowment. His greatest service to the university was in the development of one of the finest medical centers in the country. He raised a total of fifteen million dollars for the endowment and buildings of the medical school, and made vast improvements in its operation. The Carnegie Corporation termed it "unexcelled by any in the country."

In the meantime, Brookings' interests and activities turned increasingly to the newly emerging private foundations and to governmental activities on the federal level. It was in this area that he was to leave his most important and lasting imprint on American society. His first step in this direction came in 1910, when he was appointed one of the first trustees of the newly organized Carnegie Endowment for International Peace, dedicated to the abolition of international war. In 1916 Brookings organized the Institute for Governmental Research, the first of three groups he founded which would later be merged into the Brookings Institution. The Institute was "to conduct scientific investigations into the theory and practice of governmental administration" in order to develop and publicize "the most scientific practical principles and procedures that should obtain in the conduct of public affairs." Seeing the methods and procedures of business as being superior to those of government, Brookings and his associates were certain that the conduct of government could be improved by the introduction of business methods.

America's entrance into World War I in 1917 retarded the development of the Institute, but broadened Brookings' experience by bringing him into direct contact with government decision-making as a member of the War Industries Board. Being named a commissioner of finished products, Brookings became a close associate of the WIB's chairman, Bernard Baruch.* He organized a series of commodity committees, seeking to coordinate supply and demand for a number of products by opening channels of communication to the military bureaus and promising reliable information on industrial capacity in return for forecasts of military requirements, but he had little success in securing the cooperation of either buyers or sellers. When the WIB was reorganized in 1918, Brookings became chairman of the Price Fixing Committee, designed to establish a centralized, stable federal price policy. Brookings had no power to impose any arbitrary price settlements; all he could do was to urge trade leaders to organize the industry more effectively, form a small negotiating group, and try to come to some agreement on a sensible schedule of prices. As the war progressed, Brookings became attracted to a problem far more complicated than fixing prices on industrial raw materials and military purchases. He and Baruch ultimately began to look for ways to stabilize the country's entire industrial structure. This goal could not be achieved during the war, but would provide the impetus for much of Brookings' foundation activity after that time.

After the war Brookings not only continued and expanded the activities of the Institute for Governmental Research, but also established two new organizations: the Institute for Economics in 1922, and the Robert Brookings Graduate School of Economics and Government in 1924. Four years later these three organizations were merged to form the Brookings Institute for Government Research. These concerns had a major impact, either individually or collectively, upon the development of public policy and research during the 1920s and after. In 1921 the Institute for Government Research achieved its first major objective — the creation of the Bureau of the Budget within the federal government. The Budget and Accounting Act of 1921 provided for the first time a full view of all expenditures and all probable revenue of the nation. After the act was passed, President Harding asked the Institute to play the major technical role in bringing the system into operation. The Institute of Economics focused its research specifically on economic questions, making recommendations to those in policy making situations. With the Graduate School of Economics and Government, students who had completed at least one full year in economics and politics were offered training in studies in the control of a developing industrial society. These agencies and foundations were the product of a growing integration of business and the state during the twentieth century. Although they were reformist in nature, they were primarily interested in maintaining the stability of the system. And stability was increasingly defined in terms of efficiency, of greater control, of greater centralization, of closer cooperation between business and government. By removing "politics" from policy-making they could then arrive at rational, "pure" decisions, while at the same time reducing the effectiveness of representative democracy.

Brookings wrote two books on economics: *Industrial Ownership* in 1926, and *Economic Democracy* in 1929. He married Isabel Valle January of St. Louis in 1927. (**A.** *DAB; NCAB*, 33:156; *New York Times*, November 16, 1932; *Who Was Who*, vol. 1; Herman Hagedorn, *Brookings: A Biography*, 1936; **B.** David W. Eakins, "The Origins of Corporate Liberal Policy Research, 1916–1922 . . ." and Michael A. Lutzker, "The Formation of the Carnegie Endowment for International Peace . . . ," both in Jerry Israel, ed., *Building the Organizational Society*, 1972; Robert D. Cuff, *The War Industries Board*, 1973; Charles A. H. Thompson, *The Institute for Governmental Research*, 1956.)

THE BROWN FAMILY OF BALTIMORE: Alexander Brown (November 17, 1764–April 3, 1834); **James Brown Sr.** (February 4, 1791–November 1, 1877); **George Brown** (April 17, 1787–August 26, 1859); **John A. Brown** (May 21, 1788–December 21, 1872); **John Crosby Brown** (May 22, 1838–June 25, 1907); **James Brown II** (April 28, 1863–June 9, 1935); **George S. Brown** (May 7, 1834–May 19, 1890); **James M. Brown** (December 8, 1820–July 19, 1890). International bankers, Brown Brothers and Company.

Alexander Brown was born in County Antrim, Ireland, son of William Brown and Martha Margueretta Davison. His father owned a small, but successful, linen store in Belfast. Alexander immigrated to Baltimore in 1800 with his wife and eldest son, William. Upon arrival, Alexander became an importer of Irish linen and from this developed one of the greatest business and banking firms in the entire country. His sons were integral in the development and growth of this enterprise. William went to Liverpool in 1809 and established the firm of Brown, Shipley and Company; John A. Brown went to Philadelphia and organized Brown Brothers and Company; and James established Brown Brothers and Company in New York City. Alexander stayed in Baltimore as head of the entire concern.

The modest linen business Alexander had started grew into an export business as well. They began exporting cotton to Great Britain, and branched out into tobacco. From this base they moved naturally into international banking. Their family and business connections in England gave the Baltimore firm an extremely advantageous position to handle matters of this sort. The change of the firm from mercantile activities to banking was inevitable and swift. Alexander also became a ship owner, and was a masterful handler of the shipping trade at a time when it was very slow and hazardous. After 1824 the firm began to grow very rapidly. Alexander was also involved with many of the progressive movements in Baltimore, including the Baltimore and Ohio Railroad. At the time of his death his wealth stood at two million dollars and his firm, Alexander Brown and Son, was the oldest banking house in the United States. He married Grace Davison and had four sons.

George Brown was born in Ireland and was Alexander's second son. He came to Baltimore in 1802 and soon after joined his father's firm. His early interests, however, lay outside banking, and in 1827 he met with twenty-five other leading citizens of Baltimore to begin the organization of the Baltimore and Ohio Railroad. He was made treasurer of the company and, with his father, virtually supervised construction of the road. In 1831–1832 he stimulated Ross Winans to design and construct the first eight wheeled car, forerunner of the modern railway car, to supersede the modified stagecoaches then in use. He was treasurer of the road until 1834, when he took over the family banking firm, serving in that capacity until his death, a quarter of a century later. He was a Presbyterian and married Isabella McLanahan in 1818.

John A. Brown, Alexander's third son, was born and educated in Ireland and came to America in 1802. He soon joined the family firm, and in 1818 went to Philadelphia to establish a branch there. This became Brown Brothers and Company, the first American branch of the house. He was the most conservative of the four sons of Alexander Brown and retired in 1837 after the panic of that year had impaired his health. He was a Presbyterian and married Isabella Patrick of Ireland in 1813. She died in 1820. Three years later he married Grace Brown, daughter of Dr. George Brown of Baltimore.

James Brown, Alexander's youngest son, was also born in Ireland and came to America in 1802. At an early age he became a member of the family firm. In 1825, when his father felt it was time to establish a branch in New York City, because of the opening of the Erie Canal, James was sent there to begin business under the name of Brown Brothers and Company.

The Boston branch grew out of the New York firm and was given the same name. James made his bank one of the most influential in the country. He guided it through the financial crises of 1837 and 1857 and during the Civil War. He was a member of the Chamber of Commerce of New York State from 1827 until his death and an early trustee of New York Life Insurance Company. He married Louisa Kirkland Benedict in 1817 and Eliza Maria Coe in 1831.

John Crosby Brown was a son of James Brown. He was educated in private schools and graduated from Columbia University in 1859. He was then sent to the Liverpool office of Brown, Shipley and Company, where he remained until 1862, when he returned to New York. In 1864 he became a partner in his father's firm, and also served as vice-president of United States Trust Company and of the New York Chamber of Commerce. He also had some active involvement in politics, and was a member of the Committee of Seventy which defeated Tammany Hall in 1894. He was a Presbyterian and married Mary F. Adams of New York in 1864. They had six children: William Adams Brown became a minister; James Crosby Brown Jr. joined Brown Brothers and Company of Philadelphia; and T. M. Brown joined Brown Brothers and Co. of New York. They also had three daughters.

James Brown II was the son of George Hunter Brown and Rachel Blandings Wheely. He was educated in prep schools in Europe and graduated from Columbia University in 1883. He then joined Brown Brothers and Company, spending several years in England and on the Continent. In 1899 he was made a partner, serving also as a partner in Brown, Shipley and Company, until 1919. He arranged a loan of $1,500,000 from the United States government to Nicaragua in 1919 to reform the country's currency and to construct the Pacific Railway. From 1913 to 1924 he was president of the new National Bank of Nicaragua. In 1914 he was made a member of a committee of three to represent the United States at a banking conference with Great Britain, and in 1915 he initiated negotiations with the Canadian government for floating a $220,000,000 loan in New York City, along with J. P. Morgan* and a consortium of French banks. He also organized the American Foreign Securities Company with J. P. Morgan in 1916 to give loans to France. In 1919 he attended the peace conference in Paris, and conferred with French officials on fiscal affairs. In 1920 he succeeded Eugene Delano as senior member of Brown Brothers and Company, which in 1931 became Brown Brothers, Harris. Later it merged with W. A. Harriman Company to become Brown Brothers Harriman and Company. He was an active participant in the creation of the New York Port Authority, and served as president of the New York Chamber of Commerce from 1932 to 1934, retiring from active business in the latter year. He married Adele Quartly in 1888 and had three daughters, one of whom married Robert A. Lovett.

George S. Brown was educated at McNaley Institute and joined the family banking house. He became head of the firm in 1859, serving until his death thirty-one years later. He was also president of the Baltimore and Havana Steamship Company. He married Harriet Eaton of New York in 1857. **James M. Brown** was born in Baltimore, son of Stewart Brown, and was educated in the public schools until age fourteen. He then entered the family banking firm, being sent to New York, where he was trained for ten years. In 1877 he became head of the firm until he died thirteen years later. He married a daughter of Waldron B. Post and had four children. (**A.** *DAB; NCAB*, 1:474; 8:14; 15:159; 31:148; F. R. Kent, *The Story of Alexander Brown and Sons*, 1925. **B.** E. J. Perkins, *Financing Anglo-American Trade: The House of Brown*, 1975.)

THE BROWN FAMILY OF CLEVELAND: Fayette Brown (December 7, 1823–January 20, 1910); **Alexander Ephraim Brown** (May 14, 1852–April 26, 1911); **Harvey Huntington Brown** (1848–August 2, 1923); **Alexander Cushing Brown** (1885–   ). Manufacturers, Brown Hoisting Machines.

Fayette Brown was born in Trumbull County, Ohio, son of Ephraim Brown and Mary Huntington. His father was a merchant in Connecticut, and came to Ohio in 1815, becoming a merchant in the new territory, organizing the Ashtabula and Trumbull Turnpike Company and serving several terms in the general assembly of Ohio as a Jeffersonian Republican. Fayette was educated in the public school of Gambia County and at Jefferson College in Pennsylvania. When he was eighteen he left home to enter the drygoods store of his elder brother, Alexander, in Pittsburgh. He became a partner in 1845 and remained there until 1851. In the latter year he formed a partnership with George Mygott in a banking firm in Cleveland, where he remained for the next ten years. In 1861 he became paymaster for the Union Army for one year, achieving the rank of major. He then became general agent and manager of the Jackson Iron Company, where he remained until 1888. He became one of the leading iron manufacturers of the area during this period, also owning the rolling mill of Brown, Bonnell and Company in Youngstown from 1883 to 1892. He retired in 1905.

He had secured four patents during these years, two for hoisting apparatus in connection with the charging of blast furnaces and two for improvements in blast furnace design. He also became interested in Great Lakes shipping and built up a large fleet of lake steamers, especially for the transportation of iron ore. He was the first to bring ore by boat from the Lake Superior district to Cleveland. In 1880, with his son, Alexander E. Brown, he organized the Brown Hoisting Machine Company. He was also president of Union Steel Screw Company, the National Chemical Company, and G. C. Kulman Car Company, and a member of H. H. Brown Company, dealers in iron ore. He married Cornelia Curtis of Pittsburgh in 1847 and had four children.

Alexander E. Brown was born in Cleveland and educated in public schools in the city. In 1869 he entered the Brooklyn Polytechnic Institute, graduating in 1872 with a degree in engineering. He joined the U.S. Geological Survey for six months in the Yellowstone region. Subsequently he became chief engineer of the Massilon Iron Bridge Company and from 1875 to 1878 was employed as a engineer in construction work and as a superintendent of iron mines in the Lake Superior region. From 1878 to 1879 he served as a mechanical engineer for the Brush Electric Company of Cleveland.

In 1879 he made his most important invention for handling coal and iron ore at Great Lakes ports, and received a patent on it in the next year. He and his father then organized the Brown Hoisting Machine Company in 1880, with Alexander as vice-president and general manager. When his father died in 1910, he was named president. As a result of his achievement, the construction of lake boats for the transportation of bulky materials was revolutionized. Before his invention loads could not exceed 1,200 tons. After his invention loads of 8,000, 10,000, and even 12,000 tons could be used. His machines made it possible to unload a 12,000 ton vessel as quickly as a 500 ton ore carrier could be unloaded before. Then, in 1883, he built the first bridge tramway, which brought about the increased use of electricity in ore handling. In 1889 he developed blast furnace hoists and cantilever cranes which he installed at Jones and Laughlin in Pittsburgh. In 1890 he built a coal storage plant at Buffalo, New York, with a traveling tramway inside to handle coal. In 1893 he designed a machine to dredge the Chicago drainage canal, and also built the first cantilever shipbuilding crane and trestle.

He was a Republican and Episcopalian and married Carrie M. Barnett, daughter of General James Barnett of Cleveland, in 1877. He had one daughter and one son, **Alexander Cushing Brown**, who was born in Cleveland and graduated from Yale University in 1907. He joined Brown Hoisting Machine as a machinist in 1909, being promoted to vice-president and general manager in 1916. In 1925 he succeeded his father as president. He also served as president of the Cleveland Chamber of Commerce, and joined Cleveland-Cliffs Company in 1934 as a vice-president. He was named president of that giant concern in 1947. In later years Brown Hoisting Machine was renamed the Industrial Brown-Hoist Corporation. He also served as a director of a large number of companies, including Ohio Bell Telephone; Buckeye Steel Castings; Cliffs-Dow Chemical Company; Mesaba Cliffs Mining Company; Cliffs Power and Light; and Ogelbay, Norton Company.

Harvey H. Brown was born in Cleveland, the younger son of Fayette Brown. He became the senior partner in the iron ore firm of Harvey H. Brown and Company, which his father organized in 1879. He served in that position until he retired in 1922. He was also president of Stewart Furnace

Company, a blast furnace in Sharon, Pennsylvania, which he and his father purchased in 1888. In addition, he served, successively, as treasurer, president, and then chairman of the board of Brown Hoisting Machine Company. He had five children: Fayette II, who was a partner in Harvey H. Brown and Company, and Harvey H. Jr., who was with Brown Hoisting Machine; and three daughters. (**A.** *DAB; NCAB*, 33:342; American Society of Mechanical Engineers, *Transactions*, 31:1176–77; *Iron Age*, January 27, 1910; May 4, 1911; August 9, 1923; *Mining and Metallurgy*, September, 1923; E. M. Avery, *A History of Cleveland and Its Environs*, 2 vols, 1918. **B.** Harlan Hatcher, *A Century of Iron and Men*, 1950; S. P. Orth, *A History of Cleveland, Ohio*, 2 vols., 1910.)

THE BROWN FAMILY OF PROVIDENCE, RHODE ISLAND: Nicholas Brown I (July 28, 1729–May 29, 1791); **Nicholas Brown II** (April 4, 1769–September 27, 1841); **Joseph Brown** (December 3/14, 1733–December 3, 1785); **Moses Brown** (September 12/23, 1738–September 7, 1836); **John Brown** (January 27, 1736–September 20, 1803). Colonial merchants in international trade.

Nicholas Brown I was born in Providence, Rhode Island, son of James and Hope Brown. His father and his uncle, Obadiah, had established a general store in Providence and by 1739 controlled eight vessels in the West Indies trade. But James died in that year and the business was carried on by Obadiah and James' sons until Obadiah died in 1762. Between 1762 and the outbreak of the Revolution, ventures were extended from the West Indies to London, Marseilles, Nantes, Copenhagen, and Hamburg. Meantime, at home they began to develop domestic manufacture. They brought about changes in the spermaceti candle business, advancing it from the household to the factory stage of production, by gathering all those who had previously been working in their homes into a building erected for this purpose on the outskirts of Providence. They then engaged in a bitter competitive struggle over spermaceti oil with Jewish manufacturers of Newport. In 1761 they agreed to form a "union"—the United Company of Spermaceti Candle Manufacturers of Providence and Newport—with associates in Boston and Philadelphia. In 1763 the association was renewed with the Browns as the leading members. They fixed the prices of oil, prevented the establishment of new factories, and designated and limited the dealers in oil. It stood as the earliest monopolistic combination in America.

In 1764 they established an iron manufactory in Rhode Island to utilize ore from the Cranston pits. "Furnace Hope" was erected at Scituate and produced cannon during the Revolution. They also became interested in distilling and were large shareholders in successful privateering ventures. Nicholas became strongly involved on the side of the patriot cause during the Revolution and was an equally staunch advocate of the new federal constitution in 1787. He was a Baptist and married Rhoda Jenckes of Providence in 1762. She died in 1783, and two years later he married Avis Binney of Boston. His son, **Nicholas II**, was born in Providence and graduated from Rhode Island College. He joined his father's firm, which became Brown and Benson, and then Benson and Ives, during the 1790s. They were engaged in commerce on the high seas until they sold their last remaining ship in 1838. In 1804 Nicholas II purchased water rights on the Blackwater River and established a cotton manufacturing firm, controlling water power in the area. He also bought large amounts of land in Ohio during the early nineteenth century. After the Civil War the land became extremely valuable as urban properties in the growing midwestern cities. He was treasurer of Brown University from 1796 to 1825 and endowed a professorship at the university. In 1823 he erected Hope College and in 1834, Manning Hall. His gifts totaled $160,000. He was a Baptist and married Ann Carter in 1791. In 1801 he married Mary Bowen Stelle. His son, John Carter Brown (1797–1874), was a noted bibliophile and assembled an excellent library, which he donated to Brown University.

Joseph Brown was born in Providence, the second of James Brown's sons. At an early age he entered his family's store and was closely involved with the venture during its rise to an institution of international standing. But he was more interested in science than business, and was put in charge of "Furnace Hope" in Scituate, Rhode Island, where he remained involved for the rest of his life. He served several years in the Rhode Island assembly. In 1759 he married Elizabeth Power and had three children.

John Brown, the third son of James Brown, was born in Providence and entered the family business as a youth. Around 1770 he withdrew from the concern due to disagreements with Nicholas, and set up business on his own account. In 1772 he was a member of a party which boarded and burned the British armed schooner, the *Gaspe*, in Narragansett Bay. He was arrested for the deed, but saved by his younger brother, Moses. Afterward, John and Nicholas served the Revolutionary cause by supplying Continental troops with clothing and munitions, and by manufacturing cannon. John was a vigorous opponent of the Stamp Act and supported the Revolutionary cause throughout the war. He was also a major factor in the adoption of the federal Constitution by Rhode Island and was elected to Congress, but never went to serve his term. In 1787 the firm of Brown and Francis, with his son, John Francis, was formed. They sent out the first Providence vessel to engage in the East India and China trade. With his brothers, John helped bring Rhode Island College to Providence from Warren, Rhode Island, and he laid the cornerstone for the first building of Brown University. He married Sarah Smith in 1760 and had six children.

Moses Brown was James Brown's youngest son. His father died when he was only one year old, and he was raised by his mother. He left school at age thirteen and went to work with uncle Obadiah Brown. In 1763 he was admitted to his brother's firm, but retired from that in 1773, when his wife died. He never recovered from that shock. He became a Quaker, freed his slaves, and helped start the Rhode Island Abolition Society. After the Revolutionary War he was one of the first in the country to become interested in cotton manufacture, and in 1787 purchased a cording machine, which he set up under the management of his son-in-law, William Almy, and a young relative, Smith Brown. The firm became known as Brown and Almy. Moses Brown had built a spinning jenny and a carding machine, and had copied a model of an Arkwright frame. But the jenny and card did not work well, and the spinning frame was a complete failure. At that time (1798), he was approached by Samuel Slater,* an English artisan who had served an apprenticeship in a cotton mill equipped with Arkwright machinery. He had familiarized himself with the machinery, and now offered to reproduce it for Brown. The two men negotiated a contract for Slater to build two carding machines and a spinning frame in return for half the profits of the business and a half-interest in the machinery. Almy and Brown were to act as purchasing and sales agents for the mill on a commission basis. A year later the mill was in operation, requiring only nine children, supervised by Slater, to run the mill. Later, as the mill expanded, Slater kept costs low by hiring families, as was done in England, and paying them partly in due bills on Almy and Brown's store. This mill was the beginning of the modern textile industry in the United States, and was a seedbed for the spread of the industry northward and westward. Directly or indirectly, Almy, Brown, and Slater fathered most of the twenty-seven cotton mills which were found in New England in 1809.

Moses married his cousin, Anna Brown, in 1764, and she died in 1773. Six years later he married Mary Olney, who died in 1798; and in 1799 he married Phoebe Lockwood, who died in 1808. His son, Obadiah Brown II (1771-1822) was born in Providence and educated at the Friend's Yearly Meeting School in Providence. He became a major factor in his father's cotton manufacturing firm, Brown and Almy. In 1798 he married Dorcas Hadwer of Newport. When he died he left $100,000 to Brown University. (**A.** *DAB; NCAB*, 8:27; 21:381; 8:28; 2:327; 10:99; *Who Was Who*, vol. H; J. B. Hedges, *The Browns of Providence Plantation*, 1952; **B.** Caroline F. Ware, *Early New England Cotton Manufacture*, 1931.)

BROWN, F. DONALDSON (February 1, 1885–October 2, 1965). Executive, DuPont and General Motors. Born in Baltimore, Maryland, son of John Wilcox Brown and Ellen Turner. He received a bachelor of science degree at Virginia Polytechnic Institute in 1902 and pursued post-graduate studies in engineering at Cornell. He then joined the electrical department of the Baltimore and Ohio Railroad in 1903, where he remained for one year. From 1904 to 1908 he was general manager of the Baltimore subsidiary of

Sprague Electric. In the latter year he joined the sales department of E. I. DuPont de Nemours and Company. In 1912 he was placed on Hamilton Barksdale's* staff in the general manager's office, and in 1914 became one of John J. Raskob's* assistants in the treasurer's office. It was while in these positions that Brown developed techniques for calculating the return on investment which continues to be in use by the DuPont company to the present day and which revolutionized corporate information flow. The technique which he devised related the rate of return on capital invested to turnover of capital and to the volume of sales as well as to profit. To do this, Brown broke down costs, investment, sales, and so forth into their component parts. The significance of his formula was that it provided executives at both central and departmental headquarters with an accurate standard with which to appraise each operating unit's performance, locate the sources of deficiencies, and adjust plans and policies.

He became treasurer and member of the executive committee at DuPont in 1918, serving in that capacity until 1921. He was then a director of the corporation from 1921 to 1946. In 1921 he was made a vice-president of General Motors Corporation, which had recently been acquired by the DuPont* interests. Brown was in charge of finance for the company from that year until 1937. The same techniques he had developed at DuPont were also instituted at GM. His pioneering achievements at General Motors did much to ensure the ultimate success of this venture. Brown and his financial staff carried out their work in two stages. In 1921 and 1922, they concentrated on developing data and procedures which would be essential to the general office if it was to obtain some sort of administrative surveillance over the many divisions. They began by building informational procedures to control the purchasing and production schedules of each division. Next, they devised methods for the more systematic allocation of capital and other resources and for the more effective use of existing supplies of cash. After 1922, Brown and his staff concentrated more on refining their data and on perfecting their information and methods. They were particularly concerned with the problem of predicting future conditions on which current output was based and on which current performance was evaluated, rather than on past or present performance. Brown became chairman of the finance committee and vice-chairman of the board at General Motors from 1937 to 1946. He married Greta duPont Barksdale in 1916 and had six children. (Alfred D. Chandler Jr., *Strategy and Structure*, 1962; Ernest Dale, "DuPont: Pioneer in Systematic Management," *Administrative Science Quarterly*, July, 1957; *New York Times*, October 11, 1965; *Who Was Who*, vol. 4.)

BROWN, GEORGE RUFUS (May 12, 1898–   ). and **Herman Brown** (November 10, 1892–November 15, 1962). Construction company executives, Brown and Root. **Herman Brown** was born in Belton, Texas, son of Riney

Louis Brown and Lucy Wilson King. He attended the University of Texas in 1911-1912. Two years later, he became a partner in the construction firm of Brown and Root, Incorporated. He was a partner from 1914 to 1929, and president of the concern from 1929 to 1962. Over the years Brown and Root became one of the largest construction companies in the world, relying heavily on government, especially federal government, contracts. It also developed subsidiaries that included hotels, oil and gas producing properties, paper mills, mines, real estate concerns, office buildings, and a dude ranch. During World War II, a shipbuilding subsidiary constructed more than 350 combat craft for the U.S. Navy. In 1962 Brown and Root received a $43,000,000 contract from the National Science Foundation to drill a hole at the bottom of the Pacific Ocean called "Manhole Project." They were to drill through five miles of the earth's crust to the outermost part of the core, or mantle, of the earth. The project ran into considerable technical difficulties and the U.S. Senate held up funds pending a full report on the contract.

George Rufus Brown was born in Belton, Texas, and educated at Rice University and the Colorado School of Mines. He was for many years a partner with his brother in Brown and Root, and acted as chairman of the board of the firm after the latter's death. He was also chairman of the finance committee of the Texas Eastern Transmission Corporation until he retired in 1974. Both he and his brother were directors of First National City Bank of Houston and Brown Securities Corporation. George was also a director of ITT. He married Alice Pratt in 1925 and had three children. Both brothers lived in Houston. (*New York Times*, November 16, 1962; *Who Was Who*, vol. 4; *Who's Who in America, 1978-79*.)

BROWN, LEWIS HARRIS (February 13, 1894–February 26, 1951). Manufacturer, Johns-Manville Corporation. Born in Creston, Iowa, son of Lewis Henry Brown and Arminta Cole. He attended local schools and worked on neighboring farms to help put himself through school. He received a bachelor's degree from the State University of Iowa in 1915. After graduation he went to work for Ft. Wayne Corrugated Paper Company, beginning as a member of the sales department. At the outbreak of World War I, he was assistant sales manager of the company, but enlisted in the army, serving until 1919. Then he joined the personnel department of Montgomery Ward's Chicago branch. Within eight years he was assistant general manager of all Montgomery Ward plants. When Ward's president, T. F. Merseles, became president of Johns-Manville in 1927, he took Brown with him into the new organization as his assistant.

Just two years later, in 1929, Brown was elected president of Johns-Manville. In this position he instituted collective bargaining and established the eight hour day and forty hour week for management. He also began the practice of surveying employees' attitudes to determine future policies. In addition, he instituted the idea of annual and semi-annual financial reports to stockholders in 1938, and established a series of twelve regional meetings in 1941. He remained president of Johns-Manville until 1946, when he became chairman of the board and chief executive officer. He served in the latter position until 1951. He was also chairman of Johns-Manville Company of Canada and other subsidiaries.

During his management of the company, Johns-Manville became the world's largest producer of asbestos building materials, insulations, and allied products. The company received a big boost particularly from the demands of World War II. They constructed the Kansas Ordnance Plant in 1941 and operated it until 1945. After 1942 Brown was advisor to the chief of the Army Ordnance Department, and in 1946 received the Medal of Merit, a presidential citation. In 1945 Brown inaugurated a $50,000,000 reorganization of Johns-Manville, splitting it into six divisions: industrial products; building products; Celitodice; asbestos fiber; Canadian products; and an international division.

In 1947, at the request of Gen. Lucius D. Clay, Brown spent two months in Europe studying the problems of the economic recovery of Germany and Western Europe. On his return he submitted a 247 page report which urged the ending of reparations; the curtailment of de-Nazification (except for top Nazis); permission for Germany to re-establish their export trade; the institution of a central bank for West Germany; and the provision of a new currency for Germany. Earlier, in the 1930s, he helped draft the National Housing Act, and put the amortization principle into legislation. He married Mary C. Alle in 1918 and had three daughters. (*Current Biography*, October, 1947; *Who Was Who*, vol. 3.)

BROWNE, WILLIAM WASHINGTON (?-?). Black banker and capitalist, Richmond, Virginia. Born in Habershaw County, Georgia, to slave parents. Very little is known of his early life. He escaped to Wisconsin during the Civil War and served in the Union Army, returning to the South during Reconstruction as a Methodist preacher and politician. After several years of travel he came to Richmond, where in 1881 he organized the Grand United Order of the True Reformers. This was established as a mutual benefit society which he hoped would break down crime, poverty, and licentiousness among the newly freed blacks in the South. The Order began with 100 members and a capital of $150. In 1883 they got a charter from the City of Richmond, with Browne as Grand Worthy Master. The chief purpose of the Order was to provide a mutual benefit fund for its members. The corporation was empowered to hold real estate, the value of which was not to exceed $25,000. In 1888 this was increased to $500,000. The Order was established with a solemn ritual, lavish regalia, and an annual convention in Richmond with a colorful parade, which was designed to attract new members in search of a sense of community, dignity, and importance in the chaotic society of the New South.

Browne's wife set up a company to supply uniforms and regalia to the Order, and it grew rapidly between 1881 and 1901. By the latter year, death claims and sick benefits paid out amounted to $606,000 and $1,500,000, respectively. The membership was over 50,000 and it owned real estate worth $203,000. In 1887 the officials of the Order decided that the organization should have its own bank. The decision was reached as a result of a racial clash that followed a lynching at Drake's Branch, in Charlotte County. They felt they needed a depository for the funds of the Order and its branches that would be safe from whites. So the Savings Bank of the Grand Fountain United Order of True Reformers was chartered by the Virginia legislature in 1888 and began business in 1889. They took in $1,200 in deposits on the first day.

The Order of True Reformers also organized the Reformer's Mercantile and Industrial Association sometime before 1900, to set up and operate a chain of stores, erect a local hotel, conduct a newspaper and printing business, and buy and sell land. The money for conducting these services was furnished by the bank and each store operated at a heavy loss. An Old Folk's Home was chartered in 1898 to provide a home for aged blacks. They also established the Westham Farm, to raise and market agricultural products and to develop a self-contained Negro community. In all these transactions, the purposes of the bank were always subordinate to the broader designs and purposes of the Order. This was one of the fundamental causes of the bank's failure in 1910.

By 1900 the total deposits of the bank had reached $235,873.65, but by 1909 they were only $223,002.68. The bank had reached a peak of $350,858.19 in deposits in 1901. The earning assets of the bank in the early years were mostly mortgages, and in the later years lay almost entirely in loans and discounts. The tendency to expand loans disproportionately to deposits was strikingly persistent, and the two great weaknesses of the bank were a small volume of deposits in proportion to capital and a disproportionate expansion of loans. The bank's largest debtor when it failed was the Reformer's Mercantile and Industrial Association. By 1909 the loans were nearly twice as high as the deposits. Although the bank owned a large amount of real estate in several Virginia cities, Baltimore, Cincinnati, Washington, D.C., and Louisville, Kentucky, most was located in declining black areas, which did not help its investment portfolio. The word of the receivers when the bank failed was: "The Order wrecked the Bank." The bank was undoubtedly mismanaged, and some of its officers were criminally negligent and dishonest, but it nonetheless stands as the first all-Negro bank in America. (**A.** D. W. Davis, *William Washington Browne*, 1910. **B.** A. L. Harris, *The Negro as Capitalist*, 1936; Booker T. Washington, *The Story of the Negro*, 2 vols., 1909–10; W. B. Weare, *Black Business in the New South*.)

BUDD, EDWARD GOWEN (December 28, 1870–November 30, 1946). Manufacturer, E. G. Budd Company. Born in Smyrna, Delaware, the youngest child of Henry George Budd and Caroline Kettell. His father was justice of the peace in the area. Edward Budd was educated in the public schools, graduating from high school in 1887. He worked briefly as a machinist's apprentice at the Taylor Iron Works in Smyrna before moving to Philadelphia, where he spent his entire business career. In his new home he worked as a machinist's apprentice in the shops of Bement, Miles and Company, subsequently becoming drafting office foreman of the hydraulic press design group. During this time he took evening courses at the University of Pennsylvania and Franklin Institute.

In 1899 Budd became factory manager of the American Pulley Company. His role in the design and fabrication of an innovative sheet metal pulley gave him insight into the capability of press and die-formed sheet steel stampings as an alternative to forgings and castings. He drew from this experience the impetus for his later pioneering contributions as a manufacturer of transportation equipment. In 1902 he became general manager of the Hale and Kilburn Company, a leading manufacturer of railroad car seats and interior trimming for Pullman and other firms. The all-steel passenger car was then being developed to replace the earlier wooden coaches. Instead of using castings and forgings, Budd introduced pressed steel parts joined by oxyacetylene welding. Under Budd's supervision, Hale and Kilburn in 1909 manufactured pressed steel panels for auto bodies used by the Hupp Motor Car Company. Budd then submitted to the business manager of Hale and Kilburn a proposal for constructing all-steel auto bodies on a commercial basis, but the proposal was rejected and he resigned in 1912.

In that year, with the help of two outside investors, he organized the Edward G. Budd Manufacturing Company, with himself as president. The initial capital was $100,000, but this was increased to $500,000 within the first year. Shortages of capital, however, remained a problem, and a large stamping press had to be housed outdoors, under a large circus tent, due to the small size of the rented plant. Underfinancing would be a recurring problem for Budd during the next twenty-five years. The firm was originally organized to produce sheet metal stampings, but before long it added a line of sheet truck and auto bodies. At first, there was little interest shown by auto manufacturers, but in 1912 General Motors ordered welded all-steel touring car and roadster bodies for the Oakland Motor Company. Three years later Budd became the exclusive supplier of car bodies to the newly formed Dodge Brothers auto firm. They became his largest customer and allowed him to move into expanded quarters. Other customers included Willys-Overland, Studebaker, Cadillac, and Franklin.

During World War I, Budd made a variety of military equipment, including army truck bodies, mobile field kitchens, helmets, shells, and bombs.

He returned to automotive work after the war and added an all-steel sedan body to his line. At this time he waived his patents to the all-steel body, which allowed larger competitors, such as Fisher, Briggs, and Murray, to enter the field. The acquisition of new accounts, among them Ford and Chrysler, encouraged him to open a body division in Detroit in 1925. Earlier, in 1916, he had established a separate Budd Wheel Corporation, which in 1921 became Budd Wheel Company. That firm began to manufacture the tapered steel disk wheel for Michelin of France in 1919 and became a leading supplier for makers of trucks, buses, and passenger cars.

The depression of the 1930s, with its severe restriction of automobile production, led him into his next pioneering venture, the fabrication of stainless steel. In 1931 he built the first stainless steel airplane, and constructed the Pioneer Zephyr for the Chicago, Burlington and Quincy Railroad. By 1941 he had sold nearly 500 lightweight railway passenger cars. During World War II, the Budd facilities were fully converted to the production of wartime equipment. They were the original maker of the Bazooka projectile and the rifle grenade, and turned out millions of fragmentation bombs and shells. In 1946 the Edward G. Budd Manufacturing Company and Budd Wheel Company were merged into the Budd Company.

He was a Methodist and a Republican and married Mary Louis Wright of Philadelphia in 1899. They had five children, one of whom, Edward G. Jr., succeeded his father in the business. (*NCAB*, 36:17-19; 56:345; G. L. Kellog, "The Life and Work of Edward Gowen Budd," *Journal of the Franklin Institute*, May 1949.)

BUDD, RALPH (August 20, 1879-February 2, 1962). Railway executive, Great Northern Railroad and Chicago, Burlington and Quincy Railroad. Born in Waterloo, Iowa, son of Charles Wesley Budd and Mary Ann Warner. He received a bachelor's degree in civil engineering from Highland Park College in Des Moines, Iowa, in 1899, and began his career as a draftsman with the Chicago and Great Western Railroad. In 1902, after rising to the position of assistant engineer, he became roadmaster on the Chicago, Rock Island and Pacific Railroad and the divisional engineer of that company's line between St. Louis and Kansas City. In 1905 he returned to the Chicago and Great Western as divisional engineer, located in Chicago. In 1906, John F. Stevens, who had been vice-president of the Rock Island system, but was now chief engineer of the Panama Canal, appointed Budd chief engineer of the Panama Railway. He served in that position until 1909. During this time he relocated and almost completed the present Panama Railway and rehabilitated and enlarged the old Panama Railway. In 1909 Budd rejoined Stevens with the James J. Hill* railway interests in the Northwest, serving as chief engineer of the Oregon Truck Railway, the Spokane, Portland and Seattle Railway, and the Spokane and Inland Railway.

Then, in 1913, Hill appointed him chief engineer on the Great Northern

Railway, with the additional title of assistant to the president. He was elected executive vice-president in 1918, and succeeded Louis W. Hill as president of the line in 1919. At that time Budd was the youngest railway president in the country. When he took over, the system had 8,000 miles of track, and he made constant improvements in facilities and undertook new projects. The most dramatic of these was a tunnel in the Cascade Mountains in 1926–1928, at a cost of $25,000,000. This one tunnel eliminated the use of six shorter tunnels. In 1930 he spent three months in Russia at the invitation of that country's government, making a comprehensive survey of its railroads. Upon his return, he directed the expansion of the Great Northern system from Klamath Falls, Oregon, to California, where it connected to an extension of the Western Pacific Railroad. That was the most important piece of railway construction in the country in that year, and established a new all-rail through route from the Pacific Northwest and San Francisco.

In 1932 he was appointed president of the Chicago, Burlington and Quincy Railroad. With this road he introduced the new, lighter weight diesel trains. These were the new Zephyr trains of stainless steel, which were ordered from the E. G. Budd Manufacturing Company, and Budd's was the first railroad in the country to adopt them. They were put into daily service in 1934, between Lincoln, Omaha, and Kansas City. In 1935, the Twin Zepher was opened between Chicago and Minneapolis–St. Paul, and the Mark Twain Zephyr from St. Louis and Hannibal to Burlington. By 1940 he had twelve such trains.

In that year Budd was appointed transportation commissioner on the advisory commission to the Council on National Defense. He did much to bring about a close association between railroads and the military during the country's first efforts towards mobilization. In 1942 he resumed his duties as president of the Chicago, Burlington and Quincy, where he remained until 1949. He served as a director of the company until he died. He married Georgia Anna Marshall of Des Moines, Iowa, in 1901, and they had three children. His youngest son, John Marshall Budd (b. 1907), became president of the Great Northern Railroad in 1951. The elder Budd was a Republican and an Episcopalian and lived all of his later life in Chicago. (*NCAB*, F:63; J:137; *Who Was Who*, vol. 4.)

BULKELEY, MORGAN GARDNER (December 26, 1837–November 6, 1922). Politician and insurance executive, Aetna Life Insurance Company. Born in East Haddam, Connecticut, son of Judge Eliphalet Adams Bulkeley and Lydia S. Morgan. His ancestors had come to Concord, Massachusetts, from England in the 1630s. When he was eight years old, his family moved to Hartford, Connecticut, where his father became president of Aetna Insurance Company, judge of the police court, commissioner of the school board, a founder of the Republican party in the state, and speaker of the

House in the state legislature. At age fifteen, Bulkeley left the Hartford public schools to take a job as an errand boy at his uncle's store in Brooklyn, New York. He became a partner of the concern in short order, but his work was interrupted by his enlistment in the Civil War.

In 1873, upon the death of his father, he returned to Hartford, where he helped found the United States Bank, serving as its first president. In 1879 he was elected the third president in the history of the Aetna Life Insurance Company, in which position he continued until his death. Under his management, the Aetna became one of America's soundest financial institutions. Its assets rose from $25,000,000 in 1879 to over $200 million in 1922. During the same span of time, the number of employees rose from 29 to 1,500. He also established the Aetna Casualty and Surety Company and the Automobile Insurance Company of Hartford, both of which were subsidiaries of the parent company.

Bulkeley also had a profound interest in politics, entering public life at an early age. In Brooklyn, he was on the Republican general committee for King's County, and in Hartford, he immediately involved himself in municipal politics upon his arrival. Starting as a councilman, he passed from alderman to president of the court of the common council. He was elected mayor in 1880, serving four terms. In 1888 he was selected governor of the state by the state legislature. He also served a second term, beginning in 1890, but his administration was beset by constitutional wrangles with the Democrats. He could make no appointments, the legislature could make no laws, and no state appropriations were forthcoming. So, the state financed its operations with funds provided from Bulkeley's private fortune and from Aetna. From 1905 to 1911, Bulkeley served as U.S. senator and was often at odds with President Theodore Roosevelt during these years. He particularly opposed him in the "Brownsville Affair" and the Philippine tariff issue. He also opposed Roosevelt's movement toward federal regulation of the insurance industry, and was victorious on this issue.

Bulkeley served as treasurer and president of the National Trotting Association for thirty years, organized numerous baseball teams, and was president of the National Baseball League when it was formed in 1876. He married Fannie Briggs Houghton in 1885 and had two sons and one daughter. (*DAB; NCAB*, 10:345; *New York Times*, November 7, 1922; F. W. Chapman, *The Bulkeley Family*, 1875.)

BULOVA, ARDE (October 24, 1889–March 19, 1958). Watch manufacturer, Bulova Watch Company. Born in New York City, son of Joseph Bulova and Bertha Eisner. His father came to the United States from Bohemia (which later became part of Czechoslovakia) at the age of eighteen, settling in New York City. Arde Bulova was educated in the public schools of the city and began his business career in 1905 as a salesman for the J. Bulova Company, a small jewelry manufacturing concern founded by his father in 1875. The business prospered during these years and was incorporated in 1911 under the same name. His father served as president, and the son as vice-president and treasurer. In 1923 the business was re-incorporated as the Bulova Watch Company. In 1930 Arde was elected chairman of the board, which he remained for the rest of his life.

When he joined the firm in 1905, the jewelry operations were carried on in a small plant in New York City. In 1911 he arranged for establishment of a plant in Providence, Rhode Island. Two years later, the business was expanded to include the importing, assembly, and selling of fine watches. In 1919 a plant was established in Bienne, Switzerland, to manufacture watch movements. A plant was then built in Woodside, New York, for the manufacture and assembly of watch parts, but most parts continued to be imported from Switzerland. Year by year, however, new manufacturing departments were added in the U.S. By 1942 the Woodside plant was manufacturing all parts for watch movements except mainsprings, hair-springs, and jewel bearings. After World War II the plant also undertook to produce, on a mass production basis, every part incorporated in watch movements, with the exception of jewel bearings.

In the 1930s Bulova Watch began to acquire a number of subsidiaries: Sag Harbor (New York) Guild, Incorporated, Westfield Watch Company, a plant at Lac-on-Villiers, France, and Bulova Watch Company, Canada, Ltd., among others. Plants were built in Valley Stream, New York, in 1941 and Jackson Heights, Michigan, in 1952. In the latter year, Woodside operations were moved to a new modern factory at Bulova Park, Flushing, New York. The executive offices were also transferred there at this time. When Bulova started watch operations its lines included men's pocket and wrist watches, as well as all types of watches for women. During the ensuing years the company exercised a profound influence on the art of watchmaking. Bulova, believing that a watch must be easy to maintain and service, was responsible for instituting numerous manufacturing processes that permitted the standardization of parts and movements. He invented many of the improvements that were incorporated in his company's prod-ucts and designed a considerable number of special tools, gauges, and complicated machines required to produce parts.

Bulova was also interested in the radio industry from its infancy, and during the 1930s began to manufacture receiving sets. In 1956 the company began to manufacture electric razors. When World War II broke out, Bulova Company assumed a substantial role in the national defense effort, manufacturing military watches and timepieces, and such precision devices as aviation instruments, time fuses, parts for torpedoes, and fire control equipment, as well as jewel bearings. The company performed a similar task during the Korean Conflict, which also impelled Bulova to operate a fundamental research and development laboratory—the Bulova Research and Development Laboratories. They were set up at Woodside as a self-contained entity manned by engineers and scientists. Their tasks were steadily expanded over the years for research on guided missiles, instrumentation, electronics, military fuses, camera systems, camera aperture controls, infrared sensing devices, gyroscopes, and munitions. In 1953 Gen. Omar N. Bradley was made chairman of the board of the laboratories.

From the beginning, Bulova's products were sold only through licensed jewelers, and by 1957 the company was supplying products to some 18,000 stores in the United States and Canada. During the 1930s the company extended many months of credit to its customers, which led to the establishment of credit jewelry stores. Beginning in the 1920s Bulova conducted its advertising on a national scale, and Arde Bulova's interest in the radio industry led him to become a pioneer in advertising through that medium. He inaugurated the first radio spot advertisements in 1926, and with the advent of television, adapted them to that medium. In the last year of his involvement with the company, assets were $46,021,471, sales were $76,235,129, and it had a work force of 5,000.

One of Arde Bulova's most enlightened and innovative policies was his decision to hire the handicapped at the firm. They were given preferential hiring treatment, and a school was set up for the rehabilitation of disabled World War II veterans—the Joseph Bulova School of Watchmaking, opened at the Woodside plant in 1945. By 1958, 578 men and women had graduated from the school. All costs were borne by the Bulova Watch Foundation. In 1955 Arde Bulova was appointed chairman of the President's Commission on Employment of the Physically Handicapped. He held a financial interest in a number of radio stations and properties, including WOV, WNEW, and WWRL in New York City. In 1952 he married Ilcana Marie Kevcia Pociovolosteanu of Roumania. (*NCAB*, 49:541.)

BURNS, WILLIAM JOHN (October 19, 1861–April 14, 1932). Detective and security guard agency executive, William J. Burns National Detective Agency. Born in Baltimore, Maryland, the son of Michael Burns and Bridget Trakey. While he was still a child, the family moved to Zanesville, Ohio. His father was a merchant tailor, who later moved the family to Columbus, Ohio. William Burns was educated in parochial schools and a business college before he entered his father's business. Later, when his father was elected police commissioner of Columbus, William seized the opportunity to try his skill at detective work. He proved to be highly proficient at it, and in 1885 the state hired him to investigate election frauds. In 1889 he joined the U.S. Secret Service, stationed first in St. Louis, Missouri, and then in Washington, D.C. His specialty was in detecting and apprehending counterfeiters.

In 1903 the Department of the Interior sent Burns to investigate gigantic land frauds in the far west states of Washington, Oregon, and California. He turned up incriminating evidence on a number of state and federal officials, including U.S. Senator John H. Michelet. He was then called to San Francisco, California, and for three years probed the political corruption of "Boss" Abe Ruef, who was sent to the penitentiary as a result. In 1909, with his son, Raymond, he founded the William J. Burns National Detective Agency in New York City. Branches were also established in other cities, and he was given the contract for the 12,000 member banks of the American Bankers Association.

In 1910 Burns was hired to bring to justice the dynamiters of the Los Angeles *Times* building, and investigated the Atlantic City, New Jersey, and Detroit, Michigan, municipal graft cases in 1912. In 1914, he presented evidence to prove the innocence of Leo Frank, who had been charged with murder in Marietta, Georgia. As a result, he was nearly lynched by a mob in that city. Burns was also caught on the wrong side of the law on several occasions—one of which involved his illegal entry into a lawyer's office to make copies of letters for a client.

In 1921 he was named chief of the Federal Bureau of Investigation, but did not do well in the position and gave it up in 1924 to return to his detective agency. During the last years of his life he lived in Sarasota, Florida, where he was president of the Chamber of Commerce and head of the anti-Mosquito League. The detective agency continued to grow under his guidance and that of his son and successors, becoming the world's largest detective and security agency.

He was a Catholic and a Republican and married Annie M. Ressler of Columbus, Ohio, in 1880. They had two sons and two daughters. (*DAB*.)

BURPEE, WASHINGTON ATLEE (April 5, 1858–November 26, 1915) and **David Burpee** (April 5, 1893–   ). Seedmen, W. A. Burpee Company. **W. Atlee Burpee** was born in Sheffield, New Brunswick, Canada, son of David Burpee and Anne Catharine Atlee. His family moved to the U.S., settling in Philadelphia, where Burpee was educated at Friend's Central School and at the University of Pennsylvania. In 1876 he left college and opened a store in the city in association with G. S. Benson Jr., dealing in seeds, pigeons, and poultry. Shortly after that he went into business on his own, under the title of W. Atlee Burpee and Company. He was the first seedman to make a big success of the mail order business, and he did it by sticking absolutely to the truth in advertising. Backed by reliable products and progressive business methods, the firm grew steadily, and at the time of his death had 300 employees and handled nearly 3,000 orders daily.

He very early saw the desirability of conducting field trials for his crops. These were first instituted at the eastern end of Long Island, but about 1888 he purchased a large farm at Doylestown, Pennsylvania, which since then has been the chief proving grounds. Later, he purchased a farm near Swedesboro, New Jersey, where the soil was favorable for the growing of special varieties of tomatoes, eggplants, peppers, squashes, and certain flower seeds. He also purchased land in Lompoc, California, for cultivating sweet peas.

But these farms only raised a fraction of the seeds sold by the Burpee Company. The firm had contracts with growers in England, France, Germany, and Holland to supply its needs also. In 1890 Burpee introduced the original large bush lima bean, and has been instrumental in the improvement of cabbages, sweet corn, and squashes, and in introducing many notable varieties of tomatoes, culinary peas, onions, lettuces, and celery. Among flowers he was especially noted for his sweet peas, with which he did an enormous business. He had many other business interests and was president of the American Seed Trade Association for many years. He was also vice-president of the National Sweet Pea Society and a Life Member of the Royal Horticultural Society of England and the Societe Nationale Horticole of France. He married Blanche Simons of Philadelphia in 1892. They had two sons, David and W. Atlee Jr.

David Burpee was born in Philadelphia and educated at Blight School in the city, Doylestown High School, and the Culver Military Academy. He then pursued a course in agriculture at Cornell University. He left before completing his course, however, because of his father's illness. Joining the family business, he became head of the firm in 1915. When the firm was incorporated in 1917, he was named president. Through the years, the firm had increased the productivity and improved the taste of many vegetables, and since 1945 has created hybrid cantaloupe, cucumber, zucchini, squash, early squash, seven types of hybrid tomatoes, two types of hybrid watermelon, and two types of hybrid onion.

In 1916, when rising food prices threatened many large cities, the Burpee Company established demonstration war gardens in the East, and people were taught how to produce food in their backyards, which helped increase the firm's business significantly. Exclusively a mail order house, in 1936 it issued 1,000,000 catalogs annually. The enormous business has always been headquartered in Philadelphia, where orders are handled in a series of buildings containing the most modern equipment for handling, cleaning, and packing seeds. More than 420 persons were employed to handle the more than 20,000 orders daily during the peak spring season.

Toward the end of World War II, the company sent over 1,000,000 pounds of vegetables to the Allies under the U.S. lend-lease program. By 1959, about ten per cent of the business was in exports. By this time it was reputed to be the largest seed catalog mail order house in the world, and had branch houses in Clinton, Iowa, Riverside, California, and Sanford, Florida. More than fifty flowers and vegetables which have been introduced by the company have won All-American awards. When David Burpee took over as president in 1917, sales were $900,000; by 1959 they were over $6,000,000. He established the Burpee Fellowship in Genetics at Bucknell

College, was chairman of the board of James Vick's Seeds, Incorporated, and, since 1951, president of the Luther Burbank Seed Company. He is a Republican and married Lois Torrence of Norwalk, Connecticut, in 1938. They have a son and a daughter. (*NCAB*, 16:286; I:243; *Who's Who in America, 1978-79*.)

BURROUGHS, WILLIAM SEWARD (January 28, 1855-September 15, 1898). Inventor and manufacturer, Burroughs Adding Machine Company. Born in Auburn, New York, son of Edward and Ellen Julia Burroughs. His father was a model maker for castings and new inventions, but never did very well financially. William Burroughs had a limited education in the Auburn schools, and went to work at an early age. He was first employed in a bank, and later in stores and lumber goods. In his early manhood he engaged in one or two commercial enterprises, and at age 20 moved to St. Louis, where he worked in his father's model shop. He was later employed by the Future Great Manufacturing Company and by a manufacturer of woodworking machines. These brought him into contact with many inventions. In early 1884, he secured financial help from Thomas B. Metcalf, and by 1885, working in his father's shop, had made an ingenious mechanical device without commercial value. Having learned his lesson, he now decided to make something useful.

He organized the American Arithometer Company, capitalized at $100,000, with Metcalf and two other St. Louis businessmen. After Burroughs had produced a model of what was to become the adding machine, a contract was made with the Boyer Machine Company of St. Louis, to build fifty machines. These were completed in 1887, but could not stand up under usage, so they were scrapped. Finally, in 1892, he had a usable machine and received a patent on it. By 1895, 284 machines had been sold, the patents were sold in England for $200,000, and the capital of the company was increased to $500,000. Unfortunately, on the very eve of the company's success, Burroughs died, with Joseph Boyer* becoming president of the concern. In 1900, 1,500 adding machines were sold; 2,000 in 1901; 3,000 in 1902; and 4,500 in 1903. In 1905 the Burroughs Adding Machine Company was created to succeed the Arithometer Company, and the company was moved to Detroit. By 1913 the company had 2,500 employees and annual sales exceeding $8 million, more than that of all its competitors together, and was sending Burroughs machines around the world.

Burroughs married Ida Selaver in 1879 and had four children. His grandson, also named William S. Burroughs, achieved success in another field. A novelist, he was author of the highly successful *Naked Lunch*. (**A.** *DAB*, Supplement 1; *NCAB*, 27:383; *Current Biography*, November, 1971; *Who Was Who*, vol. H. **B.** Daniel Boorstin, *The Americans: The Democratic Experience*, 1973.)

BUSCH, ADOLPHUS (July 10, 1831–October 10, 1913). Brewer, Anheuser-Busch Brewery. Born Mainz-on-the-Rhine, Germany, youngest of twenty-one children of Ulrich Busch, a well-to-do dealer in wines and brewer's supplies. His mother, Barbara Pfeiffer, was his father's second wife. Adolphus was educated at the Gymnasium at Mainz, the academy at Darmstadt, and the high school of Brussels. He then worked for his father, and later for a mercantile house in Cologne. In 1857 he followed his relatives to the U.S., going to St. Louis, Missouri. On his father's death in 1859, he used his inheritance to set up a brewer's supply store with his brother, Ulrich. One of their customers was the proprietor of a Bavarian brewery in St. Louis, Eberhard Anheuser. In 1861, Anheuser's two daughters, Lilly and Anna, were married in a double ceremony to Ulrich and Adolphus. Soon afterward, Adolphus became a partner of his father-in-law, leaving for a time to serve as a corporal in the Civil War.

In 1875 the brewery was incorporated with capital of $240,000, and the name was changed from E. Anheuser and Company Brewing Association to Anheuser-Busch Brewing Association in 1879. In that same year Anheuser died, and Adolphus Busch became president of the firm. Also, about 1875, the brewery added to its line of products a beer which was light in color, pronounced in hop flavor, and not as sweet or heavy as prevailing beers. It was called "Budweiser" by Carl Conrad and soon became the brewery's specialty. Busch also put his laboratory to work on "pasteurization," which made it possible for him to ship malted beer to distant places without refrigeration. He used his skills as a commercial organizer and as a salesman to transform a local brewery into an internationally famous institution. He centered on four areas: a standard pale beer; Budweiser; "Faust" Beer; and the more expensive "Michelob." His products won many awards and gold medals.

The Busch plant grew until it consisted of 110 buildings on 70 acres, employing 6,000 workers, and producing 1,600,000 barrels of beer per year. To supply the brewery, Busch established one of the largest glass bottle works, developed railroads, owned coal mines in Illinois, acquired a major interest in the St. Louis Refrigerated Car Company, and set up a series of ice plants in major cities throughout the Southwest. He also acquired sole American rights to the manufacture of the diesel engine and established the Busch-Sulzer Diesel Engine Company near the brewery. This became a leading engineering laboratory and factory. He was also a bank president and erected the Hotel Adolphus in Dallas, Texas, for $1,000,000 and a sixteen story brick office building in the same city. He established many philanthropies and created the Crop Improvement Bureau in Chicago to improve the grain crop. He and his wife had fourteen children, of whom nine reached adulthood.

His eldest son, August Anheuser Busch (1865–1934), entered the brewery in 1889, and became first vice-president in 1894. After his father's death in

1913, he became president of the firm, which became Anheuser-Busch Incorporated in 1919. He held that position until his death. He guided the company through prohibition and depression and developed Bevo, a non-alcoholic beer. This was not successful, however, and he tried everything he could to end the prohibition amendment. In the meantime he created about twenty new industries to utilize the extensive manufacturing and distribution facilities of the company, especially corn products, malt products, and yeasts. He married Alice Zisemann and had four children. One of his sons, August A. Busch Jr., took over direction of the brewery and also became owner of the St. Louis Cardinals National League baseball team. Although Budweiser lost its number one position among American beers to Schlitz beer in the 1950s, it had regained its lead by the 1960s, increasing its market share from 6.8 percent in 1950 to 26 percent in 1979. The firm is presently directed by August A. Busch III, and had sales of $2.8 billion in 1979. (*DAB*, Supplement 1; *NCAB*, 12:23; 38:450; *New York Times*, October 11, 1913; *Who Was Who*, vol. 1.)

BUTTERFIELD, JOHN (November 18, 1801–November 14, 1869). Western stagecoach operator, American Express Company. Born in Berne, New York, son of Daniel Butterfield. John Butterfield had brief periods of schooling, but soon became a stagecoach driver. He rose from that position to a partnership in the firm, and soon most of the stage lines of western New York were under his control. He also became interested in packet boats on the Erie Canal, steam boats on Lake Ontario, and plank roads in the region. He organized the street railway of Utica, New York, and also helped organize the New York, Albany and Buffalo Telegraph Company. Although not an originator of the express business, he was one of the first to see the possibilities of such service.

In 1849, he formed the express company of Butterfield, Wasson and Company. When Congress in 1857 established the first transcontinental stage line, the Butterfield company was awarded the contract at $600,000 annually. This new stage line was called the American Express Company, and was to become the largest stagecoach line in America, extending from St. Louis, via Tucson and Los Angeles to San Francisco. It was 2,800 miles long, and coaches were to be run semi-weekly each way on a twenty-five day schedule. Butterfield was also president of the Overland Mail Company, in which he displayed his executive ability. The planning and establishment of this service was maintained with outstanding success.

During these years of his western success, Butterfield continued to live in Utica, New York, where he built the Butterfield Hotel and Butterfield Block. He was also elected mayor of the city in 1865. He married Malinda Harriet Baker in 1822. They had nine children, one of whom, Daniel Butterfield, became a general during the Civil War and later entered business. (**A.** *DAB; NCAB*, 22:61; **B.** Roscoe P. and Margaret Conkling, *The*

Butterfield Overland Mail, 1857-1869, 1947; Leroy R. Hofer, *The Overland Mail*, 1926; Ralph Moody, *Stagecoach West*, 1967; Henry P. Walker, *The Wagonmasters*, 1966.)

BUTTERICK, EBENEZER (May 29, 1826–March 31, 1903) and **Ellen Augusta (Pollard) Butterick** (d. 1871). Sewing pattern manufacturers, E. Butterick and Company. **Ebenezer Butterick** was born in Sterling, Massachusetts, son of Francis Butterick and Ruhamah Buss. His father was a carpenter. Ebenezer became a tailor and shirtmaker and married **Ellen Augusta Pollard**. In 1859, he and Ellen conceived the idea of a set of graded shirt patterns, by which it would be possible to reproduce these garments in unlimited quantities. In 1863, their first patterns, cut from stiff paper, were put on the market. The product was instantly successful and the demand was great, so Butterfield moved his plant in that year to Fitchburg, Massachusetts, where there were better facilities for manufacturing and distribution.

At the suggestion of Ellen Butterick that mothers would welcome patterns from which to make clothes for their children, Ebenezer added to his shirt patterns a graded set of patterns for boy's suits. The first juvenile patterns were for "Garibaldi Suits," modeled after the uniform worn by the Italian hero. These became enormously popular, so the factory was moved from their home to an unused academy. In 1864 headquarters were opened in New York City. Patterns now began to be made of tissue paper, and the firm specialized in children's suits. In short order they began to expand into women's fashions, at the suggestion of an agent of the company, J. W. Wilder. In 1867 E. Butterick and Company was established, with Ebenezer Butterick, J. W. Wilder, and A. W. Pollard as the principals. Wilder, however, became the active and controlling member of the firm.

They also established a magazine with fashion reports to stimulate the sale of patterns, called the *Metropolitan*. In 1871 the company sold 6,000,000 patterns, and by 1876 had branches in London, Paris, Berlin, and Vienna. The business was reorganized in 1881 and renamed the Butterick Publications Company, with Wilder as president and Ebenezer Butterick as secretary. He remained with the firm until 1894, when he retired. He and his wife had one child, Mary Ellen Butterick. (*DAB; NCAB*, 13:231; *New York Times*, April 1, 1903.)

BYRD, WILLIAM (1652–December 4, 1704) and **William Byrd II** (1674-1744). Colonial planters, merchants, speculators, and politicians. **William Byrd** was born in England, son of John Byrd, a London goldsmith of modest means, and Grace Stegg. William Byrd came to Virginia while he was quite young, and because of him his uncle, Thomas Stegg, was able to acquire land on both sides of the James River in 1671. This is the site of the present city of Richmond. Byrd's advancement in Virginia was rapid. In

1676 he joined forces with Nathaniel Bacon, the rebel, but later made peace with Governor Berkeley, serving as a member of the House of Burgesses from 1677 to 1682. A year later he entered the Council of State, and in 1688 became auditor general of Virginia. In 1691 he moved to Westover, Virginia, and in 1703 became president of the Council.

William Byrd's wealth grew from his involvement in tobacco trading, and his success depended largely on his ability to secure slave labor. Byrd imported large numbers of African slaves for his own use, and some for sale to neighboring farmers. For his tobacco, which he shipped to England, he received in return all manner of manufactured goods—cloth, hats, iron work, brandy, horse collars, and especially indentured servants. From Barbados he imported slaves, rum, sugar, molasses, and ginger. In return he sent out corn, flour, and pipe staves. He was also deeply engaged in the fur trade, owning a 400 mile tract of land southwest to the Catawba, over which he sent rough wooden wagons laden with articles to exchange for pelts. This was a dangerous business, with seven of his employees killed over a two year period. Byrd was often selected by the colony to deal with Indians on its business, was part-owner of several merchantmen, and speculated in land.

In 1673 Byrd married Mary Harsmanden, daughter of Warden Harsmanden, a Royalist refugee. Among their children was **William Byrd II**. He was born at James River, Virginia, and because his father's frontier plantation was peopled mostly by black slaves, was sent to England for his education. He later studied law at Middle Temple in London, being admitted to the bar in 1692. In that same year he returned to Virginia, securing election to the House of Burgesses. In 1697 he returned to England to defend Sir Edmund Andros against charges of hostility to the Anglican Church and as an agent for the colony. Upon his father's death in 1704 young William returned to Virginia to manage the sprawling family estate.

In 1709 William II was appointed to the Council of State, which at that time acted as the Supreme Court of Virginia, and served on it for the rest of his life. During the early years of his service he found himself embroiled in a series of controversies. He first clashed with a group of wealthy planters whose power was centered in the Council. He tried to put an end to the monopolizing of vast tracts of land by enforcing the collection of quit rents. Circumstances, however, soon found him allied with these very planters against the royal governor, Alexander Spotswood. Spotswood attempted to establish a separate court to act as a supreme court in the colony, intending to staff it with men who were not members of the Council. Byrd went to England in 1715 to present the colonists' case, managing to secure Spotswood's removal for usurping colonial judicial power. Byrd then remained in England as agent for Virginia.

In 1726 William Byrd II returned permanently to Virginia, and during the next several years would greatly enlarge the family estate, which stood at

179,000 acres at the time of his death. Although he was a fairly careful plantation manager, he lived an elegant and expensive lifestyle and was more than once so pressed with debt that he had to sell land and slaves to satisfy creditors. With his extensive landowning interests on the frontier, he became deeply interested in Western expansion, and was one of the first to recognize the peril posed by the French to expansion into the Ohio area. In 1728 he was a commissioner to establish the boundary between Virginia and North Carolina, and in 1743-1744 served as president of the Council of State. Throughout his life Byrd retained a careful balance between his commitments to the crown's interests in the colony, and the interests of his fellow planters. He was especially effective as the colonial assembly's agent in England in disputing the royal authority as expressed by Spotswood. He married Lucy Parke, daughter of General Daniel Parke, in 1706. After she died in 1716 he married Maria Taylor. William Byrd II's greatest fame, however, lies in his writings. Several of his essays were published posthumously in the *Westover Manuscripts* (1841), and his intimate diary, discovered and published after his death, offers a revealing portrait of southern plantation life. In an otherwise poorly documented time and place, his diaries and writings provide an insight into a stratified colonial society involved in the slow transition toward home rule and eventual independence.

If William Byrd I typified the business acumen of wealthy seventeenth century Virginia planters, William Byrd II typified the grace, charm, and culture, and the rather more lax business methods of Virginians of the eighteenth century. (*DAB; EAB; NCAB*, 7:27; J. S. Bassett ed., *The Writings of Col. William Byrd*, 1901; Pierre Marambaud, *William Byrd of Westover, 1674-1744*, 1971; Louis B. Wright, *The Prose Works of William Byrd of Westover: Narratives of a Colonial Virginian*, 1940.)

C

CABLE, RANSOM R. (1834–November 12, 1909). Railroad executive, Rock Island Railroad. Born in Athens County, Ohio, he moved to Rock Island, Illinois, as a child. At an early age he became interested in the railroad business and became president of the Rockford, Rock Island and St. Louis Railroad in 1870. He was elected a director of the Chicago, Rock Island and Pacific Railway in 1877, also serving as assistant to the president. In 1883 he became president of the line, serving until 1898. From 1898 to 1902 he was chairman of the board. In the latter year he retired and was succeeded by Daniel G. Reid.* He was also chairman of the board of the Burlington, Cedar Rapids and North Railroad and president of the Rock Island and Peoria Railroad. In his early years he had been involved in the coal mining business in Rock Island.

After Cable took over the Rock Island, the road grew rapidly to become a large integrated system that ranged from Chicago to Kansas City, Denver, and Fort Worth. It was generally recognized as one of the strongest of the railway systems built during the late nineteenth century, and Cable is acknowledged as one of the soundest of the railroad executives of that period. He was married and had two sons and two daughters. (**A.** *Who Was Who*, vol. 1; *New York Times*, November 13, 1909. **B.** Alfred D. Chandler Jr., *The Visible Hand*, 1977; Stuart Daggert, *Railway Reorganization*, 1908; Julius Grodinsky, *Transcontinental Railway Strategy*, 1962.)

CABOT, GEORGE (January 16, 1752–April 18, 1823). Shipowner and merchant. Born in Salem, Massachusetts, son of Joseph Cabot, a successful merchant. George was one of eleven children and entered Harvard College. He took an active part in the "Rebellion of 1766" at the college, and was a member of the committee chosen to deal with college authorities. He withdrew from the school in 1768. He then joined his brothers, John and Andrew Cabot of Beverly, Massachusetts—who were carrying on their father's rum, fish, and iron trade with the southern colonies—as a cabin boy on one of their ships. On his eighteenth birthday he became the skipper of his brother's schooner, *Sally*, and in the next year became captain of the new schooner, *Premium*.

In 1774 George married his double first cousin, Elizabeth Higginson, acquiring a one-sixth interest in her family's distillery, and was entrusted with one of their best ships. About 1777 he gave up active seafaring and was taken into his brother's firm, which during the Revolutionary War owned and operated at least forty privateers. Their armed merchantmen traded with Spain, and kept their proceeds in that country, so that unlike most privateering firms, they were able to retain their profits until peace was concluded. In 1784 Cabot's ships were the first to carry the American flag to St. Petersburg, Florida, and in the same year George became a director of the Massachusetts Bank, the state's first bank. He was a leading promoter in 1788 of the Essex Bridge Company and the Beverley Cotton Manufactory. In 1785 he formed a partnership with his brother-in-law, Joseph Lee, which was so profitable that he retired from active business in ten years.

In 1778 he began to take an active part in politics with a group of Essex County merchants and lawyers who became members of the Federalist party. He was a member of the Concord Convention of 1779 where he vainly argued against price-fixing. In 1783 he was named state senator from Essex County, and was a strong advocate for the new federal Constitution in 1787. In 1791 he became a United States senator from Massachusetts, and served as a close advisor to Alexander Hamilton* and as a director of the U.S. Bank. He resigned his seat in the Senate in 1796 and retired to private life. In 1803 he became president of the Boston branch of the U.S. Bank, and in 1809 president of the Boston Marine Insurance Company. He was called the "Federalist Sage" of Boston and was part of the "Essex Junto" of the Cabot, Lowell,* Lee, Higginson,* and Jackson* families who had moved to Boston after the Revolution. For over a generation these families frequently intermarried, helped one another in business, and formed a solid political bloc, coming to be regarded as the typical Boston "Brahmins." (**A.** *DAB; NCAB*, 2:5; *Who Was Who*, vol. H. **B.** Kenneth W. Porter, *The Jacksons and the Lees*, 1937.)

CALHOUN, PATRICK (March 21, 1856–June 16, 1943) and **John C. Calhoun II** (July 9, 1843–December 18, 1918). Financiers and developers of "New South." **John C. Calhoun II** was born in Demopolis, Alabama, son of Andrew Pickens Calhoun, and grandson of John C. Calhoun. He was educated at local schools until he entered the Civil War by organizing a cavalry troop. He continued in the service until the end of the war. After the war he found his home devastated and the entire family fortune swept away. He thereupon decided to become a planter.

In 1866 Calhoun established a partnership with James R. Rowell of Montgomery, Alabama, for the purpose of colonizing Negroes in the Yazoo Valley of Mississippi, to work plantation lands on the cooperative system. This was very successful, and after one year, he sold out to his partner for $10,000. He then went to Arkansas, where he repeated the enterprise on a larger scale. He inaugurated a migration movement of more than 5,000 blacks into the Mississippi Valley from the Carolinas, Georgia, and Alabama. For fifteen years he was thus engaged in the first practical method to assist freedmen to achieve citizenship and land ownership. In 1884 he disposed of his plantation interests and moved to New York City, becoming prominent on Wall Street. In that same year he organized a combination to take control of the Richmond Terminal Railroad properties, which later absorbed the Richmond and Danville and East Tennessee Railway systems, and led to a movement to obtain control of the Central Railroad and Banking Company of Georgia. He was the principal owner of the Baltimore Coal Mining and Railroad Company and controlled coal fields in New Brunswick. He married Linnie Adams of Lexington, Kentucky, grandniece of Richard Johnson, vice-president of the United States from 1837 to 1841. They had three sons and one daughter.

Patrick Calhoun was born near Pendleton, South Carolina, on the plantation of his grandfather, John C. Calhoun. He was the son of Andrew Pickens Calhoun and his second wife, Margaret Mario Green, daughter of Duff Green. He was educated in country schools near the plantation, and studied law with his grandfather, Duff Green. Calhoun was admitted to the Georgia bar at age nineteen, but moved to St. Louis, Missouri, in 1876 to practice there. His health was not good, however, so he retired to the Arkansas plantation of his brother, John C. Calhoun II. About 1878 he went to Atlanta, Georgia, to resume his legal career, specializing in corporate law. He quickly acquired a lucrative practice and a wide circle of business contacts. He was a senior partner in the law firm of Calhoun, King and Spaulding from 1887 to 1894, but also organized the Calhoun Land Company during this time to raise cotton in the Mississippi Valley. Later, he acquired extensive properties in South Carolina and Texas. His other enterprises included oil, railroads, manufacturing, and mining. Between 1887 and 1893, he was a member of a syndicate, with his brother, controlling the Richmond Terminal, a holding company for several railroad properties. His law firm served as general counsel for Richmond Terminal and two of its subsidiary railroads. In 1892 he resigned as counsel and was ousted from the board of directors in a struggle for control. Two years later he acted for J. P. Morgan Company in buying the now bankrupt Richmond Terminal, and consolidated it into the Southern Railroad System.

After 1894 he gave up the practice of law and turned his full attention to business affairs, leaving the South. He developed and reorganized street railway properties in Pittsburgh, Pennsylvania, Baltimore, Maryland, and St. Louis, Missouri. He lived in New York City for a time, and then moved to Cleveland, Ohio, in 1896. In that city he developed a section of Cleveland Heights known as Euclid Heights, where he lived. After the turn of the century, he entered the business life of San Francisco, where he helped amalgamate the street railways into the United Railways of San Francisco. He became president of that concern in 1906. He gave political boss Abe Ruef a bribe of $200,000 to secure approval for construction of an overhead trolley network, and was indicted for bribery in 1907, following William J. Burn's* investigation. His trial in 1909 resulted in a hung jury and the case was dismissed in 1911.

But Calhoun's financial position was now tenuous. He claimed to have lost $2,500,000 in the San Francisco earthquake of 1906, in addition to heavy legal expenses for his trial. During a 1907 transit strike he broke the power of the carmen's union only by importing strike-breakers and provoking bloody riots. Then, in 1912, the California Railway Commission investigation revealed that Calhoun had juggled the books of his company, losing about $1,200,000 of the stockholders' money. New York investors forced him to resign in 1913. At that point he largely resigned from active business, but made heavy investments in real estate ventures, all of which failed. He moved to New York, virtually penniless, having existed on his wife's funds for two years. He later became involved in the development of California oil fields. He was a Democrat and married Sarah Porter William in 1885. They had eight children. (**A.** *DAB*, Supplement 3; *NCAB*, 13:506; 34:231; *New York Times*, June 18, 1943; *Who Was Who*, vols. 1 and 2; A. S. Salley Jr., "The Calhoun Family of South Carolina," *South Carolina Historical and Genealogical Magazine*, 1906. **B.** Maury Klein, *The Great Richmond Terminal*, 1970.)

CALLAWAY, FULLER EARLE (July 12, 1870–February 12, 1928) and **Cason Jewell Callaway** (b. 1894). Textile manufacturers, Callaway Textile Mills. **Fuller Callaway** was born in La Grange, Georgia, son of Abner Reeves Callaway and Sarah Jane Howard. Both his father and grandfather were Baptist ministers, and his father was also a professor at Southern Female College at La Grange. Fuller was educated in the city schools of La Grange, and as a youth became an errand boy in a local dry goods store. In 1888, he borrowed capital to start a five and ten cent store in La Grange which grew into a department store and wholesale dry goods business.

Twelve years later, in 1900, he engaged in cotton manufacturing in a company he organized with several associates—the Unity Cotton Mills of La Grange. He served as treasurer of the concern. In 1902 he was appointed to reorganize the unsuccessful Milstead Manufacturing Company. He made a success of the operation, and it became the second unit in a group of manufacturing, financial, and allied corporations which were built up by Callaway. In 1905 he became chairman of a commission that was building a branch of the Atlanta, Birmingham and Atlantic Railroad through La Grange. This project was a boon to La Grange and the Callaway enterprises.

Before his death, his enterprises consisted of twelve cotton mills and at least a dozen other enterprises: Unity Cotton Mills, Unity Spinning Mills, Holland Cotton Mills, Valley Rug Mills, Oakleaf Mills, and Valley Waste Mills, all of La Grange; the Milstead Manufacturing Company of Georgia, the Manchester (Georgia) Cotton Mills, J. T. Perkins Company of Brooklyn, New York, and the Truline Company of Roanoke, Alabama, along with Milstead Railroad, La Grange Development, Silbury Warehouse, La Grange

Electric Ginnery, Callaway's Department Stores, La Grange Insurance Agency, and the Callaway Mills of New York, a selling agency. These enterprises were all founded and developed by Fuller Callaway, and were among the leading industrial groups in the United States. The cotton mills had 6,000 employees and used over 100,000 bales of cotton per year. They shipped their product all over the world and had sales of $25,000,000 annually.

His were the first of the large textile organizations to establish their own selling organization to the finishing trade, and later to organize mills for completing the product and selling directly to the ultimate consumer. He did much social and educational work for his employees, providing homes, schools, churches, and community hotels for men and women. He instituted profit-sharing, group insurance, medical and nursing services, greenhouses, paved streets, and so forth. There were no labor problems in the Callaway mills during his tenure. He also served as president of the American Cotton Manufacturers Association in 1917-1918, and as vice-president of the World Cotton Conference in 1924. Locally, he served on the La Grange city council for twelve years, and was a member of the Georgia Railway Commission in 1907-1908. In 1917 he undertook, at the request of the Department of the Interior, to secure the cooperation of mine owners and producers in Alabama and Georgia to increase the production of pyrites for war purposes. Later, he was a member of the National Industrial Conference Board. He married Ida Jane Cason of Jewell, Georgia, and had two sons, Cason Jewell and Fuller E. Jr. He was a Baptist and a Democrat.

Cason Jewell Callaway was born in La Grange, Georgia, and educated at Bingham School in Asheville, North Carolina. He attended the University of Virginia for a time and in 1912-1913 was at the Eastman School of Business in Poughkeepsie, New York. He then entered his father's mills. During his early years with the firm, he was often on the road selling the company's products. In 1915 he organized the Valley Waste Mills, based upon an idea he developed for grading waste. They became the nation's largest manufacturer of industrial wiping cloths. After 1919 he took over the management and main responsibility for the mills from his father, serving during the next quarter century as treasurer, president, and chairman of the board. He was also an officer of many of its constituent companies.

In 1922 C. J. Callaway was primarily responsible for the establishment of Callaway Mills, the New York selling agency, and was president and director of that from its inception to 1935. In 1928 he became official head of the entire organization. In 1925 he organized the Canvas Cotton Products Manufacturing Company (later Calumet Cotton Mills) and was president of this for four years. In 1929 he sold out all of his stocks and concentrated his efforts on pulling the Callaway Mills through the depression, and they showed a profit in each year. In 1932 he consolidated all the firms, except Valley Waste Mills and Callaway Mills, Incorporated, into a new corporation, Callaway Mills of La Grange. He served as its president, and brought together seven mills with 2,656 looms, 138,360 spindles, and 856 cards. They employed 4,927 and were capitalized at $4,158,000. He was president of this until 1935 and chairman of the board until 1938.

Later he established the Callaway Community Foundation to run the mills and they ceased to be operated for profit. Instead, the proceeds went for the purposes of supporting charitable and community enterprises, especially educational and religious activities. He was chairman of the Textile Benefit Association from 1919 to 1938, and served on the boards of a large number of corporations, including U.S. Steel, Chemical Corn Exchange Bank, Shell Oil, and others. He purchased 30,000 acres of old, worn-out farmland in Harris County, Georgia, in order to restore it to fertility for use in crop production. This was called Blue Springs Farm. Later he set up another corporation to help restore 100 worn-out small farms in Georgia. He paid $30 an acre for the land, and $70 an acre to build up the soil. He had some success with the program.

He served on the Textile Code Authority of the NRA in the 1930s, and visited Japan in 1936-1937 and persuaded her to accept a quota on her exports of cotton goods. During World War II he served on the War Advisory Council of Businessmen and was a close personal friend of Franklin Roosevelt. Like his father, he was a Baptist and a Democrat, and a delegate to the Democratic National Convention in 1940. He married Virginia Hollis Hord in 1920, and had three children. (*NCAB*, 53:33; 21:154; 47:510; *Who's Who in Commerce and Industry*, 1955.)

CANDEE, LEVERETT (June 1, 1795–November 27, 1863). Merchant and pioneer rubber manufacturer, Candee and Company. Born in Oxford, Connecticut, son of John Candee and Sarah Benham. His father was a Revolutionary War veteran and later a member of the Connecticut state legislature. Leverett received a meager education in district schools and went to New Haven at age fifteen when he secured employment with Captain Gad Peck, a merchant prominent in foreign trade. His next position was with Root and Atwater, dealers in dry goods, thus beginning his twenty-five year connection with the dry goods business. With two fellow clerks, James E. P. Dean and William Cutler, he organized the firm of Candee, Dean and Cutler, which took over the business of their employers. Retiring from this business in 1833, he moved to New York City, where he was partner for two years in a firm of jobbers and commission merchants in the dry goods field. He returned to New Haven in 1835 and entered a partnership with Timothy Lester and Abraham Murdoch in a general merchandise and commission business. Upon dissolution of that firm, Candee was engaged for several years in the manufacture of book paper at

Westville, Connecticut, with the firm Candee, Page and Lester, but this was unsuccessful. Its failure in 1842 wiped out the fortune Candee had accumulated over a quarter of a century.

He then turned to the manufacture of elastic suspenders. This venture aroused his interest in rubber, and he attempted in that year (1842) to manufacture rubber shoes. Charles Goodyear then offered him a license to use the vulcanization process he had developed, and it was confirmed and extended upon the granting of a patent. Candee's venture was backed financially by Henry Lucian Hotchkiss of New Haven. He commenced the manufacture of rubber shoes at Hamden, Connecticut, being the first person in the world to manufacture rubber overshoes under the Goodyear patent. The first overshoes he produced were exceedingly crude, and the early years of manufacture were taken up with improving the product and building a market. By the late 1840s, the firm was solidly established, and a new impetus to its prosperity was given in 1852 by court decisions which upheld the Goodyear patent.

In that same year the firm was organized as Candee and Company, with capital of $200,000 and four partners: the Hotchkiss brothers, Timothy Lester, and Candee. Candee was the actual manager of the concern, and except for one year, served as its president. He retired shortly before his death in 1863. He married Jane Caroline Tomlinson and had one son. (**A.** *DAB.* **B.** Howard and Ralph Wolf, *Rubber: A Story of Greed*, 1936; and Ralph F. Wolf, *Indian Rubber Man: The Story of Charles Goodyear*, 1939.)

CANDLER, ASA GRIGGS (December 30, 1851–March 12, 1929). Soft drink manufacturer, Coca-Cola Company. Born on a farm near Villa Rica, in Carroll County, Georgia, the son of Samuel Charles Candler, a country merchant and farmer, and Martha Beall. It was a large family, eleven girls and seven boys, and in addition to Asa, several of the boys went on to become prominent in Georgia: Warren A. became a bishop in the Methodist Episcopal Church; John S. served on the Georgia Supreme Court; and Milton A. held a seat in the U.S. Congress. Asa spent his early years on the farm, receiving a good education at local academies, but never attended college. He had planned on becoming a physician, studying medicine under a private tutor, but became a trained pharmacist instead.

Candler went to Atlanta in 1873, securing a position with George J. Howard, a druggist. Four years later, with Marcellus B. Hallman, he established the drug firm of Hallman and Candler. During these years he had sold a patent medicine concocted by John Styth Pemberton, another Atlanta pharmacist, which was touted as a cureall for headaches, sluggishness, indigestion, and throbbing temples resulting from over-indulgence. In 1886 the ailing Pemberton sold Candler a part interest in the nostrum, called Coca-Cola, and a year later Candler took full control of the company. In 1892 the Coca-Cola Company, Incorporated was organized, with Candler as president and major stockholder. He had considerable difficulty in financing its early operations, but the breakthrough came when Candler realized the potential of his syrup as a simple soda fountain drink rather than as a miracle drug. He sent salesmen across the country instructing druggists what to do with a keg of Coca-Cola. Considerable sums were invested in advertising, with painted Coca-Cola signs going up on barns all over the country. The Coca-Cola legend was also put on trays, Japanese fans, bookmarks, and glasses. By 1895 Coke was sold in every state and territory in the United States, with the syrup produced in satellite plants in Chicago, Dallas, and Los Angeles. By 1898 it had moved into Canada, Hawaii, and Mexico.

During the early years Candler was content to make and sell his syrup, resisting ideas of bottling it. In 1899 he signed a contract giving two Chattanooga lawyers the rights to bottle Coca-Cola in virtually the entire United States for one dollar. The Chattanooga group set itself up as middlemen who bought the syrup from Coca-Cola Company and resold it to local bottlers across the country. It was in this way that the franchise system which remains the basis of the Coca-Cola business was born. Candler's problems with the federal government began in 1909, when the Secretary of Agriculture, under the provisions of the Pure Food and Drug Act, filed suit against Coca-Cola. The case was carried to the Supreme Court, which remanded it for trial in the federal court of eastern Tennessee. The issue was whether the amount of caffeine contained in Coca-Cola was detrimental to health. A judgement of forfeiture was entered against the company in 1917, and it was ordered to pay cash to the court, causing the Candler family to sell the company to the Georgia financier, Ernest Woodruff, for $25 million. Asa Candler remained as president of the firm until 1916, when he was succeeded by his son, Charles Howard Candler, who retained that post until after the company was sold.

During the early years of the twentieth century Asa Candler had increasingly turned his attention to real estate and the affairs of the city of Atlanta. In 1907, when a real estate panic threatened, he bought one million dollars worth of homes and resold them to people of moderate incomes for 10 percent down and 100 payments at low interest. He also gave Emory University its land and a large part of its endowment. After serving as president of the Atlanta Chamber of Commerce in 1908–1909, he resigned the presidency of Coca-Cola to run for mayor of Atlanta on a reform ticket. Serving in 1917–1918, he did much to reorganize the city's administration and untangle its finances. During the early years of World War I, when cotton prices were severely depressed, Candler offered to lend farmers six cents a pound on all cotton stored in warehouses. This cost him over thirty million dollars, and he had to construct a forty acre warehouse to hold it all. When the prices went up, the producers marketed the cotton, and paid back the loan. He was also one of the largest property owners in the city of

Atlanta and in 1905 organized the Central Bank and Trust Company, serving as its president until it was merged with Citizen's and Southern Bank in 1929. A staunch Methodist, Candler gave a great deal of money to his church, and was twice married: to Lucy Howard, daughter of his former employer, in 1875; and later to Mrs. Mary L. Reagin. He had six children.

His eldest son, Charles Howard Candler (1878–1957) joined Coca-Cola in 1899 and became president of the firm in 1916. He remained a director of the company after it was sold to the Woodruff interests, serving until his death in 1957. He was also president of Asa G. Candler Jr. Incorporated, a realty holding company. Another son, Asa G. Candler Jr. (1880–1953) spent most of his time managing the family's vast real estate interests, and also constructed the Hartwell (Georgia) Cotton Mill, one of the largest plants of its type in the country. (**A.** *DAB; NCAB*, 31:9; 46:454; 47:534; *New York Times*, March 29, 1929; *Who Was Who*, vol. 1; Charles H. Candler, *Asa Griggs Candler*, 1950. **B.** E. J. Kahn Jr., *The Big Drink*, 1960; Milton Moskowitz et al., eds., *Everybody's Business*, 1980; John J. Riley, *A History of the Soft Drink Industry*, 1972.)

CANNON, JAMES WILLIAM (April 25, 1852–December 19, 1921) and **Charles A. Cannon** (November 29, 1892–April 2, 1971). Textile manufacturers, Cannon Mills Company. **James W. Cannon** was born in Mecklenburg County, North Carolina, son of Joseph Allison Cannon, a planter, and Eliza Long. James attended private schools, and at age fourteen went to work in a store in Charlotte, North Carolina. He then obtained employment at Concord, North Carolina, with the firm of Cannon, Fetzer and Wadsworth, a mercantile establishment in which his brother was a partner. Before he reached his majority, James became a member of the firm, which not only operated a general store, but acted as a cotton buyer, banker, counselor, and director of the community.

In 1887 Cannon became interested in textile manufacturing and withdrew from his brother's firm. He erected a mill to manufacture coarse cotton yarns called the Cannon Manufacturing Company, and he was secretary-treasurer and active manager of the concern. It was capitalized at $75,000. This led to the establishment of other mills, and to the manufacture of a completed fabric—"Cannon Cloth"—which was woven at the Cannon Mills and soon became popular throughout the South. He then decided to manufacture cotton towels as the ideal instrument for the development of his business. In 1898 his enlarged mill produced the first towel ever finished in the South.

About 1906, Cannon decided to build a mill exclusively for the manufacture of towels. He built Kannopolis, the largest unincorporated town in the world. It was placed in operation in 1908 and could manufacture more towels than any single group of mills. Kannopolis was also recognized as a model mill city. The Cannon Mills manufactured a variety of cotton cloth into muslin and percale sheets and pillow cases, tire fabrics, and women's hosiery. At the time of his death there were twelve mills which employed 15,000 workers and had sales of $40,000,000 annually. The mills at Kannopolis alone manufactured 300,000 towels daily. In his mill town, he built schools, churches, dormitories for single women operatives, and parks.

He was a Presbyterian and an independent in politics. He married Mary Ella Bost of North Carolina, and they had nine children. His youngest son, **Charles Albert Cannon**, was born in Concord, North Carolina, and quit college in 1911 to go to work in his father's mills. At age nineteen he became manager of the family-owned Barringer Manufacturing Company in Rockwell, North Carolina. In 1916 he became a vice-president of Cannon Manufacturing Company, and president of Cannon Mills in 1921, upon the death of his father. Two years later, he was named head of Cannon Mills, Incorporated, New York City, the firm's selling agent.

Charles Cannon pioneered a number of industry advances: national consumer advertising, the Cannon trademark sewn into each towel, pastel colors, the wrapping of products in clear plastic, style shows, and matching towel ensembles. He also extended the company's line to include sheets, hosiery, bedspreads, draperies, decorative fabrics, and blankets. The firm's income in 1970 was $305 million. He also played a leading role in the American Cotton Textile Association, and helped his father found Kannopolis, a modern barony which was in a class by itself. Since his father had insisted that the town remain unincorporated, it had no legal existence as a municipality. Thus, it had no charter, no mayor, no town council, even though in 1970 it had a population of 36,000.

Charles Cannon and his father ran Kannopolis as a model town, hiring a Chicago architectural group to draft a master plan for the thirty-five acre business district. It was transformed into a Georgian village that resembled a movie set. Charles Cannon dominated Kannopolis and Cabarrus County during his lifetime, and was a major political power in the state. He served on the State Highway Commission and the State Public Works Commission. His candidates for public office in Cabarrus County invariably won, and he did not lose his first state-wide contest until 1958. In 1970, Ralph Nader did a television documentary on Cannon on the Public Broadcasting System. Unions found Cannon to be an adamant foe, and despite repeated efforts, did not succeed in organizing his mills. He was, however, generous to numerous medical and educational causes. He also stepped in twice to save the credit standing of the state of North Carolina. When he died in 1971, Cannon had 17 plants with 24,000 workers. He married Ruth Louise Coltrane of Concord, North Carolina, in 1912. They had four children. (*NCAB*, 33:309; *New York Times*, April 3, 1971; *Who Was Who*, vol. 5.)

CAPONE, ALPHONSE (January 17, 1899–January 25, 1947). Crime boss and illegal liquor distributor. Born in Brooklyn, New York, son of Gabriel Capone (Caponi) and Teresa Rioli, both of whom had emigrated from Naples, Italy, in 1893. His father was a small shopkeeper. Al Capone was educated in the Brooklyn public schools until age fourteen. He held various odd jobs, joined a street gang, and was arrested on several charges, including suspicion of murder. While working as a bartender and bouncer, he received a knife would on the face that would earn him the nickname "Scarface."

In late 1919 or 1920, Capone moved to Chicago to join John Torrio, a former New Yorker, then rising in the Chicago underworld. Torrio had succeeded his uncle, James ("Big Jim") Colosimo, and with considerable entrepreneurial ability, began to build a major bootlegging organization. Capone rapidly moved into a leadership position. He became manager of the Four Deuces, a combination saloon, gambling den, whorehouse, and headquarters for the Torrio businesses. Central to these enterprises was a system of liquor distributors in the Chicago Loop, the Levee, and the suburbs. He also invested in breweries and distilleries, and easily established corrupt relations with the politicians and police in the city.

In the spring of 1924, when the Torrio syndicate decided to extend its influence into suburban Cicero, Capone began to capture headlines which would bring him international notoriety. He led the gunmen who controlled the Cicero polls on election day, and in a shootout with police, Capone's brother, Frank, was killed. The Capone syndicate won, and the Torrio organization coordinated bootlegging and gambling in Cicero. Meanwhile, in Chicago itself, rivalries were breaking out in the underworld. A series of gangland killings led to the critical wounding of Torrio in 1925, with Capone taking temporary charge of the organization. Torrio then took an extended European "vacation" and Capone, at age twenty-six, became the leading figure in a coalition of entrepreneurs who operated a major bootlegging and entertainment syndicate.

Much of Capone's reputation stemmed from a series of publicized beer wars that from 1923 to 1930 left hundreds dead in the streets of Chicago and suburbs. Capone's organization was strengthened by the decimation of rival gangs, and he became known as a ruthless and remorseless assassin. The most famous of these killings was the "St. Valentine's Day Massacre" in 1929, in which seven members of the North Side Gang were machine-gunned in a garage by Capone gunmen. Failure to convict anyone of the killings did much to establish Chicago's reputation as a lawless city, and made Capone the symbol of a lawless decade.

Capone's syndicate grew and prospered, but Capone himself was never as important to its operation as the myth made him out to be. Basically the organization was operated through partnerships, the senior partners being Al Capone, his brother, Frank, Frank Nitti, and Jack Guzik. The syndicate began expanding into gambling operations in the late 1920s and soon they were as important as bootlegging. By 1928, several labor racketeers had become associated with Capone, and he moved into that area also. But after that time Capone seldom supervised the day-to-day operations of the organization. He moved to Florida that winter, and two years later was arrested in Philadelphia for carrying a concealed weapon. He was sentenced to one year in jail. Then, in 1931, he was indicted for income tax fraud, and for conspiracy to violate federal prohibition laws. He was found guilty on three counts and sentenced to eleven years in jail, plus a fine of $80,000. At age thirty-two his career was over, but not his reputation. The coalition of gunmen and entrepreneurs survived his departure, and continued for years to be known as the Capone Organization.

Capone served one year in the Cook County Jail, where his lifestyle was lavish, and then was transferred to the federal penitentiary at Atlanta, Georgia, and later to Alcatraz. In 1938 he was found to have syphilis of the brain and was released from prison in 1939. He retired to Miami. He married Mary Coughlin in 1918 and had one son. (**A.** *DAB*, Supplement 4; Wilson and Pitman, *Encyclopedia of Murder*; John Kobler, *Capone*, 1971. **B.** Jack McPhaw, *Johnny Torrio*, 1970.)

CARLISLE, FLOYD LESLIE (March 5, 1881–November 9, 1942). Paper manufacturer and utility company executive, St. Regis Paper Company, Niagara Hudson Power, and Consolidated Edison. Born in Watertown, New York, son of William Sylvanus Carlisle and Catharine Rose Burdick. His father was an expert mechanic in the local Davis Sewing Machine Company, and moved with it to Dayton, Ohio. Floyd Carlisle was educated in the public schools in Watertown and Dayton and graduated from Cornell University in 1903. He then read law and was admitted to the New York bar in 1905. He practiced law with his brother for five years and in 1910 merged two Watertown banks to form the Northern New York Trust Company. He served as its president until 1922. In 1916 he organized a syndicate of local businessmen to purchase the St. Regis Paper Company, and was president of that from 1916 to 1934.

Since St. Regis used waterpower, Carlisle began to move into that field, partly on his own, and partly on behalf of his company. He began to acquire water power sites and small electric companies, and in 1920 these were consolidated as the Northern New York Utilities Corporation. He then began a rapid program of expansion. He formed his own investment house, F. L. Carlisle and Company, and for a time was associated with the maverick utility financier, Howard Hopson.* After 1927 he broke with Hopson, and joined forces with J. P. Morgan Jr.* His own holdings were merged with those of others in 1929 to form the Niagara Hudson Power Company, of which he was board chairman. He then began the interconnection of the huge power resources of Niagara Falls with the great markets of New York City.

He was also made president of Consolidated Gas Company, which held together a sprawling network of electric utilities in and around New York City. These were brought together as Consolidated Edison. Between Niagara Hudson and Consolidated Edison, Carlisle controlled about three quarters of the electrical supply in the state. During the depression of the 1930s, utility companies fell into disrepute and several utility executives were indicted—Hopson, Samuel Insull,* and W. B. Foshay. So Morgan executives sought to cover themselves by seeing that only "bad" utility companies (that is, non-Morgan concerns) were punished. Thus, Carlisle became a reformer and advised the New Deal in its crusade against the power industry. He was instrumental in the organization in 1933, of the Edison Electric Institute, whose purpose was avowedly to purge the industry of evils and reform it from within. But holding companies (*all* holding companies) were banned in the industry in a federal act in 1935 and the concentrated power of the House of Morgan was broken by the bank acts of that period.

During the years of Carlisle's utility involvement, St. Regis Paper also prospered. It became one of the largest producers of paper in the United States, while Niagara Hudson Power at the same time became the largest producer of power in the country. Mr. Carlisle was an Episcopalian and a Democrat and married Edna May Rogers in 1912. They had four children. (*DAB*, Supplement 2; *NCAB*, F:302; 31:391; *New York Times*, November 14, 1942; *Who Was Who*, vol. 2.)

CARNEGIE, ANDREW MORRISON (November 25, 1835–August 11, 1919). Steel manufacturer, Carnegie Steel Company. Born in Dumferline, Scotland, son of William Carnegie, a handloom weaver, and Margaret Morrison. During the years of the early nineteenth century technological innovations were making handloom weaving obsolete, so his father was often without work and the family was desperately poor. In response to this William Carnegie became a radical Chartist and labor agitator who was often described as one of the most troublesome street orators in Dumferline. Because of these difficulties, the family immigrated to the United States in 1848. William Carnegie had hoped to find a position as a handloom weaver in America, but was disappointed, ending up as a laborer in a cotton textile mill in Pittsburgh. To help ends meet, Andrew Carnegie took a job in the same mill as a bobbin boy for $1.20 a week. His mother also took in washing, and worked for Henry Phipps, the shoemaker next door. Andrew's next job was as a stoker in the furnace room at the cotton mill, and at age fifteen he joined the telegraph office as a messenger boy. He later became an operator, securing a position with the Pennsylvania Railroad.

Carnegie soon caught the eye of Thomas Scott,* who had recently been appointed superintendent of the road's western division. He appointed Carnegie his secretary and personal telegrapher; this was to prove a profitable association for both men. During his twelve years with the Pennsylvania Railroad, Carnegie assimilated the managerial skills, grasped the economic principles, and cemented the personal relationships that enabled him to become a successful manager, capitalist, and entrepreneur. The railroads had been the pioneers of modern management and bureaucratic structures, and at that time the Pennsylvania Railroad was recognized as the leader in these developments. Carnegie worked for the road during the years when the administrative structure was developed, and he was later to play an instrumental role as superintendent of the western division during unprecedented growth in traffic. When Scott became vice-president of the Pennsylvania in 1859, he appointed Carnegie as his replacement as superintendent of the western division, still a relative youth of twenty-four years of age. He performed well as superintendent because he thoroughly understood the management procedures that had been developed. He also proved himself a daring innovator. He cleared wrecks by burning the cars that blocked the line, or by laying new tracks around them. He appointed the first night train dispatchers to facilitate twenty-four hour movements, and persuaded his superiors to keep all telegraph stations open around the clock. He succeeded so well that he was offered the post of general superintendent in 1865, but turned it down because he had decided to leave the railroad.

During his years with the Pennsylvania, his association with Thomas Scott also gave him an apprenticeship as a capitalist and financier. In 1856 Scott persuaded him to buy ten shares of Adams Express Company stock for $600, lending the money. Carnegie soon received his first ten dollar dividend check, and a whole new world was opened to him. From this modest beginning he began to build his fortune. By 1863 his investment ventures provided him with an outside income of over $45,000 a year, and by 1868 he owned assets worth $400,000 which paid him over $56,000 a year. The first of his major investments was in the Woodruff Sleeping Car Company, receiving a one-eighth share for acting as agent for Scott and Edgar Thomson.* With virtually no cash investment, he made nearly $20,000 a year from his holdings for some twenty years. His next major investment came in 1861 when he participated in the formation of the Columbia Oil Company, allying himself with William Coleman, a Pittsburgh ironmaster. Carnegie invested some $11,000 in the venture, which would eventually earn him over one million dollars. His most satisfying investment, however, was in the Keystone Bridge Company, even though it was less remunerative. Carnegie, Scott, Thomson, and other Pennsylvania officials had opened the firm in 1862 to build iron railroad bridges. When Carnegie left the Pennsylvania Railroad in 1865 it was to assume management of the bridge works, which he felt had an exciting future. Exploiting his railroad contacts, Carnegie built Keystone into the largest and most prosperous bridge company in the United States. His most exciting and profitable contracts were for bridges that spanned the Mississippi and Missouri rivers, building the first major bridge across the former river. Designed by James Eads, it was the largest steel arch bridge in the world, with a center span of 520 feet; the bridge is still in use.

After leaving the railroad, Carnegie also acted as a bond salesman and speculator on a grand scale. He engaged in manipulating stock in Western Union and Union Pacific, and in alliance with Thomas Scott became a promoter of stocks and bonds, selling $30 million in Europe in the five years between 1867 and 1872. Many of these bonds later faulted, and the buyers lost a great portion of their money. But Carnegie himself retained their confidence, and was later to sell further bond issues to the same sources. In 1872, however, he retired from the bond business, and began construction of what was to become Carnegie Steel. Although he had achieved great wealth in speculation, he had simply acted as the agent of Scott and Thomson, and had built nothing tangible. He now turned to manufacturing as a means of producing something of substance.

In 1864, with Andrew Kloman and Henry Phipps Jr.,* Carnegie had purchased a one-sixth interest in the Iron City Forge of Pittsburgh, an axle making concern. This soon became the Union Iron Mills, with Kloman being forced out of the partnership. Carnegie's primary motive with the founding of Union Iron was to create a reliable and cheap source of beams and plates for Keystone Bridge. In this manner he integrated two successive stages of manufacture vertically under a single controlling head. This was Carnegie's first major innovation in manufacturing, coming in an industry which as yet was largely unintegrated. Although he was not a practical ironmaster, his greatest contribution to the iron industry lay in his introduction of the more rigid accounting and bookkeeping methods he had learned in the railroad field. In the existing bookkeeping practice in the iron industry, the cost of each of the various processes was unknown, using only "lump" accounting procedures. Carnegie's first step was to implement methods of cost control whereby he could keep track of what every department was doing, and compare one department with another. Bringing cost-based pricing and management to manufacturing was a major innovation on Carnegie's part, and he was later to greatly expand the system when he organized his new Bessemer steel works in the 1870s.

In 1872 Carnegie began to contract his various interests and concentrate them on a single project—his new steel-rail rolling mill. Designed by Alexander Holley,* it was the first newly built and organized Bessemer plant in America, and was completed in 1875. In organizing his steel company, Carnegie put together a structure similar to the one he had worked in on the Pennsylvania Railroad. To provide the technical expertise in steel-making he appointed the country's most accomplished steel-maker, Captain William R. Jones,* as general superintendent to oversee day-to-day work of the superintendents in charge of other departments. As general manager he appointed William P. Shinn, a highly competent railroad manager. It was Shinn who coordinated the various parts of the firm and created an effective unit of production.

Shinn's major achievement was the development of statistical data needed for coordination and control. He introduced the voucher system of accounting, which had not previously been used in manufacturing. By this method, each department listed the amount and cost of materials and labor used on each order as it passed through the sub-unit. This information permitted Shinn to send Carnegie monthly, and later daily, statements providing data on the cost of ore, limestone, coal, coke, pig iron, and so forth. These cost sheets were Carnegie's primary instrument of control and costs were his major obsession. As he commented, "Watch the costs and the profits will take care of themselves." He compared the current costs of each department with those of previous months, and if possible with those of other enterprises. (In fact, one of the major reasons Carnegie joined the Bessemer Pool—made up of all companies producing Bessemer steel rails—was to get a chance to look at competitors' figures.)

By 1880 Carnegie's cost sheets were far more detailed and more accurate than the cost controls in the other leading industries of the day. He used them to evaluate the performance of department managers, foremen, and workers, and to check on the quality and mix of raw materials. They were also used to evaluate improvements in processes and products and to make decisions on developing by-products. In pricing they were an invaluable tool for non-standardized products like bridges. Carnegie Steel would not accept a contract until its costs were carefully estimated and until options had been obtained on the basic materials of coke and ore. Carnegie's technological and organizational innovations reaped huge dividends. Carnegie's prices were lower and profits higher than those of any other producer in the industry. As soon as the Edgar Thomson Works opened in 1875 it recorded profits of $9.50 a ton. In 1878 the rail mill had profits of $401,000, or 31 percent of equity, which rose to $2 million in 1880. As the business expanded, profits grew larger. At the end of the 1890s, Carnegie's operations had profits of $20 million, and in 1900 they stood at $40 million.

These profits were generated not only by his organizational and accounting advancements, but were produced in tandem with Carnegie's unceasing innovations on the technical side. Although he said that "pioneering don't pay," he was, in fact, one of the industry's most energetic and successful innovators. Besides his full scale entrance into Bessemer steel production in the 1870s, at a time when other producers had simply grafted Bessemer converters to existing iron plants, he introduced the basic open hearth furnace to replace the Bessemer operations in the 1890s. The open hearth process produced a better grade of steel at a lower cost, and his competitors were again left behind. Also, during these years he brought Henry Clay Frick* into partnership, thereby gaining control of Frick's massive holdings of coke fields in Pennsylvania. Enhancing the vertical integration of the company, the move further increased the power and efficiency of the Carnegie operation. This was just part of the prolific vertical integration Carnegie achieved with his firm. He purchased his own sources of iron ore, and built his own fleet of steamships to carry the ore, and a company railroad to transport ore and coke to the mills.

During the 1890s, however, friction began to grow among the Carnegie officials, especially between Carnegie and Frick. Some of this grew out of bitterness surrounding the violent Homestead Strike in 1892, and some out of their differing philosophies of business management. In any event, by 1901 Carnegie was amenable to selling his giant firm. When J. P. Morgan* set up a financing coalition to purchase his business, along with others, Carnegie sold his 58 percent of Carnegie Steel to the new U.S. Steel Company for $250 million in five percent-fifty year gold bonds. Carnegie then began to set up benefactions in order to give away large portions of his fortune, in accordance with the precepts of his *Gospel of Wealth* (1889). In 1901 he formed the Carnegie Corporation of New York, capitalized at $125 million, to support and develop his various charities. It could spend only the income on the five percent bonds. In addition, he gave $60 million to public library buildings, $29 million to the Carnegie Foundation for the Advancement of Teaching, $22 million to Carnegie Institute of Technology, and $22 million to the Carnegie Institute of Washington, in addition to several others. The Carnegie family was left with about $25 million when the benefactions were concluded.

Andrew Carnegie married Louise Whitfield in 1887 and they had one daughter. He was a Swedenborgian and a member of the Republican party. (**A.** *DAB; NCAB*, 9:151; 41:585; *New York Times*, August 12, 1919; *Who Was Who*, vol. 1; *Iron Age*, August 14, 1919; J. W. Jordan, ed., *Encyclopedia of Pennsylvania Biography*, vol. 11, 184–186; *Journal of the Iron and Steel Institute*, vol. 100, 451–452; Andrew Carnegie, *Autobiography of Andrew Carnegie*, 1920; *Triumphant Democracy*, 1886; and *Gospel of Wealth*, 1889; Andrew Hacker, *The World of Andrew Carnegie*, 1968; Alvin G. Harlow, *Andrew Carnegie*, 1953; Burton J. Hendrick, *Life of Andrew Carnegie*, 2 vols., 1932; Harold C. Livesay, *Andrew Carnegie and the Rise of Big Business*, 1975; Joseph F. Wall, *Andrew Carnegie*, 1970; John K. Winkler, *Incredible Carnegie*, 1931. **B.** J. H. Bridge, *Inside History of the Carnegie Steel Company*, 1903; Herbert Casson, *The Romance of Steel*, 1907; Alfred D. Chandler Jr., *The Visible Hand*, 1977.)

CARR, JULIAN SHAKESPERE (October 12, 1845–April 29, 1924). Tobacco and cotton textile manufacturer, Durham Tobacco Company and Durham Hosiery Mills. Born in Chapel Hill, North Carolina, son of John Wesley Carr and Eliza P. Bulloch. His father was a merchant and planter and county court judge. Julian Carr was educated in the local area and enlisted in the Confederate cavalry at the outbreak of the Civil War. After the war he attended the University of North Carolina. He then began his business career as a tobacconist, and in association with Col. W. T. Blackwell, purchased a $4,000 interest in the Bull Durham Smoking Tobacco Company. They formed the Blackwell Durham Tobacco Company, which was the foundation of the tobacco industry in Durham, North Carolina. Carr became president of the concern when it was incorporated, serving in that capacity until it was sold to American Tobacco Company in 1904 for $4,000,000. Thereafter, he devoted himself chiefly to the manufacture of cotton and to banking.

He was owner and president of the Durham Hosiery Mills, with mills in Durham, High Point, Chapel Hill, and Goldsboro, North Carolina. It was the largest group of plants producing hosiery in the world. At the time of his death there was a total of fourteen mills with 4,000 employees. He also owned and operated the Occoneechee Farm, one of the best known stock and grain farms in the state, and was president of Ormond Mining Company of Bessemer City and the North Carolina Bessemer Company. He organized and was president of the First National Bank of Durham, president of the Durham and Roxboro Railroad, the Durham and Charlottesville Railroad, Durham Electric Light Company, and the Commonwealth Cotton Factory in Durham. He was also vice-president of the Durham Cotton Manufacturing Company and the Greensboro Blast Furnace Company.

He was a Methodist and succeeded in getting Trinity College located in Durham, and started the endowment for the Greensboro Female College. He also gave liberally to Negro colleges, churches, and schools. He was a staunch Democrat and a delegate to fourteen national Democratic conventions. During World War I he was on the staff of Herbert Hoover,* food administrator, as a "dollar-a-year" man. He married Nannie Graham Parrish of Durham in 1873 and had six children. Two of his sons succeeded their father in his business interests. Julian S. Carr Jr. (1878-1922) became secretary and treasurer of the Durham Hosiery Mills in 1900, and president in 1910, serving in that position until his death. Claiborn McDowell Carr (1884-   ) was treasurer of the mills from 1905 to 1922. He then became president of the firm from 1922 to 1928, when he was named vice-president of American Enka Corporation, manufacturers of rayon yarns. He was also chairman of the First National Bank of Durham from 1824 to 1933. (*NCAB*, 17:125; 40:259; F:216; *New York Times*, April 30, 1924; March 18, 1922; *Who Was Who*, vol. 1.)

CARRIER, WILLIS HAVILAND (November 26, 1876–October 7, 1950). Inventor and manufacturer of air conditioning units, Carrier Corporation. Born in Angola, New York, son of Duane Williams Carrier and Elizabeth Haviland. He graduated from Cornell University with a degree in electrical engineering in 1901 and entered the employ of the Buffalo Forge Company as a research engineer. He became chief engineer at the company in 1906. Continuing in that position until 1915, he then organized, with Irving Lyle and others, the Carrier Engineering Corporation. He was vice-president of this company until 1930. In that year Carrier Engineering, York Heating and Ventilating, and Brunswick and Knoeshell Company were merged, forming the Carrier Corporation. He was chairman of the board of this organization, which engaged in the manufacture of air conditioning equipment. It had two plants in Newark, New Jersey, and one each in Allentown, Pennsylvania, Bridgeport, Pennsylvania, and New Brunswick, New Jersey. These were closed in 1937 and all operations were consolidated in a single plant in Syracuse, New York, with fifty-one acres of floor space. Its products consisted basically of numerous inventions in the field of mechanical refrigeration which have resulted from Carrier's experiments.

In his early working career Carrier designed for the Sackett-Wilhelm Lithography and Publishing Company a system which maintained 55 percent relative humidity in the building throughout the year, at a temperature of seventy degrees in winter and eighty degrees in summer. He next developed more flexible and efficient temperature controls. In 1904 he invented a central station spray apparatus in which a very fine mist of water was heated for humidification and cooled for dehumidification. In 1906 he developed the dew point control, a system of regulating relative humidity by altering at the apparatus the temperature at which moisture begins to condense. Concurrently, he undertook research to improve the design of air distribution systems, and by 1907 Carrier systems had been installed in several cotton mills and other plants. Later in that year, the Buffalo Forge Company established a wholly owned subsidiary, the Carrier Air Conditioning Company, to engineer and market complete systems. For six years he was vice-president of the subsidiary, and chief engineer and director of research for the parent firm. The Carrier equipment was installed in several industries: tobacco, rayon, rubber, paper, pharmaceuticals, and food processing.

In 1914 Buffalo Forge decided to limit itself to manufacturing and withdrew from the engineering business. Carrier then formed the Carrier Engineering Corporation. Basic to the success of this company was Carrier's development of a radical new refrigeration machine—the centrifugal compressor—which used safe, non-toxic refrigerants and could serve large installations cheaply. This opened the way for a system whose objective was human comfort. Carrier installed an air conditioning system in the J. L. Hudson Department Store in Detroit in 1924, and in the House and Senate chambers in 1928-1929. By 1930 more than 300 theaters had been air conditioned by his company. The depression of the 1930s forced Carrier to fight for the firm's survival, and to cut costs and streamline operations. All facilities were concentrated in a single plant in Syracuse. He then turned his attention to the problem of air conditioning high rise buildings, and by

1939 had developed a system in which conditioned air from a central station was piped through small steel conduits at high velocity to individual rooms. The industry flourished during and after World War II, but a heart attack forced him to retire in 1948.

He was a Presbyterian and a Republican and was married three times: first to Edith Claire Seymour of Gloversville, New York, who died in 1912, then, to Jennie Tiffit Martin of Angola, New York, who died in 1939. In 1941 he married Edith Marsh Wise. He had two adopted sons. (**A.** *DAB*, Supplement 4; *NCAB*, E:24; *New York Times*, October 8, 1950; *Who Was Who*, vol. 3; M. Ingels, *W. H. Carrier: Father of Air Conditioning*, 1927. **B.** Carrier Engineering Corporation, *The Story of Manufactured Weather*, 1919; Carrier Corp., *Twenty-Five Years of Air Conditioning*, 1947.)

CARROLL, CHARLES (September 17, 1737–November 14, 1832). Large landowner and entrepreneur in Revolutionary Maryland. Born at Annapolis, Maryland, son of Charles Carroll and Elizabeth Brooke. His father was a native of Ireland, who came to Maryland in 1715, where he acquired an immense estate. His son was educated by the Jesuits, and from 1748 to 1754 in France. Then he went to school in Rheims and Paris. After his schooling was completed, he spent several years in London. At age twenty-eight, he returned to Maryland, and took up the development of a 10,000 acre tract in Frederick County, known as Carrollton Manor.

He became very involved in the Revolutionary agitation in succeeding years, and in 1774 was active in the non-importation proceedings. In 1776 he agreed to seek a union between Canada and the colonies against Great Britain. He was a delegate to the Maryland Convention of 1776 and voted to separate from Great Britain. He was then elected to the Continental Congress and signed the Declaration of Independence in that year. He represented Maryland as a senator in the first federal congress, until he resigned in 1792. After that, he served in the Maryland State Senate until 1800.

After that time, he devoted most of his energies to his business activities. His estate developed rapidly until it had between 70,000 and 80,000 acres of land in Maryland, Pennsylvania, and New York. He was a member of the Potomac Company and the Chesapeake and Ohio Canal Company, which was organized in 1823. He was also on the first board of directors of the Baltimore and Ohio Railroad. When he died he was reputed to be the richest man in the United States. He married his cousin, Mary Darnall, in 1768. He was a Roman Catholic. (*DAB*; K. M. Rowland, *The Life of Charles Carroll of Carrollton, 1737–1832*, 2 vols., 1918; E. H. Smith, *Charles Carroll of Carrollton*, 1942.)

CARTER, AMON GILLES (December 11, 1879–June 23, 1955). Texas entrepreneur in publishing, broadcasting, oil, and airlines. Born in Crafton,

Texas, son of William Henry Carter, a blacksmith, and Josephine Ream. Amon Carter was educated in the public schools until he was twelve years old, when he went to work selling newspapers and lunches to railroad passengers. He was then employed in Bowie, Texas, and in an ice cream parlor in Norman, Oklahoma. His next job was with the American Copying Company of Chicago, selling enlarged portraits throughout the United States. In 1899 he went to San Francisco, California, where he engaged in advertising work with the Barnhart and Swasey advertising agency. He returned to Texas in 1905, where he first sold advertising and later sold office supplies in Ft. Worth. In 1906 he became advertising manager of the *Ft. Worth Star*, and business manager in 1907. In that year he helped to negotiate a merger of the *Star* with its afternoon competitor, the *Telegram*, and became vice-president of the new Fort Worth *Star-Telegram*. In 1923 he became president and publisher of the paper, serving in these positions until 1952, when he retired to become chairman of the board. He increased the circulation of the paper from 5,000 to 250,000 during these years.

He also entered the radio and television fields, forming one of the earliest radio stations in the country, WBAP, Ft. Worth, in 1922, and its television affiliate, WBAP-TV in 1948. He was also active in the oil business, and in 1935 drilled an exploratory well in Lea County, New Mexico. Two years later he drilled the discovery well in the Wasso lease in Gaines and Yoakum counties, Texas. He sold his interest in the Gaines County section in 1947 for $16,500,000 to establish the Amon G. Carter Foundation. He was also a director of American Airlines from its founding in 1930, and was one of the largest stockholders in the company. He was responsible for the airline establishing its southwest headquarters in Ft. Worth. Carter was a great advocate of aviation in his newspaper and invited aviation manufacturers to locate in the city. During World War II he was instrumental in getting a bomber plant established in the city, which later became the Convair Division of General Dynamics Corp. He was also personally responsible for getting the helicopter branch of Bell Aircraft located in Ft. Worth. As a result of his efforts, Ft. Worth was second only to California in aircraft production in the country. He also succeeded in getting many other plants to locate in the city: Montgomery Ward, Chicago Pneumatic, the Chevrolet Division of General Motors, and others.

He helped to found Texas Technological College in Lubbock, and was chairman of its board of trustees from 1923 to 1927. He also supported Texas Christian University, the YMCA Baptist Camp, and many other causes. He was a director of the American Petroleum Institute from 1936 to 1955 and of the Air Power League from 1946 to 1955. He was a Presbyterian and a Democrat. He was married three times. His first wife was Zetta Thomas, of Bowie, Texas, whom he married in 1902. They were divorced in 1917, and the following year he married Neretta Burton of Ft. Worth. They were divorced in 1941, and six years later he took his third wife,

Minnie (Meachum) Smith of Ft. Worth. He had one son and two daughters. (*NCAB*, 43:486.)

CARTER, ROBERT (1663–August 4, 1732). Colonial Virginia planter and merchant. Born in Lancaster County, Virginia, son of John Carter and Sarah Ludlow. His father came from England in 1649, and by his death in 1669 had accumulated considerable wealth and had become prominent in the politics of the colony. Robert Carter was educated by private tutors. Inheriting his father's estate, he became one of the chief landowners of the Northern Neck (the Chesapeake Bay, bounded by the Potomac and Rappahannock rivers), and held local offices of colonel and commander-in-chief of Lancaster County. In 1702 he became agent for the Fairfaxes, proprietors of the Northern Neck, serving them until 1722–1723. This was a highly strategic position for the acquisition of a fortune, and he made the most of it. At his death he was one of the wealthiest men in the colonies, owning 300,000 acres of land, 1,000 slaves, and 10,000 pounds. He was a friend and benefactor of William and Mary College, and a trustee and member of the board of visitors there. He built Christ Church in Lancaster County at his own expense. He was referred to as "King Carter."

He was also intimately involved in politics. At age 28 he entered the colonial assembly as a burgess for Lancaster County, serving 1691–1692 and 1695–1699. He was chosen speaker of the assemblage in 1696 and 1699. In the latter year he was advanced to the Council, and made Colonial Treasurer for six years. He was also acting governor of Virginia for a few months. He married Judith Armistead, who died in 1699, and Elizabeth Landon of England, who died in 1710. His children were among the First Families of Virginia. (*DAB; NCAB*, 13:388; Louis Morton, *Robert Carter of Nomini Hall: A Virginia Tobacco Planter of the Eighteenth Century*, 1941.)

CASE, JEROME INCREASE (December 11, 1818–December 22, 1891). Agricultural implement manufacturer, J. I. Case Company. Born in Williamstown, Oswego County, New York, son of Caleb Case and Deborah Jackson, who were among the pioneers from the eastern part of the state. Jerome worked on the farm as soon as he was old enough, and attended school when he could. He became very interested in machinery, and, at age sixteen, conducted a threshing machine business for five years. He then went to an academy in Mexico, New York, for a year, when he decided to go west and start another threshing machine business. He purchased six threshers on credit, and took these to Racine, Wisconsin, in 1842. He found buyers for five of the machines, and kept the sixth to make a living. Then, in 1844, while in Rochester, Wisconsin, he designed, built, and put into practical operation a combined thresher and separator. This eliminated the fanning mill. He rented a small shop in Racine to build the machine, and after three difficult years, it was generally accepted by buyers. He now had acquired sufficient capital to erect his own manufacturing plant.

His business grew rapidly due to the fact that he was a practical thresher, which had great advertising value. His plant became the largest west of Buffalo, and within ten years was producing 1,600 machines annually. In 1863 he took three former employees into the firm to form the J. I. Case Company, and in 1880 it was incorporated as the J. I. Case Threshing Machine Company. He also formed the J. I. Case Plow Works, and in 1871 established the Manufacturers National Bank of Racine. He was president of these companies and served on the board of trustees of Northwestern Mutual Life Insurance Company in Milwaukee. He was later identified with national banks in Minnesota, South Dakota, and California.

Case was also involved in politics, serving twice as mayor of Racine (1856–1859), and as state senator for one term. He married Lydia A. Bull of Yorkville, Wisconsin, in 1849 and they had three daughters and one son. (*DAB; Who Was Who*, vol. H.)

CASSATT, ALEXANDER JOHNSTON (December 8, 1839–December 28, 1906). Railroad Executive, Pennsylvania Railroad. Born in Pittsburgh, Pennsylvania, son of Robert S. Cassatt and Katharine Kelso Johnston. His father was a banker and a man of great influence in business and political affairs in western Pennsylvania, serving as the first mayor of Allegheny City, Pennsylvania. Alexander Cassatt began his education in the public schools of Pittsburgh, and then went with his family to Europe, where he continued his schooling, attending Darmstadt University. When he returned to the United States, he enrolled in Rensselaer Polytechnic Institute in Troy, New York, receiving his degree in civil engineering in 1859. He served an engineering apprenticeship, and in 1861 went to Philadelphia to join the Pennsylvania Railroad.

Cassatt worked under Colonel Thomas A. Scott,* the general manager, with whom he received invaluable training. This led to his rapid advancement through the engineering depatment. By 1870 he was general superintendent of the road. He was one of the first railway managers to see the immense possibilities of the air brake, and was responsible for its testing and adoption. In 1873 he became general manager of all Pennsylvania lines east of Pittsburgh and Erie, just at the time when the line was changing from a locally oriented state line to a massive system covering most of the principal traffic points east of the Mississippi and north of the Ohio River. In 1874 he was elected third vice-president in charge of transportation and traffic. It was at this time that the Philadelphia, Wilmington and Delaware Railroad was purchased, and Cassatt was responsible for securing it in competition with the Baltimore and Ohio Railroad. In 1880 he was made first vice-president, but in 1882 he retired, retaining only a directorship.

He remained in the railroad business, however, associating himself with Scott in the construction of the New York, Philadelphia and Norfolk

Railroad, serving as its president from 1885 to 1899. In the latter year he was called to the presidency of the Pennsylvania Railroad, holding that office until his death six years later. He cleaned up the major traffic difficulties on the line and improved its physical property and operations. This meant a vast increase of lines, stations, equipment and facilities—revision and elimination of grades, elevation of track, electrification, and all that goes with an efficient railway system. During his administration, earnings nearly doubled, and traffic density increased by 50 percent. He also established a pension fund to provide for retirement from active service, and a broadening of the relief fund to include superannuation. Twice he voluntarily advanced the wages of men receiving less than $200 per month by 10 percent.

Cassatt's greatest achievement was the solution of the rebate problem. Rebates had been endemic during the depression of the 1890s, and by 1899 average freight rates had reached their lowest point in the history of the company. The railroads had, in effect, put themselves at the mercy of shippers in their desperation to secure business. His plan was that of purchasing a sufficient amount of stock in competing railroads to give a voice in management, and was known as "community of interest." It involved an agreement with the New York Central to buy some stock in the Reading Railroad, with the Pennsylvania Railroad investing in the Baltimore and Ohio, the Chesapeake and Ohio, and the Norfolk and Western. The Baltimore and Ohio, in turn, bought into the Reading. Thus the strategic roads were interlocked and able to present a united front to the industrial combinations. The roads then announced that there would be no further rebates. Andrew Carnegie* was especially angry at this, and threatened to build his own road to the seaboard. In 1903 the Elkins Anti-Rebate law was passed, largely at the insistence of the Pennsylvania Railroad and Cassatt. The "community of interest" idea was later struck down by the Supreme Court, but represented a bold advance for its time. Cassatt was an advocate of the power of railway commissions to set rates and supported the Hepburn Act. He also constructed Pennsylvania Terminal in New York City, the most gigantic railroad enterprise undertaken to that time.

He married Lois Buchanan, the niece of President James Buchanan, in 1869. They had four children. (**A.** *DAB; NCAB*, 13:336; *New York Times*, January 1, 1907; *Who Was Who*, vol. 1, Patricia Davis, *A. J. Cassatt*, 1979. **B.** George H. Burgess and Miles C. Kennedy, *Centennial History of the Pennsylvania Railroad*, 1949.)

CATES, LOUIS SHATTUCK (December 20, 1881–October 29, 1959). Mining executive, Phelps-Dodge Company. Born in Boston, Massachusetts, son of Edwin Wallace Cates and Emily Allen Johnson. He was educated at the public schools of Boston, and graduated from the Massachusetts Institute of Technology in 1902. He then joined National Steel and Wire Company for a short time. While on a trip to Mexico, he secured a lease for some New York interests on a portion of the famous La Palmillo Mine. Returning to the United States in 1903, he entered the employ of Boston Consolidated Mining Company as a timekeeper of its mine in Bingham Canyon, Utah. He advanced rapidly in the firm, becoming general manager of mine and mills in 1910. When the company was acquired by the Utah Copper Company in that year, Cates became engineer of mines for the latter organization. Then he was placed in charge of mines for the Ray (Arizona) Consolidated Copper Company. During his years as general manager of the firm, from 1913 to 1922, the Ray mine was transformed from a failure into a successful property. Meanwhile, in 1919, he had been made assistant general manager of the Utah Copper Company and a subsidiary, the Bingham and Garfield Railroad, in Salt Lake City, Utah. In 1922 he became general manager of Utah Copper Company, and in the following year vice-president and general manager of both that company and its subsidiary.

Cates electrified the open pit operations of Utah Copper and remodeled its concentration plant. In 1930 he succeeded Walter Davis as president of Phelps-Dodge Corporation, one of the leading metal producers in the world. He remained in this position until 1947, when he became chairman of the board. In the year he became president of Phelps-Dodge, the company acquired control of Nichols Copper Company and National Electric Products Company. In 1931 he acquired the property and assets of the Calumet and Arizona Mining Company, and in 1935 purchased the United Verde Copper Company. With these acquisitions, Phelps-Dodge became an integrated operation in the copper industry, including mining, melting, smelting, refining, fabricating, and marketing of copper both as a metal and in manufactured products.

In 1937 he began a five year program of capital expenditures, the most important aspect of which was the opening and equipping of the Moncrief, Arizona, open pit mine, a large low-grade copper bearing ore body, at an initial cost of $35 million. Production began in 1942, making the capacity of the Phelps-Dodge open pit mines 70,000 tons per day. In 1930 the capital stock of the company stood at $30 million, with 8,000 employees, and sales of $39 million. In 1949, capital stock was $127 million, with 15,000 employees and assets of $510 million. During World War II, the operation of the company was devoted almost entirely to war production.

Cates was married three times: to Helen Mar Gillespie of Salt Lake City in 1905; to Eleanor Louise (Cahill) Christianson of San Francisco in 1926; and to Ethel (Chesbrough) Lewis of Toledo, Ohio. He had one daughter. (**A.** *NCAB*, H:290; 47:101. **B.** Robert Glass Cleland, *A History of Phelps-Dodge*, 1952.)

CHANDLER, HARRY (May 17, 1864–September 23, 1944). Newspaper publisher and land developer, *Los Angeles Times*. Born Landaff, New Hampshire, son of Moses Knight Chandler, a farmer, and Emma Jane Little. His family had been in New England since 1637, and Harry Chandler was educated in the district school in Lisbon, New Hampshire, planning to enter Dartmouth in 1882. Illness prevented this, and his family sent him to southern California to recover. He lived in a tent in the San Fernando Valley, near Los Angeles, where he broke horses and harvested fruit for a farmer for a share of the crop. In 1885 Chandler began his newspaper career as a clerk in the circulation department of the *Los Angeles Times*, owned by Harrison Gray Otis.* Without Otis' knowledge he began taking over the circulation lists, setting up his own delivery and collection procedures, and buying stock in the *Times*. When Chandler's first wife died in 1892, he proceeded to marry Otis' daughter, Marion, shortly afterward being appointed business manager of the paper.

Although Chandler was to build the *Times* into perhaps the most powerful and successful newspaper on the West Coast, the paper was largely the instrument of his and his friends' commercial interests, particularly their mammoth land development operations. At a very early stage Chandler became involved in several speculative real estate ventures in Southern California and Mexico. His newspaper provided him with invaluable contacts, and about 1899 he bought up land in the Colorado desert, above and below the Mexican border. In 1902 he formed two corporations: The California-Mexico Land and Cattle Company, which managed 1,000 acres of land in the Imperial Valley; and the Colorado River Land Company, a Mexican subsidiary which controlled his syndicate's holdings south of the border. The latter company became more important, acquiring more than 800,000 acres of land in the Mexicali Valley. By 1931 the company had spent $12 million developing this region, most of which was leased to tenant farmers engaged in the raising of cotton. The firm built canals and ditches, constructed roads and levees, and leveled extensive portions of the land. Huge profits were made on the venture, despite the fact that the Mexican government finally expropriated most of the land.

At the same time, Chandler and his associates were expanding their realty interests in the San Fernando Valley near Los Angeles. The key to the development of this area was the provision of an adequate water supply, and Chandler was the prime force behind the *Times*' successful campaign in the early 1900s to bring the water resources of Owen's Valley in the Sierras to Los Angeles. Under Chandler's prodding, the city water board mounted two bond issues in 1903 and 1907, totaling $24.5 million. By these the city acquired Owen's Valley land over the opposition of many local residents and constructed a viaduct 233 miles in length to bring the water to the upper end of the San Fernando Valley. In the meantime, Chandler, along with Otis and Moses H. Sherman, had been quietly buying up large ranches in the area, which sold at very low prices because of the lack of water. Forming the Surburban Homes Company, they subdivided the 60 million acres they had purchased into residential and industrial properties (now serviced by the new water supply), which sold for $17 million over a seven year period. They built a 22 mile highway, Sherman Way, to connect the new development to Los Angeles, and most of the San Fernando Valley was annexed to the city of Los Angeles in 1915. These real estate developments, and others, earned Chandler the title of "California's landlord."

Since the basis of his great fortune was in real estate, Chandler also used the *Times* to generally boost the economic potential of the area. Chandler owned vast amounts of land, but to subdivide and sell this land profitably, sparsely settled Southern California needed people. Perhaps his most important journalistic achievement was his use of the press to promote the qualities of Southern California. He sent out promotional mail in winter editions of the *Times* to persons in the central states. Arriving in the dead of winter, the paper pointed out how pleasant the climate in Southern California was at that time, and the availability of good land, jobs, and homes. It is estimated that over the years hundreds of thousands of Midwesterners were lured to Southern California because of his efforts. In appreciation, the Realty Board in 1921 voted him Los Angeles' "Most Useful Citizen." To provide jobs, he helped lure the movie colony to California, and the aviation industry came to California in the early twenties because Chandler had given Donald Douglas* a check for $1,500 and helped him get similar contributions from nine other businessmen. This enabled Douglas to bring his fledgling aircraft company to Los Angeles. Chandler spearheaded the *Times'* campaign for construction of a manmade harbor in the San Pedro-Wilmington area of Los Angeles, which soon became one of the leading ports on the West Coast. Among his other activities Chandler campaigned for the establishment of the Union Railroad station in Los Angeles, organized a syndicate in 1928 to purchase the federal government's Pacific shipping fleet, built the Biltmore Hotel, and started KHJ, the city's first radio station. All of this greatly enhanced the attractiveness of Los Angeles to industries and home owners, and greatly increased the value of Chandler's land holdings.

Although Chandler's primary interests were with land development and other commercial activities, he built the *Times* into a large and powerful newspaper. When Otis died in 1907, Chandler became president of the *Times*, and during the next twenty years greatly expanded its operations. By 1941 the paper had a daily circulation of 320,000, with 615,000 on Sundays. He was particularly successful in attracting advertising to the paper, so that for three straight years during the early 1920s the *Times* led all other American newspapers in advertising space and amount of classified ads. He added a *Sunday Magazine*, and the *Times* was the first newspaper to institute a motion picture page. Yet as an economic entity the *Times* had never been important to Harry Chandler, and when his son took over the paper in 1941, he found it in a desperate financial situation. Within ten years he had rebuilt it to become one of the most profitable newspapers in America.

Chandler's great crisis with the *Times* came shortly after he took over from Otis. He was strongly opposed to organized labor and campaigned for the open shop in all major industries in California. He helped organize the militantly anti-union Merchants and Manufacturers Association, which for three years determined the economic and political policies championed by the city's business interests. In 1910 the *Times* building was blown up by a bomb tied to a gas main under Chandler's desk. Twenty employees were killed, but Chandler had already left the office. Three union officials were indicted for the offense, and Chandler used the incident and the ensuing trial to greatly increase the popularity of the *Times* in Los Angeles. One element of Chandler's success in avoiding the unionization of the *Times* itself was his benevolent employment practices. He paid higher wages than the union rates, seldom discharged loyal employees, and rewarded seniority. His was the first newspaper in the country to establish a personnel department and one of the first to adopt the forty hour work week. In the early 1920s he established a group insurance plan for his company.

Chandler was a major leader of the conservative faction of Southern California Republicans. He waged a life-long fight with Hiram Johnson, the leader of the liberal wing of the party, and during the 1930s was a constant critic of the New Deal, opposing the construction of Boulder Dam and fighting numerous measures calling for public ownership of utilities and transportation. In all of this the *Times* was used as the mouthpiece for his own personal brand of politics, with little or no pretense of non-partisanship. A member of the Congregational Church, he was a trustee of the California Institute of Technology and Stanford University. He married his first wife, Magdalena Schladar, in 1888, and had eight children. His son, Norman (1899–1973) took control of the *Times* and the other Chandler interests during the 1940s. He was succeeded by his son, Otis Chandler, who is presently publisher of the paper. (**A.** *DAB*, Supplement 3; *NCAB*, 40:498. **B.** Robert Gottlieb and Irene Wolt, *Thinking Big*, 1977; David Halberstam, *The Powers That Be*, 1979.)

CHAPIN, ROY DIKEMAN (February 23, 1880–February 16, 1936). Automobile executive, Hudson Motor Company. Born in Lansing, Michigan, son of Edward Cornelius Chapin and Ella King. His father was a well-to-do lawyer. From 1899 to 1901 Roy Chapin was a student at the University of Michigan. In the latter year he left to join Olds Motor Works. His first job was to take pictures of test cars and be generally useful, at $35 per month. In that same year he drove an Oldsmobile from Detroit to New York City, the first time the trip had been made by automobile, which gained him a great deal of publicity. By 1904 he had been made the company's sales manager. But his great ambition was to become head of his own auto company. So, in 1906, he and Howard E. Coffin,* a fellow Olds employee from the University of Michigan, left the Olds organization and began to build a car designed by Coffin. Other officers of the concern were Frederick O. Byrne and James J. Brady, and their first financial backer was Edwin R. Thomas, an auto manufacturer in Buffalo, New York. The firm was established as the E. R. Thomas Detroit Company, with Chapin as general manager.

The arrangement was unsatisfactory, however, as they were too dependent upon Thomas' good will. So, in 1908, they brought in Hugh R. Chalmers, who bought out Thomas, and the firm became Chalmers-Detroit Motor Company, with Chalmers as president. Then, a year later, Chapin and Coffin, with Roscoe R. Jackson, got financial backing from Joseph L. Hudson,* a Detroit department store magnate, to organize the Hudson Motor Car Company, and sold out Chalmers-Detroit to Chalmers for $700,000. Chapin became president of Hudson Motor Car Company, with Jackson as general manager and Coffin as chief designer. They were very successful from the beginning. During World War I, Chapin was called to Washington as chairman of the highway transportation committee of the Council of National Defense. In this post he worked vigorously to develop the use of the motor vehicle to relieve congestion on the railroads.

After the war, Chapin returned to Hudson Motors to carry out three major steps. First, in 1919 he introduced the "Essex," a popularly priced car that was an immediate success. Second, in 1922 he offered closed cars at virtually the same price as the touring car. Most other automobile companies quickly conformed to this practice, and the touring car rapidly disappeared. Third, also in 1922, he organized the company's finances with the aid of the brokerage firm of Hornblower and Weeks. In the process, the original stockholders, who had paid in $100,000 in 1910, received $16,000,000 in new stock and $7,000,000 in cash. In 1923 Chapin turned over the presidency to Jackson and became chairman of the board. He was also named vice-president of the Lincoln Highway Association, chairman of the board of the Good Roads Committee of the Automobile Board of Trade, and chairman of the highway transportation committee of the International Chamber of Commerce. He also served as president of the latter organization in 1930.

In July, 1932, he was appointed Secretary of Commerce, serving until March, 1933. At that time two major preoccupations concerned the administration. The first was the necessity to find some means to stimulate the depression economy into a pre-election "take-off," and the second concerned revision of anti-trust policies. As Secretary of Commerce, Chapin became involved with both aims, although his primary interest lay with the former. When he accepted the Commerce post, he became immediately involved in helping Walter Teagle,* head of the National Share-the-Work Committee, to develop a nation-wide share-the-work campaign. They sent out 335,000 letters at Commerce Department expense to employers urging support of the movement. Chapin also strongly encouraged James H. Rand* of Remington Rand in his plan for re-employment. Rand proposed that industries place orders six months in advance to stimulate the economy, and Chapin pushed hard for its acceptance even after Hoover's* defeat. The same groups and individuals he had allied with on the re-employment campaigns (the United States Chamber of Commerce, the National Association of Manufacturers, Walter Teagle, Matthew Sloan, James H. Rand, and others), were also deeply involved during this time promoting a lifting of the restrictions of the anti-trust laws. Although Chapin gave the group his tacit cooperation on this matter, he had little real interest in the activity, preferring to focus his attention on the re-employment efforts.

In the spring of 1933 Chapin resumed the presidency of Hudson Motor Company, which was drifting into receivership at the time. Within a few months he had succeeded in putting the company in reasonably good financial condition, and at the same time he tried to salvage the Guardian Trust Company of Detroit. During the late 1930s he became a strong opponent of the New Deal, being especially critical of the code and labor policies of the National Recovery Act. He married Inez Trediman of Savannah, Georgia, in 1914 and they had six children. (**A.** *DAB*, Supplement 2; *NCAB*, D:400; 34:14; *Who Was Who*, vol. 1; *New York Times*, February 17, 1936; John C. Long, *Roy D. Chapin*, 1945. **B.** Robert F. Himmelberg, *The Origins of the National Recovery Administration*, 1976.)

CHENEY, BENJAMIN PIERCE (August 12, 1815–July 23, 1895). Expressman, Cheney Express and American Express. Born in Hillsborough, New Hampshire, son of Jesse Cheney and Alice Steele. His father was a blacksmith, and his ancestors were among the first settlers of the state. Cheney completed his education at age ten, when he went to work in his father's blacksmith shop. After two years he went to Francestown, where he was employed in a tavern and then in a store. At sixteen he purchased his time from his father and began his career in the transportation business by driving a stage between Nashua and Exeter, New Hampshire, covering a distance of fifty miles a day for six years. In 1836 he was sent to Boston as an agent.

In 1842, in partnership with Nathaniel White and Nashua and William Walker, he established Cheney and Company Express between Boston and Montreal. The route was covered by rail to Concord, New Hampshire, by four horse team to Montpelier, Vermont, by messenger on the stage to Burlington, Vermont, and finally by boat to Montreal. The venture was successful, and at the end of ten years Cheney bought out Fisk and Rice's express operation over the Fitchburg road to Burlington, which was the first of several companies to be consolidated with Cheney's. Further consolidation resulted eventually in the formation of the U.S. and Canada Express Company, which covered the northern New England states. After thirty-seven years in the business, he merged with American Express Company, becoming one of its largest stockholders, treasurer, and a member of its board of directors for the rest of his life.

Cheney was also a pioneer in promoting the Northern Pacific Railroad and the Atchison, Topeka and Santa Fe Railroad. He was interested in the "Overland Mail" to San Francisco, California, and in the Wells, Fargo Express Company. In all these ventures he amassed a great fortune. In addition to these activities, he was involved in the Vermont Central Railroad, and was a founder of the Market National Bank of Boston and of American Loan and Trust Company. Although he never held political office, he was a life-long friend of Daniel Webster, a Whig. He married Elizabeth Stickney Clapp of Boston in 1865, and they had four children. His son, Benjamin P. Cheney Jr., worked with his father in the management of his various interests, and assumed control of the holdings in 1895. He was especially involved in railway manufacture, and was president of the San Diego California Land and Town Company. He later suffered heavy losses and retired from active business. (*DAB; NCAB*, 10:213; 32:173.)

CHESEBROUGH, ROBERT AUGUSTUS (January 9, 1837–September 8, 1935). Petroleum products manufacturer, Chesebrough Manufacturing Company. Born in London, England, son of Henry Augustus Chesebrough and Marion Maxwell Woodhull, both of whom were native Americans. His ancestors had come to America in 1631, founding Stonington, Connecticut. His grandfather, Robert Chesebrough, founded the Fulton Bank in New York City. Robert A. Chesebrough was educated in private schools in New York and at the Friend's Academy. In 1850 he began the refining of crude oil distilled from cannel coal in Brooklyn, New York. By 1861 he had turned his attention to the manufacture of kerosene and lubricating oils. He was the first to use crude oil under burners and stills for refining oils. In 1870 he produced a petroleum jelly, which he called "Vaseline," and registered the trademark.

In 1875 Chesebrough organized the Chesebrough Manufacturing Company, of which he was president until 1908. The firm began with the manufacture of kerosene, but after 1881 confined itself to the manufacture of vaseline, soon developing world-wide sales. In that year he erected an office building in New York City, later becoming active in real estate and acquired large tracts of property in and about New York City. In the Battery district, with his son, William H. Chesebrough, he transformed plots covered by old warehouses, saloons, and tenements into an important steamship and office center known as the Chesebrough buildings. He was also influential in moving the immigration center from the old Castle Gardens to a new station at Ellis Island, and got the erection of a new U.S. Customs House on the Bowling Green.

Chesebrough also developed large tracts of land in the Bronx, later occupied by the yards of the New York, New Hampshire and Hartford Railroad Company. In 1872 he built the South Boulevard Horse Railroad from the Harlem River to 149th Street; he later converted it to an electric railroad. He was the founder of the New York Realty Exchange, and an author of dramas and plays. An Episcopalian and a Republican, he married Margaret McCredy of New Rochelle, New York, in 1854. They had four children. (*NCAB*, B:515; 25:311.)

CHESTER, COLBY MITCHELL (July 23, 1877–September 26, 1965). Food company executive, General Foods. Born in Annapolis, Maryland, son of Rear Admiral Colby M. Chester and Malarcia Antoinette Tremaine. He was educated at Mohegan Lake School in Peekskill, New York, and St. John's College in Annapolis. He received a Ph.B. at Sheffield Scientific School at Yale in 1897, and a B.A. at Yale a year later. In 1900 he graduated from New York Law School. In 1900–1901 he was in the U.S. Navy, serving on his father's ship.

In 1901 Chester entered a law office in Bridgeport, Connecticut, and a year later organized his own firm. In 1904 he became treasurer of Manning, Maxwell and Moore, a railroad and industrial supply company. After seven years he returned to corporate law work in New York City, continuing this until World War I, when he served as a major in the army. After the war, in 1919, Chester was made assistant treasurer of the Postum Cereal Company. He rapidly moved up the corporate ladder, becoming treasurer, vice-president, and, in 1924, president. When he assumed that post he led the re-organization of the company which culminated in the 1929 merger with fifteen other food companies to form General Foods Corporation. He was president of this concern until 1935, when he became chairman of the board until 1943. Following that, he was chairman of the executive committee until 1946 and honorary chairman until 1958.

During his presidency the corporation's annual sales increased from $25 million in 1924 to $120 million in 1935. When he became president, the firm manufactured Postum, Instant Postum, Post Toasties, Baker's Chocolate and Coconut, Log Cabin Syrup, Swan's Down Cake Flour, Jell-O, Minute Tapioca, Hellmann's Mayonnaise, and other cereals and products. In 1927 he entered into an agreement to manufacture Sanka Coffee, with the Sanka Coffee Corporation, and in 1928 acquired the Cheek-Neal Coffee Company of Nashville, Tennessee, makers of Maxwell House Coffee. The Certo Corporation was acquired in 1929, and in the same year the Frosted Foods Company, Incorporated was acquired. Two years later the Dunlop Milling Company was added, and in 1932, Baker-Bennett-Day Incorporated was formed to consolidate Bennett-Day Importing Company with the edible nut department of Franklin Baker Company.

During these years, Chester was also chairman of the board of Manning, Maxwell and Moore, Incorporated, Zonite Products Corporation, and Lehigh Valley Railroad Company, and director of the New Jersey, Indiana, and Illinois Railroad, 20th Century Fox Films Corporation, Chase Manhattan Bank, and Manufacturers Hanover Trust Company. He served as chairman of the American Enterprise Association and director of the Freedom's Foundation, Incorporated. He was a president and director of the National Association of Manufacturers, and very involved with its activities.

A Congregationalist and a Republican, he married Jessie Campbell Moore in 1904. They had three children. (*DAB*, Supplement 1; *NCAB*, 52:435; 33:185; E. L. Fisch, *Lawyers in Industry*, 1956.)

CHISHOLM FAMILY–Henry Chisholm (April 22, 1822–May 9, 1881); **William Chisholm I** (August 12, 1825–January 10, 1908); **William Chisholm II** (May 22, 1843–December 6, 1905); **Stewart Henry Chisholm** (December 21, 1846–October 8, 1933); **Wilson B. Chisholm** (1848–March 10, 1914). **Henry Chisholm** was born in Scotland, the son of Stewart Chisholm, a mining contractor who died when Henry was ten years old. Henry had little formal education and went to work at an early age, serving as an apprentice carpenter at age 12. He remained in this position until he was seventeen, when he became a journeyman carpenter for three years. He then immigrated to Montreal, Canada, in 1842, where he lived for the next seven years, working as a carpenter and contractor.

In 1850, at age twenty-eight, Henry Chisholm came to Cleveland, Ohio, where he spent three years building the brickworks for the Cleveland and Pittsburgh Railroad Company. He then received many offers to construct piers and docks in the area. By 1857 he had accumulated a modest fortune of $25,000, allowing him to enter the iron and steel industry, forming Chisholm, Jones and Company. Later it became Stone, Chisholm and Jones. He erected blast furnaces in 1859 and established a rolling mill in Chicago, another blast furnace in Indiana, and ore fields near Lake Superior and in Missouri.

In 1864 Henry Chisholm organized the Cleveland Rolling Mill Company, and bought the Lake Shore Rolling Mill. One year later he started the second Bessemer steel firm in the United States, with an annual capacity of 20,000 tons. This was increased to 150,000 tons over the years. The firm employed 6,000 men and was capitalized at $12,000,000, manufacturing steel rails and other steel products. In 1871 he organized the Union Rolling Mill of Chicago, and erected a rolling mill at Decatur, Illinois, worth $25 million. He was called the "father of the Cleveland steel trade," and did much to formulate the manufacturing policy of the city. A Baptist, he married Jean Allen of Dumferlein, Scotland, and had five sons and three daughters.

William Chisholm I was born in Scotland, brother of Henry. He came to Canada in 1847, living in Montreal before coming to Cleveland in the early 1850s. He became the superintendent in his brother's Cleveland Rolling Mill, and then opened the Chisholm Steel Shovel Works, serving as president of that until he died. He also founded the Union Steel Screw Company, which was later consolidated with National Screw and Tack Company. He married Catharine Allen of Dumferlein, Scotland (sister of his brother's wife) and had one son and one daughter. His son, Henry Arnott Chisholm (1851–1920), worked in Cleveland Rolling Mill until 1877, when he became a partner in his father's firm. He served as superintendent of this until his father died in 1908, then becoming president and general manager. In 1910 the firm was incorporated as William Chisholm Sons Incorporated. He retired in 1912. He was also vice-president of Union Steel Screw Company.

William Chisholm II was born in Montreal, Canada, son of Henry Chisholm. He went with his father to Cleveland in 1850 and was educated at Philadelphia Polytechnic Institute for four years. In 1863 he was sent to Chicago as president and manager of the Union Rolling Mill. In 1880 he returned to Cleveland to manage the Cleveland Rolling Mill while his father traveled in Europe. When his father died in 1881, William became president and manager of the firm until it was sold to American Steel and Wire Company. After the sale he retired from active business. He also served as vice-president of Union Steel Screw and was a director of several other companies. He married Henrietta Stone, daughter of A. A. Stone of Chicago. They had two children, including Alvah Stone Chisholm (1871–1919), who entered Cleveland Rolling Mill in 1894 and stayed on as assistant to the president of American Steel and Wire Company after the sale.

Stewart Henry Chisholm was born in Montreal, son of Henry. He came to Cleveland in 1850, and was educated in the city's public schools. He then joined Stone, Chisholm and Jones, becoming vice-president of Cleveland Rolling Mills, and later vice-president of American Steel and Wire Company. He also served as president of Chisholm and Moore Manufacturing Company, manufacturers of chain hoists and malleable castings, and of the Long Arm System Company. He was one of the organizers, along with John W. Gates* and others, of the American Steel and Wire Company of Illinois in 1898, and later of American Steel and Wire of New Jersey. He organized H. P. Nail Company of Cleveland and was president of American Grass Twine Company. He retired in 1900. A Baptist, he married Henrietta Kelley of Ohio in 1896, and Mrs. Henry P. Card. He had three sons, including Wilson K. Chisholm, who became treasurer of Chisholm and Moore.

Wilson B. Chisholm was born in Montreal, son of Henry, and came to Cleveland in 1850. He was educated in Cleveland's public schools, and for fifteen years was vice-president and manager of Cleveland Rolling Mill and president of Champion Rivet Company. He was also a large stockholder in Chisholm and Moore Manufacturing Company. He retired in 1902. He married Nellie Brainard and had five children. (**A.** *NCAB*, 18:247; 28:451; *Iron Age*, March 22, 1899; January 16, 1908; May 14, 1914; August 28, 1919; October 14, 1920; October 12, 1933; E. K. Avery, *A History of Cleveland and its Environs*, 3 vols., 1918; *Biographical Cyclopedia of the State of Ohio*, 1876. **B.** Herbert A. Casson, *The Romance of Steel*, 1907; S. P. Orth, *A History of Cleveland, Ohio*, 3 vols., 1910.)

CHISUM, JOHN SIMPSON (August 15, 1824–December 23, 1884). Texas cattleman. Born in Hardeman County, Tennessee, son of Claiborne C. and Lucy Chisum. The family moved to Texas in 1837. John Chisum had little formal education, and went to work at an early age. He became a contractor and builder in Paris, Texas, and for eight years was county clerk of Lamar County. In 1854, with a partner, he started in the cattle business in that county, but three years later moved to Denton County, where he remained until 1863. In that year, he drove a herd, estimated at 10,000 head, into Concho County, where he engaged in business with a number of other men on shares.

Chisum was the first of the Texas cattlemen to shift his operation to the ranges of New Mexico. In the late fall of 1866 he drove a herd up the Pecos to Basque Grande, about thirty miles north of Roswell, New Mexico. The next spring he disposed of the herd to government contractors for the Navajo, Mescalero, and Apache reservations. He then formed an association with Charles Goodnight* by which for three years he continued to drive cattle north from Texas to Basque Grande, with Goodnight contracting for their sale in Colorado and Wyoming. Indian raids were frequent, and later came white "rustlers," but despite heavy losses Chisum prospered. In 1873 he made South Spring his home, establishing a ranch there. His herds multiplied and at their peak he had between 60,000 and 100,000 head. He was the largest individual cattle owner in America, and perhaps in the world.

Chisum was also involved, at least indirectly, in the Lincoln County War of 1878–1879. He evidently hired "Billy the Kid," using his services in the war. The latter's evolution into a cattle thief and killer brought Chisum to the front of the movement to end lawlessness in New Mexico. He was instrumental in getting Pat Garrett elected sheriff in 1880, and Garrett later killed Billy the Kid. Chisum remained unmarried, and died in Eureka Spring, Arkansas, leaving an estate of a half million dollars. (**A.** *DAB; NCAB*, 22:78. **B.** T. J. Cauley, "Early Business Methods in the Texas Cattle Industry," *Journal of Economic and Business History*, 1932; E. E. Dale, *The Range Cattle Industry*, 1930; Ernest S. Osgood, *The Day of the Cattleman*, 1929.)

CHOUTEAU, JEAN PIERRE (October 10, 1758–July 10, 1849); **Pierre Chouteau** (January 11, 1789–September 6, 1865); and **Auguste Pierre Chouteau** (May 7, 1786–December 23, 1838). Fur traders, St. Louis, Missouri, Fur Company and Pierre Chouteau, Jr. Fur Company.

Jean Pierre Chouteau was born in New Orleans, Louisiana. He became a famous fur trader in Missouri, holding a monopoly of the Osage fur trade from 1794 to 1802, when it was transferred to Manuel Lisa.* Chouteau was then appointed by President Jefferson as U.S. agent to the Osages, a government territory within Lisa's monopoly. In 1809 he joined with Lisa, William Clark, and eight others in the formation of the St. Louis, Missouri, Fur Company. This was the first important organization formed to exploit the beaver region of the West. But the company did not thrive, and was dissolved in 1814. Chouteau also had several trading houses in the lower Mississippi region and made frequent trips to the frontier. By 1870, however, he lived in semi-retirement on a plantation outside St. Louis. He married Pelagie Kirserea in 1783 and Brigitta Saucier in 1794 and had one son and one daughter. His brother, Rene Auguste Chouteau (1749–1829) was one of the founders, with Pierre LeClerc, of a village on the Mississippi River which grew to become St. Louis. He became the wealthiest citizen of that city and its largest landowner.

Pierre Chouteau was born in St. Louis, son of Jean Pierre. He was educated in the village schools and before age sixteen became a clerk in his father's store. In 1808 he went with Julien Dubuque to the lead mines on the upper Mississippi, remaining there for two years as superintendent. In 1809 he joined in an expedition for the St. Louis, Missouri, Fur Company, and a year later, at age twenty-one, went into business on his own account. Three years later he formed a partnership with his brother-in-law, Bartholomew Berthold, in the Indian trade and general merchandise business. This partnership lasted until 1831, when Chouteau became a member of the firm of Bernard Pratte and Company, later Pratte, Chouteau and Company. This firm was an agency of the Western Department of the American Fur Company for a number of years, and in 1834 purchased the Western Department. Four years later this became Pierre Chouteau Jr. and Company, remaining in business for more than twenty years. As his business expanded, Chouteau was drawn into other fields and his business operations became very extensive. His trading area extended over the entire area watered by the upper Mississippi and Missouri rivers, as well as the tributaries of the latter. In 1843 he joined the American Iron Company to work the Iron Mountain deposits in St. Francois County, Missouri, and in 1850 the firm of Chouteau, Harrison and Valle was formed to operate a rolling mill in North St. Louis. He was also one of the original incorporators of the Ohio and Mississippi Railroad in 1851. He married his cousin, Emilie Gratiot, in 1814.

Auguste Pierre Chouteau was born in St. Louis, another son of Jean

Pierre. He graduated from West Point Military Academy in 1806, serving as an aide to Gen. James Wilkinson for a short time on the southwestern frontier before resigning from the army in 1807. He became one of the ten original partners of the St. Louis Missouri, Fur Company. After serving in the War of 1812 as a captain of the territorial militia, he conducted a trading and trapping expedition in the upper Arkansas region, meeting with great success until 1817. In that year he was captured by Spanish soldiers and imprisoned for forty-eight days in Santa Fe. After his return, he traded for a time with the Osage Indians in western Missouri and Kansas. In 1823 he bought the trading house of Brand and Barbour, and spent the greater part of his remaining days in this activity. He married his cousin, Sophie Labbadia, in 1814, and had one son and five daughters. He also had an Indian wife with several children. He was heavily in debt when he died and after his demise Indian and white creditors seized his property. (**A.** *DAB; NCAB*, 13:469; 12:19. **B.** Paul C. Phillips, *The Fur Trade*, 2 vols., 1961.)

CHRYSLER, WALTER PERCY (April 2, 1875–August 18, 1940). Automobile manufacturer, Chrysler Corporation. Born in Wamego, Kansas, son of Henry Chrysler and Anna Marie Breyman. His father had been born in Canada of German ancestry, and was a Union Pacific Railway engineer. Walter Chrysler went to public schools and high school in Ellis, Kansas, and then took a job in a grocery store. Next, he followed in his brother's footsteps as an apprentice machinist in the Union Pacific shops. After completing his apprenticeship, he began to travel, moving from one western railway shop to another, riding frequent trains, and building up a reputation as an extraordinarily able mechanic. At age twenty-six he was made round-house foreman at the Salt Lake City, Utah shops of the Denver, Rio Grande and Western Railroad.

By the time he was thirty-four, he had reached the top money bracket for a machinist, as superintendent of motive power on the Chicago and Great Western Railroad, with a salary of $350 per month. After a quarrel with the company president in 1910, he quit and took a position with American Locomotive Company. Within two years he had become works manager of this concern, at $8,000 per year. Meanwhile, he became an automobile enthusiast, and in 1908 bought a Locomobile for $5,000 (despite the fact his salary was only $4,200 per year at the time). He then began to study the auto, and in 1912 got an opportunity to become works manager of the Buick Motor Company, the most important division of General Motors Company at the time. He went to Buick for only $6,000 per year, even though American Locomotive offered him $12,000 per year to stay. This was a key decision of his career, for it not only brought him into the fledgling auto industry, but gave him the opportunity to move up into the highest ranks of management, something less likely to occur in the more highly bureaucratized and established railroad industry.

Chrysler introduced new processes of big metal production into the Buick shops, which were still being run by carriage makers when he arrived. In 1916 he was made president of Buick, at $50,000 per year, mostly in stock. But he did not get on well with the president of General Motors, William C. Durant,* so he resigned from this position in 1920. These were exceptionally difficult years for the automobile industry, and many of the auto companies were saved in 1920 and 1921 only by massive bank loans. Thus, in 1921, Chrysler was persuaded to undertake a two year reorganization of the Willys Overland Company, at a salary of $1,000,000 per year. At the same time he became chairman of the reorganization and management committee of the Maxwell Motor Company, and later also assumed the presidency of that organization. While he was producing Maxwells, he was working with designers to create a car which would bear his name and would present many new innovations to the industry and the consumer. Two of the most significant of these features were four wheel hydraulic brakes and a high compression motor.

The new car was ready in January of 1924, and was able to attract the necessary banker's support, so in 1925 the Maxwell Motor Company, with profits of over $4,000,000, became the Chrysler Corporation. Three years later, in 1928, he purchased the Dodge Brothers Company from Dillon Read for its manufacturing facilities, which would have cost Chrysler $75 million to build. Dodge had the requisite plants and a famous line of cars, but lacked aggressive leadership. With the acquisition of Dodge, Chrysler was now in a position to challenge Ford and General Motors for supremacy in the automobile industry. He introduced the Plymouth and De Soto lines, the former designed to compete with Ford and Chevrolet. During the 1930s Chrysler and his engineering staff continued to develop countless innovations to lead the auto industry. In 1935 Chrysler retired as president to become board chairman, with the company now out of debt and standing in second place in the industry in volume of production. During these years, the innovations he pioneered included parallel spring suspension, oil purifier, full pressure lubrication for moderate priced cars, crank case ventilation, high frequency valve springs, inner strut pistons, rubber engine mountings, fully counter-balanced crank shafts, balanced road wheels, and many others. By the time of his death, the Chrysler Corporation employed 60,000 to 65,000 persons in factories in Detroit, Newcastle and Evansville, Indiana, London, England, and Antwerp, Belgium. He also built the Chrysler Building in New York City which, at 77 stories in 1930, was the tallest building in the city at that time.

Walter Chrysler was raised a Methodist, but became an Episcopalian, and married his boyhood sweetheart, Della Vesta Forker of Ellis, Kansas. They had two sons and two daughters. (A. *DAB*, Supplement 2; *NCAB*, D:89; *New York Times*, August 19, 1940; *Current Biography*, October,

1940; *Who Was Who*, vol. 1; Walter O. Chrysler, *Life of an American Workman*, 1950. **B.** John B. Rae, *The American Automobile Manufacturers*, 1959.)

CLAFLIN, HORACE BINGHAM (December 18, 1811–November 14, 1885) and **John Claflin** (July 24, 1850–June 11, 1938). Merchants, H. B. Claflin and Company and United Dry Goods Company. **Horace Claflin** was born in Medford, Massachusetts, son of John Claflin and Lydia Miller. His father owned a country store and was a large landowner in the area. Horace Claflin was educated at the common schools and Milford Academy. In 1834 his father loaned him $1,000 with which to start a business in Worcester, Massachusetts, then a small town. He prospered, and within five years had a trade of $200,000 per year. In 1843 he went to New York City, where he engaged in the wholesale dry goods business. He was again highly successful, but was hit very hard by the outbreak of the Civil War, when he was left with one million dollars in debts owed to the house by southern creditors. Yet he was able to survive this crisis and that of the panic of 1873. Throughout all this, his business continued to grow rapidly, rivaling that of A. T. Stewart,* and in one year surpassed $70 million in value.

Claflin had been a pioneer in making the jobbing house a manufacturer, as well as an importer and distributor of merchandise. In 1853 he built the Trinity Building, at 111 Broadway, and moved his business there, and in 1861 moved to even larger quarters at Worth and Church streets. He was a Republican, and a presidential elector for that party in 1872. But in 1884 he worked for the election of a Democrat, Grover Cleveland. He married Agnes Sorge of South Carolina.

John Claflin was born in Brooklyn, New York, son of H. B. Claflin. He was educated in the public schools of New York, and graduated from the City College of New York in 1869. He traveled extensively until 1870, when he entered his father's dry goods firm. He became head of the company upon his father's death in 1885, managing it until 1914. He greatly expanded the business and established an integrated merchandising concern with many functions and a wide geographic scope. The firm was incorporated in 1890 as H. B. Claflin and Company, with a capitalization of $9 million. Later, to consolidate his interests, he organized a series of holding companies—Associated Merchants Company in 1900; United Mercantile Company in 1903; and United Dry Goods Company in 1909. He expanded the wholesale business to include thirteen warehouses across the nation, and also had a thriving import-export business abroad. Claflin had more than two dozen retail stores in the United States, as well as a large manufactory of sheets and pillowcases.

His vigorous policies and practices characterized the wholesale operations. He enlarged the variety of goods sold, at an early stage adding notions, novelties, and ladies' ready to wear clothing, to such staple articles as yard goods. A large departmentalized sales force solicited trade. The five divisions of the credit department each collected a variety of information on the designated geographic areas, and the advertising department continuously carried on extensive campaigns. To facilitate national advertising, the company adopted its own brand names; to stimulate wholesale sales it encouraged buying in advance of the season, made special offers based upon advantageous purchases, ran semi-annual clearance sales, and emphasized service to its customers.

Despite its many successes, the company went into receivership in 1914. The problem lay with an over-extension of credit in financing its retail subsidiaries, and payment of dividends in excess of earnings to bolster its stock market position. At the same time, general economic conditions were difficult and banks had tightened credit. Wholesale trade was also changing—the direct purchase from manufacturers of national brands by retailers was becoming more common and there was increased competition, especially from jobbers in regional areas, which narrowed the market.

John Claflin turned over the major portion of his private fortune to meet the claims of creditors, but the business never recovered, and in 1926 Claflin's Incorporated was voluntarily liquidated. He was a director of several life and fire insurance companies, and six large banks. He was also president of the Chamber of Commerce of the State of New York. At its height in the early twentieth century, his firm was the leading dry goods concern in the United States, and had 1,100 employees. He married Mrs. Elizabeth (Stewart) Dunn in 1890, and had three children. (*DAB*, Supplement 2; *NCAB*, 3:228; 3:229.)

CLAIBORNE, WILLIAM (c. 1587–c. 1677). Manorial planter and merchant. Born in England, the son of Edmund Claiborne, lord of the manor of Cleburne in Westmoreland County. The manor had been in family hands since at least 1086. In 1621 William Claiborne was appointed surveyor for the colony of Virginia. Four years later he was appointed secretary of state for the colony and a member of the Council. He served until 1637, and again from 1652 to 1660. In 1642 King Charles appointed him treasurer of the colony. He led an expedition against the Indians in 1629 and again in 1646. In recognition of his services he was granted large tracts of land. With a governor's license, he was active in the Indian trade along the shore of the Chesapeake in 1627 and 1628.

In 1629 he became associated with Claberry and Company, a firm of London merchants, and obtained a commission signed by William Alexander, secretary of state for Scotland, which licensed him to trade for corn, furs, and other commodities in all parts of New England and Nova Scotia, where a patent had not previously been granted to allow others sole trade. He returned to Virginia in 1631 with licenses and set up a trading settlement on Kent Island in the Chesapeake Bay. He purchased the island from the

Indians, stocked it with cattle and hogs, planted corn and tobacco, and served as a representative in the Virginia House of Burgesses. Upon the arrival of the Maryland colonists under Lord Baltimore, in 1634, Claiborne spurned an offer by the proprietor to provide him benefits in exchange for recognition of Baltimore's proprietary jurisdiction over his island.

Lord Baltimore ordered Claiborne arrested for inciting the Indians against the Maryland colonists. Petty warfare followed, with both sides petitioning the king. At the same time Claiborne had a falling out with his London associates, and in 1637 departed for England for an accounting. While he was gone, the governor of Maryland reduced the island to submission. In 1638, the Commissioner of Plantations decided wholly in favor of Lord Baltimore. During the next decade, when anti-Catholic feeling was strong in Maryland, Claiborne and Richard Ingle incited an insurrection, drove Governor Calvert into Virginia, and held the province from 1644 to 1646. In 1651 Claiborne was appointed a member of a commission of the Puritan Parliament for the government of "the plantation within the Bay of the Chesapeke," and from 1652 to 1657 the affairs of Maryland were subject to control by this body. Claiborne never regained control of his island, and one of the last records of his career was a petition in 1676 to King Charles II for it.

He also founded Palmer Island at the mouth of the Susquehanna River and established a trading post there. He was married and had three children, two sons and one daughter. (*DAB; NCAB*, 11:421; Nathaniel C. Hale, *Virginia Venturer: William Claiborne, 1600–1677*, 1951.)

CLARK, CATHARINE TAFT (1907–   ). Food processor, Brownberry Ovens. Born in Whitewater, Wisconsin, daughter of Warren Taft and Clara West. Her father ran a garage and had the only automobile in the town. Before that he had retailed and repaired bicycles, and later owned the first movie theater. He died when she was still a young girl, so her mother had to take in washing in order to support the family. Catharine Clark was educated in the public schools of Whitewater and went to work helping to send her brother through college. She moved to Milwaukee, where she worked in the personnel department of a department store, being the only member of the department with a high school education. During this time she met her husband, Russell Clark, a graduate of the University of Wisconsin, who was earning his M.B.A. at Harvard. When he graduated two years later, he went to Chicago to work for the Northern Trust Company. Then, during the depths of the depression he changed jobs, and they were married and settled in Oconomowoc, Wisconsin. Catharine continued in the personnel department after their marriage until she had her first child in 1935.

While she was home raising her children, Catharine found that a local baker sold bread which she found particularly good. She approached the man, Mr. Marsh, and stated that she wished to purchase his wheat bread recipe. He agreed to sell, so she rented a store, purchased an old beer delivery truck and began what eventually became Brownberry Ovens. Necessary equipment was obtained from Marsh, and her first mixer made twelve loaves at one time. She quickly outgrew her equipment, mortgaged her home to raise capital, and got a couple of friends to put cash into the venture. The business was organized in 1946. She designed a "Brownberry Ovens" label, and hired her former housekeeper and the former handyman of the family to help her in the business. Every other day the handyman drove to Milwaukee to make deliveries in the secondhand beer truck. Russell kept the simple books of the operation in his spare time, and six months later they bought some larger equipment secondhand in northern Michigan. This enabled them to produce in larger quantities.

A major reason for the ultimate success of her operation was that she offered distinctive baked goods free of preservatives or artificial ingredients, well before consumers considered such problems. Most importantly, however, the product was delicious. While Catharine worked at the bakery, her mother was at home with her school age girls. When the time came to market the product to new outlets, Catharine and Russell would go out and sell bread on Saturdays. Although her products were marketed only in the Midwest, since without preservatives they could not be shipped long distances, Brownberry Ovens showed a sizable profit after several years. At that point Catharine decided to invest the earnings in advertising. She took photos and presented them to a Milwaukee advertising agency, and her first advertising campaign was begun in the *Milwaukee Journal*. She also launched a campaign to teach people to bake bread at home and wrote *Bread Baking: The How and Why Book*, distributed by Brownberry.

During the first four years the company either doubled or more than doubled its previous year's sales. The total workforce grew from two employees in 1946 to 72 in 1954. In 1972 she sold Brownberry Ovens to the Peavy Corporation for $12 million. By this time the company distributed twelve different breads, a half dozen rolls, and a variety of stuffings and croutons to the north-central Midwest, especially the Twin Cities, Wisconsin, and Chicago. In the last year before the sale, Brownberry netted $250,000. After the sale Catharine retired and moved to San Francisco, California, though she continued to work two weeks of every month at the Brownberry headquarters in Oconomowoc, and served as chairman of the board. (Louise Riel McCoy, *Millionaresses: Self Made Women of America*, 1978.)

CLARK, EDWARD (December 19, 1811–October 14, 1882). Lawyer and entrepreneur, Singer Sewing Machine Company. Born in Athens, Greene County, New York, the son of a pottery manufacturer. He was educated at Williams College and studied law with Ambrose L. Jordan at Hudson, New York. In 1833 he began the practice of law in Poughkeepsie, New York, coming to New York City three years later. In 1854 he began his association with a restless Yankee machinist, Isaac Merritt Singer.

Singer, at age 39, had borrowed forty dollars for capital and made the first sewing machine in Boston in 1850. He was soon granted a patent and began to manufacture and sell the machines. He was then sued by Elias Howe, who had gotten a patent on a sewing machine in 1846. For help in the litigation, Singer turned to the New York law firm of Jordan and Clark. Ambrose Jordan, the senior partner, was state's attorney general. His son-in-law and junior partner was Edward Clark. For a one-third interest in the company, Clark agreed to fight the legal battles, later buying another one-third with Singer. They then became equal partners in I. M. Singer and Company, organized in 1851. Singer remained in charge of manufacturing and Clark took charge of finances and sales as well as legal matters.

Clark and other lawyers ended the "sewing machine war" by organizing the Singer Machine Combination, America's first patent pool. Manufacturing was licensed at $15 a machine, and twenty-four companies were licensed. The combination expired in 1877 when the last of the patents lapsed. The earliest machines were heavy devices for tailors and harness makers, but by 1856 the leading companies were making lighter machines for home use. These enabled the housewife to do in one hour what took fourteen hours by hand. The great obstacle was the price of $125 or more. Clark attacked this problem with a trade-in allowance for old machines and the barter of machines for advertising. Most importantly, however, he established the principle of installment buying, which the Singer Company pioneered, becoming its foremost proponent.

Installment sales kept Singer going in the panic of 1857, since only five dollars was now needed to place a new Singer sewing machine in the home. The rest was to be paid in small monthly payments. If the purchaser failed to make the payment, the machine was repossessed. Even Clark became apprehensive over the rapid success of this procedure, but their losses were slight. Installment buying quickly became the mainstay of Singer's sales in the United States and soon was instituted in Great Britain and many other countries under the term "home-purchase."

After the incorporation of the business in 1863, Singer left the management of the business to Clark and spent most of his time in Europe, where he died in 1875. Clark then became president of the company until he died. Singer established its own factory in 1867, and became a maker-to-user manufacturer, remaining so ever since. They began overseas manufacture in the same year in Glasgow, Scotland, and in 1882 the largest of all Singer plants was erected there. In 1873 Singer machines began to be manufactured in Montreal, and in the same year a large plant in Elizabethtown, New Jersey, was completed. All United States manufacturing operations were then shifted there. By 1965 the Singer Company had factories in 29 countries and world wide sales offices which sold direct to the user. In that year they sold $642 million in products, including $534 million in items related to sewing. They also produced business machines and industrial products. Clark was also heavily involved in real estate development in New York City, owning large numbers of apartments and dwellings. He had resided in Cooperstown, New York, since 1854 and left an estate of over $25 million. He had three sons. (**A.** *Who Was Who*, vol. 1; *New York Times*, October 17, 1882. **B.** Daniel M. Boorstin, *The Americans: The Democratic Experiment*, 1973; Robert B. Davies, "Peacefully Working to Conquer the World: The Singer Manufacturing Company in Foreign Markets," *Business History Review*, Autumn, 1969; Andrew B. Jack, "The Channels of Distribution for Innovation: The Singer Sewing Machine in America," *Explorations in Entrepreneurial History*, February, 1957; Tom Mahoney and Leonard Sloan, *The Great Merchants*, 1955.)

CLARK, WILLIAM ANDREWS (January 8, 1839–March 2, 1925). Montana mining operator, entrepreneur, and politician. Born in Fayette County, Pennsylvania, son of John Clark and Mary Andrews. His father was a farmer and Clark's boyhood was spent on the farm, with only short sessions of schooling in the winters. In 1856 the family moved to Iowa, and he was educated at an academy in Birmingham, later studying law at Iowa Wesleyan College. In 1856 he went to Missouri to teach school and when the Civil War broke out, devastating the state, he drove a team to Colorado and began working in gold quartz mines there. In 1863 he went to Bannock, Montana, attracted by reports of rich discoveries of gold on Grasshopper Creek. He soon joined a stampede to Horse Prairie Creek, where he washed out $1,500 in gold. With this for capital, he shipped in a load of provisions from Salt Lake City and started a store in Virginia City. There was a heavy demand for tobacco in Virginia City, and the price was high, so Clark went in search of a supply, finding it in Boise, Idaho. He purchased several hundred pounds and hauled the cargo to Last Chance Gulch (now Helena) where he sold it at a good profit. In 1866 he went on horseback to the Pacific Coast and bought a large stock of goods, which he took to a new store at the mining camp of Elk City, Montana.

In 1867 he received the concession for carrying the mails between Missoula, Montana, and Walla Walla, Washington. This was a hazardous enterprise through mountains and Indian territory, but he made a success of it and became quite wealthy. He then entered into a partnership with R. W. Donnell of New York and S. E. Larabie of Montana in banking and wholesale merchandise. The firm's first bank was established at Deer Lodge in 1870, with another at Butte in 1877. In 1872 he began moving into mining, purchasing the Original, Colua, Mountain Chief, and Ganbette mining claims at Butte. He then went to the School of Mines at Columbia University for one year to study mining. Upon his return he built the "Old Dexter" stamp mill, the first of its kind in Butte, and formed the Colorado and Montana Smelting Company, building the first smelter in Butte. He also established the huge Butte Reduction Works, acquired the greatest of the Butte mines, and extended his mining interests to Arizona, where he purchased the United Verde Mine and its smelter.

He also built the San Pedro, Los Angeles and Salt Lake Railroad and sold it to the Union Pacific, of which he became a director. He organized the Los Alamitos Sugar Company and built a large sugar factory near Los Angeles. Clark early became interested in Montana politics. He was a leader of the state's mining interests, but an implacable foe of Marcus Daly,* a fellow Montana mining tycoon. Both men were Democrats and fought to control that party in the state, with their rivalry dominating the mining and political history of Montana in the 1880s and 1890s. Clark began his political career as president of the state's constitutional convention in 1884, and in 1888 he was nominated for Congress. He was defeated by Daly in his bid, and in 1889 presided over a convention to frame a constitution for the new state. Clark was endorsed by the legislature. In 1893 he was again a candidate for the position, against the open and bitter opposition of Daly. The legislature was deadlocked, and adjourned without naming a senator. Their next war was over the site of the new state capital, with Daly wanting Anaconda and Clark, Helena. Clark was the victor in this battle.

In 1899 Clark was finally elected to the U.S. Senate by the legislature, but because of accusations of electoral fraud, the Senate refused to seat him. He resigned the position, but two years later was again elected to the Senate, this time without much opposition. While there he became a major opponent of President Roosevelt's conservation policies. His business interests also continued to expand throughout these years of political strife. In Montana he owned large tracts of timber land, and built a dam, a power plant, a saw mill, a flour mill, a street railway, and a water and electrical system in Missoula, and power service to towns in Bitter Root Valley. He established the first water system and electric light plant in Butte, and at one time owned a number of Montana newspapers, including the *Miner* of Butte.

He was married twice. His first wife was Kate L. Stauffer, from his old home in Pennsylvania, whom he married in 1869. In 1901 he took his second wife, Anna E. LaChapelle of Butte. He had eight children, six girls and two boys. One of his sons, William A. Clark Jr. (1877-1934), joined his father's enterprises, becoming president of many of the companies. In 1928 he sold his Montana holdings and retired to philanthropy. (**A.** *DAB; NCAB*, 21:10; 25:301; *Who Was Who*, vol. 1. **B.** C. B. Glasscock, *The War of the Copper Kings*, 1966; William D. Mangam, *The Clarks: An American Phenomenon*, 1941; Richard H. Peterson, *The Bonanza Kings*, 1977.)

CLARKE, RICHARD (May 1, 1711-February 27, 1795). Colonial Merchant, Boston, Massachusetts. Born in Boston, son of William Clarke and Hannah

Appleton. He graduated from Harvard in 1729. Clarke engaged in mercantile activities, becoming one of the most prominent merchants in the city. His firm, Richard Clarke and Sons, with his two sons, Jonathan and Isaac, was a major mercantile element at the time of the Revolution. Jonathan in 1773 was stationed in London, and the company was a factor for the East India Company, and was among the consignees of the tea which was dumped into Boston Harbor in 1773.

Richard and his sons received a letter ordering them to appear at the Liberty Tree to make public their resignation as factors of the East India Company. They met with other consignees, including Thomas Hutchinson, Benjamin Faneuil and Jonathan Winslow at Clarke's warehouse on King Street. A mob of about 500 gathered at the Liberty Tree and some of these then went to the warehouse. Nine were sent in as emissaries to induce the merchants to yield. But the merchants refused, so the mob attempted to storm the building. They were repulsed. When Jonathan came back from England a mob again attacked the Clarke's home. The Clarke firm at first refused to sign the non-importation agreement, but later consented. They were also one of the signers of an address to Gen. Gage. Since Clarke's daughter Susannah had married the artist John Singleton Copley and was living in England, Richard Clarke decided to move there and lived at the Copley home until he died. He joined the Loyalist Club of London with one of his sons. (*DAB*.)

CLAYTON, WILLIAM LOCKHART (February 7, 1880–February 8, 1966) Cotton factor, Anderson, Clayton and Company. Born Tupelo, Mississippi, son of James Monroe Clayton and Fletcher Burdine. His father was a railway conductor and cotton buyer who moved his family to Jackson, Tennessee, in 1886. William Clayton was educated there in the public schools. At age thirteen he went to work in the office of the clerk and master of the chancery court in Jackson, and later became deputy clerk and master. He also became the court reporter and did general stenographic work. In 1895 he went to St. Louis, Missouri, as secretary to Jerome Hill of the Jerome Hill Cotton Company. In the next year Hill took him to New York City, where he remained for eight years as an employee of the American Cotton Company, which Hill had helped to organize. Clayton rose to become assistant general manager of the concern. He resigned in 1904 to join his brother-in-law, Frank Anderson, and the latter's brother, Monroe Dunaway Anderson, in organizing the firm of Anderson, Clayton and Company, cotton merchants, with offices in Oklahoma City, Oklahoma. His brother, Benjamin Clayton, also became a partner in 1905.

In 1916 the headquarters of the firm was moved to Houston, Texas, where Anderson and Clayton grew into the world's largest cotton trading organization, with branches in Dallas, New Orleans, Atlanta, Savannah, Memphis, Mobile, Boston, and Los Angeles. On the New York City market they operated through an affiliate, Anderson, Clayton and Fleming. Anderson and Clayton grew rapidly by taking over the gins, branches, and business from the firm for which Clayton had formerly worked when that firm went bankrupt. During World War I the firm handled one million bales of cotton a year. Before World War II the volume per year had reached $220 million, and the company was marketing 15 percent of the total American cotton crop.

Clayton was partner and board chairman of the firm during this period, but withdrew in 1940 to enter government service as chief of the economic and financial section of the office of the coordinator of Inter-American Affairs. He remained at this for ten weeks, when he was appointed deputy federal loan administrator. In this position he had charge of the foreign procurement program of strategic and critical materials of certain subsidiaries of the Reconstruction Finance Corporation. He was also chairman of the board of the U.S. Commerce Company of the Rubber Development Corp., another subsidiary of the R.F.C. In 1942 he was appointed assistant secretary of commerce, serving until 1944. In the latter year he was made assistant secretary of state for economic affairs, coordinating extensive State Department activities for postwar reconstruction. In 1946 he was appointed an alternate governor of the International Monetary Fund and the International Bank for Reconstruction and Development. In these governmental positions he opposed high tariffs, cartels, and government interference generally. He was also in favor of a generous import and export policy for the U.S. and was a leading negotiator of the Anglo-American financial and commercial agreement of 1945. In August, 1946 he was appointed undersecretary of state for economic affairs.

During the period, Anderson, Clayton continued to expand. From its warehouse during the war, more than one-fifth of the Texas cotton crop was shipped each year to ports all over the world. The firm did twice as much business as its nearest competitor, with over two million bales per year. The company also had problems with governmental investigations of its activities in the 1920s and 1930s. Most of these were spearheaded by Senator Ellison E. "Cotton Ed" Smith of South Carolina, who expressed a wish to "pin something on Clayton." But nothing incriminating was ever found.

Clayton continued to serve in various governmental positions during the 1930s. He was a Democrat, but a conservative who had opposed most New Deal measures. He also wrote several books during the 1950s, including *Road to Peace*, 1955; *What Price Oil*, 1958; and *We Are Losing the Cold War*, 1954. He served as president of the Texas Cotton Association in 1920. A Methodist and then a Baptist, he married Susan Vaugh of Clinton, Kentucky, in 1907. They had four daughters. (**A.** *NCAB*, G:328; *Current Biography*, April, 1944; March, 1966; *New York Times*, February 9, 1966; *Fortune*, November, 1945; Ellen Clayton Gorwand, *Will Clayton*, 1958.

B. Harold G. Woodman, *King Cotton's Retainers*, 1968.)

CLEMENT, MARTIN WITHINGTON (December 5, 1881–August 30, 1966) Railroad executive, Pennsylvania Railroad. Born in Sunbury, Pennsylvania, son of Charles Maxwell Clement and Alice Virginia Withington. His ancestor, James Clement, came from England in 1660, and was one of the founders of Haddonfield, New Jersey. Martin Clement's father was a lawyer. Martin was educated in the local schools and obtained a bachelor's degree from Trinity College in Hartford, Connecticut, in 1901, majoring in civil engineering. He then joined the Pennsylvania Railroad as a rodman for the principal assistant engineer of a subsidiary, United New Jersey Railroad and Coal Company. They surveyed the floor of the Hudson River from New Jersey to New York City for the tunnel to make possible the building of Penn Station. He was then transitman and assistant supervisor until 1910, when he was promoted to supervisor of the office of general manager of the Pennsylvania Railroad Company in Philadelphia.

In 1913 he was transferred in a similar capacity to New York City, and then to Pittsburgh. A year later he was made division engineer of the New York, Philadelphia and Norfolk Railroad until 1918. In that year he was appointed superintendent of freight transportation of the Pennsylvania Railroad's eastern lines. Four months later he was acting superintendent of passenger transportation, during the time the railroad was operated by the federal government. After a return to private ownership control in 1920, Clement was appointed general superintendent of the Lake Division, with headquarters in Cleveland. After three years he was promoted to general manager of the central region, with offices in Pittsburgh. In 1925 he returned to Philadelphia as assistant vice-president in charge of operations, and was elected a director four years later. In 1933 he was named vice-president, and two years later became president of the Pennsylvania Railroad Company, succeeding W. W. Atterbury. As president he was head of the largest railway network in the world. He retired as president in 1948, remaining chairman of the board until 1951. He continued on the board of directors until 1957, when he retired from active business.

Throughout his career Clement was constantly interested in innovations in railway management and developments that would improve operations and service. One of his major achievements, at a cost of $200 million, was the electrification of the lines from New York City to Philadelphia, Baltimore, Washington, and Harrisburg. Although this was done during the depression, the Pennsylvania Railroad did not miss a dividend during this period. At least part of the reason for this was the willingness of Clement to use the resources of the federal government to partially finance these ventures. By borrowing money from the Public Works Administration in the late 1930s, over 21,000 cars were built for the road during this period.

With the outbreak of war in Europe in 1939, Clement announced that the Pennsylvania would spend $17 million for new locomotives, cars, and rails, and set about repairing 17,500 freight cars which had previously been set aside for retirement. This allowed the road to meet the rapidly expanding demands of the government and private sector during World War II. Operating revenues, which had been only $367,812,000 when Clement took over in 1935, soared to a peak of over one billion dollars in 1944. Net income increased proportionately, rising from nearly $24 million in 1935 to almost $65 million in 1944, with a peak of over $101 million in 1941. Nevertheless, in 1946, for the first time in its one hundred year history, the Pennsylvania had a deficit and did not declare a dividend. Clement blamed government regulations for the loss, and claimed that wear and tear on the railroads was aggravated by intensive use during the war. He felt the government was tardy in approving increases in rates that would have made proper renewal of rolling stock possible. Critics, on the other hand, stated that his accounting department was backward and that the railroad should not have declared profits (which were taxed at high wartime levels) and should have put aside a reserve for replacement of worn-out equipment after World War II. The official historians of the Pennsylvania Railroad, however, point out that the federal government's tax authorities would not allow reserves for maintenance to be deducted for tax purposes. The only advantage the Pennsylvania received was to be able to amortize the cost of war "plants" over 60 months or the duration of the war, whichever was shorter.

Despite these problems, Clement did manage to reduce the fixed interest obligation of the system and the fixed annual charges which the road had been required to pay. Economic conditions during the war favored this, but he had begun the procedure several years prior to the war. Funded debt reached a peak in 1937 as a result of his massive electrification projects, but by 1945 it was 15 percent below the 1937 peak, and this was accomplished in the face of additions to the property account of more than $200 million. At the end of the war the Pennsylvania controlled 6 percent of the railway mileage in the United States, but over 20 percent of the country's passengers and 11 percent of its freight. During this time Clement was involved in the development of modernized passenger cars, and helped reorganize freight handling so that shippers were given faster service. Local freight trains were abolished and replaced by motor trucks which carried shipments from outlying districts, depositing them at central freight depots.

Clement was president and director of all Pennsylvania Railroad subsidiaries, was on the board of managers of Girard Trust and the Philadelphia Saving Fund Society and was a trustee of Penn Mutual Life Insurance Company. He was an Episcopalian and a Republican and married Irene Harrison Higbie of New York City in 1910. She died in 1929, and two years later he married Elizabeth S. Wallace of Philadelphia. He had four children. (**A.** *NCAB*, 53:373; *Current Biography*, November, 1946; *New York Times*,

August 31, 1966; *Who Was Who*, vol. 4. **B.** George H. Burgess and Miles C. Kennedy, *Centennial History of the Pennsylvania Railroad Company*, 1949.)

CLEWS, HENRY (August 14, 1834–January 31, 1923). Wall Street financier, Henry Clews and Company. Born in Staffordshire, England, son of James Clews, a potter. Henry and his father came to visit the United States in 1850, the elder Clews intending to establish a china plant there. While on their visit, Henry persuaded his father to place him in business in New York City. He got a job as a clerk with the firm of Wilson G. Hunt and Company, one of the largest importers of woolen goods in New York. He remained there for eight years, but was always more interested in the financial than mercantile side of the business.

In 1858 Clews opened an office on Wall Street as a note broker and private banker in a firm called Stout, Clews and Mason, developing a very strong reputation in the United States and Europe in the years before the Civil War. But it was Civil War finance which offered to Clews a great opportunity for a large turnover and substantial profits. The Secretary of the Treasury, Salmon P. Chase, gave much business to the firm, which by now had become Livermore, Clews and Mason. It ranked second only to Cooke and Company in the amount of government bonds taken and disposed of to investors. The company continued to grow rapidly after the war. In 1877 it became Henry Clews and Company, and in 1882 it was moved to Broad Street, where it remained for forty-one years.

The company abstained from commitment to new promotions, flotations, and the like. The business was steadily conducted along conservative, limited lines, although on a very large scale. Clews also published a weekly circular which for years was widely known as the authoritative interpretation and forecast of market conditions. At one time he acted as currency advisor to the government of Japan. He wrote two books, *Fifty Years of Wall Street* (1908) and *Wall Street Point of View* (1900).

The great strength of his business in the late nineteenth century was as a negotiator of railroad loans in the United States and Europe. During the 1890s its business was more extensive than any other firm in the U.S. In 1874 he married a grandneice of President Madison, Lucy Madison Worthington of Kentucky. He was a Republican. (*DAB; NCAB*, I:373; *New York Times*, February 1, 1923.)

CLYDE, WILLIAM PANCOAST (November 11, 1839–November 18, 1923). Steamship and railway entrepreneur, Clyde Line and Richmond and Danville Railroad System. Born in Claymont, Delaware, son of Thomas Clyde and Rebecca Pancoast. His father was a native of Scotland who came to America in 1820, settling in Chester, Pennsylvania. He was a civil and marine engineer who was associated with the Swedish engineer, John Ericsson, in the introduction of the screw propeller for steam vessels. In

1844 he built and operated the *John S. McKin*, sailing between New York City and Charleston, South Carolina. This was the first screw propeller steamship in the United States and the first vessel of the Clyde Line, which was to become the largest American coastwise steamship company. It had twenty-two steamships and serviced every important port on the Atlantic Coast except Baltimore and Savannah.

William P. Clyde entered Trinity College in 1860, but on account of the Civil War left to join the "Philadelphia Greys," serving until the end of the war. He then became associated with his father as a shipbuilder and operator. At age thirty-four he became president of the Pacific Mail Steamship Company, which dominated the Pacific Coast like his father's company dominated the Atlantic Coast. William Clyde was a bold and aggressive shipping operator and adopted many steamship improvements. In 1871 he built the first compound engine ever constructed in the United States and placed it in the *George W. Clyde*. In 1886 he built the first triple expanded engine in the country and placed it in the steamer *Iroquois*.

For many years he was an important factor in steamship transportation between New York and San Francisco, as well as running the Panama Railroad. He was also active in the development of railroads in the southern states, for a time controlling the Richmond and Danville Railroad System. Working with Calvin Brice,* George O. Seney, and John Inman,* he developed the Richmond and Danville, the East Tennessee, and then the Central of Georgia into a single system. Although the Terminal ended in bankruptcy, the venture spurred its neighbors to build their interregional systems. He was an Episcopalian and a Republican and married Emeline Field Hill of Philadelphia in 1865. They had seven children. (**A.** *NCAB*, 20:57. **B.** Alfred D. Chandler Jr., *The Visible Hand*, 1977; Maury Klein, *The Great Richmond Terminal*, 1970.)

COFFIN, CHARLES ALBERT (December 30, 1844–July 14, 1926). Electrical manufacturer, General Electric Company. Born in Somerset, Massachusetts, son of Albert Coffin and Anstrus Varney. He graduated from an academy in Bloomfield, Maine. His family had come to Massachusetts in 1642, and he started his business career with an uncle, Charles E. Coffin of Lynn, Massachusetts, a shoe manufacturer. Soon afterward he helped found the firm of Coffin and Clough, a shoe manufacturing establishment, also located at Lynn.

In 1883 Charles A. Coffin became a member of the Lynn syndicate formed for the purchase of the American Electric Company of New Britain, Connecticut, the head of which was Elihu Thomson. The plant was moved to Lynn, and the name changed to the Thomson-Houston Electric Company. Coffin knew little about electrical matters at this time, but had a genius for organization and the ability to surround himself with the best associates in the technical field. The technical expertise was provided by Thomson, Edwin J. Houston, and E. W. Rice.

In 1892 the Thomson-Houston Company was consolidated with the Edison General Electric Company of New York, in which all the interests and activities of Thomas Edison's* incandescent lamp development had been merged. Coffin was elected president of the new firm, called General Electric Company. He held this office until 1913, and from 1913 to 1922 was chairman of the board. The growth of the company under his leadership was phenomenal.

While with Thomson-Houston, Coffin in four years had completed a national network of sales offices. In 1886 he began to move into the production of other electrical products besides arc lights, including a complete incandescent system, a line of direct current motors, railway motors, and alternating generators and transformers. He did so both by internal expansion and by the acquisition, largely through the exchange of stock, of four small companies. When Coffin became head of the new consolidation, he amalgamated the organizations of the two companies into a single centralized structure. Nearly all of the twenty subsidiaries were then liquidated. He concentrated production at three major works: lamp production continued to be carried on in Harrison, New Jersey; Schenectady manufactured heavy specialized machinery, such as large generators, motors and turbines; and the plant at Lynn turned out smaller mass-produced products including arc lights, small motors, and meters. The Thomson-Houston sales organization became the core of the new sales department, and the company's volume grew very rapidly, so that by 1895 they had 10,000 customers and processed 140,000 separate orders.

Coffin's major accomplishments in the late 1890s involved negotiation of a patent agreement with Westinghouse Electric and the creation of a research laboratory. Westinghouse and General Electric had long been accustomed to giving patent guarantees on all equipment. They were willing to accept complete responsibility for patent infringement suits against the equipment purchaser. By the mid-1890s, however, guarantees could no longer be made by both companies on all kinds of equipment. The solution to the patent impasse was a cross-licensing agreement which permitted the two companies to produce full lines of good quality equipment and to continue to carry on their normal price–product competition. The agreement became effective in 1896; it was to run for fifteen years and be administered by a board of patent control which had two members each from General Electric and Westinghouse. A fifth member, from outside the industry, was available to arbitrate in case of a deadlock. The patent agreement called for the pooling of patents and the manufacture of patented equipment by both companies, with exceptions for railway equipment in favor of Westinghouse and incandescent lighting in favor of General Electric. With basic patents in all the main lines of equipment, General Electric and Westinghouse were in a very powerful patent position relative to smaller companies who were unable to make strong patent guarantees. In 1895 Coffin established a standardizing laboratory for General Electric as a whole, and in 1901 he and his associates created a full-scale research laboratory. This laboratory not only contributed to electrical development, but also to the advancement of pure science. Coffin supported the work of company engineers in the development of the Curtis steam turbine, which revolutionized the primary power sources in electric light and power stations. During Coffin's tenure with General Electric, capitalization grew from $35 million to $184 million, and the number of employees increased from 4,000 to 70,000.

During World War I Coffin created the War Relief Clearing House and worked for the Red Cross. He was of Quaker heritage, and married Caroline Russell of Holbrook, Massachusetts, in 1872. They had three children. (**A.** DAB; NCAB, 20:20;1 Who Was Who, vol. 1. **B.** Kendall Birr, Pioneering in Industrial Research: The Story of the General Electric Research Laboratory, 1957; Alfred D. Chandler Jr., The Visible Hand, 1977; John W. Hammond, Men and Volts: The Story of General Electric, 1941; Harold C. Passer, The Electrical Manufacturers, 1875-1900, 1953; and "The Development of Large Scale Organization: Electrical Manufacturing Around 1900," Journal of Economic History, Fall, 1952.)

COFFIN, HOWARD EARLE (September 6, 1873-November 21, 1937). Automaker and airline executive, Hudson Motor Company and United Air Lines. Born on a farm near Milton, Ohio, son of Julius Vestel Coffin and Sarah Elma Jones. He was educated in area schools and worked his way through the University of Michigan. He entered the school in 1893, left in 1896 to work as a letter carrier and postal clerk, and returned from 1900 to 1902. He did not finish, but was awarded a degree from the school of engineering in 1911 in recognition of his achievements. During his last two years of college he experimented with both gasoline and steam automobiles.

In 1902 Coffin joined the Olds Motor Works, owned by Ransome E. Olds,* as head of the experimental department, becoming chief engineer in 1905. A year later he left the Olds organization, and with Roy D. Chapin* started to develop a car of Coffin's design. He was vice-president and chief engineer of the E. R. Thomas Detroit Company and its successor, the Chalmers-Detroit Motor Company, until he and Chapin obtained the independence they sought with the funding of the Hudson Motor Car Company in 1910. The success of the latter firm was due largely to the engineering talents of Coffin along with the executive and sales ability of Chapin.

During World War I Coffin entered government service with the Naval Consulting Board, an advisory group headed by Thomas A. Edison.* He conducted an important nation-wide inventory of plants capable of war production. In 1916 he was appointed by President Wilson to the advisory committee of the newly created Council of National Defense, and in

1917-1918 headed the council of National Defense, and in 1917-1918 headed the council's Aircraft Board. His principal achievement in this position was to supervise the development of the Liberty Motor. After the war he continued to advise the government on aeronautical matters, and in 1925 served on the Morrow Board to establish a long-term policy for aviation. In 1919 he was named president of the Society of Automotive Engineers, and was a major contributor to its program of technical standardization in the industry.

By the end of the war, Coffin's major interest was in aviation rather than automobiles, and after 1920 he acted only as a consultant at Hudson, although he retained the title of vice-president until 1930. He was a founder of the National Aeronautical Association and was its president in 1923. In this position he promoted the technical standardization in that industry and worked out a system for cross-licensing of patents similar to that in the automobile industry. He was also a founder of the National Air Transport Company, Incorporated (later United Air Lines), and served as its president from 1925 to 1928, and as chairman of the board from 1928 to 1930. In 1930 he retired and moved to a new home near Sea Island, Georgia. There he became chairman of the Sea Island Company, which was engaged in real estate development. He also became involved in the cotton industry as chairman of the board of the Southeastern Cottons, Incorporated.

Coffin was a Quaker and a Republican. A close friend of Herbert Hoover,* he was a virulent opponent of the New Deal, which he thought was a socialist conspiracy. He married Matilda Vary Allen of Battle Creek, Michigan, in 1907. She died in 1923, and he married Gladys Baker of New York. He had no children. (**A.** *NCAB*, 30:31; *New York Times*, November 24, 1937; *Who Was Who*, vol. 1. **B.** R. C. Epstein, *The Automobile Industry*, 1928; Charles Kelly Jr., *The Sky's the Limit*, 1963; E. D. Kennedy, *The Automobile Industry*, 1941; John B. Rae, *Climb to Greatness*, 1968; and *American Automobile Manufacturers*, 1959; Robert Sobel, *The Age of Giant Corporations*, 1972.)

THE COKER FAMILY: James Lide Coker (January 3, 1837–June 25, 1918); **James Lide Coker Jr.** (November 23, 1863–December 23, 1931); **David Robert Coker** (November 20, 1870–November 28, 1938); **Charles Westfield Coker** (July 13, 1877–November 21, 1931); **James Lide Coker III** (July 21, 1904–February 16, 1961); **Robert Richardson Coker** (September 6, 1905–   ); **Charles Westfield Coker Jr.** (August 15, 1906–   ). South Carolina merchants, industrialists, and agriculturalists.

James Lide Coker was born on a large plantation near Society Hill, South Carolina, son of Caleb Coker and Hannah Lide. He was educated at the local academy and the South Carolina Military Academy in Charleston, South Carolina. He then entered Harvard in 1857 for special work in soil analysis and plant development, studying with Louis Agassiz and Asa Gray.

After he completed the course, his father gave him a substantial estate near Hartsville, South Carolina, and he returned to undertake actual farming. He also organized an agricultural society for the dissemination of scientific ideas. At the outbreak of the Civil War, Coker volunteered and became a captain of a cavalry unit for two years in Virginia. He was then transferred to Tennessee, where he was wounded at Lookout Mountain. Promoted to major, he was captured and then paroled in 1864, when he returned to his ruined plantation. Although he had a brief fling in the state legislature from 1864 to 1866, he turned his full attention to business.

Coker continued to farm his estate with uniform success during the next fifty years, but also, in 1866, opened a small country store at Hartsville, which grew in time into one of the largest department stores in the state. From 1874 to 1881 he was a member of Norwood and Coker, dealers at Charleston in cotton and naval supplies, and in 1884 organized the Darlington National Bank. In 1887 he built a small railroad from Darlington to Hartsville which was later purchased by the Atlantic Coast Line. In the same year, with his son, James L. Jr., he organized the Carolina Fiber Company, the first company to make wood pulp from the pine wood so common in that section of the South. A few years later he organized the Southern Novelty Company, to manufacture from paper the cones and parallel tubes used by yarn mills for shipping the yarn. During the 1890s he organized the Hartsville Cotton Mill, the Hartsville Cotton Seed Oil Mill, and the Bank of Hartsville. With his son, David R., he developed one of the South's principal experimental agencies for seed listing and plant development.

During these years, Coker accumulated one of the largest private fortunes in the history of South Carolina, and was the state's most versatile businessman and its foremost philanthropist. In 1905 he gave $600,000 for the establishment of a college for women in Hartsville, called Coker College. He served as president of Carolina Fiber Company from 1890 to 1918. He married Susan Stout of Alabama in 1860, and they had seven children.

James Lide Coker Jr., his eldest son, was educated at Richmond College in Virginia and Stevens Institute of Technology in New Jersey, receiving a degree in mechanical engineering in 1888. In 1890 he organized the Carolina Fiber Company with his father, serving as its vice-president until 1918, and as president until his death thirteen years later. After World War I there was a greatly increased demand for a stronger and darker colored Kraft paper, and in 1925–1926 he made the first commercial installation for the manufacture of pulp from black gum wood by a semi-chemical process developed by the U.S. Department of Agriculture. He was also involved with his father and brother, Charles W., from 1904 to 1908 in the manufacture of textile cones and tubes made of paper. This resulted in the organization of Sonoco Products Company to produce them. In addition, he was president of the Estate Land and Securities Company, and director of several of the family businesses. He married Vivien Gay and had two daughters and one son.

David Robert Coker was born in Hartsville and was educated in the public schools there. He received a bachelor's degree from the University of South Carolina. After college, he entered J. L. Coker and Company, general merchants. Under his direction, the firm grew rapidly after 1889, becoming the largest department store in the eastern section of South Carolina. He resigned in 1897 due to ill health. He then became interested in scientific plant breeding, and in 1900 organized Coker's Pedigreed Seed Company, of which he was president for thirty-eight years. The company exerted an important influence on the improvement of agriculture in South Carolina and the Southeast generally, originating new varieties of cotton, a highly productive type of wheat, new varieties of corn, and many others. In 1918 he became president of J. L. Coker Company and partner in Coker Cotton, and vice-president of Sonoco Products and Hartsville Cotton Oil Mill. From 1897 to 1899 he was mayor of Hartsville, and during World War I was federal food administrator in Hartsville. He was a Democrat and married Jessie Ruth Richardson of South Carolina in 1894, and Margaret May Roper in 1915. He had eight children.

Charles Westfield Coker was born in Hartsville, son of James L. He was educated at Bethel Military Institute in Virginia and studied for a time at Furman University. In 1899 he joined his father in the Southern Novelty Company as treasurer and salesman. The company grew rapidly, and in 1917 began making its own paper. In 1918, he became president of the concern, which was renamed Sonoco Products in 1924. Charles Coker was responsible for the introduction of the Sonoco seamless cone and tube, the "Dytex" tube for package dying, and various important methods of manufacturing. It was the largest plant of its kind in the world. He was also chairman of a national commission in 1929 to assist in the standardization of paper cones and tubes under the U.S. Bureau of Standards. He served as mayor of Hartsville in 1903 and from 1917 to 1919, and as state senator in 1930. He was a Democrat. He married Carrie Lide of South Carolina and had two sons, James Lide III and Charles W. Jr.

James Lide Coker III was born in Hartsville, graduating from the University of North Carolina in 1926 and receiving an M.B.A. from Harvard in 1928. He then entered Sonoco Products as assistant treasurer and purchasing agent. He became president of the company in 1931. From that year until 1940, he increased the annual sales of the company from $1,500,000 to $5,000,000, and increased the number of employees from 500 to more than 1,500. In 1935 he established a paper plant at Mystic, Connecticut, and another at Lowell, Massachusetts. Also, in 1933, he set up a plant at Brantford, Ontario. In 1938 a large paper mill was erected at Garwood, New Jersey. In 1940 James L. Coker III was elected president of the National Fiber Cone and Tube Association. He was an Episcopalian and a

Democrat and married Elizabeth Boatwright of South Carolina. He had two children.

Charles W. Coker Jr. was born in Hartsville and graduated from the University of South Carolina in 1928, also attending Harvard Business School for one year. He joined his brother and father at Sonoco Products in 1930, becoming vice-president and then executive vice-president from 1934 to 1961. Upon his brother's death in 1961, he became president, serving until 1970, when he was named chairman of the board. He married Elizabeth Howard in 1931 and had two children.

Robert Richardson Coker was born in Hartsville, son of David R. Coker. He was educated in the public schools of the town and at Webb School in Tennessee. He graduated from the University of South Carolina in 1928, when he joined his father's Coker Pedigreed Seed Company, becoming sales manager and director in 1935 and president in 1951. The firm had 250 employees, including farm labor and college-trained experts. It was capitalized at one million dollars and farmed nearly 50,000 acres. Since 1940 he was also president of J. L. Coker and Company, the family department store, which was capitalized at $750,000, and had annual sales of one million dollars. He was a member of the agricultural research committee of the U.S. Department of Agriculture from 1946 to 1952, and a member of the Agricultural Mobilization Policy Board in 1951–1952. He also served as vice-president of the National Cotton Council from 1940 to 1945 and on the National Agricultural Advisory Board in 1953. He organized the National Council of Commercial Plant Breeders and served as its president from 1959 to 1960. He married Lois Walters of Idaho and had three children. (*DAB; NCAB*, 17:21; 23:77; 29:99; F:106; J:129; *Who's Who in America, 1978-79*.)

COLGATE FAMILY: William Colgate (January 25, 1783–March 25, 1857); **Samuel Colgate** (March 22, 1822–April 23, 1897); **Gilbert Colgate** (December 15, 1858–January 5, 1933); **Samuel Bayard Colgate** (April 4, 1898–October 8, 1963). Soap, perfume and toiletry manufacturers, Colgate, Palmolive-Peet Company.

William Colgate was born in Hollisbourne, England, son of Robert Colgate and Sarah Bowles. His father was a supporter of the French Revolution who was threatened with arrest in 1795, so the family immigrated to Baltimore, Maryland, in that year. His father bought a farm there, but later lost it through a defect in the title. William received a smattering of education in England and America, and at fifteen went to work for a tallow chandler. In 1804 he moved to New York City, where he worked for Slidell and Company, the city's largest tallow chandlers, becoming business manager of the firm within a short time. In 1806 he started his own establishment, which became very successful, and in 1812 began the manufacture of starch on an extensive scale. It became one of the largest plants of its kind in America, but was later abandoned.

During the first thirty-five years of its operation the Colgate Company, like other American soap manufacturers, concentrated on manufacturing laundry soap, since finer quality soaps were made by a secret process in England and France. After Chevreal's discovery in 1841, revealing the true principles of saponification, Colgate moved rapidly into the production of quality hand soaps, greatly transforming the industry and prompting the manufacture of many new varieties of toilet and shaving soaps. In 1820 the headquarters of the firm had been moved to Jersey City, New Jersey, and in 1850 a large factory for the manufacture of "fancy soaps" was established there.

Over the years William Colgate gave a great deal of money to charitable concerns, especially in the areas of education, religion, and temperance. He was a liberal supporter of the Hamilton Literary and Theological Seminary, which in 1890 became Colgate University, and in 1816 helped organize the American Bible Society under the auspices of the Baptist Church. He served on the board of this organization for twenty years, until 1835, when he resigned to help organize the American and Foreign Bible Society, serving as its treasurer for three years. In 1838 he withdrew from the Baptist Church. He married Mary Gilbert in 1811, and they had three sons. One of his sons, Samuel, joined his father in the soap business, while Robert became president of the Atlantic White Lead Works of Brooklyn, and the eldest, James B. (1818–1904), organized James B. Colgate Company, which conducted one of the largest specie and bullion businesses in the United States at the time. He was also a founder of the New York Gold Exchange and a vice-president of the Bank of New York.

Samuel Colgate was born in New York City and educated in private schools there. At sixteen he entered his father's soap business, assuming control of the firm upon the latter's death in 1857. During the forty years he ran the firm it became the largest soap manufacturer in the United States, marketing over one hundred different types of toilet soaps. During the 1880s, however, Colgate began facing stiff competition from Procter and Gamble, formerly a small Cincinnati soap manufacturer which had developed "Ivory Soap" in 1879. Using the new continuous-process machinery for the manufacture of soap, along with the development of a national advertising campaign and a network of sales offices to market its product, Procter and Gamble soon pushed Colgate out of the top spot. This forced Colgate, along with other American soap manufacturers, to build an integrated enterprise similar to Procter and Gamble's, and to engage in large-scale national advertising of their products. By the end of his tenure, the Colgate plant had 800 employees, with eight immense boiling kettles, each with a capacity of 600,000 pounds. His greatest innovation, however, was the introduction of Colgate toothpaste in jars in 1877. For eighty years Colgate Dental Cream was the largest selling toothpaste in the world, aided by extensive advertising and an international network of sales organizations.

Like his father, Samuel Colgate was a Baptist, a church deacon, and Sunday School superintendent in North Orange, New Jersey. He married Elizabeth Ann Morse, sister of Samuel F. B. Morse, in 1852. All four of his sons, Richard, Gilbert, Sidney, and Austin, became partners in the firm, but it was Gilbert Colgate who had the most important impact on the company's development. **Gilbert Colgate** was born in Orange, New Jersey, and graduated from Yale University in 1883. In that year he entered Colgate and Company, holding various positions between 1883 and 1896. In the latter year he became a partner in the firm, advancing to first vice-president in 1908, president in 1920, and chairman of the board in 1928. It was during the years of World War I that Colgate allied with two other large soap and toiletry manufacturers and began a massive expansion into foreign markets. Colgate was one of the earliest multinational firms, establishing sixteen foreign subsidiaries between 1914 and 1933. After World War I they consolidated with B. J. Johnson, a Milwaukee soap manufacturer who had made his Palmolive soap the largest selling brand in America in the early years of the twentieth century, and the Peet Company, soap manufacturers of Kansas City, forming Colgate, Palmolive-Peet Company, with assets of $63 million. During these years the volume of business of the firm increased twenty-five-fold, and it became the second largest manufacturer of soap and toiletry articles in the United States. From 1922 to 1924 Gilbert Colgate was president of the American Perfumers Association. A Presbyterian, he married Florence Buckingham Hall of Buffalo, New York, in 1888. They had four children.

Samuel Bayard Colgate was born in Orange, New Jersey, son of Sidney Morse Colgate and nephew of Gilbert Colgate. He was educated at Hill School in Pottstown, Pennsylvania, and attended Yale University in 1917–1918. In 1922 he joined the family business, serving as manager of advertising until 1928, when he was named vice-president and member of the executive committee of the newly formed Colgate, Palmolive-Peet Company. In 1933 S. Bayard Colgate was elected president of the firm, serving until 1938, when he became chairman of the board. He held the latter position until 1952, when he was named honorary chairman until 1959. Despite the fact that his tenure as president of the company encompassed the years of the deepest economic depression in the United States, he was able to expand its operations significantly. When he assumed the presidency the firm had annual sales of $62 million, and by 1938 this had increased to over $100 million. After World War II, however, the firm's fortunes began to slip dramatically. When detergents replaced soaps after the war, Colgate was slow to convert and lost ground to Procter and Gamble that it was never able to make up. Next Procter and Gamble came up with the fluoride ingredient for its Crest toothpaste, winning the endorsement of the American Dental Association. This enabled Procter and Gamble to knock Colgate

Dental Cream down from its perch as the best selling toothpaste in America, a position it had held for eighty years. It took Colgate years to learn how to make a fluoride toothpaste, and it never did get back into first place. By 1979 Colgate had sales of $4.5 billion, and ranked second in sales of toothpaste, soap and detergent, and shaving cream to Procter and Gamble. It had 56,000 employees worldwide.

S. Bayard Colgate was also interested in the brokerage house of Spencer, Trask and Company from 1931 to 1938, and was a partner in James B. Colgate and Company in 1939-1941. He was a trustee of the National Industrial Conference Board (1946-1956) and of the Committee for Economic Development (1944-1963). He was a trustee of Colgate University (1930-1963), and on the board of Junior Achievement from 1953 to 1963. A Presbyterian and a Republican, he married Anne Louise Burr in 1924. They were divorced in 1946, and in that year he married Angele Beatrice (Shaw) McHenry of Macon, Georgia. He had one son, Austin Bayard Colgate. (**A.** *DAB; NCAB*, 13:159; 26:343. **B.** Samuel Colgate, "American Soap Industry," in C. M. Depew, ed., *One Hundred Years of American Commerce*, 1895; Alfred D. Chandler Jr., *The Visible Hand*, 1977; Milton Moskowitz et al., eds., *Everybody's Business*, 1980.)

COLLINS, EDWARD KNIGHT (August 5, 1802-January 22, 1878). Packet ship operator, United States Mail Steamship Company—"Collins Line". Born in Truro, Massachusetts, son of Captain Israel Gross Collins and Mary Ann Knight. His father was a ship's captain who married his wife in England. They came to Truro, and she died five months after the birth of Edward. He was educated in the area, and at age fifteen went to New York City, where he lived the rest of his life. Edward first served as a clerk in the house of McCrea and Slidell, and went to the West Indies as supercargo on a joint venture. Then he and his father conducted a general commission business. During this time Edward began to be involved in the management of packet lines. He took over and improved the line to Vera Cruz, and in 1831 secured control of the New Orleans line. In 1836 he started his "Dramatic Line" from New York to England, so called because the ships were named after famous actors. This venture made him one of the wealthiest men in New York.

Quite early Collins became convinced that steam would soon replace sails, but he was unable to convince President Van Buren of the need for a steam navy, or any navy, for that matter. In 1847 he and his partners, James and Stewart Brown, made a contract with the postmaster general. They were to build, under naval supervision, five steamships of specified size which were to make twenty round trips annually, carrying mails between New York and Liverpool. They received $385,000 annually for the ten years of this undertaking. Five weeks later they organized the United States Mail Steamship Company, known as the "Collins Line." They spent two years building four ships which were larger, faster, and more splendid than anything afloat, averaging 2,800 tons and 1,500 horsepower. Service began in 1850 and attracted the cream of the passenger trade. It also forced a radical revolution in the British freight rates, and in 1852 Congress increased their subsidy to $858,000 per year.

Then came a series of disasters, caused perhaps by excessive speed. In 1854 the *Arctic* collided in the fog with a small French steamer off Cape Race. It sank with all aboard, including Collins' wife, son, and daughter. But service continued, and in 1853 the *Adriatic* was launched at 4,114 tons. In 1856 the *Pacific* sailed from Liverpool and was never heard from again. Then, in 1856, the extra subsidy granted by Congress in 1852 was withdrawn, and a contract was given to Commodore Vanderbilt* to run a rival line. The panic of 1857 hastened the end of the company, and in 1858 the three remaining ships were sold at auction for $50,000 to satisfy creditors. Collins then turned to the development of coal and iron properties in Ohio. He married Mary Ann Woodruff and Mrs. Sarah Brown. He had three sons. (**A.** *DAB; NCAB*, 23:126. **B.** John G. B. Hutchins, *The American Maritime Industries and Public Policy, 1789-1914*, 1941; John H. Morrison, *History of American Steam Navigation*, 1958.)

COLT, SAMUEL (July 19, 1814–January 10, 1862). Gun manufacturer and inventor, Colt Firearms Company. Born in Hartford, Connecticut, son of Christopher Colt and Sarah Caldwell. His father was a manufacturer of cotton and woolen fabrics. The concern had been very prosperous, but when Samuel was seven years old the business failed and his mother died of consumption. For the first three years after his mother's death, Samuel lived with an aunt and seldom went to school. In 1824, at age ten, he went to Ware, Massachusetts, to work in his father's dyeing and bleaching factory. He also attended school and worked on various farms. At thirteen he was sent to preparatory school at Amherst, Massachusetts, but was dismissed for disciplinary reasons in 1830. He was thereupon sent to sea as an ordinary seaman, taking a one year voyage to India and back. He then returned to his father's bleaching establishment and began to acquire a strong interest in the chemical side of the business. He left after a year and spent three months traveling as "Dr. Coult," giving popular lectures on chemistry and laughing gas.

Colt had always been interested in explosives and firearms, and soon began to work on perfecting a revolving barrel firearm. In 1832 he sent the idea to the U.S. Patent Office, and a year later constructed a pistol factory in Baltimore. He went to England and France in 1835, gaining patents on his invention there. Upon his return in 1836, he secured his first U.S. patent, for the revolving pistol. He formed a company to manufacture the revolver at Patterson, New Jersey, and was able to secure wide acceptance of the firearm by individual purchasers, but could not get the U.S. Navy to accept it. In 1837–1838 he spent the winter in the swamps of Florida, where he saw the value of his revolver proved in the wars against the Seminole, and was also able to sell quantities of the guns to the Texas Rangers in the War for Texas Independence. But the inability to secure a U.S. government contract doomed the company, and it failed in 1842. Thereupon, he lost all patent rights to others and began work on a submarine battery developed to blow up a ship in motion by electrical batteries controlled from shore. He also engaged in submarine telegraphy, and put in operation for the U.S. Navy a system from New York to Coney Island in 1843.

At the outbreak of the Mexican War he received an order for 1,000 pistols from the federal government, and began to manufacture them at Whitneyville, near New Haven, Connecticut. He bought back his patent rights, and in 1848 began to manufacture in three buildings in Hartford. The business grew rapidly, and between 1845 and 1855 he built an immense armory at Hartford which he directed until he died. Over the years Colt's Armory was an important training ground for many celebrated American machinists. He married Elizabeth H. Jarvis of Middletown, Connecticut, in 1856, and they had three children. After Colt's death, his wife ran the affairs of his great estate and proved herself a successful businesswoman. (**A.** *DAB; NCAB*, 6:175. **B.** E. A. Belden, *A History of the Colt Revolver*, 1940; W. B. Edwards, *The Story of Colt's Revolver*, 1953.)

COLT, SAMUEL POMEROY (January 10, 1852–August 13, 1921). Rubber manufacturer, United States Rubber Company. Born in Paterson, New Jersey, son of Christopher Colt and Theodora G. DeWolf, and brother of U.S. Senator L. Baron Bradford Colt. Samuel P. Colt graduated from Massachusetts Institute of Technology in 1873, spent a year traveling in Europe, and graduated from Columbia University Law School in 1876. He then set up private practice in Providence, Rhode Island, while also involved in politics as a member of the state's general assembly from 1876 to 1879 and as assistant attorney general from 1879 to 1885. During this same time he also became interested in the manufacture of rubber.

In 1888 Colt reorganized the National Rubber Company, and four years later consolidated it and a number of other rubber companies into the U.S. Rubber Company. On being named president, he decided to transform U.S. Rubber into a modern industrial corporation. In marketing he called for a major expansion of the branch stores that did the company's wholesaling and appointed a manager with a separate office at sales headquarters to administer these units. In purchasing he formed the General Rubber Company in 1904 to buy crude rubber. The latter organization had offices in Liverpool and London and the rubber-growing areas in Brazil and the West Indies. In 1909 the company obtained the first of its rubber plantations in Sumatra. Five years earlier, the company decided to produce its own sulphuric acid plant for its rubber reclaiming processes and to have its own fleet of tank cars.

Once Colt and his managers had accomplished their goals of vertical integration and administrative centralization, they turned to diversification as a way to fully utilize their existing facilities and organization. The production of belting, hose, insulating and flooring materials, sheeting and other industrial rubber products, and above all, tires for the new automobile market promised a different and steadier demand than that for footwear. To this end, Colt purchased the Rubber Goods Manufacturing Company in 1905. This company handled the marketing of all non-footwear items, including tires. Then, as the demand for tires boomed, the sales network was greatly expanded. In 1912 the firm set up a separate central development department, which took over administration of the company's chemical activities. It soon set up central research laboratories, and extended its functions to include research in rubber growing and crude rubber processing, as well as product improvement.

The growth of the company under Colt's management, as indicated by the above transitions, was rapid. Its capital stock was increased in 1905 from $50 million to $75 million, and it employed over 20,000 people in its plants in Massachusetts, Rhode Island, and Connecticut. He remained president of the corporation until 1918, then acted as chairman of the board until 1921. He also founded Imperial Trust of Providence, serving as its president from 1887 to 1908, and as chairman of the board from 1908 to 1921. He was a Republican and married Elizabeth M. Bullock of Rhode Island. They had two sons. (**A.** *NCAB*, 15:408; *New York Times*, August 14, 1921; *Who Was Who*, vol. 4. **B.** Glenn D. Babcock, *History of the United States Rubber Company*, 1966; Alfred D. Chandler Jr., *The Visible Hand*, 1977.)

CONE FAMILY: Moses Herman Cone (June 29, 1857–December 8, 1908); **Caesar Cone** (April 22, 1859–March 1, 1917); and **Herman Cone II** (May 2, 1895–December 10, 1955). Textile manufacturers, Cone Mills Corporation.

Moses Herman Cone was born in Jonesboro, Tennessee, son of Herman Cone, a native of Bavaria, and Helen Guggenheim, whose parents had emigrated from Germany. Moses' father was a merchant in Jonesboro, and after 1870, in Baltimore, Maryland. After two partnerships in the latter city in the wholesale grocery business, his father started his own business, H. Cone and Sons, which he ran with his four eldest sons. Moses was educated in the public schools of Jonesboro and Baltimore, and entered his father's business, which was largely engaged in the southern wholesale trade at this time. Among their customers were many southern cotton mills which maintained mill villages and company-owned stores for trade with their operatives. The connection of the Cones with the southern cotton factories began with their incidental acceptance of bale goods by the wholesale grocers in lieu of payment of accounts by mill stores. Gradually the mills came to ask the Baltimore firm to sell their products on a commission.

Moses was struck by the lack of standardization and the difficulty of marketing what was known as "Negro Plaids," a favorite product of the southern mills. He spent the year 1890, a depression year for the cotton goods trade, in the first significant attempt to combine the southern mills into a selling organization intended to control the product to the extent of making goods more uniform and improving the styles. The Cone Export and Commission Company was founded in 1891, with offices in New York City. After a time, about forty mills in the Carolinas, Georgia, and other southern states joined the venture. The wholesale grocery firm in Baltimore was thereupon dissolved, and Herman Cone joined with his sons in the new business. The Cones then began to acquire interests in southern cotton mills, the first one being located at Asheville, North Carolina. In 1893 head offices were set up at Greensboro, North Carolina, and in 1895 Moses and his brother Caesar began the erection of denim mills in the town. Before long these became the largest of their kind in the world. Moses was Jewish and married Bertha M. Linden of Baltimore in 1888.

Caesar Cone was also born in Jonesboro, son of Herman Cone. He was educated in the public schools there and in Baltimore. At age fifteen he entered his father's grocery concern. He remained there until 1891 when he moved to New York City to head the Cone Export and Commission Company, which he and Moses had founded. He remained there four years, then he moved to Greensboro, North Carolina, becoming president of Proximity Manufacturing Company, makers of cotton goods. In 1900, with Moses Cone and Emanuel and Herman Sternberger, he established the Revolution Flannel Mill in Greensboro. The Proximity Mills began as a small plant with 240 employees, but achieved tremendous growth through the acquisition in 1905, of the giant White Oak Mills, the largest denim mill in the world. He was also interested in many smaller concerns throughout the South. He was Jewish and married Jeanette Siegel of New York City. They had three sons, the eldest being Herman Cone II. **Herman Cone II** was born in New York City and educated in the public schools of Greensboro. He spent two years at the University of North Carolina, leaving school in 1914 to become a salesman for the family firm. In 1917 he was named treasurer of the Proximity Manufacturing Company, becoming president in 1938. He served in that position until 1950, when he became chairman of the board until his death. In 1950 he consolidated all the Cone's firms under one corporation, Cone Mill Corporation, with eighteen plants, including the huge White Oak plant in Greensboro, which continued to be the largest denim manufacturer in the world. The company employed 15,000 persons in 1950 and had sales of $163 million. Herman was president of the American Cotton Manufacturers Association in 1942 and of the North Carolina Cotton Manufacturers Association in 1937. He also served as chairman of the Cotton Textile Institute in 1943. He married Louise

Wolf of New York City and they had two sons. He was a Jew and a Democrat. (*DAB; NCAB*, 49:470; 50:614.)

CONVERSE FAMILY: James Coggswell Converse (September 23, 1807–1891); **Edmund Winchester Converse** (June 12, 1825–January 6, 1894); **Edmund Coggswell Converse** (November 7, 1849–April 4, 1921). Tube manufacturers, National Tube Company.

James C. Converse was born in Weathersfield, Vermont, son of James Converse and Mehitabelle Coggswell. His father was a minister, and young Converse was educated in the village schools until he was fifteen years of age. In 1823 he was sent to Keene, New Hampshire, to be fitted for college, but he decided against attending. He went into business as a clerk in West Townshend, Vermont, for one year, when he went to Boston. By 1832 he had become a junior partner in the firm of Farrington and Converse. Four years later he formed Blanchard, Converse and Company, which was engaged in the southern and western trade. He was a leader in the movement in 1852 to organize the Boston Board of Trade, serving as its vice-president from 1860 to 1863, and as president from 1863 to 1865. In 1868 he was a delegate to the National Board of Trade. He also served as chairman of the Board of State Railroad Commissions from 1869 to 1873. In the latter year he organized the National Tube Works in Boston, which was later moved to McKeesport, Pennsylvania. He served as its president from 1873 to 1877. James Converse married Sarah Peabody in 1834 and had five children. His daughter Anna married John H. Flagler* and his son Edmund C. became an executive at National Tube.

Edmund W. Converse was born in Weathersfield, Vermont, son of James and brother of James C. He went to Boston at age seventeen to enter his brother's dry goods house, becoming a partner in it after a short time. He also became head of the firm of Converse, Stanton and Cullen in Boston. In 1877 he succeeded his brother as president of National Tube Works, serving in that position until 1893. In the last year of his presidency, the firm was consolidated with various other tube manufacturing companies to form National Tube Company, with a capitalization of $11,500,000. He was also president of the Connecticut Mills of Fall River, Massachusetts, and a member of the State Drainage Commission. He married Charlotte Augusta (Shepard) Albree of Boston in 1854. They had seven children. His granddaughter, Louise Converse, married Junius Spencer Morgan Jr.

Edmund C. Converse was born in Boston and educated at Boston Latin School, from which he graduated in 1869. He then went to work as an apprentice at National Tube Works in McKeesport, Pennsylvania. In 1882 he was granted a patent for his invention of lock-joints for tubing, one of the most significant developments in the industry. He also had several other patents on various improvements in tubing. The company's tubing was renowned as the best on the market for water and gas systems, and his inventions brought millions of dollars of orders to the firm. He became general manager of the company in 1889, and played a leading role with his uncle in 1892 in bringing about the consolidation of the tube manufacturing industry. A year later he became president of the National Tube Company. In 1899, with William Nelson Cromwell,* he acted as agent for J. P. Morgan* and Company in the merger of twenty iron and steel tube companies and other concerns into a new National Tube Company, incorporated at $80,000,000. When U.S. Steel was organized in 1901, he retired and went into banking. He was president of Liberty National Bank from 1903 to 1907, of Bankers Trust Company from 1903 to 1913, and of Astor Trust from its organization in 1907 until its merger with Bankers Trust in 1917. He was also a director of a large number of corporations, including, American Bank Note Company; National Supply Company; Standard Seamless Tube; Washington Trust Company; and Bowling Green Trust Company. In 1912 he endowed a chair of banking at the graduate school of business at Harvard for $125,000, and in 1915 gave $250,000 for a new library at Amherst. He married Jessie MacDonough Green in 1879. She died in 1912, and in 1914 he married Mary Edith Dunshee of New York. He had two children. (*DAB; NCAB*; John Jay Putnam, *Family History in the Line of Joseph Converse of Bedford, Mass.*, 1897; *New York Times*, April 5, 1921; *Iron Age*, April 11, 1901; April 7, 1921; Frederick A. Virkus, ed., *American Compendium of Genealogy*, 7 vols., 1925ff, vol. 1.)

CONWAY, CARLE COTTER (December 19, 1877–August 19, 1959). Can manufacturer, Continental Can Company. Born in Oak Park, Illinois, son of Edwin Stapleton Conway and Sarah Judson Rogers. His father was a native of Canada and vice-president of W. W. Kimball Company, pioneer piano manufacturers of Chicago. Carle Conway graduated from Yale University in 1899, and began his career with W. W. Kimball Company as a salesman. In 1905, with his brother, he organized the Conway Company of New Jersey, a holding company which acquired the interests of the Hallett and Davis Piano Company of Boston, and in 1908 the Simplix Player Action Company of Worcester, Massachusetts.

In 1927 the Conway Company became an investment corporation, having disposed of the piano business. It acquired an interest in the Continental Can Company in 1908, and Carle became vice-president and member of the executive committee of that company in 1913. He was named first vice-president in 1923 and president three years later. He remained in that position for thirty-three years. After 1928 Continental Can absorbed nine can manufacturing companies, ranking second in the world only to American Can Company. It operated thirty plants for the manufacture of cans at strategic sites throughout the United States, plus a tin plate mill at Canonsburg, Pennsylvania, and a research department in Chicago.

He married Sylvia Gifford Norton, daughter of Edwin Norton,* a New

York can manufacturer, in 1900. He took a second wife, Helen Patricia Flynn, in 1940. He had four children. (**A.** *NCAB*, C:249; *New York Times*, August 20, 1959; *Who Was Who*, vol. 3. **B.** James W. McKie, *Tin Cans and Tin Plate*, 1959.)

COOKE, JAY (August 10, 1821–February 16, 1905). Investment banker, Jay Cooke and Company, Philadelphia. Born at Sandusky, Ohio, son of Eleutheros Cooke and Martha Carswell. His father was a lawyer who also served in the U.S. Congress. Jay Cooke was educated in his home town, and gained employment as a clerk while still quite young. In 1836 he secured a position in St. Louis, Missouri, but his employers were ruined by the Panic of 1837, so he left after a few months. He next became a clerk on a local packet line in Philadelphia. In 1839 he joined the banking house of E. W. Clark and Company, where he remained for eighteen years, retiring after the Panic of 1857.

In 1861 he formed his own banking firm, Jay Cooke and Company, which until 1873 was one of the most widely known banking houses in the country. His brother, Henry David Cooke, a journalist and banker in Ohio, knew Governor Salmon P. Chase of Ohio quite well. When Chase was appointed in 1861 as Secretary of the Treasury, he gave Jay Cooke entrée to the federal government. Chase depended upon Cooke's banking house to raise funds for the government during the war by bond sales. In very short order in 1861 Cooke was able to get $50 million advanced to the government by bankers in New York and Philadelphia. A year later he opened an office in Washington, D.C., to take care of the government's business, and by 1864 had distributed loans of $500 million in 6 percent, five and twenty bonds. Over 600,000 citizens had taken shares in the public debt in a massive campaign organized by Cooke.

In 1865 Cooke was again appointed "fiscal agent" of the Treasury Department, and this time sold $600 million in bonds. After the war, Cooke returned to general banking, establishing a branch in New York in 1866, and one in London in 1870 with ex-Secretary of the Treasury Hugh McCulloch as resident partner. He was particularly attracted during these years to the profit to be made from a Pacific railroad over a northern route from Duluth, Minnesota, to Tacoma, Washington, which would connect the navigation of the Great Lakes with the navigation of the Pacific. Before the project could be completed, Jay Cooke and Company was compelled to close its doors on September 18, 1873, which brought about a general panic and large-scale depression.

Despite the ultimate failure of his banking house, Jay Cooke stands as one of the most important and innovative bankers of his period. Besides his crucial role in government finance during the Civil War, he was also the first to form a modern underwriting syndicate in the United States to sell the bonds of the Pennsylvania Railroad. He arranged for eight financial houses to guarantee the sale of a block of bonds, with each member of the syndicate accepting responsibility to sell an agreed-upon amount. The syndicate paid all the costs of distribution, including advertising.

He was an Episcopalian and a Republican and married Dorothea Elizabeth Allen in 1844. They had four children, including Rev. Henry E. Cooke, an Episcopal minister, and Jay Cooke Jr., who became a banker. His grandson, Jay Cooke III (1897-1963) became an investment counselor, heading the firm of Cooke and Bieler Incorporated in Philadelphia from 1940 to 1963. He was also prominent in Republican politics in Pennsylvania. (**A.** *DAB; NCAB*, 1:253; 51:122; *New York Times*, February 17, 1905; *Who Was Who*, vol. 1; Henrietta Larson, *Jay Cooke, Private Banker*, 1936; E. P. Oberholtzer, *Jay Cooke*, 2 vols., 1907. **B.** Alfred D. Chandler, *The Visible Hand*, 1977; Fritz Redlich, *The Molding of American Banking*, 2 vols., 1951.)

COOLIDGE FAMILY: Thomas Jefferson Coolidge (August 26, 1831–November 17, 1920); **Thomas Jefferson Coolidge Jr.** (March 15, 1863–April 14, 1912); **Thomas Jefferson Coolidge III** (September 17, 1893–August 6, 1959); **William Appleton Coolidge** (October 22, 1901–   ). Boston financiers and entrepreneurs, Atchison, Topeka and Santa Fe Railroad; Old Colony Trust; United Fruit Company; and Minute Maid Corporation.

T. Jefferson Coolidge was born in Boston, son of Joseph Coolidge Jr. and Eleanor Wayles Randolph. His father's family had been in Massachusetts since 1630 and his mother was descended from Thomas Jefferson. He was educated in boarding schools in London, Geneva, and Dresden, and at age sixteen entered Harvard, graduating in 1850. He then devoted himself to the acquisition of wealth, beginning his career in foreign commerce and mercantile affairs. After the crash of 1857 he was persuaded by his father-in-law, William Appleton, to accept the treasurership of the Boott Mills, thereupon embarking upon a life-long career in the cotton textile industry of New England. He served as treasurer of the Lawrence Manufacturing Company and of the Amoskeag Mills, and was director of several banks in the area. He also served as president of the Atchison, Topeka and Santa Fe Railroad.

Coolidge had extensive public service and political interests. He served as member of the first park commission of the city, which laid out the park system of Boston. In 1889 he was a member of the Pan-American Congress, and in 1892, Minister to France. Four years later he was a member of the Massachusetts Taxation Commission, and in 1898 was appointed to the Joint High Commission of the United States, Great Britain, Canada, and Newfoundland to settle the question of the Alaskan boundary, fisheries, destruction of fur seals, armaments on the lakes, and transportation of goods in bond. He married Hetty Sullivan Appleton of Boston in 1852 and had three daughters and one son, **T. Jefferson Coolidge Jr.**

The younger Coolidge was born in Boston and graduated from Harvard in 1884. He then spent a year in travel around the world, and for the next two years took graduate courses at Harvard. His business career began in 1887 when he entered the employ of Bay State Trust Company of Boston. Three years later he organized the Old Colony Trust Company, becoming its first president. He served in that position until 1904, when he resigned due to ill health. He was then chairman of the board and later chairman of the executive committee. Old Colony Trust grew to be the largest institution of its kind in New England. He also served as president of Bay State Trust from 1902 to 1911, and of Lawrence Manufacturing Company.

Coolidge was also instrumental in the organization of the United Fruit Company, and associated with Charles T. Yerkes* in the building of the London, England, subway system. In addition, he was deeply involved in railroad reorganization, taking an active part in the affairs of the Union Pacific; Oregon Short Line; New York and New England; Wisconsin Central; and Seaboard Airline railroads. He served as a director of American Bell Telephone, General Electric, Amoskeag Manufacturing, and Edison Electric Illumination. He married Clara Amory of Boston in 1891 and had four sons, including **T. Jefferson Coolidge III** and **William Appleton Coolidge**.

T. Jefferson Coolidge III was born in Boston and educated at St. Mark's School. He graduated from Harvard in 1913, and served two years in the Massachusetts militia before being sent to France as a major in the army during World War I. In 1921 he joined Old Colony Trust, serving as vice-president until 1929, chairman of the board from 1937 to 1940, and chairman of the trust committee until he died.

He was also vice-president of the First National Bank of Boston from 1929 to 1934, when he was appointed special assistant to the Secretary of the Treasury of the United States, and then Under-Secretary of the Treasury until 1936. His service was terminated when he became an outspoken critic of the New Deal. He was a director of United Fruit Company until 1925, and served as chairman of the board from 1938 to 1958. He was also chairman of the Baystate Corporation and director of many other companies. An Episcopalian and a Republican, he married Catharine Luhn of Pittsburgh in 1927. They had two sons and one daughter.

William Appleton Coolidge was born in Boston and educated at the Miss Fiske School, the Nobley Greenough School, and St. Mark's. He graduated from Harvard in 1924, and received a bachelor's and master's degree at Balliol College, Oxford, in 1927, and a law degree at Harvard in 1936. Prior to receiving his law degree, in 1927, he joined the Boston investment house of Jackson and Curtis, which later became Paine, Webber, Jackson and Curtis. He was made a partner in 1930 and a special partner in 1933, serving until 1947. After he was admitted to the Massachusetts bar in 1936, he also practiced law as an associate of the Boston law firm of Ropes, Grey, Boyden, and Perkins until 1941.

In 1940 he was one of the founders of Enterprise Associates, a small group of men who invested in small business. In the same year he formed the National Research Corporation in Brookline, Massachusetts, to manufacture high vacuum equipment. The firm became a leading producer of superconductors and of capacitor grade tantalum powder, and a manufacturer of Tarlatum mill products. In 1963 this firm became a subsidiary of the Norton Company, of Worcester, Massachusetts, and Coolidge became a director of the latter in the same year. In 1945 National Research Associates started the Minute Maid Corporation in Plymouth, Florida, and he was director of that from 1947 until 1960, when it was purchased by Coca-Cola. He then became a director of the latter firm. Enterprise Associates formed Kaman Aircraft and Servco Corporation of America.

During World War II he worked in the office of the Undersecretary of the Navy, and served in the finance section of the Office of Production and Material, making advance payments and guaranteed loans to contractors. An Episcopalian and a Republican, he was unmarried. (*DAB; NCAB*, 12:58; 27:148; 47:531; L:54; *New York Times*, April 16, 1912; November 18, 1920; *Who Was Who*, vol. 1.)

COOPER, MARK ANTHONY (April 20, 1800–March 17, 1885). Early Georgia entrepreneur. Born in Hancock County, Georgia, son of Thomas Cooper and Mary Cooper. His father was from a Virginia family which migrated to Georgia. Mark Cooper was educated in private academies and attended the University of Georgia and the University of South Carolina, graduating from the latter institution in 1819. He then studied law and was admitted to the bar in Eatonton, Georgia, in 1821. His primary interest, however, lay in business rather than law.

He was one of the few in the early years who saw the possibilities of the natural resources of Georgia, other than farming. In 1833 he organized a cotton mill company, and erected near Eatonton the second water driven cotton factory in the state, capitalized at $50,000. In 1835 he sold his stock and moved to Columbus, Georgia, to organize a bank, capitalized at $200,000. He also became a member of the state legislature in that year, where he advocated charters for railroads. One was granted to the Georgia Banking and Railroad Company to build a road connecting Augusta with Atlanta. Later, he was an important factor in the building of the East and West Railroad in northwest Georgia.

His work as a developer spread from cotton milling, banking, and railroads to the production of iron. He purchased an interest in a small furnace near Etawah in Bartow County, renovated and extended the plant, and added a rolling mill and rail factory. He built a four-mile railroad, the Western and Atlantic, to Chattanooga, developed coal mines, and erected a flour mill. His business interests encompassed 12,000 acres and he became the sole owner of the entire property.

In 1836 he served as a major in the Seminole War, and in 1839 was elected to the U.S. Congress as a Whig. In 1840, however, he switched with John C. Calhoun to the Democratic Party. He was then elected to the next two congresses. In 1843 he resigned to run for the governorship, but was defeated. He married Mary Evelina Flournoy in 1821, but she died a few months later. He then married Sophronia A. R. Randle. They had seven daughters and three sons, two of whom were killed in the Civil War. (*DAB*; W. F. Northern, *Men of Mark in Georgia*, vol. 2., 1910.)

COOPER, PETER (February 12, 1791–April 4, 1883). Iron manufacturer, Trenton Iron Works. Born in New York City, son of John Cooper and Margaret Campbell. His family had been in the area since 1662, and his father was a hatter, brewer, storekeeper and brickmaker. He was aided in all these ventures by his son, Peter, who was well experienced by age sixteen. Peter Cooper had only one year of formal education, and at age seventeen was apprenticed to John Woodward, a New York coach maker. Cooper remained there four years and then Woodward offered to aid him in starting his own business. Peter declined and found employment first in the manufacture of cloth shearing machines and as a traveling salesman, and then as owner of new cloth shearing machines. He did well in business until the close of the War of 1812, when profits fell. He then sold out and organized a retail grocery store in New York City.

His next venture was to purchase a glue factory in New York City, and he was soon supplying the American market with American-made glue and Isinglass. He won a monopoly of the trade in that line, but was very frugal and did all of the work in the plant by himself to save money. Later, he entrusted part of his business to his son, Edward, and son-in-law, Abram S. Hewitt.* In 1828 he set up an iron works in Baltimore with two partners. They bought 3,000 acres for $10,000 within the city limits and erected the Canton Iron Works there. Cooper then designed new locomotives for the failing Baltimore and Ohio Railroad—the "Tom Thumb" and the "Teakettle"—which were the first steam locomotives built in America.

He sold the iron works in 1836 for stock in the Baltimore and Ohio Railroad, which he soon sold for five times what he paid for it. He then expanded his business to include wire manufacture at Trenton, New Jersey; blast furnaces, a rolling mill, and a glue factory in New York City; foundries in Ringwood, New Jersey, and Durham, Pennsylvania; and iron mines in northern New Jersey. In 1854 he rolled the first structural iron for fireproof buildings, for which he won the Bessemer Gold Medal in 1870. He also served as president of the New York, Newfoundland and London Telegraph Company, and was a chief supporter of Cyrus Field* in his endeavors to lay a cable across the Atlantic Ocean. Cooper also became president of the North American Telegraph Company, which at one time controlled more than one-half of the telegraph lines in the country.

In addition to his entrepreneurial activities, he was also an inventor and a philanthropist. He invented washing machines and machines for mortising hubs and for propelling ferry boats by compressed air. In politics, he served on the board of aldermen of New York, where he supported paid police and fire departments, sanitary water, and public schools. He was a supporter of the Greenback Party and was its presidential candidate in 1876. Between 1857 and 1859, he established Cooper Union in New York for the advancement of science and art. He married Sarah Bedele of Hempstead, Long Island, in 1813. They had six children, but only one, Edward, survived to adulthood.

Edward Cooper (1824–1905) was born in New York City and educated in the public schools and at Columbia University. He helped his father and college friend and brother-in-law, Abram S. Hewitt, organize the iron and steel manufacturing firm of Cooper, Hewitt and Company. Edward became an expert metallurgist, developing the regenerative hot blast stove for blast furnaces. This greatly increased output and lowered the cost of production. He was also a director of U.S. Trust Company, American Sulphur Company, and New Jersey Iron and Steel. He was intimately involved in municipal politics as a reform Democrat. He backed Samuel Tilden to oust the Tweed ring as a member of the Committee of Seventy, and in 1879 was a coalition candidate for mayor and was elected. He married Cornelia Redmond. (**A.** *DAB; NCAB*, 3:114; *New York Times*, April 5, 1883; February 26, 1905; *Who Was Who*, vol. H.; R. W. Raymond, *Peter Cooper*, 1901; American Institute of Mining Engineers, *Transactions*, 1907. **B.** Allan Nevins, *Abram S. Hewitt, With Some Account of Peter Cooper*, 1935.)

COPLEY, IRA CLIFTON (October 25, 1864–November 2, 1947). Public utilities and publishing executive. Born in Copley Township, Knox County, Illinois, son of Ira Birdsall Copley, a farmer, and Ellen Madeline Whiting. His father had migrated to Illinois from New York State in 1854. Because young Ira was blinded by scarlet fever at age two, the family moved to Aurora, Illinois, to be near an eye specialist. Here the elder Copley became part owner and manager of the troubled Aurora Gas Light Company. Young Ira regained his vision after four years, but it remained impaired for the rest of his life. He graduated from high school in 1881 and attended Francis Jennings Seminary until 1883. He received a bachelor's degree from Yale in 1887 and a law degree from Union College of Law in Chicago in 1889. He was admitted to the bar in Illinois, but never practiced.

Shortly after graduation he was called home to help run his father's ailing gas company. He revived the utility by marketing gas as a fuel rather than as an illuminant. Building on this success, he went on to acquire other utilities in Illinois, which were merged in 1905 into the Western United Gas and Electric Company, of which he was president. Over the next two decades Copley purchased more gas and electric companies and streetcar lines. In 1914 he organized a firm to market coke and coal. His utilities empire was consolidated in 1921 into the Western Utility Corporation.

Copley also built parallel careers in publishing and politics. He purchased his first newspaper, the *Aurora Beacon*, in 1905. By 1913 he owned papers in Elgin and Joliet, Illinois. In 1926 he sold his interest in the Western United Corporation to an investment firm, and two years later—at age 63—he bought 24 Southern California newspapers, including the *San Diego Union* and the *San Diego Evening Tribune*, at a cost of $7.5 million. He established the Copley Press, Incorporated, serving as its president from 1928 to 1942. In 1939 he brought his Illinois papers into the corporation. His actions hastened the spread of newspaper monopolies. He preferred to operate in medium-sized cities, and by the time of his death, all his papers, save one in San Diego, were in one-publisher cities.

Copley was also one of the few men to find the key to the successful management of a large group of newspapers. He recognized that each community had a distinct identity and refused to do "mass thinking" for his chain. He thus gave his publishers considerable authority and insisted that they publish all local news impartially. He was thus quite successful in the transference of managerial techniques from one industry—utilities—to another, publishing. Copley represents two significant phenomena in twentieth century business: first, the growth of combinations in public utilities and publishing in the 1920s—what some analysts refer to as the "second merger movement"; and, second, the managerial initiatives of decentralization common to firms after 1925. The latter were particularly evident in his publishing empire.

Copley's political career began as early as 1894, when he was a member of the Republican State Central Committee in Illinois and a lieutenant colonel in the Illinois National Guard. He served on the Illinois Park Commission from 1894 to 1898, and as an aide to Gov. Charles S. Deneen from 1905 to 1913. In 1910 he was elected to the first of six consecutive terms in the U.S. House of Representatives. A political liberal, he supported Theodore Roosevelt in 1912, and ran as a Progressive in 1914. He was defeated for renomination in the Republican primary of 1922 by farmer unrest and antiprohibition sentiment. A Unitarian and then an Episcopalian, he married Edith Straker of Los Angeles in 1892. She died in 1929 and two years later he married Mrs. Chloe (Davidson) Warly. He had two adopted sons, James Strohn, who succeeded his father as head of Copley Press, Incorporated, and William Nelson. (*DAB*, Supplement 5; *NCAB*, 36:118; Walter S. J. Swanson, *The Thin Gold Watch*, 1964.)

CORBIN, AUSTIN (July 11, 1827–June 4, 1896) and **Daniel Chase Corbin** (October 1, 1832–June 29, 1918). Bankers, financiers and transportation entrepreneurs, Iowa, New York and Far West.

Austin Corbin was born in Newport, New Hampshire, son of Austin Corbin and Mary Chase. They were a well-to-do, old New England family, but Austin had little in the way of formal education beyond the area's common schools. At age twenty he found employment in a Boston store, and later entered Harvard Law School, from which he graduated in 1849. He only practiced law for a short time, however.

In 1851 he went to Davenport, Iowa, where three years later he opened a bank. He was very successful during the period of "wild cat" banking prior to the Civil War and survived the Panic of 1857. He then induced friends in the East to loan money with Iowa farm lands as security and built up a large business in this manner. In 1863 he organized the First National Bank of Davenport, and in 1865 he moved to New York City, where he organized Austin Corbin and Company, which after 1874 became Corbin Banking Company.

Corbin very early saw the advantages of Coney Island as an ocean resort near New York City, but knew that the transportation between Manhattan and the beach on Long Island was a problem. He constructed the New York and Manhattan Beach Railroad in 1876–1877 and then set about to redevelop the east end of Coney Island as the fashionable Manhattan Beach resort area. He built two stylish hotels, the Manhattan Beach (1877) and the Oriental (1880). Involved with him in this enterprise was his brother, Daniel Chase Corbin. From 1886 to 1888 he rehabilitated the Philadelphia and Reading Railroad. He married Hannah M. Wheeler in 1853 and had one son and one daughter.

Daniel Chase Corbin was born in Newport, New Hampshire, and educated in the common schools there. In 1852 he secured a government contract for surveying lands in Iowa. In 1858 he began a similar operation in Nebraska, purchasing much land there. Then he became interested in the early mining development in Colorado, moving to Denver in 1862. There he secured important contracts for supplying the quartermaster department at Ft. Laramie, Wyoming, and operated wagon trains from the Missouri River via Denver to Salt Lake City, Utah. Three years later he moved to Helena, Montana, where for the next ten years he engaged in the mercantile business and in banking as cashier and part owner of the First National Bank.

In 1876 Daniel Corbin moved to New York City, and until 1882 was associated with his brother in the financing and management of the Manhattan Beach Railroad. In the latter year he returned to the Northwest, where he was attracted to the silver discoveries in the Coeur d'Alene district. In 1886 he constructed one of the first concentrating plants in the region. About the same time he became interested in the transportation problems of the area and organized the Coeur d'Alene Railroad and Navigation Company. The firm operated steam boats and constructed a railroad, which was completed in 1887. A year later he sold it to the Northern Pacific Railroad.

He moved to Spokane, Washington, in 1889 to begin construction of the

Spokane Falls and Northern Railroad, which was absorbed ten years later by the Great Northern Railroad. He was also active in British Columbia mining, organizing the Corbin Coal and Coke Company to handle the properties there. He tried to develop the sugar beet industry in Spokane, but failed at this venture. In 1905 he began construction of the Spokane International Railroad to Eastport, Idaho, which connected with the Canadian Pacific Railroad in British Columbia. He was one of the first to grasp the strategic importance of Spokane's site. He married Louise M. Jackson of Iowa in 1860. She died in 1900, and seven years later he married Mrs. Anna (Larsen) Peterson. (**A.** *DAB; New York Times*, June 5, 1896. **B.** John F. Kasson, *Amusing The Million*, 1978.)

CORLISS, GEORGE HENRY (June 2, 1817–February 21, 1888). Engine manufacturer, Corliss, Nightingale and Company. Born in Easton, Washington County, New York, son of Hiram Corliss, a doctor and surgeon, and Susan Sheldon. When George was eight years old the family moved to Greenwich, New York, where he was educated until age fourteen. He then entered the employ of William Mowry and Son as their general storekeeper. He advanced to clerk, bookkeeper, salesman, and official inspector and measurer of cloth turned out by their factory. After four years his father sent him to Castleton Academy in Vermont, where he remained for three years; then he returned to Greenwich where he opened a store of his own. At that time he also designed a crude machine which improved the method of sewing heavy boots, receiving a U.S. patent on this in 1842.

In 1844 he went to Providence, Rhode Island, to market his invention, where Fairbanks, Bancroft and Company, a machine and engine building firm, undertook to assist him. They offered him a position as a draftsman, which he accepted. He sold out his store in Greenwich, and moved to Providence. In less than one year he was admitted to partnership in the firm. Within one more year he was revolutionizing the construction and operation of steam engines for the company. His first ideas were formulated in 1846, and his first patent was granted in 1849 and reissued in 1851. In 1848 he left Fairbanks, Bancroft and joined John Barstown and E. J. Nightingale of Providence, organizing a new company, Corliss, Nightingale and Company. They built the first engine embodying the Corliss feature, consisting of rotary valves and a governor which, by a system of levers, controlled the valves and the admission of steam to the engine cylinder. They purchased land in Providence to erect a factory, which was completed in 1856. Corliss was president of the company and directed all the business activities as well as the technical inventions and improvements. The business grew at a prodigious rate during the next several years.

Perhaps Corliss' most important, and certainly most symbolic, achievement was his construction of the giant Corliss steam engine for Machinery Hall at the Philadelphia Centennial Exhibition in 1876; it was the largest and most powerful engine that had ever been built to that time. The engine was installed at the exhibition to provide power for all the lathes, grinders, drills, weaving machines, printing presses, and other machinery. Although the machine weighed 1,700,000 pounds, it worked almost as quietly and with as little vibration as a fine watch. Unlike most other engines of this type, the Corliss engine had an almost severe design, and many worried that it would disappoint the general public. But standing in the center of a twelve acre building, towering forty feet above its platform, it had a profound impact on visitors, and was the single most talked about exhibit at the show.

Corliss was a Republican and a representative of North Providence in the General Assembly of Rhode Island from 1868 to 1870 and a presidential elector in 1876. A member of the Congregational Church, he married Phoebe R. Frost of Canterbury, Connecticut, in 1839. She died in 1859 and seven years later he married Emily A. Shaw of Newburyport, Massachusetts. His son, George Frost Corliss (1841–1927), represented his father's interests in Europe for a number of years, but poor health prevented an extensive business career. He lived most of his life in Nice, France. (**A.** *DAB; NCAB*, 10:394; 22:355. **B.** John A. Kouwenhouven, *Made In America*, 1948.)

CORNELL, EZRA (January 11, 1807–December 9, 1874). Telegraph pioneer, Western Union. Born at Westchester Landing, on the Bronx River in New York, son of Elijah Cornell and Eunice Barnard. His family was of New England Quaker stock, and his father was a farmer and pottery maker. Business was poor, however, so the family moved to DePeyster in Madison County, New York, in 1819. Ezra attended village school there, helped to manage his father's farm and earthenware manufacturing shop, and learned carpentry. At age eighteen, he set out for himself, working as a laborer and mechanic at Syracuse and Homer, New York. In 1828 he went to Ithaca where he secured employment as a carpenter and millwright. Making this his life-long home, he became general manager of the flouring and plaster mills of J. B. Beebe. Here he planned and built an enlarged flouring mill and devised many mechanical improvements, but the conversion of the mills into a woolen factory in 1841 cost him his job.

Cornell then came into contact with F. O. J. Smith, editor of the *Maine Farmer* and member of Congress, who was interested in Samuel F. B. Morse's magnetic telegraph. He hired Cornell to develop a machine and lay the pipe to hold the telegraph cable to be laid from Washington, D.C., to Baltimore, Maryland, under contract from the federal government. The concept did not work, so they erected wires on poles. Cornell thus became one of the chief figures in the field of telegraphy. He helped organize the Magnetic Telegraph Company to connect New York and Washington, and in 1845 built the line from the Hudson River to Philadelphia. He then built a New York to Albany line on which he made $6,000, his first large profit.

In 1847 he founded the Erie and Michigan Telegraph Company, which linked Buffalo, Cleveland, Detroit, Chicago, and Milwaukee. The New York and Erie Telegraphy Company, which connected New York City and Dunkirk, was also developed. He rapidly added subsidiary lines, especially in the Middle West, and in 1855 he and others formed the Western Union Telegraph Company, a consolidation of several major and minor systems. The company extended its operations to most parts of the United States and Canada. He served as a director of Western Union for twenty years, and was to a limited degree active in the management of the concern. He was its largest stockholder for fifteen years, collecting dividends of over $100,000 per year.

Cornell then turned his attention to public affairs, in 1863 building a public library for Ithaca. In 1862 he was president of the State Agricultural Society, and for six years after 1861 sat in the state legislature. In 1862 he endowed Cornell University with the assistance of the Morrill Land Grant. He married Mary Ann Wood in 1831, and his son, Alonzo B. Cornell, became governor of New York. (**A.** *DAB; NCAB*, 4:475; Philip Dorf, *The Builder...* , 1952. **B.** Elisha P. Douglass, *The Coming of Age of American Business*, 1971; Paul W. Gates, *The Wisconsin Pine Lands of Cornell University*, 1943; Robert L. Thompson, *Wiring a Continent: The History of the Telegraph Industry in the United States*, 1947.)

CORNING, ERASTUS (December 17, 1794–April 9, 1872). Merchant and financier, New York Central Railroad. Born in Norwich, Connecticut, son of Bliss Corning and Lucinda Smith. His ancestors had been in New England since 1641. Erastus served an apprenticeship in business as a clerk in the hardware store of an uncle, Benjamin Smith, in Troy, New York. In 1814 he moved to Albany where he began manufacturing iron. He started in a small way in a partnership in a hardware store, then purchased a small foundry and rolling mill for making nails. In 1837 he associated with John F. Winslow, a metalworking genius, and the business became one of the most extensive in the country.

At an early stage Corning became involved with the development of railroads. He was one of the principal promoters of a railroad company to extend the Mohawk and Hudson Railroad to Utica, a distance of about 78 miles. He was one of the thirteen original directors of the company and the firm's first and only president. He served for twenty years, until the line became part of the New York Central in 1853. In 1851 Corning applied to the state legislature for permission to consolidate two or more companies into a single company, and received their permission in 1853. When the consolidation was finished, the New York Central Railroad was created, and he was elected its first president, serving until 1864. He was a director for a few years after that, and ceased his connection with the firm in 1867. He was also a director of the Michigan Central Railroad for several years, and of the Hudson River Railroad from 1849 to 1863.

In 1835 he established the Corning Land Company for the purpose of establishing a commercial center at the head of navigation of the Chemung River. The village of Corning was named in his honor. A railroad was built south to the Pennsylvania coal regions to divert traffic to the new Chemung Canal, and from there to the Erie Canal and the Hudson River to New York City.

Corning was elected mayor of Albany four times, and was state senator from 1842 to 1846 as a Democrat. He was also a U.S. Congressman from 1857 to 1859 and from 1861 to 1863. (*DAB; New York Times*, April 10, 1872; *Who Was Who*, vol. H; Irene D. Neu, *Erastus Corning: Merchant and Financier*, 1960.)

CORTELYOU, GEORGE B. (July 26, 1862–October 23, 1940). Public official and public utilities executive, Consolidated Edison of New York. Born in New York City, son of Peter Crolius Cortelyou and Rose Seary. The Cortelyous were a well-established middle-class urban family who had come to Manhattan before 1660. His father and grandfather were both substantial businessmen. George Cortelyou was educated at Hempstead Institute on Long Island, and graduated from Massachusetts State Normal School in 1882. Then, while teaching in Cambridge, Massachusetts, he took courses at the New England Conservatory of Music in Boston. In 1883 he returned to New York City, studied stenography, and became a law reporter, while also serving as a prep school principal.

He began to advance rapidly with his stenographic background, becoming private secretary to the surveyor for the Port of New York, and then going to Washington, D.C., as secretary to the fourth assistant postmaster general. In 1895 he was appointed stenographer to President Grover Cleveland, in the same year receiving a law degree from Georgetown University. In 1900 he was appointed to the newly created post of Secretary to the President (Theodore Roosevelt). In 1902 he was made head of the newly created Department of Commerce and Labor, with the responsibility of organizing the department and setting up broad policy. He was particularly interested in expanding the services of the government to businessmen, especially in providing marketing informaton. He also advised the president on controversial domestic issues. In 1904 he was elected chairman of the Republican National Committee, and managed President Roosevelt's campaign. After the election he was appointed Postmaster General. Being more concerned with the efficient administration of the department than patronage, he conducted a major reorganization of the service. In 1907 he was appointed Secretary of the Treasury. His major contribution to the Treasury Department was the official use he made of its central banking functions to meet the financial panic in 1907. He then concentrated on legislation to establish a central banking system.

Cortelyou left the Cabinet in 1909 to become president of New York Consolidated Edison (later Consolidated Edison Company). In that year Consolidated Edison controlled all of the power and light business of Manhattan. By 1928 it had control of the services in all of greater New York. Cortelyou concerned himself mainly with the development of new markets for gas and electric power, with the systematic and thorough training of employees, and with the provision of legal, insurance, and pension benefits. He was also president of the National Electric Power Association and its successor, the Edison Electric Institute. He retired in 1935 to his estate in Huntington, Long Island. He married Lilly Morris Hinds, daughter of the president of Hampstead Institute, in 1885. They had five children. (*DAB*, Supplement 2; *NCAB*, 14:18.)

COUCH, HARVEY CROWLEY (August 21, 1877–July 30, 1941). Utilities executive in Arkansas. Born in Calhoun, Arkansas, son of Thomas Gratham Couch, a farmer, and Marie Heard. The family had moved west from Georgia, and Harvey was educated in a one-room school house in Calhoun and at the Southwestern Academy in nearby Magnolia, Arkansas. He worked briefly at his uncle's drug store, and in 1897 took a job as mail clerk on the Cotton Belt Railroad. In 1903 he set up a system of interconnected telephone exchanges in small towns along the railway lines. With this start, he resigned his railroad job in 1905 and steadily built his network until 1910, when he had over fifty exchanges with 1,500 miles of lines. In 1911 he sold the property to the Bell Corporation for about one million dollars.

Couch then acquired electric and water properties in Arkadelphia, Arkansas, bought a power plant in nearby Magnolia, and in 1913 organized the Arkansas Power Company. In the following year he reorganized it as the Arkansas Light and Power Company, using methods typical of other utilities of the period to expand his business over the next few years. He obtained franchise rights through political influence, and built up markets by promoting and attracting industry. He raised capital through local banks and private subscriptions—reviving a "booster spirit" which had been dead since the days of railway promotion. He then established financial connections in New York City and sold bonds through investment banking houses there.

His principal innovation in the power industry involved his approach to the highly seasonal nature of power demands in the South. Traditionally the demands were very heavy in winter, then dropped off to practically nothing in the other three seasons. So he created summer demand by promoting the use of electrical power for irrigation in the Arkansas and Louisiana rice fields, and fall demand by persuading cotton gin owners to electrify their operations. In both cases he was able to persuade equipment manufacturers to extend liberal credit terms for making purchases.

Couch also was named Federal Fuel Administrator of Arkansas during World War I. By 1925 he operated an extensive, integrated electrical system that served most of Arkansas and much of northern Louisiana and western Mississippi. In that same year he sold out to Electric Bond Share Company, headed by Sidney Z. Mitchell.* He was a Methodist and a Democrat, and married Jessie Johnson of Athens, Louisiana, in 1904. They had five children. His eldest son, Harvey C. Couch Jr. (1908–   ) became president of the First National Bank in Conway, Arkansas, holding that position until 1947. He was also vice-president of the Union National Bank in Little Rock from 1939 to 1950 and president of the Columbia Corporation and Pine Realty of Little Rock. (*DAB*, Supplement 3; *NCAB*, 51:190.)

COUPER, JAMES HAMILTON (March 4, 1794–June 3, 1866). Georgia sugar and rice planter. He was the son of John Couper and Rebecca Maxwell, and was born on his father's plantation in Georgia. His father had acquired an extensive tract of land called "Hopeton" on the south bank of the Altamaha River, sixteen miles from Brunswick, Georgia. This was a plantation of about 2,000 acres, and he owned another plantation on St. Simon's Island. A native of Scotland, James Couper's father became a wealthy and influential citizen in the state. James was well educated and graduated from Yale in 1814. He spent some time in Holland studying methods of water control by dikes, and afterwards came back to Georgia to manage the Hopeton estate. His father's business failed in 1826, and his partner, James Hamilton, assumed all of John Couper's liabilities in return for a one-half interest in the Hopeton estate, and remained as manager of the whole enterprise. James Couper was also interested in his father's lands on St. Simon's Island and acquired other interests in his own right. He had supervision of 1,500 slaves and management of extensive properties owned by others, in addition to his own extensive plantations.

Couper's major distinction derives from the fact that he was one of the first American planters to conduct his operations on the basis of scientific research and experimentation. His diking and drainage system at Hopeton became the model followed by all rice planters, and he experimented with cotton, but shifted to sugar cane as his supplementary crop. In 1839 he erected the most complete and modern sugar mill in the South at Hopeton. Afterwards, however, he and most other Georgia planters virtually abandoned sugar growing for rice.

Couper made extensive experimentation in the production of olive oil, and grew olives on the St. Simon's Island plantation. He was also a pioneer in the crushing of cotton seed for oil. In 1834 he was operating two such mills, one at Natchez, Mississippi, and one at Mobile, Alabama. He also introduced Bermuda grass to Georgia, now the principal grass of the state.

The outbreak of the Civil War badly disrupted his life. His slaves were freed and the plantation fell into decay as the forest and water reclaimed the coastal acres. All five of his sons were in the Confederate army, with two dying in the service. (**A.** *DAB.* **B.** Duncan C. Heyward, *Seed From Madagascar*, 1937; J. Carlyle Sitterson, *Sugar Country: The Cane Sugar Industry in the South*, 1953.)

COUZENS, JAMES (August 26, 1872–October 22, 1936). Automobile company executive, Ford Motor Company. Born in Chatham, Ontario, Canada, son of Joseph Couzens and Emma Cleft. They had immigrated to Canada from England a short time before his birth. His father worked in a small grocery in Chatham and as a common laborer in a soap factory. Later, he set up his own soap factory but never made more than a modest income from it. As a boy, James worked at a variety of odd jobs, and after completing public grammar schools, went to high school, transferring after two years to the Chatham Business College. He also worked as a newsboy on the small Erie and Huron Railroad.

In 1890, after a year in his father's soap works, he went to Detroit and obtained a job as a checker with the Michigan Central Railroad. He was soon promoted to clerk in the freight house. In 1895 he went to work for the Malcomson Fuel Company as an assistant bookkeeper and office boy. The owner, Alex Y. Malcomson, was a friend of Henry Ford,* who asked Malcomson in 1902 for financial help in making his third attempt at an automobile venture. In the creation of Ford Motor Company, Malcomson put up the largest share of the original capital and enlisted other investors. Couzens also participated in the venture, buying $2,500 worth of stock with the assistance of Malcomson. He was then appointed business manager of the company. Within four years Malcomson was forced out by Ford, and Couzens became a partner, in fact if not legally, from 1903 to 1915. He was chiefly responsible for the concept and implementation of the five dollar a day wage plan adopted in 1914. In 1915 he held 11 percent of the company's stock, more than anyone except Ford himself. When he sold out to Ford in 1919, he received $29,308,857 for himself and $691,142 for his estate. Earlier, in 1915, he had resigned as business manager because of personal differences with Ford.

Couzens acted as Detroit Street Railroad Commissioner from 1913 to 1915, and sought, unsuccessfully, to bring about municipal ownership of the street car lines. In 1916 he was appointed police commissioner of Detroit, and in 1918 was elected mayor of the city, being re-elected in 1921. As mayor he set up an unprecedented public works program and municipal ownership of the local transportation system. He was a Republican, and in 1922 was appointed to the U.S. Senate seat by the Governor of Michigan. In the Senate he allied himself with Sen. Robert M. LaFollette, and was in general revolt against the Harding administration. He especially opposed the tax program proposed by Secretary of the Treasury, Andrew W. Mellon.* Couzens was a champion of high income taxes on the rich and low or no income taxes on the poor. Mellon then brought suit against Couzens and other former holders of Ford Motor Company stock on charges that they had not paid enough income taxes on the sale of their stock in 1919. Couzens was able to prove, however, that he overpaid his taxes by $900,000. He was re-elected in 1924 and 1930.

He was also a major philanthropist, giving two million dollars to the Children's Hospital of Detroit and several other ventures. He became a strong supporter of the New Deal in 1933, but was defeated in his bid for re-election to the Senate in 1936. He married Margaret Ann Manning of Detroit in 1898, and they had six children. He organized Highland Park State Bank in 1907, acting as its president, and also organized the Bank of Detroit, serving as president of the latter institution from 1916 to 1923. In 1933 he organized the First National Bank of Birmingham, Michigan, and the Wabeek State Bank in Detroit. He was also president of Rogers Shoe Company and director of Detroit Truck Company and the old Detroit National Bank.

His son, Frank Couzens (1902–1950) headed a construction firm in Detroit until 1941. Like his father, he was heavily involved in municipal politics, becoming mayor of the city in 1933, and serving until 1938. He then was with Wabeek State Bank until his death. He was a Roman Catholic. (**A.** *DAB*, Supplement 3; *NCAB*, 30:32; 39:444; *New York Times*, October 23, 1936; January 31, 1937; *Who Was Who*, vol. 1; Henry Barnard, *Independent Man: The Life of Sen. James Couzens*, 1958. **B.** A. Nevins and F. E. Hill, *Ford: The Times, The Man and the Company*, 1954.)

COWLES FAMILY: Gardner Cowles (February 28, 1861–February 28, 1946); **Gardner ("Mike") Cowles Jr.** (January 31, 1903–   ); **John Cowles** (December 14, 1898–February 25, 1983). Newspaper and magazine publishers and broadcasters, Cowles Publications and Cowles Broadcasting.

Gardner Cowles was born in Oskaloosa, Iowa, son of William Fletcher Cowles and Maria Elizabeth La Markin. His father was a Methodist clergyman and collector of internal revenue for the fourth district in Iowa. Gardner was educated in public schools in Muscatine and Mt. Pleasant, Iowa, and studied at Grinnell College. He graduated from Iowa Wesleyan College in 1882, and got a master's degree there in 1885. Before doing his advanced study, he spent two years as superintendent of schools at Algona, Iowa, where in 1883–1884 he was also editor of the *Algona Republican*, a weekly newspaper. In the latter year he became a rural mail contractor and engaged in the banking and real estate fields.

Cowles' publishing career began in 1903 when, at the urging of Harvey Ingham, a one-time competitor as a newspaper editor in Algona, Cowles bought a major interest in the *Des Moines Register and Leader*. This was a morning newspaper which had been founded in 1849, and was the smallest of Des Moines' three dailies, with a circulation of only 16,000, and a debt of

$180,000. Cowles set out to make it a publication with a state-wide following. By 1906 there were 25,000 readers, and two years later he purchased the Des Moines *Evening Tribune*, a small afternoon daily. He changed the name of the publishing firm to the *Register and Tribune*, of which he was president and treasurer. By 1913, the circulation of the *Register and Tribune* was 22,000 in a city with a population of 100,000, with another 33,000 readers outside the city. In 1924 he acquired from the Scripps-Howard chain the Des Moines *News*, which had been founded in 1881, and in 1937 he purchased the Des Moines *Capitol*, thus absorbing his evening competitors. Cowles now became chairman of the board, with his son, Gardner Jr., becoming president. The Cowles' three newspapers were the only ones in the city, and had immense political influence.

In 1928 he founded the Cowles Broadcasting Company to operate KRNT (Des Moines), WNAX (Yankton, South Dakota) and WOL (Washington, D.C.). Cowles Magazines was founded in 1937 as publishers of *Look* magazine, which had a national circulation of 2,600,000 at the time of Cowles' death. For a number of years prior to 1930 Cowles was director of the Iowa–Des Moines National Bank and Trust and the North-West Bank Corporation. In 1932–1933 he was a director of the Reconstruction Finance Corporation. He was a Methodist and a Republican, and served in the state legislature from 1899 to 1903. In 1884 he married Florence Maud Call of Algona, and they had six children. His eldest son, Russell Cowles, became a prominent artist.

Gardner ("Mike") Cowles Jr. was born in Algona, educated at Phillips-Exeter and graduated from Harvard in 1925. He then became city editor of the Des Moines *Register and Tribune*. By 1926 he was news director, in the next year associate managing editor, and in 1931 executive editor. He instituted the technique of covering Iowa and Middle Western news by airplane for news and pictures, and started George Gallup on his polling career. Gallup had been a journalism instructor at the University of Iowa, and Mike Cowles set him to work measuring "reader interest" in the *Register and Tribune*. The surveys showed that readers liked pictures rather than type, so the picture story concept was developed, which made the *Register and Tribune* very popular.

Mike Cowles was also primarily responsible for putting the family into the radio business. He first bought a small station in Ft. Dodge, Iowa, and another in a small Iowa town. He then moved both to Des Moines. By the mid-1950s, the Cowles chain covered all of the midwestern states. He was president of the Iowa Broadcasting Company and the South Dakota Broadcasting Company. In 1935, he and his brother John purchased the Minneapolis *Star*, for one million dollars. In a few years they came to control all of the newspapers in Minneapolis as well as Des Moines. At about the same time they also began to bring out a weekly picture magazine called *Look*. In 1939 Mike became associate publisher of the Des Moines *Register and*

Tribune, while remaining executive editor. In 1942 Mike Cowles became Deputy Director of the Office of War Information, causing much dissension from the writers in the ranks because of his policies. He resigned in 1943. He married Helen Curtiss and Lois Thornburg and had three children.

John Cowles was born in Algona, and moved to Minneapolis, Minnesota, in 1935 when the family bought the Minneapolis *Star*; he became its publisher in 1941. He was also chairman of the board of the Des Moines *Register and Tribune*, Cowles Magazines, and Cowles Broadcasting. His first job had been in the advertising department of the Des Moines paper, and when he went to the *Star*, he doubled its circulation between 1935 and 1939. He then bought the Minneapolis *Journal* for $2,200,000, and in 1941 purchased the morning *Tribune*. He married Elizabeth Manly Bates in 1923, and had four children. His son, John Cowles Jr. (b. 1929), has been with the Minneapolis *Star and Tribune* since 1953, and was president (1965–1968) and chairman of the board (1968–1972) of *Harper's Magazine*. (*DAB*, Supplement 4; *NCAB*, 36:270; 16:272; *Current Biography*, June, 1943; 1954.)

COXE, TENCH (May 22, 1755–July 16, 1824). Economist and public official. Born in Philadelphia, Pennsylvania, son of William Coxe, a merchant, and Mary Francis. Both families had long been prominent in Pennsylvania. His paternal grandfather, Daniel Coxe, was a noted colonial lawyer, legislator, and jurist, and his maternal grandfather, Tench Francis, was a prominent lawyer who once served as Attorney-General of the province of Pennsylvania. Tench Coxe was educated at the College of Philadelphia (later the University of Pennsylvania). He studied law for a time but later engaged in business with his father and others, becoming a partner in the firm of Coxe, Furman and Coxe.

Throughout most of the revolutionary struggles with Britain, Coxe remained a Loyalist but after he was arrested for these sympathies he turned his sympathies to the patriot cause and was paroled. He was a member of the Annapolis Convention in 1786 and the Continental Congress in 1788. He supported the adoption of the Constitution in 1787 with the publication of a pamphlet entitled *An Examination of the Constitution of the United States*, and remained a strong Federalist until the late 1790s. In 1789 he was made Assistant Secretary of the Treasury, and from 1792 to 1797 served as Commissioner of Revenue, until he was removed by President Adams. At that point he joined the Republican party and campaigned for the election of Thomas Jefferson in 1800. In 1803 he was named surveyor of public supplies, holding that post until it was abolished in 1812.

While in the Treasury Department Coxe was a close ally of Alexander Hamilton.* In their relationship Hamilton was the master strategist and Coxe the able tactician. Coxe made contributions to numerous reports that Hamilton submitted to Congress during these years, playing a particularly significant role in the important reports on a national bank and manufactures. Coxe had opposed the rechartering of the Bank of North America, but only on the grounds that it was not sufficiently accountable to the public. Thus he was quite ready and willing to support Hamilton's plans to convert it into a truly national bank, with full accountability. Although there has been a great deal of debate among historians concerning the extent of Coxe's influence on the *Report on Manufactures*, the most recent evidence indicates that he was the single individual whose influence was most decisive on Hamilton. Coxe provided Hamilton with a bright picture of the current state and future prospects of manufactures, both in Pennsylvania and in the nation as a whole, but also pointed out critical problems such as the shortage of labor.

Much of the information Coxe accumulated for the *Report on Manufactures* was the result of the voluminous writings on economics he had been producing for a number of years. In 1787 he published a pamphlet entitled *An Inquiry into the Principles on Which a Commercial System for the United States Should be Founded*, and two years later brought out a book called *Observations on the Agriculture, Manufactures, and Commerce of the United States*. This was followed in 1791 by *A Brief Examination of Lord Sheffield's Observations on the Commerce of the United States*, and in 1792 by *Reflections on the State of the Union*. In 1810 he published *Statement of the Arts and Manufactures of the United States in 1810*, an exhaustive industrial census of the United States.

All his life Coxe was active in the promotion of the agricultural and industrial development of the United States. In 1775 he became a member of the United Company of Philadelphia for Promoting American Manufactures, and in 1787 was named president of the Pennsylvania Society for the Encouragement of Manufacture and Useful Arts. He was one of the first leaders in the introduction of cotton growing in the South, and was very active in the promotion of cotton manufacture, attempting to bring Richard Arkwright's machinery to the United States without success. He was also among the earliest to become aware of the mineral resources of central and western Pennsylvania and purchased extensive tracts of land in the coal regions. He had little success in the development of coal mining, but his grandson, Eckley Brinton Coxe (1839–1895), was an outstanding mining engineer who took up development of the family coal lands and organized the firm of Coxe Brothers and Company. Later this became the Cross Creek Coal Company, and in 1890 Eckley B. Coxe organized and was president of the Delaware, Susquehanna and Schuylkill Railroad Company.

Coxe's basic economic concept was the doctrine of a balanced system of national economy. In this system he ascribed a leading place to agriculture because of the vast agricultural resources of the United States, but felt that both commerce and manufactures had important roles to play. In his writings he centered most of his attention on manufacturing. In his view, the establishment and development of manufacturing was essential to the maximum population, prosperity, and power of the young nation. He felt that the development of manufacturing would rectify the unfavorable balance of trade and make possible the retention of an adequate supply of money in the country; stabilize the market and improve the price of agricultural produce; increase the volume and profitability of commerce; and cause the importation of productive equipment rather than manufactured consumer goods. For the development of its manufacturing resources, Coxe pointed out the many great benefits enjoyed by America, but also recognized the dearness of labor, for which he recommended the use of labor-saving devices.

Unlike Hamilton, Coxe was not a staunch protectionist. Nor was he a free-trader like Albert Gallatin. He represented a transition from the free trade to the protective school of American economic thought. His reasons for differing with Hamilton on the benefits of protectionism were threefold: first, he did not believe it was necessary to the establishment and development of manufacturing industries in the United States; second, he feared high tariffs would encourage smuggling and a general decline in morality; and, third, he felt it would impose an unfair burden on mercantile and agricultural classes. In all of his writings Coxe was an untiring advocate of a well-balanced, largely self-sufficient national economy. He judged other ideas and policies on this objective, and his support for a national bank and a strong central government came because they would, in his view, contribute to his goal of a system of national economy which would promote the general interest of the country with the least injury to particular persons and sections.

Coxe married Catherine McCall of Philadelphia and Rebecca Coxe of New Jersey. His son, Charles Sidney Coxe, became district attorney and judge of the district court of Philadelphia. (**A.** *DAB; NCAB*, 6:14; *Who Was Who*, vol. 4; Henry Simpson, *Lives of Eminent Philadelphians*, 1859; Jacob E. Cooke, *Tench Coxe and the Early Republic*, 1978; "Tench Coxe, Alexander Hamilton and the Encouragement of American Manufacturers," *William and Mary Quarterly*, 1975, 369–392; Alexander duBin, *The Coxe Family*, 1936; Harold Hutcheson, *Tench Coxe: A Study in American Economic Development*, 1938. **B.** Joseph Dorfman, *The Economic Mind in American Civilization*, 4 vols., 1946–59; Leo Marx, *The Machine in the Garden*, 1964; Virgle Glenn Wilhite, *Founders of American Economic Thought*, 1958.)

CRAMP, WILLIAM (September 22, 1807–July 6, 1879) and **Charles Henry Cramp** (May 9, 1828–June 6, 1913). Shipbuilders, William Cramp Shipbuilding Company. **William Cramp** was born in Kensington, a section of Philadelphia, and was a descendent of Johannes Krampf, of Baden, Germany, who settled in Philadelphia in 1703. William received a good elementary education, and then studied with Samuel Grice, the leading American naval architect of the time.

At age 23, in 1830, he established the William Cramp Shipbuilding Company, which was to construct many important sailing and steam vessels. Under his direction the company was provided with modern mechanical devices, and came to be considered one of the best equipped shipyards in the country. He managed the firm through the enormous transition in construction and design of vessels which occurred during these years. First, wooden vessels were replaced by iron, and then iron by steel. These changes involved the installation of new machinery, a new industrial organization, and a new science of naval architecture. He was one of the first to foresee this change, and his aggressiveness enabled him to cope with the situation. By 1870 he had taken several of his sons into the organization, and he incorporated the concern as William Cramp and Sons Ship and Engine Building Company.

Over the years he constructed 207 vessels of all sorts, both merchant and naval. He built war vessels for Russia and Venezuela and the U.S. government gave him several contracts. He was president of the firm until he died, when he was succeeded by his son, Charles H. Cramp. He married Sophia Miller of Philadelphia in 1827.

Charles H. Cramp was born in Philadelphia and educated in the public schools. He worked in his uncle's shipyard for two years. In 1846 he entered the employ of his father and became an expert shipbuilder. In 1879 he became president of the company until he retired in 1903, at the age of 75. He continued as chairman of the board until he died in 1913. Charles Cramp was one of the leading naval architects of his day. The shipyard he inherited from his father was still relatively small, but he soon developed it into one of the most extensive and complete in the U.S. Many important merchant and naval vessels were constructed there, including the steamships *St. Louis* and *St. Paul*, among the fastest vessels of their day, and *Kroonland* and *Finland*, among the largest built up to that time. Among others he constructed the U.S.S. *Maine*, which was blown up in Havana Harbor.

The company also became a pioneer in engine development. The first triple expansion engine ever constructed in America was installed in the yacht *Peerless*. It also built the first vessel to be powered by three propellers. He married two sisters, Hannah Ann Cox in 1850, and Amy Jane Cox in 1870. He brought six sons into the shipbuilding business. (*DAB; NCAB*, 5:253–54; *New York Times*, June 7, 1913; *Who Was Who*, vol. H and vol. 1.)

CRANE, RICHARD TELLER (May 15, 1832–January 8, 1912) and **Richard Teller Crane Jr.** (November 6, 1873–November 7, 1931). Plumbing manufacturers, The Crane Company. **Richard T. Crane** was born in Paterson, New Jersey, son of Timothy Batchford Crane and Maria Ryerson. His family had settled in New England in 1655. His father had been born in Dunbar, Massachusetts, and was a mechanic and builder who had suffered financial reverses in the Panic of 1837. As a result of his father's misfortunes, young Richard became an operator in a cotton mill at the age of nine. He was variously employed until 1847, when he secured a position in the brass and bell foundry of John Benson of Brooklyn, New York. After mastering the brass business, Crane entered the employ of the Taylor Printing Press Works, and from there went to Robert Hoe and Company, also manufacturers of printing presses. He lost his position there in 1854.

In that year he went to Chicago, where his uncle, Martin Ryerson, lived. He erected a brass foundry in his uncle's lumber yard, which was the beginning of a business that developed into one of the largest of its kind in the world. His first products were brass couplings and copper points for lighting rods. He was soon joined in this venture by his brother, Charles S. Crane, who remained in the business until 1871. The original R. T. Crane and Brother was incorporated in 1865 as the Northwestern Manufacturing Company, and in 1872 as Crane Brothers Manufacturing Company, becoming the Crane Company in 1890. He early added wrought iron pipe and fittings to his product line, and later began to manufacture pulleys and shafting, steam engines, steam pumps, and elevators. At one time he controlled about 95 percent of the elevator business in the United States. He dropped these lines and began to manufacture pipe fittings and connections exclusively.

Richard Crane was married three times: in 1857 to Mary Josephine Prentice of Lockport, New York; to her sister, Eliza Ann Prentice, in 1889; and to Emily Sprague Hutchins in 1903. He had nine children. His eldest son, Charles Richard Crane (1858–1939) joined his father's business, becoming vice-president in 1894 and president in 1912. Ill health, due to malaria contracted as a youth, however, caused him to sell out to his brother in 1914.

Richard T. Crane Jr. was born in Chicago and educated at Tilden School in that city and at Hill School. He graduated from Sheffield Scientific School at Yale in 1895. The following year he joined his father's business; he worked first in the iron and brass foundry, and was later in charge of city sales. He was made second vice-president in 1898, first vice-president in 1912, and president in 1914. He remained in that position until he died. Under his leadership the Crane Company experienced the greatest expansion in its history, developing into an organization with factories, branch houses, sales offices, and exhibition rooms in 200 cities throughout the world. The company had more than 20,000 employees. He married Florence Higinbottom of Chicago in 1904. They had one daughter and one son. His nephew, Charles R. Crane II (1892–1954), son of Herbert Prentice Crane, was a vice-president of Crane from 1925 to 1945. (*DAB*, Supplement 2; *NCAB*, 26:450; 30:221.)

CRAVATH, PAUL DRENNAN (July 14, 1861–July 1, 1940). Wall Street lawyer. Born in Berlin Heights, Ohio, son of Erastus Milo Cravath and Ruthanna Jackson. His father was a prominent Congregational clergyman who devoted his life to the education of blacks as an official of the American Missionary Association and as founder and first president of Fisk University in Nashville, Tennessee. The family lived in Cincinnati from 1866 to 1870 and in New York City from 1870 to 1875. Paul Cravath was educated at Brooklyn Polytechnic Institute until age fourteen, when he went on a tour of Europe with the Fisk Jubilee Singers to raise money for the university. When he returned, he went to Oberlin College, graduating in 1882. He then began to study law in the office of Frank B. Kellogg in Minneapolis, Minnesota. After working for a time for a subsidiary of Standard Oil Company to earn money for law school, he attended Columbia Law School, graduating in 1886.

He joined the New York City law firm of Carter, Hornblower and Byrne. The senior partner, William S. Carter, was a pioneer in the organization of the modern law office. He wanted an office made up primarily of young graduates recruited annually from the law schools who would spend a few years there before undertaking their own careers. This became known as the "Cravath System." Also in the firm was a Columbia classmate, Charles Evans Hughes. Both he and Cravath became partners, and the firm became Carter, Hughes, and Cravath. The firm's practice was primarily in the dry goods trade, but Cravath brought in Westinghouse, Bethlehem Steel and other large manufacturers, a number of railroads, and the investment banking firm of Kuhn, Loeb and Company.

Cravath then started his own firm of Cravath and Houston. His effectiveness came from his quiet and firm grasp of the new business problems and his ability to organize and direct the legal task forces necessary to deal with them. In 1917 he was appointed by President Wilson as a member of the House Mission to Paris and spent two years in Europe. He was awarded the Distinguished Service Medal for his work. He supported the Council on Foreign Relations after the War. He was a Republican and married Agnes Huntington, an opera singer, in 1892. They had one daughter, Vera. (*DAB*, Supplement 2; *NCAB*, 11:115; C:110; *Current Biography*, August, 1940; *Who Was Who*, vol. 1.)

CRAWFORD, GEORGE WASHINGTON (June 4, 1861–April 6, 1935). Oil and gas company pioneer, Treat and Crawford. Born in Emlenton, Venango County, Pennsylvania, son of Ebenezer Crawford and Elizabeth Wilson. He was educated in the public schools and at Eastman Business College in Poughkeepsie, New York. Crawford went to work at age nineteen in the oil and gas fields in the Venango area. Later, he conducted a hardware and oil and gas well supply company in Bolivar, Allegheny County, New York. He returned to Emlenton and joined his father and brothers in the operation of a system of oil pipelines extending from the oil fields to railway landing points; this concern was called E. Crawford and Sons. During 1891 through 1893 he was with U.S. Pipeline Company, and in 1893 joined his brother-in-law, Milo Calvin Treat, in Treat and Crawford, which became prominent in the oil and gas industry. He remained with the firm until 1925.

The firm's first operation in 1893 was in the Corning (Ohio) field, where natural gas was developed. They formed the Corning Natural Gas Company, and in the next several years Crawford and his company organized several other gas companies. In 1902 he formed the Ohio Fuel Supply Company to centralize the firm's extensive gas interests in Ohio, with Crawford as president. In 1916 he organized and became president of the United Fuel Gas Company, which acquired gas plants for various cities in West Virginia, Kentucky, and Ohio. The Ohio Fuel Corporation was formed in 1924 with Crawford as president. With this company a consolidated system was established which extended through the states of Indiana, Ohio, Kentucky, West Virginia, and Pennsylvania. In 1926 he formed the Columbia Gas and Electric Company and was president of that. This latter consolidation brought under one management properties valued at five hundred million dollars, and produced one of the leading public service systems in the United States.

Treat and Crawford also participated in the early development of the mid-continent oil and gas field, forming various companies in the Indian and Oklahoma Territories. In 1909 they organized the Lone Star Gas Company, which in 1926 became Lone Star Gas Corporation, serving 300,000 customers. In 1909 they formed the Penn-Mex Fuel Company, and leased 162,000 acres of oil and gas land in the United States and Mexico. These were sold to Sinclair Oil in 1932. Crawford was president of the firm until then. In 1916 he helped to organize the Tropical Oil Company, which was engaged in oil development in the Republic of Columbia. He was vice-president of this until 1920, when it merged with International Petroleum of Canada. He was also chairman of the board of Western Public Service Corporation, incorporated in 1928 to deliver natural gas to southwest Wyoming, northern Colorado, and eastern Utah.

He was a Republican and a Presbyterian and married Annie Laurie Warmack of St. Louis, Missouri, in 1927. They had one daughter. (*NCAB*, 28:188.)

CROCKER, CHARLES F. (September 16, 1822–August 14, 1888); **William Henry Crocker** (January 13, 1861–September 23, 1937); and **William Willard Crocker** (June 29, 1893–August 11, 1964). Railroad builders and bankers, Southern Pacific Railroad and Crocker National Bank.

Charles Crocker was born in Troy, New York, son of Isaac Crocker and Eliza Wright. His father was a merchant. Charles Crocker had few educational advantages and at an early age went to work to support his family. In 1836 the family moved to Marshall County, Indiana, and soon after Crocker began to earn his own living, first as a farm hand, then in a sawmill, and then as an apprentice in an iron forge. In 1845 he discovered a bed of iron ore in Marshall County and established a forge known as Charles Crocker Company. When gold was discovered in California, he sold the business and led a band of men, including two younger brothers, by the overland route to the Pacific Coast, arriving in 1850. In 1852 he gave up mining and opened a store in Sacramento. By 1851 he was one of the wealthiest and most prominent men in the city, and in 1855 was elected to the city council.

In 1860 Crocker was elected to the state legislature, and soon afterward became associated with Leland Stanford,* Collis P. Huntington,* and Mark Hopkins* (known thereafter as the "Big Four"), fellow Sacramento merchants, in the building of the Central Pacific Railroad across the Sierra Nevada to connect with the Union Pacific Railroad being constructed eastward from Omaha, Nebraska. A self-trained engineer, Crocker took charge of the actual construction of the line, leaving financing and general policy development to his associates. Labor was scarce in the West because most men were seeking their own fortune rather than a mere job, and the labor problem seemed insuperable until Crocker began importing Chinese coolies by the thousands. Few believed that the Chinese, who weighed, on the average, no more than 110 pounds, could stand up under the rough railroad work in the high Sierras. But Crocker first tried fifty as an experiment, found they could do the work, and soon was hiring them by the hundreds, importing many directly from Canton. Supplies were also a problem, since they were scarce and high priced, and getting them to the widely dispersed 12,000 workers became a major problem. For five years (1864–1869) the work went on, under terribly difficult circumstances. When the last spike was driven at Promontory Point in 1869, however, the Big Four were major proprietors of an immensely valuable railroad which had been constructed almost entirely at government expense in the form of land grants and loans.

The Central Pacific, however, was merely the cornerstone of a massive transportation and land empire that the Big Four began to construct. The Central Pacific bought up all existing roads in the state, built the California and Oregon Railroad to the north and the San Joaquin Valley road to the south, with the latter line becoming part of the Southern Pacific. They then took up a land grant to build a railroad from San Francisco to New Orleans via Los Angeles. As part of a vast transportation monopoly on the West Coast, they owned the steamship line connecting Sacramento and San Francisco, monopolized dock facilities at Oakland, and formed an ocean steamship line which competed with the Pacific Mail. This allowed the four men to dominate the entire business climate of California for a number of years, and set the stage for titanic battles between the Southern Pacific and other business interests, particularly newly emergent groups in Los Angeles and San Francisco. In 1886 Charles Crocker was seriously injured in a carriage accident and never fully recovered. He married Mary Ann Deming. They had three sons and a daughter, and left them a fortune of over $40 million.

William H. Crocker was born in Sacramento, California, son of Charles Crocker. He was educated at Phillips Academy at Andover, Massachusetts, and graduated from Sheffield Scientific School at Yale in 1882. In the next year he entered the banking business in partnership with his father and Ralph C. Woolworth, under the firm name of Crocker-Woolworth and Company. In 1886 it became the Crocker-Woolworth National Bank. William was made cashier, advancing to the presidency on the death of Woolworth. In 1906 it became the Crocker National Bank and First National Bank of San Francisco. He continued as president until 1936, when he was suc-ceeded by his son, William W. Crocker. He remained as chairman of the board until his death, however.

W. H. Crocker was also president of Crocker Investment Company, Provident Securities, and Crocker Estate Company, and director of many others. The Crocker estate erected the Crocker, Alexander, Underwood, Chancery, and Rosenthal buildings in San Francisco. After the earthquake in 1906, he played a large and important part in the rehabilitation of the city, going to New York City and personally arranging for loans amounting to millions of dollars. He helped finance the restoration of many public and private buildings, including the Palace Hotel; the Pacific Union, Olympic, and Bohemian Clubs; and Commercial Building; the Masonic and Scottish Rite Temples; the YMCA; and the California Academy of Sciences buildings.

In 1911 W. H. Crocker was elected first vice-president and director of the Panama Pacific International Exposition of 1915. From 1908 until his death he was a regent of the University of California, and was chairman of the board in 1928. In 1937 he contributed funds to erect a building for a cyclotron and the laboratory devoted to the study of radiation in relation to medical science. He was first president and a constant supporter of the Community Chest and had many philanthropies. A Republican and Episcopalian, he married Ethel Willard Sperry of Stockton, California, in 1886. They had four children, including William W. Crocker.

William W. Crocker was born in San Francisco and educated at Groton, earning his bachelor's degree at Yale in 1915. He studied law in 1916 at Harvard. He then served in World War I, and after the war entered Bankers Trust Company, in New York City. In 1919 he returned to San Francisco to begin his career with the Crocker First National Bank. He served as vice-president from 1919 to 1936. He then was president until 1950, when he became chairman of the board. He continued in that position until 1956, when Crocker merged with the Anglo-California National Bank to form the Crocker-Anglo National Bank. In 1962 he was named honorary chairman of the bank, which was then called the Crocker-Citizen's National Bank.

When he became president of the bank in 1936, it had deposits of some $133 million, resources of over $148.5 million, and 364 employees. By 1950, it had deposits of $340.6 million, resources of $378.4 million, and 620 employees. He was also president of Crocker Estate Company, Provident Investment Company, Crocker Land Company, Merced Water Company, and Provident Securities Company, and director of many others. An Episcopalian and a Republican, he was married three times. In 1923 he married Ruth Hobart of San Mateo, California. They were divorced in 1949, and in the same year he married Gertrude (Hopkins) Parrott. In 1960, he married Elizabeth (Fullerton) Coleman of Miami, Oklahoma. He had a son and a daughter. (**A.** *DAB; NCAB*, 36:122; 52:225; *New York Times*, August 15, 1888; *Who Was Who*, vol. H. **B.** Stuart Daggert, *Chapters on the History of the Southern Pacific*, 1922; Matthew Josephson, *The Robber Barons*, 1934; Oscar Lewis, *The Big Four: The Story of Huntington, Stanford, Hopkins and Crocker*, 1938; John Moody, *The Railroad Builders*, 1919.)

CROOKS, RAMSAY (January 2, 1787–June 6, 1859). Fur industry executive, American Fur Company. Born in Greenoch, Scotland, son of William Crooks and Margaret Ramsay. At age sixteen he emigrated to Montreal, Canada, and at once entered the fur trade. As a clerk of Robert Dickson he went to St. Louis, Missouri, in 1806. A year later he formed a partnership with Robert McClellan, and that fall, with eighty men, set out for the Upper Missouri. But on learning of the defeat of a party by Indians, they turned back and established a trading post near the present site of Calhoun, Nebraska. Two years later, with forty men, they started to follow the great expedition of the St. Louis Missouri Fur Company northward, but ran into hostile Sioux, and so gave up the venture. In 1810 the partnership was dissolved and Crooks went back to Canada. Here he bought five shares in John Jacob Astor's* Pacific Fur Company, which was recruiting men for a journey to Astoria.

Crooks then accompanied the expedition the following spring, but in the Blue Mountains of Oregon, worn out with illness and hunger, he and five others were left behind. Finally, in May, 1812, he and a companion arrived in Astoria. Four days later he relinquished his shares, and in June started his return with a party of seven. After many dangers and extreme deprivation, they reached St. Louis in April, 1813. But Crooks remained in close association with Astor's American Fur Company, which in 1816 bought out the American interest of the Northwest Company. He was appointed general manager of the American Fur Company in 1817, and three years later visited Astor in Europe and arranged for the next four years' campaign. It was due to his persistence and urging that Astor established the Western Department of the company, in St. Louis in 1822. Crooks acted as virtual head of the fur company until the time of Astor's retirement in 1834.

Every year he had to make the long and arduous journey to Mackinaw, after going on to St. Louis. He formulated the policies of the company, and with an extraordinary grasp of detail managed its business through the whole field of its operations. When Astor sold out, Crooks bought the Northern Department, of which he became president, continuing the name of the American Fur Company. He remained as president of the company until he died at his home in New York City. He was also president of the Mohawk and Hudson Railroad Company, serving until 1835, and a trustee of Astor Library. He married Marianne Pelogie Emilie Protte, of the Chouteau* family of St. Louis. This union greatly enhanced Crooks' standing in that fur metropolis. (**A.** *DAB*. **B.** Hiram M. Chittenden, *The American Fur Trade of the Far West*, 3 volumes, 1902; Kenneth W. Porter, *John Jacob Astor, Businessman*, 2 volumes, 1931.)

CROMWELL, WILLIAM NELSON (January 17, 1854–July 19, 1948). Wall Street lawyer, Sullivan and Cromwell. Born in Brooklyn, New York, son of John Nelson Cromwell, an army officer, and Sarah M. Brokaw. The family soon moved to Peoria, Illinois, and in the fall of 1861 his father left for the Civil War. He was killed at Vicksburg. The family returned to Brooklyn where Cromwell was educated in the public schools and worked for several years as an accountant in a railroad office to support his younger brother and mother. In 1874 he secured an accounting job with the New York law firm of Sullivan, Kobbe and Fowler. With the encouragement of the firm's senior partner, Algernon S. Sullivan, he attended Columbia Law School on the side, being admitted to the bar in 1876.

In 1879 he became a partner in the Sullivan firm, with a one-third interest. When Sullivan died in 1887, Cromwell became senior partner. Under his leadership the firm prospered and grew, employing twelve lawyers and six stenographers by 1902. He specialized in business law, and the firm excelled in supplying legal advice to increasingly complex organizations trying to reach rapidly expanding markets. He handled the consolidation of sixteen of the largest tube manufacturing concerns into the National Tube Company in 1899, which was capitalized at $80 million, and worked with E. H. Harriman* on a two year proxy battle against Stuyvesant Fish* for control of the Illinois Central Railroad. This case was brought to a successful conclusion in 1908.

His first major breakthrough, however, had come in 1896, at the time of the reorganization of the Northern Pacific Railroad. He was retained by J. P. Morgan and Company and helped put into effect the plan for the fundamental reorganization of the railroad. He also played a leading role a few years later in the organization of United States Steel Company. He reorganized the Brazilian Railroads for French and English interests. For the sake of economic rationality, he urged corporations to make full public disclosure of their assets to win and hold the confidence of the investing public. He also established the so-called Cromwell Plan for salvaging enterprises in distress. He was often called the "physician of Wall Street" for this work. The essence of his plan was to arrange a voluntary agreement of the creditors within the framework of the New York State insolvency laws, so the firm could reorganize itself and fulfill its obligations, without a sacrifice sale. It was originally developed in 1891 to save a failing New York brokerage house, and was subsequently used for many others, especially during the panic of 1907.

He also represented various European banks and bond syndicates in the United States, and played a part in streamlining the flow of European capital to the United States before World War I. He represented France's New Panama Canal Company in 1896 and did eight years of intensive lobbying, negotiations, and public relations work, promoting a plan of the Colombian government to allow the canal company to sell its Panamanian property to the United States for $40 million. After World War I he retired from private legal practice, and was a resident for long periods of time in France. His firm had subordinate offices in Paris, Berlin, Buenos Aires, Manila, and Shanghai at various times.

He was an Episcopalian and a Republican, and married Jennie Osgood Nichols in 1878. They had no children. (*DAB*, Supplement 4; *NCAB*, 42:314; *New York* Times, July 20, 1948; *Who Was Who*, vol. 2.)

CROWELL, HENRY PARSONS (January 27, 1855–October 23, 1944). Breakfast food manufacturer, Quaker Oats Company. Born in Cleveland, Ohio, the son of Henry Luther Crowell and Ann Eliza Parsons. They were both natives of Connecticut who moved to Cleveland in 1853. Henry P. Crowell was educated at Greylock Institute in Massachusetts until 1872. It was not until two years later, in 1874, that he was employed as a clerk in the wholesale shoe firm of Crowell and Childs, of which his father was senior partner prior to his death. But the younger Crowell, finding his health impaired, spent the next seven years traveling throughout the western United States. During this period he purchased and sold two farms in South Dakota, the second comprising 17,000 acres, which he had operated from 1878 to 1881. Then he returned to Cleveland and purchased the Quaker Mill at Ravenna, Ohio, where he resided until 1888.

In 1887, in association with a number of other millers, he formed the Consolidated Oatmeal Company, of which he was president. The company was shortlived, and in the same year the American Cereal Company of West Virginia was formed as a holding company with offices in Chicago. Crowell moved to the latter city in 1888. In 1891 a further consolidation of millers took place with the merger of American Cereal Company of West Virginia and a number of rival companies to form the American Cereal Company of Akron, Ohio, of which Crowell was vice-president from 1891 to 1898, and president from 1899 to 1901. But his goal of an association of millers operating under one trade name and having a central authority and capital stock was not reached until the millers in the American Cereal Company in 1901 formed the Quaker Oats Company, of which he was president from 1901 to 1922, and chairman of the board from 1922 to 1942. After the latter year he served as honorary chairman until his death.

Throughout this entire period Crowell had been a major innovator in cereal, especially the oatmeal aspect of it. As early as 1882 he had built a mill that was the first in the world "to maintain under one roof operations to grade, clean, hull, cut, package, and ship oatmeal to interstate markets in a continuous process that in some aspects anticipated the modern assembly line" (Marquette). Another of Crowell's major contributions was his concept for the packaging and marketing of oatmeal. While the older and larger producers at the time continued to market oatmeal in the traditional manner of selling in bulk through wholesalers, Crowell packaged and then advertised his brand, Quaker Oats, nationally as a breakfast cereal, a product which was new to American tastes. In advertising Quaker Oats, Crowell's staff used box-top premiums, prizes, testimonials, scientific endorsements, and the like. The company set up a number of sales offices in the United States and abroad. Their managers were expected not only to maintain contact with jobbers, but also to schedule flows from the factory to the jobbers. At the same time Crowell built a buying organization that soon came to include the "fieldmen" who purchased directly from the farmers in the grain-growing states and buyers who had seats on the Minneapolis and Chicago grain exchanges. After the Quaker Oats consolidation was established in 1901, production was concentrated at two giant plants—one at Akron and the other at Cedar Rapids—each using improved continuous-process machinery. After the turn of the century, to make fuller use of its marketing and purchasing facilities, the company added new lines to wheat cereals, farina, hominy, corn meal, specialized baby foods, and animal feed.

By the time of his death, Quaker Oats was a $250,000,000 enterprise, with twelve large plants and many smaller establishments, and more than eighty grain elevators in the United States and Canada. It was engaged in buying, selling, dealing in, and manufacturing cereals and cereal products, flour, and commercial mixed feeds on an international scale. The net sales in 1942 were $85 million. The firm maintained subsidiaries in England, Germany, France, Denmark, and Holland, and its products included Quaker Oats, Mother's Oats, Puffed Wheat and Puffed Rice, Aunt Jemima Pancake Flour, Muffets, macaroni, spaghetti, cornmeal, and stock and poultry feeds. Crowell also organized and was chairman of the Perfection Stove Company of Cleveland, which he founded in 1888. It was set up to manufacture a new type of oil stove and prospered from the start. It ultimately had a plant that covered over twenty-seven acres and employed 1,800 persons.

Crowell, a Presbyterian and a Republican, was in large measure responsible for the strengthening and development of the Moody Bible Institute of Chicago. He was president of its board of trustees from 1904 to 1944. He also owned a Hereford ranch of over 35,000 acres in Wyoming. He married Lillie Wick of Cleveland in 1882. After she died in 1885, he married Susan B. Coleman of Cleveland. He had one daughter and one son. His son, Henry Coleman Crowell (1897–1965) was an executive with the Moody Bible Institute from 1939 to 1965. (**A.** *NCAB*, 33:417; *Who Was Who*, vols. 2 & 4; Richard E. Day, *The Breakfast Table Autocrat: The Life and Times of Henry Parsons Crowell*, 1946. **B.** Alfred D. Chandler Jr., *The Visible Hand*, 1977; Arthur E. Marquette, *Brands, Trademarks and Good Will*, 1967; Walter D. Teague, *Flour for Man's Bread*, 1952; Harrison J. Thornton, *The History of the Quaker Oats Company*, 1933.)

CROWN, HENRY (June 13, 1896–   ). Building materials and defense production entrepreneur, Materials Service Corporation and General Dynamics Corporation. Born in Chicago, Illinois, son of Arie Crown and Ida Curdon. His father was a Lithuanian immigrant who worked most of his life in sweatshops as a suspender maker. The family was very poor, and his two older brothers, Sol and Irving, always had to work to make ends meet. Henry also had to quit school at age fourteen to take a clerical job with the Chicago Firebrick Company. After he mixed up an order, his brother Sol, the sales manager, was forced to fire him. In 1912 he took a job with the Union Drop Forge Company, where he learned much about wrought iron and metal works, and also went to night school where he studied bookkeeping and commercial subjects. Four years later his brother Sol established a steel brokerage company, known as S. A. Crown and Company, and Henry put up a modest amount of money, becoming a partner along with another brother, Irving.

In 1919 the three brothers invested $10,000 to expand their facilities and reorganize them as the Material Services Corporation. Henry first served as treasurer of the company, and in 1921 became president and general manager. During their first year of operation, sales of sand and gravel amounted to $218,000, with net earnings of $7,000. But Crown expanded the enterprise until Materials Service Corporation dominated the Chicago market, enjoying a steady stream of credit on unsecured loans due to the confidence of bankers in him. He built up a fleet of trucks, shipped materials cheaply by way of the Lockport-Chicago Canal, and kept profits low. By bidding low in a market where building costs were always kept high by a group of entrenched suppliers, Crown captured many contracts; even during the depression Crown won enough government contracts to keep the company going. It soon became the leading construction supply firm in the Midwest, doing millions of dollars of business a year.

In 1941 he became chairman of the board of Material Service Corporation and other members of the family took over the active management. By this time he had amassed a large fortune and had a reputation for philanthropy. During World War II he was made a colonel in the Army Corps of Engineers, and at the end of the war began investing in real estate, railroads, sugar plantations, and coal mines. He poured millions of dollars into the mechanization of his coal mines, which had an annual capacity of over 600,000 tons. He sold his New York real estate for the United Nations headquarters, making a profit of $600,000 in a few months. He also bought bonds in the Chicago, Rock Island and Pacific Railroad and the Seaboard Airline Railroad, making large profits on both. In the 1950s Crown made his most important real estate acquisition in the Chicago area, for $2,500,000 becoming sole owner of the nineteen-story Chicago Mercantile Building and a major stockholder in Hilton Hotels Corporation, which was on the threshold of expanding its chain of properties. In 1952 he purchased the largest operating interest in the Empire State Building in New York City, buying 24 percent of the stock for three million dollars. He then became chairman of the new Empire State Building Corporation. By 1954 he and his family had exclusive rights to the building, which they had purchased for $49,500,000. He modernized the building, making it into a prestigious property again, and sold it in 1961 for $65,000,000.

Throughout all these ventures, he still regarded the Material Service Corporation as the keystone of his empire. By this time, besides dealing in sand and gravel, it was the largest cement distributor in the world, and also became involved in the production of coal, lime, and clinker dolomite. The firm netted $45 million in 1951, on sales of $115 million. In 1960 the Material Service Corporation was merged with General Dynamics Corporation, builder of atomic submarines, missiles, and supersonic bombers. The Material Service Division was established as an autonomous unit of the General Dynamics Corporation, with Crown as chairman, and as director and chairman of the executive committee of the parent corporation.

By 1960 General Dynamics was no longer the largest defense contractor in the United States, and its earnings had slid downward. After its commercial jet program failed, losses were $40 million in 1961. Crown was opposed by management in his plans for centralizing operations and eliminating the duplication of autonomous divisions, and his position deteriorated further in 1965–1966 when the board of directors overrode his protests and used its option to buy out Crown for $100,000,000. This created a severe financial drain on the company, and Crown announced his resignation from the board in 1966.

In 1966, with the $100 million from General Dynamics, Crown organized his own firm to invest the family wealth. He put the money into solid corporations, including two Chicago banks, Pennzoil, Swift and Company, the St. Louis and San Francisco Railroad, and others. He also began buying back into General Dynamics, and by 1970 had acquired over 10 percent of the company, which shortly increased to 18 percent. He was again named to the board of directors and became chairman of the new executive committee to ward off a proxy fight. His first concern on returning to the management of General Dynamics was to determine the fate of the F-111 military fighter, which had turned into a fiasco for the company. He installed a new management team in 1971, and the firm was soon operating in the black.

General Dynamics, under Crown's influence, has continued as the number one defense contractor in the United States and, more than any other aerospace company, is dependent on the Pentagon. Government defense contracts continue to account for two-thirds of its four billion dollar sales. Its Electric Boat Division makes submarines in Groton, Connecticut; the Quincy, Massachusetts, ship yard makes tankers; the F-16 fighter jet is made in Fort Worth, Texas; and the Tomahawk cruise missile comes out of San Diego, California. In addition, tactical weapons are made in California, lime in Chicago, and telecommunications equipment in Florida and Missouri. With headquarters in St. Louis, Missouri, General Dynamics has over 77,000 employees.

Crown married Rebecca Kranz in 1920, and she died in 1943. Three years later he married Gladys Kay. He had three sons, Robert, Lester, and John Jacob. Lester (b. 1928) became an officer in the family's Marblehead Lime Company from 1950 to 1965, and was also vice-president of Material Service Corporation from 1953 to 1966, and president after 1970. He also served as executive vice-president of General Dynamics from 1960 to 1966, and as a director after 1970. Lester was vice-president of Henry Crown and Company in 1966–1967, and president of that concern after 1969. He was also a partner in the New York Yankees American League baseball team after 1973. (**A.** *Current Biography*, 1972; *Who's Who in America*, 1978–79. **B.** Charles D. Bright, *The Jet Makers*, 1978; Milton Moskowitz et al., *Everybody's Business*, 1980; Victor Perlo, *Militarism and Industry*, 1963; Herman Steckler, *The Structure and Performance of the Aerospace Industry*, 1965.)

CUDAHY FAMILY: Michael Cudahy (December 7, 1841–November 27, 1910); **John Cudahy** (1843-1915); *Patrick Cudahy* (1849–July 25, 1918); **Edward A. Cudahy** (February 1, 1859-1941); **Edward A. Cudahy Jr.** (1885-1966); and **Michael Francis Cudahy** (1886–May 20, 1970). Meat packers, Cudahy Brothers Company.

Michael Cudahy was born in County Kilkenny, Ireland, son of Patrick Cudahy and Elizabeth Shaw. He came to America with his parents in 1849. They made their home in Milwaukee, and at age fourteen Michael left grammar school and entered the employ of Layton and Plankinton, meat packers. He advanced rapidly in the business, and later worked for another meat packer, Edward Raddis, until 1866, when the business was terminated. In that year he became a private meat inspector for Layton and Company, and three years later was made superintendent in charge of the packing house of Plankinton, Armour at Milwaukee. In 1875 he was made a partner in the firm of Armour and Company of Chicago, assuming control of the company's plant operations at the Union Stockyards as general superintendent. His outstanding contribution to the development of the meat packing operation was the epoch-making innovation of the summer curing of meats under refrigeration from 1870 to 1880. Although it was Gustavus F. Swift* who pioneered in the development of refrigeration in transportation with the refrigerated car, it was Cudahy and Armour* who made the greatest developments in using refrigeration on the production side of the meat packing business. Before it had been largely a winter business, but the process of refrigeration revolutionized the industry so that it could be carried on continuously throughout the year. The refrigeration process prevented the premature decay of perishable products, lengthened the period of consumption, and greatly increased production, enabling the owner to market his products at will. Cudahy's part was that of a captain of industry who understood the significance of a new scientific development and made possible its application to commerce.

He set up stationary refrigeration units, or "coolers," in every packing plant, then refrigeration was added to transportation in the middle 1870s with the refrigerated car. Cudahy's contribution was mainly on the production side, although he was also a leader on the transportation side. Then, in 1887, Philip D. Armour,* Michael Cudahy, and his brother, Edward A. Cudahy, purchased a small packing plant in South Omaha, Nebraska, and began a new business there called Armour-Cudahy Packing Company. At that time there were only two small packers in Omaha, where the business was confined to the British market. The Cudahy brothers shrewdly saw opportunities in packing there for the domestic market, especially in hogs. They later developed extensive foreign outlets as well.

In 1890 Michael Cudahy sold his interests in the Chicago Armour business to Armour and Company, and, in turn, purchased Armour's interest in Armour-Cudahy, which was renamed Cudahy Packing Company. He remained president of this concern until he died. In the early twentieth century, the firm was capitalized at $7 million and had 57 branch houses throughout the nation. He was also president of North American Transportation and Trading Company. A Roman Catholic and a Democrat, he was a trustee of Catholic University of America. He married Catharine Sullivan of Cedarburg, Wisconsin, in 1866 and they had seven children. His eldest daughter, Elizabeth, married William P. Nelson, of the Chicago meat packing family.

John Cudahy, brother of Michael, was born in Ireland and entered the meat packing house of Edward Raddis in 1857. He remained there until age nineteen when he joined Plankinton and Armour Company for a short time. He was a nursery foreman until 1870, when he returned to the meat packing industry with Layton and Company for three years. In 1875 he moved to Chicago to form a partnership with E. D. Chapin in Chapin and Company, Packers. In 1880, Chapin withdrew while Cudahy continued the firm. He also became involved with his brother, Patrick, in a meat packing concern, Cudahy Brothers, Milwaukee, which had succeeded the business of John Plankinton in 1889. He married Mary Nalona of Bridgeport, Connecticut, and Margaret F. O'Neill of Chicago. He had four daughters.

Patrick Cudahy was born in Ireland, a brother of Michael and John Cudahy, and at age twelve became a delivery boy for a Milwaukee grocer. At fourteen he entered Raddis Packing Company, and later worked for Layton and Company, Lyman and Wooley, and Plankinton and Armour, becoming superintendent of the latter firm in 1874 and partner in 1876. In that year he and his brother, John, bought controlling interest in the firm, which in 1888 became Cudahy Brothers, and moved to Cudahy, Wisconsin. He remained as president of the concern until 1915. He was a Roman Catholic and a Democrat. His son, John Cudahy Jr. (1889-1943), was a lawyer and rancher and was involved in real estate. He was named Minister to Ireland from 1937 to 1939, and Ambassador to Belgium in 1939-1940.

Edward A. Cudahy was born in Milwaukee, brother of Michael, John, and Patrick. In 1875 he went to Chicago where he entered the Armour Packing Company. In 1887 he went to Omaha, Nebraska, where he helped to establish the Armour-Cudahy Packing Company with P. D. Armour and his brother, Michael. The firm became one of the largest of its kind in the world, marketing the "Rex" brand of hams. The plant had ninety acres of floor space and had branch plants in Sioux City, Iowa, Kansas City, Missouri, and Los Angeles, California. In 1910 he succeeded Michael as president of Cudahy Brothers, and three years later turned management over to a nephew, Joseph M. Cudahy. In 1915 he again assumed the presidency of the company, remaining in that position until 1926. He was then chairman of the board until he died in 1941. He married Elizabeth Murphy of Milwaukee and had five children.

Edward A. Cudahy Jr., son of Edward A., entered the meat packing business and became president of Cudahy Packing Company from 1926 to 1944. He was then chairman from 1944 to 1962. He was also president of Red Wing Company until 1961. He was a Roman Catholic. **Michael Francis Cudahy**, son of Patrick Cudahy, entered the meat packing business in 1910. He was with Cudahy Brothers Company all of his life, and chairman of the concern from 1960 to 1969. He changed its name to Patrick Cudahy, Incorporated. (**A.** *DAB; NCAB*, 11:385; 35:24; *Who Was Who*, vols. 1, 2, 4, 5. **B.** Oscar E. Anderson Jr., *Refrigeration in America*, 1953; R. A. Clemen, *The American Livestock and Meat Industry*, 1923; Mary Yeager Kujovich, "The Refrigerator Car and the Growth of the American Dressed Beef Industry," *Business History Review*, 1970.)

CUFFE, PAUL (January 17, 1759-?). Black shipowner and merchant. Born in Dartmouth, Massachusetts, son of a man who had purchased his freedom in 1746 and his Indian wife. When Paul was seven years old, his parents bought 120 acres of land in or near Dartmouth for 650 Spanish dollars. They were farmers and raised a family of ten children. The land, however, was infertile, and Paul turned his attention to the sea at an early age. At sixteen years of age he set sail as a common seaman on a whaler bound for the Gulf of Mexico. A second trip took him to the West Indies. On a third voyage, during the American Revolution, he was captured by the British and detained for three months in New York City.

Four years later he and his brother, David, built a vessel designed for trading along the Connecticut coast. On both their first and second voyages their cargoes were captured by privateers, but a third voyage turned a profit. On a fourth trip, Paul sailed a covered boat and had a hired man aboard. Later, he acquired the *Surfish*, a twenty ton vessel, and made two trips to Newfoundland. In 1793 he built the *Mary*, a forty-two ton schooner, for another whaling voyage. Using the profits from this venture, he built a sixty-nine ton vessel called the *Ranger*. Two expeditions to the Chesapeake netted a clear profit.

In 1797 Cuffe purchased a farm on the Westport River for $3,500 and constructed a wharf and warehouse to accommodate his growing cargoes. By 1800 he had purchased a one-half interest in the *Hero*, a 162 ton barque, and in 1806 he further enlarged his tonnage by adding a three-quarters interest in the *Alpha*, a ship of 268 tons, and a one-half interest in the *Traveler*, a 109 ton brigantine. With a crew of sailors he voyaged to Wilmington, Savannah, and then across the Atlantic to Sweden, returning with a cargo to Philadelphia.

In 1811 Cuffe set sail for the Guinea Coast in Africa. He remained in Sierra Leone for three months, attending to missionary activities with an almost fanatical devotion, and exploring the country to determine opportunities for freed American blacks for colonization and trade. He hoped to encourage trade relations between Sierra Leone, America, and England, but the War of 1812 interrupted his plans for investment and development. In 1815, however, he made a fresh start. In that year, he launched the *Traveler* with a cargo of tobacco, soap, candles, naval stores, flour, and iron. There were thirty-eight passengers on board, and the cost of the expedition was $5,183.96. Contributions from the passengers amounted to only a little more than $1,000, and Cuffe made up the deficit out of profits from the sale of cargo. He purchased gumwood at $100 a ton for the return voyage and sold it in Albany, Poughkeepsie, and New York City. His trips to Africa were financial failures, but were continued due to his zeal for racial improvement. Nevertheless, from his fishing expeditions, coastwise trading, ocean shipping, and miscellaneous business activities, he accumulated a fortune at the time of his death of some $20,000. (A. L. Harris, *The Negro as Capitalist*, 1936; N. N. Sherwood, "Paul Cuffe," *Journal of Negro History*, vol. 8.)

CULLEN, HUGH ROY (July 3, 1881–July 4, 1957). Texas oil operator. Born in Denton County, Texas, son of Cicero Cullen and Louise Beck. His grandfather had emigrated from Georgia to Texas and fought in the Texas-Mexican War. He later became a judge and state senator, and introduced the bill into the state legislature that established the public educational system of the state. Hugh Cullen's father was a cattleman. Hugh Cullen was educated in the public schools for only three years, and started working at age twelve. When he was seventeen he entered the cattle business, becoming a buyer or factor operating in Texas and Oklahoma. In 1904 he entered into business for himself in Houston, later acquiring a seat on the Houston Cotton Exchange. He continued in that business until 1917.

In that year Cullen entered the oil business as an independent operator. He always remained an independent, while at the same time cooperating with others in the joint ownership and operation of various properties. His associates in various ventures were J. M. West, the Humble Oil and Refining Company, and Gulf Refining Company. He was also president of Quintana Petroleum Company, an operating company serving other oil corporations. He was always a "wildcatter," and was responsible for the discovery of a number of major oil fields. The first was the Pierce Junction Field in Harris County, Texas. Others were the Blue Ridge Field extension in Harrison County, the Thompson Field in Ft. Bend County, the Tom O'Conner Field in Refugio County, and the Washburn Field in La Salle County. Most important was his discovery at Humble, Texas, of an oil-bearing stratum running from Mexico to the Mississippi.

By the mid-1950s he owned some 350 producing wells with an annual production of about 3,000,000 barrels of oil. He was also a director of the Second National Bank of Houston and a large stockholder of the First National Bank of Houston. He has been called the "father" of the University of Houston; he served as chairman of its board of regents, and in 1948 donated to it oil royalties of several million dollars. He has also been president and supporter of the Houston Symphony, and vice-president of the Independent Petroleum Association and the Mid-Continent Oil and Gas Association. It is estimated that he has given away about 93 percent of his estimated $250 million fortune.

Called the "King of the Texas Wildcatters," Cullen was one of the pioneers of the oil business who discovered millions of barrels of oil. He established the Cullen Foundation in 1947 to aid educational, medical, and charitable institutions. The foundation receives the income from 18,511 acres of oil-bearing lands worth $160,000,000. He was a Democrat, but opposed Franklin Roosevelt in the 1930s and supported Eisenhower in 1952. He married Lillie Granz of Schulenburg, Texas, in 1903. They had five children. (*NCAB*, 47:42; G:437; *Current Biography*, 1955, 1957; E. W. Kilman and T. Wright, *Hugh Roy Cullen*, 1954.)

CULLEN, RICHARD J. (1872–November 13, 1948). Paper manufacturer, International Paper Company. He was born in Canada, and as a young mechanical engineer went to work in the engineering department of the Riordan Paper Mills, Ltd., later part of Canadian-International Paper Company. After working on the reconstruction of a pulp mill at Nerritton, Ontario, he designed and supervised the construction of the Riordan Mill at Hawkesbury, Ontario. In 1909 he came to the United States, as manager of the Cushnoc Paper Company in Augusta, Maine. A few years later he became vice-president and general manager of the Louisiana Fibreboard Company of Bogalusa, Louisiana. He designed the plant of the Century Roofing Company in New Orleans, and later designed and built the Bastrop Pulp and Paper Company at Bastrop, Louisiana, for the manufacture of Kraft pulp and paper. He also designed and built the Louisiana Pulp and Paper Company mill in Bogalusa.

These two companies were purchased by the International Paper Company, and Cullen became president of the Southern International Paper Company, a subsidiary. He was also vice-president of the parent company, International Paper, and had direct charge of the Southern Kraft Corporation until 1935. During this time he had become interested in the possibilities of mass producing an all-Kraft board for shipping cartons. Board of this type had been produced in limited quantities, but large-scale production was not attempted until the construction of International Paper's Panama City plant in Florida, which was designed by Cullen and opened in 1931. The plant had a capacity of 900 tons per day.

In 1936 Cullen succeeded Archibald R. Graustein as president of International Paper. Seven years later he was elected to the newly created post of chairman of the corporation. He held that position until he died in 1948. He was also chairman of the International Envelope Company and director of Canadian International Paper Company. Cullen is recognized as the pioneer in the development of Kraft paper and of the paper industry generally in the South. He was one of the first to open up the resources of the southern woodlands as the raw material for making Kraft paper, and he was also one of the first to promote the possibilities of the mass production of Kraft container board on Fourdrenier machines. (*New York Times*, November 14, 1948.)

CULLINAN, JOSEPH STEPHEN (December 31, 1860–March 11, 1937). Oil producer, Texas Company (Texaco). Born in Sharon, Pennsylvania, son of John Francis Cullinan and Mary Consadine, natives of Ireland who emigrated from County Clare. His father was an oil field worker who never did well financially. As a consequence, Joseph left school at age twelve to help support the family. They were then living in Oil Creek, Pennsylvania, where his parents had moved when he was eight years old. He drifted into oil field work, and joined the Standard Oil Company in 1882, where he got his first experience drilling, laying pipe lines, assembling tank "farms" and constructing refineries. He had risen to the position of manager of its natural gas interest when he resigned in 1896 to establish his own business, the Petroleum Iron Works at Washington, Pennsylvania, to manufacture oil tanks.

Cullinan's reputation was such that upon the discovery of oil at Consecara, Texas, he was asked by city officials to survey the field's possibilities. There, with the financial backing of Calvin N. Payne and Henry Clay Folger, both Standard Oil officials, he established in 1897 the first pipeline and refining company in Texas, J. S. Cullinan and Company; the predecessor of the Magnolia Petroleum Company. Though primarily a producer of illuminating oil, he and his brother, Dr. M. D. Cullinan, demonstrated the practicality of oil as a locomotive fuel on a St. Louis and Southwestern Railway engine. Other experiments provided the basis for later methods of asphalt and bitulithic paving.

The discovery of oil in the famous Spindletop Field in Beaumont, Texas, in 1901 presented greater opportunities, and Cullinan sold out at Consecara to go to Beaumont where he formed, on paper, a $50,000 corporation, the Texas Fuel Company, to refine and market the new-found oil. He also organized the Producers Oil Company, based on thirteen acres of Spindletop, to give the first company an assured source of fuel. The Texas Fuel Company went into operation in 1902, but proved too small, and its assets were transferred to a new corporation, the Texas Company, capitalized at $3,000,000. The firm's only advantage over its rivals was Cullinan's reputation as a successful oil man. Under his presidency, Texaco began expanding. After only eight months, it had invested $652,040 and was committed to additional heavy outlays.

The company was saved from the effects of the sudden failure of Spindletop production only by the timely Sour Lake discovery and Cullinan's ability to raise an additional one million dollars to take up an option there. Each succeeding major strike found Cullinan strategically located. His willingness to gamble was well illustrated by his decision to risk six million dollars on a pipeline from the great Oklahoma Glen Pool at a time when the company's assets were less than eight million dollars. The Texas Company was virtually a one-man show during Cullinan's presidency, with him running it from the field. When the board of directors moved the company's headquarters from Texas to New York in 1913, he resigned. By then, Texaco had over 4 percent of the nation's production, five refineries, and a fleet of freight cars and ocean-going tankers; it was capitalized at $30 million, and had assets of some $60 million.

Oil still remained Cullinan's primary occupation, and in 1914 he formed the Farmer's Oil Company, which was consolidated with other interests in

1916 into a holding company, the American Republic Corporation. It was originally capitalized at $30,000, but by 1927 had assets of $74 million, and at its height controlled nearly two million acres of oil land and had twenty subsidiary companies. But Cullinan still had time and energy enough to become president of Galena-Signal Oil Company in 1919. In 1927 a powerful group of stockholders unsuccessfully challenged his leadership of American Republic Corporation.

Cullinan was also very concerned about the industry's overproduction in the 1920s, and in 1928 proposed various solutions, including federal control of the oil fields, with the appointment of Herbert Hoover* or some other person as an "energy czar," and a program to coordinate the efforts of numerous control agencies. He turned the presidency of American Republic over to his son in 1928, but was one of the two receivers when the company was placed in receivership in 1932. When that was lifted in 1934, he became president again until 1936. He was one of the original members of the Food Administration during World War I, and remained a close friend of Herbert Hoover. During the 1930s he served on the National Advisory Committee of the American Liberty League. He married Lucie Haln of Lima, Ohio, in 1891, and they had five children. One of his sons, Craig Francis Cullinan (1894–   ), was president of American Petroleum Company of Texas from 1920 to 1926, vice-president of American Republic Corporation from 1926 to 1928, and president of the firm from 1928 to 1932. He was then president of American Petroleum Company from 1932 to 1936, when he again assumed the presidency of American Republic Corporation until 1950. (**A.** *DAB*, Supplement 2; *Who Was Who*, vol. 1; John O. King, *Joseph Stephen Cullinan*, 1970. **B.** Richard O'Conner, *The Oil Barons*, 1971; James Presley, *The Rise of the Texas Oilmen*, 1978; Anthony Sampson, *The Seven Sisters*, 1975.)

CULLMAN, JOSEPH FREDERICK III (April 9, 1912–   ). Tobacco company executive, Philip Morris. Born in New York City, son of Joseph F. Cullman Jr. and Frances Nathan Wolff. His great-grandfather, Ferdinand Cullman, came to the United States from Germany in 1848. Young Cullman was educated at Hotchkiss School and graduated from Yale University in 1935. During the summers he sold cigars in New York City for Webster Tobacco Company, which his father had acquired in the crash of 1929. In 1935 he was employed briefly as a clerk in a Schutte cigar store in New York, and then gained further experience in the tobacco industry by working in the Uppmann Cigar Factory in Havana, Cuba. Following that, he served in World War II, and in 1946 became vice-president of Benson and Hedges, tobacconists of New York City. He held this post until 1953, when he was made executive vice-president. Controlling interest in the Benson and Hedges company had been purchased by Cullman Brothers, Incorporated in 1941 for about $850,000. The latter corporation was an investment firm in which his father was a partner.

Benson and Hedges had increased greatly in value by 1954 when Cullman Brothers, Incorporated traded its interest to Philip Morris, Incorporated for stock valued at $22.4 million. In return, Philip Morris acquired Benson and Hedges and Parliament cigarette brands, as well as twenty lesser known brands, and Cullman became a vice-president of Philip Morris. In the next year he was made executive vice-president, and at the end of 1957 was named president and chief executive officer. In 1967 he became chairman of the board and chief executive officer, in which position he still served in 1979.

Under his guidance Philip Morris' sales rose from $440 million to $2.6 billion in 1973, and profits increased from $17.4 million to $148.6 million. Unit production in American factories was increased from more than 42 billion cigarettes in 1957 to more than 150 billion in 1973. He spent $45 million in capital expenditures in the first five years of his presidency in modernizing Philip Morris' manufacturing establishment, replacing nearly all its cigarette-making equipment with the most efficient machines available.

A program of corporate diversification was also begun in 1957, when the company acquired Milprint, Incorporated of Milwaukee, Wisconsin, a basic supplier of packaging material to the industry, and its subsidiary, Nicolet Paper Company, DePere, Wisconsin. In 1958 Philip Morris acquired Polymer Industries, Springfield, Connecticut, a chemical firm specializing in packaging adhesives and finishing chemicals. Two years later they acquired A. S. R. Products, Company, Staunton, Virginia, and in 1961, reestablished the American Safety Razor Company in Staunton as a division. Subsequent acquisitions included Miller Brewing Company in 1970; and the Mission Viejo Company of California, a land development company, in 1972.

Despite these achievements, it was in cigarette marketing that Cullman made his major contribution to the growth of Philip Morris. Shortly after he was named executive vice-president in 1955, he assumed the task of capturing the filter-tip market with Marlboro cigarettes. For thirty years Marlboros had been a premium priced cigarette appealing mainly to women. He converted them into a popularly priced, full-flavored filter-tip with a new brand appeal intended to attract men to the product. He developed a new Marlboro package, with a red and white flip-top box, the first major packaging innovation in the cigarette industry in a half a century. The new brand image was initially established through the "Marlboro Man"—a tattooed outdoorsman. With this image, Cullman created one of the most durable and memorable themes in advertising. Experiencing phenomenal growth over the next few years, Marlboro became the best selling brand of cigarettes in the world in 1972. During this same time, other Philip Morris brands also moved up rapidly in their respective categories. Parliament became a leader in the high filtration segment, Benson and Hedges 100's was a leader in the one hundred millimeter category, and Virginia Slims was the best selling brand designed for women.

Cullman also directed the company's international expansion, and in 1972 Philip Morris was the world's largest exporter of cigarettes and the second largest publicly held cigarette company in the world. In 1955 he had become the first president of the company's newly formed international division, Philip Morris Overseas, and he held this position until 1957. Four years later it became Philip Morris International, which marketed more than 140 brands of cigarettes in 162 countries and territories. In 1958 it acquired Benson and Hedges (Canada) Ltd., and in 1960 completed construction of a new plant near Toronto, Ontario. In 1959 it acquired a substantial interest in C. A. Tabacalena Nacional Venezuela, which was amalgamated with Philip Morris' C. A. Venezalona de Tobaca in 1961. The company's other foreign affiliates include companies in West Germany, Sweden, Belgium, England, Switzerland, the Canary Islands, Nigeria, Australia, India, Pakistan, Argentina, and Brazil.

Cullman was also a director of IBM World Trade Corporation, Bankers Trust Company, Ford Motor Company, Braniff Airways, and Levi Strauss and Company. He was a member of the Tobacco Institute, and from 1968 to 1972 was chairman of the organization and served as the chief spokesman of the tobacco industry. Of the Jewish faith, he married Susan Lehman, a daughter of Harold M. Lehman of New York City, in 1935. They had one daughter. His brother, Edgar M. Cullman (b. 1918) was president of Culbro Corporation, a diversified consumer products company. His cousin, Hugh Cullman (b. 1923) has been vice-president of Philip Morris since 1966, and president of Philip Morris International since 1967. His uncle, Howard S. Cullman (b. 1891) was earlier president of Cullman Brothers, and became a Port Authority Commissioner in New York. (**A.** *NCAB*, M:169. **B.** Mira Wilkins, *The Emergence of Multinational Enterprise*, 1970.)

CURTIS, CYRUS HERMANN KOTZSCHMAN (June 18, 1850–June 7, 1933). Publisher, Curtis Publishing Company. Born in Portland, Maine, son of Cyrus Libby Curtis and Samone Ann Cummings. Young Curtis was forced to leave high school after his first year because of the loss of the family home and possessions in the great Portland fire of 1866. He worked as an errand boy until he was nineteen, when he obtained a job as a salesman for a dry goods store in Boston. Curtis next went into the newspaper advertising business with the *Travelers Guide* and then with the *Boston Times* and *Independent*. In 1872, with very little capital, he established the *Peoples Ledger*, a weekly that featured a complete story in each issue rather than serialization, which was then the rage. Each story was a reprint of one that had first appeared some thirty years earlier. He continued this operation for six years, taking it to Philadelphia in 1876 because of the cheaper printing costs there. Two years later he sold it and became advertising manager of the weekly edition of the *Philadelphia Press*. In 1879 he began publication of the *Tribune and Farmer*, a four-page weekly with a subscription rate of fifty cents a year.

While running the *Tribune and Farmer*, Curtis established a department devoted to subjects of interest to women, which was written by his wife. This became so successful that in 1883 he decided to publish it as a separate monthly supplement to his magazine. The first issue of the *Ladies Journal and Practical Housekeeper* appeared in December, 1883. It contained an illustrated serial, articles on flower culture, fashion notes, advice on the care of children, and articles on cooking, needlework, and handicrafts. The supplement, under the editorship of Mrs. Curtis, was immediately successful. While it had taken five years for the *Tribune and Farmer* to reach a circulation of 48,000, the *Ladies' Home Journal*, as it came to be called, had 25,000 subscribers by the end of its first year. Curtis therefore decided to sell his interest in the *Tribune and Farmer* and devoted all his attention to the new magazine.

Curtis then put into operation a series of policies that would make the *Journal* an astounding success and would become the basis of success for mass circulation magazines in the future. He first went after well-known contributors for the *Journal*, and his great coup was securing the services of Louisa M. Alcott, which attracted other popular authors to the new magazine. He advertised the new magazine extensively, securing a large amount of credit from the advertising agency of N. W. Ayer and Son for this purpose. Within six months the circulation of the *Ladies' Home Journal* had reached 50,000. In another six months it reached 100,000. With circulation at 700,000, he enlarged the magazine to twice its former size and raised subscriptions to one dollar a year, deliberately losing thousands of subscribers in order to stabilize circulation and consolidate his gains. He continued to spend massive amounts of money on advertising, investing more than a half a million dollars in it during the *Journal*'s first five years of existence.

In 1889 Curtis hired Edward W. Bok (1863–1930), a Dutch-born former employee of Charles Scribner's Sons in New York, as editor of the *Journal*. Becoming the youngest and highest paid magazine editor of the time, Bok took over the *Journal* in the midst of great publicity and fanfare. For the next thirty years Bok was to guide the editorial fortunes of *Ladies' Home Journal*, making it a "great clearing house of information" for women. Continuing in the traditions of Curtis, Bok obtained writings by William Dean Howells, Mark Twain, Bret Harte, and others for the magazine, making it well known for its high literary standards. He also published serious articles by outstanding public figures such as Grover Cleveland, William H. Harrison, Theodore Roosevelt, William Howard Taft, and Woodrow Wilson. Bok involved the *Journal* in many of the most controversial issues of the day, including woman's suffrage, municipal reform, sex, and venereal disease. The latter subject, breaking a long-standing taboo in

Victorian America, cost the *Journal* many subscribers, but Curtis stuck by his editor.

Curtis had a rare ability for choosing capable editors, then leaving them alone to run the magazine. When advertisers, subscribers, and friends put pressure on Curtis to stop the *Journal*'s articles on sex, he gave them all the same reply: "Go talk to Mr. Bok about it. He is the editor." He also spared no expense in getting his editors the finest materials to work with. He approved Bok's request for new four-color printing presses costing $800,000 without even bothering to read the cost statement Bok had prepared for him. By 1893 the circulation of the *Journal* had reached a record-breaking one million, and when Curtis died, forty years later, it stood at over two and a half million.

In 1897 Curtis purchased the *Saturday Evening Post* for only $1,000. A venerable and prestigious journal, the *Post* had been losing money for a number of years and had only 2,000 subscribers in 1897. It was the nearly unanimous opinion of other publishers and editors at the time that Curtis had made a bad mistake in buying the *Post*. Nonetheless, Curtis over the next five years poured over $1.25 million into the *Post*, engaging in extensive advertising and paying top prices for literary contributions. As with the *Journal*, Curtis had the foresight and good luck to hire a dynamic and promotive-minded editor for the *Saturday Evening Post*. He had hired George Horace Lorimer (1867–1937) as an interim editor in 1897, but two years later made him editor-in-chief, a post he would retain until 1936. Lorimer was the son of George Claude Lorimer, one of the most powerful Baptist evangelical ministers in America. Young Lorimer had earlier been closely associated with Philip D. Armour* in his packing house, and retained a life-long love of business.

The major competitors of the *Post* in 1899 were *Harper's Weekly, Frank Leslie's*, and *Colliers*, each of which sold for ten cents and was concerned almost solely with the news, news pictures, and politics in competition with the newspapers. The *Post* cut its price to five cents and made no attempt to compete with these magazines or with newspapers. Instead, Lorimer and Curtis determined that Americans would read and like a certain type of story, certain types of articles, and a soothing, somewhat humorous type of reporting. Making its primary appeal to the intelligent businessman, the *Post* eschewed both the sensational and the intellectual. The businessman and his family were given action stories; romances; stories of business; the life stories of successful men in action; articles on economic and political subjects that were at once informing and entertaining; comments on current events; and a bit of serious and sentimental poetry. Lorimer's ambitious master plan was to create a magazine that would interpret America to itself, and he hired prominent writers (as had been done at *Ladies' Home Journal*) for this task.

Under the guidance of Curtis and Lorimer, *Saturday Evening Post* became the largest-selling weekly magazine in the world, with circulation rising from 2,000 in 1899 to more than three million by 1937. For years it was virtually without a serious competitor, and it was seen and read everywhere. Its influence was pervasive and measurable, and the magazine was continually improved. The *Post*, as did other Curtis publications, essentially glorified the middle classes of America, especially the small businessman and his family. Its success was due as much to its failure to criticize as to its ability to report and portray. Curtis himself was a product of the middle class, and he and his magazines naturally catered to those groups which he knew and understood and with which he was at home. The *Post* upheld free enterprise and competition and the right of the individual to work for profit. It saw monopolistic control, whether by business, labor, or the government, as dangerous and undemocratic. To a large extent Curtis and Lorimer succeeded in their master plan, as the *Post* reflected the United States of the first half of the twentieth century to itself, with all its strengths and weaknesses.

The *Ladies' Home Journal* and the *Saturday Evening Post* made Curtis Publishing Company into the wealthiest and most successful magazine publishers in the world. At one time they took in $2 out of every $5 spent on national advertising magazines, and in doing so they contributed substantially to the development of the low-priced, mass-circulation periodical. Curtis had demonstrated more vividly than any other publisher the principle on which most large circulations of the twentieth century were based: that by selling a magazine for less than its cost of production, a publisher could become wealthy on the advertising which a large circulation attracted. All of his publishing ventures, however, were not financially successful. In 1911 he acquired the *Country Gentleman*. At the time the few national farm magazines did not cover the business side of farming, and Curtis thought that a business magazine for farmers, who were becoming increasingly more scientific and businesslike, would have the same broad appeal as his earlier ventures. It took six years and an investment of some two million dollars to put *Country Gentleman* on a sound financial footing, but it never became a big money-maker. In 1913 Curtis acquired the historic Philadelphia *Public Ledger*, and founded an evening edition with it. To these he added the *Philadelphia Inquirer* and the New York *Evening Post*; but none of these acquisitions proved to be successful, and all were sold after losing enormous amounts of money.

Another of Curtis' great contributions to his company and to magazine publishing in general was his recognition of the important part that advertising was to play in the American economy. As evidence of this recognition, Curtis Publishing Company engaged in much of the pioneer work in market research. In 1911 Curtis hired Charles C. Parlin,* a Wisconsin high school principal, and established a Division of Commercial Research in the company's advertising department. The idea was to provide advertisers with knowledge of where their markets lay, how they were constituted, and how best to reach them. This, of course, would help establish the value of the Curtis magazines for reaching and retaining these markets. The first studies were comprehensive reports on entire industries, with Parlin issuing a 460-page report on agricultural implements in 1911. This was followed by a multi-volume department store study in 1912 and a survey of the automobile industry in 1914. Others followed. This kind of "commercial research" was new and welcomed by business, which had few other sources of dependable information at that time.

Curtis resigned as president of Curtis Publications in 1932, being succeeded by Lorimer, but remained chairman of the board until he died. He gave two million dollars to Franklin Institute, $1.25 million to Drexel Industries, and another million to the University of Pennsylvania, among others. Politically, he was an ultraconservative, but had little active interest in politics. A Unitarian, he married Louisa Knapp of Boston in 1878. She died in 1910, and in that same year he married Mrs. Kate Stanwood Cutter Pillsbury of Milwaukee, Wisconsin. His daughter, Mary Louise, married Edward W. Bok.

Curtis, Bok, and Lorimer all died in the 1930s and with their death the vitality was sapped from Curtis publications. In 1942 *Life* magazine passed *Saturday Evening Post* in circulation, and during the 1950s *Ladies' Home Journal* began losing its market share to newer and more dynamic women's magazines. In 1929 the *Post* and *Journal* together carried 40 percent of all U.S. magazine advertising, but by the 1960s the company was losing money heavily. Finally, in 1968, Curtis sold the *Journal*, and in 1969 ceased publication of the *Post*. In the former year its losses had reached $20 million and Curtis Publications was delisted by the New York Stock Exchange. A Curtis director called it the "greatest corporate disaster in American history." (**A.** *DAB*, Supplements 1 and 2; *NCAB*, 24:26; *New York Times*, June 7, 1933; *Who Was Who*, vol. 1; Edward W. Bok, *A Man From Maine*, 1923. **B.** Frank L. Mott, *A History of American Magazines*, 5 vols., pp. 1938ff; Theodore Peterson, *Magazines in the Twentieth Century*, 1964; John Tebbel, *George Horace Lorimer and the* Saturday Evening Post, 1948; James P. Wood, *Magazines in the United States*, 3rd. ed., 1971.)

CURTISS, GLENN HAMMOND (May 21, 1878–July 23, 1930). Pioneer aircraft inventor and manufacturer, Curtiss-Wright Aircraft. Born in Hammondsport, New York, son of Frank R. Curtiss and Lia Andrews. His father sold and mended harnesses; he died when Glenn was six years old. Young Curtiss completed grammar school in the local public school, and then worked in Rochester, New York, as a messenger boy in a telegraph company, and at stenciling in the Kodak Company. He took up bicycle racing, and for three years won every race he entered. He then turned to the motorcycle. In 1902 he established the G. H. Curtiss Manufacturing

Company at Hammondsport to make and sell motors, motorcycles, and accessories. In the next few years he continued to win motorcycle races and establish land speed records.

About this time his interest in aeronautics was aroused by Thomas Scott Baldwin, a dirigible balloonist who gave Curtiss an order for a motor. For several years Curtiss did a considerable business with balloonists. Baldwin moved his balloon plant to Hammondsport, and the two men built the first army dirigible, which was tested in 1905 with Curtiss as engineer and Baldwin as pilot. The craft was accepted by the government. Curtiss then turned his attention to airplanes, his interest having been generated from a meeting with Alexander Graham Bell in Nova Scotia. In 1907, Bell and his wife founded the Aerial Experiment Association at Hammondsport, with Curtiss as director of experiments. Curtiss built an airplane there, the *June Bug*, which was flown in 1908, winning him the *Scientific American* trophy.

In 1910, at Atlantic City, New Jersey, by dropping oranges from the airplane instead of bombs Curtiss demonstrated the potential use of the airplane in war. In the next year he established a flying school for army and navy officers at San Diego, California, and later schools at Hammondsport and Miami, Florida. About this time he made his first attempt to develop a sea plane, and he was successful in 1911. The U.S. Navy bought two of these planes, and later England, Germany, Italy, France, and Russia did so. In 1912 he invented the flying boat, and in the same year built the first heavier-than-air flying craft designed for transatlantic flight. In 1913 he was awarded the Langley Medal by the Smithsonian Institution for his hydroplane.

Curtiss' most noteworthy invention was the aileron, a device for maintaining the lateral balance of the airplane. But the Wright Brothers contended that it violated their patent, and a long court fight ensued. Curtiss was granted a patent on it in 1911, but the dispute did not end until 1917. World War I brought mass production to the aircraft industry for the first time, and more than 5,000 "Jennies," Curtiss' standard airplanes, were made during these years. The Curtiss plant was enormously expanded, and the Curtiss Aeroplane and Motor Company, with Curtiss as chairman of the board, was established. At the time it was America's greatest aircraft laboratory, and was located in Garden City, Long Island. It was here that he developed the *Wasp*, holder of the world's records for speed, climb, and altitude.

With the end of the war the government, despite the protests of aircraft manufacturers, decided to sell off its surplus airplanes. This dealt a crippling blow to the industry, and after that time Curtiss' connection with his companies was slight. He turned his attention to real estate near Miami, Florida, and the development of Hialeah Country Club Estates. In 1929 the Curtiss Company merged with the Wright Aeronautical Company to form the Curtiss-Wright Company. He was a director of this until his death. He married Lena P. Neff of Hammondsport in 1898 and they had two children. (**A.** *DAB*, Supplement 1; *NCAB*, 22:195; *New York Times*, July 24, 1930;

Who Was Who, vol. 1. **B.** G. R. Simonson, *History of the American Aircraft Industry*, 1968.)

CUSHING, JOHN PERKINS (April 22, 1787–April 12, 1862). China merchant. Born in Boston, Massachusetts, son of Robert Cushing and Ann Maynard Perkins. His ancestors had been in Massachusetts since 1638. Early in life Cushing became a clerk in the mercantile firm of Perkins and Company, established by his uncles, James and Thomas Hansayd Perkins,* for carrying on trade with China and the Northwest Coast. In 1803 Cushing accompanied Ephraim Bumstead, the oldest apprentice in the firm, on a voyage to Canton, China. Bumstead was taken ill and returned home, so Cushing, at age sixteen, was left, to carry on the business in China. Perkins allowed him to act as resident agent for the company there, and he was known as "Ku-Shing" in China. He was soon admitted to a partnership in the business and became the wealthiest and most respected foreign merchant in the country.

Tea and silk were in heavy demand in the United States; in return for these the Chinese took furs and candlewood. Cushing remained in China for nearly thirty years, amassing a fortune which was colossal for the time. He returned to Boston in 1830, in ill health, and built a large mansion in the city, with seven Chinese servants, a superb wine cellar, and elegant gardens. He then started to invest in banks, canals, and factories, and then in railroads. Since there was an enormous demand for capital at the time, Cushing was in a position to have a major influence on future developments. He hired a fellow China merchant, William Sturgis,* as an advisor on his investments, and tripled his already impressive fortune before he died. In 1851 it was estimated that he had an estate of some two million dollars.

·On his return to Boston he married Mary Louise Gardiner, daughter of Rev. John S. J. Gardiner, rector of Trinity Church in Boston. (**A.** *DAB; Who Was Who*, vol. H. **B.** Tyler Dennett, *Americans in Eastern Asia*, 1941; Foster Rhea Dulles, *The Old China Trade*, 1930; Ben Seligman, *The Potentates*, 1971.)

CUTTEN, ARTHUR (July 6, 1870–June 24, 1936). Stock market speculator. Born in Guelph, Ontario, Canada, son of Walter Hoyt Cutten and Annie MacFadden. He was educated in Guelph and came to the United States in 1888, at age eighteen. Settling in Chicago, he became a bookkeeper, and by 1896 had accumulated $600, which he invested in a seat on the Board of Trade. His great speculations began in the years after World War I, and during that time his activities were on a scale comparable to that of other great speculators, Jack Cudahy,* Norman B. Ream,* and Philip Armour.*

His first early success came in 1924, when he made a profit of about two million dollars. He then transferred his attention to the stock exchange and became one of the group known as "the big ten" who, with another syndicate, were reputed to have bought and sold half the stocks turned over on the New York Exchange on some of the important trading days. Despite his successes, he insisted on being called a "cash merchant and dirt farmer," not a speculator. He owned an 800,000 acre estate in the western suburbs of Chicago, but preferred to call it a farm that paid its own way.

Cutten was one of the fastest traders in the grain pit of Chicago. He did his own trading, and frequently had a half dozen houses trading for him at the same time. Within ten years after joining the Board of Trade he was a millionaire, with most of his big deals on the bull rather than the bear side of the market. All these speculative actions were planned from a small office near the Board of Trade in Chicago. His name did not even appear on the door. He was reputed to have lost as much as $50 million in the Crash of 1929. This was exaggerated, but he did say he was down to his last $17 million after the crash. A banking commission investigating the stock market in 1933 found that he and his colleagues shared $12 million from a deal in Continental Oil securities.

His activities were so great that, together with other giants of finance, he came before a Senate committee, and in 1935 was found guilty of violating the Grain Futures Act. He was suspended from trading on the grain markets for two years. He was also declared to have made false reports of his holdings and to have concealed his position in the market in 1930 and 1931, in order to manipulate the price of grain and thereby reap large profits. Cutten fought the decision and won out later that year when the Supreme Court ruled out the previous verdict; he was restored to all activities. It was estimated that he made more than $100 million in his various speculations. He was one of the boldest traders in grain, a man who took gains and losses with equanimity and who preferred to keep in the background. He was a director of Sinclair Oil, Baldwin Locomotive, Standard Oil of Indiana, Continental Chicago Corporation, and the Merchants and Manufacturers Securities Company.

He claimed to have many philanthropies in Guelph, and was a trustee of Northwestern University. He married Maude Boomer of Chicago in 1906. Despite his long association with the grain market, he had no love for it. He said, "If I had a son I would keep him away from the market. . . . There are so many wrecks down there." (**A.** *New York Times*, June 25, 1936. **B.** Robert Sobel, *The Great Bull Market: Wall Street in the 1920's.*)

D

DALY, MARCUS (December 5, 1841–November 12, 1900). Copper mining magnate, Anaconda Copper Company. Born in Ireland, son of Luke and Mary Daly. His parents were very poor and he had little opportunity for formal education. At age fifteen he came to America, working for a while around New York and then going to California, where he toiled as a miner with a pick and shovel. But it was not long before he became an expert on mining practices, and after a time he entered the service of James G. Fair* and of John W. Mackay* in Nevada. While working there, his ability attracted the attention of Walker Brothers, and in 1876 they sent him to Butte, Montana. There he purchased the Alice silver mine in partnership with them, soon selling his interest for $30,000. He subsequently went to California to get aid from friends there for mining prospects he had discovered in Montana. He induced George Hearst* and others to share his convictions and they bought the Anaconda silver mine. The silver gave out quickly, but underneath it was a rich vein of copper. Daly closed the mine and quickly bought up others in the neighborhood, and then started the great copper mining operations which were to make Butte and the Anaconda Copper Company famous.

Daly rapidly expanded his activities in Montana. He mined coal for his furnaces and acquired huge tracts of timber where he cut the wood for his mines. He built a railway from Butte to Anaconda, established banks, built power plants and irrigation systems, and encouraged enterprises. During a span of twenty years he developed an enormous fortune. By the 1890s the development of electric power and light had created a demand for copper that made Butte one of the world's leading copper centers. But Daly's dramatic feud with William A. Clark* attracted more publicity during this period. At first the two men had been fast friends, but the latter's decision to run for Congress in 1888 brought on a bitter battle.

Daly had established the *Anaconda Standard* and made it into the best newspaper in the state. Both Daly and Clark were Democrats, and both built up powerful political machines composed of their employees and businessmen who were dependent upon their enterprises. Daly had tried for ten years to thwart Clark's political ambitions, and with his newspaper played a major role in Clark's election defeat in 1888. Then, in 1893, he prevented his election as U.S. senator. When Clark was finally elected to the U.S. Senate in 1899, Daly gave $25,000 to carry on the fight to the Senate Committee on Elections, claiming fraud on Clark's part. This forced Clark's resignation and intensified the bitterness between the two men. Meanwhile, Daly gave lavishly to any cause he favored. He funded the first Democratic campaign in Montana with a donation of $40,000, and spent over a half million dollars to make Anaconda the state capital, with Clark pushing for Helena. Clark won that battle. In 1896 Daly gave $50,000 to William Jennings Bryan's campaign for the presidency.

Daly built a home in the upper Bitter Root Valley and developed one of the finest ranches in the West. He also gave a start to fruit growing in the valley. His last achievement was the combination of a number of mining and lumber companies into the Amalgamated Copper Company, capitalized at $75 million. He married Margaret Evans in 1872. (**A.** *DAB; New York Times*, November 13, 1900; *Who Was Who*, vol. 1; H. Minar Shoebotham, *Anaconda: Life of Marcus Daly, Copper King*, 1956. **B.** C. B. Glasscock, *The War of the Copper Kings*, 1935; Richard Peterson, *The Bonanza Kings*, 1977.)

DANFORTH, WILLIAM H. (September 10, 1870–December 24, 1955). Cereals manufacturer, Ralston-Purina Company. Born in Charleston, Missouri, son of Albert Hampton Danforth and Rebecca Lynn. He was educated in area schools and received a degree in mechanical engineering from Washington University in St. Louis in 1892. His father had told him to "get into a business that fills a need for lots of people, something they need all year round in good times and bad," so in 1894 Danforth opened a feed business near the St. Louis levee. In the store he bought grains from area farmers, mixed them in 175 pound bags, and sold them back to farmers as feed for their horses and mules. This was the basis of the Ralston-Purina Company, which over the next several years would develop mills in St. Louis and 32 other cities in the United States and Canada.

A major reason for the rapid growth of Ralston-Purina was Danforth's promotional genius. Purina in the company's name was coined from an early Danforth slogan, "Where Purity is Paramount"; another of his early slogans was "If Chicken Chowder won't make your hens lay, they must be roosters." The Ralston in the company name came from a Dr. Ralston, who headed a prominent health club at the turn of the century. Danforth got him to endorse a wheat cereal for the company, and his name was incorporated in the firm's standard. In later years Danforth developed the famous Chow brand name, which came out of his experiences as a representative of the YMCA ministering to troops in France during World War I. Noticing the enthusiastic reception of the troops to "chow call," he replaced the word feed with chow on his return. The firm's famous checkerboard logo also came from Danforth's personal experience. He grew up near a family in which the children always wore clothes their mother made from a checkerboard material, giving them a distinctive appearance. Danforth felt the checkerboard pattern would distinctively identify his products in a similar manner, so it went on everything the company produced. Danforth even occasionally wore a red checkerboard jacket to work, with matching socks.

Danforth retired from active management of Ralston-Purina in 1932, turning the reins over to his son Donald. The great growth of the firm, however, came after World War II, and particularly after Danforth's death in 1955. During these years it became the world's largest producer of commercial feeds for poultry and livestock, and in recent years has also become king of the pet food market. Agricultural products accounted for about one-half of the firm's sales in 1979, with another 20 percent from pet foods. Most of the rest of the sales came from distribution to restaurants and from a grocery products line that includes Chicken of the Sea tuna, Chex cereals, and Ry Krisp and Bremner crackers and cookies. The great bonanza for Ralston-Purina in the pet food market came with the shift from moist items packed in cans toward dry goods. Purina Dog Chow and Cat Chow both became world market leaders. The company had sales of $4.6 billion in 1979, making it the sixth largest food processor in the United States. But it was number one in animal feeds and dog and cat foods, having some 70,000 employees.

Danforth also made a wide reputation for himself and his firm as enlightened exponents of liberal labor policies. In the early years his interest in employees' welfare largely took the form of leading his workers in prayer and calisthenics every day, but in later years the company installed full-scale employee benefits which were a model for the industry. After 1932 Danforth devoted most of his time to the Danforth Foundation, which he and his wife had established in 1927. The foundation has gained wide respect from analysts for the calibre of its giving. Waldemar A. Neilson, in his book on major foundations, called it "creative, socially pertinent, and professionally competent." In its early years the foundation gave much of its funds to religious education, and more recently became a major supporter of black colleges. It also took the lead in urban redevelopment in St. Louis. Danforth helped form the Christian Carolers Association in St. Louis in 1911, and was its president for 40 years. He was also president of the American Youth Foundation, and a director of the First National Bank of St. Louis, the St. Louis Union Trust Company, New York Life Insurance Company, and the Illinois Terminal Railroad. A deeply religious man, he taught Sunday School at his local church for a number of years. He married Ada Bush in 1894 and they had a daughter and a son, the latter of whom succeeded him as head of Ralston-Purina. His three grandsons are all prominent in the affairs of St. Louis: Donald Danforth Jr. is president of Danforth Agri-Resources, Incorporated, a family investment company; William H. Danforth II is chancellor of Washington University; and John Danforth is U.S. senator from Missouri. (**A.** *New York Times*, December 25, 1955; *Who Was Who*, vol. 3. **B.** Milton Moskowitz et al., *Everybody's Business*, 1980; Waldemar A. Nielson, *The Big Foundations*, 1972.)

DAVIS, ARTHUR VINING (May 30, 1867–November 17, 1962). Aluminum manufacturer, Aluminum Company of America (Alcoa). Born in Sharon, Massachusetts, son of Rev. Derley B. Davis and Mary F. Vining. He was educated at Hyde Park, Massachusetts, and Roxbury Latin School in Boston, and graduated from Amherst College in 1888. After graduation he took a job with a new company that was planning to produce a new light metal, regarded at that time as a more or less mystical substance. On Thanksgiving Day, 1888, he and Charles Martin Hall, the discoverer of the process, poured out commercial aluminum, which they hoped to sell at two dollars a pound, in 1,000 pound lots. The original company was known as the Pittsburgh Reduction Company, acquiring the Alcoa name in 1908. Its growth continued steadily, and with the discovery of new uses for aluminum — such as the vast market in the aviation field alone — production soared and the price decreased. What sold for two dollars in 1888 sold for eighteen cents in 1951.

Davis flooded the country with aluminum pots and pans when other companies displayed no interest in manufacturing household utensils. Davis made them himself, hired three college students, and sent them out to peddle their wares to businessmen. He became president of Alcoa in 1910, and chairman of the board in 1928. At one time he was also president of U.S. Aluminum Company and the Aluminum Ore Company.

Alcoa's domination of the aluminum industry had the company in continual conflict with the federal government. In 1913 Davis admitted to a House inquiry committee that an international agreement covered the aluminum industry. In 1924 and 1926 charges of illegal combinations and lawsuits bedeviled the company, and Davis stated in 1924 that Alcoa actually consisted of Andrew W.* and Richard B. Mellon.* From 1913 until 1937, when the government filed its antitrust suit to force Alcoa executives to divest their holdings in the Aluminum Company, Ltd. of Canada, the company faced incessant challenges from the government. For the Canadian company, Davis created a model town in northern Canada for working families. A giant dam was built at Keragami on the Saguenay River to provide power for the Duke Price Paper Mills and for the new $100 million aluminum plant at Arvida. A town of detached houses was built and sold to employees at moderate prices and low interest rates.

Davis worked closely with the U.S. government during both world wars to see that there would be no shortage of aluminum. He played a prominent role in the aluminum production drive during World War II, and helped attain an output vital to the Allied achievement of air superiority. For this work he got a Presidential Certificate of Merit. His fortune at one time was estimated at $350 million, and after 1948 he acquired vast real estate holdings in Florida. He resigned as chairman and director of Alcoa in 1957, at age 90. During the remaining years of his life he devoted himself to the expansion of his Florida real estate interests.

His enterprises reportedly stimulated the greatest Florida boom since World War II. His purchases of 125,000 acres included one-eighth of Dade County. He also bought 30,000 acres on Eleuthera Island in the Bahamas, where he developed a resort. He owned an ice cream plant, vegetable farms, a cement plant, a road building company, a steel fabricating plant, a furniture plant, and an airline. He purchased the Boca Raton Hotel and Club for $22.5 million, and property in Sarasota on the Gulf Coast for $13.5 million. He was a director of Union Trust of Pittsburgh, Logan Trust Company of New Kensington, Pennsylvania, Pennsylvania Water and Power Company, Mellon National Bank and Trust, Aluminum Goods Manufacturing Company, Canada Life Assurance Company, Bucyrus-Erie Corporation, American Brake Shoe Company, and the Waldorf-Astoria Hotel Corporation.

Davis married Florence Holman in 1896. She passed away in 1908, and four years later he married Mrs. Elizabeth Hawkins Weiman, who died in 1933. He was a Republican and an Episcopalian. (**A.** *New York Times*, November 18, 1962; May 9, 1964; July 7, 1967; *Who Was Who*, vols. 4 and 5. **B.** Charles Carr, *Alcoa: An American Enterprise*, 1952.)

DAVIS, CHARLES STROUT (February 2, 1877–July 2, 1954). Auto parts manufacturer, Borg-Warner Corporation. Born in Terre Haute, Indiana, son of Daniel Nicholas Davis and Margaret Deith Hyde. His father was employed in the rolling mill and coal mining industries of the Middle West. Charles Davis graduated from Harvard in 1899, and for eighteen months was on the editorial staff of the *New York Times*. In 1901 he returned to Indiana to join his father in the Davis Coal Company, miners and wholesalers of coal. He remained there until 1907 when he became secretary-treasurer of Glascock Brothers, which he had helped to organize. The firm made bottle coolers and dispensers in Muncie, Indiana. In 1918 Davis became president of the firm, and remained as chairman of the board until his death. In 1919 he was named secretary-treasurer of the Warner Gear Company of Muncie, which made transmissions, differentials, and steering gears for automobiles.

This company was merged with fourteen other manufacturers of auto parts in 1928 to form the Borg-Warner Corporation, of which he was chairman of the board in 1928–1929 and president until 1950. He then served as chairman of the board again until his death. During his presidency he greatly expanded the company's operations until it controlled twenty-seven subsidiaries and operated thirty manufacturing plants in eight states, Canada, and England. It produced gear shafts, overdrives, and fully automated transmissions for the auto industry, along with a complete line of household appliances under the name Norge. It also produced aircraft and farm equipment parts and military equipment. From 1928 to 1950 the assets of the firm grew from $19 million to $161 million, the working capital from $14 million to $92 million, and the net earnings from $7 million to $29 million.

A Baptist and a Republican, Davis was president of the social service bureau of Muncie from 1920 to 1923. In 1904 he married Florence Grace Johnson, daughter of Abbott Livingston Johnson, one of the founders of Warner Gear Company. They had three children. (*NCAB*, D:345; 44:564; *Who Was Who*, vol. 3.)

DAVIS, FRANCIS BREESE JR. (September 16, 1883–December 22, 1962). Chemical and rubber company executive, DuPont and United States Rubber. Born in Ft. Edward, New York, son of Francis Breese Davis and Julia Underwood. He was educated at an academy in Glens Falls, New York, and graduated from Sheffield Scientific School at Yale in 1906. For a short time he worked in the office of the city engineer of New Haven, Connecticut, and then with Empire Engineering Corporation, on construction of a section of the New York State Barge Canal. From 1907 to 1909 he was employed in the maintenance of right-of-way department of the Philadelphia, Baltimore and Washington Railroad, a subsidiary of the Pennsylvania Railroad.

In the latter year, Mr. Davis joined DuPont as a construction engineer at the Berlin Black Powder factory, near Noosic, Pennsylvania. In 1911 he transferred to the engineering department of the DuPont headquarters in Wilmington, Delaware. Two years later he was made superintendent of the company's sporting powder division, and after the outbreak of World War I he was successively placed in charge of construction of a gun cotton factory at Hopewell, Virginia, and the building of the Old Hickory factory near Nashville, Tennessee, and was engaged in the operation of the DuPont smokeless powder factory in New Jersey. After the war he became vice-president of DuPont Chemical Company and had the task of disposing of many DuPont factories that had been built during the war to meet military needs. In 1921 he was made assistant general manager of the Saginaw Division of General Motors, but a year later came back to DuPont as general manager of the Pyrolic division, which manufactured plastics. In 1923 he was made president of a DuPont subsidiary, the DuPont Viscaloid Company, into which Pyrolic was merged. He continued in this position until 1929, while also president of Celastic Corporation and associate chairman of the board of the parent DuPont Company and several DuPont subsidiaries.

In 1929 Davis was elected president and chairman of the board of the U.S. Rubber Company, which had been purchased by the duPonts* in 1927. He remained in that position until 1942, and was chairman of the board until 1949. U.S. Rubber had been incorporated in 1892 as a merger of ten companies in the Northeastern area engaged in the production of rubber footwear. In 1905 it acquired the Rubber Goods Manufacturing Company, which had been formed from an amalgamation of twenty companies manufacturing automobile tires and mechanical goods. The company expanded very rapidly after that under the direction of Samuel P. Colt.* In 1917 it began to manufacture U.S. Keds, rubber-soled canvas shoes which became a major product of the company. In 1928 its sales were $193 million, but it suffered a net loss of $10 million due to the collapse of the world crude rubber market.

Despite the great growth of U.S. Rubber over the years, it had done little to perfect a management structure, allowing each of the companies it had taken over to continue operating as functionally and legally separate entities. Little attention had been paid to long-term strategy or organizational structure. When Davis took over as president for the duPonts in 1929, he was instructed to dispose of certain unprofitable lines and to bring forth a managerial reorganization of the giant company. Drawing upon his experience at DuPont, Davis adopted the multi-divisional structure that had been used so effectively there. After 1930, United States Rubber had separate multidepartmental operating divisions for tires, footwear, industrial products, sundries, and chemicals, and a department for the sale of crude rubber and liquid latex, another to market finished products overseas, and a third to manage rubber plantations. At the same time he instituted a general office with general executives and staff specialists as well as financial and statistical systems and controls similar to those of DuPont and General Motors. All of this greatly enhanced the profitability of U.S. Rubber; Davis reduced the debt by $40 million in five years, and in 1935 a profit of $2 million was earned, the first in seven years. In 1934 U.S. Rubber introduced a foam rubber cushion material, Kaylon, and manufactured elastic fiber under the name of Lastex. In 1938 it developed a rayon cord for use in tire manufacture. When Davis resigned as president in 1942, it had net sales of over $290 million, and had paid dividends continually for five years. The debt had been reduced by nearly $100 million. In 1967 the company changed its name to Uniroyal. It had sales of $2.6 billion in 1979. A Republican, Davis married Jean Raybold of Wilmington, Delaware, in 1913. They had one daughter. (**A.** *NCAB*, 32:277; 51:249; *Who Was Who*, vol. 4. **B.** Glenn D. Babcock, *History of the United States Rubber Company*, 1966; Alfred D. Chandler Jr., *Strategy and Structure*, 1962; and *The Visible Hand*, 1977.)

DAVISON, HENRY POMEROY (June 13, 1867–May 6, 1922). Banker, J. P. Morgan and Company and Bankers Trust Company. Born in Troy, Bradford County, Pennsylvania, son of George B. Davison and Henrietta Pomeroy. He was educated in Troy until he was fifteen years old, when he entered the Greylock Institute in Williamstown, Massachusetts, for five years. He also began teaching school in Troy, during intervals in his schooling and for three years afterward. He then went to work in a bank in

Troy owned by his mother's brothers. At age twenty-one he applied for a job in a New York City bank, but failed to get it. For the next three years he was employed in a bank in Bridgeport, Connecticut, rising to a tellership. In 1891 a new bank, the Astor Place, opened in New York City, and Davison was hired as a teller after his third interview. After thwarting a bank robber, he was appointed assistant cashier of the Liberty National Bank in 1894, and within five years was president of the institution.

It was while serving at Liberty National Bank that he conceived a plan that resulted in the formation of the Bankers Trust Company, intended to serve as a depository for the funds of national banks and insurance companies. In 1902 he was invited to become vice-president and director of the First National Bank, where he soon received recognition from J. P. Morgan Jr.,* who frequently consulted him during the financial crisis of 1907. Davison had an important role in determining the actions of New York's banks during this crisis. Soon afterward, he became a partner in J. P. Morgan and Company, and in 1908 joined the Monetary Commission, headed by Senator Nelson W. Aldrich.* This commission drew up the "Jekyl Island" report, which resulted in the creation of the Federal Reserve System.

While a Morgan partner, Davison conducted the negotiations by which the firm and allied banking interests acquired control of the Guaranty Trust Company, which became the largest trust company in the United States. Davison also spent several weeks in London in 1915 with British officials, resulting in J. P. Morgan and Company being named the purchasing agent for the British government. The French government also decided to coordinate its purchases through the Morgan office, and both governments made the House of Morgan their fiscal agent in the United States, entrusting them at the outset with the task of selling to American investors a half-billion dollar issue of Anglo-French bonds, the largest issue of securities ever floated in the country to that time. During World War I, Davison was appointed head of the Red Cross War Council by President Wilson from 1917 to 1919. He raised $115 million for the Red Cross in 1917 and another $170 million in 1918.

He married Kate Trubee of Bridgeport, Connecticut, in 1893, and they had two daughters and two sons. Their eldest son, Frederick T. Davison (b. 1896), became a prominent New York City lawyer. The younger son, Henry P. Davison Jr. (1898–1961), graduated from Yale in 1920 and joined J. P. Morgan and Company two years later. He remained with the company until 1959, serving as a partner from 1929 to 1940, vice-president from 1940 to 1953, senior vice-president from 1953 to 1955, and president from 1955 to 1959. He married Anne Stillman, and they had five children. He was a Republican and an Episcopalian. (**A.** *DAB; NCAB*, 20:88; *New York Times*, May 8, 1922; *Who Was Who*, vol. 1; Thomas W. Lamont, *Henry P. Davison*, 1933. **B.** Vincent P. Carosso, *Investment Banking in America*, 1970; Lewis Corey, *The House of Morgan*, 1930.)

DEBARDELEBEN, HENRY FAIRCHILD (July 22, 1840–December 6, 1910) and **Henry Ticknor DeBardeleben** (January 2, 1874–November 2, 1948). **Henry F. DeBardeleben** was born on his father's cotton plantation in Alabama, son of Henry DeBardeleben and Jennie Fairchild. His father had migrated to Alabama from South Carolina, and died when young Henry was ten years old. Henry then moved with his mother to Montgomery, Alabama, where the boy secured work in a grocery store. When he was sixteen he became the ward of Daniel Pratt,* the first great industrial magnate of Alabama, whose plants were at Prattsville, near Montgomery. Young DeBardeleben lived in the Pratt mansion and attended school. Later, he was made "boss" of the teamsters and foreman of the lumber yard, and superintendent of the gin factory. At the outbreak of the Civil War, he joined the Prattsville Dragoons and served in the Pensacola and Shiloh campaigns.

In 1872, when Pratt, the wealthiest man in the state, turned his attention toward the district surrounding Birmingham, Alabama, which had been founded in the previous year, he bought a controlling interest in the Red Mountain Iron and Coal Company. He then undertook the construction of the Oxmoor furnaces and development of the Helena Mines, of which he made DeBardeleben manager, even though he knew nothing about ironmaking. The Panic of 1873 temporarily closed the works, and Pratt died in that same year, making DeBardeleben the richest man in the district.

In 1877 J. W. Sloss* and T. H. Aldrich interested him in the great Browne seam of coal west of Birmingham. He joined them in the Eureka Coal Company, doubling the capital, and changed the name of the seam to "Pratt." A year later the company was reorganized as the Pratt Coal and Coke Company, with DeBardeleben as president. With T. T. Hillman* he built the Alice furnaces in 1879 through 1881, naming them for his eldest daughter. Fearing that he had tuberculosis in 1881, he sold his holdings and went to Mexico, but returned to Birmingham the next year. At that time, with W. T. Underwood, he built the Mary Pratt Furnace, named for his second daughter. Illness attacked him again, and he went to Texas, where he met David Roberts, who joined him in 1886 to form the DeBardeleben Coal and Iron Company. He also organized the DeBardeleben and Pickard Land Company. These interests were capitalized at $2.5 million, and founded the town of Bessemer, Alabama, ten miles west of Birmingham, near the Red Mountain iron seam. Here four furnaces and an iron mill were built. The firm held 150,000 acres of mineral lands, and the venture was the greatest up to that time in the South. In 1887 all his property was consolidated into the DeBardeleben Coal and Iron Company, capitalized at $13 million. In 1891 the company was taken over by the Tennessee Coal, Iron and Railroad Company, of which DeBardeleben was made vice-president. After three years he went to New York City and tried to take control of the company; he failed, and lost his entire fortune, save some $75,000.

Then, with his sons Henry and Charles DeBardeleben, he explored new fields and started mining at Margaret in St. Clair County, Alabama, and in the Acton basin, southeast of Birmingham. DeBardeleben's Red Mountain iron seam, with the Pratt coal seam, was the basis for the industrial development of Birmingham. He was the first to succeed in making pig iron in the city, cheaper than that made elsewhere. He built the first coal road in Alabama, and aided T. H. Aldrich in exploring and exploiting the Montevallo coal fields. He also attracted other monied men to Birmingham, getting the Louisville and Nashville Railroad to spend $30 million on the Mineral Railroad there. He induced J. W. Sloss to build furnaces, and joined with T. T. Hillman in the erection of others. He was called the "King of the Southern Iron World." He remained president of the Alabama Fuel and Iron Company until his death, and was connected for a time with the Birmingham Rolling Mills and the Birmingham National Bank.

A Methodist and a Democrat, he married Ellen Pratt, daughter of Daniel Pratt, in 1863. She died in 1894, and in 1898 he married Katherine McCrossin of Birmingham. He had seven children, including four sons. Several of his sons, including Henry Ticknor DeBardeleben, joined him in the business.

Henry T. DeBardeleben was born in Birmingham and educated at Howard College there and at Alabama Polytechnic Institute, graduating in 1892. He also studied for a year at Eastman Business College in Poughkeepsie, New York. He then became superintendent of Alice Furnace division of Tennessee Coal, Iron and Railroad in 1894–1895; of Watts Iron and Steel Syndicate, 1896–1898; of Gracie Woodward Iron Company in 1896; of Woodward Iron Company in 1897–1898; and of Red River Furnace Company from 1899 to 1904. In the latter year he became manager of the Alice Creek, Tennessee, furnaces and ore mines of the Bon Air Coal and Iron Company, and in 1907 became vice-president and general manager of Woodstock Iron and Steel Corporation of Anniston, Alabama. In 1909–1910 he was president of Russellville (Alabama) Iron Ore and Metal Company and also vice-president and director of Alabama Fuel and Iron Company, which had been founded by his father. He held both these positions until he died in 1948.

In 1910 he was also president of the Maryland Coal and Coke Company, which became DeBardeleben Coal Company, Incorporated in 1915. In 1922 that firm was merged with Empire Coal Company and Carona Coal Company, both of Birmingham, into the DeBardeleben Coal Corporation. Henry T. DeBardeleben was president of that firm from its organization until 1947, when he became chairman of the board. In 1940 the DeBardeleben Coal Corporation acquired a by-product plant at Holt, Alabama, which operated as a division of the company. In 1946 Coyles Lines, Incorporated of New Orleans, Louisiana, was created from its marine division.

At the time of his death, the DeBardeleben Coal Corporation owned

100,627 acres of coal lands in Walker, Cullman, and Fayette counties, Alabama, and also engaged in the mining and sale of bituminous coal, with a capacity in excess of one million tons per year. It also operated retail coal yards in Birmingham. Gross sales in 1948 were $10.5 million, and it employed 1,500 persons. Henry T. served as vice-president and director of the National Coal Association.

An Episcopalian and a Republican, he married Julie Thomas of Atlanta, Georgia, in 1896; she died in 1910. He then married Dorie Drane of Clarksville, Tennessee. They had three sons and two daughters. One of his sons, Newton Hanson DeBardeleben (b. 1915), was a lawyer and then joined DeBardeleben Coal Corporation in 1948. He was named president of the firm in 1949, serving until 1962, when the company was sold. He then became vice-president of the First National Bank of Birmingham. (**A.** *DAB;* *NCAB*, 37:320; K:124; *Who Was Who*, vols. H and 4. **B.** Ethel M. Armes, *The Story of Coal and Iron in Alabama*, 1910.)

DEBOW, JAMES DUNWOODY BROWNSON (July 10, 1820–February 27, 1867). Business publicist and analyst for the South, *DeBow's Review*. Born in Charleston, South Carolina, son of Garret DeBow and the former Miss Norton. His father was a native of New Jersey who was once a prosperous merchant, but was financially ruined shortly before his death. James DeBow was left an orphan while still quite young, and used a small inheritance to enter a mercantile house in Charleston. Here he saved his money for seven years in order to attend Cokesbury Institute, and entered the College of Charleston, graduating in 1843. He then devoted a year to reading law and was admitted to the bar. He was not successful at this career, however, being a poor speaker.

DeBow began to send essays to the *Southern Quarterly Review*, published in Charleston. In 1845 he was one of those chosen to attend the Memphis Convention, which considered principally projects of internal improvement in the South, and the extent to which the federal government should aid construction. DeBow decided to found a monthly magazine devoted to social and business matters. He left Charleston for New Orleans, Louisiana, in early 1846 to begin publishing the *Commercial Review of the South and Southwest*. He had trouble getting contributors and there were almost no subscribers, and the *Review* suspended publication eighteen months later. DeBow then came to the attention of Maunsel White*, who had made a fortune in sugar planting and merchandise. He loaned DeBow money to resume publication, and though he continued to struggle for some time, within two years he had the largest circulation of any magazine published in the South.

In 1848 DeBow was appointed to a chair in political economy at the University of Louisiana at New Orleans; the chair had been endowed for him by Maunsel White, but he had no students. Later he was made head of the new Louisiana Bureau of Statistics, but the office went out of existence after one year. He was then appointed superintendent of the United States Census of 1850. In 1854 the U.S. Senate published his *Statistical View of the United States.*

His journal, later called *DeBow's Review*, was very influential throughout the South. He was an outspoken partisan of the South prior to the Civil War and an admirer of John C. Calhoun, but he also retained some nationalistic sentiments. He believed deeply in the moral right of slavery and the inferiority of blacks. He was an important contributor to a series of commercial conventions held in the South prior to the Civil War, especially with respect to building a southern transcontinental railroad, direct trade between the South and Europe, and a canal through South America. During the Civil War, the confederate government made him its chief agent for the purchase and sale of cotton. He revived the *Review* after the war (it was published until 1880), and was president of the Tennessee Pacific Railroad, a paper project for a transcontinental railroad through the South. He married Caroline Poe of Georgetown, D.C., in 1854, and Martha E. Johns in 1860. He had three children. (**A.** *DAB*; Otis C. Skipper, *J. D. B. DeBow, Magazinist of the Old South*, 1958. **B.** Herbert Wender, *Southern Commercial Conventions, 1837-1859*, 1930.)

DEEDS, EDWARD ANDREW (March 12, 1874–June 1, 1960). Automotive parts and cash register manufacturer, Delco and National Cash Register. He was educated at the Granville (Ohio) Academy and later graduated from Denison University. While at college, he operated the electric light and water plants of the town and university and was janitor at the university science building. He next took a special course in electrical engineering at Cornell University and in 1898 became a draftsman for the Tresher Electrical Company of Dayton, Ohio, a manufacturer of electrical motors. Within one year he had become chief engineer and superintendent. In 1900 he went to the National Cash Register Company as a cost and maintenance engineer, and while there he designed and built a large power plant for the company and electrified the plant. Deeds left National Cash Register in 1901 and for the next two years was engaged in designing a plant and automatic electric baking machines for the Shredded Wheat Company of Niagara Falls, New York. He returned to NCR in 1903 as assistant general manager, later becoming vice-president in charge of engineering and production. Under his direction, the company established plants in Canada, England, France, Germany, and Italy. He resigned in 1914 to give time to other interests, but returned in 1931 as chairman of the board and executive committee. During the first four years of his chairmanship, the firm's combined domestic and overseas sales more than doubled. In 1937 he succeeded Frederick B. Patterson as president of the company, also retaining the chairmanship. During his presidency he was instrumental in expanding the Toronto, Ontario, plant and amalgamating with Krupp Cash Register in Germany and the Fujiyama interests in Japan. He retired as president in 1940, and in 1957 was named honorary chairman of the board.

In 1904, while assistant general manager at NCR, Deeds employed Charles F. Kettering,* who invented the first automatically operated cash register. Deeds developed a torque motor which permitted electrical operation of business machines. It was this light and powerful motor that became the basis for successful development by Deeds and Kettering of the automobile ignition and starting system which superseded the hand crank. The patent was issued in Kettering's name. The two men gave the name Delco to the new mechanism, taken from the initials of the Dayton Engineering Laboratories Company, which they had formed to manufacture the system. Deeds was president of the company until 1916, when the firm was sold to General Motors.

In the same year Deeds and Kettering formed the Domestic Engineering Company, with Deeds as president, to manufacture the Delco-Light, a self-contained electrical power plant of simple and compact design for use in farmhouses, hotels, schools, churches, and rural and isolated areas. This unit came to be used around the world. The original $800,000 capitalization of Domestic Engineering Company was increased in 1918 to $3.5 million. Sales grew from $2.5 million in 1916 to $20 million in 1919. This company also eventually merged with General Motors. In the 1920s Deeds was president of Smith Engineering Company, manufacturers of gas products, and of the Domestic Building Company, formed to develop sites in Moraine City, a suburb of Dayton.

In 1922 Deeds helped organize over 100 Cuban sugar firms into a single concern—the General Sugar Company, which later became Vertientes-Camaguey Sugar Company—and he was its president and chairman of the board until 1946. In 1927 he became president of the Niles-Bement-Pond Company (later Pratt and Whitney Company, Incorporated) with headquarters in New York. He remained in this position until 1943, when he retired. He was also director of some twenty-eight other United States corporations.

During World War I Deeds served as a member of the Aircraft Production Board and while in charge of its activities laid the foundation for producing the Liberty Motor. In 1917–1918 he served in the Army Signal Corps. In 1918 there was criticism of the slow progress of aircraft production, and President Wilson had Charles Evans Hughes investigate. He recommended that Deeds should be judged by court martial due to certain transactions in which he was involved, but Deeds was acquitted. He was a Baptist and married Edith Walton of Dayton. They had two sons. (**A.** *NCAB*, A:327; 49:40. **B.** Isaac F. Marcossen, *Wherever Men Trade*, 1945.)

DEERE, JOHN (February 7, 1804–May 17, 1886) and **Charles Henry Deere** (March 28, 1837–October 29, 1907). Agricultural implement manufacturers, Deere and Company. **John Deere** was born in Rutland, Vermont, son of William Ronald Deere and Sarah Yates. His father was previously a native of England and his mother was the daughter of a British army officer who served during the American Revolution and then settled in Connecticut. John Deere was educated in the common schools of his home town and at age seventeen was apprenticed for four years to learn the blacksmith's trade with Capt. Benjamin Lawrence of Middlebury, Vermont. During the next twelve years he worked as a blacksmith in various towns of his native state. In 1837, at age 33, he went West, taking his tool kit with him. He headed for Illinois and eventually settled at Grand Detour, where he set up a blacksmith shop, sending back for his wife and children in the following year. Soon after his arrival he found that plows brought out from the East were not satisfactory for the prairie soils. So Deere set to work to make plow improvements. Within a year three new plows were made by Deere and his partner.

The excellent work of these new plows aroused considerable interest, and they sold rapidly. But Deere continued to experiment to determine the proper curvature of the steel moldboard that would be most effective for scouring not only new land, but old and sticky bottom land as well. Ten improved plows were made in 1839, and in 1840 a second anvil was added to the shop and forty plows were produced. The business continued to develop until 1846, when the annual output was over 1,000 plows. At this time, Deere was convinced that Grand Detour was poorly situated, and he sold out to his partner and moved to Moline, Illinois, where he organized a new company.

By then, Deere had concluded that the greatest obstacle to further development of the plow was the quality of steel plate available. Steel of high enough quality could only be obtained in England, so he ordered sufficient English steel for fifty plows, which he distributed throughout the country for testing. These were successful, so he opened negotiations in Pittsburgh for the manufacture of steel plate. This brought about the first manufacture of plow steel in the United States by William Woods at the steel works of Jones and Quigg in 1846–1847. Ten years later Deere's annual output had risen to 10,000 plows. In 1858 he took his son, Charles H. Deere, and in 1863 his son-in-law, Stephen H. Velie, into partnership. In 1868 the firm was incorporated as Deere and Company, with John Deere as president, Charles Deere as vice-president, and Velie as secretary. John Deere continued as active president until his final illness, when his son succeeded him. He married Damaris Lamb of Granville, Connecticut, in 1827. She died in 1865, and two years later he married Lucinda Lamb, younger sister of his first wife.

Charles Henry Deere was born in Hancock, Addison County, Vermont. He was educated in the public schools of Grand Detour and Moline, Illinois, and at academies at Davenport, Iowa, and Galesburg, Illinois, and at Bell's Commercial School in Chicago. He then became assistant book-keeper in his father's plow factory, advancing to bookkeeper, purchaser, salesman, and demonstrator. In 1858 he was admitted to partnership. After the Civil War wagons, carriages, and a full line of farming implements were added to the output of the Deere company. In 1868, when the firm was incorporated, Charles Deere became vice-president, succeeding to the presidency upon the death of his father in 1888.

As president, Charles H. Deere inaugurated several important changes and improvements in the marketing of Deere products. Formerly the company had marketed its products through independent jobbers, who sold them to similarly independent dealers. Charles Deere broadened this system to include branch houses placed in strategic locations which served an ever-increasing number of dealers directly, thereby cutting out the independent jobber. By the time of his death there were fifteen branch houses in the United States and Canada. He also originated the policy of arranging a complete line of farm equipment for distribution by each branch house, a move which led eventually to the acquisition of factories to make a complete line of farming equipment under the Deere name. In 1877 the firm of Deere and Company was formed for the sole purpose of supplying a John Deere corn planter for distribution by John Deere dealers. Similarly, the John Deere Buggy Company of St. Louis, Ft. Smith Wagon Company, Ft. Smith, Arkansas, Velie Saddling Company, and Union Malleable Iron Company were organized to broaden the scope of the Deere line to corn planters, sulky plows, gang plows, and spike tooth harrows, in addition to their basic line.

Charles Deere was also president of Deere-Marscer Company, Moline Water Power Company, Union Malleable Iron, Velie Saddlery, Ft. Smith Wagon, People's Savings Bank and Trust Company, Deere and Webber Company of Minneapolis, Deere Implement of San Francisco, and ten John Deere Plow Companies, operating in Omaha, Kansas City, St. Louis, Dallas, Oklahoma City, Denver, Baltimore, Indianapolis, Portland, Oregon, and New Orleans. He also had extensive real estate holdings in Moline, New York City, and Chicago.

A Republican, he was a presidential elector for Harrison. He married Mary Little Dickinson of Chicago in 1862. They had two daughters. Their eldest, Anna, married William Dwight Wiman, and the youngest, Katharine Mary, married William Butterworth. Both sons-in-law became prominent in the management of Deere and Company in the twentieth century. Butterworth (1864–1936) joined Deere and Company in 1892 and succeeded his father-in-law as president in 1907. He served in this position until 1928, when he became chairman of the board until his death. Since 1837 Deere has had only five chief executives—all related by blood or marriage to the Deere family.

During the twentieth century Deere became America's number one farm equipment manufacturer, selling more than $3.5 billion worth of tractors, plows, combines, and the like to farmers all over the world, and becoming one of the country's fastest growing industrial corporations. The firm's advancement has come from the close relationship they developed with Midwestern farmers, and their uncanny ability to know in advance what these farmers wanted. During the Great Depression of the 1930s, Deere continued to extend credit to their customers on their most expensive equipment, even though it often took years to collect on debts they had written off in the mid-1930s. The policy resulted in repeat business and business from sons of old customers. Some farmers in the Midwest say that if John Deere sold underwear, they'd buy it. After World War II they were the first to notice the trend in farming away from labor and toward heavy machinery. They capitalized on the trend by pouring twice as much money into research and development as their competitors. By the mid-1960s Deere had surpassed International Harvester as the nation's top farm equipment manufacturer. (**A.** *DAB; NCAB*, 20:63; 28:252, 253; *Who Was Who*, vol. H. **B.** Roger Burlingame, *March of the Iron Men*, 1938; *Fortune*, 1976; Milton Moskowitz et al., *Everybody's Business*, 1980.)

DEERING, WILLIAM (April 25, 1826–December 9, 1913). Agricultural implement manufacturer, William Deering and Company. Born South Paris, Maine, son of James Deering and Eliza Moore, both members of old Puritan families. His father was a woolen clothing manufacturer. William was educated in public schools and graduated from Rendfield Seminary in 1844. He then studied medicine with Dr. Barrows in Fryeburg, Maine, but decided to enter his father's manufacturing establishment instead. He remained there for several years, serving as manager. During the next few years he became interested in western farming lands, but on the death of his wife in 1856 returned to South Paris, where he opened a dry goods store. After a number of years he organized a wholesale commission dry goods business, Deering, Millikin and Company, in 1865, with headquarters in Portland, Maine, and offices in New York City. Deering was directing head of the firm for five years.

In the meantime, an old Maine friend and Methodist preacher, Elijah H. Gammon, who had been in Illinois for many years, interested Deering in the manufacture of agricultural machinery, especially the hand binding harvester. Gammon purchased the rights to manufacture a harvester designed by Charles W. and William W. Marsh, and Deering gave up his wholesale business to go to Plano, Illinois, to join Gammon as a partner. Deering invested $40,000 in the venture, and owing to his persistent and tireless management, the harvester trade was pushed out into channels that it had hitherto been unable to reach. A year later the manufacture of a Gordon wire binder was undertaken, against the advice of Gammon, but Deering saw clearly the need for a harvesting machine with automatic binding.

In 1879 Deering became sole owner of the business, and he made another bold move by beginning the manufacture of a twine binder invented by John F. Appleby. At this point Deering moved to a new and larger establishment in Chicago. The venture almost failed, due to the difficulty in finding a twine which would adapt to use on the binder. He at last persuaded Edwin H. Fitler, a Philadelphia rope manufacturer, to undertake experiments for him, and eventually produced a single strand manila twine that made the binder successful. After 1880 the business progressed steadily, and each year the shops were enlarged and new departments were added. It soon became the largest agricultural implement factory in the world, employing about 9,000 operatives. In 1883 it was incorporated as William Deering and Company, with sons Charles W. and James E. Deering, and son-in-law Richard F. Howe in the management with him. Later the name was changed to the Deering Manufacturing Company. In 1901 Deering retired, and a year later the company was merged with the International Harvester Company of Chicago. He was a director of Metropolitan Bank of Chicago and a trustee of Northwestern University.

Deering married Abby Reed Barbour in 1849, but she died two years later. In 1856 he married Clara Hamilton. He had two sons and one daughter. His eldest son, Charles Deering (1852–1927), entered the family business in 1881, serving until 1902, when the company was sold to International Harvester. He then served as chairman of the board of that company from 1904 to 1916, when he retired to become an art patron. The younger son, James E. Deering (1859–1925), entered Deering Company in 1880, remaining there until 1902. He then became a vice-president of International Harvester until 1919, and remained a director until he died. (**A.** *DAB; NCAB*, 11:268; 33:112; 20:449; *Who Was Who*, vol. 1. **B.** William T. Hutchinson, *Cyrus Hall McCormick*, 2 volumes, 1930, 1935; Cyrus Hall McCormick III, *The Century of the Reaper*, 1933; Helen M. Kramer, "Harvesters and High Finance: Formation of the International Harvester Company," *Business History Review*, 1964.)

DEGOLYER, EVERETTE LEE (October 9, 1886–December 14, 1956). Geophysical engineer and petroleum exploration company executive, Geophysical Research Corporation. Born in Greensburg, Kansas, son of John William DeGoyler, a mineral prospector, and Narcissa Kagy. Everette was educated in the public schools of Joplin, Missouri, and at the prep school of the University of Oklahoma, graduating from that university in 1911. Long before graduation he began to work in his chosen field. In 1906 he worked with the Oklahoma Geological Survey, and that summer worked as a camp cook with the United States Geological Survey. The next two years he worked with the survey as a field assistant in Wyoming, Colorado, and Montana. In 1909 he joined the Mexican corporation, La Compania Mexicana de Petrolie ed Aquila S.A. (Mexican Eagle Oil Company), which had been organized by the British engineering firm of S. Pearson and Sons, Ltd. In 1912 he became chief geologist and chief of its land department. Two years later he severed active participation with the company to establish his own consulting engineering offices in Oklahoma, serving as a consultant to his former employers until 1916. In that year he moved his headquarters to New York City.

In 1918 DeGoyler went to London to direct negotiations for the sale of Aquila Company to the Royal Dutch Shell Corporation, and then was commissioned to organize the Amerada Petroleum Corporation to operate in the United States and Canada. Amerada was financed by Lord Cowdroy of the Rycade Oil Company to concentrate on the salt dome lands bordering on the Gulf of Mexico. In 1919 DeGoyler gave up private practice and became vice-president and general manager of Amerada, as well as its affiliated corporations, Amerada Corporation and Amerada Refining. From 1929 to 1932 he served as chairman of the board of all three companies. He was also vice-president and general manager of Rycade Oil Company from 1923 to 1926, and president and general manager from 1926 to 1941.

In 1925 he organized the Geophysical Research Corporation as a subsidiary of Amerada, to design and manufacture seismic equipment and engage in seismic explorations. He was president of this also until he resigned from all Amerada interests in 1932. He then moved to Dallas, Texas, where he established Core Laboratories, Incorporated to examine core and other samples of wells for the oil industry. With J. C. Karcher and Eugene McDonald he established the Geophysical Service, Incorporated, a seismic contracting company. Also in 1932, he founded the oil-finding company, Atlantic Royalty Corporation, of which he was president from its inception until 1950. In 1923 he founded the Filmont Corporation for the same purpose; he was president until 1939.

With Lewis MacNaughton as partner, DeGolyer reorganized his own consulting practice as DeGolyer and MacNaughton in 1936, with headquarters in Dallas. He was with this firm for the rest of his life. His final organizational undertaking was the founding in 1936 of Isotopes, Incorporated, a firm designed to adapt radioactive isotopes to industrial use; he was also president of this organization.

During all these years, his achievements in oil exploration were striking. While with the Mexican Eagle Oil Company DeGolyer brought in a well at Patrera de Llano, in the center of what was to become the Golden Lane, one of the most prolific sources of oil in the world. At the end of 1910 he brought in the Patrera de Llano number four, regarded as the world's largest and most spectacular well, with a capacity of 110,000 barrels daily, and a cumulative production which exceeded 100 million barrels. When he resigned as president of Amerada in 1929 to become chairman, the company's holdings comprised 1,252,127 acres in Oklahoma, Kansas, Louisiana,

Arkansas, New Mexico, California, and Texas, with 600 producing oil wells, 20 gas wells, and 35 well drillings. It operated 11 casinghead gasoline plants. At the close of 1928 its assets were $22,623,397 and gross revenues were $14,746,503.

In 1922, at DeGolyer's instigation, Rycade Oil Company made a survey of the famous Spindletop oil field in Texas. This was the first geophysical survey of an oilfield in the United States. Two years later Rycade discovered a new salt dome by its new techniques at Nash, Texas, and in 1926 completed a producing well there, making it the first field to be discovered by geophysical methods. DeGolyer also pioneered in the use of seismic equipment and surveys in the 1920s and 1930s. At the time of his retirement from Amerada in 1932, he gradually transferred his operations to the frontiers of the oil industry, then marked by oil field development in the Southwest and the salt dome province encircling the Gulf of Mexico. He financed his own prospecting oil wells, and set up one enterprise after another. In 1934 his company, Atlantic Royalty Corporation, with Geophysical Service Incorporated, discovered Oil Ocean, which was developed into one of the Gulf Coast's largest oil and gas fields. They also organized the Coronada Exploration Corporation. DeGolyer sold Atlantic in 1950 and Geophysical Services Incorporated before he died.

He was the originator of applied geophysics in the United States and was known as the father of American geophysics. He advanced refraction surveying to its highest perfection and reduced reflection surveying to practice. In addition he was a pioneer in the use of the modern magnetometer in this country and the use of seismography for geologic exploration. In 1942-1943 he was deputy administrator for the Petroleum Administration for the War Department, and headed its mission to Mexico in 1942, and a mission of the Department of the Interior to the Middle West in 1943-1944. He was also chief of the technical advisory committee to Franklin Roosevelt at the Tehran Conference. From 1947 to 1952 he was on the U.S. Military Petroleum Advisory Board, and a member of the Petroleum Council from 1946 until his death. He was founder of the American Association of Petroleum Geologists and a celebrated book collector in the history of science. DeGolyer married Virginia Goodrich of Norman, Oklahoma, in 1910 and they had four children. (**A.** *NCAB*, D:356; 43:12; *Who Was Who*, vol. 3; Lon Tinkle, *Mr. De*, 1970. **B.** Anthony Sampson, *The Seven Sisters*, 1975.)

DELMONICO, LORENZO (March 13, 1813–September 3, 1881). Restaurateur, Delmonico's. Born in Marengo, Switzerland, son of a small farmer. Lorenzo had very little formal education, and at age nineteen left his native village and immigrated to America, landing in New York City. He joined his two uncles, John and Peter Delmonico, who had preceded him there. John, the eldest, had been master of a sailing vessel trading between

Cuba and the United States, but in 1825 gave that up to become a dealer in wines in the city. Peter had started a small confectionary and catering business, and took his young nephew into partnership. Lorenzo soon suggested a new departure in the business, one which would make the name Delmonico internationally famous. His idea was to open a restaurant in downtown New York City which would provide foods cooked and served in the European manner of the day. He especially advocated the use of salads, which were virtually unknown in America at the time.

Lorenzo soon won international recognition as a leader in gastronomy. Without much capital and at first without influential friends, within twenty years he made New York known the world over as a center of gracious dining. He prepared dishes which few New Yorkers had ever tasted, but usually he just made obvious use of items formerly overlooked by Americans. Soon experienced cooks from Parisian kitchens were coming to New York and offering Delmonico their services. The first Delmonico Restaurant, on William Street, was destroyed by the Great Fire of 1835, and was succeeded by a new one on Broad Street; later it was moved to Beaver Street and then back to William Street.

About the same time, Lorenzo purchased more than 200 acres of land within the city limits of what later became the City of Brooklyn, and began farming operations modeled on those in Switzerland. John Delmonico died in 1842, and in 1848 Lorenzo became sole proprietor of the firm. From 1846 to 1856 a Delmonico Hotel was conducted at 21-25 Broadway, and from 1855 to 1875 the principal Delmonico restaurant was at Broadway and Charles. In the first year of the Civil War, a new restaurant was opened up at 14th Street and Broadway Avenue, and the year 1876 began the career of the famous Delmonico Restaurant at Broadway and 26th Street. During this time, Lorenzo brought his brother Siro and other members of the family from Switzerland, and all took places in the organization. The restaurant continued to grow during this time, becoming the greatest of its kind in existence.

In 1861, through unfortunate investments in oil stocks, Delmonico lost $500,000, which was made up in a few years out of the profits of the restaurants. He founded a public school in his native village, and gave liberally to the Roman Catholic Church in New York. He married a widow, Mme. Miege, in 1856. (*DAB*.)

DEMOREST, ELLEN CURTIS (November 15, 1824–August 10, 1898). Publisher, clothing patterns and fashion magazines, *Demorest's Illustrated Monthly Magazine*. Born in Schuylerville, Saratoga County, New York, daughter of Henry D. Curtis and Electo Abel. Her father was a farmer and owner of a men's hat factory. Ellen, or Nell, as she was called, attended a local school and Schuylerville Academy. At age eighteen her father helped her set up a millinery shop in Saratoga Springs. She prospered there, and moved her shop to Troy, then a leading millinery center. Eventually she moved it to New York City, where she settled in the Williamsburg section of Brooklyn.

There she met her husband-to-be, William Demorest, a native of Brighton, New York, who had established himself in New York City as a dry goods merchant, but he went bankrupt at the time of their marriage. They then went to Philadelphia to make a new start. The couple's rise to fortune came one day when Mrs. Demorest saw her black maid cut out a dress from a crude brown paper pattern. From this Nell conceived the idea of accurate patterns, mass-produced on thin tissue paper, for home dressmakers. Her husband set about to promote the idea, moving the family back to New York City, where they began to manufacture patterns. In the fall of 1860, they launched a quarterly magazine, *Mme. Demorest's Mirror of Fashions*, featuring colored plates like those in *Godey's Lady's Book*, with a pattern stapled to each number. At the same time Nell opened her Emporium of Fashions, a private dressmaking and millinery establishment on Broadway, catering to the wealthy. Both ventures were immediately successful. They soon employed skilled dress designers to create the patterns, and imported models from London and Paris which Nell's sister, Kate Curtis, adapted to the more conservative American tastes. Distributed by a countrywide network of local agencies, the patterns became a familiar sight in American homes.

In 1864 the magazine became *Demorest's Illustrated Monthly Magazine and Mme. Demorest's Mirror of Fashion*, with a circulation of 60,000. Nell Demorest's twice-yearly openings became a social event, and by the mid-1860s she was the acknowledged dictator of American fashion. The family's interests soon expanded. William Demorest marketed dressmaking gadgets and a new sewing machine with a tucking attachment. At the same time he established a "purchasing bureau" to fill mail orders for all kinds of merchandise and profited in Manhattan real estate dealings. He also undertook several publishing ventures which made him editor-in-chief of five different magazines with a combined circulation of over one million. He was interested in temperance reform, while Nell was concerned with Negro welfare and worked on enlarging employment opportunities for women. She employed over 200 women in the family business, especially widows.

In 1872 Nell joined with Susan A. King, who had made a fortune in real estate in New York, to form the Women's Tea Company, sending a clipper ship to the Orient to bring back tea. The venture was a modest success. She was also a founder in 1868 of Sorosis, the pioneer New York woman's club. The Demorest enterprises reached their peak in the 1870s, with agents all over the United States as well as an office in Paris, under son Henry's direction. In 1876 three million patterns were distributed through 1,500 agencies. But they had failed to patent their invention, and the product was eventually swamped by competition from Ebenezer Butterick's* patterns and his *Delineator* magazine. William retired in 1885 to run for governor of New York on the Prohibition ticket, and devoted full time to the temperance movement while his sons carried on the magazine. Nell Demorest withdrew from the pattern business in 1887 and it was sold soon after. William died in 1895, and Nell lived the remaining three years of her life as an invalid. She began life as a member of the Congregational Church, but became a Christian Scientist. Nell and William had four children, two sons and two daughters. (*NAW*; Isabel Ross, *Crusades and Crinolines*, 1963.)

DENNISON, CHARLES SUMNER (June 20, 1858–August 22, 1912). and **Henry Sturgis Dennison** (March 4, 1877–February 29, 1952). Manufacturers of stationery, Dennison Manufacturing Company. **Charles S. Dennison** was born in Newtonville, Massachusetts, son of Eliphalet Wharf Dennison and Lydia Ann Beals. He was educated in public schools in Newton, Massachusetts, Highland Military Academy, and Massachusetts Institute of Technology. In 1878 he entered the employ of the family's Dennison Manufacturing Company, Framingham, Massachusetts, working in the machine ship. Two years later he was sent to New York City to work in the company store. In 1884, when the London office was established, he took charge of the business there. He was recalled in 1887 and made purchasing agent, and in 1893 was elected a member of the board of directors. Later he served as treasurer for sixteen years and as vice-president for three years, and in 1909 was elected president until he died in 1912.

The Dennison Manufacturing Company had been started in 1843 by his uncle, Aaron Lufkin Dennison, a watchmaker who was finding it difficult to obtain boxes for his watches. Aaron Dennison, known as the "father of American watchmaking," was at that time engaged in the factory manufacture of watches, the first such attempt in America. Although he was later forced into bankruptcy with the venture, the firm went on to become American Waltham Watch Company, which was then the largest watch company in America. He set up his father, Andrew Dennison, a shoemaker, in the box-making business in New Brunswick, Maine. Shortly thereafter, Andrew and Aaron devised a paper box-making machine for cutting and scoring cardboard and greatly increased the activities of the business. Aaron returned to watchmaking, and his brother, Eliphalet W. Dennison, joined the family business in 1849. Six years later he became the sole owner, and in 1863 formed the partnership of Dennison and Company. In that same year, Eliphalet Dennison invented a new kind of shipping tag, with the hole in the tag reinforced by a paper washer on each side. With this innovation the Dennison business grew rapidly. He incorporated the business in 1878 and retired in 1886, when he was succeeded by his son, Henry Beals Dennison.

During the 1880s, while Charles S. Dennison was a member of the firm, the merchandise line was expanded rapidly, as other types of fine boxes, shipping and merchandise tags, gummed labels and papers, stationer's goods, and tissue paper were added. They also introduced crepe paper to America, first importing it from England, and then manufacturing it in their own plant. Following this, they began to market Christmas wrapping papers, seals, and tags, and later began to market for other holidays. The Dennison operations were finally consolidated in a large factory in Framingham, Mass. in 1897–1898, with branch offices in New York, Philadelphia, and Chicago.

During Charles S. Dennison's presidency, the annual sales of the company increased from $4,723,000 to $5,252,000 in just three years, and a program of developing export sales was launched, with a subsidiary established in Great Britain. He was a Republican member of the Newton City Council from 1903 to 1906. A Unitarian, he married Mary Rosabelle French of Boston in 1883. He had three daughters.

Henry S. Dennison was born in Boston, Massachusetts, son of Henry Beals Dennison and Emma Stanley. His father was president of Dennison Manufacturing from 1886 to 1892, but was ejected from the presidency in the latter year because of his alcoholism. Henry S. graduated from Harvard University in 1899 and joined the family business. He worked for two years at various production jobs, and was subsequently made foreman of the sealing wax department. After a time he was transferred to the works' manager's office, where he took an active part in developing cost and accounting practices. He became manager of the works in 1906, and a director in 1909. He served as purchasing agent from 1910 to 1913, and became treasurer in 1912. He was elected president of the company in 1912, serving in that position until he died in 1952.

Henry S. Dennison became an early practitioner of scientific management and industrial relations techniques, and was an advocate of Taylorism. He was also a pioneer advocate among the capitalist class of unemployment insurance and a leading corporate "liberal" during the 1920s and 30s. His introduction to some of these ideas came in 1900 when he visited Dayton, Ohio, to observe National Cash Register Company's well-publicized welfare programs. Although he was repelled by the excessive paternalism at NCR under John H. Patterson's* aegis, he nonetheless complimented the firm's management for their "intelligently unselfish" attitudes. A year later Dennison set up an NCR-style suggestion/bonus system. During the next five years a factory clinic, employee cafeteria, library, social club, and savings bank were organized at the firm.

Despite these reforms, Dennison had little interest in broader Progressive Era reforms and was quite conservative on the issue of wage increases for the majority of workers. In 1911, however, he initiated a considerably more ambitious reorganization of his firm's operations. His twin goals were to end absentee stockholder control over company policy and to incorporate all "active managers" into a collectivity that could gradually assume all rights and powers of full ownership. With his uncle, Charles, he established a "Management Industrial Partner" program, in which absentee stockholders were issued preferred (non-voting) stock, and managers, as long as they were working for the company, controlled voting stock, with which they could exercise a strong voice in the determination of company policy. Thus, Dennison created an industrial program that predated by some ten years the ideas to be expressed by Thorstein Veblen in his *Engineers and the Price System* (1921). Dennison's dream was to build an expert management team to collectively own and operate a self-financing business.

These ideas, which Dennison felt would create a finely engineered organization run along the most "scientific" principles of workmanship and personnel relations, brought him into close sympathy with the disciples of Frederick Winslow Taylor.* He formed a close association with Boston-area Taylorites such as Henry P. Kendall,* and by 1916 was an active participant in the affairs of the Taylor Society. In 1913 Dennison was appointed to serve on the Massachusetts State Pension Commission, along with Magnus W. Alexander, future founder of the National Industrial Conference Board. Conversations with trade union leaders at the pension commission hearings caused Dennison to augment management training programs at his firm and to restrict powers of foremen. All welfare projects were placed under the control of an "employment manager," and strong efforts were made to even out irregularities in production schedules in order to avoid layoffs. In 1916 Dennison Company established the first employer-initiated unemployment insurance system in the United States.

When Dennison served as president of the newly organized Boston Chamber of Commerce (1912–1916), he was brought into contact with Edward* and Lincoln Filene.* He came under the influence of their ideas of "profit-sharing," and in 1915 Dennison, Kendall, A. W. Burritt, and Edwin F. Gay produced a book on the subject called *Profit Sharing: Its Principles and Practice.* The study concluded that profit sharing systems which had earlier tried to operate along cooperative lines were merely idealistic dreams. Instead they advocated indeterminate bonus systems confined to managers and foremen, feeling that the masses of workers were not informed or responsible enough to comprehend the spirit or operation of such programs.

With the outbreak of World War I Edwin Gay hired Dennison as his assistant to run the Planning and Statistics section of the War Industries Board. This caused Dennison to break with his normally Republican politics and endorse the policies of Woodrow Wilson. It also began his increasingly close association with the federal government as an official and unofficial advisor in the 1920s and 30s. In 1920 he attended several "national industrial conferences" called to deal with the "labor problem" and Red Scare of that time. At these conferences Dennison took a distinctly more liberal line than his corporate counterparts, declaring that individual employees had no parity of bargaining power with employers. He felt collective bargaining was necessary for labor to achieve a viable independence, and this could be achieved either through trade unions or works councils. During the war Dennison had set up works councils in his plants along lines suggested by the War Industries Board. Despite these views, Dennison continued to focus his principal attentions on a favored managerial class rather than on the mass of workers. From 1919 to 1921 Dennison was president of the Taylor Society and was involved with the Twentieth Century Fund and the International Management Institute at Geneva, Switzerland. He also became an active member of the National Bureau of Economic Research and the Social Science Research Council. He was a member of President Harding's unemployment commission in 1921, Herbert Hoover's* committee on recent economic changes in 1928-1929, and the Wickersham Committee on Prohibition Law Enforcement of 1930. He was also director of welfare work for the U.S. Post Office from 1922 to 1928, setting up works councils, credit unions, and a scientific management program there.

The stock market crash of 1929 decimated the welfare programs at Dennison Company as unemployment insurance funds were exhausted, company profits were virtually nonexistent, and wages, salaries and employee roles were being steadily cut. By 1932 Dennison was convinced that voluntary efforts among businesses had not succeeded in dealing successfully with the problem. In the future he felt that capitalists must set up planning organizations which included the federal government as a major partner, although he felt that partnership, not coercion should be the basis of decision-making. In 1931 he was a member of the United States Chamber of Commerce's Committee on the Continuity of Business, which recommended cartelization and price-fixing to stimulate economic recovery. In these ideas Dennison developed an increasingly close association with Gerard Swope* of General Electric, and helped mediate between business and government after the passage of the National Industrial Recovery Act in 1933. In the late 1930s Dennison also began working with John Kenneth Galbraith, then a young economics professor at Harvard. In 1938 Dennison, Lincoln Filene, and others published *Towards Full Employment*, which advocated using the taxation system to increase consumption and decrease savings. In the same year he and Galbraith brought out *Modern Capital and Business Policy*, which spelled out the dangers of oligopoly, price-fixing, and industrial self-regulation, advocating programs for the governmental regulation of business—stark testimony to how far Dennison's thinking had progressed during the depression decade.

During the years of his management, the Dennison Company generally continued to prosper. From 1917 to 1951 the company's net capital increased from nearly six million dollars to over fifteen million and its sales grew from $3,481,000 to $37,375,000. Dennison also pursued an active policy of integrating the manufacturing, marketing, and financial divisions of the company, along with improving its human relations. In 1930 a line of price-marking machines was developed. After his death, however, the Dennison Company began to dismantle his reform programs. By 1965 Dennison Corporation was a "normal corporation," complete with absentee control and stock speculation by management personnel. In 1958 a craft union called the first strike against the firm in over forty years and in 1971 a majority of workers voted to affiliate with the AFL-CIO. Dennison married Mary Tyler Thurber of Plymouth, Massachusetts, in 1901. She died in 1936, and in 1944 he married Gertrude (Bement) Petri. He had four children. (**A.** *DAB; DAB*, Supplement 1; *NCAB*, 39:254; 50:52; *New York Times*, March 1, 1952; *Who Was Who*, vols. 1, 3, 5; James T. Dennison, *Henry S. Dennison: New England Industrialist*, 1955. **B.** Henry S. Dennison, "Decision-Making at the Top Executive Level," *American Economic Review*, 1951; Kim McQuaid, "Henry S. Dennison and the Science of Industrial Reform," *American Journal of Economics and Sociology*, 1977; David F. Noble, *America By Design*, 1977.)

DEPEW, CHAUNCEY MITCHELL (April 23, 1834–April 5, 1928). Lawyer, politician, and railway executive, New York Central Railroad. Born in Peekskill, Westchester County, New York, son of Isaac Depew and Martha Mitchell. His father was a successful entrepreneur involved in river transportation. Chauncey was educated at a private school and then took a high school course at Peekskill Academy. He graduated from Yale in 1856, and entered the law office of Edward Wells in Peekskill, where he studied for two years. In 1858 he was admitted to the bar and began private practice in his native village. The Depew family had long been Democrats, but Chauncey Depew joined the Republican party soon after its founding, serving in the state legislature in 1862 and 1863. He was the Republican nominee for speaker in the latter year, but lost out in a deal for legislative support for the Republican candidacy for the U.S. Senate. In 1863 he was elected Secretary of State of New York.

In 1866 he was offered the position as first minister from the United States to Japan, but instead accepted a job as attorney for the Vanderbilts'* Hudson River and Harlem Railroad lines. He handled political contacts for his employer with great tact and skill, and in 1872, at the Vanderbilts' behest, took a hand in securing Horace Greeley's nomination to the Independent Republican ticket, and he himself ran for lieutenant governor of New York. Both he and Greeley were defeated.

The major portion of Depew's duties for the Vanderbilts concerned legislation, and he smoothed the way for his clients at Albany. In 1874 he became a director in the Vanderbilt system, and in 1875 its general counsel. In 1882 he became second vice-president of the New York Central and Hudson Railroad, and three years later, its president. During his term of office, which lasted thirteen years, he brought about the absorption of the rival West Shore System, and for a time was the president of that road. When he became president the road had 993 miles of line and earned $24,429,441. When he resigned as president thirteen years later, it had 2,650 miles of line and earnings were $47,484,632. Great improvements were made in the property; equipment was increased from 492 passenger cars to 1188 cars, and freight cars from 24,744 to 42,485; and average train load increased from 188 tons to 304 tons. The increased mileage was achieved primarily by consolidation. Besides the West Shore Railroad, he also acquired the Beech Creek Railroad in 1890, the Rome, Watertown and Ogdensburg Railroad in 1891, and subsidiaries of the Lake Shore and Michigan Southern and the Michigan Central railroads in 1898. In between political involvements, he remained chairman of the board of New York Central until his death, devoting 62 years of his long life to the Vanderbilt system.

In 1881 Depew became a candidate for the U.S. Senate, but withdrew his name. In 1888 the state Republican party endorsed him for president, but he got only nine votes at the Republican convention. Then, in 1899, he was elected to the U.S. Senate from New York, resigning his position with the New York Central, although remaining chairman of the board. In 1905 he was re-elected and served another full term. A small scandal arose in that year when it was disclosed that he received a $20,000 annual retainer from the Equitable Life Assurance Society, but he promised to give it up, and the issue was settled. He held a large number of directorates during his lifetime, especially among railroads, Western Union Telegraph, and various bridge companies. Depew won great fame as a public speaker and compiled *One Hundred Years of American Commerce*, which was published in 1895.

He married Elsie A. Hegeman, sister of John R. Hegeman,* head of Metropolitan Life Insurance Company. They had two children. (**A.** *DAB; NCAB*, 23:96; *New York Times*, April 5, 1928; *Who Was Who*, vol. 1. **B.** Alvin F. Harlow, *The Road of the Century: The New York Central Railroad*, 1947.)

DEPEYSTER, ABRAHAM (July 8, 1657–August 2, 1728). Colonial merchant and land owner. Born New Amsterdam (New York), son of Johannes DePeyster and Cornelia Lubberts. His father was a native of Haarlem, from a long line of goldsmiths of considerable wealth. He immigrated to New Amsterdam prior to 1649 and became one of the most substantial citizens in the city. Abraham enlarged on the possessions inherited from his father, and became an enterprising merchant, "importing in his own ships." He built warehouses near the dock, and acquired a large tract of land north of the Wall (the present Wall Street) which was then known as the "Great Garden of Col. De Peyster." He built a house near the East River Shore in 1695, one of the finest in the city. He also gave loans to the city when it was struggling under financial burdens, and was alderman in 1685, mayor for four successive terms (1691-1694), colonel of the local militia, member of the Governor's Council (1695-1702, 1709, 1710-22), acting governor for a short time, deputy auditor general (1701), and receiver general of the port (1708). He also served as Justice of the Supreme Court from 1698 to 1702 and as chief justice in 1701.

He played a major role in developing a better system to care for the city's poor. He went to Holland in 1684 and married Catharine dePeyster, a kinsman. They had eight sons and five daughters. His son became treasurer of the province in 1721, succeeding to a position held by his father from 1706 to 1721. (*DAB; NCAB*, 2:44.)

DERBY FAMILY: Richard Derby (September, 1712-November 9, 1783); **Elias Hasket Derby** (August 16, 1739-September 8, 1799); **Elias Hasket Derby Jr.** (January 10, 1766-September 16, 1826); **Elias Hasket Derby III** (September 24, 1803-March 31, 1880). Salem merchants and railroad executive.

Richard Derby was born in Salem, Massachusetts, son of Richard Derby and Martha Hasket. His grandfather, Roger Derby, was a Quaker who had come to Salem from England in 1671 and became engaged in trade. He accumulated a fairly large fortune which he willed to his two sons, Samuel and Richard, father of the present subject. Young Richard went to sea at an early age, and at age twenty-four became captain of the sloop *Ranger*, trading between Salem and the West Indies. After sailing for a number of years in the employ of Salem merchants, he acquired a vessel of his own. By means of successful trading he was enabled by age forty-five to retire from the sea and set himself up as a merchant.

He began building up a thriving commerce with Spain, and at the same time sent his ships to the West Indies, exchanging New England fish, lumber, and farm products for rum and sugar. Because of almost continual wars pitting Britain against France and Spain, Derby's ships were harassed by all three powers. During this period several were captured, but so great were the profits made by those that evaded capture that he began to amass a considerable fortune. To take care of some of the increasing business he built the Derby Wharf in Salem Harbor, and was recognized as one of the most influential men of the community. He lived in a fine mansion near the head of Derby Wharf.

The British Acts of Trade and Navigation sorely disrupted his business in the 1760s and 1770s, and he became an active patriot. In 1775 he headed a band of citizens who met British troops at the entrance to the town to seize cannon and ammunition. Backing down from the confrontation, the British captain withdrew his troops. About this time Richard withdrew from active business and turned management of his affairs over to his second son, Elias Hasket Derby. He married Mary Hodges of Salem in 1735 and they had three sons and three daughters. She died in 1770, and a year later he married Mrs. Sarah (Langley) Mersey of Salem.

Elias Hasket Derby was born in Salem, and at the outbreak of the Revolutionary War, having taken over his father's business, he outfitted a number of his ships as privateers. The spoils brought in by these vessels, together with the proceeds of a number of successful trading ventures made him one of the wealthiest merchants in New England at the close of the Revolution. He took advantage of the new circumstances to embark upon extensive commerce with many parts of the world. In 1784 he dispatched his ship *Light Horse* from Salem to St. Petersburg, Russia, with a cargo of West Indies sugar. A year later he sent his ship *Grand Turk* to the Cape of Good Hope on a trading voyage, and in 1786 dispatched her to the Isle of France in the Indian Ocean. From there she went to China, being the first New England ship to reach the Orient. His vessels also found their way to Bolivia, Rangoon, Calcutta, Bombay, and Canton. But his most lucrative trade was with the Isle of France on Mauritius, a small island in the Indian Ocean, where he exchanged the products of New England for the exotic commodities of the East. Toward the end of his career he profited greatly during the Napoleonic Wars, when neutral ships were in demand for the carrying trade.

His success lay in his farseeing initiative as a trader and partly in the superior type of men he employed as captains and supercargoes. They were given a large share of the profits, and many became quite wealthy. Some of the principal family fortunes in New England were founded by men who sailed in Derby ships. Derby himself never went to sea, but had a thorough knowledge of ships, and most of his fleet was built under his own supervision. Of all the vessels he dispatched to the ends of the earth only one was ever lost, other than those captured.

Although he never held political office, he freely gave of guns, ammunition, and supplies to the Continental Army during the Revolutionary War, and after the conflict took an active interest in the original tariff acts. It was largely through his advice that the bonded warehouse system was adopted by the federal government. He bought a large farm on the outskirts of Salem where he experimented with many new plants brought by his ships from abroad. In 1797 he built a magnificent mansion in Salem, the first in the town. When he died he left one of the largest fortunes ever amassed in America to that time. He married Elizabeth Crowninshield in 1761, daughter of one of the leading merchants in Salem. They had four sons and three daughters. Their eldest son was Elias Hasket Derby Jr.

E. H. Derby Jr. was born in Salem and attended Harvard for two years. He subsequently spent several years in the counting house of the family business, and received thorough instruction in navigation under old captain Jonathan Archer before taking several voyages as captain's clerk. Finally, in 1787, he made a voyage as a supercargo of the brig *Rose* to the

West Indies. A few months later he sailed on the *Grand Turk* for the Isle of France, and did not return to Salem until 1790. He also visited Barbary, Madras, and Calcutta, adding $100,000 to the Derby fortune. In 1799 he sailed from Salem in the *Mount Vernon*, a new ship of 355 tons armed with twenty guns, for the Mediterranean. This added another $100,000 to the family coffers. He returned to Salem in 1800, after his father had died, and took over the business.

Things did not go well for him after that time, however. There was a great deal of wrangling over his father's will, since E. H. Jr. received a double portion; the family became a subject of gossip and scandal as he quarreled with his brother-in-law, Nathaniel West. Derby also became embroiled in the violent factional politics of Salem, and his reduced income was not sufficient to maintain the magnificent Derby mansion. In 1809, in an attempt to restore his fortune, he made a voyage to Rio de Janeiro and London in the *Mount Vernon*, but it was a failure. He then moved to Londonderry, New Hampshire, where he was the first to import merino sheep to the United States. He married Lucy Brown and they had four daughters and five sons. His eldest son was Elias Hasket Derby III.

E. H. Derby III was born in Salem, and educated at Dr. Stearns Academy in Medford, Massachusetts, Pinkerton Academy in Londonderry, New Hampshire, and Boston Latin School. He graduated from Harvard in 1821 and read law in the office of Daniel Webster. He was admitted to the bar in 1827, and soon won distinction as a railway lawyer. In the process he acquired an extensive knowledge of railway operation, and for some years was president of the Old Colony Railroad and director of several others. He worked to extend various lines, and secured the completion of the Hoosac Tunnel. He also did much writing for newspapers on a wide range of business and economic matters. He amassed a considerable fortune during his lifetime. He married Eloise Lloyd Strong of Long Island and they had seven children. (**A.** *DAB; NCAB*, 5:32; *Who Was Who*, vol. H.; James D. Phillips, *The Life and Times of Richard Derby*, 1929. **B.** R. D. Paine, *The Ships and Sailors of Old Salem*, 1908; C. E. Trow, *Old Shipmaster of Salem*, 1905.)

DEWOLF, JAMES (March 18, 1764–December 21, 1837). Slavetrader and politician. Born in Bristol County, Rhode Island, son of Mark A. DeWolf and Abigail Potter. Both his father and his uncle, Simeon Potter, were seafaring men who had become interested in slave trading in French Guinea. The family was very poor, however, and James and his brother hoed corn on their father's farm until, tiring of that, they walked to Providence and sailed out on one of Potter's privateers. This was during the American Revolution, and the sea was infested with pirates who became even more audacious after the onset of the French Revolution. James DeWolf had many wild experiences, fought in several naval battles, was captured twice, and was imprisoned once. As a result he became a man of great force and indomitable energy with few ethical distinctions about what he was doing.

His earliest voyages were made to Africa, where he seized and transported Africans as slaves to the West Indies. Providence merchants of the highest commercial and social standing backed him in the trade, and he had no qualms of conscience concerning it. He often went to Southern ports personally to supervise the sale of the captives. As long as the slave trade was flourishing his ships were engaged in it, and he was always careful to follow the lines of largest profit. Later, some of his ships turned to fur trading on the Northwest Coast, then to whaling, and finally even went to China. His principal trade, however, was always with the West Indies.

In 1804, when South Carolina threw open its ports to the importation of slaves because of the threatened national prohibition, DeWolf leaped to their aid, and 10 of the 203 vessels that entered Charleston between 1804 and 1808 were his. During the Napoleonic Wars he suffered heavily from British impressment of his seamen, and was a strong advocate of war with England. Eleven days after the declaration of the War of 1812 he offered to the government, at his own expense, an armed brig of 160 tons, with eighteen guns and 120 men. The ship was named the *Yankee*, and was immensely successful, making six cruises in less than three years and capturing more than five million dollars of British property.

At the close of the War of 1812 he sensed the coming development of manufactures in the United States, and gradually withdrew from shipping. Even before this he had already established one of the earliest cotton mills in the United States at Coventry, Rhode Island, in 1812. For thirty years he also represented the town of Bristol in the Rhode Island legislature, becoming speaker of the house. In 1821 he was elected to the United States Senate, where he became a strong advocate of the protection of growing new industries, and opposed the extension of slavery to Missouri and the West. His interest was no longer in the American slave, but in white American mill workers, whom he felt needed the guarantee of free land for free white men in the West. He resigned his Senate seat in 1825 and returned to the Rhode Island legislature. He owned a great estate in Bristol of over 1,000 acres with a stately mansion. He married Nancy Bradford. (**A.** *DAB; NCAB*, 8:348. **B.** John R. Spears, *The American Slave Trade*, 1900.)

DICK, ALFRED BLAKE (April 16, 1856–August 15, 1934) and **Alfred Blake Dick Jr.** (February 11, 1894–October 24, 1954). Office equipment and supply manufacturers, A. B. Dick and Company. **Alfred B. Dick** was born in Bureau County, Illinois, son of Adam Dick and Rebecca Wible. In 1863 he moved with his parents to Galesburg, Illinois, where he was educated in the public schools. His early business education (1872–1879) was obtained with George W. Brown and Company, manufacturers of agricultural equipment in Galesburg. In the latter year he joined Deere and Manson Company in Moline, Illinois, also becoming a partner in the Moline Lumber Company. In 1883 he went to Chicago, where he organized the lumber firm of A. B. Dick and Company. The firm was incorporated a year later with Dick as president, treasurer, and principal factor in its management until shortly before his death.

In the operation of his lumber business Dick conceived the idea of sending daily inquiry sheets to mills and lumber yards as a means of compiling a stock inventory showing where he could draw supplies that his own yard did not have on hand. The labor involved in hand-writing these sheets prompted him to seek some means of duplicating the originals. After much experimentation he succeeded in devising a wax-covered sheet of paper, called an "automatic stencil," upon which, with a stylus, he could write form letters. These, by means of ink applied by a hand roller in a flat bed press, could be duplicated hundreds of times. From Thomas A. Edison* he secured permission to use a patent for an electric pen for the multiple reproduction of original writings to complete his process. Edison also supplied a device for coating the wax stencil sheets and invested a substantial sum in the new enterprise. The new device was therefore called the Edison-Dick Mimeograph.

The A. B. Dick Company sold its lumber interests in 1887 and thereafter concentrated on the manufacture and marketing of the mimeograph. Over the years the machine was improved; it was adapted to typewriting, a rotary mimeo machine was developed, stencil fabric was perfected, and finally electricity was applied as motive power. By the time of the elder Dick's death the machine had become virtually indispensable to every sort of public and private institution, and A. B. Dick Company had become internationally known. It employed 1,700 workers and had branches in practically every large city in the United States, with sales agents throughout the world. Like producers of other complex machinery (Burroughs Company and International Business Machines among others), A. B. Dick Company had to develop their own marketing mechanisms. In the late 1890s they began to market their product on a national scale, and by the late 1960s still dominated the manufacture of mimeograph machines.

Alfred Dick was a trustee of Lake Forest College from 1904 to 1921, and director of the Guda Company, the National Bank of the Republic, and the National City Bank of Chicago. He married Alice Sheldon Matthews of Galesburg in 1881. She died in 1885, and seven years later he married Mary Henrietta Matthews, sister of his first wife. He had a daughter and four sons, including **Alfred B. Dick Jr.** Young Dick was born in Chicago and graduated from Yale University in 1915. He entered his father's company as a clerk and salesman, served in the U.S. Navy during World War I, and after the war was appointed vice-president and treasurer of the firm. He was elected president and treasurer upon his father's death in 1934, serving in those offices until 1947, when he became chairman of the board. Under his direction during World War II, about 50 percent of the company's facilities were devoted to war materials production, including bomb sighting heads, requiring the finest type of precision workmanship. When the war ended he launched a new production program, introducing the 400 series of A. B. Dick Mimeographs.

In order to consolidate production under one roof, the company moved in 1949 to a new plant at Miles, Illinois. During the early 1950s, A. B. Dick began to expand their line of office machines, introducing a folding machine and entering the lithograph field with a complete line of supplies. They also began producing impression paper and spirit duplicating fluid at about the same time, becoming one of the few companies in the office supply business to offer a complete line of supplies for the three forms of office duplicating: mimeo, spirit, and offset.

A. B. Dick Jr. was a director of the New York Central Railroad, Northern Illinois Gas Company, Public Service Company of Northern Illinois, Commonwealth Edison, Marshall Field and Company, Northern Trust Company, and the First National Bank of Lake Forest, Illinois. He helped to found Lake Forest Hospital, and was alderman in Lake Forest for several years, as well as mayor of the town from 1928 to 1930. A Presbyterian and a Republican, he married Helen Aldrich of Lake Forest in 1917. They had a son and a daughter. Their son, Alfred Blake Dick III (b. 1918), joined A. B. Dick Company in 1939, advancing to the presidency in 1947. He served in that position until 1961, when he was named chairman of the board. (**A.** *NCAB*, 34:206; 45:226; *New York Times*, October 26, 1954; *Who Was Who*, vol. 1. **B.** Daniel M. Boorstin, *The Americans: The Democratic Experience*, 1973.)

DILLON, CLARENCE DOUGLAS (August 21, 1909–   ). Investment banker and public official, Dillon, Read and Company. Born in Geneva, Switzerland, son of Clarence Dillon and Ann McElder Douglass. His parents were visiting in Europe at the time. He was educated at Groton School, and graduated from Harvard in 1931. After completing his studies he joined his father's investment firm, Dillon, Read and Company, in New York City, being elected vice-president and director in 1938. In 1940 he was called to Washington to help establish a statistical control center for the U.S. Navy. Later in that same year he was commissioned an ensign in the naval reserve, and in the spring of 1941 was called to active duty, serving until 1945. He had a number of special assignments in Washington during the war, and spent one year at the naval air station in Seattle, Washington, followed by eighteen months of sea duty.

After the war he returned to Dillon, Read as chairman of the board of directors from 1946 to 1953, and as president of the United States and

Foreign Securities Corporation. He also served as president of the United States and International Securities Corporation, a subsidiary of the latter. From 1947 to 1953 he was a director of Amerada Petroleum Corporation. After 1953 he devoted himself to public service exclusively.

From 1953 to 1957 he was United States Ambassador to France, and since 1957 has played a major role in determining America's foreign and domestic policies. In 1957 he was called upon to reorganize and centralize the various economic functions of the State Department; he was Deputy Undersecretary of State for economic affairs in 1958-1959, and Undersecretary of State in 1959-1960. In 1959 he helped establish the Inter-American Development Bank, designed to promote economic development in Latin America. His most significant achievement with the State Department was in persuading the six nations of the European Common Market and the seven nations of the European Free Trade Association to join together in the Organization for Economic Cooperation and Development. In 1960 he was named by President Kennedy as Secretary of the Treasury, and he headed the American mission to the conference at Punta del Este, Uruguay in 1961. The Alliance for Progress was launched at this meeting.

The firm of Dillon, Read and Company had evolved when his father, who had joined the banking firm of William A. Read and Company, became president of the firm in 1916. In 1920 it became Dillon, Read and Company, and Clarence Dillon launched one of the most spectacular financial operations of the 1920s. He had organized the U.S. and Foreign Securities Corporation and the U.S. and International Securities Corporation in 1924 as publicly owned investment trust concerns with far-flung domestic and foreign holdings in chemicals, metals, natural gas, oil, and public utilities. By 1951 these corporations had a net income of $4,712,414. After conclusion of his public service activities, C. Douglas Dillon became president and director of U.S. and International Securities from 1967 to 1971, and chairman of the board after 1971. He also became chairman of the executive committee of Dillon, Read after 1971. In addition to those duties, he served as chairman of the Rockefeller Foundation from 1972 and of the Brookings Institution from 1970, and as president of the Metropolitan Museum of Art from 1970. Quite obviously, Mr. Dillon's business and public service careers have nicely dovetailed in a mutually beneficial fashion. This has caused some analysts to identify him as a key member of a new "ruling" or "governing" class, dominant in financial institutions, governmental affairs, and powerful private foundations.

A Republican and a close friend of John Foster Dulles, he is an Episcopalian, and married Phyllis Chess Ellsworth of Boston in 1931. They have a son and a daughter. (**A.** *NCAB*, J:39; *Current Biography*, April, 1953; *Who's Who in America*, 1978-79. **B.** G. William Domhoff, *Who Rules America?*, 1967; and *The Governing Circles*, 1970.)

DILLON, SIDNEY (May 7, 1812–June 9, 1892). Railroad construction contractor and financier, Union Pacific Railroad. Born in Northampton, Montgomery County, New York, son of Timothy Dillon. His family had resided near his birthplace for several generations, but were very poor, and Sidney received only a meager education. At age seven he began work as a water boy on the Mohawk and Hudson Railroad from Albany to Schenectady, and when this road was finished he took a similar position on the Rensselaer and Saratoga Railroad. Later, he acted as overseer and then foreman on several other railroad construction projects in the Northeast.

Finally he decided to enter business for himself, although he had little capital. He made a bid for the construction of what became the Boston and Albany Railroad. The bid was accepted and the work was satisfactorily completed in 1840. This was the beginning of a contracting career of unusual extent and success. During the next thirty years he built thousands of miles of railroads in all parts of the country, either individually or in association with other contractors. Among those he partially constructed were: Rutland and Burlington; Central Railroad of New Jersey; Philadelphia and Erie; Morris and Essex; the Pennsylvania; the New Orleans, Mobile, and Chattanooga; and the Canada Southern. He also built for Cornelius Vanderbilt* the tunnel from Grand Central Station on 42nd Street in New York to the Harlem River.

The greatest enterprise of his life was the construction of the Union Pacific Railroad, with which he became actively associated through the purchase of stock in the Credit Mobilier. He was one of the original contractors and the directing authority for subsidiary contractors. During the next four years he took an active part in the construction of railway track, taking part in the laying of the ceremonial last rail in 1869. He served as a director of Union Pacific for eight years (1864–1872) and as president for nearly twelve years (1874–1884 and 1890–1892). At the time of his death he was chairman of the board.

In 1870 he was chiefly known as a financier. He had accumulated a large fortune which lay principally in investments in railroad securities. Much of this accumulation resulted from his early policy of taking as part payment for construction shares of stock in the companies for which he worked. He became actively associated with Jay Gould* in many of the properties controlled by the latter. He was a director of Western Union Telegraph Company, Manhattan Elevated Railroad Company, the Missouri Pacific Railroad, and several other transportation organizations. He married Hannah Smith of Amherst, Massachusetts, in 1841, and they had two daughters. (**A.** *DAB; New York Times,* June 10, 1892; *Who Was Who,* vol. H. **B.** Robert G. Athearn, *Union Pacific Country,* 1971; Robert W. Fogel, *The Union Pacific Railroad: A Case of Premature Enterprise,* 1960; Matthew Josephson, *The Robber Barons,* 1934; James McCague, *Moguls and Iron Men,* 1964; Stephen Salsbury, *The State, the Investor and the Railroad: The Boston* *and Albany, 1825-1867*, 1967; Nelson Trottman, *History of the Union Pacific*, 1923.)

DISNEY, ROY (June 24, 1893–December 20, 1971) and **Walter Elias Disney** (December 5, 1901–December 15, 1964). Motion picture and entertainment company executives, Walt Disney Productions. Roy and Walt Disney were born in Chicago, Illinois, sons of Elias Disney and Flora Call. Their father was a native of Canada whose family had moved to Kansas in the 1870s. Elias Disney tried a number of jobs and ventures during his career, none of which was successful. He attempted citrus fruit growing in Florida, was a carpenter at the Columbia Exposition in Chicago, ran a small contracting business for several years in that city, and in 1906 moved the family to a small eight acre farm near Merceline, Kansas. In 1910 he was forced to sell the farm and moved to Kansas City, where he purchased a Kansas City *Star* newspaper route of 3,000 customers. Still later he returned to Chicago as head of maintenance and construction in a jelly factory. The boys were educated in the public schools of Merceline and Kansas City.

While **Roy Disney** was in school he helped his father on the farm and later assisted him with his newspaper route in Kansas City. He graduated from high school in 1911 and worked as a clerk at the First National Bank of Kansas City from 1914 to 1917. During the next two years Roy served as a petty officer aboard a cargo ship plying between New York and Paris, and later aboard a cruiser. Roy resumed his position at the bank in 1919 but, being in ill health, he went West in 1920 to recuperate. As a youth **Walt Disney** delivered newspapers and wrote a weekly sketch for a local barber in return for twenty-five cents or a free haircut. During the summer of 1917 he sold magazines and candy aboard a Kansas City to Chicago train. After his family returned to Chicago, Walt continued his education at McKinley High School there, also taking a course in photography and studying evenings at the Chicago Academy of Fine Arts. In 1918 he enlisted for war service in France as an ambulance driver for the Red Cross, and after the war returned to Kansas City, finally securing a job as a commercial artist with the Gray Advertising Company. During this time he continued to practice his cartooning, and in 1920 was hired as an apprentice cartoonist for the magazine *Film Advertising*. He remained at this job for two years, and through it his interest in film was aroused. Experimenting in a studio above his father's garage, he succeeded in turning out a cartoon for showing in local theaters. In 1923 he decided to join his brother Roy in Hollywood, leaving Kansas City with forty dollars and sketches for an animated cartoon of *Alice in Cartoonland*, which combined a living girl with animated cartoon figures. Upon arrival in California, Walt persuaded Roy to assist him in his new venture as a cartoonist.

The two brothers formed a partnership with $290 in savings and $500 borrowed from an uncle. They converted a small garage into a studio and produced a series of *Alice* cartoons over the next three years. In 1926 they contracted with Universal Studios to have Walt direct the *Oswald the Rabbit* cartoons for the next two years. During this same time he was working on the creation of the cartoon character Mickey Mouse, which was designed by his friend and assistant, Ub Iwerks. In 1928 they brought out an animated sound cartoon, *Steamboat Willie*, starring Mickey Mouse. The cartoon was an instant success, and within the next ten years Mickey Mouse, with a supporting cast of Minnie Mouse, Pluto, and Donald Duck, achieved international stardom in over one hundred cartoons.

During these years Roy Disney handled the financial and administrative end of the business, freeing Walt to pursue the creative side. Walt, however, soon realized he had little talent as a cartoonist, and left the actual designing and drawing of the cartoons to employees. Walt's creativity lay more in the overall vision and direction of the films and other later enterprises. Sincerely treasuring a set of Middle Western middle-class values, he ensured that these values were portrayed in his films, unerringly striking the pulse of "middle America" and eschewing the avant garde. By combining talents, the Disney brothers built an entertainment empire, first as innovators in the animated cartoon medium, then as producers of live action films and television programs for family audiences, and later as creators and builders of world famous amusement centers. In 1929, at Roy Disney's insistence, the business was incorporated as Walt Disney Productions, with Walt as president and Roy as vice-president.

In 1929 Walt began the "Silly Symphony" series, which introduced the *Three Little Pigs* in 1933. A year later he began work on *Snow White and the Seven Dwarfs*, the first feature-length animated cartoon ever attempted. The venture took an outlay of $1.6 million and three years to complete, but grossed over $8 million in a short time, holding the record as the film industry's biggest moneymaker until *Gone With the Wind*, four years later. Disney Productions built a new fifty-one acre studio in Burbank in 1939, the same year that *Ferdinand the Bull* was released. This was followed by *Fantasia* in 1940, *Dumbo* in 1941, and *Bambi* in 1942. Despite the critical success of these ventures (winning three Academy Awards during these years), and the fact that the films did well in the theaters, Disney's meticulous attention to detail and perfection made these full-length animated cartoons very costly to produce. As a result, Disney studios went through a severe financial crisis in the late 1930s and early 1940s, forcing it to make a public stock offering in 1940.

The fortunes of Disney studios at this critical juncture were largely saved by the federal government, which gave Disney contracts for training and propaganda films during the war. This allowed the studio to continue functioning and to keep its crisis largely hidden, and gave the Disneys a head start in planning for diversification of the firm's activities, first in the nature of the company's motion picture productions, then in its overall activities. Although the studio produced another full-length animated cartoon, *Song of the South*, in 1947, it increasingly turned its efforts to less expensive nature documentaries and live-action films. It was also one of the first Hollywood studios to move into television, but unlike the others, Disney refused to sell his films to the networks, retaining control over his own product. In 1950 the Disneys brought their cartoon characters to the television screen for the first time, and a year later a new series of Mickey Mouse cartoons was inaugurated. The company also began producing a number of Mickey Mouse and Silly Symphony books and syndicated comic books at about this time. In 1954 Walt and Roy founded Disneyland as the base of their television productions. They produced *Disneyland T.V.* and the *Mickey Mouse Club Show* on ABC-TV from 1954 to 1961; the television show *Zorro*, which appeared in 1957; *Walt Disney Presents* from 1958 to 1961; and *Walt Disney's Wonderful World of Color*, which began its long run (twenty years as of this writing) on NBC-TV in 1961.

As a capstone for all this, in 1954 the Disney brothers created the amusement and entertainment center, Disneyland, in Anaheim, California, the first of America's "theme" or "atmospheric" parks. This was followed some ten years later by Walt Disney World in Orlando, Florida. They also developed the Celebrity Sports Center in Denver, Colorado, in 1962, and in 1965 obtained rights from the U.S. Forest Service to develop a $35 million year-round ski resort at Mineral King in the Sierra Nevada range of California. This latter move was resisted by conservation groups and challenged in court by the Sierra Club. Disneyland and its clone, Disneyworld, became instant and phenomenal successes. While the former park was being constructed in 1954 Disney liberally advertised its progress on his aptly named *Disneyland* television show, and the results were apparent in the attendance at Disneyland. In its first six months of existence slightly more than a million people visited the park, and in 1956, its first full year of operation, about three million people passed through its gates, producing gross revenues of $10 million. Thereafter, word of mouth and Disney's publicity machinery spread the news of the glories of Disneyland, and the park itself soon generated the capital to finance a vast expansion of all of Walt Disney's enterprises.

The reasons for the fabulous success of Disneyland and other theme parks in contemporary America are complex and much debated. Partly the success comes from the park's ability to appeal to a wide spectrum of age groups. Having the popular Disney cartoon characters and "tame" rides for smaller children combined with more exciting rides for adults and teenagers makes it an ideal family outing. But the source of its success probably lies deeper in the American psyche. Most visitors to the park comment on its cleanliness and orderliness, and Disney himself had a life-long passion to order, control, and keep clean any environment he inhabited. Thus there is a compulsion to keep the park perfectly clean and orderly at all times. All day sanitation men prowl the streets, picking up litter. Every night each street and walkway is thoroughly hosed down, and crews armed with putty knives get down on their hands and knees to scrape up discarded chewing gum. The staff itself is as well scrubbed as the grounds and is exceptionally well mannered and polite. Further, the park is "safe"; a steep admission fee to the park, along with the fact that it can only be entered via a monorail, helps ensure a "respectable" clientele. The safety factor is enhanced by the park's own police, largely moonlighting schoolteachers, who make sure rowdyism is nipped in the bud. For Americans whose urban environments are increasingly unclean and unsafe, Disneyland and Disneyworld are like nostalgic havens in a world gone mad.

Until the opening of Disneyland, the Disney studios remained a very small business among the Hollywood giants. In 1954, however, they grossed more than $10 million, and after that sales and earnings shot sharply upwards, going over $100 million in 1965. Profits in 1966 reached $12,392,000. By this time Walt and Roy Disney and their associates had found a proven formula of appeal and had managed to adapt it to every medium of communication known to man. They had even invented a new and unique medium all their own—Disneyland. All the parts of the great Disney machine—movies, television, book and song publication, merchandising, and Disneyland—interlock and are mutually reciprocating. And all are aimed at the most vulnerable part of an adult's psyche—his feelings for children. As Richard Schickel has commented, "as capitalism it is a work of genius; as culture it is mostly a horror." Disney has been criticized for shattering the two most valuable things about childhood—its secrets and its silences—and replacing them with a banal predictability that everyone is forced to share. Yet this same predictability was probably the reason for his great success among the masses. Disney created a world of fantasy, keeping its frets and doubts and inner troubles to itself. To people nostalgic for a romantic past, for an escape from the realities of the present, for simple humor and morally "safe" entertainment, the Disney brothers filled a clear need.

Although Walt Disney was often attacked for his political conservatism by liberal commentators, and although he supported the Republican party of his friends George Murphy and Ronald Reagan, he had little active interest in politics. If he had any politics at all, they were the politics of nostalgia, and his instinct throughout his life was to wall himself off from the affairs of nations and governments—a characteristic shared by his films and other entertainment successes. Roy Disney married Edna Francis in 1925 and they had one son. Walt Disney marred Lillian Marie Bounds of Lewiston, Idaho, one of his first office employees, and they had two daughters. (*NCAB*, E:70; 57:391; *Current Biography*, August, 1940; April, 1952; February, 1967; *New York Times*, December 16, 1966; *Fortune*, May,

1966; *Who Was Who*, vol. 4; R. D. Feild, *The Art of Walt Disney*, 1942; Diane Disney Miller, *The Story of Walt Disney*, 1957; Richard Schickel, *The Disney Version*, 1968.)

DISSTON, HENRY (May 23, 1819–March 16, 1878). Saw manufacturer, H. Disston and Sons. Born in Tewkesbury, England, son of Thomas Disston and Ann Harrod. His father was a mechanic experienced in the manufacture of lace-making machines. The father brought Henry and his sister to America when the boy was fourteen years old (1833). Three days after arriving in Philadelphia his father died, so Henry became a sawmaker's apprentice. In 1840 he started a small business with capital of $350. The saw industry was still in the handicraft stage, was dependent upon imported steel, and was confronted with the competition of superior English workmanship.

Henry Disston's significance was twofold: first, he was an innovator in technology; second, he transformed a small, struggling industry into one that entered worldwide competition and conquered world markets. As early as 1844 he made use of steam power in his saw factory. Another early innovation was the conversion of waste steel into ingots in place of reshipment to England. He evolved the formula for the manufacture of the highest grade crucible steel demanded by the peculiar strains to which saws are subjected, and was freed from imported steel.

During the Civil War he adapted the plant to produce war supplies, and built a rolling mill to make metal plates. He set up an experimental sawmill to determine the types of saws best suited to various kinds of timber and the varying needs of woodcutting. He worked on the conservation of lumber by reducing the thickness of saws. Greater speed and driving power were made possible by improvements in the quality of steel and in the models of saws. Disston was unusually gifted as a mechanic and inventor, and this was demonstrated in the constant improvements in products and plant equipment.

The expansion of the business continued until at length the works produced all types of saws from the largest circular saw to the smallest keyhole saw. They also produced a great number of files, knives, screwdrivers, trowels, and so forth. By establishing agencies in various places, he contributed greatly to the tendency of manufacturers to supplant the mercantile factor in the industrial group. In 1871 the Disston Factory at Tacony, Pennsylvania, near Philadelphia, was opened. The establishment included a tract of several hundred acres and a factory town rapidly grew up around it, with workers' houses partly financed by the company.

He was a Republican and a Presbyterian, and married Amanda Bickley in 1844. They had no children. He then married Mary Sillman of New Jersey, and they had five sons: Hamilton, Albert H., Horace C., William, and Jacob S. Disston. The Disston works was a family business in the fullest sense of the term, with Henry bringing all his sons, plus several of his brothers, into the business. His brother Charles (1823–1895) was with the firm for forty-three years; Thomas (1832–1897) joined the firm in 1848; and Samuel (1838–1908) was a selling representative for the firm for many years.

Of Henry's sons, Hamilton (1844–1896), the eldest, succeeded his father as head of the firm, serving until his death. He also formed the Disston Land Company in 1880, which purchased 4,000,000 acres of land from the state of Florida. It was swamp land which he improved for $2.5 million and opened for settlement. This transaction was later to play a prominent role in the Populist campaign of that state. William Disston (1849–1915) succeeded Hamilton as president in 1896, serving until his death in 1915. William's son, William Dunlop Disston (b. 1859) also became president of Disston Saw. His son, William D. Disston Jr. (b. 1888) became a vice-president of the firm in 1913, serving for the rest of his life. Jacob S. Disston (1862–1938), Henry's youngest son, was a director of Disston Saw for his entire adult life. He was also involved in banking in Tacony and Philadelphia. His son, Jacob S. Disston Jr. (b. 1895) became a vice-president at Disston in 1933, rising to the presidency in 1947. He was followed into the firm by his son, Jacob S. Disston III (b. 1919), the fourth generation in management in the family. (**A.** *DAB; NCAB,* 6:146; 18:75; 28:468; *Encyclopedia of Contemporary Biography,* vol. 2, 29–32; John W. Jordan, ed., *Encyclopedia of Pennsylvania Biography,* 31 vols., 1914–63, 9:122; 27:219; 29:21; *Iron Age,* March 21, 1878; December 12, 1895; May 7, 1896; November 25, 1897; July 2, 1908; April 8, 1915. **B.** E. P. Oberholtzer, *Philadelphia: A History,* 4 vols., 1912, 4:426; C. Vann Woodward, *Origins of the New South,* 1951, 117.)

DOAN FAMILY: see The Dow and Doan Families.

DODD, SAMUEL CALVIN TATE (February 20, 1836–January 30, 1907). Corporate lawyer, Standard Oil Company. Born in Franklin, Venango County, Pennsylvania, son of Levi L. Dodd and Julia Parker. His father was a cabinetmaker and carpenter. Young Dodd was educated in the schools of Franklin, working as an errand boy and printer's devil to earn money for his college education. He graduated in 1857 from Jefferson College (now Washington and Jefferson) at Canonsburg, Pennsylvania. He then studied law in Franklin for two years and was admitted to the bar in 1859, the year oil was discovered in western Pennsylvania. His entire subsequent career was to be shaped by that fortuitous event. A vast influx of capital and business came upon the heels of the great discovery and he found himself immediately involved in the complications and competition growing out of the boom.

He gave his attention mainly to corporate law and equity. Dodd also had strong ideas concerning the wastefulness of the cut-throat competition of the oil producers of the early boom period, and even at an early period felt that consolidation was desirable. Nevertheless, the 1870s found him fighting the battles of the independent oil men of his home region against John D. Rockefeller,* and he acquired a considerable reputation as an anti-rebate lawyer. In 1872 and 1873 he was a delegate to the Pennsylvania constitutional convention, where he fathered the anti-rebate clause which was written into the constitution. During this period he served as counsel for numerous oil operators and transportation companies, especially the transportation companies from which the United Pipe Lines were later formed.

In 1881 Dodd became general solicitor for the Standard Oil Company, moving to New York City. He had an unusual relationship with the company, since he felt that in order to give it the best legal advice, he should occupy a detached, almost judicial position. Therefore he refused to allow Rockefeller to place to his credit for gradual payment a block of stock that would have made him a millionaire many times. His salary was never more than $25,000, and he left an estate worth less than $300,000. Dodd always stood somewhat aloof from Rockefeller and other Standard Oil magnates.

Dodd's principal reputation rests upon his involvement in the organization in 1882 of the Standard Oil Trust, and he is sometimes called the "father of the trusts." The obvious move for Standard Oil to have made in order to reduce the competition in the oil fields was to form a single large legal and administrative consolidation of these companies. In order to do that one proposal was to appeal to the Pennsylvania legislature for a special charter. This, they felt, would bring needless negative publicity and possibly negative results. So Dodd conceived the idea of creating a "corporation of corporations," which could serve as a legal mechanism to bypass existing state laws. Under the trust agreement that he drew up, the voting stocks of some forty companies were placed in the hands of trustees. The trust instrument authorized an office of nine trustees to "exercise general supervision over the affairs of the several Standard Oil Companies." At the same time state-chartered subsidiaries were formed to take over the properties of the alliance operating in one state. As local enterprises they were not subject to restrictions or excessive taxes levied on "foreign" corporations. The trust experiment was kept secret for six years, and it was Dodd's task to officiate at both its birth and at its demise.

In 1892 a judicial decision in Ohio declared the purposes of the Standard Oil Trust "to establish a virtual monopoly of the business of producing petroleum . . . and to control . . . the price . . . contrary to the policy of our state." Fortunately for Standard Oil, the state of New Jersey in 1889 had revised its corporation laws, limiting the taxes that could be levied on a corporation to a small percentage upon its capitalization. Furthermore, New Jersey had aided incorporation by putting few limitations on the purposes of a corporation. Corporations with a New Jersey charter could own real estate in other states and carry on business there, and own stocks in other corporations. This authorization to serve as a holding company enabled a New Jersey corporation to act as a centralizing agency in combination policy. Dodd directed the creation of the Standard Oil Company of New Jersey, purchasing from the Trust its refineries, shipping works, and other factories. In 1899 he drew up the plans for the organization of a great holding company under the same name, increasing the capital stock from ten million to one hundred ten million dollars. The organization of this holding company signaled the final triumph of the corporation. Dodd continued as legal advisor of the company until 1905, when he retired from active service to Standard Oil, although he retained the title of counsel until his death.

Dodd opposed the early interpretation of the Sherman Anti-trust Act which penalized all combinations in restraint of trade, arguing that only unreasonable combinations should be banned. Ironically, his view was adopted by the Supreme Court in 1911 in *Standard Oil of New Jersey v. the United States*, which dissolved the holding company he had created. Despite the fact that Standard Oil was broken up into constituent units by this decision, the court established the principle of "reasonableness" as the operative doctrine after this time. Dodd was a firm believer in the federal incorporation of business companies, and favored a constitutional amendment to make this possible.

A Democrat in his early career, Dodd later became an independent in politics. He was a Presbyterian and married Mary E. Green of Waterford, Pennsylvania, in 1860, and Melvina E. Smith in 1877. He had three sons and a daughter. (**A.** *DAB; NCAB*, 24:264; *Who Was Who*, vol. 1; S. C. T. Dodd, *Memoirs, Written For His Children*, 1907. **B.** James C. Bonbright and Gardner C. Means, *The Holding Company*, 1932; Alfred D. Chandler Jr., *The Visible Hand*, 1977; David Freeman Hawke, *John D.*, 1980; Ralph W. and Muriel E. Hidy, *Pioneering in Big Business*, 1955; Edward C. Kirkland, *Industry Comes of Age*, 1961; William Letwin, *Law and Economic Policy in America: The Evolution of the Sherman Act*, 1965; Alan Nevins, *A Study of Power*, 1953; William J. Ripley, *Trusts, Pools and Corporations*, 1905; Ida M. Tarbell, *History of the Standard Oil Company*, 2 vols., 1904; Hans B. Thorelli, *Federal Anti-Trust Policy*, 1954; Harold F. Williamson and Arnold R. Daum, *The American Petroleum Industry*, 1959.)

DODGE FAMILY: William Earl Dodge (September 4, 1805–February 9, 1883); **William E. Dodge Jr.** (February 15, 1832–1903); **Cleveland Hoadley Dodge** (January 26, 1860–June 24, 1926). Mining Company Executives, Phelps Dodge Corporation. **William E. Dodge** was born in Hartford, Connecticut, son of David Low Dodge and Sarah Cleveland. His family had been in New England since 1638, and his father had joined with his wife's cousins, the Higginsons, in the Boston dry goods trade. After prospering in his own mercantile business in the area, he went to New York City in 1809, where he started a jobbing concern, again in partnership with the Higginsons. The firm suffered heavy losses during the Napoleonic Wars and was soon dissolved. In 1813 David Low Dodge became head of Bozrah Manufacturing Company, which erected the first cotton mill in the state of Connecticut.

William E. Dodge was educated in Norwich, Connecticut, New York City, and Mendham, New Jersey. At thirteen he began to work in his father's wholesale dry goods firm in New York, and a year later was employed as a clerk in the country store connected with his father's factory in New York. At age twenty-one he went into the dry goods business on his own account. In 1828 he married Melissa Phelps, daughter of Anson G. Phelps,* a prominent New York merchant. Phelps was engaged in the export of cotton and the import of metals in his business, and in 1833 Dodge retired from his own dry goods business to join Phelps in organizing Phelps Dodge and Company, which for two generations was to hold a prominent place as a dealer in copper and other metals.

The Phelps Dodge Company was to play an important part in the development of Lake Superior copper and Pennsylvania iron, and established a rolling mill at Derby, Connecticut, and manufacturing operations in the village of Ansonia, Connecticut. Dodge was a founder of the Lackawanna Iron and Coal Company at Scranton, Pennsylvania, with additional iron and steel works in Oxford Furnace, New Jersey, Illinois, and Virginia. He also purchased extensive woodlands near Williamsport, Pennsylvania. Phelps Dodge, however, reached its position of eminence in the copper industry by its exploitation of large bodies of copper ore in Arizona. A Detroit mining promoter, attracted to the region, developed claims and started mining and smelting on a regular basis. In need of further capital, he solicited a loan in 1880 from William Dodge. Dodge then engaged a Canadian-born mining engineer, James Douglas, to investigate the properties. On the basis of Douglas' glowing report, Dodge started investing in Arizona. Over the next three decades the Phelps Dodge firm committed an increasing amount of capital to copper mining and smelting enterprises there, all of which were managed by Douglas. By 1910 the company had completely abandoned the import-export business and had become one of the largest copper producers in the nation.

William E. Dodge was a large investor in several railroads, including the Erie, Lackawanna, Jersey Central, and Texas Central. He was one of the organizers of the YMCA in America and played a prominent role in the Evangelical Alliance and temperance reform. From 1865 until his death he was president of the National Temperance Society, and he proposed a national commission of inquiry into the liquor traffic. An antislavery man, he was a member of the unsuccessful Peace Conference at Washington, D.C., in February, 1861. After the outbreak of the Civil War he helped arm and equip Union soldiers in West Virginia and East Tennessee. A Presbyterian and a Republican, he and his wife had one son, **William E. Dodge Jr.**, and five daughters.

Young Dodge became a partner in Phelps Dodge and took over direction of the enterprise after his father's death. It was during the years of his administration that the firm underwent its vast expansion in the copper mining industry. A Presbyterian and president of the Evangelical Alliance, he married Sarah Hoadley in 1854. They had a son and a daughter. Their son, **Cleveland H. Dodge**, graduated from Princeton in 1879 and received a master of arts degree there in 1882. In the following year he was named a partner at Phelps Dodge, and became a vice-president in 1908 when it was incorporated with capital of $50 million. In that year Phelps Dodge took over the complete ownership of the Copper Queen Consolidated Mining Company, Detroit Copper and Mining Company, Montezuma Copper Company, and the Stag Canon Fuel Company. In the same year it purchased the El Paso and Northeastern Railroad. Annual production of copper at Phelps Dodge increased from 115 million pounds in 1908 to 208 million pounds in 1925. Cleveland H. Dodge remained as vice-president and then chairman of the board of the firm until he died. He married Grace Parrish in 1883, and they had four children. Their eldest son, Cleveland Earl Dodge (b. 1888) was named a vice-president of Phelps Dodge in 1924 and remained with the company throughout his life. By 1957 the annual sales of the firm were in excess of $300 million, and copper production stood at 500 million pounds. He married Pauline Morgan, and they had three children. His eldest son, Cleveland E. Dodge Jr. (b. 1922) became a director of Phelps Dodge, but his principal business interests lay with Dodge Industries in Hoosick, New York.

Grace Hoadley Dodge (1856–1914), daughter of William E. Dodge Jr., was well known for her philanthropic, charity, and reform work in New York City for over thirty years. She was president of the Working Girls Society, treasurer of Teacher's College, president of the national board of the YMCA of the United States, and a disciple of Dwight L. Moody, the evangelist. (**A.** *DAB; NCAB*, 3:174; 13:352; 20:171; 18:310; 26:407; 1:116; *Who Was Who*, vol. H; *Who's Who in America, 1978–79; New York Times*, February 13, 1883; Richard Lowitt, *A Merchant Prince of the Nineteenth Century*, 1954. **B.** Robert Glass Cleland, *A History of the Phelps Dodge Company*, 1952.)

DOHENY, EDWARD LAURENCE (August 10, 1856–September 8, 1935). Oil producer, Mexican Oil Company of California. Born near Fond du Lac, Wisconsin, son of Patrick Doheny, of Irish extraction, and Eleanor Elizabeth Quigley, a native of Newfoundland. After some schooling, Edward Doheny left home at age sixteen to drive mules for the government's geological survey of the boundary line between Arizona and New Mexico. In this position he picked up the rudiments of surveying, but was not attracted to that profession, so he began prospecting for gold in western mountains. At one time or another over a period of twenty years of prospecting he enjoyed a modest prosperity.

In 1893 he was walking on a street in Los Angeles, California, with little money in his pocket, when he saw a wagonload of what looked like dark earth pass by, driven by a black man. The driver told him it was "brea," a Mexican word for pitch, which was used by some small factories for fuel. He indicated that he had dug it near Westlake Park. Doheny felt that it was oil-soaked earth so he went to the spot and found an oily excretion from the soil. He and an old prospector friend, Charles A. Canfield, leased a vacant lot nearby and began digging with a pick and shovel. After digging some distance down, they hired a driller, who at 225 feet brought in a well that produced 45 barrels of oil per day. This started the oil boom in Los Angeles, and within five years there were 2,500 wells in the city. Doheny convinced the Santa Fe Railroad to convert an engine yard into an oil burner for demonstration purposes. A. A. Robinson, head of the Mexican Central Railroad, saw it and suggested to Doheny in 1900 that he prospect for oil near Tampico, Mexico, promising a contract with the railroad for oil if he found it.

Doheny took leases on 250,000 acres near Tampico, but when he brought in his first oil well, he found that there had been a change in management at the Mexican Central Railroad, and its promise to buy oil was repudiated. Since there was overproduction of oil in the United States at that time, Doheny was left without a market, so he began to produce asphalt from his find. He laid about one-half of the asphalt paving in Mexico City. Shortly after that, the automobile began to create a rapidly growing demand for gasoline, and Doheny organized the Mexican Petroleum Company of California in the United States, with capital of $10 million. This firm became dominant in the Tampico field, and later the Tuxpan district, where a lighter oil of higher gasoline content was found. The Standard Oil Company also had large interests in these two fields.

Doheny was very close to the Diaz government in Mexico, but when he brought British interests into his company Diaz was displeased, so Doheny supported his overthrow in the Revolution of 1910. The stock of Doheny's company fluctuated so wildly on the exchange during this period that he was called before the Governors of the New York Stock Exchange to explain. He convinced them that he had not been manipulating it. In 1922 he procured from the U.S. government a contract to build a large naval fuel station at Pearl Harbor, Hawaii, and seven months later received drilling rights to 32,000 acres of naval oil reserve land at Elk Hills, Colorado. Later the public was to learn that he had sent Albert B. Fall, the Secretary of the Interior, $100,000 in cash. Doheny claimed it was a loan, but Fall and Doheny were indicted in 1925 for bribery. The trial went on for years. In 1926 they were acquitted of conspiracy charges, but in 1930 Fall was convicted of receiving a bribe, even though Doheny was judged innocent of giving it. The government, however, cancelled Doheny's oil leases, and he was forced to make restitution of the profits he had gained from them.

Doheny's reputation was blackened by the incident, and little else is usually remembered about him. In spite of those scandalous dealings, however, it was he who largely made Mexico into the second largest producer of oil at that time. He constructed a refinery at Tampico Terminal with a capacity of 130,000 barrels of crude oil daily, most of which was sent to the United States, Great Britain, and South America. In 1911 he acquired the Calorie Company, which distributed petroleum and its products in South America. In 1915 he formed the Mexican Petroleum Corporation to distribute Mexican oil in the U.S., and a year later the Pan American Oil Company of California. In 1925 he sold his Mexican oil interests to Standard Oil of Indiana, and later sold off the rest of his oil interests outside the state of California. He donated one million dollars to the University of Southern California for a library in memory of his son.

A Roman Catholic and a Democrat, he married Carrie Estelle Betzhold of Marshalltown, Iowa, in 1900. They had one son, Edward L. Doheny Jr., who was killed by a servant in 1929. (**A.** *DAB*, Supplement 1; *NCAB*, 29:238. **B.** Burl Noggle, *Teapot Dome: Oil and Politics in the 1920's*, 1962.)

DOHERTY, HENRY LATHAM (May 15, 1870–December 26, 1939). Utility Executive and Oil Producer, Cities Service Oil Company. Born in Columbus, Ohio, son of Frank Doherty and Anna McIlvaine. His father was a college-trained engineer and superintendent of the water works in Columbus. When he died in 1882 he left the family in a very poor financial situation, so Henry was forced to leave school at age twelve, becoming an office boy for the Columbus Gas Company. He worked his way up from this post, and was one of the first to realize that the proper strategy of the gas companies, faced with increasing competition from electric light companies, was to develop new uses for gas, such as cooking. In 1896, the parent company in New York—Emerson, McMillan and Company, bankers—sent Doherty to Madison, Wisconsin, on the first of a series of troubleshooting missions. Before long he was chief engineer and general manager of all the McMillan properties, which he reorganized into a formal holding company called the American Light and Traction Company. He also served as president of the National Electric Light Association in 1901–1902.

In 1905 Doherty formed his own company, Henry L. Doherty and Company, to render engineering and financial services to utility companies. In 1910 he bought three operating companies and put them under a holding company called Cities Service. It rapidly expanded when fifty-three operating companies were acquired in 1913. Many of these firms were in deep financial trouble, but he rescued them by what he called the "Doherty Formula." That was defined as acquire, rebuild, merge, refinance, infuse new life and new organization, and move on to the next field. . . . Doherty soon went from manufacturing gas, to natural gas and drilling for natural gas, to oil. He constructed the first long-distance large-diameter high pressure gas pipeline from Amarillo, Texas, to Chicago in 1931. He was also among the first users of underground storage to meet seasonal peaks in the use of gas.

Doherty also fought for years for rational conservation policies within the oil industry, and pushed for legislation requiring unit operation of oil pools. All of the rapid expansion that his firm had undergone required more capital than Doherty was able to get from earnings or bankers. He was able to get some financing in Europe prior to World War I, but mostly he relied on selling his own stocks and debentures through a network of branch offices of Henry L. Doherty and Company, using high pressure methods on his employees and customers. Some of these practices were declared illegal by the Securities Act of 1933 and the Public Utilities Holding Company Act of 1935.

Doherty also invested heavily in real estate during the 1920s, especially buying Wall Street office buildings and Florida resort hotels. He built Cities Service into one of the largest enterprises of its kind in the U.S.; with subsidiaries it had assets of over $1,288,000,000 in 1932, and controlled more than 200 electric power, artificial and natural gas, and oil properties in thirty-three states and several foreign countries. The physical assets of the firm included 5,500 producing oil wells, 900 miles of oil pipeline, an oil refining capacity of 36,000 barrels daily, storage capacity of 20 million barrels, 300 tank cars, a fleet of seven tankers, 1,700 natural gas wells, 8,400 miles of natural gas pipelines, 2,000 miles of artificial gas pipelines, and 3,160,850 acres of leased oil and gas lands. Its equipment was sufficient to supply its customers with 1,587,517,000 kilowatt hours of electrical current and 122,466,300,000 cubic feet of gas. Its gross earnings were about $200 million per year.

In 1919 Doherty helped found the American Petroleum Institute, and was vice-president of the organization from 1919 to 1924, and a director until 1931. He was also president of several regional utility associations. He married Mrs. Grace Eames in 1929 and adopted her daughter from a previous marriage. (*DAB*, Supplement 2; *NCAB*, 4334:11; *New York Times*, December 27, 1939.)

DOLAN, THOMAS (October 27, 1834–June 12, 1914). Utility company executive, United Gas Improvement Company. Born in Montgomery County, Pennsylvania, of obscure ancestry. His education was limited to a few years in the public schools. Dolan began his business career at age fifteen, when he became a salesman in a store. At twenty-two his connections with the wholesale knitting goods business began. During the early years of the Civil War he successfully reorganized a factory under the firm name of the Keystone Knitting Mills, gaining a virtual monopoly in his particular branch of the industry. He reorganized the business to manufacture, in turn, knit goods, worsted shawls, and worsted coating goods. He was one of the very first manufacturers to introduce electrical power into the factory.

In 1882 Dolan became a director of the United Gas Improvement Company of Philadelphia. From that point, he expanded his activities in the field of public utilities until his interests extended over a large part of the industry. In this manner he became a national figure in the early development of the gas and electric lighting and power industry. In 1892 he became president of United Gas Improvement, and in 1897 secured a thirty year lease of the city's gas lighting system. In 1905, however, the city decided to negotiate for a new lease, which created a political storm with Dolan in the center. It was widely believed by the public that the political organization in control of the city was proposing to mortgage or "rob" the city's future for the sake of ready money for corrupt use. But city officials went ahead and opened negotiations for a new lease. As adopted, the new lease extended to 1980, instead of 1927, and payments to the public were to amount to $25,000,000. But the mayor vetoed the council's bill, so Dolan wrote to the city and said his company had lost interest in the deal.

Dolan was a pioneer in the development of modern interlocking directorates, was one of the organizers and first president of the Manufacturer's Club of Philadelphia, and served as president of the National Association of Manufacturers. His knitting mills remained among the largest manufacturing establishments in Philadelphia, and he was also president of the Quaker City Dye Works. He was a Republican and vice-president of the Union League Club. (*DAB; NCAB*, 2:158; *Who Was Who*, vol. 1; *New York Times*, June 13, 1914.)

DONAHUE, PETER (January 11, 1822–November 26, 1885). Machine works owner and public utilities executive, Union Iron Works, San Francisco. Born in Glasgow, Scotland, of Irish parents, his early life was one of hardship and little schooling. When he was eleven years of age, his parents immigrated to the United States, settling in Mattawan, New York, where he worked first in a factory and then on a farm. About 1837 his parents moved to Paterson, New Jersey, and there Peter was apprenticed to learn the craft of machinist and millwright. His younger brothers, James and Michael, learned the related trades of iron casting and moulding. Peter returned to New York in 1845 and found employment in the construction of a gunboat for the Peruvian government, then accompanied the completed vessel to Peru as assistant engineer. He remained in that capacity until 1849, when he embarked for the gold fields of California. Enroute the ship's machinery broke down, but Donahue repaired it and the owner rewarded him with $1,000. He then hunted for gold for six months before giving up and returning to San Francisco, where his two brothers were now located.

The three Donahues opened a crude blacksmith and boilermaking shop, the first iron works and machine shop in California. Subsequently, they expanded it into the great Union Iron Works, named for the works in Paterson, New Jersey, where Peter had learned his trade. They made the first castings in California and also repaired engines; constructed quartz mills, mining machines, and mining pumps; and erected gas works. In 1852 and 1856 Michael and James sold their interests in the firm to Peter, who carried on the business in his own name for a time. He built ships for the United States government, which were the first government vessels produced on the West Coast. He also manufactured the first printing press made in California, and in 1865 built the first locomotive in the state. By 1863 he was so involved in other enterprises that he was unable to exercise personal supervision over the mechanical side of the business. Thus, he entered a new partnership with H. J. Booth and C. S. Higgins, as Donahue, Booth and Company. Two years later he sold out to the H. J. Booth Company.

Donahue was also a pioneer in the development of public utilities in California. In 1852 he organized the first gas company for street lighting in San Francisco, and was president of that firm for twenty years. In 1862 he organized the Omnibus Street Railway, the first street car line in the city, and was president of that for many years. In 1860 he was treasurer of the San Francisco and San Jose Railroad, holding two-thirds of its stock. Ten years later it was sold to the Central Pacific for $3,250,000. In 1862 he became one of the charter members of the Union Pacific Railroad Company, and in 1870 he acquired a controlling interest in the San Francisco and Humboldt Railroad, out of which he created the San Francisco and North Pacific Railroad.

He married Mary Jane Maguire in 1852, and they had four children. Later he married Annie Dawney. His son, Mervyn, succeeded him as president of the San Francisco and Northern Pacific Railroad. (*DAB; NCAB*, 7:180.)

DONNELL FAMILY: James C. Donnell (April 20, 1854-January 10, 1927); **Otto Dewey Donnell** (September 26, 1883-April 9, 1961); **James C. Donnell II** (b. June 30, 1910); **John Randolph Donnell** (b. June 22, 1912). Oil producers, Ohio Oil Company and Marathon Oil Company.

James C. Donnell was born in County Armagh, Ireland, son of James Donnell and Elizabeth Doyle. Two years after his birth, his family came to the United States, settling in Waterford, Pennsylvania. Young James Donnell's career in the oil industry began at age eighteen, hauling crude oil out of a refinery at Titusville, Pennsylvania. Upon the opening of the Bradford oil field he went into business for himself, securing leases at Red Rock and Dallas City, Pennsylvania, and later at Allentown and Bolivar, New York. He then transferred his activities to the Lima Oil Field in Ohio, becoming associated with the Standard Oil Company, for which he drilled the first large Indiana gas well in 1887. Two years later, when Standard Oil acquired control of the Ohio Oil Company, which had been organized at Lima, Ohio, in 1887, Donnell was made a director of the company and manager of its field operations. In 1900 he was elected vice-president and general manager, devoting his efforts to the development of new oil fields. In 1901 the offices were moved to Findlay, Ohio.

When Standard Oil Co. was dissolved by the U.S. Supreme Court in 1911 on trust violations, Donnell succeeded John D. Archbold* as president of Ohio Oil, remaining in that position for the rest of his life. The scope of Ohio Oil Company's operations was extended to include sixteen states and Mexico during his presidency. In 1915 he organized the Illinois Pipeline Company, capitalized at $20 million, to operate the pipeline transportation company of the Ohio Oil Company. Petroleum refining was added in 1924 when he secured control of the Lincoln Oil Refining Company at Robinson, Ill. At the time of his death, the assets of Ohio Oil were $108 million, and net income stood at $17 million. The firm owned or operated under lease 5,000,000 acres of oil and gas producing lands, and some 42,000 wells were drilled under his direction.

Besides his duties with Ohio Oil, Donnell was also active in the affairs of the parent company until its dissolution. In 1908 he assisted Archbold in the reorganization of Standard Oil of California, and in that of the Romano-American Oil Company of Roumania in 1906. He was president of the First National Bank of Findlay from 1908 to 1915, and the leading citizen of the city. He married Sara Elizabeth Flynn of Buffalo, New York, in 1886, and had two children, Elizabeth and Otto D. Donnell.

Otto D. Donnell was educated in the public schools of Findlay, Ohio, and received a bachelor's degree in mechanical engineering at Case School of Applied Science in 1906. He then entered the employ of Ohio Oil Company as a mechanical engineer in the pipeline department at Marshall, Illinois. He was named a director of the company in 1911, second vice-president and assistant general manager in 1913, first vice-president and treasurer in 1926, and president and general manager upon the death of his father in 1927. He continued in that position until 1948 when he was succeeded by his son, James C. Donnell II. In 1927, when he assumed the presidency, the company had assets of $104,454,746, and produced crude oil at wells in Ohio, Indiana, Oklahoma, Kansas, Texas, Louisiana, and Mexico. To a lesser extent it operated refineries and a number of bulk and service stations. The net profit in 1927 was $7 million.

Under Otto Donnell's direction, a program of expansion was started in 1930, with the purchase of a major interest in the Transcontinental Oil Company, the Michigan properties of Weber Oil Company, properties of the Producer's Oil Company and Producer's Gas Market, as well as real estate holdings of the First Central Realty Company. The latter included twenty-three service stations and five station sites, and all the assets of the

Sonny Service Company, with seven service stations. In 1936 a former subsidiary, Marathon Oil Company, was absorbed into the parent company. By 1948 the company owned or leased 240,626 acres, with a total of 7,876 producing wells, and another 2,420,574 acres of undeveloped land in oil and gas producing fields in several states. It operated 5,700 miles of gathering and trunk pipelines and five refineries, distributed through 3,500 bulk plants and service stations. It had assets of $203,389,193, gross oil production of 38,800,000 barrels, and a profit of $68 million.

Otto Donnell was also president of the Mexican Oil Company, Western Public Service Company, and Mountain Fuel Supply Company. When the First National Bank of Findlay had to close its doors in 1930, he took a leading role in the reorganization of the bank and served as chairman of the board for several years. He was a Presbyterian and a Republican, and married Glenn McClelland of Findlay in 1909. He had three sons, James C. II, John R., and Otto D. Jr.

James C. Donnell II was born in Findlay, Ohio, and graduated from Princeton University in 1932. After graduation he became manager of crude oil sales for Marathon Oil company, serving until 1936. In the latter year he was named a director, rising to the vice-presidency in 1937, and the presidency in 1948. His tenure as president lasted until 1972, when he became chairman of the board until 1975. He married Dolly Louise DeVine in 1932. They have one daughter. His brother, **John Randolph Donnell** (b. 1912), was with Marathon Oil after 1938. He rose to be senior vice-president of finance and planning and president of Marathon International Oil Company from 1961 to 1967. He also served as chairman of the board of the First National Bank of Findlay after 1947. (**A.** *DAB; NCAB,* 24:429; 51:17; *Who's Who in America, 1978-79.* **B.** Hartzell Spence, *Portrait in Oil, 1962.)*

DONNELLY, NELL QUINLAN (1889-   ). Women's Clothing manufacturer, Donnelly Garment Company. Nell Quinlan was born on a Kansas farm, youngest of twelve children. She was educated at a Parsons, Kansas, convent, high school, and business school. She then got a job as a stenographer in Kansas City. At age seventeen she married Paul Donnelly, a man who lived in the same rooming house and who also worked as a stenographer. Nell Donnelly had a great passion to go to college, and Paul saved money and sent her to Lindenwood College near St. Louis. The only married student in the school, she graduated in 1909.

For the next seven years she was a housekeeper, but had no children to help fill her time. Finding it difficult to buy inexpensive but fashionable house dresses, she began to design a dozen "dress aprons," which she persuaded the buyer at George B. Peck Dry Goods Store in Kansas City to put on sale as a test. All were sold by noon of that day, and a dozen more were ordered. Her husband, Paul, gave her $1,270 from their savings to establish a factory in their house. Nell installed two power machines in the attic and hired two girls to help with the production. The business was later moved to a location nearer downtown Kansas City department stores. The venture proved to be so successful that Paul quit his job as credit manager of the Barton Shoe Company to become president of Donnelly Garment Company. Nell served as secretary and treasurer of the organization. Paul handled all the financial strategy for the company and Nell designed the dresses, hired the workers, and supervised the selling.

The company prospered during the 1920s, grossing as much as $3.5 million per year. Nell also put her signature on the product, shortening it to Nelly Don, and the company managed to survive well during the depression of the 1930s. During this time, however, she ran into personal difficulties. In 1931 she and her black chauffeur were kidnapped and held for $75,000 ransom. Through the intercession of their lawyer, Senator James A. Reed, they were released in thirty-four hours without paying the ransom. A year later, however, Nell Donnelly divorced her husband and married her seventy-two year old lawyer. She later had a son by her second husband.

Nell retained control of Donnelly Garment Company after the divorce and became its president. She retained that position until the mid-1940s, when she sold her interest for more than one million dollars. She continued with the company, however, until she retired in 1954. (Caroline Bird, *Enterprising Women*, 1976; *Fortune*, September, 1935.)

DORRANCE, JOHN THOMPSON (November 11, 1873–September 21, 1930) and **Arthur Calbraith Dorrance** (1893–September 22, 1946). Food processors, Campbell Soup Company. **John T. Dorrance** was born in Bristol, Pennsylvania, son of John Dorrance and Elizabeth Cottingham Thompson. Educated in prep schools and Rugby Academy in Philadelphia, he graduated from Massachusetts Institute of Technology in 1895. He then went to the University of Goettingen, where he received his Ph.D. in chemistry in 1897. A brilliant chemist, he received offers to teach chemistry at Goettingen, Columbia University, Cornell University, and Bryn Mawr College, but decided to enter the business world instead. He went to work in 1897 for the Joseph Campbell Preserve Company in Philadelphia, where his uncle, Arthur Dorrance, was a partner. In 1899 John Dorrance invented the process for making condensed soup, a soup from which the water has been removed. At that time three companies were making canned soup in America, but they were unable to achieve wide distribution because they shipped it in bulky, water-heavy cans. Campbell's condensed product became an instant success, aided by the firm's extensive advertising campaign. They began advertising on New York City streetcars in 1899, and five years later were selling sixteen million cans of soup a year. Campbell's ran their first national ad in *Good Housekeeping* in 1905, and six years later penetrated the market in California, becoming one of the first American companies to achieve nation-wide distribution of a brand name food product.

John Dorrance was named a vice-president of the firm in 1900, and fourteen years later became president and general manager. A year later (1915) he purchased the firm's first subsidiary, the Franco-American Food Company of Jersey City, New Jersey, the first company in America to pack soup. He served as president of Campbell's until his death in 1930, and was also a director of the Pennsylvania Railroad, Reading Railroad, Philadelphia and Camden Ferry Company, Prudential Life Insurance, and the National Bank of Commerce in New York. An Episcopalian, he married Ethel Mollinckodt of Baltimore, and they had a son and four daughters.

His brother, **Arthur C. Dorrance** was also born in Bristol, Pennsylvania, was educated at Episcopal Academy there, and graduated from Massachusetts Institute of Technology in 1914 in chemical engineering. During his summer vacations while in college he worked in various departments of Campbell Soup, and after graduation took a job in the Camden, New Jersey, plant of the firm. In 1917 he was named president of the firm's subsidiary, Franco-American Foods. He served as a captain in the United States Army during World War I, and after the war became assistant general manager of Campbell Soup, advancing to general manager in 1928. Upon the death of his brother in 1930 he was elected president, serving in that position until his death. He was a director of many companies, including Camden Safe Deposit and Trust Company, the Reserve Bank of Philadelphia, Philadelphia National Bank, Lehigh Valley Railroad, Guaranty Trust Company of New York, and Bell Telephone of Pennsylvania; he was on the board of managers of Girard Trust Company, and was a trustee of Penn Mutual Life Insurance. After 1935 he was a trustee of MIT and he founded Camden County Community Chest in 1942. He served as first president and member of the executive council of the National Canner's Association from 1930 to 1940. An Episcopalian, he was married and had two sons.

The present head of Campbell's Soup is John T. Dorrance Jr., son of the elder John T. Dorrance. Although the Dorrance family has generally eschewed the public eye, and relatively little is known of either the company or the family, John Dorrance Jr. is a recluse rivaling Howard Hughes.* Virtually nothing has been written about him or what he does, he never grants interviews, and his photograph has never even appeared on the company's annual report. Under his direction, however, Campbell's has made some significant advances in recent years. In 1955 it purchased the C. A. Swanson Company, frozen food packers in Omaha, and acquired Pepperidge Farm of Norwalk, Connecticut, in 1961. During the 1970s it entered the dog food, restaurant, garden, chocolate, and pickle business, the latter via the acquisition of Vlasic Foods, a Michigan packer of pickles, relishes, peppers, and sauerkraut. By 1979, Campbell's Soup had $2.2 billion in sales, ranking seventeenth among food processors in the United States, but first in soups, frozen dinners, canned spaghetti, and pickles. (**A.** *Who Was Who*, vol. 1; *New York Times*, September 22, 1930; September 23, 1946. **B.** Earl C. May, *The Canning Clan*, 1937; Milton Moskowitz et al., *Everybody's Business*, 1980.)

DOUBLEDAY FAMILY: Frank Doubleday (January 8, 1862–January 30, 1934); **Nelson Doubleday** (June 16, 1889–January 11, 1949); **Nelson Doubleday Jr.** (b. 1933). Publishers, Doubleday and Company.

Frank Doubleday was born in Brooklyn, New York, son of William Edwards Doubleday and Ellen M. Dickinson. His father, who had been born in Binghamton, New York, became a merchant in New York City. Educated at Brooklyn Polytechnic Institute, Frank Doubleday left school at age fifteen to work at Charles Scribner's Sons. He remained with Scribner's for twenty years, becoming manager of *Scribner's Magazine* when it was founded in 1887. In 1897 he left Scribner's to found, with Samuel Sidney McClure, the publishing firm Doubleday and McClure Company. In 1900 he took in as partners Walter Hines Page, William H. Lanier (son of Sidney Lanier), John Leslie Thompson, and Samuel A. Everett, and organized the firm of Doubleday Page and Company. Frank Doubleday was a partner of the firm until 1927, when it absorbed the George H. Doran Company to form Doubleday and Doran and Company, Incorporated. He served as chairman of the board until his death.

In 1900, with Page, he founded *World's Work*, a monthly magazine devoted to politics and practical affairs, with Page as editor until 1913. The magazine's special interest was the South. Doubleday also published *Country Life in America, Garden and Home Builder* (later *American Home*), *Short Stories West*, and *Frontier*. In 1910 the publishing house was moved to Garden City, Long Island, and in 1923 a subsidiary organization was instituted known as Garden City Publishing Company, Incorporated. Other subsidiaries which were developed included: Doubleday-Doran Book Shops, Incorporated, The Crime Club Incorporated, Doubleday and Doran Incorporated (Canada), and Sun Dial Press, Incorporated. In 1920 he acquired William Heinemann Company of London, with a new publishing plant in that country. The authors published by Doubleday included: Frank Norris, Henry George, Hamlin Garland, Rudyard Kipling, Joseph Conrad, O. Henry, Booth Tarkington, Sinclair Lewis, Ellen Glasgow, Edna Ferber, and Kathleen Norris. Despite these literary successes, Frank Doubleday was known as the first of the "business oriented" publishers, and his partner, George Doran, said he was "by practice and extraction ruthlessly Prussian."

Frank Doubleday was married twice: to Neltje De Graff in 1886, who died in 1918, and in the latter year to Florence Van Wyck. He had a daughter, Dorothy, and a son, Nelson. **Nelson Doubleday** was born in Brooklyn, and grew up in Oyster Bay, New York. He was educated at Friend's School in New York City, and Holbrook Military Academy in

Ossining, New York, where he graduated in 1908. He then attended New York University for two years, but dropped out to pursue a career in book publishing and merchandising.

Nelson Doubleday did not join the family publishing firm until he had established himself independently. In 1910 he had started a "deferred subscription" business by which individuals could purchase unsold copies of current periodicals which had been returned to the publishers. With the profits from this venture, he began to publish books under his own imprint. In 1916 he sold his father an interest in his enterprises, and two years later, after service in World War I, joined Doubleday, Page and Company as a junior partner. He rose rapidly in the organization, becoming vice-president in 1922 and president in 1928, a year after the merger with Doran Company. Upon his father's death in 1934, he became chairman of the board of Doubleday, Doran Company, Incorporated as well.

Nelson Doubleday concentrated on the mass production of inexpensive books and their distribution to the broadest possible market. Production was handled at the firm's Country Life Press in Garden City, Long Island, and distribution was carried out through department stores and other high volume outlets and through a variety of direct mail book clubs and reprint divisions controlled by the parent company. These included the Dollar Book Club, Garden City Reprints, the Famous Author Series, the Crime Club, Sun Dial Press, Windward House, the Mystery Guild, and Doubleday Junior Books.

The company also owned a chain of twenty-six retail book stores, and in 1934 acquired full ownership of the Literary Guild of America, a book club which alone generated sales of one million books a year. A managerial genius, Nelson Doubleday exercised close supervision of these various enterprises and subdivisions, readily terminating any that proved unprofitable. In 1937 he moved the business and editorial offices from Garden City to New York City's Rockefeller Center. The books Doubleday favored were those best adapted to mass market distribution—popular fiction by Edna Ferber, Kenneth Roberts, and Daphne du Maurier; inspirational, reference and "how to" books; and cheap reprints of classics and best sellers.

By 1947 Doubleday and Company was the largest publishing house in America, with annual sales of over thirty million books. Nelson Doubleday enthusiastically embraced modern advertising techniques and market strategies already well established in other lines of endeavor, but new to the book trade. The publishing industry still clung to a rather genteel and elitist pattern in the 1930s, and Nelson's comment that "I sell books, I don't read them," did not endear him to older line publishers. In 1946 he resigned the presidency of Doubleday and Company to Douglas Black but continued as chairman of the board until his death.

He married Martha Jewett Nicholson of Providence, Rhode Island, in 1916, and they were divorced in 1931. A year later he married Ellen George

(McCarter) Violett of Rumson, New Jersey. By his second wife he had two children, Nelson Jr. and Neltje. **Nelson Doubleday Jr.** graduated from Princeton in 1954, joining Doubleday and Company after his graduation. Two years later he joined the United States Air Force, serving until 1959, when he returned to Doubleday as executive vice-president, secretary, and director of the trade publications division. Later, he became head of the company, and in 1980 purchased control of the New York Mets, National League baseball team. As he was a direct descendent of Abner Doubleday, the supposed inventor of baseball, the purchase had nostalgic connotations.

Doubleday remains a private, family-owned company, with Nelson Doubleday Jr. holding 51 percent of the stock. It is also extraordinarily tight-lipped about its operations to the point where the *New York Times* called it the "Sphinx of Publishing." Nevertheless, Doubleday is probably the nation's largest publisher of hardbound "trade" books, and about 35 percent of its profits continue to emanate from book clubs. Sales in 1979 amounted to $351 million. (**A.** *DAB*, Supplements 1 and 4; *NCAB*, 13:400; 37:36; *New York Times*, January 12, 1947; July 15, 1979; *Who's Who in America, 1978-79.* **B.** Charles Madison, *Book Publishing in America*, 1966.)

DOUGLAS, DONALD WILLS (April 6, 1892–1981) and **Donald Wills Douglas Jr.** (July 3, 1917–   ). Aircraft manufacturers, McDonnell-Douglas Aircraft Company. **Donald W. Douglas** was born in Brooklyn, New York, son of William Edward Douglas and Dorothy Locker. His great-grandfather had immigrated to America from Scotland in 1813, and his father was a bank cashier. Donald Douglas was educated at Trinity Chapel School in New York City and entered the United States Naval Academy in 1909. While a midshipman he witnessed a demonstration flight by the Wright Brothers which sparked his interest in aviation. He resigned from the naval academy in 1912, enrolling in Massachusetts Institute of Technology, where he graduated in 1914. He was their first graduate in aeronautical engineering; he remained at the university for a year after graduation as a teaching assistant and aided in the construction of the first wind tunnel. In 1915 he joined the Connecticut Aircraft Company in New Haven as a consultant, working on the first dirigible built for the U.S. Navy.

He subsequently became chief engineer of the Glenn L. Martin* Company, airplane manufacturers in Los Angeles, California. In 1916 he was appointed chief engineer of the aviation section of the U.S. Signal Corps, but after the U.S. entered World War I he returned to Glenn L. Martin Company, then located in Cleveland, Ohio, and assisted in the building of the Martin bomber, the first completely American-designed plane constructed during the war. In 1920, with the financial backing of David L. Davis, he organized the Davis-Douglas Company in Los Angeles to build a plane for non-stop transcontinental flight from Los Angeles to New York. The plane's motor failed on a trial run, and Davis-Douglas Company was dissolved. Later,

Douglas built a number of torpedo planes for the U.S. Navy and, after that order was filled, organized the Douglas Company, capitalized at $100,000.

As president of the new company, he began building transport planes that incorporated new standards of safety. In 1928 the name of the company was changed to the Douglas Aircraft Company, Incorporated, of which he was president. The firm expanded very rapidly, developing and constructing military planes of all types and civilian transport planes which served airline routes in fifty-seven countries prior to World War II. Douglas' great breakthrough came in the early 1930s with the development of the company's famous series of planes, the Douglas Commercial (DC). He introduced the DC-1 in 1931, but the series got off the ground in 1933, with an order from Trans World Airlines for 40 DC-2s. Shortly thereafter he developed the DC-3, known as the "immortal," since it was so perfect aerodynamically that engineers claimed it could glide if the engines failed. Airlines eventually bought 448 DC-3s, and they were steady sellers on the used plane market for years. A DC-4 became the first presidential aircraft, ordered for Franklin D. Roosevelt, while a DC-6 was used by Harry Truman.

Douglas Aircraft was also one of the largest producers of planes for the U.S. Army and Navy and U.S. allies abroad. In 1941 the company completed the first of the B-19 bombers for the U.S. Army, the largest and most formidable aircraft that had been built to that time. Douglas Aircraft opened huge plants at Santa Monica, El Segundo, and Long Beach, California, and in Tulsa, Oklahoma. By 1941 his factories in Southern California alone employed more than 29,000 persons. Douglas won the Collier Air Medal in 1936 and the Guggenheim Gold Medal in 1940. An Episcopalian, he married Charlotte Ogg of Marion, Indiana, in 1916. They had four sons and a daughter.

Their eldest son was **Donald Wills Douglas Jr.**, who was born in Washington, D.C., and educated in the public schools of Santa Monica, California. He attended Stanford University from 1934 to 1938 and Curtiss-Wright Technical Institute in 1939. In the latter year he became an engineer for Douglas Aircraft. In 1943 he was named director of the firm's testing division, and supervised the tests of many Douglas planes. Five years later he became director of contract administration and was placed in charge of the firm's research laboratories in Santa Monica. Upon the retirement of his father in 1957 he became president of the company.

Under his leadership Douglas Aircraft has undergone extensive changes. In 1958 the firm's first jet transport, the DC-8, made its maiden flight, going into commercial service later that same year. Despite the plane's success, it came on the market well after the introduction of Boeing's 707. As a result American Airlines, a major Douglas customer, ordered Boeing's 707 after being persuaded that the plane was faster and less expensive to operate than the Douglas version. This gave Boeing a lead in jet aircraft it was never to relinquish, and created a major crisis for Douglas. In 1961 he consolidated all of the West Coast operations into two divisions—the aircraft division and the missile and space systems division. This enabled him as president to maintain direct control over both facets of the company. In 1965 the DC-9, a short to medium range transport plane, was introduced, and the company continued to develop military aircraft and Nike missiles (which had been begun in 1951) for the U.S. government. The company was also largely involved in the space program, and in 1965 was awarded a contract to build the manned orbiting laboratory for the U.S. Air Force. Douglas' missiles have also been used as the first stage of most space explorations.

None of this, however, was enough to compensate for the loss of the commercial jet market to Boeing. By 1966 the company was losing money and accepted proposals for a merger with McDonnell Aircraft of St. Louis. The latter firm was primarily a manufacturer of military aircraft, and was particularly successful in the production of jet fighters. The takeover of Douglas was generally hailed as a beneficial merger for both companies, since the consolidated firm was seen as stronger than either of the companies could have hoped to become individually. In the first years after the takeover this proved to be an accurate forecast. McDonnell-Douglas became the second largest supplier to the Defense Department, with sales of over $5 billion in 1979, and Boeing had miscalculated on the demand for its 747 jumbo jet, for which there were few orders in the first years after its introduction. McDonnell-Douglas' answer to the 747 was the DC-10, a flexible, wide-bodied "airbus" which sold very well in the early years. But a series of crashes, capped by the crash of a DC-10 at O'Hare Airport in Chicago in 1979, killing 273 persons in the nation's worst air disaster, disclosed serious design flaws in the aircraft. Presently the firm wonders if it will ever sell enough of the DC-10s to cover their cost.

Donald Douglas Jr. married Molly McIntosh in 1939 and they were divorced in 1950. The following year he married Jean Cooper. He has two daughters. Despite the great success and major contributions of Douglas Aircraft over the years, its most signal contribution remains the DC-3 aircraft in the 1930s. This plane enabled the airline industry to at least partially break away from its dependence on government airmail contracts for survival, since it was the first plane which made it possible for the airlines to haul passengers, and only passengers, at a profit. This allowed airline passenger traffic to grow rapidly during the 1930s. (**A.** *NCAB*, F:70; K:1; *Current Biography*, November, 1941; December, 1950. **B.** Lloyd Morris and Kendall Smith, *Ceiling Unlimited*, 1953; Victor Perlo, *Militarism and Industry*, 1963; John B. Rae, *Climb to Greatness: The American Aircraft Industry, 1920–1960*, 1968; G. R. Simonson, *History of the American Aircraft Industry*, 1968; Robert Sobel, *Age of the Giant Corporations*, 1972; Herman Streckler, *The Structure and Performance of the Aerospace Industry*, 1965.)

THE DOW AND DOAN FAMILIES: Herbert Henry Dow (February 26, 1866–October 15, 1930); **Willard Henry Dow** (January 4, 1897–March 31, 1949); **Leland Doan** (November 9, 1894–April 4, 1974); **Herbert Dow Doan** (September 5, 1922–   ). Chemical manufacturers, Dow Chemical Company.

Herbert H. Dow was born in Belleville, Ontario, Canada, son of Joseph Henry Dow and Sarah Bunnell. The family was of New England ancestry, having come to Watertown, Massachusetts, in 1637. Soon after his birth, the family returned to New England, settling in Birmingham (Derby), Connecticut. Later they moved to Cleveland, Ohio, where his father became a master mechanic at the Chisholm Shovel Works. Herbert Dow was educated at Case School of Applied Science, graduating in 1888. He did his thesis on Ohio brines, and presented a paper at a meeting of the American Association for the Advancement of Science at Cleveland that summer. In conducting research for the paper, he found that lithium occurred in large concentrations in the Ohio brine fields but that it was not found in those of Michigan, and that bromine was more concentrated in the brines of Canton, Ohio, and Midland, Michigan. Thus began his interest in the products contained in brines, which became the foundation of his industry.

In 1889 he served as professor of chemistry and technology at the Homeopathic Hospital College in Cleveland, and in the same year developed and patented a method for obtaining bromine by blowing air through slightly electrolyzed brine. The next year he secured financial support and organized a small company for work with Canton, Ohio, brines. This venture failed, but he made improvements in the process which were continued at Midland Chemical Company, formed in 1890 at Midland, Michigan. The new company was able to succeed for two reasons: first, the Dow process achieved the removal of bromine from brine without the need for evaporating the brine to the point of salt separation, thus avoiding a by-product, common salt, which would flood the market; and second, only a small amount of fuel was required and could be supplied at the lowest possible cost, utilizing wastes of the nearby lumber industry. In 1892 he installed a direct current generator, the first commercially successful installation of an electrochemical plant in America.

Dow's next venture was a company to electrolyze brine for the production of chlorine. Experiments began in Navarre, Ohio, in 1895, but were moved to Midland in 1896. A year later they were absorbed by the newly founded Dow Chemical Company. The new company manufactured bleaching powder as its principal product, and in 1900 purchased the Midland Chemical Company. The growth of Dow Chemical Company over the years was marked by the development of chemical compounds that were produced, one after another, as a result of Dow's determination to utilize all values to be found in the brines from which he worked. His interest in horticulture was enhanced when the company took up the manufacture of insecticides as a natural result of the quest for a broader outlet for chlorine. He was also interested in pharmaceuticals and salicylates.

The magnesium chloride found in the brine was used in the form of oxychloride for stucco, and by 1918 the electrolysis of magnesium chloride was under production on a small scale to yield magnesium metal. An intensive study was made of the alloys of magnesium; these alloys were given the name Dowmetal, and large-scale production of light metals followed. The development of a process of electrometric chemical control involved the first commercial application of the principles involved, and played a guiding role in the automatic handling of ocean brines for a continuous supply of chemical products by the Dow methods.

The company introduced the first synthetic indigo process in the Western hemisphere, followed by a full line of brominated indigos. Synthetic phenol and aniline were also perfected. The extraction of iodine, first from Louisiana brines, and then from the brine of California petroleum, was the first production of that important element in the United States. In 1930 Herbert Dow was awarded the Perkin medal by the Society of the Chemical industry.

During World War I Herbert Dow served on the advisory committee of the Council for National Defense, and the Dow Chemical Company produced large quantities of mustard gas and other war chemicals for the government. At the time of his death, Dow Chemical produced more than 200 products, which were sold in the U.S., Canada, and some foreign countries. It had plants in Midland and Mt. Pleasant, Michigan, Long Beach, California, and Wilmington, North Carolina. Affiliated companies included Midland Ammonia Company, Dowell, Incorporated, and Ethyl-Dow Chemical Company.

A Presbyterian, he married Grace A. Ball of Midland, Michigan, in 1892. They had seven children, including Ruth Dow, who married Leland Doan, and **Willard H. Dow**. Young Dow was educated in the public schools of Midland, Michigan, and received his bachelor's degree from the University of Michigan in 1919. He then joined his father's chemical company as a chemical engineer. Three years later he was named a director and four years after that became assistant general manager. Upon his father's death in 1930 he became president and general manager, and in 1941 was also elected chairman of the board.

Willard Dow brought his organizational ability to Dow Chemical to greatly expand the company his father had founded. He was responsible for acquiring a string of affiliated companies, including a 75 percent interest in Midland Ammonia Company in 1930, forming Dowell Incorporated, in 1932, and, most importantly, joining with Ethyl Gas Corporation in 1933 to form Ethyl-Dow Corporation. In 1935 he joined with Cleveland-Cliffs Iron Company to form the Cliffs-Dow Chemical Company, and in the same year acquired the Great Western Electro-Chemical Company. Dow Magnesium

Corporation, a wholly owned subsidiary, was formed in 1941 to build and operate magnesium plants for the U.S. government, and Dow Chemical of Canada, Ltd. was formed in 1942 to manufacture styrene for Canadian rubber producers. In 1943 the Dow-Corning Corporation was formed with Corning Glass Works.

By the time of his death, Dow Chemical turned out 500 products, 40 percent being chemicals used by industry, 25 percent were magnesium products, 10 percent pharmaceuticals, and the remaining 25 percent included plastics such as styron and a saran, as well as Dowicide. All of these were built on a base of brine, whose vast deposits at Midland, Michigan, were expected to last 500,000 years. The Dow Chemical Company almost totally dominated the small town of Midland, which had a population of 12,000 in 1944, 6,000 of whom worked for Dow. The company's headquarters had 400 buildings on 800 acres, and had assets of $250 million. During World War II Willard Dow was a member of the chemical advisory commission of the Joint Army and Navy Munitions Board and of the advisory board of the U.S. Army Chemical Warfare Service. A Presbyterian and a Republican, he was awarded the Gold Medal of the American Institute of Chemists in 1944. He married Martha L. Pratt of Midland in 1921, and had two children, Helen Adeline and Herbert Henry Dow II.

Leland Ira Doan was born in North Bend, Nebraska, son of Ira Doan and Hester Spencer. He was educated at the University of Michigan from 1913 to 1916. In 1917 he married Ruth Alden Dow, daughter of Herbert H. Dow, and in that same year entered the employ of Dow Chemical, beginning in the sales department. He moved up to assistant sales manager, general sales manager, and from 1938 to 1947 was vice-president and secretary. In the latter year he was named president of Dow Chemical, serving until 1962, when he became chairman of the executive committee until 1970. He was a director from 1935 to 1972.

Leland Doan's father had been a physician, and at the University of Michigan Leland had specialized in chemical engineering. When he joined the sales staff at Dow, he found the sales functions were concentrated in the hands of just a few people. In order to expand these activities he established a number of branch offices, with a corps of salesmen in each of the company's specialities. As one method of promoting sales he catalogued information about prospective customers, including even their hobbies. As he moved up the sales ladder at the firm he developed markets for new products such as magnesium plastics and pharmaceuticals. Then, when Willard Dow was killed in a plane crash in 1949, Leland Doan became his successor. During his presidency Doan was responsible for the company's greatest diversification and expansion.

The rapid expansion in the decade before Doan assumed the presidency necessitated administrative changes when he came into office, so that the positions of president, chairman, and general manager, which had been simultaneously held by Willard Dow, were broken up. Doan delegated authority to department heads and began building up a larger sales force trained to become market and production analysts who could then help Dow's industrial customers plan their sales. Doan announced a $25 million program of expansion and directed his energies toward plastics. He also constructed an ammonia plant at Freeport, Texas; expanded the Freeport Velasco plant; purchased a steel casting plant in Madison, Illinois, to be converted to the rolling of magnesium sheets; and constructed a plant for the production of plastics near New London, Connecticut. In 1951 he announced plans for new plant facilities at a cost of about $100 million over the next several years.

One of his major projects was to increase the civilian demand for magnesium. In order to expand its export sales, the Dow Company formed two new exporting companies, the Dow Chemical Inter-American Ltd. for exports in the Western hemisphere, and the Dow Chemical International Ltd. for exports to other countries. Dow's sales for 1952 were $407,155,799, compared to $340,000,000 the previous year. A Presbyterian and a Republican, he and Ruth Dow had two sons, Leland Alden Doan and Herbert Dow Doan, and a daughter, Dorothy Doan. His second wife was Mildred Mellus, whom he married in 1950.

Herbert Dow Doan was born in Midland, Michigan, and educated at Cranbrook Prep School from 1941 to 1947. He received his degree in chemical engineering at Cornell University in 1949. In 1950 he joined the technical services and development division of Dow Chemical, becoming a purchasing analyst in 1951. He was then named executive in charge of research from 1953 to 1956, and manager of the chemistry department from 1956 to 1960. In the latter year he was named executive vice-president, serving until 1962. From 1962 to 1971 he was president of Dow Chemical. After retiring as president, he continued as director. He then became a partner in Doan Associates, Midland, and chairman of Doan Resources Corporation. He is married with four children.

Dow Chemical has been the fastest-growing and most profitable chemical company during the past twenty-five years. During the 1970s it passed rivals Monsanto and Union Carbide to become DuPont's closest competitor in the industry. Even more impressive, Dow reaped higher profits than all its rivals, including DuPont, despite smaller sales. In 1979 the firm had sales of $9.3 billion, with profits of $784 million. It has the reputation of being one of the best-managed companies in the world and has made phenomenal gains in one of the most competitive industries in America. During the Vietnam War Dow Chemical was attacked by antiwar groups for making napalm. Although the firm made no apology for their actions on this score, they did quietly allow themselves to be outbid on the defense contract when it came up for renewal. (**A.** *DAB*, Supplement 1; *NCAB*, 24:12; 37:21; *Current Biography*, February, 1944, 1952, 1974; *New York*

Times, April 5, 1974; *Who Was Who*, vol. 6; *Who's Who in America, 1978-79*. B. R. P. Dow, *The Book of Dow*, 1929; Dan Whitehead, *The Dow Story*, 1968.)

DREW, DANIEL (July 29, 1797–September 18, 1879). Financier, Erie Railroad. Born in Carmel, New York, son of Gilbert Drew and Catharine Muchelworth. His father owned a one hundred acre stock farm. Daniel had only a meager education, and at age fifteen was left by his father's death to make his own way. He earned one hundred dollars as a substitute in the War of 1812, serving for twelve months. After that he became a cattle drover and horse trader, collecting livestock in the Hudson and Mohawk valleys and driving them to New York City. His training made him sharp-witted, grasping, and unscrupulous, though this was sometimes tempered with sanctimoniousness. He soon became a preeminent cattle buyer, and with the help of capital supplied by Henry Astor* extended his operations westward. He became the first to drive cattle from Ohio, Kentucky, and Illinois across the Alleghenies.

In 1829 Drew took up permanent residence in New York City, making his Bull's Head Tavern at Third Avenue and Twenty-fourth Street, with yards for 1,500 cattle, the principal headquarters and exchange for drovers. During 1834 he went into the steamboat business in competition with Cornelius Vanderbilt,* reducing the fare from Albany to New York from three dollars to one dollar. He was quite successful, and when the Hudson River Railroad opened in 1852 he held undaunted to his line. For twenty-two years he also controlled the Stonington Line in Long Island Sound and established profitable steamboat services on Lake Champlain.

Having accumulated a great deal of capital, he entered Wall Street in 1844, forming the house of Drew, Robinson and Company, which for ten years did a large stockbroking and banking business. When the death of his partner dissolved the firm he became one of the boldest and craftiest of the independent operators on the street. His connection with the Erie Railroad began in 1853, and in 1857 he forced his election as a director. This enabled him to manipulate the Erie stock and he did so shamelessly, becoming the first of that type of speculative director. But in the famous Harlem Railroad corner with Cornelius Vanderbilt and John Tobin, planned in 1864, he was outwitted, losing several million dollars. This left him eager for revenge.

Drew's greatest business battle was the "Erie War" with Vanderbilt from 1866 to 1868. He was treasurer of the hard-pressed line, and in 1866 advanced it $3.5 million, taking 28,000 shares of unissued stocks and bonds for $3 million convertible into stock. He simultaneously unloaded 28,000 shares on a rising bull market, making enormous profits. Vanderbilt determined to get control of the line, and made an alliance with Boston speculators who held stock in the company. He then threatened court proceedings and frightened Drew and his allies, Jay Gould* and James Fisk,* into a treaty of peace. But Drew was still dangerous, and the crisis came in 1868 when Vanderbilt, with the aid of a court injunction to stop the Erie from printing more stock, tried to corner Drew. Drew, Gould, and Fisk succeeded despite the court in dumping 50,000 shares of newly printed stock on the market, depressing the price from 83 to 71, and bilked Vanderbilt out of millions. The judge then ordered the arrest of the trio and they retreated with six million in cash to Taylor's Hotel in Jersey City, New Jersey, which they fortified. The conflict was transferred to the courts and the New York state legislature. Gould brought about passage of a bill legalizing the stock issue, and Vanderbilt consented to a peace plan by which the plundered wreck of the Erie was handed over to Gould and Fisk. Drew, Gould, and Fisk then used their gains for an assault on bank credit, stock prices, and foreign exchange that ruined thousands of investors. In 1870 Drew's bank folded, and he was the victim of a coup by Gould and Fisk, who sold Erie stock in England to produce an unexpected rise in its stock price. This cost Drew one and one-half million dollars. His descent thereafter was rapid, with further losses in the Panic of 1873 and the resulting failure of Kenyon, Cox and Company, a firm in which he was largely interested. He filed for bankruptcy in 1876, with liabilities of over one million dollars. In 1866 he helped found Drew University.

He married Roxanna Mead in 1822, and had a son, William H. Drew. (A. *DAB; NCAB*, 11:502; 7:218; *New York Times*, September 20, 1879; *Who Was Who*, vol. H. **B.** Charles Francis and Henry Adams, *The Chapters of Erie*, 1886.)

DREXEL, JOSEPH WILLIAM (January 24, 1833–March 25, 1888) and **Anthony Joseph Drexel** (September 13, 1826–June 30, 1893). Bankers, Drexel and Company and Drexel and Morgan. **Joseph W. Drexel** was born in Philadelphia, son of Francis Martin Drexel (1792–1863) and Catharine Hookey. His father had been born in the Austrian Tyrol, and was the son of a well-to-do merchant. Francis Drexel came to America in 1817, working for ten years in Philadelphia as a portrait artist. He subsequently went to South America to paint portraits and amassed considerable wealth trafficking in currency. In 1837 he opened a brokerage house in Louisville, Kentucky, and the next year opened one in Philadelphia. There he amassed great wealth, and also engaged in far western banking during the California gold rush. Joseph W. Drexel was educated in the Philadelphia schools and by his own father. He first represented his father's banking firm in Germany, and in 1864 entered into banking in Chicago. Two years later, upon the death of his father, he returned to Philadelphia. In 1867 he became one of the partners in the banking firm of Drexel, Harjis and Company of Paris, and four years later became associated with J. P. Morgan* in the firms of Drexel, Morgan and Company of New York and Drexel and Company of Philadelphia. Thereafter his principal activities were oriented toward New

York City, where he became connected with a large number of financial institutions.

As a businessman, Joseph Drexel's chief significance lay in his serving as a connecting link between the larger banking and brokerage institutions of Philadelphia and New York, and between these and European investment bankers. He vastly increased his fortune by the promotion of more stable industrial enterprises, as well as by handling great quantities of securities issued by national and local governments. In 1876 he withdrew from active business to pursue philanthropic interests.

Anthony J. Drexel was born in Philadelphia and at thirteen entered his father's brokerage firm. His education was largely confined to these offices and his father's tutelage at home. He was made a member of the firm of Drexel and Company in 1847. His father's death in 1863 coincided with a major turning point in the national banking system and of the firm itself. Connections were established with the banking houses of San Francisco, New York, London, and Paris. The handling of the flood of investment securities connected with national and local public debts, the building of railroads, the development of mining, the growth of the factory system, and the improvement of urban real estate led to the transformation of the firm into essentially a house of investment bankers. During this period A. J. Drexel was the directing genius of the firm, and when his older brother died in 1885 he was left with the entire supervision of its affairs.

He built a magnificent new bank and office building and was heavily involved in real estate operations in Philadelphia and vicinity, adding greatly to his fortune. He also became connected with the publishing business, as part owner of the *Public Ledger* in association with George W. Childs. He became a noted philanthropist, founding the Drexel Institute in Philadelphia in 1892. He gave three million dollars to the school, which emphasized technology, free scholarships, low tuition, night classes, public lectures and concerts, and an unrestricted admissions policy in regard to religion, race, sex, and social class.

Joseph W. Drexel married Lucy Wharton of Philadelphia in 1865, and Anthony J. Drexel married Ellen Rozet of Philadelphia. (**A.** *DAB; NCAB*, 2:273 and 366; *New York Times*, July 1, 1893; *Who Was Who*, vol. H. **B.** Frederick Lewis Allen, *The Great Pierpont Morgan*, 1949; Vincent P. Carroso, *Investment Banking in America*, 1970; Fritz Redlich, *The Molding of American Banking*, 2 vols., 1951.)

DREYFUS, CAMILLE (November 11, 1878–September 27, 1956). Chemical manufacturer, Celanese Corporation. Born in Basel, Switzerland, son of Abraham Dreyfus and Henrietta Wahl. His father was a banker. He was educated in his home town and at the University of Basel, receiving an M.A. and Ph.D. before leaving in 1902. He continued his studies at the Sorbonne in Paris until 1906. After working in Basel to gain experience, in

1910 he and Dr. Henry Dreyfus established their own chemical laboratory in the same city. There they began the manufacture of cellulose acetate, the first nonflammable type of celluloid. One-half of their production went into motion picture film, and the other half into toiletry articles. Meanwhile, they continued to try to make a fiber from the cellulose acetate. They were successful in their quest, but before it could be marketed commercially World War I intervened.

A solution of cellulose acetate was used for military purposes on airplane wings to retard fire on the wooden framework covered with silk when it was hit by incendiary "tracer" bullets. In 1914 Great Britain invited Dreyfus to come to that country and constructed a large plant for him outside London. When the United States entered the war, Dreyfus was asked by the Secretary of War, Newton Baker, to establish a plant in the United States. The American Cellulose and Chemical Manufacturing Company was incorporated in 1918 with Dreyfus as president. The construction of a small plant was begun at Cumberland, Maryland, but before it was completed the war was over and the military market had vanished.

Dreyfus spent the next six years perfecting his cellulose acetate fiber and the methods for producing it. In December, 1924, the first "celanese," as the yarn was named, was manufactured in the Cumberland plant. The name of the corporation was changed to the Celanese Corporation of America, with Dreyfus retaining the presidency. J. P. Morgan* and Company became associated with the firm in 1926 as underwriter of its stock issue. The company showed a profit every year after 1925, and had its first really big year in 1939. The firm had grown by 700 percent in the ten years after 1929, with a new plant built near Pearisburg, Virginia, and a labor force of 12,000. It held 233 patents in the U.S. by 1940, most of which were concerned with the production of celluloid acetate.

In 1932 the company began experiments to produce acetic acid, which had formerly been purchased from chemical companies, and during World War II the War Production Board decided that Celanese should participate in the wartime chemical program. They authorized the construction of a plant in Bishop, Texas, which was not completed until the war's end. It was then converted to the production of chemicals for use by Celanese and for sale to other companies. In addition to acetic acid and acetic anhydride for production of cellulose acetate, the company also made formaldehyde, methanol, propyl alcohol, and trioxane. Celanese Mexicana, S.A., a Mexican affiliate, was organized in 1944, with Dreyfus as president. In 1945 he was elected chairman of the board of Celanese, but continued to act as executive head of the company.

During the years of his presidency, Celanese Corporation became a leading producer of cellulose acetate fiber and a variety of cellulose acetate fabrics suitable for use in home decoration and both civilian and military wearing apparel. It also produced woven and knitted fabrics, and introduced warp-knit rayon to the United States, becoming its largest manufacturer. It also became the third largest producer of viscose in the country. With the end of World War II it also began the production of plastics, including plastic film for packaging purposes. In 1954 Celanese introduced a new synthetic fiber, Annel, and also had developed polyester resin, combined with glass fibers.

Of Jewish heritage, Mr. Dreyfus married Jean Tennyson, a singer, in 1931. (*Current Biography*, 1955; *Who Was Who*, vol. 3.)

DRYDEN, JOHN FAIRFIELD (August 7, 1839–November 24, 1911). Life insurance executive, Prudential Life Insurance Company. Born on a farm, at Temple Mills, near Farmington, Maine, son of John Dryden and Elizabeth Butterfield. His ancestors had come to New England in the seventeenth century. John F. Dryden was educated at Yale, which he entered in 1861, but ill health forced him to quit before graduating. After he left Yale he became interested in life insurance, especially as related to a practical solution of the economic problems of the poor. He made a careful study of the Prudential Assurance Company of London, which had met with considerable success in writing industrial insurance.

In 1873 he settled in Newark, New Jersey, and secured the cooperation of a small group of men, including Leslie D. Ward, a young physician, and Noah F. Blanchard, a leading leather manufacturer. He wrote the first policy of the Prudential Friendly Society on November 10, 1875. This was a poor time to start because of the depression and at first the new company did not do well at all. Dryden persevered, and in 1878 it became the Prudential Insurance Company. Under his leadership the firm advanced to the foremost place among the life insurance companies of the world. The secret of his success was his clear grasp of fundamental principles, combined with an indefatigable industry and remarkable capacity for details. He has been called the "Father of Industrial Insurance in America."

Dryden was secretary of the company for six years, and in 1881 was elected president. By 1899 the firm's receipts were over $17 million. In 1875 less than 2 percent of the American people had their lives insured; by 1899 this had risen to over 17 percent. By this time there were twelve companies insuring lives on the industrial plan, with total policies of over one billion dollars. Industrial insurance was offered in small units to families too poor to afford the policies of the established life companies. Its success depended upon a unique marketing system developed in England. Agents were assigned a certain number of blocks in working class areas of large cities where they not only sold insurance by door-to-door solicitation, but also made weekly collection of premiums, which amounted to about ten cents apiece. Personal collection was considered an essential element of the system because of the assumption that the poor would not make the payments on their own volition and could not accumulate the surplus for even a low yearly premium. The cost of industrial insurance was necessarily greater than regular life policies, but it appeared to be the only way in which life insurance could be afforded by the working class.

John Dryden was also vice-president of Fidelity Trust of Newark, and director of Merchants National Bank in that city, and of U.S. Casualty Company of New York. A Republican, he was elected in 1902 to the U.S. Senate, but in 1907 he was denied renomination by powerful forces in the state party. In 1864 he married Cynthia Jennings Fairchild and had a son and a daughter. (**A.** *DAB; NCAB*, 9:415; *New York Times*, November 26, 1911; *Who Was Who*, vol. 1. **B.** William H. A. Carr, *From Three Cents a Week...*, 1975; Elisha P. Douglass, *The Coming of Age of American Business*, 1971; J. Owen Stalson, *Marketing Life Insurance*, 1942.)

DUER, WILLIAM (March 18, 1747–May 7, 1799). Financier and land speculator, Bank of New York. Born in Devonshire, England, son of John Duer and Frances Frye. His father was quite wealthy, owning plantations in Antigua and Dominica. William Duer was educated at Eton and commissioned as an ensign in the British army. He was appointed aide-de-camp to Lord Clive, and accompanied him when he returned to India as Governor of Bengal in 1764. Duer was not able to withstand the climate, however, and returned to England. Shortly thereafter, upon his father's death, he inherited a share of the paternal plantations and went to the West Indies. In 1868, having obtained a contract to supply masts and spars for the British navy, he visited New York for the purpose of purchasing timber. There he met Philip Schuyler of Albany, on whose advice he purchased an extensive tract of timberland on the Hudson River above Saratoga, New York, and established large sawmills there. He also made other investments. In 1773 he went to England, settled his affairs in that country, and upon his return made the province of New York his home.

Duer soon joined with the patriot cause and in 1775 was a delegate to the Provincial Congress, also being appointed deputy adjutant general of the New York troops, with the rank of colonel. In 1776 he was a delegate to the New York Constitutional Convention, and helped draft the constitution for the new state. In the same year he acted on the Committee for Public Safety and in 1777 was chosen as a delegate from New York to the Continental Congress. In the same year he was appointed first judge of commons pleas of Washington County, New York, serving until 1786. A signer of the Articles of Confederation, he resigned from Congress in 1779 to attend to his private affairs.

Duer then became immersed in a variety of commercial and financial projects. He was engaged in furnishing supplies to the army, holding some of the largest contracts. By the close of the war he was a very rich man. It was due to his efforts that in 1784 the Bank of New York was founded. In 1786 he was appointed secretary to the Board of the Treasury, and established his residency in New York City permanently. He was also elected a member of the state assembly at this time. In 1787 he was an investor in the Scioto speculation, with he and his associates securing the right to purchase from the United States a huge tract of western lands, which they in turn designed to sell to capitalists chiefly in France and Holland. He was also involved in the attempt to establish an international banking house which was intended to supplant the great Dutch firms in the handling of loans and commercial business generally. In 1789 the Department of the Treasury was organized and Duer was appointed assistant secretary under his close friend Alexander Hamilton.* He resigned six months later, and subsequently both he and Hamilton were involved in a funding scandal.

Thereafter Duer was continuously engaged in speculation on a large scale, involving purchases of lands in Massachusetts, Maine, and Vermont, contracts for army supplies during the Indian troubles of 1791, a project for a national manufacturing society in New Jersey, and large dealings in stocks. He finally became hopelessly insolvent and was arrested for debt in 1792. He was sent to prison, which caused one of the greatest financial panics in the history of New York. He remained in prison until he died. He married Catharine Alexander, daughter of Major General William Alexander (Lord Sterling), in 1779. His son, William Alexander Duer, was chief justice of the Supreme Court of the City of New York. (**A.** *DAB; NCAB*, 7:503; *Who Was Who*, vol. H; Joseph S. Davis, "William Duer, Entrepreneur," in *Essays in the Earlier History of American Corporations*, 2 vols., 1917. **B.** Bernard Mason, "Entrepreneurial Activity in New York During the Revolution," *Business History Review*, 1966.)

DUKE, JAMES BUCHANAN (December 23, 1856–October 10, 1925). Tobacco manufacturer, American Tobacco Company. Born on his father's small farm near Durham, North Carolina, son of Washington Duke and Artelia Roney. His mother died when he was an infant, and the family was soon plunged into poverty brought on by the Civil War. He was educated in a log house at Harden's and later at Pisgah Church. When his father returned from the Confederate army, life resumed on the home farm, which had been scoured clean by the invading Union armies. As later mythology put it, a small quantity of bright leaf tobacco had been overlooked, and this was seized upon as their only hope. The tobacco was put in packages labeled "Pro Boro Publico," blind mules were hitched to a wagon, and they struck out for the southern portion of North Carolina, where tobacco was scarce. There they met with ready sales, so they purchased more leaf tobacco, built a larger log house for manufacture, and found themselves prospering in their new venture. They sold 125,000 pounds in 1872 and had become one of the most substantial producers in the local industry. During these years his father and his brothers, Brodie Leonidus Duke (1846–1919) and

Samuel T. Duke, were the main factors in the company.

James and another of the younger brothers, Benjamin Newton Duke (1855–1929), were educated for a time at the academy in Durham, North Carolina. Here James proved himself to be quite adept with numbers and was sent to boarding school in Guilford County, but returned home after the first term. He then completed a business course at Eastman Business College in Poughkeepsie, New York, in record time. At fourteen he was made manager of the young black boys who labored in the tobacco factory, and four years later became a member of the firm of W. Duke and Sons. At the same time he became the company's traveling salesman. Seven years later, at age twenty-five, he became president.

In the same year that he assumed the presidency, the Dukes began the manufacture of cigarettes, for which the local "bright" leaf tobacco was especially adapted. James Duke soon replaced the hand workers with the new Bonsack machines which, with the aid of William T. O'Brien, he had perfected. When the law was passed reducing the government tax on cigarettes by two-thirds, Duke immediately reduced the price of his product from ten cents to five cents a pack two months in advance of the implementation of the act. This bold stroke, coupled with wide advertising, gave Duke's firm a lead over all others. A new period began in 1884 when he left Durham to set up a branch factory in New York City. His firm now invaded the northern and western markets and, largely through pouring hundreds of thousands of dollars into advertising of every form, came to furnish one-half of the country's cigarettes by 1889.

Soon the five principal cigarette manufacturing companies were engaged in the celebrated "tobacco war" in which competition and advertising concessions ruined profits. The older companies finally offered to buy Duke out, but this was his signal to force the fighting even harder, and in 1890 all were joined together in the American Tobacco Company, capitalized at $25 million, with James Duke as president. In 1895 the combination began to aggressively absorb companies making other kinds of tobacco products, such as chewing tobacco and snuff. At about this time an attempt by other capitalists to oust Duke failed.

In 1898 a combination of plug tobacco manufacturers was formed with Duke as president; it was capitalized at $75 million. But Duke was still eager for other mergers, and with Oliver H. Payne, P. A. B. Widener,* Grant B. Schley, William C. Whitney,* Richard J. Reynolds,* and Thomas Fortune Ryan,* he formed the American Snuff Company in 1900 and the American Cigar Company in 1901, and entered the retail field with the United Cigar Stores Company. In 1901 the Consolidated Tobacco Company was formed as a holding company to concentrate control of the American and Continental. But after the Northern Securities decision by the Supreme Court the holding company was discontinued, and the three were merged under the original name of the American Tobacco Company.

Duke's major failure during these years was his move into the cigar industry. Expecting to conquer that field with the same methods he had used with cigarettes, even including the creation of an extensive nation-wide retailing organization, American Tobacco never obtained more than 14 percent of the nation's cigar trade. What he failed to realize was that American Tobacco could make little use of its existing organization to make and sell cigars. The processes of both production and distribution were different. Cigars were produced by skilled workmen in small batches, and their leaf came from Cuba, Puerto Rico, and scattered areas in the northeastern United States. It was cured differently from other types of tobacco, and finally, cigars had traditionally been sold by their makers in small lots to retailers, with each brand and taste appealing to a different type of customer. Administrative coordination, therefore, did not reduce costs, nor could massive advertising bring about American Tobacco's dominance in the cigar business.

During this same time Duke began to enlarge his company's overseas trade. In this venture he was initially successful. His first step was to challenge his foremost competitor in Britain, W. D. and H. O. Wills, by purchasing Ogden's Ltd. for over $5 million. Wills countered this move by carrying out a merger of thirteen British tobacco firms to form the Imperial Tobacco Company. Imperial threatened to open a factory in America, and after some brief and sharp skirmishes, Imperial agreed to limit its sales to Great Britain, and American Tobacco confined itself to America. The trade with the rest of the world was the province of the newly created British American Tobacco Company, in which American held two-thirds and Imperial one-third of the $5.2 million worth of stock issued. In addition, American received 14 percent of Imperial's stock by the sale of Ogden's, making it the second largest stockholder in Imperial. Duke became chair-man of the board of British American Tobacco, and until he retired in 1923 devoted most of his time and attention to enlarging British American's trade.

Meanwhile, back in the United States, the Supreme Court ordered American Tobacco dissolved as a combination in restraint of trade. Duke bore the chief responsibility for the difficult task of setting up the constitu-ent elements of the combination—American, along with R. J. Reynolds, Liggett and Myers, and P. Lorillard—to operate as competitors once more. He continued to serve as president of American Tobacco until 1912, when he transferred his interest to British American. Since British American was largely controlled by Duke and the stockholders of American Tobacco, the worldwide tobacco business remained largely in the hands of Duke and other Americans despite the Supreme Court decision.

In 1904 James Duke had turned to the development of the water power of the Southern Piedmont. In the next year the Southern Power Company was formed, which in twenty years came to supply power to over 300 cotton mills and other factories and cities. In 1924 he created a trust fund, mostly of holdings in Southern Power (which had earlier been merged with Duke Power Company), worth $100 million to set up Duke University in North Carolina. At the time of his death the power company operated fifteen hydroelectric and steam power plants with a total capacity of 831,000 horsepower. He was president and principal owner of this organization until his demise. He also organized and was president of Duke-Price Power Company Ltd. of Canada, which constructed a 360,000 horsepower hydro plant in Quebec, one of the largest single water power developments in North America. More than one-half of its output was used to operate extensive newsprint paper mills.

James Duke was a Methodist and a Democrat, and married Mrs. William D. McCready of New York City in 1904. They were divorced in 1905 and two years later he married Mrs. Nanaline Inman of Atlanta. They had one daughter, Doris Duke. His brother, Brodie Leonidus Duke, had sold a large part of his tobacco company holdings upon the death of his father in 1905. He then lost and regained a large fortune several times through speculations. Another brother, Benjamin Newton Duke, was one of the directors of American Tobacco, but after 1911 devoted his capital to a variety of other enterprises. He was president of the Citizen's National Bank in Durham, head of the the Durham and Southern Railroad, and became heavily involved in the Southern Power Company, in cotton manufacturing, and in real estate. He married Sarah Pearson Angier of Durham and had two sons and one daughter. His daughter, Mary, married Anthony J. Drexel Jr.* of Philadelphia, and his grandson, Angier Biddle Duke (b. 1915), became a prominent diplomat with the State Department and in 1961 was appointed chief of protocol for the State Department. (**A.** *DAB; NCAB,* 17:382; 21:11; 18:196; *New York Times,* October 12, 1925; October 14, 1925; *Who Was Who,* vol. 1; Robert F. Durden, *The Dukes of Durham, 1865-1929,* 1975; John B. Jenkins, *James B. Duke, Master Builder,* 1929; John K. Winkler, *Tobacco Tycoon: The Story of James Buchanan Duke,* 1942. **B.** Alfred D. Chandler Jr., *The Visible Hand,* 1977; Maurice Corina, *Trust in Tobacco,* 1975; P. Glenn Porter, "The Origins of the American Tobacco Company," *Business History Review,* 1969; Richard Tennant, *The American Cigarette Industry,* 1950; Nannie Tilley, *The Bright Tobacco Industry, 1860-1929,* 1948.)

DUN, ROBERT GRAHAM (August 7, 1826–November 10, 1900). Credit rating service, R. G. Dun and Company. Born in Chillicothe, Ohio, son of Robert Dun and Lucy Worthum Angus. His parents had immigrated to America from Scotland. R. G. Dun was educated at a local academy in Chillicothe and his first job was in a store in the town. At twenty-one he became the proprietor of a small local business. Then in 1850 his brother-in-law, Benjamin Douglass, gave him the opportunity to join the organization of Tappan and Douglass, "The Mercantile Agency" of New York City.

The firm had been organized by Lewis Tappan* after the Panic of 1837, and was the first of its kind in the country. At first its service consisted of simply supplying facts relating to the credit standing of country store-keepers to a few wholesale firms in New York City, which paid annual subscriptions to cover the cost of obtaining such information. Under the management of Douglass, however, the scope of the service was being expanded.

Dun's first major success was achieved in dealing with the personnel of the central office. He quickly won the interest and loyalty of his colleagues, which in the later development of the business was an important factor. In 1854 the firm was reorganized as B. Douglass and Company, with Dun as a partner. On the withdrawal of Douglass from the company in 1859, Dun became the sole owner, although profits were shared with various associ-ates who were known to the public as partners in the enterprise. The New York office operated as Dun, Boyd and Company and later, Dun, Barlow and Company. At the outbreak of the Civil War in 1861, R. G. Dun and Company had branches in the principal cities of the country, including several in the South. The firm was not able to grow during the war, but at its conclusion it experienced unparalleled growth and adaptation to rapid changes in business methods. In this period Dun's managerial abilities were severely tested. He and his associates shaped the company policy to fit with the changing demands of business, taking advantage at the same time of every new device in the mechanics of the trade that seemed to promise increased efficiency in the service they were rendering.

The problem of reaching distant states promptly and receiving informa-tion from them in time to be of service was an especially vexing problem. R. G. Dun and Company had to develop new methods to deal with the new problems. It was among the first to make large use of the typewriter for communicating with subscribers, and the publishing activities of the house were expanded with the increasing business. As early as 1859 the first series of reference books appeared. To meet these demands the company erected its own printing plant, employing several hundred persons. In 1893 *Dun's Review*, containing a weekly report of business conditions, was inaugurated. Before long offices were opened in Paris, Germany, Australia, and South Africa, and nearly everywhere else. In total it had about 140 offices in the United States and abroad. Even as early as the 1870s Dun's agency employed over 10,000 reporters or investigators and received daily requests for infor-mation totalling 5,000.

Robert Dun married Elizabeth Douglass, sister of Benjamin Douglass, and Mary D. Bradford of Milwaukee. (**A.** *DAB; NCAB*, 24:429; *New York Times*, November 11, 1900; *Who Was Who*, vol. 1. **B.** *Dun and Bradstreet: The Story of an Idea*, 1966; James Madison, "The Evolution of Commer-cial Credit Reporting in Nineteenth Century America," *Business History*

Review, 1974; E. N. Vose, *Seventy-Five Years of the Mercantile Agency, R. G. Dun and Co., 1841-1916*, 1916; Bertram Wyatt-Brown, "God and Dun and Bradstreet, 1841-1851," *Business History Review*, 1966; and *Lewis Tappan and the Evangelical War Against Slavery*, 1969.)

THE DUPONT FAMILY: Eleuthere Irenee duPont (June 24, 1771–October 31, 1834); **Henry duPont** (August 8, 1812–August 8, 1889); **Alfred Irenee duPont** (May 12, 1864–April 29, 1935); **Thomas Coleman duPont** (December 11, 1863–November 11, 1930); **Lammot duPont** (October 12, 1880–July 24, 1954); **Pierre Samuel duPont** (January 15, 1870–April 5, 1954). Gunpowder and chemical manufacturers and financiers, duPont Corporation and General Motors.

(Eleuthere) Irenee duPont was born in Paris, France, son of Pierre Samuel duPont de Nemours, celebrated member of the physiocratic school of economists and an active participant in French public affairs. Turgot was his godfather, and gave him his baptismal names. His mother was Nicole Charlotte Marie Louise LeDee. Irenee was raised on his father's estate and was an indifferent student under private tutors. In 1788 Lavoisier, his father's close friend and chief of the royal powder works, took Irenee into the laboratory at Essonne, promising the boy his own post some day. In 1791, however, abrupt changes took place in Irenee's life. In that year he married Sophie Madelaine Dalmas, despite his father's violent objections, and Lavoisier lost his directorship of the powder works, forcing Irenee to leave also. The son then took active charge of his father's large printing house in Paris, established earlier in the year to bolster the conservative cause. Both father and son suffered several imprisonments for their activities. In 1797 the Jacobins suppressed the publishing business of the duPonts and the father decided that the fortunes (and fortune) of the family should be cast in America. His eldest son Victor had gone there about a decade earlier, and the family had strong ties with many American statesmen.

The elder duPont established a company to exploit land in the valley of the James River in western Virginia, and with Irenee, his wife and three children, and other close relatives left for America, arriving in 1800 at Newport, Rhode Island. They subsequently moved to New York City when Thomas Jefferson advised that their land investments be delayed. Thus, a part of the company's capital was used to establish a commission business in New York City, but it did not prove to be profitable. Irenee then hit upon a project which offered a greater return. He had been impressed with the poor quality and high price of American gunpowder, and concluded that an expertly run establishment, even though small, would return a profit of $10,000 per year. He returned to France for three months at the beginning of 1801 to secure machinery and designs for the manufacture of powder and received assistance from the government works at Essonne. Two-thirds of the necessary capital was subscribed by his father's company. Irenee purchased a farm on the Brandywine River, four miles from Wilmington, Delaware, where there had formerly been a cotton mill operated by water power.

In 1802 Irenee and his family settled in a little log house on the property and pushed forward the construction of the mill, despite many discouraging aspects, particularly the lack of capital. By 1804 the powder was ready for sale, and Thomas Jefferson, then president, promised orders from the federal government. Sales in that year amounted to $10,000; the next year they were $33,000, and by 1807 were $43,000. For the first six years profits averaged about $7,000 per year. By 1811 the profits were more than $40,000, and Irenee and Peter Bauduy invested in a woolen mill near the powder works, to be conducted by Peter's older brother, Victor. The War of 1812 then put the powder business in an assured position, and duPont became a principal supplier of powder to the federal government. He also supplied large quantities to the American Fur Company and to South American countries.

Irenee was made a director of the Bank of the United States and had a strong interest in agriculture. In addition, he was active in the American Colonization Society. His manufacturing establishment was semi-feudal in nature, with the workers being housed on the property and fed from the farm.

Henry duPont, Irenee's second son, was born at Eleutherian Mills, near Wilmington, Delaware. He was educated at Mt. Airy Military School in Germantown, Pennsylvania, from 1823 to 1829. He then entered West Point, where he graduated in 1833. He served as a second lieutenant in the artillery in the Creek country of Alabama, but resigned in 1834 to join his father's gunpowder works. He had served in the mill for sixteen years when, in 1850 (on the death of his brother, Alfred Victor, who had been president since their father's death in 1834), he became head of the firm. His partners were his brother, Alexis, and a nephew, Irenee duPont.

The great profits redounding to the company as a result of the Crimean War in 1854 helped Henry in his policy of progressive management. Both his older brother, Alfred, and his father had continued the semi-feudal management traditions when they headed the company. But when Henry took over a new economic era was dawning, and he adjusted his policies to it. Also, in 1857 Lamont duPont was granted a patent which enabled the firm to use nitrate of soda from Peru (which was much cheaper than India's saltpeter) in the manufacture of blasting powder. In 1859 the company bought mills on Big Wapwallopen Creek, Luzerne County, Pennsylvania, near large coal mining markets, for the manufacture of blasting powder, partially solving an old problem of transportation.

In that same year Henry duPont had experiments conducted in the making of hexagonal cakes of powder of large grain for big guns; but the work was interrupted and was not resumed for fifteen years, when it was notably successful. The firm refused to furnish powder to Virginia when that state's loyalty was in doubt prior to the Civil War, and in 1861 Henry was appointed a major general of the Delaware forces and put down disaffection in the state. The firm was made an agent of the government in purchasing enormous supplies of saltpeter (an essential ingredient for its powder-making) in England, but it also lost its trade in the South, and because of fear of capture, was prohibited from shipping powder from New York or Philadelphia. This meant that the West Indies, Mexico, and even for a time, California, went unsupplied. Independent mills were established in California in 1861 to meet the needs of miners there. DuPont supplied the army and navy with powder at low prices during the war, despite high taxes and slow remittances on the part of the government.

The depression of the 1870s brought about consolidation in the powder business, with duPont buying a controlling interest in the Hazard Powder Company in 1876 and in the California Powder Works in the same year. The firm discontinued experiments in "high explosives" after 1865, and not until 1876 did it begin the manufacture of Hercules Powder. Henry refused to produce Nobel's dynamite, but his nephew took up its manufacture by setting up Repauno Dynamite Company. Henry devoted most of his attention to the finances of the company, and conducted an enormous correspondence with 500 agents and half a dozen affiliated companies; he wrote by hand 6,000 letters a year, refusing the aid of a stenographer. He married Louisa Gerhard in 1837.

Alfred Irenee duPont was born near Wilmington, Delaware, son of Eleuthere Irenee duPont II and Charlotte Henderson, and grandson of E. I. duPont I. Both his parents died when he was thirteen, and at age twenty he left his course at Massachusetts Institute of Technology to enter one of the family's plants. Four years later, in 1888, he aided in the construction of a large blasting powder plant near Keokuk, Iowa. The following year he spent time in France, Germany, England, and Belgium, studying, at the request of the U.S. Ordance Department, a new brown or prismatic powder then being developed in Europe. As a result of these investigations, the duPonts contracted for the right to manufacture this powder in America.

When Eugene duPont, who had succeeded Henry as head of the company, died in 1902 there seemed to be no one to take his place, so the partners decided to offer the business to Laflin and Rand, a competitor, for $12 million. But Alfred said he would buy the company. He had induced his cousin, Thomas Coleman duPont, to enter the firm as an executive, and another cousin, Pierre S. duPont, was to be treasurer. Alfred himself was the technician, and the three cousins took over the company at a cost to themselves of $3,000. The firm was capitalized at $20 million, and they took more than $8 million of the new stock for their organization fees. All this was pledged as security on the other $12 million, which was the purchase price of the old company. During the rapid growth of the business that followed, Alfred designed new machines and developed the prismatic powder used by the U.S. in large-calibre guns. In 1914 Pierre purchased Coleman's share of the stock, and this move was fought by Alfred in the courts. He was unsuccessful, and despite the fact that he remained the largest stockholder next to Pierre, he was ousted from the company in 1915.

At the close of World War I Alfred organized the Nemours Trading Corporation to sell American goods in Europe, but when the economic collapse hit Europe in the 1920s he lost millions. He also owned the Wilmington *Morning News* from 1911 to 1920, and a variety of other interests, including radium mines in Colorado. In 1916 he purchased control of Delaware Trust Company and developed a chain of banks throughout the state. In 1929 he became the principal owner of a group of Florida banks and was also one of the largest individual investors in Florida real estate. He was an advocate of social security for the aged, and set up his own plan for 1,100 of the needy poor in Delaware.

An Episcopalian, he married Bessie Gardner of New Haven, Connecticut, in 1887. They were divorced in 1906, and a year later he married his second cousin, Alicia Bradford Maddox of Wilmington. She died in 1920, and in the next year he married Jessie D. Ball of Virginia. He had three daughters and a son.

Thomas Coleman duPont was the son of Antoine Bidermann duPont and Ellen Susan Coleman. His father had left the family powder business in Delaware and went to Kentucky, where he acquired interests in a paper mill, coal mines, and street railways. Coleman duPont was educated at an Ohio college for a short time, but was not a good student. He then went to M.I.T. where he met his cousin, Alfred duPont. After graduating in 1885 he was sent by his father to his western Kentucky coal mines to learn that business. He dug coal, drove and shod mules, and became superintendent of the enterprise. He developed the Central Coal and Iron Company into a major enterprise in the state.

In 1893 Coleman became manager of the Johnson Steel Company, a street railway rail plant in Johnstown, Pennsylvania, owned by Tom Johnson of Cleveland. Then, after a few years he bought the Johnson Street Railway Company, making it into a profitable venture. He then resigned from the steel company and formed an organization to promote street railways in other parts of the country. In 1902 his cousin Alfred urged him to head a reorganization of the duPont business, and he accepted. Shortly afterward he and Pierre began a series of significant financial maneuvers in keeping with the general thrust of the merger movement of the time.

The duPont Company already owned all the stock of Hercules Powder Company, a majority of the stock in another company, 50 percent of yet another, and minority holdings in fifteen more. Coleman, with Pierre, arranged to buy control of Laflin and Reed, their largest competitor, and of

Moosic Powder Company. They then organized holding companies to own each, and paid for the stock with the bonds of the holding company, thus giving the duPonts control without spending any of their own money, outside the $3,000 organization fees. Pierre, aided by John J. Raskob,* organized a super holding company, E. I. duPont de Nemours Company of New Jersey, with capital of $50,000,000, to control all the other companies. They continued organizing and consolidating the units at a rapid pace, until the duPonts controlled all plants in the country that made military powder, and were producing 90 percent of all explosives used in the United States. In four years the stocks of more than one hundred corporations had been acquired, of which sixty-four were eliminated. In the first decade of Coleman's presidency the duPont profits were $50 million. In 1907 the United States government filed an antitrust suit against the duPont concern, and in 1912 the court ordered the divorce of the two companies. But the effect on the company was not serious.

Meanwhile, Coleman had been engaging in personal ventures elsewhere. He obtained a controlling interest in the Equitable Life Assurance Society, and began erecting what was then the largest office building in New York to house it. In 1914, needing money for the $30 million Equitable Life Building, and tiring of the powder business, he offered to sell a large block of his stock back to the company. His cousins, Alfred and William, demurred at the price, but Pierre S. duPont, with a small group of kinsmen, secretly bought Coleman's entire holdings. Coleman then began to invest more heavily in hotels, controlling the McAlpin, the old Waldorf-Astoria, the Claridge, the Martinique, the Savoy Plaza, and the Sherry Netherland in New York City; the Windsor in Montreal; the Bellevue-Stratford in Philadelphia; and the Willard in Washington, D.C.

In 1908 he became a member of the Republican National Committee. Eight years later he tried for the U.S. Senate, but lost the race due to the opposition of his cousin Alfred's Delaware newspapers. In 1921 he was appointed to the U.S. Senate to fill out an unexpired term, and in 1924 was elected to a full term. He resigned in 1928 due to ill health. In 1889 he married a cousin, Alice duPont of Wilmington, and they had five children.

Pierre S. duPont was born in New Castle County, Delaware, son of Lammot duPont and Mary Belin. He was the grandson of Alfred Victor duPont and great-grandson of the founder of the family in America. His father was an able chemist and businessman who had functioned as Henry duPont's right hand man. He had left the company, however, when Henry had refused to move into the production of dynamite. Pierre was educated at William Penn Charter School in Philadelphia and graduated from Massachusetts Institute of Technology in 1890. He then joined the duPont company at the Wilmington plant, two years later becoming assistant superintendent of the company's factory in New Jersey. That factory manufactured smokeless gunpowder and gun cotton. There he and Francis G. duPont developed a new principle in the gelatinating and granulating of nitro cellulose which was patented. Under this formula the duPont smokeless shotgun powder was manufactured at the plant after 1894. He left duPont in 1899 and joined Coleman, becoming president of the Johnson Steel Company, which was in process of liquidation. He spent three years developing the sale of the company's other interests, which included street railways and large realty holdings in Lorain, Ohio. In 1902 he joined with his cousins, Alfred and Coleman duPont, in the complicated purchase of the duPont company. He was named treasurer of the new concern and handled the financial organization of the new consolidated companies.

In 1915 he headed a group that purchased the interest of Coleman duPont in the company, and he became chairman of the finance committee and president of the corporation. He served as chairman of the finance committee until 1926, and as chairman of the board from 1919 to 1940. From the latter year until his death in 1954 he was a member of the finance committee and a director. The group that purchased Coleman's interest was the Christiana Securities Company, of which Pierre was president from 1915 to 1919, and a director for the rest of his life. His presidency at duPont covered the period of World War I, during which time a program of great expansion was inaugurated and carried out in order to fill orders for munitions from the Allied countries and from the United States. In a short time the capacity of the company was increased from 12 million pounds per year to one million daily.

DuPont's own plants were augmented by numerous additional units erected for the U.S. government in various parts of the country, the most important of which were a smokeless powder plant in Nashville, Tennessee, a guncotton plant in Hopewell, Virginia, a factory for loading shells in Virginia, a TNT plant in Wisconsin, and acid and nitrating plants in Indian Head, Maryland. The company produced nearly one and one-half billion pounds of military explosives during the war, and its workers reached a peak of 86,000.

After the war the resources of the duPont company were applied to new fields: the firm developed Duco pyroxylic lacquer, new plastics, cellophane, improved rayon, neoprene synthetic rubber, nylon, and many other new materials, with explosives becoming a relatively minor aspect of the business. It acquired many other companies, including an interest in General Motors during 1918-1919. Pierre duPont served as president of the latter firm from 1920 to 1923, and as chairman of the board until 1929. He remained on its board of directors until 1944. He was also a director of a large number of other firms.

Pierre duPont's contributions to American industry generally, and to the explosives, chemical and automobile industries in particular, were profound. First, he and Coleman duPont, with the assistance of John J. Raskob, totally reorganized the structure of the explosives industry. At duPont, they centralized the administration of production under three operating departments: black powder, high explosives, and smokeless powder. They replaced the older selling agencies by an international network of offices administered by a central sales department, and set up a large buying organization that within a few years operated nitrate beds in Chile and its own extensive shipping and transportation facilities. They also developed a department to manage a modern research laboratory, and Pierre developed new methods of assets accounting, of capital allocation, of financial forecasting, and of determining the rate of return on capital invested that have became standard procedures in American industry.

Pierre retired as president of duPont in 1919, turning duties over to his brother Irenee, but in the next year assumed the presidency of General Motors. In 1917, at John Raskob's urging, he had invested $25 million of his war profits in General Motors. After the war, Raskob joined William C. Durant* in Detroit, and together they embarked on a massive expansion program. But a steep postwar recession brought the company close to bankruptcy, and Durant retired. Pierre duPont then reorganized General Motors' operating structures and marketing strategies, relying heavily on Alfred P. Sloan* in carrying this out. The two set up a top management office, consisting of a number of the general executives without day-to-day operational responsibilities and a large financial and advisory staff to evaluate, coordinate, and plan for the operation of the many divisions. Pierre brought in experienced managers from duPont to institute accounting and statistical control procedures that he had developed earlier. In marketing, duPont's strategy was essentially to bracket the market, to have each auto division sell its products in each major price class. In 1923 he turned the presidency over to Sloan to complete the reforms and became chairman of the board. General Motors experienced phenomenal growth in the next decade, selling more cars than Ford and showing a profit record which was the best in the industry. He retired from the board chairmanship in 1929.

During the 1930s Pierre duPont became involved in various aspects of local and national politics. Serving as tax commissioner of Delaware from 1925 to 1937 and from 1944 to 1949, he was also on the state liquor commission from 1933 to 1938. On the national level, he was named to the advisory board of the NRA in 933, and then the NRA National Labor Board. He returned to his Republican party sympathies in 1934, however, and founded and funded the Liberty League, a major anti-New Deal organization. An Episcopalian, he married Alice Belin. They had no children.

Lammot duPont, Pierre's younger brother, was born near Wilmington, Delaware. His father died in an explosion when he was four years old, and he was raised by his older brother. He graduated from Massachusetts Institute of Technology as a civil engineer in 1901 and became a draftsman for U.S. Steel Company. A year later, upon reorganization of the company by Pierre, Coleman, and Alfred, he took a job in the duPont company's black powder mills at the urging of his brother. In 1915 he became superintendent of the black powder department, and a vice-president of the company. During the war, the duPont firm also began to expand into other fields, such as paint, dyes, artificial leather, celluloid, and chemicals. Lammot was put in charge of these developments. In 1926 he succeeded Irenee as president of DuPont Company, an office in which he served until 1940, when he became chairman of the board, a position that he held until 1948.

His tenure as president was significant in the development of the company. By the end of World War I the firm had ceased to be primarily an explosives manufacturer, and had become a broad-based chemical company, a change that Lammot, as head of the miscellaneous manufacturing division, had helped to bring about. He was early committed to large expenditures for research and development, and encouraged work on the creation of artificial fibers that led, in the 1930s, to the invention of nylon, which revolutionized the textile industry. Other major discoveries of the company during his presidency were neoprene (the first general purpose synthetic rubber), Orlon, and Dacron. The DuPont Company remained highly profitable during the depression of the 1930s, and during World War II its engineering staff took a major part in atomic research and contracted for the government the Harford Atomic Works in Washington State. He was also chairman of the board of General Motors from 1931 to 1937, but rode a bicycle six miles to work each day.

A Republican, he had supported Franklin Roosevelt in 1932 because he promised to balance the budget. But he quickly lost faith in the New Deal and became a supporter, with his brother Pierre, of the American Liberty League. He especially resented the 1934 Nye Commission investigating the World War I munitions makers, and vigorously defended the company. He was married four times: in 1903 to Natalie Wilson, who died in 1918; in 1920 to Bertha Taylor, who died in 1928; in 1930 to Caroline Hyrson Stollenwerck, from whom he was later divorced; and in 1933 to Margaret A. Flett. He had ten children. (**A.** *DAB; DAB*, Supplements 1, 3, and 5; *NCAB*, 6:456; 457; 25:25; 22:2; 31:446; 56:322; A:310; *New York Times*, January 1, 1929; November 12, 1930; April 6, 1954; July 25, 1952; *Current Biography*, September, 1940; May, 1954; *Who Was Who*, vols. H; 1; 3; W. Carr, *The duPonts of Delaware*, 1964; Alfred D. Chandler Jr. and Stephen Salsbury, *Pierre S. duPont and the Making of the Modern Corporation*, 1971; M. Dorian, *The duPonts From Gunpowder to Nylon*, 1962; Marquis James, *Alfred I. duPont—The Family Rebel*, 1941; Leonard Mosley, *Blood Relations*, 1978; John K. Winkler, *The DuPont Dynasty*, 1935. **B.** Alfred D. Chandler Jr., *Strategy and Structure*, 1962; Ernest Dale, *The Great Organizers*, 1960; Bessie G. duPont, *E. I. duPont de Nemours and Company: A History, 1802-1902*, 1920; W. S. Dutton, *duPont*, 1942; Thomas Johnson,

"Managerial Accounting in the Early Integrated Industrial: E. I. duPont de Nemours Powder Company, 1903–1912," *Business History Review*, 1975; Michael Massouh, "Technological and Managerial Innovation: The Johnson Company, 1883–1898," *Business History Review*, 1976; Alfred P. Sloan Jr., *My Years at General Motors*, 1964; Arthur P. Van Gerlder and Hugo Schlatter, *History of the Explosives Industry in America*, 1927; Gerard C. Zilg, *DuPont: Behind the Nylon Curtain*, 1974.)

DURANT, THOMAS CLARK (February 6, 1820–October 5, 1885). Financier and railway executive, Union Pacific Railroad. Born in Lee, Massachusetts, son of Thomas Durant and Sybil Wright, both members of old New England families. T. C. Durant received his medical degree from Albany Medical College in 1840, but soon abandoned the practice of medicine, joining his uncle in the mercantile firm of Durant, Lathrop and Company, exporters of flour and grain. He was given charge of the firm's New York office, where he rapidly gained a reputation as a daring and successful speculator in stocks. Becoming interested in developments in the West, in 1851 he joined with Henry Farnum* in construction of the Michigan Southern Railroad. They also contracted to build the Chicago, Rock Island and Pacific Railroad and the Mississippi and Missouri Railroad.

About 1860 Durant began to survey for a railroad to the Pacific, to travel through what appeared on the maps at the time as the "Great American Desert"—an area thought to be populated only by prairie dogs and Indians. The Republican platform in 1860 had promised the building of a transcontinental railroad through this region, and Durant, together with a few associates, convinced Congress to sweeten the pot for the railroad's eventual builders with sizable land grants, loans, and a federal bond issue. With a liberal dispensation of bribes to members of Congress, Durant secured passage of the Pacific Railway Act of 1862, creating the Union Pacific Railroad and offering ten square miles of the supposedly worthless land in the Great American Desert for every mile of track built. The act fixed the capital of the Union Pacific at $100 million, but permitted organization of the company when only $2 million had been subscribed. By the fall of 1863 the company was formally organized, with General John A. Dix as president and Durant as vice-president; but Dix never took an active interest in the company, while Durant remained the motive force behind the organization.

Ground was broken for the new line on December 2, 1863, at Omaha, Nebraska; but labor was scarce, the connecting rail line east across Iowa was far from completion, and new stock subscriptions were slow in appearing. By 1864 the building contractors associated with the line had stopped construction after only a few miles were completed and refused to do more until they received more money. Durant was undaunted by this turn of events. He simply returned to Congress and convinced them to amend the 1862 act, doubling the size of the land grants to the Union Pacific and allowing the company to offer their own bond issues. At the same time Durant, along with Oakes* and Oliver Ames* and other New England capitalists, secured the charter of the Credit Mobilier, which took over the builder's contracts, agreeing to take securities issued by the road in lieu of cash payment for construction.

The Credit Mobilier, of which Durant was chief stockholder and president, became a fabulous moneymaking machine. Although construction estimates for construction of the first 500 miles of road were pegged at $30,000 a mile, Credit Mobilier contracted with Union Pacific to do the work for $60,000 a mile. With the signing of this contract the Union Pacific's chief engineer, Peter A. Dey, resigned in disgust. He was replaced by General Grenville M. Dodge, an equally competent engineer, but one who was more amenable to the ways of Durant and the corrupt construction companies. Corrupt or not, the Credit Mobilier supplied the necessary incentive and helped provide the requisite funds to build the Union Pacific. By September, 1866, some 180 miles of track had been laid, and by the end of the year the base construction camp was at North Platte, Nebraska, 293 miles west of Omaha. The rapid pace of construction captured the public's imagination. The Central Pacific was starting simultaneously from California, and the·two were to link up at some yet unspecified point. Because the federal loans and land grants depended on track mileage, the two companies staged a vigorous race to lay the most track. Each offered enormous wages for the times and cut corners wherever possible to save time.

By 1869, when the two railroads were finally linked in the Golden Spike ceremony at Promontory Point, Utah, the Union Pacific had been granted more than 18,000 square miles of territory—an amount of land equal to the combined areas of Vermont and New Hampshire. Some of this was sold to settlers along the way in the hope that the cheap land would increase railroad business; but most was kept by the railroad. The completion of the line in 1869 was followed by months and years of rebuilding the jerry-built road—relocating, regrading, and reconstructing much of it. The Union Pacific had captured the nation's imagination; it had made its backers, including Durant, fabulously wealthy; and it did provide an important transcontinental linkage for the American economy. There is some question, however, about the economic efficacy of the road. Critics at the time chastised its shoddy building practices and wastefulness; later economic historians have asserted that it was a premature enterprise, built far ahead of demand and unable to stimulate adequate demand once it was built, making it an enormously expensive white elephant for a number of years.

Meanwhile there was a power struggle brewing within Credit Mobilier and the Union Pacific that was to explode in a major national scandal in 1872. From 1866 to 1869 the Ames brothers and the "New England Crowd" contested Durant and his "New York Crowd" for control of the Union Pacific. They managed to oust Durant as a director of Credit Mobilier in

1867, but he remained as director of the Union Pacific. Oliver Ames became president of Union Pacific in 1868, succeeding Dix, while at the same time his brother Oakes, a member of Congress, was distributing shares of Credit Mobilier stock among influential members of that body. The subsequent congressional investigation implicated vice-president Schuyler Colfax, Speaker James G. Blaine, and James A. Garfield. In the meantime, Durant and George Francis Train, his eccentric crony, had managed to defraud Union Pacific investors of some $23 million through the exorbitant markups they charged the road for materials used in construction. By the 1890s, thanks to Credit Mobilier, Durant, and the other scandals and mismanagement on the road, along with the fact that it was unable to generate sufficient business along its line, the Union Pacific was bankrupt. E. H. Harriman* bought the road at auction just prior to the turn of the century. In the years to follow he built the Union Pacific into one of America's premier railroads.

Durant himself was crippled financially by the Panic of 1873, but still retained a vast expanse of land in the Adirondacks as the base of a considerable fortune. He married Heloise Hannah Timbrel of England in 1847. (A. *DAB; Who Was Who*, vol. H. **B.** Robert G. Athearn, *Union Pacific Country*, 1971; John P. Davis, *The Union Pacific Railroad*, 1894; Robert Fogel, *The Union Pacific Railroad: A Case of Premature Enterprise*, 1960; Wesley S. Griswold, *A Work of Giants*, 1962; Arthur M. Johnson and Barry E. Supple, *Boston Capitalists and Western Railroads*, 1967; James McCague, *Moguls and Iron Men*, 1964; Milton Moscowitz et al., *Everybody's Business*, 1980; John F. Stover, *American Railroads*, 1961.)

DURANT, WILLIAM CRAPO (December 8, 1861–March 18, 1947). Automobile manufacturer, General Motors and Durant Motor Company. Born in Boston, Massachusetts, son of William Clark Durant and Rebecca Folger Crapo. Little is known about his father, but he appears to have been a drifter from New Hampshire who married into a wealthy family. His mother was the daughter of Henry Haviland Crapo of New Bedford, Massachusetts, who made a fortune in whaling and then moved to Michigan where he became a successful lumberman and Governor of Michigan from 1865 to 1869. Durant was raised in his grandfather's home in Flint, Michigan. He left high school at age sixteen to work in his grandfather's lumberyard, but soon took a variety of jobs, mainly in selling. At twenty he became manager of the Flint Water Works.

Since Flint was one of the leading centers of carriage and wagon manufacture, Durant was inevitably drawn into that business. He took his first major step in 1885 by buying the patent rights to a two-wheeled cart for fifty dollars and organizing, with J. Dallas Dort, the Flint Road Car Company, renamed the Durant-Dort Carriage Company one year later. The company rapidly became one of the country's leading manufacturers of horse-drawn vehicles, with fourteen plants in the United States and Canada and a maximum annual production of 150,000 carriages. It purchased extensive hickory forests in Mississippi and Arkansas for a source of hardwood, and separate companies were organized for the manufacture of parts and accessories: Imperial Wheel Company, Flint Axle Works, and Bluff (Arkansas) Spoke Company. Its production methods anticipated the assembly system that later characterized the American auto industry, with separate plants making the parts and assembly at the main factory in Flint. Durant continued his association with the firm until 1914.

Durant also moved into the automobile business in 1904 when a fellow carriage manufacturer, James H. Whiting, decided he could no longer afford to support David D. Buick's effort to put the Buick car into production and pursuaded Durant to buy him out. Durant did not possess the technical skill of the other automotive pioneers, but he was an energetic promoter and an excellent administrator when he concentrated on the management of a single company. With a basically good design to sell, he quickly made the Buick Motor Car Company the largest auto manufacturer in the United States.

But the expanding market in automobiles was being contested by hundreds of small companies, and the attrition rate was very high. Durant became convinced that the formula for success lay in creating a large organization making a variety of models and controlling its own sources of parts. To this end he tried in 1908 to merge Buick with its three principal competitors: Ford, Maxwell-Briscoe, and Reo. The plan failed when Henry Ford* and Ransom E. Olds* demanded three million in cash for their companies. Durant's next move was to charter the General Motors Company of New Jersey in September of that year. It acquired a number of motor vehicle firms—Buick, Cadillac, Oakland (later Pontiac), and Oldsmobile, and several parts manufacturers. Durant then caused the Weston-Mott Axle Company to move from Utica, New York, to Flint and financed Albert Champion's project for making porcelain spark plugs.

General Motors soon ran into financial problems. Durant, ever the optimist, had produced more autos than he could sell immediately, thus getting caught with a cash flow problem, since he did not have enough cash from the sale of autos to pay his suppliers and workers. He was forced to turn to a group of New York and Boston bankers to bail the company out, but since the banking community viewed him as a speculator and a visionary, he was forced out of active management of the firm. In 1910 General Motors passed under the control of a banker's trust headed by James J. Storrow* of Boston's Lee, Higginson and Company.

Durant, however, was not to be sidetracked. In 1911 he joined with Louis Chevrolet, a Swiss-born mechanic and racing driver, in a new automobile venture, organized as the Chevrolet Motor Car Company. This firm entered the popular-priced car market so successfully that Durant was able to start swapping Chevrolet stock for GM stock. By 1916 he had picked up enough shares of GM to oust the bankers and recover the company. In the meantime, in 1914, he had interested John J. Raskob* and then Pierre S. duPont* to join him in his automobile ventures. It was with their financial backing that he was able to acquire the requisite shares of GM stock to oust Storrow and regain control of General Motors. During this same time Durant organized the United Motors Corporation (1916), a holding company for a group of auto parts manufacturers including the Hyatt Roller Bearing Company and the Dayton Engineering Laboratories Company (Delco), with the important result that Alfred P. Sloan Jr.* and Charles F. Kettering* were brought into the GM management. At Pierre duPont's insistence, a new General Motors Corporation was chartered in Delaware in 1916 to absorb United Motors and to rectify the anomoly of having GM technically controlled by Chevrolet.

Durant again launched an ambitious program of expansion for GM; the Fisher Body Company was acquired in 1919, and in the same year the General Motors Acceptance Corporation was created to assist in financing dealers. The building of the General Motors Center in Detroit was also begun. The firm became a manufacturer of refrigerators when Durant bought control of the Guardian Refrigerator Company and later sold it to GM under the name of Frigidaire. Durant, however, allowed his energies to be so dispersed that he was able to give the sprawling GM structure neither coherent organization or consistent management. His determination to run all aspects of GM cost the company some of its best executives: Henry M. Leland, president of Cadillac, resigned in 1917, and Walter P. Chrysler,* president of Buick, left in 1920. Alfred P. Sloan also threatened to resign.

The depression of 1920 created a financial crisis for GM and Durant. In the fall of 1920 the market for automobiles had collapsed, and the company, with poor central management procedures, had allowed division heads to greatly outrun demand, resulting in some $80 million in inventories which had to be written off. As the price of GM stock declined sharply, Durant sought to bolster it by making large purchases on margin and soon became overextended. At this point Pierre duPont moved to preserve the solvency of GM by paying off Durant's debts in return for control of a large block of his GM stock. As part of the deal, Durant resigned as president of GM and was replaced by Pierre duPont. All of this was done with the sanction and urging of the banking house of J. P. Morgan and Company.

Early in 1921 Durant returned to the auto industry by raising seven million dollars among friends and organizing the Durant Motor Company. It acquired various minor companies and produced some well known cars—Durant, Flint, and the Star. But it was not a success, losing money even during the peak of the boom period for cars in the twenties. Thus, it was not able to survive the Crash in 1929, and was liquidated in 1933. Two years later, Durant filed for bankruptcy, with liabilities of nearly one million dollars and assets of only $250 (his clothes). Yet his promotional zeal was undiminished. Ever the innovator, he opened a supermarket in Asbury Park, New Jersey, in 1936, one of the very first in the nation, and in 1940 returned to Flint to launch a chain of bowling alleys designed for family recreation. The coming of the war, however, blocked the project, and shortly afterward his health broke down.

A Republican, he was first an Episcopalian and then a Presbyterian. He married Clara Miller Pitt in 1885 and they were divorced in 1908. In 1916 he married Catharine Lederer. He had a son and a daughter. (**A.** *DAB*, Supplement 4; *NCAB*, 36:16; *New York Times*, March 19, 1947; *Who Was Who*, vol. 2; Lawrence R. Gurstin, *Billy Durant*, 1973. **B.** Alfred D. Chandler Jr., *Strategy and Structure*, 1962; *Giant Enterprise*, 1964; and with Stephen A. Salsbury, *Pierre S. DuPont and the Making of the Modern Corporation*, 1971; John B. Rae, *American Automobile Manufacturers*, 1959; Alfred P. Sloan Jr., *My Years with General Motors*, 1969; Bernard A. Weisberger, *The Dream Machine*, 1979.)

DURFEE, ZOHETH SHERMAN (April 22, 1831–June 8, 1880). Steel manufacturer, Kelly Pneumatic Process Company. Born in New Bedford, Massachusetts, son of Thomas Durfee and Delight Sherman. He was educated at Friend's Academy in New Bedford, and in his early youth learned the blacksmith's trade. Later he was associated with his father and uncle in that business. Becoming interested in the process of manufacturing steel directly from pig iron with an invention of Joseph Dixon, Durfee, with the sponsorship of New Bedford capitalists, undertook investigations of various processes for the manufacture of iron and steel. This led him to believe that William Kelly of Kentucky was the true inventor of the "Bessemer Process." On the basis of this belief, in partnership with Captain E. B. Ward of Detroit, he obtained control of Kelly's patents in 1861. In the same year he went to Europe to study the Bessemer process and to purchase, if possible, Bessemer's rights in the U.S. He failed to accomplish the latter project.

Upon his return to the U.S. he organized a company called Ward and Durfee in 1862 to protect use of the Kelly patents. He invited William F. Durfee, a cousin, to assist in erecting an experimental plant at Wyandotte, Michigan, for the manufacture of pneumatic steel. In May, 1863, they and their partners organized the Kelly Pneumatic Process Company. During his visit to England in 1861, Durfee had become familiar with an invention by Robert Mushet for using spiegileisen as a recarburizing agent, and was convinced that it was essential to the successful conduct of the Kelly and Bessemer processes. In 1863 he was sent to England to secure control of Mushet's patent in the U.S., and was successful in doing so in 1864. While he was in England the experimental works at Wyandotte made its first blow under the supervision of W. F. Durfee—producing the first Bessemer steel made in the United States.

In 1865, at Troy, New York, a plant built by Alexander L. Holley* began to manufacture steel under Bessemer's patents, and in 1866 the two interests were combined in the Pneumatic Steel Association, a joint stock company organized in New York in which was vested the ownership of both the Kelly and Bessemer patents. Z. S. Durfee served as secretary-treasurer of this company, holding the office until his death. He was also superintendent for a time prior to 1868 of the steel works of Winslow and Griswold in Troy.

Durfee originated the idea of using the cupola instead of the reverberation furnace for melting pig iron from the converter charge, a practice which became universal. He guarded Kelly's business interests and did more than any other person to get the rights of Kelly recognized in the United States. He also obtained numerous patents for steel manufacture. He was raised a free will Baptist. (**A.** *DAB; NCAB*, 6:190; *Who Was Who*, vol. H. **B.** Douglas Alan Fisher, *The Epic of Steel*, 1963; Stewart H. Holbrook, *Iron Brew*, 1939.)

DWIGHT, EDMUND (November 28, 1780–April 1, 1849). Cotton manufacturer, Boston and Springfield Manufacturing Company and Chicopee Manufacturing Company. Born in Springfield, Massachusetts, son of Jonathan Dwight and Margaret Ashley, and a descendent of John Dwight, who settled in Dedham, Massachusetts, in 1635. His father had come to Springfield at an early age and had become a leading merchant in the city. Although the family was prosperous, Edmund was brought up to work on the family farm and store. He graduated from Yale College in 1799 and then read law in the office of Fisher Ames in Dedham. Upon completion of his studies, however, he decided on a career in business rather than law. His association with Ames served him well, nonetheless, as it brought him into contact with the best society of Boston and many of the keenest minds of eastern Massachusetts, which would be invaluable to him in his later dealings.

His father gave him his inheritance early, and Edmund spent 1802-1804 traveling abroad. Returning to America, he associated himself with his father and brothers, whose business interests now included banking enterprises and branch stores in several towns. Edmund still found time to represent the town of Springfield in the General Court from 1810 to 1813 and in 1815, and his keen interest in politics continued throughout his life. After marrying Mary Harrison Eliot, daughter of Samuel Eliot, a prominent merchant of Boston, he moved to that city in 1816.

After arriving in Boston, he established a partnership with James K. Mills and became one of the foremost entrepreneurs in laying the foundation for New England manufacture. He was the directing hand in the establishment of three manufacturing centers in Chicopee Falls, Chicopee, and Holyoke, all set up in the Connecticut Valley, where he had lived for many years. In 1822 he and his brother, Jonathan, purchased most of the land later occupied by the village of Chicopee Falls, built a dam to harness the power of the river, and by 1831 had erected four cotton mills operating under the name of the Boston and Springfield Manufacturing Company, and then of the Chicopee Manufacturing Company. The first named company in 1825 bought the water rights and land later covered by the city of Chicopee. These rights were distributed by the Springfield Canal Company, organized in 1831. Along the canal operated by the company Dwight himself built huge mills and induced other manufacturers to establish themselves in the area.

Through the Hadley Falls Company Dwight secured the water rights and built the dam and canals upon which the manufacturing of Holyoke was based. By 1841 his company had the principal direction of cotton mills, machine shops, and calico printing works, employing about 3,000 persons. Outside of manufacturing, his chief business interest was in the organization of the Western Railroad from Worcester to Albany. He was a member of the first board of directors from 1836 to 1839, and was elected a director by the legislature on the part of the state in 1842. Until his death he continued on the board as a representative of either the state or of the stockholders. He also served as president of the road in 1843.

Dwight was also involved in educational reform; he was at the center of a group who devised the School Law of 1837, and became a member of the Board of Education established by this law. The law gave the board broad powers to collect information and distribute school funds. He served as secretary of the board for sixteen years. It was he who paid Horace Mann's salary. He also gave $10,000 to establish a system of normal schools. His son, Edmund, became a merchant in Boston. (**A.** *DAB; NCAB*, 12:341. **B.** Constance M. Green, *Holyoke, Massachusetts: A Case History of the Industrial Revolution in America*, 1939; Robert K. Lamb, "The Entrepreneur and the Community," in William Miller ed., *Men in Business*, 1952; Vera Schlakman, *Economic History of a Factory Town: A Study of Chicopee, Massachusetts*, 1935; Caroline F. Ware, *Early New England Cotton Manufacture*, 1931.)

DYMOND, JOHN (May 3, 1836–March 5, 1922). Sugar planter, association leader and publisher, *The Louisiana Planter and Sugar Manufacturer*. Born in Canada, son of Richard Dymond and Anne Hawkens, Cornish immigrants to that country. His father was a Methodist preacher and later a merchant. While he was still a child his family moved to Zanesville, Ohio, where he was educated in the public schools and at Zanesville Academy, and graduated from Bartlett's College in Cincinnati, Ohio, in 1857. He worked for a time in his father's store before leaving in the spring of 1860 for New York City, where he secured a position as a traveling salesman.

In 1863 he became a broker in New York in the firm of Dymond and Lally, which three years later opened a branch house in New Orleans, doing a large business in Louisiana sugar and molasses as well as in imported sugar and coffee. In the fall of 1868 the firm purchased the "Belair" and the "Fairview," sugar plantations on the Mississippi River, thirty miles below New Orleans. Dymond thus began his career as a planter, gradually withdrawing from his city business. In 1877 he led the movement resulting in the creation of the Louisiana Sugar Planters Association, and from 1887 to 1897 was its president. He was also one of the leaders in urging the importance of research work in the culture and manufacture of sugar. This was culminated by the organization of the Louisiana Scientific Agriculture Association, of which he was president until his death, and the establishment of the Audubon Sugar Experiment Station.

When sugar planters formed a corporation in 1888 to publish the *Louisiana Planter and Sugar Manufacturer*, Dymond was chosen its managing editor, general manager, and president, serving for thirty-four years. He was quick to grasp new ideas in laborsaving devices and to lend aid in their development. He helped to introduce the Mallon stable digger and McDonald hydraulics. He also introduced double and triple milling in grinding the cane, the redivivus or multiple effect evaporation, and the so-called dry vacuum in vacuum boiling. He installed the first nine roller mill ever erected in Louisiana, and he patented a sulphur machine and the shelf on a cascade machine, which became universal in its use. He was the first man in the sugar industry to weigh sugar cane received at the mill as a basis for a comprehensive system of cost determination at the mill by weight.

His sugar plantations in 1866 comprised more than 6,000 acres, and grew to have more than 10,000 acres under cultivation, with an average annual output of plantation sugar of nearly 3,000,000 pounds. His sugar manufacturing house had a capacity for 250 tons. He was also involved in Democratic politics as a delegate to the Democratic National Convention in 1888, and as a member of its platform committee. In that position he opposed the party's free trade ideas. He was also involved in local politics, as president of the police jury of Plaquemines Parish and chief executive on the Levee Boards. He led the movement in the 1890s to return the parish to white control.

After his "Belair" sugar house burned down in 1907, he sold two of his large plantations and gradually turned his attention to other matters. He served as president of the Louisiana Press Association from 1900 to 1909, and of the National Editorial Association from 1906 to 1906. After 1907 he went to New Orleans, where he edited the *Southern Farmer* and the *Trade Index of New Orleans*, and published the *Louisiana Planter and Sugar Manufacturer*.

Born a Methodist, he became a Unitarian and married Mary Elizabeth Cassidy of Zanesville in 1862. They had six children. One of his sons, John Dymond Jr., became a prominent lawyer in the state prior to his death in 1932. (*DAB; NCAB*, 25:350.)

E

EASTMAN, GEORGE (July 12, 1854–March 12, 1932). Photographic equipment manufacturer, Eastman Kodak Company. Born in Waterville, New York, only son of George Washington Eastman and Maria Kilbourn. His family had come to America in 1628, and his father was a penmanship teacher who went to Rochester in 1842, establishing the city's first commercial college. He did not move his family there until 1860, two years before his death. By taking in boarders, Eastman's mother was able to maintain the family's modest living standard. After seven years in the public schools, George Eastman secured his first job at an insurance office. In 1874 he became junior bookkeeper at the Rochester Savings Bank, where rapid advancement gave him a salary of $1,400 by 1876. By the time he was twenty-one, he had saved over $3,000.

In 1877, at age twenty-three, he spent $94 on photographic equipment and began to develop prints. He also began some experiments to reduce the size and weight of outdoor photographic equipment, but was too frugal to devote much money to his hobby. By 1879 he was ready to embark upon his business career. Patents were secured in Europe and America on his coating machine, which was an improved process of preparing gelatin dry plates for use in photography. In 1880 he began the manufacture of dry plates in partnership with Henry A. Strong, who supplied some of the funds to equip the third floor factory. Eastman shortly afterward left his bank job to devote full time to his new enterprise.

He began his search for a transparent and flexible film in 1884. His first success was in the preparation of paper-backed film, which was patented in that year, leading to the reorganization of Eastman Dry Plate Company as the Eastman Dry Plate and Film Company with a capitalization of $200,000. Half of this came from Eastman and Strong, and half of it was new capital. The first commercial film, put into production a year later, was cut in narrow strips and wound on a roller device. Film rolls sufficient for 100 exposures were mounted in a small box camera, and the Kodak, priced at $25, was placed on the market in 1885. It was introduced by a national advertising campaign which said, "You push the button, we do the rest." The first Kodaks had to be returned to the factory for development.

Still not satisfied with the paper-backed film, Eastman employed a young chemist, Henry M. Reichenbach, to prepare a transparent film, one of the first industrial research assignments in the country. An order from Thomas A. Edison* for film to be used in his experimental motion picture camera emphasized the urgency of the research, and in 1887 Reichenbach prepared a suitable film by adding camphor, fusel oil, and amyl acetate to a solution of nitro cellulose in wood alcohol. Patents were secured shortly afterward. The 1890s witnessed Eastman's emergence as an industrialist of the first order. The Eastman Company, organized in 1890 with a capital of one million dollars, was reorganized two years later as Eastman Kodak Company with capital of five million dollars. Despite the panic of the 1890s, it was reorganized again in 1898 at $8 million, a transaction that netted Eastman a profit of $969,000 as promoter. A remarkable expansion followed, and capital doubled every few years as the decades passed. Daylight-loading film was introduced in 1891, a pocket Kodak hit the market in 1895, and a new cheap camera, priced as low as five dollars, was introduced in the following year. All these went a long way towards making photography a mass market hobby, to be practiced by the average man on the street.

Eastman Kodak also developed a stronger film for Edison's popular movie camera. The original factory on State Street in Rochester was expanded and a new plant known as Kodak Park, on spacious grounds north of the city, was developed. The number of employees had reached 3,000 by 1900, and a branch plant was opened in Harrow, England. This growth brought a host of new problems, however. Eastman generally made decisions independently of his board of directors, and sacked any associates who did not agree with him. He discharged Reichenbach and his two assistants in 1892 when he discovered that they were attempting to form a rival company, and later brought suit against them. Meanwhile the growing complexity of the organization compelled him to seek executives for the various departments and to enlarge his research staff. In order to develop employee and executive loyalty, in 1899 he distributed $175,585 in profits among his executives and older employees. In 1911 he set up an employee benefit fund of $500,000, but refused to allow his employees to bargain collectively. In 1912 he declared the first wage dividend, a bonus of 2 percent on the wages received in the previous five years. Safety appliances, a medical department, shorter hours, and social as well as lunch room facilities were introduced as Eastman sought to decrease turnover in the plant, discourage strikes, and head off minimum wage legislation. His program for the sale of Eastman stocks at par value to older employees, begun in 1917, climaxed his efforts to cement the loyalty of the company's employees, who numbered over 15,000 by 1920.

During these years Eastman also had a series of successful battles for control of the marketplace. He had absorbed several rivals prior to 1898, but others had still remained. A combination of leading photographic manufacturers in Europe in that year prompted Eastman to buy out all the photographic paper producers in America, and to contract with the European combine for all its paper shipped to the U.S. Exclusive contracts were negotiated with most of the distributors of photographic supplies, further checking competition in the amateur field. At the same time, developments in the motion picture industry were controlled by an agreement with Edison assuring the latter's royalties for the use of his camera, and securing the film market for Eastman.

Before long, however, Eastman encountered strong antimonopoly forces. An attempt to form an international cartel in 1908 was balked by French law, and an alliance between the leading French and German firms provided vigorous competition until Eastman acquired Pathe's film production plant in 1927. Meanwhile, his control of 75 to 80 percent of the American output gave him a virtual monopoly over the home industry. Moderate price reductions were frequently adopted with the object of expanding the market, but an average profit of 171 percent was realized on the products sold in 1912. Investigations were launched by the attorney general's office, and the firm was adjudged in violation of the antitrust laws in 1915. The case was appealed and ultimately dismissed after several of the subsidiary companies were sold off and other practices modified. During World War I Eastman put his plant at the disposal of the government for war production, refusing to accept unusual profits for war work. The company ultimately cancelled bills or returned payments that totaled a third of a million dollars.

Before his death, Eastman Kodak had manufacturing plants in Rochester; Kingsport, Tennessee; Harrow, England; Vincennes, France; Germany; Australia; and Hungary. The main plant at Kodak Park in Rochester had 120 buildings covering 480 acres, with its own water supply, power and light system, and fire department. There were 7,000 employees at this plant alone at the time of his death, and 2,500 at the other Rochester plant. He retired as president in 1923 and served as chairman of the board until his death. He also had become one of America's leading philanthropists, giving money in the early years to M.I.T. and the University of Rochester. Half of his vast fortune was disposed of in 1924, and in 1932 most of the remaining money was also given away. In total he dispensed over $75 million. He committed suicide in 1932, leaving a note which said, "My work is done, why wait?" He never married. (**A.** *DAB*, Supplement 1; *NCAB*, 26:32; *New York Times*, March 15, 1932; *Who Was Who*, vol. 1; C. W. Ackerman, *George Eastman*, 1930. **B.** Reese W. Jenkins, "Technology in the Market: George Eastman and the Origin of Amateur Photography," *Technology and Culture*, 1975; and *Images and Enterprise*, 1975.)

EASTMAN, JOSEPH BARTLETT (June 26, 1882–March 15, 1944). Public official, Interstate Commerce Commission, and Director of Defense Transportation. Born Katarek, New York, son of Joseph Huse Eastman, a Presbyterian minister, and Lucy King. His ancestors came to America in 1638. He was educated in his hometown, and after 1895 in Pottsville, Pennsylvania, where he attended high school. He then spent a year learning

Latin and Greek before entering Amherst College, his father's alma mater, where he received a bachelor's degree in 1904. After graduation he received a fellowship to work on the small staff of Robert A. Woods at South End House in Boston. This launched a lifelong career for Eastman in public service.

At this time several reformers, Louis Brandeis, Edward A. Filene,* and George W. Anderson, had formed the Public Franchise League to serve as a watchdog over municipal utilities. In 1905, when Brandeis suggested hiring a full-time secretary for the League, Woods recommended the twenty-three year old Eastman. For the next decade Eastman for all practical purposes *was* the League, personally and sometimes singlehandedly investigating proposed railway mergers, testifying on pending railway, gas and electric rate changes, exposing stock frauds, and preparing bills for presentation to the state legislature. In 1906 he enrolled in Boston University Law School, but dropped out in the next year, working for an uncertain salary that rarely reached $1,000 a year.

In 1913, partly as a result of his efforts, Massachusetts established a state Public Service Commission. Two years later Eastman replaced George W. Anderson on the commission when the latter was named U.S. District Attorney for the state. In 1917 President Wilson elevated Anderson to the Interstate Commerce Commission, and a year later Eastman was nominated to the I.C.C. The Senate confirmed his appointment in 1919. Eastman would remain on the board for the rest of his life, serving twice as its chairman. As a believer in the concepts of scientific management, Eastman eschewed politics and belonged to no political party.

Shortly after World War I, during which time the nation's railroad system was taken over by the Federal Railway Administration, Eastman advised against returning the railroads to private management. He believed that the railroads were in a poor credit position, and therefore could not operate efficiently without government coordination. This stance placed him in direct opposition to the railroad owners and also irritated the nation's shippers, with whom he had usually been identified. They distrusted the Federal Railway Administration, since it had sided with the railroad managers during World War I. Also, business in general feared any type of "socialism" during this period, so only organized labor supported the "Plumb Plan." Later, Eastman was also to incur the wrath of labor as he opposed many of their demands on the grounds that the railroads could not absorb the costs of them.

In 1933 Eastman was appointed Federal Coordinator of Transportation to bring some order to an industry severely damaged by the Great Depression. His efforts met with little success. He was able to effect little coordination among the railroads because they resisted his every effort. In attempting to develop a policy to maximize the public interest, Eastman transgressed upon the special interests of both labor and management, as well as upon certain jealously guarded prerogatives of other governmental agencies. His formal powers lapsed when Congress refused to renew them in 1936.

In 1941 he was appointed Director of Defense Transportation, and in this he had more success, as he now recognized the necessity to work with the principal spokesmen of the interest groups directly engaged in the transportation industry. Thus, he came to rely heavily on advice from representatives of railway management and the shipper's associations. He was an Episcopalian and never married. (*DAB*, Supplement 3; *NCAB*, D:259; 43:540; *Current Biography*, July, 1942; May, 1944; *Who Was Who*, vol. 2; Claude M. Fuess, *Joseph B. Eastman*, 1952.)

EATON, CYRUS STEPHEN (December 27, 1883–May 10, 1979). Financier and industrialist, Cleveland Trust; United Light and Power; Continental Shares; Republic Steel; Otis and Company; Chesapeake and Ohio Railroad; Goodyear Tire and Rubber; and Cleveland Cliffs Iron Mining. Born in Nova Scotia, Canada, son of Joseph Howe Eaton and Mary Adelle McPherson. Cyrus Eaton was a member of an old New England family that had come to America in 1640. In 1760 David Eaton had moved to Nova Scotia, and over the generations the family developed great influence in the area. Joseph Howe Eaton, however, was not prosperous, and Cyrus Eaton was raised in humble circumstances. At seventeen he decided to become a Baptist minister, and after graduating from Amherst Academy in Woodstock, Ontario, he visited with his uncle, the Reverend Charles A. Eaton, who was a Baptist minister in Cleveland, Ohio. While visiting there, he secured a job in a hotel, but upon being introduced to John D. Rockefeller Sr.,* a member of his uncle's congregation, Rockefeller put him to work on his Cleveland estate and also as a messenger boy in his private telegraph office. At the end of the summer Eaton planned to attend McMaster University in Toronto to get his divinity degree. Rockefeller attempted to dissuade him from these studies, telling him, "You've got what it takes to be successful in business." Eaton went on to McMaster nonetheless, graduating in 1905. During the summers he worked for Rockefeller's Cleveland gas company, and upon graduation toiled for a while as a cowboy in western Canada. A few months later he returned to Cleveland as a lay minister, and soon joined Rockefeller's enterprises.

Eaton started in business in 1907 when Rockefeller and several of his associates sent him to Manitoba to acquire franchises for a series of proposed power plants. He was successful in acquiring the franchises, but upon his return the Panic of 1907 had hit and the Rockefeller group was unwilling to continue with the project. Eaton thereupon cancelled the franchises, raised money from banks in Canada, and built a power plant at Brandon, Manitoba. This maiden venture was a success, so he built others. By consolidation and acquisition he eventually set up the Continental Gas and Electric Company, with holdings in western Canada and the midwestern

United States. He was soon worth over two million dollars, and in 1913 returned to Cleveland from Manitoba, acquiring a partnership in the investment house of Otis and Company.

During the next several years he continued to multiply his assets, and in 1919 was one of the principals involved in bringing about the consolidation of the Lake Shore and Garfield banks with the Cleveland Trust Company, which was the largest bank in the city as measured by deposits. His next step was to merge the Continental Gas and Electric Company, the Kansas City Power and Light Company, and the Columbia Power and Light Company with the United Light and Power Company. The latter firm was incorporated in Maryland in 1923 and furnished public utility service through subsidiary companies to 5.5 million people in 711 cities and towns in Illinois, Indiana, Iowa, Kansas, Michigan, Missouri, Nebraska, Ohio, Oklahoma, Tennessee, Texas, and Wisconsin, and to Brandon, Manitoba. Assets of United Light and Power in 1929 were in excess of a half billion dollars, and the company was symptomatic of the great holding company boom in the public utility industry in the 1920s. About this same time Eaton began secretly buying up shares in utilities controlled by Samuel Insull,* threatening to throw them all on the market at one time unless Insull bought them at a lofty price. Caught in a desperate situation, Insull purchased Eaton's 160,000 shares of Commonwealth Edison, People's Gas, and Public Service of Illinois. To do so, Insull was forced to run to Wall Street bankers for the first time; this was the beginning of his undoing and the genesis of one of the most infamous financial bankruptcies of all time.

Meanwhile, in 1925, Eaton moved into the steel industry. In this venture he encountered the opposition of New York bankers and Eastern financial interests, but he looked for a weak company he could take over. He found such a firm in Trumbull Steel of Warren, Ohio. It was badly in debt, and Eaton offered the firm $18 million (the precise amount of its indebtedness) and took control. In 1926 he organized and became chairman of the board of Continental Shares, Incorporated, which was formed to hold stock in firms in the public utilities industry, steel, and rubber. By the end of 1929 it had assets of over $132 billion, and in the same year he acquired United Alloy Steel Company and Central Steel Company of Massillon, Ohio, combining them into Central Alloy Steel Corporation. By 1927 his holdings in Republic Iron and Steel Company were great enough to give him control of that firm, and he merged it with Trumbull Steel. Then, in 1929, he formed an alliance with Cleveland-Cliffs Iron Company to gain control of Donner Steel Company in Buffalo, New York. The following year he merged all these firms into the Republic Steel Corporation, with assets of $331 million and a production capacity of five million ingot tons, the third largest steel company in America. During the same year he took control of Goodyear Tire and Rubber Company, which had assets of $200 million.

In 1929, however, his luck turned sour. First of all, he was hit hard by the stock market crash in October of that year and lost an estimated $100 million, leaving him nearly without liquid resources. Secondly, he became involved in a fight with Bethlehem Steel for control of Republic Steel. Although he was able to ward off the challenge by 1931, it cost him a large part of what remained of his personal fortune. By 1933 he had little left except his Cleveland securities house, Otis and Company. In that year Chase National Bank (controlled by his old friends, the Rockefellers) auctioned off his collateral to pay off the debts he had incurred in the fight against Bethlehem Steel. Within a few years, however, he was able to reestablish himself.

Eaton's first step in his financial rehabilitation came in 1932 when he allied himself with Harold L. Stuart,* head of Halsey, Stuart and Company, the Chicago investment house. Halsey, Stuart had handled the financing of Insull's empire for over a decade, and Harold Stuart had been indicted along with Insull in 1932. From 1932 to 1935 the Eaton and Stuart worked closely together, rebuilding their shattered empires. By the late 1930s they were again ready for large-scale investments. In 1938 they allied with Robert R. Young* (a former protégé of the duPonts* and Donaldson Brown*) to aid him and Allen Kirby (son of one of the founders of Woolworth's) in their bitter struggle with J. P. Morgan and Company and Kuhn, Loeb and Company for control of Allegheny Corporation and its prize holding, the Chesapeake and Ohio Railroad. These properties were the last remnants of the great transportation empire built up by the Van Swearingen* brothers in the 1920s. They, like Insull, had been ruined by the stock market crash, and had been pushed into bankruptcy by Wall Street bankers. The flash point in the struggle between Morgan and Kuhn, Loeb on one hand and Eaton, Young, and Stuart on the other came over the issue of competitive bidding. In 1938 a $30 million bond issue of the C & O came due for refunding. The New York bankers on the board assumed the issue would be underwritten through their houses, a standard practice at the time. Instead, Young obtained a commitment from Eaton and Stuart to underwrite the issue at a lower rate, with a saving to the railroad of $1.35 million. The directors reacted negatively, charging that Eaton was a man in "poor repute." Young threatened to take legal action against the directors, and they capitulated. This was the start of competitive bidding in railroad finance, and by 1942 it had been made a regulation by the Securities Exchange Commission.

In 1942 Eaton purchased the Steep Rock Iron Mines Limited in Ontario for $20,000. He then successfully negotiated a loan from the Reconstruction Finance Corporation, while the Canadian government gave him an equivalent amount for docks, roads, and a railway spur line. Steep Rock iron ore was marketed by the Cleveland Cliffs Corporation, with the Premium Iron Company, Ltd. (also organized by Eaton) acting as middleman and agreeing to purchase all Steep Rock ore for a ten year period.

Eaton was also aided in this venture by the timely assistance of John L. Lewis, who made substantial stock purchases in the Eaton enterprises with the United Mine Workers' pension fund. The quid pro quo was the unionization of Eaton's mines. This deal led to sharp questioning by a congressional committee. In 1947 Eaton's Otis and Company purchased 34,000 shares in the Cliffs Corporation, an operating and holding company with assets of $90 million.

In 1948 Eaton and Otis and Company became involved with the newly organized Kaiser-Frazer Automobile Company, organized by Henry J. Kaiser.* Eaton underwrote more than $17 million worth of stock in the company, but ordered Otis and Company to back out of the deal, since he charged that Kaiser-Frazer had misrepresented its earnings. The case went through the courts and in 1952 they ruled in favor of Eaton. He also attempted to purchase the Pullman Sleeping Car Company's interests in 1945, but was rebuffed, and in 1946 underwrote more than one million shares of the Portsmouth Steel Company, set up by Eaton to supply Kaiser-Frazer with part of their steel requirements.

During the final quarter century of his life, transportation became Eaton's major concern. In 1954 he replaced Robert Young as chairman of the Chesapeake and Ohio, holding that position until he was removed in 1973. He remained the largest single stockholder in the road, with some 115,000 shares. He also had sizable holdings and served on the boards of directors of some 40 corporations during this period, including Youngstown Sheet and Tube; Fisher Body; Sherwin-Williams Paint; Republic Steel; Inland Steel; Cleveland Cliffs Iron Company; Detroit Steel Corporation; Baltimore and Ohio Railroad; and Kansas City Light and Power. He also owned extensive public utility interests in Tokyo, Berlin, and Brazil. His fortune at his death was estimated at some $150 to $200 million, but may have been much greater.

Eaton, was a somewhat bewildering combination of the old nineteenth century entrepreneurial spirit and political liberalism and iconoclasm. He not only continually warred with Wall Street financial interests like J. P. Morgan and Company, but also wrote a number of books and articles critical of American capitalism. During the 1930s he accepted trade unionism. Rather than battling the unions, as most of his colleagues in the steel industry were doing, he recognized them and signed contracts with them. A lifelong, rock-ribbed Republican until 1930, he decided that Herbert Hoover* could not lift the country out of the depression and threw his support to Franklin Roosevelt. He continued to support FDR during the 1930s and remained at least a nominal Democrat for the rest of his life. He backed Harry Truman in 1948, coming through with a crucial $15,000 for the campaign during its closing days.

His most famous and controversial stands, however, concerned his relations with the Soviet Union and other Communist-bloc countries. He developed an active trade and personal relation with Russia during the 1950s, and was often referred to as the "Kremlin's favorite capitalist." Although many persons questioned his patriotism, he replied that "[I believe] that a nation's social and economic system is its own affair. I wouldn't want Communism here, but if the Russians want it, that's up to them." In 1954 he set up a meeting of American and Soviet atomic scientists at his home in Pugwash, Nova Scotia, in hopes that they would warn their respective governments of the perils of atomic warfare to mankind. This was the start of a series of over 40 conferences at Pugwash dedicated to easing world tensions. In 1960 Eaton was awarded the Lenin Peace Prize for these activities. Although he claims he never profited from these transactions with Russia, companies with which he was associated sold products in Eastern Europe, and members of his family, in association with the Rockefeller interests, built hotels in Prague, Budapest, Bucharest, and Warsaw. With the American-Soviet wheat deal in 1972, his railroads handled much of the American grain in the transaction.

Eaton's proudest accomplishment, however, was his role in the development of the St. Lawrence Seaway Project. His principal function was to act behind the scenes during the 1930s, obtaining the support of the Canadian government for the venture. He was a trustee of the University of Chicago and Denison University and of Harry S. Truman Library. He was also a founder of the Cleveland Museum of Natural History, and a member of the American Council of Learned Societies, the American Historical Association, and the American Academy of Political and Social Science. A Baptist, he married Margaret House in 1904, and they were divorced in 1933. In 1957 he married Anne Kinder Jones. He had seven children, two of whom died young. (**A.** *NCAB*, C:88; *Current Biography*, July, 1948; *New York Times*, December 27, 1973; May 11, 1979; *Who's Who in America*, 1978–79. **B.** Frederick Lewis Allen, *The Lords of Creation*, 1935; Matthew Josephson, *The Money Lords*, 1972.)

ECCLES, MARRINER STODDARD (September 9, 1890–December 18, 1977). Banker, food processor, and government official: First Security Corporation, Eccles Investment Company, Federal Reserve Board. Born in Logan, Utah, son of David Eccles and Ellen Stoddard. He was the eldest of twenty-two children. His father was born in Scotland in 1849, and came to America with his family in 1863, settling in Utah with a party of Mormon pioneers. David Eccles began by peddling wood and chopping logs for a sawmill. He soon had his own lumber business and over the years created a large regional financial empire in lumbering, banks, and sugar beet companies. Marriner Eccles worked for his father during the summer, tending stores, working in logging camps, and learning to be a supervisor of men. He attended Brigham Young College from 1905 to 1907, and in 1909 his father asked him to serve as a Mormon missionary in Scotland.

In 1912 his father died, leaving a fortune of $7 million to the family. In the early years his mother served as president of the family's business concerns, and in 1916 Eccles Investment Company was organized as a holding company for the family's widespread enterprises, with Ellen Stoddard Eccles as president and Marriner as vice-president and general manager. She remained president of the concern until 1928 when Marriner succeeded her in that office. During much of this time, however, he took the leading role in bringing about an expansion of the business. By 1927 he had acquired a number of banks, and had become president of the First Security Corporation, which operated twenty-six banks in Utah, Idaho, and Wyoming. He was also president of Sego Milk Products Company; the Stoddard Lumber Company; the Utah Construction Company (which was one of the firms that built Boulder Dam); and the Amalgamated Sugar Company; and director of many other corporations. All the banks and other companies were very successful, and not a single depositor in an Eccles bank lost a dollar in the Crash of 1929 or its aftermath. By 1933 the banks he controlled had assets of $60 million, Utah Construction Company was one of the oldest and largest construction companies in the United States, and Eccles owned one of the largest sheep and cattle ranches in the country.

A Republican during his early business years, Eccles had shared the party's orthodox economic philosophy. The deep depression of the early 1930s shattered his faith in the way in which the economic system was being run. He wanted answers to the problems of unemployment and insecurity that were endemic during the early years of the Great Depression. Searching for these answers, he turned in 1931 to the *Road to Plenty*, which had been written in 1928 by William Trufant Foster and Wadill Catchings. The book focused on a staple of nineteenth century economic thought, Say's law of markets. According to that law, the financing of production would by itself automatically create enough purchasing power in the economy to move all the goods produced. The implication, then, was that the needs of production should be attended to first, and demand would take care of itself. Foster and Catchings argued that Say's law overlooked two major facts of economic life. First, as industry increases its output, it does not proportionately increase its payment to the people (even Henry Ford's highly paid workers could not buy all the autos they produced). Second, Say's law overlooked the dilemma of thrift. Although corporations and individuals alike had to save, every dollar saved was a dollar subtracted from the flow of money to the potential consumer. This led to a decrease in effective consumer demand, and from there to depression. Only the federal government could offset the deficiencies in demand caused by oversaving.

With the onset of the depression, Foster argued against the conventional business demand for balancing the federal budget, calling instead for an increase in total payrolls to increase effective purchasing power. Since private enterprise was unable to fund this operation, public enterprise was the only remaining resource. Eccles supported the ideas of Foster and Catchings, and enhanced their concepts in the light of his own experiences as a banker and businessman. His recommendations for recovery would eventually far surpass Foster's in concreteness and fundamental challenge to the reasoning of the major leaders of business opinion. Eccles rejected the concept that a "lack of confidence" was the cause of the depression and that this could only be cured by returning to a balanced budget. What was to become his lifelong credo was enunciated in the following manner: "A policy of adequate government outlays at a time when private enterprise is curtailing its expenditures does not reflect a preference for an unbalanced budget. It merely reflects a desire and the need to put idle men, money and material to work. As they are put to work, and as private enterprise is stimulated to absorb the unemployed, the budget can and should be brought into balance, to offset the danger of a boom on the upswing. . . . "

Eccles began giving speeches calling for government "reflation"; for increased government spending and higher income and inheritance taxes; for federal grants to the unemployed; for federal control of the securities and stock exchanges; for child labor laws, rational planning for security, cancellation of war debts, unification of the banking system, greater transportation regulation, and so forth. This was an early blueprint of the New Deal, and all but the cancellation of war debts was adopted in principle by the Roosevelt administration. In 1933 he testified about these views before a Congressional committee, and soon thereafter was appointed Assistant Secretary of the Treasury, with responsibility for monetary and credit problems. Six months later, in November, 1934, he became chairman of the Federal Reserve Board. This unleashed a storm of protest from eastern banking interests, but his appointment was confirmed. During the next eighteen months he was one of the main authors of the Banking Act of 1935, which led to a restructuring of the Federal Reserve System, strengthening its control over monetary and credit policy. This change was strenuously opposed by the American Bankers Association, but again he was able to prevail. Later, he was to incur the wrath of organized labor when he called for lower wages to stimulate recovery. He also had continual run-ins with Henry Morgenthau, the Secretary of the Treasury. During World War II Eccles presided over a major expansion of credit for America's European allies and for domestic arms production.

Eccles had been particularly criticized during the war for cooperating with the Treasury Department in financing a $200 billion increase in the national debt. The Federal Reserve Board, because it stabilized interest rates at low levels, became known as the "Engine of Inflation." After the war Eccles advocated tight economic measures to fend off inflation, and tried to bring an end to the wartime policy of artificially low interest rates. This decision came at at time when returning servicemen and families who had been denied consumer goods during the war were eager to reap the benefits of the expanding economic system. Eccles' stance, therefore, set him at odds with Harry Truman, and when his term ended in 1948 Truman refused to reappoint him. He remained on the Board of Governors, however, until 1952.

After leaving Washington, Eccles returned to the family economic enterprises and resumed the chairmanship of First Security Corporation, a position he held until 1975, when he became honorary chairman. He was also chairman of Amalgamated Sugar and Utah International, the latter of which became a subsidiary of General Electric in 1976. By the 1960s it was estimated that he controlled one of the largest family fortunes in America. He also continued to speak out on causes he favored. He was a champion of world population control and sought closer relations with Communist China long before it became acceptable in financial circles. His most controversial stand, however, was on the Vietnam War. He was one of the first businessmen to speak out against the war, and he retained his conviction to the end. In 1972 he said, "We are told we have to have a victory in Vietnam or there will be a 'blood bath'. What do you consider 700,000 Vietnamese killed by us and our ally—not to mention the appalling civilian toll. Isn't that a 'blood bath?' . . . We are guilty. And no amount of rhetoric about a 'generation of peace' will make it go away. It will never be forgotten—or forgiven. Nor should it be."

A Democrat after 1932, Eccles' only try for elective office came in 1952 when he was an unsuccessful candidate for the U.S. Senate in Utah. A Mormon, he married Mary Campbell Young of Scotland in 1913, and Sara Madison Glassie in 1951. He had three children. (**A.** *NCAB*, E:434; *Current Biography*, April, 1941; *New York Times*, December 20, 1977; Sidney Hyman, *Marriner S. Eccles*, 1976. **B.** Marriner Eccles, *Beckoning Frontiers*, 1951.)

ECKSTEIN, OTTO (August 1, 1927-   ). Economic forecaster, Data Resources, Incorporated. Born in Ulm, Germany, son of Hugo Eckstein and Hedwig Pressberger. His father was a businessman and his brother, B. H. Eckstein, is a research chemist. The family moved to the United States in 1939. Otto Eckstein was educated in the schools of Germany, England, and New York City, graduating from Stuyvesant High School in New York City in 1946. He entered the U.S. Army as a private in that same year. After his discharge in 1947 he enrolled in Princeton University, majoring in economics, graduating *summa cum laude* in 1951. He then chose Harvard University for graduate study, getting his M.A. in 1952 and his Ph.D. in 1955. In the latter year he joined Harvard's faculty.

Having written a book, *Multiple Purpose River Development*, based on his doctoral dissertation, which called for the need for public participation in river development for economic efficiency, he at the same time served as a consultant to Resources for the Future, Incorporated from 1956 to 1959, and to the Rand Corporation from 1957 to 1966. He was also a consultant to the Committee for Economic Development in 1959, preparing *Trends in Public Expenditures in the Next Decade* for them. As technical director of the Joint Economic Committee of Congress during 1959, Eckstein also conducted an investigation of U.S. fiscal policy. From 1961 to 1964 he served as consultant to both the Treasury Department and the Council of Economic Advisors for Presidents Kennedy and Johnson. In 1964 he was appointed a member of the Council of Economic Advisors, along with Walter Heller and Gardner Ackley. In 1966 he rejoined Harvard University, which awarded him a grant to spend the year doing research at the Center for Advanced Study in the Behavioral Sciences at Stanford, California. He also served as editor of the *Review of Economics and Statistics*. From 1967 to 1969 he was a member of the National Advisory Council on Economic Opportunity, a member of the President's Commission on Income Maintenance Programs in 1968–1969, and a member of the research advisory board for economic development from 1967 to 1970. In 1975 he became Paul M. Warburg Professor of Economics at Harvard.

In the late 1960s Otto Eckstein founded Data Resources, Incorporated, which dealt in economic forecasting for industry. By 1978 it had 600 employees and revenues of $31 million. The firm makes economic predictions based on elaborate computer models and has had enormous influence on business and government at all levels. Customers pay an annual fee of $10,000 or more for its services. In 1979 Eckstein sold Data Resources, Incorporated to McGraw-Hill, Incorporated for $103 million in cash, with Eckstein making about $20 million from his DRI stock.

Otto Eckstein represents an increasingly prevalent phenomenon in American life—a growing breed of academic economists who move easily between academia, government, and private business. Although academics of this nature existed as early as the 1920s, it was only after World War II that large numbers of them began to appear, coinciding with the period when the "state" became fully committed to rationalizing the economy. He married Harriett Mirkin in 1954 and they have three children. Eckstein is a Democrat. (*Current Biography*, 1967; *Newsweek*, July 30, 1979; *Who's Who in America*, 1978–79.)

EDISON, THOMAS ALVA (February 11, 1847–October 18, 1931). Inventor and electrical equipment manufacturer, Edison General Electric Company. Born in Milan, Ohio, son of Samuel Edison and Nancy Elliott. His father was born in Canada and his grandfather, who had been a Loyalist during the American Revolution, went to Nova Scotia at the close of the war. During the Canadian Insurrection of 1837, Samuel Edison had become involved with William Lyon Mackenzie in an attempt to organize a revolt against the Canadian government. When it failed, Samuel escaped to the United States and settled in Ohio, becoming a prosperous shingle manufacturer in Milan. In 1854 he established a grain and lumber business in Port Huron, Michigan, which was also quite prosperous. Thomas Edison was slow in school and his mother taught him at home. At an early age he developed a strong interest in chemistry, and also earned money selling newspapers, magazines, tobacco, and candy on trains. It was during this time that an accident caused his lifelong deafness.

In 1863 he became a telegraph operator and wandered through the Middle West from one job to another, all the while continuing his chemical experiments. He began inventing at age sixteen, usually laborsaving devices which would increase his time for study. In 1868 he secured employment with the Western Union Telegraph Company at Boston, where he continued his experiments. In 1869 he took out a patent on a stock ticker, but a similar device had previously been invented years before by Samuel S. Laws, and had been used for some time on the New York Stock Exchange. In that same year, Edison went to New York in search of a position, being nearly penniless at the time. He was made general manager of the Law's Gold Indicator Company, at $300 per month.

In the same year he entered into a partnership with Franklin Pope and James N. Ashley, called Pope, Edison and Company, electrical engineers. They were bought out in 1870 by the Gold and Stock Telegraph Company, whose president, Marshall Lefferts, offered Edison $40,000 for the rights in certain stock ticker inventions. With this capital he started his own manufacturing business, employing fifty men. The enterprise developed into what has been called the first "invention factory," the forerunner of the great research laboratories of the twentieth century. Many of Edison's technicians later became famous on their own account, which showed his remarkable intuitive judgement of men and talent.

During the next five years he devoted himself to improvements in the telegraph. He furthered the development of an automatic telegraph invented by an Englishman, George Little, greatly increasing its speed. In 1874 he made quadreplex telegraphy possible. In 1875 he invented a resonator for the purpose of analyzing sound waves, but did not put it to use until after the inventions of Alexander Graham Bell. In 1876 he devised his carbon telephone transmitter, which became universal in its use. In that same year he moved to Menlo Park, New Jersey, where he built the laboratories that he occupied for the next decade. In 1877 he produced the phonograph, which was his most significant invention.

Contrary to popular beliefs, he did not invent the incandescent lamp. But he did make improvements in the early inventions which were vital to its common use and cheap production. He was responsible for the complex system by which widely distributed lamps were powered from a central station, which was an immense engineering achievement. By 1882 he had a system working in New York based on the famous Pearl Street Power Plant, in which the generator and auxiliary equipment were all of his own design. Most of Edison's work after 1880, however, was not in invention, but in organization and promotion. For example, in the development of the motion picture he made few original contributions, but did do much to organize the industry and standardize the technology.

In 1887 he moved his laboratories to West Orange, New Jersey, where he built a larger and more modern establishment. From these laboratories came the nearly countless products of collective invention. Edison was the guiding hand in all this, and his organizational ability showed itself in the number of commercial companies put in motion for the manufacture and sale of the Edison inventions. These companies were later consolidated into the Edison General Electric Company, which with the Thomson-Houston Company ultimately constituted the General Electric Company. Once Edison organized a company, however, he lost interest in it and his mind moved on to new fields. He lost a great deal of money trying to develop processes for the magnetic separation of iron from ore, but he did develop machinery for cement manufacture which was successful. He also worked on the storage battery which was successfully used in electric traction, and in submarines, railway signals, and train and mine lighting. He also devised a dictating machine and a mimeograph.

During World War I he was president of the Naval Consulting Board, with which he conducted much research on torpedo mechanics, flame throwers, and submarine periscopes. In 1920 he received the Distinguished Service Medal. He married Mary Stilwell in 1871, and they had three children. She died in 1884 and two years later he married Mina Miller, by whom he also had three children. (**A.** *DAB*, Supplement 1; *NCAB*, 25:1; *New York Times*, October 18, 1931; *Who Was Who*, vol. 1; Matthew Josephson: *Edison*, 1959; J. C. Martin and E. L. Dyer, *Edison: His Life and Inventions*, 1927; F. T. Miller, *Thomas A. Edison*, 1931; A. O. Tate, *Edison's Open Door*, 1938. **B.** Arthur A. Bright Jr., *The Electric Lamp Industry*, 1949; Forrest McDonald, *Insull*, 1962; Harold C. Passer, *The Electrical Manufacturers*, 1953.)

ELKINS, WILLIAM LUKENS (May 2, 1832–November 7, 1903). Public utility and traction entrepreneur, United Gas Improvement Company. Born near Wheeling, West Virginia, the youngest child of George Elkins and Susannah Howell. His father was a pioneer paper manufacturer. William Elkins was educated in the public schools of Philadelphia, Pennsylvania, where his family had moved in 1840. In 1847 he left school to begin work as a clerk in a grocery store. Five years later he went to New York City for a year, where he engaged in the produce business. Returning to Philadelphia, he formed a partnership in the same business with Peter Sayboldt under the name of Sayboldt and Elkins. As the firm prospered, it soon became necessary to keep perishable foods for long periods. To do this, Elkins built the first large refrigerator in Philadelphia. In 1860 he bought out his partner and continued the business under his own name.

Shortly after the discovery of petroleum in western Pennsylvania, he made a thorough survey of the oil region, organizing many oil companies between 1861 and 1880, and becoming an extensive operator in the industry. In 1875 he became a partner in the Standard Oil Company, but disposed of his interest in 1880. After spending some time in the oil fields, he concluded that the refining of oil for illuminating purposes offered tremendous opportunities for profit. He therefore established a small refinery in Philadelphia and acquired or built others, until he controlled the oil refining business in the city. The first gasoline made was a product of one of his refineries. In 1873 he also became engaged in the manufacture of illuminating gas. He secured a financial interest in a number of gasworks throughout the United States, and was one of the organizers of the United Gas Improvement Company. In the same year (1873) he also became interested in street railways.

Elkins was one of the organizers of the Philadelphia Traction Company, which later became the Philadelphia Rapid Transit Company. In this venture he was associated with Peter A. B. Widener* and William Kemble. The latter two men supplied the political connections and sagacity imperative for the success of a traction venture, while Elkins acted as the hard-headed businessman. This combination of business experience, access to capital, and political connections allowed the trio to dominate the traction scene in Philadelphia. In addition, the three men had extensive interests in Philadelphia suburban real estate, which attracted them to street railways. Widener and Elkins purchased large tracts of land in the northwest section of Philadelphia, later erecting 3,000 homes there. As they built their street railway in the city, they began rationalizing operations to increase productivity and profits. They purchased or leased lines on the basis of their previous business, but recognized that combination would pay off only through lowered costs and increased traffic. To attract more passengers they offered free transfers within their lines, a new service in local transit. By 1882 their roads carried almost three million passengers annually, of which one-third were transfers.

In the 1880s they were compelled to replace their horsecars with new motive power. In their search for a mechanical substitute they settled on the cable system, a highly capital-intensive venture which put even greater demands on efficient operation. This required them to make innovations in three areas: law, finance, and technology. They secured the enactment of a special motive power law that allowed them to incorporate the Philadelphia Traction Company in 1883, which they used as a holding company to complete consolidation and to facilitate the management of their properties. Because Philadelphia Traction could not own stock in other corporations, the group leased their various lines to it, granting virtually perpetual (999 year) leases. In exchange, stockholders in the leased companies received a guaranteed rental as a dividend on their stock. While this device allowed the partners to solve legal and financial problems, they still had to develop workable cable technology. This took six years of experimentation and aggravation, and only in 1889 did they finally achieve satisfactory results. By this time, however, the cable was being superseded by electric lines, and in 1892 they sought authority to electrify their lines. This again engendered a long and costly period of experimentation and rebuilding. Only by repaving virtually the entire city were they able to gain permission from the city to complete their electrification project.

In two decades Elkins and Widener had revolutionized Philadelphia's public transit system. Unified operation had brought increased service, reduced costs, rationalized lines, and a transfer system. Electricity had replaced the horse, providing greater speed, capacity, and convenience. By 1900 their lines carried more than 300 million passengers annually. In the process they had created a powerful monopoly that controlled the city's street railways. During this same time they also joined with William C. Whitney* and Thomas Fortune Ryan* in an alliance to develop New York City's transit system. Using techniques similar to those they had developed in Philadelphia (but eschewing the costly cable system), they were able to dominate the traction industry in New York in the same way. They also had interests in street railway systems in Chicago, Pittsburgh, and Baltimore. Although Elkins was not generally closely involved with politics, he did serve one term as a Republican city councilman in Philadelphia in 1876. He married Maria Louise Broomall of Chester County, Pennsylvania, in 1857. They had two sons and two daughters, and he left them a fortune of some $25 million. (**A.** *DAB; NCAB*, 9:324. **B.** Charles A. Cheape, *Moving the Masses*, 1980; Sam Bass Warner Jr., *Private City*, 1968.)

EMANUEL, VICTOR (January 31, 1898–November 26, 1960). Aircraft manufacturer and early conglomerate organizer, AVCO. Born in Dayton, Ohio, son of Albert Emanuel and Deborah Rieser. His father was a self-taught lawyer who pioneered and prospered in the utility business in Dayton. His grandfather had immigrated to the United States from Switzerland in about 1850. Victor Emanuel was educated in the public schools of Dayton and St. Mary's College (now the University of Dayton). He then entered Cornell University, where he graduated in 1918. During World War I he was with the U.S. Flying Corps, acquiring a lifelong interest in aviation. After the war he gave up his earlier plans for a teaching career and entered his father's public utility company. In 1923 his father retired and Victor, in partnership with Arthur C. Allyn of Chicago, purchased his father's interest. At the end of 1926, after the business had been expanded to include fourteen utility companies throughout the United States, Emanuel and Allyn sold the system to Samuel Insull.*

Victor lived in England for part of the time from 1927 to 1934, where he was active in stock market transactions, and became associated with the London banking firm of J. Henry Schroeder and Company. He then became involved with Alfred Lowenstein, the Belgian financier who was then planning the formation of the U.S. Electric Power Corporation. Lowenstein died before arrangements could be completed, so Emanuel, Allyn, and others carried forward his plans, gaining control of a utility empire that stretched over twenty states and was worth $1,119,000,000. Emanuel was also president of Standard Light and Power Company.

In 1939 he resigned as head of the latter company, while remaining a director, and turned his attention to the rebuilding of the Aviation Corporation, which was originally a subsidiary of the Cord Corporation, whose holdings he had purchased in 1937. Throughout World War II the Aviation Corporation and its associated companies, including Consolidated Vultee Aircraft Corporation, produced all types of military aircraft from giant bombers to liaison planes, airplane engines and propellers, aircraft carriers, cruisers, auto bodies, and precision parts. In 1944 these companies manufactured over four billion dollars worth of equipment vital to the war effort, producing 28,000 planes throughout the course of the entire war, 13 percent of the nation's military aircraft. He was also a director of the Aircraft War Production Council.

Among the affiliates of Aviation Corporation at the end of the war were Lycoming Motors, Spencer Heater Company, Republic Aircraft Products, North Aircraft Products, and American Propeller Company. It also had partial ownership of New York Shipbuilding Company and American Central Manufacturing Company. After the war Emanuel, as chairman of the board and later as president, directed the conversion of the firm from the production of aircraft and heavy goods to the manufacture of consumer goods. It was renamed the AVCO Corporation, becoming an operating rather than a holding company. In 1945 he purchased the Crosley Corporation— manufacturers of refrigerators, ranges, radios and televisions, and operators of WLW in Cincinnati—for $19,700,000. AVCO later established five television stations in the Middle West, with broadcasting as a separate division of the company. He also negotiated the purchase of the New Idea, Incorporated, which manufactured farm equipment in Ohio and Illinois. In 1947 he released control of Consolidated Vultee Aircraft Corporation to the Atlas Corporation.

By 1946 net sales of AVCO were $52,781,267 and its net profit was $14,235,339. Emanuel also acquired Bendix Home Appliances in 1950 and Horn Manufacturing Company in 1951, manufacturers of farm equipment in Ft. Dodge, Iowa. During all of this, AVCO continued to be a prime defense contractor, getting $30 million in defense contracts in 1950, which had risen to $500 million by the late 1960s. By the early 1950s AVCO had become a conglomerate, one of the earliest examples of that type. Thirty years later it remained one of the major such organizations on the scene.

Victor Emanuel married Dorothy Elizabeth Woodruff in 1920, and had two sons. (**A.** *NCAB*, I:193; *Current Biography*, May, 1951; January, 1961; *New York Times*, November 27, 1960; *Who Was Who*, vol. 4.)

EMERY, LEWIS JR. (August 10, 1839–November 19, 1924). Oil Producer, United States Pipe Line Company and Pure Oil Company. Lewis Emery Jr. was born in Cherry Creek, Chautauqua County, New York, the son of Lewis Emery and Maria Gilson. He was a descendent of John Emery, who came from England to Massachusetts in 1635. While he was a child, his father moved to Jonesville, Michigan, where he established a woolen mill. Young Lewis was educated in the schools of Jonesville and served an apprenticeship in his father's mill. In 1858 he became a school teacher in Hillsdale County, and later was the owner of a flour mill. After engaging in lumbering and farming in Illinois for a year, he was drawn to Venango County, Pennsylvania, by the discovery of oil there in 1865. He spent several months as a teamster, hauling oil from Pithole to Titusville. With his two brothers and another associate, he leased land in the area and drilled his first well, which proved to be a success. A sequence of successes and failures followed until 1874, when upon the discovery of the McKean County oil field, he moved to Bradford County, Pennsylvania, and embarked on the oil business on an extensive scale. He organized the Quintuple Oil Company, with a tract of 5,000 acres that proved to be valuable oil land. In the course of his operations he organized numerous successful companies, becoming one of the outstanding leaders in the oil industry.

Emery early became involved in the efforts to break up the system of railroad rebating by which Standard Oil Company secured a virtual monopoly on the transportation of oil to market. He was one of the organizers in 1872 of the Oil Producers Association, composed of independent operators to resist the increasing power of Standard Oil. A bill which he helped frame, declaring discriminatory railroad rates illegal, was introduced into Congress through his initiative, but the measure was defeated. Emery continued to fight in each succeeding session of Congress until 1885, when the Interstate Commerce Commission bill, which contained such provisions, was passed. He was also a member of the lower house of the Pennsylvania state legistature from 1878 to 1880 and of the state senate from 1880 to 1889. He fought his biggest legislative battle in 1878 when he assumed leadership of the opposition, and after a bitter battle lasting six weeks, secured the overwhelming defeat of bills to reimburse the Pennsylvania Railroad for $4 million in damages during the Pittsburgh strike riots of 1877. The money was to have been raised by imposing a tax of fifty cents on every barrel of oil produced in Pennsylvania. His charges of bribery resulted in the arrest and conviction of the state treasurer in this affair.

In 1890 Emery originated the first attempt on the part of independent oil refiners of Pennsylvania to build a pipeline to the Atlantic coast for the purposes of avoiding the heavy transportation charges and giving the independents shipping facilities equal to those of Standard Oil. He organized the United States Pipe Line Company, of which he became president, with a capital of $600,000. In spite of innumerable obstacles it opened a pipeline 180 miles long connecting the Bradford oil fields with a friendly railroad, the New Jersey Central, at Wilkes-Barre, Pennsylvania, and a refined line 250 miles long from Oil City, Pennsylvania, to the same point. These lines were later extended to Washington, New Jersey, from whence the oil was transported by New Jersey Central to New York City.

In 1904 he built the first oxalic acid plant in the country at Bradford at a cost of $250,000. It was operated at a loss until World War I, when German imports were ended. Then it paid a large financial reward, since it was the only supplier of the acid in the country. In addition, he engaged in wheat farming in North Dakota, and gold mining and rubber producing ventures in South America. The firms he controlled included: American Alkali and Acid Company, Emery Manufacturing Company, Emery Oil Company, Mineral Run Oil Company, Quintuple Oil Company, Selavan Oil Company, Emery Pipe Line Company, Inca Mining Company, Inca Rubber Company, Bradford Gas Company, and Emery Hardware Company. He established Pure Oil Company in the 1890s to handle marketing for independent producers. By 1900 it had become an integrated organization, selling 70 percent of its product abroad.

Lewis Emery Jr. married Elizabeth A. Caldwell of Vistula, Indiana, in 1863. She died in 1915, and two years later he married E. Leta Card of Port Hope, Ontario, Canada. He and his first wife had three sons and two daughters. One of his sons, Delavan Emery (1867-1911), became manager of the Emery Manufacturing Company, a position he held until his death.

The other son, Lewis Emery III (1878-1941), was born in Titusville, Pennsylvania, and educated in the public schools of Bradford and at Berkeley's Prep School in Boston. He graduated as a mining engineer from Massachusetts Institute of Technology in 1899. He then became involved with a number of his father's oil interests, especially Emery Manufacturing Company, which operated a refinery. In the beginning the output of the plant was only 200 barrels a month, but by construction of additional plants the output was raised consistently over the years. Following the death of his father in 1924, Lewis Emery III became president of this company, continuing in that position for three years until its properties were sold to the Tide Water Oil Company and the South Penn Oil Company. By this point its production had reached 60,000 barrels of high grade lubricating oil a month.

Lewis Emery III was also a partner in Lewis Emery Jr. and Sons, and Emery Brothers, both operating oil companies in Oklahoma and Texas, and in the Emery Oil Company of Bradford. In 1926 he became president of Mineral Run Oil Company, which had been organized in 1906, and held this office until his death, although he was not active in its affairs after 1930. He was not married.

The family were originally Presbyterians, though Lewis Emery III became an Episcopalian. They were Republicans. (**A.** *NCAB*, 20:412; 32:222; 40:167. **B.** Chester M. Destler, *Roger Sherman and the Independent Oil Men*, 1967; Arthur M. Johnson, *The Development of American Petroleum Pipelines*, 1956; Harold F. Williamson and Arnold R. Daum, *The American Petroleum Industry*, 1959.)

ENDICOTT, HENRY BRADFORD (September 11, 1853–February 12, 1920). Shoe manufacturer, Endicott and Johnson. Born in Dedham, Massachusetts, son of Augustus Bradford Endicott and Sarah Fairbanks. His ancestors had come to Massachusetts in 1658, and his father was a carpenter and a farmer who later became a bank president. Henry Endicott was educated in district schools and did dairying work on the family homestead. Subsequently he was apprenticed to a Boston plumber and worked as a clerk in the leather trade of that city. In 1875, when only twenty-two years old, he founded the firm of H. B. Endicott and Company, sheepskin merchants. Somewhat later he became treasurer of the Commonwealth Shoe and Leather Company, a connection that led to his entry into the shoe manufacturing business.

He embarked on that industry with the acquisition of the Lester Brothers Shoe Company of Lestershire, near Binghamton, New York, which was in financial difficulty. This firm laid the foundation for an enormous plant development in the village, which became known as Johnson City. He changed the name of the concern to the Lestershire Manufacturing Company, and upon taking in George F. Johnson,* the superintendent of the factory, as partner, it became known as Endicott and Johnson Company. It was incorporated as Endicott-Johnson Corporation in 1919, and Endicott was president of it until his death. At that time the firm, with factories at Johnson City and Endicott, New York, where it had large tanneries, had an output of 75,000 shoes per day. The plant had been enlarged to several times its original size, and the village of 1,700 grew to a city of 10,000, nearly all of whom were connected with the company.

In 1917 Governor McCall of Massachusetts appointed Endicott director of the Committee of Public Safety, which coordinated home defense for the American entrance into World War I. He was also a federal and state food administrator during the war. Governor McCall also appointed him official strike mediator in the state. In that position he adjudicated more than 300 labor disputes during the war, continuing his role as industrial arbitrator after the conflict ended. Among the strikes he settled were the strike of Boston elevated car men, and the threatened tie-ups of the Lawrence woolen industry and of the Lowell cotton industry. He also dealt with labor troubles at the Watertown Arsenal, the Fore River shipbuilding yards, and among trolley and shoe workers. In 1919 he was appointed by President Wilson to be one of the representatives of the public in the industrial conference held in Washington that year.

He was also successful in maintaining harmonious relations with the workers in his own plants, which were nonunion and never had a strike in the thirty-six years he ran the business. He established a successful profit-sharing program in which all his workers shared alike in the net profits, regardless of length of service or position.

He was a director of a large number of corporations, including Chase National Bank in New York, U.S. Smelting and Refining Company, United Shoe Machinery Corporation, State Street Trust of Boston, and many others. A Unitarian, he married Caroline Williams Russell of Dedham and Louisa (Clapp) Calburn of Walpole, Massachusetts. He had a daughter, Gertrude Adele, and a son, Henry Wendell Endicott (1880–1954). His son joined the shoe business in 1901 and become a vice-president in 1919, serving in that position until his demise. (*NCAB*, 19:294; *New York Times*, February 13, 1920; *Who Was Who*, vol. 1.)

ERLANGER, ABRAHAM LINCOLN (May 4, 1860–March 7, 1930). Theatrical booking agent, Theatrical Syndicate, Klaw and Erlanger. Born in Buffalo, New York, son of Jewish parents, Leopold and Regina Erlanger. He spent most of his early life in Cleveland, Ohio, receiving little or no formal education. Erlanger began his theatrical apprenticeship as a cloak-room attendant and call boy at the Academy of Music, and subsequently rose to a position of some influence in the financial management of the Euclid Opera House.

After leaving Cleveland, he traveled for a number of years as an advance agent and later as a business manager of theatrical companies sent out from New York City. During these years he discovered the terrible inefficiency of the existing system of bookings. Although both theater owners and New York production managers desired a system whereby all theaters would be filled throughout the entire season, there was no adequate machinery to do so. Instead the whole "system" was managed by a series of haphazard individual contracts and arrangements made between local theater owners and production companies. The result was that theaters stood empty part of the time and production companies went weeks without bookings.

The development of a modern centralized booking system was in large measure the work of Erlanger and his partner, Marc Klaw.* They had been advance agents on the road, and in 1886 they purchased one of the small booking agencies in New York. Two years later they drew up a formal partnership. Although they also acted as New York producers, and gained control over a chain of theaters in the South, their major contribution to the theatrical industry lay in their activities as booking agents. In 1896, in association with four other leading managers, they organized the Theatrical Syndicate to bring about changes in booking. The execution of these reforms was entrusted to Klaw and Erlanger, which was made booking agent for all the attractions presented in the theaters controlled by the Syndicate.

Erlanger was the more active of the two executives, coming to exercise a nearly autocratic control. His office became the clearinghouse for actors, producers, and managers. He worked incessantly on the endless details of routing shows across the country. With a virtual monopoly, he brooked no opposition from actors or producers. Moreover, he was able to give preferential bookings to his own productions, even over those of Charles Frohman,* another powerful Syndicate member. Erlanger's power rested on the constantly mounting revenues of the Syndicate and the security he was able to offer to the various elements of the theatrical profession. Although he suffered the wrath of critics within the industry, they had little success in their campaigns against him.

When the Syndicate fell apart, it was partly the result of the growing inability of the concern to furnish satisfactory attractions in sufficient numbers to meet the demands of such a vast chain of theaters. This was then exacerbated by the growing inroads made by the Shuberts,* a group of rival theatrical managers formerly associated with the Syndicate who began operating along similar lines. But Klaw and Erlanger continued to operate for several more years and to hold a dominant position among New York booking agents. They were also engaged in the vaudeville business for a number of years. The partnership was dissolved in 1920, but Erlanger continued as producer and manager and remained one of the dominant financial powers in the American theater. Klaw and Erlanger represent an important transition in the entertainment industry, as it evolved from a loosely organized network of locally controlled institutions to a nationally centralized industry. In this respect the movement was symptomatic of the great merger movement in American industry from 1898 to 1905. (*DAB;* *New York Times,* March 9, March 16, 1930.)

ESTAUGH, ELIZABETH HADDON (May 25, 1680–March 30, 1762). Colonial proprietor, founder of Haddonfield, New Jersey. Born in Southwick, London, England, daughter of John Haddon and Elizabeth Clark. Both her parents were Quakers; her father was a prosperous blacksmith, manufacturer, and shipowner. Elizabeth Haddon received a liberal education in England. Her father had purchased 500 acres of land in Gloucester County, West Jersey, and bought another large tract in the same county. Because of persecution for his religious views, he planned to migrate there with his entire family, and became a member of the Pennsylvania Land Company of London. But ill-health prevented him from settling there, so Elizabeth felt a strong call to go in his place. She met a young Quaker, John Estaugh, who was about to begin a ministry in America, so she left for America with him in 1701, accompanied by a housekeeper and two male servants. She had her father's power of attorney to develop the properties, and after a brief stay in Philadelphia she moved out on the properties, taking over a small house which the original proprietor had built. Somewhat enlarged it was to become known as "Old Haddonfield."

Elizabeth married John Estaugh in 1702, and after their marriage he became the legal head of the Haddon plantations, although she continued to take an active part in their management. He was also made an agent of the Pennsylvania Land Company, charged with the complicated problems of land ownership and oversight of 1,000 acres of land in which English Quakers were involved. Nevertheless, he continued his travels as a minister, not only in the colonies, but also in England, Ireland, and the West Indies. During these times Elizabeth took over management of his affairs, often aided by her nephew and by William and Francis Rawle. In 1713 she moved to another tract of land and built "New Haddonfield," and here the village of Haddonfield began to grow. John Estaugh developed and Elizabeth manufactured a healing salve which was still used in the neighborhood a century after her death. She had no children of her own, but adopted her nephew, Ebenezer Hopkins.

She gave land to the Friend's Meeting House in Haddonfield, and when her father died in 1742 most of his New Jersey holdings went to the Estaughs. In 1742 John Estaugh died in the British Virgin Islands while on a preaching mission. After his death Elizabeth managed her estates and acted as trustee for the estates of others. As a woman alone, she now had all the legal rights enjoyed by a man of property. She acted as clerk of the Women's Meeting of her church for fifty years. (*DAB; NAW.*)

EVANS, OLIVER (1755–April 15, 1819). Steam engine manufacturer and inventor, Mars Iron Works. Born in New Castle County, near Newport, Delaware, son of Charles Evans, a farmer of modest means. Oliver Evans was educated in a country school until he was fourteen, when he apprenticed himself to a wagon maker. At the same time he began to study mathematics and mechanics on his own. At seventeen he learned of the atmospheric steam engine of Thomas Newcomen, and devoted his life to the development of the steam engine and its utilization. In 1772 he built a road vehicle embodying steam power. Because of financial limitations and public ridicule, however, it would be another thirty years before he would realize his ambition.

In the meantime he continued to perfect a completely new series of water-powered mechanical devices which, when installed together, revolutionized flour milling. In 1786 Pennsylvania granted him a patent on the exclusive use of his milling machinery, and in the following year Maryland granted the same privileges, also extending its use to steam power. Millers were slow to adopt his innovations, so Evans decided to enter the milling business himself with his brothers in Wilmington, Delaware. This was the first completely automated flour mill, and for that matter was the first automated factory in the world. He patented the mill operation, and as millers increasingly adopted the technique (which became nearly universal by 1820) the royalties on this patent were one of his chief sources of income.

During these years he continued to work on the steam engine, and by 1802 had developed a working engine. At first he encountered a great deal of ridicule because of his insistence on using high-pressure steam. His breakthrough came in 1804 when he constructed a steam dredge for use in the Schuylkill River, the first engine sold in the world. This established him as a regular engine builder, the first man in the United States to make a specialty of this work. He established the Mars Iron Works in 1807, and by the time of his death 50 steam engines had been built by his firm and were in use in all the states of the Atlantic coast. In 1812 he also opened a steam engine manufactory in Pittsburgh under the supervision of his son, George Evans.

Oliver Evans belonged to the first great generation of American inventors, and is considered by many historians to be the most important of all American inventors. He pursued two careers simultaneously. First, he attempted to discover the principles of the arts and apply them to making improvements in current practice. His two great triumphs in this line were the completely automatic flour mill and the high-pressure steam engine. His second career began in 1793, when he moved to Philadelphia as a manufacturer and merchant, first of general mill supplies, later of steam engines and iron work.

Although his manufacturing activities and his royalties on the automated flour mill earned him a prosperous living, his innovative efforts were less well rewarded. The problem lay in the inadequate patent laws of the time and in the fact that his inventions were so useful that they were universally adopted. Being indispensable, they in effect became public. After years of controversies and litigation, at age 54 he burned his drawings and specifications for further inventions. His *Millwright's Guide*, published in 1795, was reprinted several times both in America and abroad, and became a great influence on generations of mill owners. (*DAB; NCAB,* 6:65; *EAB; Who Was Who,* vol. H; Greville and Dorothy Bathe, *Oliver Evans: A Chronicle of Early American Engineering,* 1935; Eugene Ferguson, *Oliver Evans,* 1981.)

EVERLEIGH, ADA (February 15, 1876–January 3, 1960) and **Minna Everleigh** (July 5 or 13, 1878–September 16, 1948). Prostitution madams, Chicago. Born in Kentucky, daughters of an attorney named Lester, they assumed the name of Everleigh early in their lives. After brief unhappy marriages, the sisters deserted their husbands and left their hometown to join a traveling theatrical troup as actresses. In 1898, having inherited $35,000, they invested in a high-class brothel in Omaha, Nebraska, near the site of the Trans-Mississippi Exposition. When the fair closed, their investment had increased to $70,000 and they went to Chicago, where the famous madam, Effie Hankins, sold them her business at 2131 South Dearborn Street.

They named their bordello the "Everleigh Club," and it became the most famous and most luxurious house of prostitution in the country. Before opening the club, the sisters recruited new girls, replaced the help with black servants, and furnished the house in an extravagant manner. The downstairs rooms were used for group entertainment, while the upstairs rooms accommodated private pleasures. At a time when one dollar for a prostitute was the norm, and twenty-five cents was not uncommon, the Everleigh Club charged ten dollars merely to enter the premises, twelve dollars for a bottle of wine, and fifty dollars for an evening with a hostess of one's choice. Nightly receipts at the club, which employed 35 to 40 girls, averaged $2,000 to $2,500.

In eleven years of operation the sisters accumulated one million dollars, along with $200,000 in furnishings, a fortune in jewels, and $25,000 in receipts outstanding. They were, indeed, the queens of the prostitution industry in the United States. The initial operation proved so successful that a "new annex" at 2133 was opened in 1902. As the years progressed, their fame allowed them to become ever more selective in their clientele. Advertising was an important business tool for the Everleighs. In 1902 the club subscribed to a one-half page advertisement in the Cook County Republican Marching Club's Eighth Annual Reception souvenir booklet. The club also published an illustrated brochure of the interior of the establishment.

Minna was the dominant figure of the two sisters and generally handled business matters, while Ada interviewed and managed the girls of the house. Both sisters were always completely proper in their manner and attire, and their fame and pretentions set them apart from their fellow madams. As the club became a success, anti-vice reforms were started to end the official policies that permitted prostitution. A municipal commission was finally set up in 1910, and its report in 1911 marked the beginning of the end for Chicago's "red light district." The Everleigh Club was a prime target and the end came when Mayor Carter H. Harrison Jr. was shown a copy of the club's illustrated brochure. Incensed by their audacity, he ordered the club closed as a signal to clear out the district.

After the club was shut down the sisters traveled in Europe for six months and then returned to Chicago. But the furor had not died down, so they moved to New York City, where they lived anonymous lives as wealthy, refined southern widows, attending poetry readings and the theater. After Minna died in 1948, Ada moved to Virginia, where she lived out the rest of her life in utter respectability. In the years of the early twentieth century, when there were few business opportunities open to women, running a house of prostitution was one of the few avenues open for entrepreneurship. This also probably accounts for the inherent respectability the two sisters were able to bring to their establishment and their own private lives. For others their business represented licentiousness; for them it was a respectable means of business opportunity. (*DAB*, Supplement 4; *NAW*.)

F

FABER, JOHN EBERHARD (December 6, 1822–March 2, 1879) and **Lothar Washington Faber** (September 27, 1861–May 12, 1943). Pencil manufacturers, Eberhard-Faber Company. **John Eberhard Faber** was born in Bavaria, son of George Leonard Faber and Albertina Fredericka Kupfer. For three generations the family had been makers of writing pencils at Stein, Bavaria. The firm was started by his great-grandfather, Caspar Faber, in 1761. His father was very prosperous and did not at first expect his son to go into the pencil business, intending for him to become a lawyer. John Faber was educated at the Gymnasium at Nuernberg, and took lectures in jurisprudence at the Universities of Erlanger and Heidelberg. He was most attracted to ancient history and literature, becoming a cultivated scholar in these areas. He migrated to America shortly after the Revolutions of 1848, starting a business in New York City; there he acted as agent for the family pencil factory at Stein, which was by then managed by his older brother, J. Lothar Faber.

During this time John Faber sold on commission various articles of stationery manufactured in Germany and England. After a time he acquired control of vast tracts of cedar forest land in Florida. He began exporting cedar wood in logs to pencil factories in Europe, and later built a sawmill at Cedar Keys, on the Gulf Coast of Florida. The mill cut the cedar logs into sizes suitable to be worked into pencils and shipped the wood in that form to European factories. Meanwhile, his pencil trade, which had grown quite large from its small beginnings, was dependent on the Bavarian factory for its finished product, even though a large part of the raw material originated in America.

Faber believed that he could manufacture the pencils in New York provided machinery could be made to offset the difference in labor costs between the U.S. and Europe. He was nearer the source of cedar wood supply, but farther from the graphite mines, which were in Bohemia. He was ready to open his first factory in 1861, but this was not a good time, since his cedar wood supplies were now in Confederate territory. He nevertheless started on a comparatively small scale and was able to meet the demands of the time. After the war the industry grew rapidly and became firmly established in the U.S. When the New York factory burned down in 1872, a larger plant was set up in the Greenpoint section of Brooklyn. Faber was the first pencil manufacturer to attach rubber tips and metallic point protectors to pencils. He extensively employed a nickel-plating process and operated a factory at Newark, New Jersey, for the making of rubber bands and erasers. He also produced pen holders. Having the distinction of being the first pencil factory in America, it also became one of the largest, employing over 1,000 persons by 1917 and operating a plant with 180,000 square feet of floor space. The factory was incorporated in 1898 as Eberhard Faber Pencil Company, with one son in charge of manufacturing and the other son in charge of the selling end.

John Faber married Jenny Hoag of Munich, Germany, in 1854, and they had two sons: J. Eberhard Faber (1859–1946) and Lothar W. Faber. John Faber joined his father's pencil company in 1876. A year later he went to Europe to learn the foreign end of the business, and to complete his education abroad. Upon his father's death in 1879 he took over the business, which he headed until 1894, when his brother became the managing head. Eberhard continued with the firm as vice-president and treasurer, and later as chairman of the board, for the balance of his life.

Lothar Washington Faber was born in New York City and was educated in private schools in that city. He graduated from the Columbia University School of Mines in 1882. In the following year he joined the family pencil business, then operated by his brother. He became a partner in 1894, and when the business was incorporated in 1898 he became president of the firm, a position which he held until his death. As head of the manufacturing end of the firm he proved himself to be a progressive manufacturer, constantly improving his line of products with the addition of fountain pens, mechanical pencils, refill leads, and other articles. He invented the clamp tip type of pencil with a removable, adjustable eraser. He was also vice-president of the Eberhard Faber Rubber Company in Newark from 1913 until his death. By the time of his death the Brooklyn factory occupied 455,000 square feet, and the Newark factory was about one-half that size.

He was a Moravian and married Anna Prieth of Newark in 1885. They had three children. (*DAB; NCAB*, 14:267; F:262; 32:138.)

FAHEY, FRANK JOSEPH (May 1, 1874–February 19, 1945). Safety razor manufacturer, Gillette Safety Razor Company. Born in Monkton, Baltimore County, Maryland, son of John Fahey and Catharine Ryan. His father was superintendent of right-of-way for the Pennsylvania Railroad. Frank Fahey was educated in the public schools of Baltimore through high school, and in 1893 entered the employ of the Cleveland, Cincinnati, Chicago and St. Louis Railroad in Cleveland, Ohio, as a clerk. Three years later he entered the Chicago office of Ware and Leland, grain brokers in the city. He later became a partner in that firm and a member of the Chicago Board of Trade. He then was made managing partner of the company, with offices in New York City, where he had a seat on the Cotton Exchange. He disposed of his interest in Ware and Leland in 1906 and became associated with the Gillette Safety Razor Company as director of Gillette Sales Company, Incorporated, the firm's sales outlet in Boston.

In 1908 he was made assistant treasurer and advertising manager of Gillette Safety Razor Company, the parent organization, which was also located in Boston. He remained associated with the firm until his retirement in 1931, serving as treasurer from 1911 to 1917, vice-president and treasurer from 1917 to 1927, and vice-president and general manager until 1931. From the time he became treasurer of the firm, he assumed the role of chief executive of the company, and under his guidance a sales organization was established which eventually distributed the company's products throughout the world. Although King Gillette* was the titular head of the company, Fahey was the driving force behind the organization and made it into an extremely profitable enterprise. The rapid expansion of the firm in the years after he joined bears this out. By 1917 the company was manufacturing 1,000,000 razors annually, compared with only 91,000 in 1904, and had established factories in England, France, Germany, and Canada.

The first of Fahey's marketing triumphs came during World War I, when Gillette peddled "Service Set" shaving kits (3.5 million razors and 36 million blades) to departing servicemen. When the soldiers returned they were confirmed Gillette customers. During the 1920s Gillette embarked on a series of promotional campaigns that spelled doom for the straight razor. Under the slogan "Shave and Save" banks across the country gave away Gillette razors to every new depositor. Hotels, restaurants, and service stations gave away razors at their opening day ceremonies.

During the 1930s Gillette became a major radio sports sponsor and later carried that tradition over to television. They sponsored the 1939 World Series, and quickly followed that with the Orange and Sugar Bowl games and the 1940 Kentucky Derby. In 1941 the firm began sponsoring a variety of different sporting events, all of which were advertised as part of Gillette's "Cavalcade of Sports." In that same year they began their long association with professional boxing by sponsoring the Joe Louis-Billy Conn heavyweight championship fight. The result of all this advertising and promotion was to make Gillette the unchallenged leader in its field. The firm faced no serious competition during Fahey's years with the company, and it was not until Wilkinson Sword introduced the first stainless steel blade in the early 1960s that they were challenged in any effective manner. They rapidly introduced their own stainless steel blade and soon won back much of the market. A greater challenge came from the Bic Company of France, which introduced their ballpoint pens in America in 1961. Gillette had dominated the ballpoint market since 1955, when they purchased the Papermate Pen Company, but Bic soon passed them in sales and now controls 60 percent of the ballpoint business. In 1975 Bic introduced a disposable razor that also cut into Gillette's sales. Nevertheless, by 1979 Gillette had sales of two billion dollars and was still the number one producer of razor blades, while standing second in deodorants, ballpoint pens, and disposable lighters.

Fahey was a director of the First National Bank of Boston from 1924 to

1931 and of Old Colony Trust from 1922 to 1927. A Republican and an Episcopalian, he married Florence Alice Meyer of Lowell, Massachusetts, in 1917. They had one son. (**A.** *NCAB*, 34:390. **B.** Alfred D. Chandler Jr., *The Visible Hand*, 1977; Milton Moskowitz et al., *Everybody's Business*, 1980.)

FAIR, JAMES GRAHAM (December 3, 1831–December 28, 1894). Nevada silver miner, Consolidated Virginia Mine. Born near Belfast, Ireland, son of James Fair, an Irishman of Scottish descent, and a Scottish woman named Graham. He was educated in Ireland and America, being brought to Illinois by his parents when he was twelve years old. At eighteen he joined in the great California Gold Rush. When he got there he did little panning for gold, but instead searched for the quartz from whence it came. Before he was thirty years of age he had a mill on the Washoe in Nevada, and thereafter became prosperous.

The Comstock Lode had been discovered before Fair reached Nevada and had yielded ore for fifteen years. But it was the kind of mining in which the individual miner, without capital or machinery, had no chance to compete, whereas the mining company and the banking interests behind it might profit both from the output of ore and from the greed of a speculative public. The San Francisco bankers controlled Nevada development until Fair and his associates, including John W. Mackey,* captured a group of their holdings, organized them around their own new Bank of Nevada, and stumbled upon the silver and gold pocket of the Consolidated Virginia Mine. This is thought to be the single most valuable ore pocket ever discovered. It was Fair's persistent pursuit of a meandering vein that led to its discovery in a rock chamber of vast dimensions. In 1873 the yield began to unsettle the market for both metals and the mine released so much silver bullion that it induced a great political controversy over the monetary use of that metal.

In the next six years they took more than $100 million worth of metal out of the mine before it was exhausted. Fair held on to his share and converted it not only into luxurious living, but into land, buildings, railroads, and other steady sources of income. In 1881 he was elected to the U.S. Senate from Nevada by the Democratic legislature in the state. He rarely participated in Senate activities during his term. In 1887 he took over active control of the Nevada Bank, which had been close to foundering.

James Fair married Theresa Rooney of Carson City, Nevada, in 1861, but they were divorced in 1883. His wife retained custody of their two daughters, both of whom married very well. Theresa married Herman Oelrichs of New York City and Virginia married William K. Vanderbilt Jr.* James Fair retained custody of his two sons, and things did not go very well on that score. His son James committed suicide, and the other son, Charles Lewis, made a youthful marriage which enraged his father. Charles Lewis and his wife were killed in an auto accident near Paris in 1902. (**A.** *DAB; NCAB*, 11:189. **B.** Dan DeQuille, *The Big Bonanza*, 1967; Oscar Lewis, *The Silver Kings: The Life and Times of Mackey, Fair, Flood, and O'Brien, Lords of the Nevada Comstock Lode*, 1967; Rodman Paul, *Mining Frontiers of the Far West*, 1963; Richard H. Peterson, *The Bonanza Kings*, 1977.)

FAIRBANKS, ERASTUS (October 28, 1792–November 20, 1864) and **Thaddeus Fairbanks** (January 17, 1797–April 12, 1886). Scale manufacturers and inventors, E. and T. Fairbanks Company. **Erastus Fairbanks** was born in Brimfield, Massachusetts, eldest of three sons of Joseph Fairbanks and Phebe Paddock. His ancestors had settled in the area in 1633. In 1815 his father moved to St. Johnsbury, Vermont, where he built a saw and grist mill. His three sons, Erastus, Thaddeus, and Joseph, extended the business by erecting a foundry and wheelwright shop, which prospered and grew into a small manufacturer of stoves, plows, and agricultural implements. The firm also began to build some of the machinery required by the hemp industry. The need for weighing wagon loads of raw materials brought into town led Thaddeus Fairbanks to devise a crude apparatus by which grappling chains suspended from a steelyard could lift a wagon from the ground and the approximate weight of the load could be determined.

Thaddeus Fairbanks was also born in Brimfield, and was educated at home by his mother and in the public schools. He was an able, natural mechanic, and he assisted his father in mill construction in 1815. As a sideline he also undertook wagon construction. In 1823, with Erastus, he established a small iron foundry in St. Johnsbury, called E. and T. Fairbanks and Company. During the next several years Thaddeus was the inventor of many new implements manufactured by the small foundry, including a cast-iron mold board plow, a cook stove, and a parlor stove. Thaddeus was also the manager in one of the hemp mills of St. Johnsbury, inventing and patenting a hemp and flax dressing machine for that industry. In 1831 he patented his platform scale.

After this time the brothers devoted all their energies to the manufacture of the new platform scales whose use rapidly became worldwide, with an ever growing demand. Erastus was the head of the firm and its chief executive, while Thaddeus handled the production end and invention. The business of the firm doubled in volume every three years from 1842 to 1857, when its growth was temporarily halted by the depression of that year. It recovered rapidly, however, and grew to a very large size in the years after the Civil War. The firm remained a partnership until 1874, when it was incorporated as the Fairbanks Scale Company. For scales alone, the company held 32 patents.

Erastus was also interested in politics and public affairs. In 1836 he was elected as a representative of St. Johnsbury to the lower house of the state legislature. In 1852 he was elected by the Whigs as governor of the state as a strong temperance advocate. He was not reelected. In 1856 he affiliated himself with the rising Republican party, and in 1860 was again elected governor, this time on that party's ticket. Becoming one of the "War governors" of the North, he helped to raise troops and equip them for war. He received no salary as governor. A member of the Congregational Church, he married Lois C. Crossman in 1815. They had eight children.

Thaddeus established the St. Johnsbury Academy in 1842, and at his death left it a very large endowment. He married Lucy Peck Barker of St. Johnsbury in 1820. His son, Henry Fairbanks (1830–1918), became a vice-president of Fairbanks Scale in 1868, serving until his death. Like his father, he made several inventions on the scale. (**A.** *DAB; NCAB*, 8:320; 10:300. **B.** Alfred D. Chandler Jr., *The Visible Hand*, 1977; *Pioneers in Industry: The Story of Fairbanks, Morse and Company*, 1945.)

FAIRBURN, WILLIAM ARMSTRONG (October 12, 1876–October 1, 1947). Match company executive and engineer, Diamond Match Company. Born in Huddersfield, England, son of Thomas William Fairburn and Elizabeth Fosdick. His father was a shipbuilder and came from an old-time seagoing family. The family immigrated to Bath, Maine, in the late 1880s; there his father was employed by the Bath Iron Works. William Fairburn was educated in the Bath public schools and became an apprentice mechanic in the local iron works. He acquired his master's papers at age eighteen. In 1896 he entered the University of Glasgow and completed in one year a two-year program in naval architecture and engineering, standing at the head of his class. Returning to Maine, he became general superintendent and naval architect for the Bath Iron Works. At twenty-three he designed the first all-steel freighter built in America. By 1900 he had become an independent engineering consultant.

Both James J. Hill,* from 1900 to 1903, and E. H. Harriman,* from 1904 to 1908, employed him to supervise the construction of cargo vessels when they expanded their railway enterprises to shipping. Fairburn pioneered in applying the diesel to railroads, urging Harriman to adopt his design for a locomotive. Meanwhile, he served as a consultant for the Sterling Company and for Babcock and Wilson, on steam boiler and marine manufacturing problems. Executives in both these companies, Ohio Columbus Barber* and Edward R. Stenttinius Sr.,* were also officers in the Diamond Match Company, which was plagued by rising manufacturing costs, losses in related manufacturing operations, and negative public attitudes towards its matches. The U.S. Bureau of Labor had publicly condemned the main ingredient of matches, white phosphorus, because it led to poisoning among production workers and children who ate the matches. Also, their handling posed a growing fire hazard. A safety match was already available in foreign markets, but it would strike only on a special surface, and the American consumer was unfamiliar with its use. Threatened with the loss of business to foreign competitors, Barber and Stenttinius placed Fairburn in charge of the Diamond Match operations in 1909 to reorganize production and to solve its marketing and public relations problems.

Fairburn represented a new breed of corporate executive, distinct from either the old founder-entrepreneur type or the banker-reorganization type. As a trained engineer, he was inclined to take a systematic approach to business based on the efficient use of technology. Fairburn brought forth a company-owned, European-developed process for match production, using sesquisulphate rather than white phosphorus of potash. He guided Diamond research chemists into opening new domestic sources, which were more expensive but allowed domestic match production to continue during World War I. After the war, however, Diamond was left with excess capacity. So Fairburn streamlined production, shutting down the most inefficient plants, reorganizing the administrative network, and diversifying into other household woodenware and paper products. This helped the firm maintain its profits throughout the 1920s and 1930s, despite competition from foreign match companies. In 1915 all of Diamond's profits had come from match sales; by 1940 only one-half of the company's revenues came from that source.

In 1920 Fairburn negotiated an agreement with Ivar Kreuger, the Swedish "match king," for marketing foreign matches. Later, Kreuger grew restive under the agreement and attempted to purchase production facilities in the United States. Fairburn was successful in containing these efforts by the reorganization and recapitalization of Diamond Match in 1930 and by selling Kreuger an interest in a Diamond-owned subsidiary. When the Kreuger empire collapsed in 1932 the threat ceased to exist. By 1937, Diamond controlled 90 percent of American match production and was closely allied with British and European match manufacturers. He was president of the firm until his death in 1947.

Fairburn was a Republican who vehemently opposed New Deal labor policies. He married Louise Ramsey of Perth Amboy, New Jersey, in 1904. They had two sons. The youngest son, Robert Gordon Fairburn (b. 1912), graduated from Princeton in 1932. He was with Best-Forster-Dixfield Company in New York City from 1932 to 1947, serving as its president from 1942 to 1947. In the latter year he succeeded his father as president of Diamond Match Company, serving in that position until 1957. He was chairman of the board until 1961. In 1957 Diamond Match Company became the Diamond Gardner Corporation and in 1959 the Diamond National Corporation, through a series of mergers. After leaving Diamond National in 1961, he became chairman of the board of Keyes, Filine Company of New York City. He was also co-owner and treasurer of the H. R. Dunham Company of Waterville, Maine. He was married three times, with two children. (A. *DAB*, Supplement 4; Herbert Manchester, *William Armstrong Fairburn*, 1940; *Fortune*, May, 1939; *NCAB*, 37:24–25; *New York Times*,

October 3, 1947. **B.** Ohio Columbus Barber, "The Match Industry," in Chauncey DePew ed., *One Hundred Years of American Commerce*, 1895; Alfred D. Chandler Jr., *The Visible Hand*, 1977; Diamond Match Company, *Commemorating the 75th Anniversary of the Diamond Match Company*, 1956; Herbert Manchester, *The Diamond Match Company*, 1935.)

FALK, OTTO HERBERT (June 15, 1865–May 21, 1940). Machinery manufacturer, Falk Corporation and Allis-Chalmers Company. Born in Wauwatosa, Wisconsin, son of Franz Falk and Louise Wahl. His father had learned the cooperage and brewing trades in his native Bavaria before immigrating to Milwaukee in 1848, settling in Wauwatosa around 1857. Franz Falk worked in Milwaukee breweries until 1856, when he formed a partnership with Frederick Goes to start the Bavarian Brewery, under the name of Goes and Falk, in Wauwatosa. In 1866 he purchased his partner's interest and operated the business alone until his death in 1882. Otto Falk was educated at the German-English Academy in Milwaukee and at Northwestern College in Watertown, Wisconsin. In 1884 he graduated from the Allen Military Academy in Chicago, which was the beginning of a notable military career.

Rising rapidly in the Wisconsin National Guard, he served as state adjutant general from 1891 to 1893, and retired from the service in 1895. As a military officer his particular skill was in dealing with labor unrest. In 1892 he was ordered by Governor George W. Peck to Merrill, Wisconsin, where he settled a strike in the lumber mills in a few days, without the use of troops. In 1893 he was sent to Ashland, Wisconsin, and within two days ended a longshoremen's strike to the apparent satisfaction of all concerned. In 1894, when the Pullman strike led to bitter clashes between railway workers and militia forces in Chicago and other Middle Western cities, Falk succeeded in avoiding violence in his state, except for a brief eruption at Spooner, Wisconsin. During the Spanish-American War he was commissioned a major and chief quartermaster of the Third Army Corps, U.S. Volunteers. In 1898 he became special inspector of the quartermaster department, with the rank of lieutenant colonel. He was discharged in 1899 and rejoined the Wisconsin National Guard, serving until 1911, with the rank of brigadier general.

During this same time, he had also begun a distinguished business career. He started at age twenty in his father's brewery, and continued in various capacities until the firm was acquired by Pabst Brewing in 1892. In 1893 he organized the Wisconsin Milling Company, serving as its general manager until 1898. In 1895 he and his brother, Herman Wahl Falk, organized the Falk Manufacturing Company, which after 1926 became the Falk Corporation, steel founders and manufacturers of special machinery. He served as vice-president of that firm until his death in 1940.

Otto Falk's major contribution to the business world, however, came through his involvement with Allis-Chalmers Manufacturing Company of West Allis, Wisconsin. The firm had its origins in the 1860s when Edward P. Allis* organized a small machine shop. Over the next several years it became one of the largest of its kind in the country, making milling machinery, sawmill and mining machinery, heavy pumps, and the famous Corliss engines. In 1901 his son, William W. Allis,* merged it with the Chalmers Company to form Allis-Chalmers Corporation. In 1904 it began producing electric and gasoline engines, and by 1910 had become the third largest manufacturer of electrical apparatus in the United States. The firm ran into financial difficulties, however, and in 1912 Otto Falk was appointed receiver for the company. Upon its reorganization as the Allis-Chalmers Manufacturing Company in 1913, he was chosen president of the firm, an office he held until 1932, when he became chairman of the board. He immediately launched Allis-Chalmers on a policy of diversification, one of the first such programs in the country. In the years prior to World War I he created a line of earth-moving and other construction machinery, including tractors, using the internal combustion engine.

After the war, Falk decided to build tractors for farmers as well as for construction contractors and companies. To meet the already stiff competition in this market, he developed a full line of agricultural implements and set up a separate marketing organization with its own branch offices. By the time of Falk's death in 1940, it had become the third largest producer of farm equipment. Nor did Falk slight Allis-Chalmers' traditional lines, as these lines continued to be advanced, both in terms of volume of sales and technological improvements.

A Republican, Otto Falk married Elizabeth A. Vogel of Milwaukee in 1901. They had two children, Elizabeth Louise and Otto Herbert Jr. His nephew, Harold Sands Falk (1883-1957) and grandnephew, Harold Frank Falk (b. 1909) both became prominent in Falk Corporation. Harold Sands Falk was the son of Otto's brother, Louis Wahl Falk, and joined Falk Corporation as an assistant superintendent in 1906. He was named vice-president and works manager in 1920, and president upon the death of his father in 1957. He was then chairman of the board and chief executive officer from 1962 to 1973, and chairman of the executive committee after that. (**A.** *DAB*, Supplement 2; *NCAB*, D:272; H:261; *Who Was Who*, vol. III; *Who's Who in America, 1978-79.* **B.** Allis Chalmers Company, *1847-1947: A Story of Men . . . and of a Great Industrial Era*, 1947; Alfred D. Chandler Jr., *Strategy and Structure*, 1962.)

FANEUIL, PETER (June 20, 1700–March 3, 1743). Colonial Boston merchant. Born in New Rochelle, New York, son of Benjamin Faneuil and Anne Bureau. His father was one of three brothers who came to America by way of Holland after the revocation of the Edict of Nantes. They were among a small number of French Huguenots who were able to bring considerable property with them to America. Benjamin Faneuil went to New Rochelle, while his brother, Andrew, went to Boston. Peter's father died when he was eighteen years old, so he went to Boston, where his uncle Andrew had become a prosperous merchant and had risen to considerable wealth. Peter engaged in business and acquired some real estate of his own, becoming a favorite of his widowed and childless uncle. Peter remained a bachelor all his life.

During his uncle's eighteen-month illness, Peter managed his business as well as his own. In 1738 Peter became executor and residuary legatee. His brother, Benjamin, who had married, was cut off with only five shillings, while Peter inherited one of the largest fortunes in the city. He continued to prosper as a merchant, enjoyed the good life, and named one of his best ships the *Jolly Bachelor.*

Peter's main claim to fame is his gift to the town of Boston, Faneuil Hall. He had long been interested in the development of a public market, but there was a division of opinion among people as to its necessity. He finally offered to donate the building, but even at that the town was hesitant. In 1740 they voted 367 yes and 360 no on the proposal. Peter died before the building was completed. At the first annual town meeting held in the new hall after its completion, the chief business was a eulogy to him. The building was almost wholly destroyed by fire in 1761, but was then rebuilt and enlarged. (*DAB; NCAB*, 1:441; *Who Was Who*, vol. H.)

FARGO, WILLIAM GEORGE (May 20, 1818–August 3, 1881). Expressman, American Express and Wells, Fargo and Company. Born in Pompey, Onondaga County, New York, son of William C. Fargo and Tacy Strong. William G. Fargo was the eldest of twelve children. His father had been born in Connecticut, and in 1807, at sixteen, had come west to Pompey, New York. At age thirteen, William G. twice a week made a mail route of thirty miles. For the next eleven years he helped in a village inn, worked in a grocery store, failed as a grocery store owner himself in Weedsport, New York, and was the first freight agent at Auburn on the newly completed Auburn and Syracuse Railroad. In 1842 he became a messenger for Pomeroy and Company, the express firm between Albany and Buffalo, and in the next year was named their agent in Buffalo. In 1844 he became an agent for Wells and Company, becoming one of the three owners of the firm. This was the first express concern west of Buffalo.

This western service was joined in 1850 with two firms operating between Albany and Buffalo to form the American Express Company, with Henry Wells* as president and Fargo as secretary. Wells had been one of the owners of the Pomeroy Company, which had operated between Albany and Buffalo, along with owning the Wells and Company lines west of Buffalo. In 1845 he had sold out to William A. Livingston, and the firm had become Livingston and Fargo. It was the interests of Wells, Fargo and Livingston, along with those of Butterfield and Wasson and Company, that were put together in 1850 to form American Express.

The service of American Express had already been extended to Chicago, Milwaukee, Cincinnati, St. Louis, Galena, and Dubuque. In 1852, to meet the demand for transportation to and from the gold diggings in California, Wells, Fargo and Company was organized for the express business in that state. Through its friendly relations with American Express Company, the new firm could offer complete transportation services to New York, Boston, and Europe. The Adams Express Company suffered financial difficulties in 1855, which left Wells, Fargo and Company in control of the field in California. Their expresses carried gold-dust, mail packages, and passengers, and conducted the necessary banking business for the communities they served. The profit realized in the express business during the Civil War led to the organization of competing companies in the postwar period, resulting in several consolidations during this time.

In the West in 1866, a general consolidation of mail stages and express companies from the Missouri to the Pacific was effected by the California legislature, and incorporated as Wells, Fargo and Company. The business was unprofitable, and with the completion of the Union Pacific Railroad, the stage lines were dropped. In 1869 a merger of Wells, Fargo and Company with the newly organized Pacific Express Company, a holdover of the Adams Express interests in California, led to overcapitalization at $15 million, later reduced to $5 million. Meanwhile, in the East, the Merchants Union Express Company became so powerful that in 1868 the American Express Company was compelled to incorporate on equal terms into the American Merchants Union Express Company, of which Fargo was president. In 1873 its name was again changed to the American Express Company. The task of retrenchment in this period of postwar deflation and relative stagnation was a major challenge to Fargo, and he accomplished it in good fashion. By 1904 the American Express Company had capital of $18 million, 4,000 offices, and used the services of 6,000 employees.

Fargo was also director and vice-president of the New York Central Railroad, and director of the Northern Pacific Railroad. He was elected mayor of Buffalo as a Democrat, serving from 1862 to 1866. He was defeated in his try for the state senate in 1871. He married Anna H. Williams of Pompey, New York, in 1840. They had three children. His two brothers, James Congdell Fargo (1829–1915) and Charles Fargo (1831–1900) were also involved in the express business. James became president of American Express after his brother's death in 1881, remaining until 1914. Although the firm had begun to offer American tourists in Europe assistance with mail forwarding, railway tickets, making hotel reservations, and finding lost baggage, James Fargo insisted that there was no money to be made in tourists and forced the company to stick to its original express interests. Since the tourist business was later to become the source of

American Express Company's great wealth and prestige, his attitude hardly showed a great deal of foresight. Charles Fargo entered the express business in 1853 and rose to become second vice-president and general manager of the western section in 1881, serving until his death in 1900. (**A.** *DAB; NCAB*, 12:44; *Who Was Who*, vols. H and 1. **B.** Alden Hatch, *American Express, 1850–1950*, 1950; Edward Hungerford, *Wells, Fargo: Advancing the American Frontier*, 1949; Oscar O. Winther, *The Transportation Frontier*, 1964; and *Express and Stage Coach Days in California*, 1936.)

FARISH, WILLIAM STAMPS (February 23, 1881–November 29, 1942). Oil producer and refiner, Humble Oil and Refining Company and Standard Oil of New Jersey. Born in Mayersville, Mississippi, son of William Stamps Farish and Catharine Maude Power. His father was a lawyer and planter who had come to Mississippi from Virginia. Young William was educated at St. Thomas Hall in Holly Springs, Mississippi, and entered the University of Mississippi, where he enrolled in the law course. He earned his law degree in 1900 and was admitted to the bar in his home state. He entered private practice in Clarksdale, Mississippi, leaving the following year for Beaumont, Texas, to look after the oil interests of an English syndicate in which his uncle was an investor.

Not long after arriving in Texas, he went into business for himself, but his first venture ended in bankruptcy and his partner's death. He promptly paid off the outstanding debts and reestablished his credit. By 1904 he had joined with another young man, Robert Lee Blaffer, in a new endeavor. Beginning as contract drillers and traders in oil leases, Blaffer and Farish soon went into the production of oil on their own. In 1905, in order to concentrate on the Humble Oil Field, they moved their offices to Houston. During this time they also entered several other ventures, especially concentrating on the new oil fields of North Texas. By 1916 Farish had become one of the leading independent oilmen in Texas.

But in 1915 Farish had run into some serious trouble. Like other Texas oil producers, he had entered into contracts with major oil companies which specified the price the buyers would pay and the maximum amount they would be required to take. He had made these contracts at a time when the price of oil was declining sharply, and a few months later found he had to sell the oil at well below the prevailing market price. As a consequence, Farish spearheaded the organization of the Gulf Coast Producers Association in 1916 in order to bring about a concerted attack on the small producers' marketing problems. As association president, he tried to arrange to sell directly to the refineries and to bypass the major companies in Texas, but quickly learned that the eastern refineries required a steady supply in large volume. To meet this requirement, he proposed that the small producers pool their oil, but he failed in this effort. At that point, he merged his holdings with those of Ross Shaw Sterling,* former governor of

Texas, and other oil producers with whom he had close business and personal relations, to form a new corporation in 1917, the Humble Oil and Refining Company.

The immediate objective of Humble Oil and Refining was to build up a large producing business, and Farish was named vice-president with overall responsibility for that end of the business. Under his direction Humble expanded rapidly, but its growth potential soon exceeded its capital resources. To remedy this problem Farish began negotiating with Standard Oil of New Jersey, selling it a one-half interest in Humble for $17 million in 1919. Jersey Standard had been stripped of its crude oil producing facilities by the Supreme Court decision of 1911, and found itself in a desperate situation by this time. Farish was astute enough to exploit this weakness, and was able to secure sufficient capital in this manner to allow Humble to develop large oil fields in Eastland County and a refinery in Baytown, Texas. On the other hand, Farish, foe of "Big Oil," had now become big oil himself. Farish was named president of Humble Oil in 1922, and over the next decade guided the growth of the firm from a loose aggregate of smaller producers into a complex and well-coordinated organization that relied heavily on scientific research and utilized advanced engineering techniques. Farish also promoted diversification and integration, supporting the development of a larger pipeline system, and the building of several more refineries, with Humble's largest and most modern at Brownsville, Texas.

At the same time, Humble became a large purchaser of crude oil, besides expanding its own production and exploration activities. It thereby not only greatly improved its own search for new oil fields and its production, but was a leader in the advances of the industry's technology. Farish early came to see the need for reform in the oil company's producing practices as well, and called for a change in the laws governing the production of oil and gas. The existing "rule of capture" gave oilmen every incentive to drain a field as rapidly as possible, with much resulting waste and instability. So he founded and became president of the American Petroleum Institute in 1926, in which position he called for reform in the producing industry's operation. At first he was in favor of self-regulation, and was chairman of a committee set up in 1927 by the Federal Oil Conservation Board to study the industry's problems and explore ways to solve them. He supported a plan by which a field's allowable production would be shared among its producers, feeling it was the fairest and most practicable system. He felt this should be regulated by state laws with market demand estimated by the federal Bureau of Mines.

Farish left Humble in 1933 to become chairman of the board of Standard Oil of New Jersey. He had served as a director of the parent firm since 1927, and was one of the firm's leading authorities on new production concepts and methods, and on the domestic oil production industry in general. In 1937 he was elected president of the firm, succeeding Walter Teagle*; he held the position until his death. He was a member of the Petroleum Industry War Council in the early days of World War II. At the time of his death Standard Oil of New Jersey had resources of $2 billion. Shortly before his death, Farish was accused, along with Walter Teagle, of engaging in treasonable activities as a result of Jersey Standard's agreement with I. G. Farben of Germany to exchange patents and research. In 1941 the U.S. Senate discovered that the agreement was still functioning, despite the ongoing war in Europe. Teagle, who made the agreement, was most vulnerable to attack, but both were broken by withering criticism from Congress and the press. Farish was still recovering from the attack eight months later when he died at Teagle's estate. Teagle resigned his position as chairman of the board of Jersey Standard a month later.

Farish was an Episcopalian and married Libbie Randon Rice of Houston, Texas. They had a daughter and a son. (**A.** *DAB*, Supplement 3; *NCAB*, 32:325; *New York Times*, November 30, 1942. **B.** George S. Gibb and E. H. Knowlton, *Standard Oil Company (New Jersey): The Resurgent Years*, 1956; Henrietta Larson, E. H. Knowlton, and C. S. Popple, *History of the Standard Oil Company (N.J.)*, 1971; Larson and Kenneth W. Porter, *History of the Humble Oil and Refining Company*, 1959; James Pressley, *A Saga of Wealth: The Rise of the Texas Oilmen*, 1978; Anthony Sampson, *The Seven Sisters*, 1975; Harold F. Williamson et al., *The American Petroleum Industry*, 1963.)

FARNUM, HENRY (November 9, 1803–October 4, 1883). Railroad contractor. Born in Scipio, Cayuga County, New York, son of Jefferson Amherst Farnum and Mercy Tracy. His ancestors had left Connecticut in the eighteenth century to establish pioneer farms further west in New York. He was born and raised on such a farm and educated in the village school. He taught himself to be a surveyor, gaining employment in that capacity on the Erie Canal from 1821 to 1824. In 1825 he went to Connecticut to take the post of assistant engineer on the construction of the Farmington Canal. He advanced to chief engineer, remaining so until 1846, when the canal was abandoned. He then acted as chief engineer and superintendent of the railroad which took the canal's place. Work on the canal brought Farnum into frequent contact with Joseph E. Sheffield,* a man of much property and wide business connections, who was a large stockholder in the canal.

The two men became associated in a plan to build a railroad from New Haven to New York, obtaining a charter in 1844. The project failed, as no one was willing to subscribe to stock in the venture and they were forced to abandon it. During the twenty-five years Farnum was with the New Haven, Northampton line, he gained a great deal of experience and a strong reputation for good work and expertise, but little money. In 1850 he was invited to Chicago, a town of 3,000 at the time, which was still looking for a railroad connection to the outside world. In a few years, the Farnum and

Sheffield firm completed the Michigan Southern Railroad, from Hillsdale, Michigan, to Chicago, providing an all-rail route to the East (1852). They next built the Chicago and Rock Island Road, giving rail connection to the Mississippi River, between 1852 and 1854. Farnum designed and built the first railroad bridge crossing the Mississippi River at Rock Island in 1855, and the firm of Farnum and Durant completed the construction of the Mississippi and Missouri Railroad as far west as Grinnell, Iowa. His bridging of the Mississippi River was resented by many railway interests and brought his firm many suits. He engaged Abraham Lincoln as his attorney in one of these suits, in which he won the famous Rock Island Bridge Case.

In his railroad building, like most contractors of the time, he had to construct everything. He not only did grading, built the bridges, and imported and laid iron rails; but also built the stations and freight houses, built the machine shops and equipped them with engines, machinery and tools, and supplied the line with rolling stock. He was paid mostly in stocks and bonds, so he had to finance as well as build the road. He also became a railroad operator, as Farnum shortly assumed the presidency of the Chicago and Rock Island, and held that position until he retired in 1863. After his retirement he traveled for several years in Europe and then returned to New Haven. He was a major benefactor of Yale College. He married Ann Sophie Whitman of Farmington, Connecticut, in 1839. (**A.** *DAB; NCAB*, 11:517; Henry W. Farnum, *Henry Farnum*, 1889. **B.** Thomas C. Cochran, *Railroad Leaders, 1843-1899*, 1953.)

FARRELL, JAMES AUGUSTINE (February 15, 1862–March 28, 1943). Steel company executive, United States Steel Company. Born in New Haven, Connecticut, son of John Guy Farrell and Catharine Whalen. His father, an Irish Catholic, had come to America from Dublin in 1848. He was, successively, a merchant, sea captain, and shipowner. James Farrell in his youth acquired a life-long love for sailing ships. When he was sixteen, his father was lost on one of his ships, and James had to leave school, going to work as a laborer in a steel wire mill in New Haven. Nine years later, in 1888, he moved to Pittsburgh, where he got a job with Pittsburgh Wire Company as a laborer. During these years, he studied at night to improve his education and tried to learn every aspect of the wire drawing trade. Impressing his employers, he was made a salesman for the firm in 1889. Within three years he was promoted to sales manager, with offices in New York.

In 1893 he was named general manager of Pittsburgh Wire, managing to keep the firm solvent during the depression of the 1890s by seeking out foreign markets, which were to that time a relatively untapped source. His knowledge of these foreign markets proved the key to his advancement. In 1899 Pittsburgh Wire was merged with the American Steel and Wire Company of New Jersey, and he was made head of the foreign sales department of that firm. When the latter company was absorbed by U.S. Steel Company in 1901, he received a similar post in the parent organization. Two years later he was named president of U.S. Steel Products Corporation, a subsidiary formed to coordinate all foreign sales of the giant concern. During his eight years in that post, he tripled the company's export business, sharply cut the cost of foreign trade, and purchased a fleet of ships to transport its growing variety of steel products.

His work with the export side of the business so impressed J. P. Morgan* and Elbert Gary* that they selected him to replace William E. Corey as president of U.S. Steel when the latter was forced to retire amidst a scandal in 1911. He held that office until he retired in 1932, continuing to serve as a director for the rest of his life. During his presidency he increased the steel output of the firm from 6 million tons to 29 million tons. After the death of Gary in 1927, the company's operations were divided, with Myron C. Taylor* as director of financial affairs, and Farrell as both head of operations and chief executive officer. When he retired in 1932, U.S. Steel owned 1,153,350 acres of coal and coke properties, and owned and operated twenty-five railroad lines with 2,964 miles of track, and 689 sailing vessels. In 1931 its gross sales were $730 million, and its employees numbered 53,619 full-time and 150,100 part-time.

Although the firm's growth was impressive in many respects while Farrell was president, he must also share with Morgan and Gary much of the blame for the steel giant's lackluster performance during the 1920s and afterward. U.S. Steel had been "born old" in 1901, and remained slow and conservative throughout the century, more interested in stabilizing prices than in developing new products and new technologies. With the new demand from the automobile industry for light sheet steel products in the 1920s, Farrell and U.S. Steel were reluctant to abandon obsolete and poorly located Pittsburgh mills. Instead of moving the mills closer to Detroit and developing new plants designed to fulfill the needs of the auto industry, they instituted a "Pittsburgh Plus" price system under which all steel was priced as if it had been made in Pittsburgh, and won a "gentleman's agreement" from the industry not to locate in Detroit. But not all companies could be persuaded to stop competing, with Republic Steel and others garnering a large share of the new auto market. The result by 1930 was that U.S. Steel's share of the market, which stood at 65 percent in 1901, had fallen to 40 percent. The onset of the depression only made things worse. U.S. Steel's operations were hit heavily by the economic slump, while other, smaller steel companies weathered the storm without major damage. Farrell was also vehemently opposed to labor unions, and during the Great Steel Strike of 1919 refused to negotiate with the union. In the mid-1930s, he watched in dismay as Myron Taylor negotiated and signed an agreement with the Steel Workers Organizing Committee of the CIO.

Farrell was chosen chairman of the foreign relations committee of the

American Iron and Steel Institute in 1911, serving until 1932. He was also for many years chairman of the National Foreign Trade Council, and served as honorary president of the Pan American Society and as honorary vice-president of the Iron and Steel Institute of Great Britain. In addition, he was vice-president of the American Iron and Steel Institute from 1914 until his death. A Roman Catholic, he married Catharine McDermott in 1889. They had five children. Both of his sons, John Joseph and James A. Farrell Jr., became prominent in the shipping business as executives of the Farrell Lines. (**A.** *DAB*, Supplement 3; *NCAB*, 32:54–55; *Iron Age*, April 1, 1943. **B.** Gertrude G. Schroeder, *The Growth of Major Steel Corporations*, 1953; Melvin Urofsky, *Big Steel and the Wilson Administration*, 1969.)

FIELD, CYRUS WEST (November 30, 1819–July 12, 1892). Developer of trans-Atlantic telegraph. Born in Stockbridge, Massachusetts, son of David Dudley Field and Submit Dickinson. His father was a prominent Congregational minister, and three of his brothers received national recognition: David Dudley Field was an eminent jurist and law reformer; Stephen J. Field was a leading justice of the United States Supreme Court; and Henry M. Field was a clergyman and author. His family had been in New England since 1629. He was educated in a careful, Puritanical way, but at age fifteen abandoned the idea of a college education and persuaded his father to allow him to leave home to seek his fortune. With eight dollars in his pocket he went to New York City, where, with an older brother to help him, he became an errand boy in the leading dry goods store of A. T. Stewart and Company on Broadway. He made very little money in the three years he worked there, so he resigned and went to Lee, Massachusetts, as an assistant to his brother Matthew, a paper manufacturer. In less than two years he started in business for himself as a paper manufacturer at Westfield, Massachusetts. Shortly afterwards he was invited to become a partner in the firm of E. Root and Company, wholesale paper dealers. In 1841 the firm failed, and although Field was only the junior partner, the burden of all the debts fell upon him. Out of this financial wreck he built the firm of Cyrus W. Field and Company, with his brother-in-law, Joseph F. Stone, as his partner.

In 1849, because of overwork, his physician advised him to take a trip to Europe. He was now, at age 33, wealthy enough to retire from his business with a fortune of $250,000, all of which had been made in less than nine years. After visiting Europe, he took a trip to South America. Then, in 1854, he met a Canadian, Frederick N. Gisborne, who was promoting a telegraph line across Newfoundland for the purpose of connecting with the fast steamers that ran between St. John's and Ireland, thus shortening by several days the transmission of important news from one side of the Atlantic to the other. Field got an idea for a cable, and contacted Samuel F. B. Morse and M. F. Maury, of the National Observatory at Washington,

D.C.. Morse and Maury had had the idea before, but were unable to get any promoter interested in it.

After a favorable government charter had been obtained, granting a fifty-year monopoly, a company of prominent New Yorkers was formed and $1.5 million was subscribed by Peter Cooper,* Wilson G. Hunt, Moses Taylor,* and Marshall O. Roberts. Two and one-half years were consumed in putting the telegraph line across Newfoundland and connecting it by cable to the mainland. A company was then organized by Field in England and capital was subscribed there. Soundings were made in the ocean, and a shallow tableland or "telegraph plateau" was discovered under Maury's direction. The British government assisted by lending a ship to help lay the cable and by guaranteeing a generous annual sum for official messages. But in Washington by this time opposition to the project arose, although a large ship was finally assigned to help out. The laying of the cable was begun in 1857 with little knowledge of how it should be done. Several miles had been laid out from Ireland when the cable broke and $500,000 of cable was lost in the Atlantic. Then the depression of 1857 hit, forcing Field's mercantile firm into bankruptcy. He was not deterred, however, and in 1858 arranged to have two ships meet in mid-ocean to splice the cable and head in opposite directions towards Ireland and Newfoundland. There were continual breakages and talk of abandoning the enterprise, but a fourth attempt was made and proved successful. A copper wire 1,950 miles long connected Trinity Bay with Valentia through water over five miles deep.

On August 16, 1858, Queen Victoria sent a message to President James Buchanan, and great celebrations were held. At about the same time the cable stopped working. Now the public began to say that the earlier messages sent had been fakes, and that the cable never worked at all. This caused Field's telegraph stock to decline sharply in value, and in the next year his New York office and warehouse burned down with substantial losses. In 1859 he again went to England to raise money for a new cable and to make repairs to the old one, but the Civil War intervened and he was forced to wait until it was over to begin anew. This time he laid a heavier and better insulated cable; but this also broke at the half-way point, so another cable was ordered. During the summer of 1866 it was successfully laid, and the cable of 1865 was recovered. In 1867 Congress awarded Field a gold medal. He then began to talk of laying a cable to Hawaii and Asia, but never followed up on it.

In 1877 he became interested in efforts then being made to establish an elevated railroad system in New York City. The present firm was in dire financial straits, so he purchased a large block of stock and served as its president without pay. He was a major factor in making the elevated lines a reality in the city. He was also a partner with Jay Gould* in the development of the Wabash Railroad and controlled the *Mail and Express*, a New York newspaper. In 1887 Gould drove him to financial ruin in a struggle to gain control of the Manhattan Railroad. When the commodity markets collapsed later that same year, Field, who had been speculating heavily, lost the rest of his fortune. He lived the final five years of his life in modest circumstances in Stockbridge, Massachusetts. He married Mary Bryan Stone of Guilford, Connecticut, in 1840. They had seven children.

The laying of the Atlantic cable was not only a bold venture which brought much publicity and great fortune to Field, but it also had dramatic effects on the development of international markets for securities and grains. Quotes "by cable" for some securities and for wheat and cotton were now speedy and continuously at hand. Prices set in England ruled at grain elevators in American prairie towns and southern country stores. In spite of its high rates ($100 for ten words initially), the cable was quickly profitable. (**A.** *DAB; NCAB*, 4:451; *New York Times*, July 13, 1892; *Who Was Who*, vol. H; Samuel Carter, *Cyrus Field*, 1968; Isabella F. Judson, *Cyrus W. Field: His Life and Work*, 1896. **B.** Elisha P. Douglass, *The Coming of Age of American Business*, 1971.)

FIELD, MARSHALL (August 18, 1834–January 16, 1906) and **Marshall Field III** (September 28, 1893–   ). Department store pioneer and publisher, Marshall Field and Company, Chicago *Sun-Times*, Parade Publications, Incorporated.

Marshall Field was born near Conway, Massachusetts, son of John Field and Fidelia Nash. His ancestors came to Massachusetts in 1629. He was educated at the district schools in Conway until age seventeen, when he left home to become a clerk in a dry goods store in Pittsfield, Massachusetts, remaining there for five years. He was offered a partnership in the business, but wanted to go West, and he left Pittsfield for Chicago in 1856. At this time the western town was still a frontier settlement with wooden sidewalks. He had no capital, so he became a clerk in the wholesale dry goods firm of Cooley, Wadsworth and Company, leading house in the city. His salary was $400 in the first year, of which he saved $200 by sleeping in the store.

He worked as a traveling salesman as well as a clerk for the company, and in his travels around the country he was impressed with the opportunity for business expansion. In 1861 he was made general manager of the store, and a year later was made a partner in the firm, now called Cooley, Farwell and Company. In 1864 Levi Z. Leiter was admitted to partnership, and the firm became Farwell, Field and Company. Then, in 1865, Potter Palmer,* who wanted to retire from the retail and wholesale business he had built up, offered it to Field and Leiter. Palmer financed the new organization of Field, Palmer and Leiter, retiring himself in 1867. Within eight years Field had become head of a successful business in which he had an interest of $260,000. He was now thirty years old, and brought his brothers, Henry and Joseph Field, into the firm. It remained Field, Leiter and Company until 1881 when, upon the withdrawal of Leiter, it became

Marshall Field and Company. The firm weathered the loss of its store and stock of goods in the Chicago Fire of 1871 and the ensuing Panic of 1873, although the store burned down again in 1877. But seemingly nothing could stop the venture's success. As early as 1868 it had sales of $12 million a year, and by 1881 they were $25 million. Before Field's death, they had reached $68 million.

Marshall Field, like A. T. Stewart* in New York and John Wanamaker* in Philadelphia, promoted a new type of merchandising. He developed a one-price store, with the price plainly marked on the item. He did not misrepresent his goods in advertising and built up a reputation for quality merchandise and fair and honest dealing. Sales were for cash, and when credit was extended payment was expected on the date due. Courtesy towards customers was the golden rule. Goods were bought from wholesalers for cash, and then a demand was created for them. Thus he was able to undersell competitors who waited for demand to appear and then had to buy goods on the open market.

Field himself had a thorough grasp of detail, had an uncanny ability to select able managers, and was skillful in handling his employees. All of this made him one of the most successful merchants of his day. His buying agencies operated on a worldwide scale, often contracting for the entire output of manufacturing plants. In 1907, the year after Marshall Field's death, a huge store was opened up in downtown Chicago, the largest in the world, with 450 department in 73 acres of space and thirteen floors. During the twentieth century Marshall Field and Company continued to be one of America's great department stores. In 1966 it had sales of over $306 million, with eight branch stores, seven in the Chicago area, and one in Wauwatosa, Wisconsin. It also owned the Frederick and Nelson store in Seattle, Washington.

Marshall Field became involved in philanthropies in Chicago, founding the Chicago Manual Training School, and donating 10 acres and $100,000 to the University of Chicago. In 1893 he gave one million dollars to the Columbian Museum at the Chicago's World's Fair, which was later developed into the Field Museum of Natural History. In his will he gave $8 million for a new building on the lakefront in Grant Park. He also gave a library to the town of Conway, where he was born. The bulk of his estate was in Chicago real estate, which he left to his grandsons, Henry and Marshall Field III, who did not come into full possession of the inheritance until 39 years after his death.

A Presbyterian, Marshall Field married Nannie Scott of Ironton, Ohio, in 1863. She died in 1896, and nine years later he married Mrs. Delia Spencer Caton. His son, Marshall Field Jr., married Albertine Huck, and their eldest son was **Marshall Field III**. The latter was educated at Eton and Cambridge University in England. He left college when the United States entered World War I, rising in rank from private to captain. After the war he was director of Chicago's "Bureau of Justice" for a time, and devoted a great deal of time to securing jobs for exservicemen. In 1919 he entered the office of Lee, Higginson and Company, in Chicago, and a year later founded his own investment firm of Marshall Field, Glare, Ward and Company, of which he was president. In 1928 it became Field, Glare and Company, with offices in New York City. He was senior partner of this firm until 1935.

He entered the world of publishing in 1940 when he became a stockholder of the New York daily, *PM*, which began publication in that year. It was a highly innovative venture, having no advertising and depending on circulation for its revenues. It was not a success, however, and absorbed all of its $2.5 million capital in one year. So Field bought out the other stockholders and became sole owner as well as president of the company. One year later he had a deficit of one million dollars, but had tripled the circulation of the previous year. Three years later *PM* announced its first profit. By 1946 he had spent $4 million on it, and although circulation was up to 165,000, the paper was discontinued.

Meanwhile, in 1941, he had established the *Chicago Sun* as a rival to the powerful *Chicago Tribune*. He was president of this paper, and it sold nearly 900,000 copies on its first day. By 1946 daily circulation was 400,000 and Sunday circulation was 450,000. The *Tribune* denied it membership in the Associated Press in 1942, but in 1945 the U.S. Supreme Court forced AP to allow the *Sun* membership. Field also became publisher of *Parade*, a weekly pictorial supplement, which in 1946 had a circulation of 3.5 million; and he was president of its parent company, Parade Publications. He owned radio stations in Chicago and Cincinnati, and purchased Pocketbooks, Incorporated, an affiliate of Simon and Schuster. It was estimated that he had a fortune of about $168 million in the 1960s.

He was married three times. In 1915 he married Evelyn Marshall of Chicago. They were divorced in 1930. In the same year he married Audrey (Jones) Coats of London, England, and they were divorced four years later. In 1936 he married Ruth (Pruyn) Phipps of New York City. He had five children. His eldest son, Marshall Field IV, succeeded him in the newspaper business. (**A.** *DAB; NCAB*, 6:104; G:85; I:38; *New York Times*, January 17, 1906; J. W. Tebbel, *The Marshall Fields*, 1947. **B.** John William Ferry, *A History of the Department Store*, 1960; Tom Mahoney and Leonard Sloan, *The Great Merchants*, 1955; Robert W. Twyman, *History of Marshall Field and Company*, 1954; Lloyd Wendt and Herman Kogan, *Give the Lady What She Wants: The Story of Marshall Field and Co.*, 1932.)

FILENE, EDWARD ALBERT (September 3, 1860–September 26, 1937) and **Lincoln Filene** (April 5, 1865–August 27, 1957). Department store executives, Filene's, Boston, and Associated Merchandising Corporation.

Edward A. Filene was born in Salem, Massachusetts, son of William

Filene and Clara Ballin. His father was a native of Posen, Prussia, who came to America in 1848, when he was eighteen years old, becoming a merchant tailor in Boston. In 1856 he opened a retail store in Salem. Later he moved to Lynn, Massachusetts, and in 1863 to New York City. Business reverses forced him to return to Lynn in 1870. Edward Filene was educated at the Lynn public schools, and for a year and a half in a German military academy. In 1881 his father liquidated several businesses specializing in women's clothing and accessories in order to open a small store in Boston. Edward decided not to enter Harvard because of his father's declining health, and assumed full charge of his father's business.

As president of Filene's, he developed sales and general policies, leaving the detail work and human relationships to his brother, Lincoln. By 1891 Filene's was a prominent Boston women's fashion specialty store, and in that year William Filene's Sons Company was organized, with full control in the hands of the two sons. As head of the firm, Edward began a series of innovations which brought him a fortune. Most famous and successful was his "Automatic Bargain Basement," in which prices automatically declined as merchandise failed to sell within a given period. In 1901 the store was moved to a new location with three times the floor space. In 1903 it was incorporated, with Edward as general manager and treasurer until 1908, when he was made president. Filene's soon became the world's largest specialty store, with the main building occupying a city block in length, in a building designed by Daniel Burnham.

Filene's also developed the concept of "cycle billing," instead of billing all customers at the end of the month, making billing a more orderly procedure. They invented the Charge-a-Plate, and were the first to develop college and high school advisory boards. By 1900, sales had passed the half million dollar mark, and in 1902 exceeded one million for the first time. When their new building was completed in 1912, 715,000 persons went through its doors within one week. This store was still in service fifty years later. Outlying branches began to be established after World War I, with taxation rather than traffic providing the initial impetus. By 1912 sales were $4,810,899, and in the next year sales rocketed to $8,466,467, with the completion of the new building. Promising young men and women were hired and systematically trained, their progress recorded and evaluated long before such personnel methods were general. Both Professor Frank Parsons, the "father of vocational guidance," and Frank B. Gilbreth,* motion study expert, were employed by Filene's at one time.

Although their innovations were unfailingly successful, the more conservative associates with whom they shared the business objected. A struggle for control of the business commenced in 1911, culminating after much litigation and bitterness in 1928, when Edward Filene was shorn of all voice in management, although he remained as president of the firm for the rest of his life. Much of the struggle was occasioned by his plan, implemented in

1911, to ultimately transfer management of the store to his employees, through the Filene Cooperative Management Association, which had been organized in 1898. It had been originally set up in that year to settle employee grievances. Filene's store was also the first to establish a minimum wage for women and girls, and in 1913 inaugurated Saturday closings during the summer, the first store in Boston to do so. In 1924 winter vacations were instituted in addition to its usual summer holiday. The Filene Employees Credit Union was also established, the prototype for credit unions throughout the country, and Edward Filene did much to make it a national movement.

Edward Filene had always been strongly attracted towards public affairs. He was first drawn to civic reform by the struggle over street car franchises in Boston in the 1890s, and he responded fully to the mood of the Progressive Era. In 1909 he called Lincoln Steffens to Boston to help him in his plan for a broad campaign for city betterment, the "Boston, 1915" movement. He was able to achieve some material improvements in schools, harbor facilities, and public health, but failed in his broader aims, partly because of his weakness as a leader. He was too impatient to explain his ideas fully, and was needlessly critical of his associates. He also undertook the lead in organizing the Boston Chamber of Commerce and the State Chamber of Commerce, to unite Boston's business groups for reform. But the most permanent of his civic achievements were the development of the credit union movement and his organization of the Twentieth Century Fund. He had pressed successfully for the organization of credit unions in Massachusetts, and employed Ray Frederick Bergergren to further the idea throughout the nation. In 1919 he organized the Cooperative League, which in the next decade became the Twentieth Century Fund, endowed with Filene's trust funds. This organization was expected to gather facts in all fields of social endeavor, but it ultimately concentrated on the economic field. In 1935 Edward Filene organized the Consumer Distribution Corporation, intended to develop consumer cooperatives, especially cooperative department stores. In the next year he set up the Good Will Fund, to conduct research and educational projects in cooperation and other public affairs enterprises. Filene was a Democrat and Jewish. He broke openly with the U.S. Chamber of Commerce in 1936, because of its attitude towards the New Deal. He never married.

Lincoln Filene was born in Boston and was educated in the public schools of Lynn until he went to work in his father's dry goods store. His task was to handle the personnel of the store, and he pioneered in many management policies for the welfare of workers. It was he who set up an employee's organization in 1901 with the power to take wage disputes to arbitration; established a profitsharing plan in 1903; and instituted the summer Saturday closings in 1912, and paid winter vacations, which were started in 1924. He was among the first to apply scientific methods and efficiency techniques in retail stores, and repeatedly emphasized the importance of frequent stock turnover.

Lincoln Filene organized the Retail Research Association in 1916 and the Associated Merchandising Corporation in 1918. The latter was a joint buying group for a large number of department stores. He was president of both until 1943, when he became honorary chairman of the board. In 1929 he led a merger of Filene's with Abraham and Straus of Brooklyn and F. R. Lazarus and Company of Cincinnati, Ohio, into the Federated Department Stores, of which he was chairman of the board until 1957. The Associated Merchandising Corporation set up buying offices in London, Paris, Brussels, Berlin, Milan, and later Florence. Eventually offices were also set up in the Orient and other places, with more stores joining in the 1920s. By 1966, Associated Merchandising Corporation had sales of three billion dollars. Edward Filene had opposed the organization of Federated Department Stores, but Lincoln, aided by vice-president Louis E. Kirstein, deposed Edward as chief executive of the company. At the time of Lincoln's death, Federated Department Stores had thirty-eight stores and branches in eleven states, with sales of more than $601 million. Filene's was one of the member units doing a business of $50 million or more yearly, and had 4,000 employees with eight branches in Massachusetts cities and one in Maine. Lincoln was chairman of Filene's until his death.

Lincoln Filene was also a founder of the American Arbitration Association, president of Massachusetts Savings Bank Insurance League in 1937, and chairman of the National Council on Trade Relations in 1933. He was also named a member of the Industrial Advisory Board of the NRA from 1933 to 1935, and a member of the advisory council of the U.S. Department of Commerce from 1933 to 1938. He established the Lincoln and Theresa Filene Foundation in 1937, and founded the Lincoln Filene Professorship of Retailing at Harvard in 1949, and Filene's Professor in Civics Education at Tufts in 1953. In 1955 he helped establish Boston's WGBH-TV, the first educational television station in the United States. He was Jewish and a Republican, and married Theresa Wells in 1895. They had two daughters. (**A.** *DAB*, Supplement 2; *NCAB*, A:319; 45:17; 421; *Biographical Encyclopedia of American Jews; Who Was Who*, vol. 1; Gerald Johnson, *Liberal's Progress*, 1948. **B.** Edward L. Bernays, *Biography of an Idea*, 1965; John William Ferry, *History of the Department Store*, 1960; Leon Harris, *The Merchant Princes*, 1979; Stacy Holmes, *Brief History of Filene's*, 1972; Tom Mahoney and Leonard Sloan, *The Great Merchants*, 1955.)

FINK, ALBERT (October 27, 1827–April 3, 1897). Railroad organizer, Southern Railway and Steamship Association, and Trunk Line Association. Born in Lauterbach, Germany, son of Andres S. Fink and Margaret Jacob. He was educated at private schools and at the polytechnic school at Darmstadt, graduating in engineering and architecture in 1848. He immigrated to the United States in 1849, entering the drafting office of the Baltimore and Ohio Railroad, under the direction of Benjamin H. Latrobe,* chief engineer of the road. He was soon placed in charge of design and erection of bridges, stations, and shops for the railroad from Grafton to Moundsville, West Virginia. During this period he invented the bridge truss which bears his name, and which was first used in a bridge over the Monongahela River at Fairmont, West Virginia, in 1852. At that time it was the largest iron railroad bridge in America. He became section engineer and later division engineer, but left the B and O in 1857 to become construction engineer of the Louisville and Nashville Railroad, at Louisville, Kentucky.

With the Louisville and Nashville he pioneered and superintended the erection of a freight and passenger station, then turned his attention to bridging the Green River south of Louisville, which attracted much publicity because of its engineering difficulties. During this same period he designed and constructed a new courthouse for the city of Louisville. In 1859 he took charge of machinery for the Louisville and Nashville and a year later became chief engineer of the road. During the Civil War much of the property of the Louisville and Nashville was destroyed, and it was his job to carry out its reconstruction. In 1865 he was promoted to general superintendent. During the next ten years he rehabilitated the line, built up businesslike relations with its competitors and connecting railroads, and as an engineer completed his crowning work, the bridge across the Ohio River at Louisville. With a length of one mile, it was the largest truss bridge in the world.

In 1869 he became vice-president and general superintendent of the road, and began his annual reports, which became classics in the analysis of the real costs of transportation. He analyzed and standardized freight rates, and established them upon an accounting and statistical basis, raising these two disciplines to the level of a science in the economics of railroad operation. His report of 1874, generally known as "The Fink Report on the Cost of Transportation" is regarded as the foundation stone of railway economics. In addition, he took an active part in the extension of the Louisville and Nashville beyond Nashville, as far as Montgomery, Alabama, which involved large-scale financing, partly negotiated in England. During the Panic of 1873, the Louisville and Nashville was one of the few railroads that continued payment of interest on its funded debt and escaped bankruptcy.

In 1875 Fink resigned, intending to retire from active life and engage in literary work on various railroad problems. But he was offered the executive directorship of the Southern Railway and Steamship Association, recently formed, with offices in Atlanta, Georgia. He had advocated its establishment as a way to curb ruinous rate-cutting and competition among the financially weak southern railroads. The Association was to allocate traffic at points where competing roads met. The allocation would be in accordance with already existing traffic patterns determined by a statistical bureau set up by the Association. Fink also presented the public with a standardized set of railroad rates on which they could depend. He was successful in bringing a fair degree of order out of chaos in that situation.

In 1877 he was again going to retire, but on the urging of the chief executives of four trunk lines entering New York City, he organized the Trunk Line Association, an effort to settle the disastrous rate war then in progress. He became its commissioner, with powers and duties similar to those he had held in Atlanta, and met with similar success. His first task was to formalize regional conventions of competing roads to meet at regularly specified times in order to determine local as well as interregional freight rates and classifications. At the same time, he developed a large staff in New York that included more than sixty clerks, to collect information on existing rates and traffic movements which the committees used in their deliberations. He also held conferences on ways to adjust and enforce rate and allocation decisions and to review complaints. He next brought the connecting lines to the West and to New England into the Association. Such formal federations of railroads quickly became the order of the day.

Yet Fink felt that these private federations would not in themselves be enough to maintain stability. So he continually urged Congress, without success, for national legislation to sanction their rulings. This failure, along with the continual breakdown of private federation agreements, caused Fink to become discouraged, and by 1884 the rate structure was in chaos. When Congress finally defined public policy toward railroad competition with the Interstate Commerce Act in 1887, it failed to sanction pooling, and in fact forbade it. Fink retired in 1889, in failing health. He was married twice, first to a Baltimore woman, and in 1869 to Sarah Hunt of Louisville. He had one daughter. (A. *DAB; NCAB*, 9:489; *New York Times*, April 4, 1897; American Society of Civil Engineers, *Transactions*, 1899; *Who Was Who*, vol. H; Albert Fink, *The Railroad Problem and Its Solution*, 1882. B. Alfred D. Chandler Jr., "The Railroads: Pioneers in Modern Corporate Management," *Business History Review*, 1965 and *The Visible Hand*, 1977; D. T. Gilchrist, "Albert Fink and the Pooling System," *Business History Review*, 1960; Maury Klein, *History of the Louisville and Nashville Railroad*, 1972.)

FIRESTONE, HARVEY SAMUEL (December 20, 1868–February 7, 1938). Rubber manufacturer, Firestone Tire and Rubber Company. Born in Columbiana, Ohio, son of Benjamin Firestone and Catharine Flickinger. The Firestones were an Alsatian family who had immigrated to the United States in 1752 and had come to Ohio in its pioneer days in 1807. Harvey grew up on his father's farm and was educated in a one-room school house. He graduated from high school and completed a brief business college course in Cleveland. After working two years as a bookkeeper and salesman, he took a position with an uncle, Clinton Firestone, at the Columbiana Buggy Company. He showed marked salesmanship ability, and by 1892 was in charge of the entire Michigan district. In 1896 the buggy company went bankrupt, and Harvey decided that his future was in rubber wheels rather than buggies. He persuaded an acquaintance to invest in his new venture, establishing a firm in Chicago in 1896. After three years it was sold to a competitor, with Firestone receiving over $40,000 in cash. In the meantime, he had acquired a patent for a method of attaching tires, and went to Akron, Ohio, where the large tire-making companies were located. These firms manufactured solid tires for buggies, and pneumatics for bicycles. The automobile industry had not yet influenced their operations. In 1900 Firestone organized the Firestone Tire and Rubber Company, joining a group which controlled a "crosswire" patent for solid tires; by putting in his own patent and $10,000 in cash, he acquired one-half the shares of a $50,000 corporation.

The new firm struggled for several years, with its tires made for it by other firms. After 1903, when it began to manufacture its own products, the firm prospered. The automobile was now becoming an important factor in the tire market, and Firestone catered to its needs, first with his solid tire, then with a special type of pneumatic tire which he developed. A large order from Henry Ford* in 1906 marked the beginning of a long and important business relationship between the two men and companies, which also led to personal friendship. Firestone offered a "dismountable rim" in 1907, which permitted the wheel and tire to be removed together and a spare substituted. He particularly promoted the popularity of his tires by having them used in automobile races, and by 1913 the company's sales reached $15 million, compared to only $100,000 in 1901. Firestone Tire and Rubber soon became one of the "Big Five" of the tire industry, which included Goodyear, Goodrich, U.S. Rubber, and Fisk.

The postwar depression of 1920-1921 left the company with a debt of $43 million, so Firestone promptly cut prices, refusing the overtures of other tire manufacturers to "stabilize" competition in the industry. With increased sales, he had completely paid off the debt by 1924. He also cut wages, but in concert with other Akron tire manufacturers, was able to forestall any organization of his workers until the 1930s. From 1918 onward, Firestone undertook to promote the use of motor driven trucks, the extension of the American highway system, and the elimination of railroad grade crossings. Meanwhile, he increased the company's capital, improved its production facilities, and in 1923 introduced the balloon tire, soon to become the standard for most types of motor vehicles.

In 1922 the British "Stevenson Plan" went into effect, restricting the production of crude rubber on plantations in British possessions throughout the world, and causing a drastic rise in prices. Joined by Henry Ford and encouraged by Secretary of Commerce Herbert Hoover,* Firestone set out to establish an American-controlled supply of crude rubber. He acquired a plantation in Liberia in 1924, and by 1926 had leased the rights to a maximum of one million acres. Sixty thousand acres had been planted by 1936, yielding over 1,000 tons of crude rubber that year. By agreement with the government of Liberia, Firestone improved the Monrovia harbor, loaned the Liberian government several million dollars, and developed a sanitary work and living site for his native employees. Although in many respects this was a valuable contribution to Liberia's economic growth, there has been consistent criticism over the years that Firestone has had too dominant a position in the country's affairs and has paid Liberian workers disgracefully low wages.

In 1928 Firestone inaugurated a plan for the establishment of "one-stop master service stores" throughout the United States to supply the public with the company's tires and gasoline, oil and batteries, and brake and general equipment service. They later also included auto supplies, and the name was changed to "auto supply and service stores." In 1942 there were 650 of these stores in operation. By the later 1930s, Firestone employed over 45,000 people, and by 1942 it had the largest rubber plantation operating under single management in the world, employing 30,000 laborers, with 80,000 acres planted. Firestone weathered the depression of 1929 without suspending dividend payments, and continued to improve his position in the trade during the 1930s. By 1937, with a capital of $108,346,054 and sales of $156,823,000, the firm showed profits of more than $9 million and supplied one-quarter of all the tires used in the United States. He had steadily improved manufacturing facilities, and by 1937, besides the Akron plant, had twelve factories in the U.S. devoted to steel, rubber, and textile products, and five plants abroad. He was president of Firestone until 1932, and chairman of the board until his death.

Despite the fact that Firestone, like Ford, was a technical innovator and a pioneer in mass production techniques, he soon lost his leadership in tire production to Goodyear, which had superior marketing and management abilities. Also like Ford, Firestone remained a family-controlled business, and prior to the depression of the 1930s did not attempt diversification of its lines. Engaging largely in vertical integration during the 1920s, Firestone acquired textile mills, steel and rim-making factories, rubber and cotton plantations, and extensive distribution facilities, including dealers and retail outlets. During the depression Firestone began to diversify, taking on auto parts, rubber and plastic items, and other lines that used its marketing organization more than its production facilities. Despite this, Firestone remained more concentrated on tire production than Goodyear or its other rivals. This dependence on tires hit Firestone hard in 1978 when the company was forced to recall more than 10 million Firestone 500 steel-belted radial tires which the National Highway Traffic Safety Administration had judged to have a safety defect. As a result the firm closed down tire plants in five cities, throwing 7,000 employees out of work. Whether it will force Firestone to further diversify its lines is still an open question.

A Republican and an Episcopalian, he was president of the Ohio Federation of Churches. He married Idabelle Smith of Jackson, Michigan, in 1895. His sons, Harvey S. Jr., Russell Allen, Leonard Kimball, Raymond Christian, and Roger Stanley, were all associated in the business with him. (**A.** *DAB*, Supplement 2; *NCAB*, C:66; 32:11; *New York Times*, February 8, 1938; *Who Was Who*, vol. 1; Alfred Lief, *Harvey Firestone*, 1951. **B.** Alfred D. Chandler Jr., *Strategy and Structure*, 1962; Harvey Firestone, *Men and Rubber*, 1926; Alfred Lief, *The Firestone Story*, 1951; Mira Wilkins, *The Emergence of Multinational Enterprise*, 1970.)

FISH, STUYVESANT (June 24, 1851–April 10, 1923). Railroad executive, Illinois Central Railroad. Born in New York City, son of Hamilton Fish and Julia Kean. His father was governor of New York and Secretary of State during the Grant administration. The Fishs were an old New York family which had come from Massachusetts in the seventeenth century. Stuyvesant was educated at the best schools in New York and graduated from Columbia University in 1871, getting an M.A. there in 1874. After graduation he became a clerk in the New York offices of the Illinois Central Railroad, then becoming secretary to the president of the road. After a short time there he entered the banking business of Morton, Bliss and Company, remaining there for five years. Wall Street did not appeal to him, and he returned to railroading.

In 1877 Fish became a director of the Illinois Central Railroad, also working at various posts in the road's financial department over the next ten years. In the mid-1880s a group of conservative and respected New York bankers, including August Belmont,* Robert Goelet, Sidney Webster, and Edward H. Harriman,* came into control of the road. They appointed Fish president of Illinois Central, with Harriman taking Fish's former position of vice-president in charge of finance. Running from Chicago to New Orleans, the Illinois Central had been built up carrying the products of the Mississippi Valley to market, with 80 percent of its freight consisting of the products of farm, forest, and mine. It was Fish's policy to extend the facilities of the line to create new traffic, thus continually building up an independent, self-contained system extending throughout this heartland and fed by various tributary lines.

Working with the road's executive committee, Fish outlined a plan calling for a highly centralized structure. Although the acting general manager had wanted a system of autonomous units similar to that of the Burlington Road, Fish and the other operating executives favored a more highly centralized structure. The new organization concentrated all decisions regarding traffic, transportation, and finance in Chicago. The three major functional departments remained quite autonomous, and even their regional subdivisions did not cover the same geographic areas. Only the president, residing in Chicago, coordinated these activities. Since nearly all the board members lived in New York and were involved in other tasks, they had little time to review past operations or plan for future ones. The plan, however, was attractive to the New York financiers. By having fewer managers, administrative costs were reduced. By having all senior executives housed in Chicago they were able to consult easily with one another and could be easily reached by New York directors. Finally, the traffic department's autonomy allowed it to adjust its schedules swiftly to meet continuing rate changes. A major innovation in administration at the time, by the turn of the century nearly all American railroads were using this type of administrative structure, rejecting the more decentralized form of the Pennsylvania Railroad.

Fish was president for nineteen years, and during this time increased the mileage and lines of the road by 175 percent. The gross receipts during this period rose 365 percent, and dividends on common stock were augmented by 227 percent. By 1906 the Illinois Central had acquired a reputation as one of the best equipped, best managed, and best financed railroads in the country. But as a railroad administrator, Fish in some respects had succeeded too well, making the line a property highly coveted by other corporations. His withdrawal as president was the climax of one of the longest and most bitterly fought contests in American railroad history, in which Fish antagonized Charles A. Peabody, President of Mutual Life Insurance, and Edward H. Harriman, a trustee of Mutual, who were both powerful directors of the Illinois Central.

The whole controversy came about over Fish's uncompromising stand, taken in 1906 when he was appointed chairman of a committee to investigate the charges preferred against officials of the Mutual Life Insurance Company, of which he was a trustee. Fish demanded a "thorough housecleaning," but this demand was not supported by his other associates on the commission. He then resigned both his commission membership and his trusteeship in the insurance company, giving the details of the quarrel to the press. Wall Street financial interests, led by Harriman, threatened his removal as president of Illinois Central, and within eight months this came to pass, as he was ousted by the board of directors. Since Harriman by this time owned 30 percent of the company, it made him the dominant factor, and although Fish took him to court over his dismissal in 1908, he was unsuccessful. Fish was active for a time in the management of Missouri Pacific Railroad, of which he was a director.

Fish was also for many years vice-president and director of the National Park Bank of New York, and trustee of New York Life Insurance Company. He was president of the American Railway Association from 1904 to 1906, and chairman of the Seventh International Railway Congress in Washington in 1905. He married Marion Graves Anton in 1876, and they had two sons and one daughter. He was an Episcopalian. (**A.** *DAB; NCAB*, 19:15; *New York Times*, April 13, 1923; *Who Was Who*, vol. 1. **B.** Alfred D. Chandler Jr., *The Visible Hand*, 1977; Thomas C. Cochran, *American Railroad Leaders*, 1953; Carlton Corliss, *Main Line of Mid-America*, 1950.)

FISHER, FREDERICK JOHN (January 2, 1878–July 14, 1941). Automobile body manufacturer, Fisher Body Company. Born in Sandusky, Ohio, eldest of seven sons of Lawrence Fisher and Margaret Theisen. His grandfather had been a wagon and carriage builder in Germany, and after coming to the United States became a merchant in Peru, Ohio. Lawrence Fisher became a blacksmith and wheelwright in Norwalk, Ohio. Fred Fisher was educated in Roman Catholic parochial schools to the eighth grade, entering the family business at fourteen. Under his father's tutelage, he became an expert carriage maker. In 1902 he went to Detroit and took a job as a draftsman with the C. R. Wilson Carriage Works, at that time the largest manufacturer of auto bodies in the city. In 1907 he became superintendent of the Wilson shops, having been joined there by his brothers, Charles T., Alfred J., Lawrence P., William A., and Edward F. Fisher. They would be associated with him in a variety of industrial and financial enterprises for some thirty-five years. Fred was the acknowledged leader of the Fisher brothers, who constituted one of the most closely knit family groups in American business history.

In 1908, with his brother Charles, Fred Fisher organized the Fisher Body Company, with capital of $50,000, establishing a plant in Detroit. The other four brothers were brought into the firm, and an uncle, Andrew Fisher, served briefly as president until the brothers purchased his interest. The business was highly successful from the very beginning. Fisher bodies were designed specifically for autos rather than being modifications of horse-drawn carriages. They were sturdier and more shock-resistant than those built by the competition. The Fishers also grasped more quickly than their competitors the possibilities of the closed car. An order for 150 closed bodies that Cadillac placed with them in 1910 was the first volume order of its kind in the United States, and led directly to the creation of the Fisher Closed Body Company in 1912. In the same year they organized the Fisher Body Company of Canada at Walkerville, Ontario. Within four years the combined profits of the Detroit and Walkerville companies had increased almost four-fold to $1,390,592.

In 1916 the three firms were merged into the Fisher Body Corporation, a holding and operating company capitalized at $6 million. It had a total annual capacity of 370,000 units, making it the largest firm of its type in the industry. The growth of the company was financed primarily by the reinvestment of profits. In 1919, General Motors, under the direction of William C. Durant,* acquired a 60 percent interest in Fisher Body, and agreed to purchase practically all its auto bodies from Fisher for the next ten years, at a price of cost plus 17.6 percent. The acquisition cost General Motors $27 million under an agreement whereby Fisher Body increased its 200,000 shares of common stock to 500,000, and sold the new issue to G.M. at $92 per share. The Fisher family, however, retained its managerial control of the firm.

After World War I, they constructed the world's largest body factory at that time at Cleveland, Ohio. Between 1922 and 1929 the firm built or acquired some twenty factories in various parts of the country. Fred Fisher joined the executive committee of G.M. in 1922, and in 1924 was made vice-president of the parent corporation and a member of the finance committee. The Fisher division was the most profitable of all of Durant's acquisitions. It yielded especially high returns in the years after World War I when the switch was made from open touring cars to closed cars. The Fisher Company made $23 million in 1923 on a volume of 417,000 bodies. By 1925 it was earning a return of 18.9 percent on its assets.

The Fishers introduced numerous innovations in body hardware and interior fittings, such as external steel panels, the rubber weather strip for windshields, side window vents, and the window regulator. They pioneered in the development of steel body presses. They were the first to use lacquer rather than paint on auto bodies. Their Fleetwood custom division, acquired in 1925, became a standard for excellence in design and craftsmanship in the industry. The trademark, "Body by Fisher," became familiar to millions of motorists.

In 1926 the minority stockholders of Fisher Body, mostly the Fisher brothers, sold their 40 percent interest to G.M. in exchange for the latter's stock, which had a market value of $130 million. Fisher Body became a division of G.M. and each of the six brothers was named to a post in the corporation or one of its subsidiaries. William was made head of Fisher Body, Lawrence head of Cadillac Division, and Fred vice-president and general manager of G.M. until he resigned in 1934. Meanwhile, the Fishers began construction of the Fisher Building in Detroit, designed by Albert Kahn.

By 1928 Fred Fisher's personal fortune was estimated at $50 million, and the combined assets of the Fisher brothers was later set at about one-half billion dollars. The Fisher brothers entered the stock market in 1926, with operations conducted through Fisher and Company, a family concern of which Fred was chairman. From 1927 to 1929, during the great bull market, the Fishers carried out several carefully planned and boldly executed financial maneuvers, frequently allying with the Wall Street operator, Arthur W. Cutten.* This brought them a national reputation as shrewd speculators. The market crash of 1929 wiped out their paper profits and soon afterward the family withdrew from such large-scale trading.

Fred Fisher was a director of some twenty corporations, including North

American Aviation, the Sperry Corporation, National Bank of Detroit, and Intercontinental Trust Company. He was a Roman Catholic and a Republican, and married Burtha Meyers in 1908. He had no children. Of the other brothers, Charles T. Fisher's son, Charles T. Fisher Jr. (1907-1958) became president of the National Bank of Detroit and director of many corporations. His son, Charles T. Fisher III (b. 1929), joined National Bank of Detroit, becoming president and chief administrative officer in 1972. He was also president of the National Detroit Corporation after 1973 and a director of General Motors, Detroit Edison, Hiram Walker, and American Airlines, among others. William A. Fisher remained head of the Fisher Body division until he retired in 1944. He died in 1969. Edward F. Fisher was a director of G.M. until he died in 1972. Lawrence P. Fisher remained a director of G.M. until his death in 1961. (**A.** *DAB*, Supplement 3; *New York Times*, July 15 and 17, 1941; *Who Was Who*, vols. 3, 4, 5; *Who's Who in America, 1978-79*. **B.** Alfred D. Chandler Jr., *Strategy and Structure*, 1962, and *Giant Enterprise*, 1964; Alfred P. Sloan Jr., *My Years With General Motors*, 1969.)

FISK, JAMES (April 1, 1834-January 7, 1872). Stockbroker and financier, Fisk and Belden and Erie Railroad. Born in Bennington, Vermont, son of James Fisk and Love B. Ryan, he later lived also in Brattleboro, Vermont. After only a rudimentary education Fisk became a waiter in a hotel, a ticket seller for the Van Amber Circus, and a salesman with his father's "traveling emporium," which he later purchased and operated himself, taking his father into his employ. Fisk next branched from peddling into a jobbing business for Jordan Marsh of Boston, entering their wholesale department in 1860 and managing large war contracts for them on a commission basis. Later he went South to buy cotton in the occupied districts for a Boston syndicate, becoming wealthy enough to start his own business. But his Boston dry goods jobbing establishment was hard hit by the postwar deflation of 1865, and later a brokerage office in New York was also a failure.

Fisk recouped his losses by acting as an agent in the sale of Daniel Drew's* steamboats to a Boston group. He subsequently returned to New York and with Drew's support founded the brokerage house of Fisk and Belden in 1866. His rise to great wealth thereafter was very rapid. Drawn into the "Erie War" between Drew and Cornelius Vanderbilt,* Fisk became a director of the Erie Railroad and helped Jay Gould* and Drew drain it of its profits and assets. It was Fisk who evaded the injunction against the issuance of more Erie stock by seizing 50,000 ready signed shares, which were then used to break Vanderbilt's attempted corner. It was also he who led the famous flight with Gould and Drew to Taylor's Hotel in Jersey City. When Drew and Vanderbilt made peace, Fisk and Gould shared control of the half-wrecked Erie Railroad.

Gould and Fisk then embarked upon a series of bold and unscrupulous ventures. They increased the Erie's stock during the summer of 1868 from $34 million to over $57 million, with part of the proceeds being used for expansion—leasing other railroads; building bridges; buying steamboats, rolling mills, and car shops; and adding new rolling stock and equipment— while the rest was used in reckless speculative forays. They launched a campaign with Drew in 1868 to tighten credit and raise the price of gold, which had a severe effect on the economies of both America and Europe, but gained them large profits. They also carried out a corner that so outraged the business community that the Erie's stock was taken off brokers' boards. This included a raid on the United States Express Company, whose stock was manipulated at will, and a raid on the Albany and Susquehanna Railroad, which resulted in a pitched battle between gangs of employees near Binghamton, New York.

These raids culminated in the famous Black Friday attempt to corner the gold market in September, 1869, an action which ruined hundreds and caused the entire business community to suffer a profound shock. The coup failed disastrously, and Fisk flatly repudiated contracts worth millions made through his responsible business partner, Belden. Fisk bought Pike's Opera House in New York City and fitted it with costly offices, at the same time producing dramas and French opera bouffe. He leased the Academy of Music and put on grand opera until the expense became too great. He controlled the Fall River and Bristol line of steamboats, and paraded as "admiral" of these fleets, placing on the Hudson River its largest ferryboat, the *James Fisk*, and engaged in a myriad lavish and expensive hobbies.

Fisk's romantic life was as notorious as his business career, and he openly kept a succession of mistresses for many years. Finally, he singled out the actress, Josie Mansfield, as his favorite; he quarreled over her and business transactions with Edward Stokes, who fatally shot Fisk in the Grand Central Hotel on January 6, 1872. He died the next day. Fisk had married Lucy D. Moore, of Springfield, Massachusetts in 1855. She survived him. (**A.** *DAB; NCAB*, 22:170; *New York Times*, January 7, 1872; *Who Was Who*, vol. H; R. H. Fuller, *Jubilee Jim*, 1928; W. A. Swanberg, *Jim Fisk: Career of an Improbable Rascal*, 1939. **B.** Charles Francis Adams Jr. and Henry Adams, *Chapters of Erie*, 1886; Matthew Josephson, *The Robber Barons*, 1934.)

FITZHUGH, WILLIAM (1651–October, 1701). Seventeenth century Virginia merchant and land speculator. Born in Bedford, England, son of Henry Fitzhugh, a lawyer. Young William probably received an excellent education in England, including training in the law. He immigrated to Virginia in 1670 and established himself on the Potomac River in what was then Stafford County, Virginia. In this area he purchased a large estate, settling down to the life of a large planter and exporter, while at the same time practicing law. He soon became one of the leading lawyers in the colony, and his agricultural and mercantile pursuits proved to be extremely profitable.

He was a member of the House of Burgesses for a number of years, and on two occasions found himself in legal entanglements in which he was charged with misrepresenting his claims for emolument, but was never brought to trial. The series of letters he left from the period 1679 to 1699, 213 in all, provides intimate insight into the business practices of a prominent Virginia capitalist of those times. The letters reveal that he married a girl who was only eleven years old, who brought him a dowry of land and slaves, which laid a firm economic foundation for his own later fortune and that of his family. He was appointed the land agent for Lord Culpeper, the proprietor of the Northern Neck of Virginia, which further enhanced his abilities in land speculation. He married Sarah Rucker of Virginia in 1674. (**A.** *DAB*; William Fitzhugh, *William Fitzhugh and his Chesapeake World: The Fitzhugh Letters and Other Documents*, ed. by Richard B. Davis, 1963; Richard B. Davis, "Chesapeake Pattern and Pole Star: William Fitzhugh and His Plantation World, 1676–1701," American Philosophical Society, *Proceedings*, 1961. **B.** Louis B. Wright, *First Gentlemen of Virginia*, 1940.)

FLAGLER, HENRY MORRISON (January 2, 1830–May 20, 1913). Oil producer, Standard Oil Company. Born in Canandaigua, New York, son of Rev. Isaac Flagler and Elizabeth Morrison. His father was an impoverished Presbyterian minister, and his ancestors were German Palatinates who came to America in about 1712. Henry Flagler was educated in district schools until he was fourteen, when he struck out on his own. He made his way to Sandusky, Ohio, and secured employment in a country store in nearby Republic, Ohio. He saved money on this job and on one at Fostoria, Ohio, where he later worked. Around 1850 he became a grain merchant at Bellevue, Ohio, also having as interest in a distillery. It was while living in Bellevue that he met John D. Rockefeller,* who was then in the produce business in Cleveland, occasionally selling grain through him. When Flagler had accumulated about $50,000, he moved to Saginaw, Michigan, to engage in the manufacture of salt, but he lost his fortune in this venture, in addition to owing almost that much more.

Flagler then moved to Cleveland, where he set himself up as a grain merchant, renewing his acquaintance with Rockefeller. In 1867 he joined the oil firm of Rockefeller and Andrews, which became Rockefeller, Andrews and Flagler. Flagler brought not only a small amount of his own money into the firm, but was instrumental in getting Stephen V. Harkness, who had made a fortune in whiskey, to invest as much as $100,000. In 1870 the firm was incorporated as the Standard Oil Company. Next to Rockefeller himself, Flagler was the strongest and most dominant figure in the organization. Throughout the stormy early years of the development of the giant organization, Flagler was active in its management, retaining his connection with it until near the end of his life, resigning as vice-president in 1908 and as a director in 1911.

It was Flagler's idea to reorganize the company in 1870 into a flexible corporation that could expand at will by increasing its capitalization and stock. In the years to follow, Rockefeller and Flagler went hand-in-hand in dealing with the various problems confronted by Standard Oil. In these dealings, it was Flagler who handled the legal aspects, making sure that Standard Oil stayed within the law of every state in which it operated. This left Rockefeller free to handle personnel. In 1879 Flagler, with Samuel C. T. Dodd,* perfected the first trust agreement, under which three men in the Cleveland office of Standard Oil would hold the stock of Standard and its affiliates in trust for the stockholders of Standard. When this proved inefficient, Flagler and Dodd created the Standard Oil Trust in 1882, which in effect changed the business structure of America.

In the late 1880s, however, Flagler's interests turned more toward railroads and land development. In 1886 he purchased the Jacksonville, St. Augustine and Halifax River Railroad in Florida, and later purchased some other short lines which he combined as the Florida East Coast Railroad. In 1892 construction was begun southwest from Daytona, reaching Palm Beach in 1894 and Miami in 1896. Meanwhile he built a string of palatial hotels along the line—the Ponce de Leon and Alcazar at St. Augustine; the Ormond at Ormond; the Royal Poinciana and the Breakers at Palm Beach; and the Royal Palm in Miami. Perhaps his greatest achievement was the extension of the railroad from Miami to Key West, through everglades and over and between 106 islands, which was completed in 1912. He also dredged the harbor in Miami and established a steamship line to Key West and another to Nassau, where he also opened hotels. His total investment in Florida exceeded $40 million.

He was married three times: to Marli Harkness in 1853; to Ida A. Shounds in 1883, from whom he was divorced in 1901; and in 1901 to Mary Lily Kenan of North Carolina. He had three children. (**A.** *DAB; NCAB*, 15:10; *Who Was Who*, vol. 1. **B.** Grace Goulder, *John D. Rockefeller: The Cleveland Years*, 1973; David Freeman Hawke, *John D.*, 1980; Ralph W. and Murial E. Hidy, *Pioneering in Big Business: 1882-1911*, 1955; Ida M. Tarbell, *History of the Standard Oil Company*, 2 vols., 1904; Harold F. Williamson and Arnold R. Daum, *The American Petroleum Industry*, 1959.)

FLEMING, ARETUS BROOKS (October 15, 1839–October 13, 1923). Coal operator, Fairmont Coal Company and Consolidation Coal Company. Born on a farm near Middleton, West Virginia (then part of Virginia), son of Benjamin F. Fleming and Rhoda Brooks. The Flemings were a prominent Scotch-Irish family who had immigrated to America in 1741, obtaining a patent to land in Pennsylvania. Aretus Fleming was educated in private schools, and in 1859 entered the University of Virginia, where he studied law. In 1860 he opened a private school in Gilmore County and began the practice of law. At the outbreak of the Civil War he returned to Fairmont, West Virginia, near his birthplace, where he served as a prosecuting attorney from 1863 to 1867. In 1865 he entered into a law partnership with Judge Alpheus Hammond. Fleming was elected to the state legislature in 1872 and reelected in 1874, becoming an active leader in the founding of the Fairmont State Normal School.

Until 1878 Fleming was attorney for the Baltimore and Ohio Railroad in Fairmont, and had been identified with coal development in the Monongahela Valley with his father-in-law, James Otis Watson, the pioneer coal operator of the region. He was also associated with J. N. Camden in the building of the Monongahela River Railroad, and in 1901 helped organize the Fairmont Coal Company, which later became the Consolidation Coal Company, acting as a director of these concerns until he retired from active business. He was also interested in the building of electric traction lines, both local and interurban, and was one of the founders of the Bank of Fairmont. Throughout his life he was recognized as the leading corporation lawyer in the state.

On December 6, 1907, a mine explosion in Monongah mines 6 and 8 of the Fairmont Coal Company killed 361 men; it was the worst mine disaster in the nation's history. The mines were regarded by experts as among the safest in the industry, and many concluded that if the Monongah mines blew up, so could any mines. This provided a stimulus for mine-safety reform and converted Fleming into a cautious reformer. Fearful that an aroused state legislature might enact costly legislation, Fleming and his fellow operators shifted the focus of the reform movement to the national government. Fleming became a strong ally of Joseph A. Holmes, director of the Bureau of Mines, in a campaign to establish coal-mining safety securely in the Geological Survey and the Bureau of Mines. Fleming was particularly chagrined at the public relations aspect of mine explosions, and did his best to minimize publicity in this area. Nor did his own mines adhere to all aspects of the newly passed West Virginia safety regulations, refusing to adopt several of the special rules required by the law. For Fleming, safety was mostly a public relations problem, and his main interest was in production and the profitability of the corporation.

Throughout his career Fleming was intimately involved in politics, and these activities were closely connected with his industrial developments. After serving in the state legislature, he became judge of the circuit court of his district until 1888. In the latter year he was Democratic candidate for governor of the state of West Virginia. The election was very close, and was thrown into the state legislature for a decision before he was finally elected to the position in 1890. As governor he attracted attention to the undeveloped mineral and timber resources of the state. He married Caroline

Margaret Watson in 1865. (**A.** *DAB; NCAB*, 12:432; *New York Times,* October 14, 1923; *Who Was Who*, vol. 1. **B.** Howard N. Eavenson, *The First Century and a Quarter of the Coal Industry*, 1942; William Graebner, *Coal Mining Safety in the Progressive Era*, 1976.)

FLINT, CHARLES RANLETT (January 24, 1850–February 12, 1934). Financier, United States Rubber Company, American Woolen Company, and others. Born in Thomaston, Maine, son of Benjamin Chapman and Sarah Tobey Flint. His mother died when he was three years old, and he was adopted by her brother, Benjamin Flint. Both his father and stepfather were in the shipbuilding business, with the firm of Chapman and Flint, organized in Maine in 1837 and later moved to New York City. Charles Flint was educated in a boarding school in Topsham and at public schools in New York. He graduated from Brooklyn Polytechnic Institute in 1868.

His apprenticeship in business began in 1868, when he became a desk clerk in New York City. During the period from 1871 to 1879 he was a partner, first in the ship-chandlery of Gilchrist, Flint and Company, and later in W. R. Grace and Company, prominent commission merchants in the South American trade. While he was engaged in this business, Flint acted as Chilean consul in New York from 1876 to 1879. Meanwhile, his firm had become a financial agent for Peru. When Peru and Chile went to war in 1879, Flint resigned his consulate and engaged in supplying war materials and guns to Peru. Becoming a free-lance businessman, he was far too individualistic to be a partner unless he was able to dominate the partnership. In 1880 he assumed the presidency of the United States Electric Company, and tried to bring about a merger of light and power interests, including those of C. F. Brush and Thomas Edison.* He was not successful in this endeavor and his firm was absorbed by the Westinghouse Electric and Manufacturing Company. In 1884 he arranged for the importation of Brazilian rubber to the United States, later becoming known as the "Rubber King of America." These activities brought Flint into close association with bankers in both America and abroad, especially J. P. Morgan and Company.

The most important part of his business career began in 1885 and lasted for more than two decades. In that year he joined the firm of Flint and Company, commission merchants of New York City, which was an offshoot of Chapman and Flint. The firm evolved from shipbuilding and ship operation to a general commission business, dealing in lumber, rubber, and general merchandise in foreign trade, and in merchant banking, having about 3,000 correspondents. In 1894 it assigned its foreign trade to Flint, Eddy and Company, and in 1899 sold its sailing vessels to Flint, Dearborn and Company. Flint's commission firm, and Flint himself, became notable for activities on behalf of foreign governments, especially providing ships, guns, and munitions in South America. A fleet of war vessels was fitted out for the Brazilian government in 1893; a Chilean ship was purchased and delivered to Japan in 1895 for use in its war against China; negotiations were carried on for the purchase of war vessels for the American government in 1898; and active aid was given to the Russian government in its war against Japan in 1905. His firm acted as agents for the sale of Wright airplanes abroad and also for Simon Lake's submarines.

Flint's second field of operations lay in consolidating large industrial units. He seldom bought into these companies, believing that it was better for the consolidation if he had no vested interests of his own. His dealings with crude rubber had brought him into contact with the manufacturers of rubber boots and shoes, among whom there was intense competition. At their request he undertook the consolidation which, as early as 1892, resulted in the United States Rubber Company. In 1906, as treasurer of U.S. Rubber, he was sent to Brussels and negotiated with King Leopold for the entire rubber output of the Belgian Congo. In 1899 he brought about the consolidations of the American Woolen Company; the Sloss-Sheffield Company; the American Chicle Company; the United States Bobbin and Shuttle Company; and several others. By 1900 he had been dubbed the "Father of Trusts" by a Chicago newspaper.

His interest in developing these consolidations rested on his belief that there would be greater economies of scale and greater stability in the larger organizations, and that the families of industrial founders would be better served by owning stock in horizontal combinations managed by financial interests, than in inheriting factories which would be mishandled by the heirs. He believed that the consolidated companies would compete with one another and that stockholders, consumers, and workers would all profit from the new organizations. His chief personal services seem to have been in discovering possible combinations, getting together the persons concerned, and suggesting terms and compromises.

Charles Flint was also the founder of the firm which ultimately became International Business Machines. In 1911 he helped organize the Computer-Tabulating-Recording Company as an umbrella for a number of firms that manufactured counting and weighing equipment, among them Hollerith's Tabulating Machine Company. Computing-Tabulating-Recording was capitalized at $6,500,000, a figure that was five times the assets of all its subsidiary companies. In 1924 the firm became IBM. Flint also helped to form Clarksburg Fuel Company, Fairmont Coal Company, Mechanical Rubber Company, National Starch Company, Sen Sen Chicle Company, and Somerset Coal Company, and was chairman of a commission that consolidated the street railways of Syracuse, New York.

Although Flint had a large income of some $50,000 per year, he had no great wealth and until his old age was quite unknown to the general public. He was an industrial capitalist who became a promoter and served on the fringes of large industrial corporations. He retired from business in 1928, but reentered when the Great Depression hit, serving until 1931, when he left office for good. He was married twice: in 1883 to Emma Kate Simmons of Troy, New York, who died in 1926; and to Charlotte Reeves of Washington, D.C. He had no children. (**A.** *DAB*, Supplement 1; *NCAB*, 37:200; *New York Times*, February 14, 1934; *Who Was Who*, vol. 1. **B.** B. D. Babcock, *History of the United States Rubber Company*, 1966; W. Rodgers, *THINK: A Biography of the Watsons and IBM*, 1969; Ben B. Seligman, *The Potentates*, 1971.)

FOLSOM, MARION BAYARD (November 23, 1893–September 28, 1976). Government official and corporation executive, Committee on Economic Development and Eastman Kodak Company. Born in McRae, Georgia, son of William Bryant Folsom, a merchant, and Margaret Jane McRae. His family had come to Massachusetts in 1638. Marion Folsom was educated in local schools and graduated from the University of Georgia in 1912. He received an M.B.A. at Harvard in 1914. Upon his graduation from Harvard he joined Eastman Kodak Company in Rochester, New York, leaving for only a brief time to serve in the army during World War I. In 1921 he was appointed special assistant to George Eastman,* becoming assistant treasurer in 1930, and treasurer of the company in 1935.

Folsom's most enduring achievement during his years at Kodak lay in the area of pensions and retirement benefits. Folsom described George Eastman as a "rugged individualist" who did not believe in pension plans. As a result, some inefficient older workers, personally acquainted with Eastman and lacking the resources to support themselves in retirement, had to be kept on the company payroll. Folsom took the lead in developing a pension plan for Kodak, and although this was not adopted until late in the 1930s, it brought him into contact with developments for a national social security program. As a member of the Advisory Board of the Committee on Economic Security in 1934–1935, he had the major responsibility for convincing his business colleagues of the efficacy of the proposed Social Security legislation. His experience at Kodak had caused him to realize that state old-age insurance could function as a surrogate, providing employees with adequate retirement incomes and thus making it possible to separate them from company payrolls.

To his business colleagues on the CES Advisory Council Folsom stressed the contribution old-age insurance could make to corporate efficiency. By encouraging employees to plan for retirement and to retire, social security would increase productivity. He also argued that old-age insurance would function to stabilize the economy by encouraging counter-cyclical spending. His arguments were persuasive, as his fellow businessmen on the Advisory Council approved the concept of old-age insurance. In 1939, as treasurer of Kodak, Folsom argued for the need to integrate social security and private pensions, thus providing greater total benefits. This would allow employers to retire older workers, thereby achieving the gains in efficiency for which the pensions had been designed. Later, as Secretary of Health, Education and Welfare during the Eisenhower administration, Folsom opposed lowering the age for women's social security benefits to age sixty-two. Despite his opposition, the measure became a law in 1956.

The desires to stabilize the economy and employment which were part of Folsom's advocacy of social security also caused him to be a supporter of unemployment insurance. Following the stock market crash in 1929, Folsom began a study of the problem of stabilizing production and employment which became known as the "Rochester Unemployment Plan". This plan led to his appointment to the Advisory Council of the CES and his assignment as a delegate to the International Labor Conference at Geneva, Switzerland, in 1936.

In 1940 Folsom was appointed a divisional executive of the National Advisory Defense Commission, serving for six months. When the Committee for Economic Development was organized under Paul G. Hoffman* in 1942, Folsom was one of the committee's original trustees. The objectives of the CED were: first, to help businessmen plan for quick reconversion and expanded production, distribution and employment after the war; and second, to help determine through objective research those economic policies that would encourage both the attainment and maintenance of high production and employment. Folsom was chairman of the CED field development division from 1942 to 1944, when he resigned to become staff director of the House of Representatives' Special Committee on Post-war Planning and Policy. He served on this committee until its work was completed in 1946. He returned to the CED, and was chosen one of its six vice-chairmen.

Folsom served as a member of the Business Advisory Council of the Department of Commerce from 1936, functioning as vice-chairman of that body for several years. From 1942 to 1948 he was a director of the United States Chamber of Commerce. When not involved in government service, Folsom continued as treasurer of Eastman Kodak, holding that post until he was appointed Secretary of Health, Education and Welfare in 1953. Upon his retirement from that position in 1958, he returned to Kodak as a member of the board of directors, serving until 1969. He was also president of Eastman Savings and Loan Association from 1957 to 1962. A Presbyterian and a Republican, he married Mary Davenport in 1918, and they had three children. (**A.** *NCAB*, I:170; *Current Biography*, January, 1950; November, 1976; *New York Times*, September 29, 1976. **B.** Grace Abbott, *From Relief to Social Security*, 1941; William Graebner, *A History of Retirement*, 1980; Lewis Meriam, *Relief and Social Security*, 1946; Edwin E. Witte, *The Development of the Social Security Act*, 1962.)

FORBES, JOHN MURRAY (February 23, 1813–October 12, 1898). Merchant in the China trade and railroad builder, Russell and Company; Michigan Central Railroad; Chicago, Burlington and Quincy Railroad; Burlington and Missouri River Railroad; Hannibal and St. Joseph Railroad. Born in Bordeaux, France, son of American parents who were vacationing abroad. His father, Ralph Bennet Forbes, was descended from John Forbes, who had emigrated from Scotland to Florida in 1764. His mother, Margaret Perkins, was the daughter of Thomas H. Perkins,* one of the most prominent merchants of colonial Boston. John Forbes was educated in local schools and at fifteen entered his uncles' counting house, J. and T. H. Perkins. The firm had been organized in 1792 by Thomas Handasyd Perkins and his brother James. They established a Canton, China branch which at a later date handed over its commission business to Russell and Company. In 1830 John M. Forbes was sent to Canton to join Russell and Company, which was then under the direction of his cousin, John Perkins Cushing.* With Forbes went Augustine Heard (1765–1868), who had been active as shipmaster and supercargo in trade with China, India, and South America. At about the same time Robert Bennet Forbes (1804–1887), John Forbes' elder brother, was given charge of Russell and Company "storeship" at Lintin, which had been developed to circumvent the efforts of Chinese authorities to halt the trade in opium.

John Forbes remained in Canton until 1833, when he left for reasons of health; but he returned the following year as supercargo for Bryant, Sturgis and Company (headed by William Sturgis,* who was related to the Perkins family by marriage). The following year Forbes accepted a partnership in Russell and Company and by his mercantile aptitude did much to advance the firm's business in China. He brought to the company the commission business of Houqua, a wealthy Hong Kong merchant, and this mercantile and personal friendship became one of the pillars of Forbes' fortune. He not only received 10 percent of the profits of the merchant's business, but later also managed large sums of Houqua's capital, much of which he later invested in America's western expansion. In 1836 Forbes left Canton for good, although he retained a financial interest in Russell and Company long after he had turned his primary attention to domestic investment. In fact, Russell and Company continued to create relationships and generate capital, both of which were important to American expansion and development. In the later 1850s, while deeply involved in western railroad development, the Forbes family continued to dominate the Canton firm in the persons of Robert B. Forbes and Paul S. Forbes, a cousin. Money from them also flowed into the western enterprises in which John M. Forbes was prominent.

Upon his return to America Forbes played a strategic role in the investment patterns of Boston's wealthy China merchants. By managing the investments of his brother and cousin and his friend Augustine Heard, as well as those of other men in his Boston circle, he was exercising control over capital that had been derived almost entirely from the China trade. Prior to 1846 he invested the capital primarily in eastern railways and other ventures. His first railroad venture was evidently a $5,000 investment in the Attica and Buffalo Railroad, on the recommendation of William Sturgis in 1843. This was soon followed by a more extensive commitment to the Philadelphia and Reading Railroad in 1845. The line was in deep financial trouble, however, and Forbes sold his stock in early 1849 after learning of the road's condition. He disapproved of the management's short-run perspective and policies, but lacked the means of influencing them. Therefore he withdrew his money. Forbes also became involved in the financing of the Philadelphia, Wilmington and Baltimore Railroad in 1846. In these investments in eastern roads, Forbes stressed that profitability lay in the long-run development of the railroad as a transportation facility and not in short-run speculative operations. He was to carry this principle over into his more spectacular western railroad enterprises.

Forbes' first move into western railroad investment, however, was motivated initially by opportunistic rather than developmental concerns. The state of Michigan had begun the Michigan Central Railroad, but had run into financing difficulties. Under the urging of James F. Joy,* a native of New Hampshire and a leading Detroit lawyer, eastern capitalists were urged to participate in the venture. In 1845 Forbes became one of a number of leading Boston financiers to join in a syndicate to purchase the Michigan Central from the state for $2 million. After an extensive legislative struggle the sale was finally approved in March, 1846. At first Forbes had seen the railroad primarily as a speculative investment, but upon agreeing to take over the presidency of the road soon after its sale, he began to think in terms of long-run developmental potential. Forbes now embarked upon a program of expansion that was the beginning of his career in railroading and was to have important consequences for the development of the American West.

One of the requirements of the sale of the Michigan Central to the Boston group was that the road be extended to Lake Michigan. In 1849 the line was completed to Buffalo, Michigan (on Lake Michigan), over 200 miles from its origin in Detroit. The next step was to extend the line to Chicago, while at the same time supplying funds for connecting links between Detroit and Buffalo through Ontario with the building of the Great Western Railroad. By the mid-1850s the Forbes group was involved in western development on a continuing basis. As they pushed westward, the logic of the concept of a railroad system, a unified transportation network as opposed to a railroad line, was beginning to emerge in their minds.

In creating this new railway network, Forbes and his Boston associates concentrated on the area between the Ohio and Missouri Rivers during the 1850s. He financed and put into operation roads from Chicago to the

Mississippi River and across Iowa, which formed the nucleus of what was later to become the Chicago, Burlington and Quincy System. One of these roads was the Hannibal and St. Joseph Railroad, to provide a route through northern Missouri between the Mississippi and Missouri Rivers. In 1852 Congress had approved a land grant of 600,000 acres for the road, but Forbes viewed federal land grants as a stimulus to construction with great suspicion. His main argument was that the lure of federal aid would spur construction of roads that were not justified by other considerations and that their inevitable collapse would discredit railroad-building and retard the development of needed roads. As he became involved in the trans-Mississippi area, however, his attitude toward federal railroad policy changed. The Hannibal and St. Joseph was badly in need of funds, and if it had not taken possession of the federal lands it probably would not have survived. Forbes, as the line's financial agent, issued bonds in Europe secured by the railroad's lands, selling about $4 million worth.

Forbes' next step in the creation of the Burlington system was the acquisition of the Burlington and Missouri River Railroad in Iowa in 1854, receiving public lands from Congress for the road in 1856. During the 1850s the Forbes group had begun to build a railroad system. They had created an integrated rail network extending from Chicago to Burlington and Quincy on the Mississippi River and organized a company to hold and manage it. Also, as individuals they had begun to take an interest in weak young roads across the Mississippi which formed logical extensions to the evolving Burlington System. During the Civil War years and immediately after, Forbes turned his attention to public affairs, but in 1873 he again became the leading figure in the management of the Burlington System, serving as president from 1878 until 1881.

In his railroad endeavors, Forbes believed in building a railroad substantially, though he would, to some extent, compromise with this principle. However, his standards of sound investment made him unwilling to be identified with a speculator's railroad. This stand was clearly demonstrated in the 1870s and 80s when he and his cousin, Charles E. Perkins,* bitterly fought Jay Gould's* attempts to control their midwestern lines. To meet the Gould challenge they consolidated the Burlington and Missouri River into the Chicago, Burlington and Quincy in 1880, and added 863 miles of operating railroad and 109 miles of new construction to the Burlington System. In that same year they took steps to take control of the Kansas City, St. Joseph and Council Bluffs Road, which would partially offset Gould's acquisition of the Missouri Pacific. They next decided to extend the line to Denver, and to acquire by lease or purchase the Burlington and Southwestern. Their final tactical move against Gould in 1882 was to acquire the Hannibal and St. Joseph, which the Burlington had relinquished a decade earlier. During the remainder of the decade, under Perkins' direction since Forbes had retired, the Burlington extended in several directions. In 1886 the Chicago, Burlington and Northern was opened to tap the spring wheat and lumber traffic at Minneapolis–St. Paul, and by the end of the decade a new line had been completed across Nebraska to Cheyenne, Wyoming, and another had been built into South Dakota. Ultimately, in 1894, a branch was extended to connect with the Northern Pacific at Billings, Montana, giving direct access from points in the Northwest to the major centers served by the Burlington in the central part of the country. The system indelibly bore the stamp of John M. Forbes' emphasis on integrity, sound management, and service as a source of profit. These were the qualities and values that had enabled the Forbes group to exert a constructive and profitable influence on the West for over half a century.

During the Civil War Forbes helped the Governor of Massachusetts put the state on a war footing and organized several regiments of black soldiers. In Washington he assisted the Department of the Navy and organized the Loyal Publication Society, an effective bureau for propaganda. He was a Republican and married Sarah Hathaway of New Bedford, Massachusetts, in 1834. They had six children, one of whom, William H. Forbes, was a financial backer and president of the Bell Telephone Company. (**A.** *DAB; NCAB*, 35:331; *Who Was Who*, vol. H; Sarah Forbes Hughes, ed., *Letters and Recollections of John Murray Forbes*, 2 vols., 1900; H. G. Pearson, *John Murray Forbes: An American Railroad Builder*, 1911. **B.** Thomas C. Cochran, *Americans in East Asia*, 1941; Foster Rhea Dulles, *The Old China Trade*, 1930; Arthur M. Johnson and Barry E. Supple, *Boston Capitalists and Western Railroads*, 1967; Richard C. Overton, *The Burlington Route*, 1965, and *Burlington West*, 1971.)

FORD, HENRY (July 30, 1863–April 7, 1947) and **Henry Ford II** (September 4, 1917–   ). Automobile manufacturers, Ford Motor Company. **Henry Ford** was born in a farmhouse in Greenfield Township (now Dearborn), Wayne County, Michigan, son of William Ford and Mary Litogot. His ancestors immigrated to the United States in 1832, becoming pioneer farmers in the frontier townships around Detroit. Henry was educated in district schools from 1871 to 1879, in the latter year going to Detroit to become a machinist at the James Flower and Bros. Machine Shop. He also took a night job in a jewelry shop, where he repaired watches. In 1880 he joined the Detroit Drydock Company, the largest shipbuilding firm in the city, and was assigned to the machine shop, where he acquired a broad knowledge of diverse types of power plants. Completing his apprenticeship in 1882, he became a road agent for the Westinghouse Engine Company, spending a year servicing steam tractors for farmers in southern Michigan. Then, from 1884 to 1886, he divided his time between operating and repairing steam engines, reluctantly helping his father on the farm, and occasionally working in Detroit factories during the winters.

In 1888 his father gave him a tract of land at Dearborn on the condition that he would abandon the machinist's trade and return to the farm. Henry then built a house on the land and made a small income selling lumber and firewood from the farm. But he did not engage in farming and used his spare time to experiment with steam and gasoline engines in a shop attached to the home. In 1891 he abandoned farming and moved to Detroit, becoming night engineer with the Edison Illuminating Company, at $45 per month. In 1893 he was transferred to the power house in downtown Detroit, becoming its chief engineer at $100 a month. During these years he continued to experiment with a gasoline engine in a small shed behind his Detroit home. About 1896 he completed a four cycle, air-cooled gasoline motor with two cylinders which would develop three to four horsepower. He mounted the engine on a chassis and body built by James W. Bishop, calling it a Quadracycle. Later in the year he sold it for $200 and began work on a second engine.

In the development of his second car, Ford received financial support from Mayor William C. Maybury of Detroit and three associates. During this time (1897–1899) he continued to work at Edison, and by 1899 had produced an operable two passenger vehicle, which established his reputation as one of the automotive pioneers of the city. In 1899, with financial support from William H. Murphy, a wealthy Detroit lumber merchant, and a group of other investors, he established the Detroit Automobile Company, capitalized at $150,000. This was the first company organized in Detroit for the manufacture of autos, but after turning out some twenty vehicles, it went out of business in the fall of 1900. To gain a wider reputation, Ford then turned to auto racing, again backed by Murphy and helped by other technicians. He built a racer with a horizontal engine capable of generating 26 horsepower and entered it in a contest held at Grosse Pointe, Michigan, in 1901. In this race he beat the more powerful and experienced Winton Motor's entry, which revived the enthusiasm of former stockholders and resulted in his firm's reorganization as the Henry Ford Company in November, 1901. The firm was capitalized at $60,000, of which more than one-half was paid in. But dissension soon broke out between Ford and the promoters, partly because he insisted on building a larger and faster car rather than concentrating on a commercial model. When Henry M. Leland was brought into the firm as consulting engineer in 1902, Ford resigned. The firm was then reorganized as the Cadillac Motor Car Company, with Leland as production manager.

Ford again turned to auto racing and began construction of two racing cars, the "Arrow" and the "999." In October, 1902, with Barney Oldfield at the wheel, "999" won the Manufacturer's Challenge Cup at the Grosse Pointe racetrack, setting a new American record. With this victory, Ford again turned his attention to creating a model car capable of competing with such popularly priced cars as Oldsmobile. Needing $3,000 in developmental costs, Ford approached Alexander W. Malcomson, a leading Detroit coal dealer, and in 1902 they formed a partnership to produce a marketable automobile. Ford agreed to contribute his designs and skills, taking charge of manufacturing, while Malcomson financed the project and agreed to handle business operations, which he delegated to a clerk, James Couzens.* Although a model was completed by December, 1902, the high incidence of failure in the infant automobile industry made investors wary. But demand picked up a few months later. Ford and Malcomson moved to larger quarters and built a second and improved model, contracting with outside suppliers, especially Dodge Brothers, for parts.

They were now able to attract a substantial number of investors, and the Ford Motor Company was incorporated in June, 1903, with a capital of $150,000, of which only $28,000 was paid in. Ford and Malcomson were the largest shareholders, with equal amounts of stock. Ford was named vice-president and general manager, Malcolmson was elected treasurer, and Couzens was made secretary. The latter handled office duties, negotiated contracts, attended to advertising, and laid the groundwork for a strong sales organization. The first Ford automobile, the Model A, was brought out in June, 1903, selling for $850. A total of 1,708 sold in the first fifteen months, so a second story was added to the plant. Higher priced B, C, and F models were offered in 1904-1905, and in early 1905 manufacturing operations were transferred to a newer and larger plant.

In the meantime, a dispute had broken out between Ford (supported by Couzens), who advocated a standardized design for a cheap car suitable for quantity production and a mass market, and Malcomson, who wanted production of a heavy, expensive luxury car. The outcome of the dispute was a significant redistribution of power in Ford Motor Company, with Malcomson in 1906 accepting Ford's offer of $175,000 for the purchase of his 255 shares of stock. During that year the other three stockholders also sold their stock, so that Ford held 585 shares, and Couzens 110. Ford was now named president, with Couzens as treasurer. Ford proceeded to translate into reality his concept of a low-cost car for mass use. His first step was the Model N of 1906-1907, which was introduced at $600, but sold at $700. They made 10,000 units of the car and it was very successful, raising the net income of the company to over one million dollars for the first time. But Ford at this time was at work on the basic elements of a "universal car." In 1908 the company increased its capital to $2 million and acquired a sixty acre tract in Highland Park, just north of Detroit, beginning construction of the largest industrial plant in Michigan. Its foreign operations were also initiated at this time, with branches in Canada and Great Britain.

The Model T was introduced in 1908, combining in a standard utility vehicle the features of lightness, durability, economy of operation, efficiency, interchangeable parts, and lower cost. Ford was responsible for the basic concept, and by 1916 he was able to reduce the price of the car to about $350 because of cost-cutting production methods. From its inception to

1927, the Model T was the sole model sold by the company, and most of the time was available only in black. Ford designed the car for rural America, and it was well-suited for travel over poor country roads. It became very popular in the untapped market of the Middle West and Plains states and rode the prosperity of agriculture's "golden age" from 1909 to 1916. Production went from 18,664 to 78,440 in 1911–1912. By 1913 there were 7,000 dealers affiliated with the company, with at least one in every town with a population over 2,000.

The Ford Motor Company became the first auto manufacturer to concentrate on a single model with a standardized chassis made of interchangeable parts. This revolutionary development imposed a new set of technological requirements which were met in the Highland Park plant between 1910 and 1914. During these years the foundations of automotive mass production and the culminating achievement of a continuously moving assembly line were laid in the plant.

These new production techniques raised output to 730,041 by 1916, averaging 2,000 cars per day. But by 1913 Ford found that the speed and monotony of the assembly line work was generating much restiveness and discontent among his workers, and he had serious problems with labor turnover. Thus, he had to give the workers incentive to submit to the new industrial discipline of the moving assembly line. So, in January, 1914, the Ford Motor Company announced a basic wage of $5 a day for all eligible workers in the Ford plants, as well as a reduction in the shift time from nine hours to eight. At this time the highest daily wage in Detroit auto factories was $1.80 for unskilled workers and $2.50 for skilled workers. Thus, his $5 a day made front-page news and turned Henry Ford into a national celebrity. The action was hailed as a landmark of labor-management relations, and he was praised as a prophet of a new industrial order and a high-consumption society. To administer the $5 wage plan, the company established the Sociological Department in 1914, which made "home visits" to determine those workers "eligible" for the $5 wage.

Despite the success of the firm, Ford continued to have disputes with his business colleagues, based upon his drive to have absolute power. He broke with Couzens in 1915, and had disputes with the Dodge Brothers over dividends from 1916 to 1919. Ford lost this battle in the courts and in 1918 resigned as president of the company, announcing plans to start a new and entirely family-owned firm to undersell the Model T. Meanwhile, he began to negotiate through third parties for the purchase of 8,300 shares of stock, comprising the full minority interest of 41.5 percent. He paid $12,500 per share, and $13,444 per share to Couzens. The Dodges received $25 million, and Couzens over $29 million; the total cost to Ford was $105,820,894.57. To finance the purchase, Ford received a credit of $75 million from a financial syndicate of three eastern banks. All Ford enterprises were then absorbed into the Ford Motor Company of Delaware in 1920, with Henry

Ford holding 55.2 percent of the stock, Clara Ford 3.1 percent, and Edsel Ford 41.7 percent. Henry Ford now had centralized authority over the entire operation.

Despite Henry Ford's highly publicized antiwar speeches and actions, with the outbreak of war between the U.S. and Germany he pledged to put his factory at the disposal of the government, and to "operate without one cent of profit." The company filled government contracts for ambulances, trucks, light trucks, Liberty aircraft motors, Eagle boats, gun caissons, shells, armor plate, and helmets. He never fulfilled his promise to return his war profits. Nominally a Republican, he enthusiastically supported Woodrow Wilson in 1916, and in 1918, at Wilson's urging, agreed to enter the Michigan race for the U.S. Senate as an advocate of the League of Nations, entering both the Republican and Democratic primaries. He became the Democratic nominee, but lost the election, which unleashed his bigotry against Jews, whom he blamed for his defeat. He began to publish the *Dearborn Independent* in 1918, which he devoted to anti-Semitic propaganda. It reached a peak circulation of 425,000 in 1923, but ceased publication at the end of 1927 with a deficit of nearly $5 million.

Ford responded to the postwar recession of 1920–1921 by sharply reducing prices on the Model T, initiating ruthless internal economies, and shutting down the plant for six weeks. When he reopened he assembled some 90,000 vehicles made of materials purchased at deflated prices. He then forced these cars on Ford dealers, who were generally able to obtain financing from local bankers. In this way, Ford was able to realize $24.7 million from the sale of cars and parts, and had saved $28 million by reducing inventories. Combined with a cash reserve, this gave him liquid assets of $87.3 million to pay off debts amounting to some $58 million. Ford then embarked on a program of vigorous growth and expansion both at home and abroad. His most innovative technological achievement was his development of the immense River Rouge plant in Dearborn, which he attempted to make into a virtually self-contained industrial city covering 1,115 acres. He built an enormous complex of blast furnaces, coke-ovens, dock facilities, the world's largest foundry, a glass plant, and other structures. He also acquired forest and iron mines in upper Michigan and coal mines in Kentucky and West Virginia to ensure his supplies. Between 1924 and 1927 the principal car-making factories at Highland Park were transferred to River Rouge. But he found that comprehensive vertical integration at River Rouge was impractical, so he began to create decentralized "village industries" in Michigan, Ohio, and other states. He also acquired a glass plant in Pennsylvania, established another in Minnesota, and developed a rubber plantation in Brazil to guarantee a rubber supply. In 1929 he purchased the Lincoln Motor Car Company at a sacrifice price, ousted the owners, Henry Leland and his son, and for the first time diversified the Ford line of cars. He also helped pioneer commercial aviation in the United

States, setting up a factory at Dearborn to manufacture the all-metal Ford monoplane—the "tin goose." He bought the Detroit, Toledo and Ironton Railroad in 1920, which he operated until 1929, when he sold it to the Pennsylvania Railroad.

In 1921 the Model T accounted for about 56 percent of all cars sold in the United States, and it continued to increase its output after that time. But since other companies were also expanding very rapidly during the 1920s, its share of the market had fallen to 45 percent by 1925. Ford answered the challenge by cutting his prices, but it didn't work. The Model T no longer satisfied the more sophisticated preferences of the cities and suburbs, where the interest was more in comfort, fashion, and style. By 1924 the principal threat to his supremacy was General Motors' Chevrolet, which cost more than the Ford, but was more stylish. Ford refused to innovate in style or adopt new technological innovations such as hydraulic brakes. By 1926 Ford production accounted for only 34 percent of auto output, so Henry Ford decided to bring out a new car. In 1927 he shut down his plants for a massive changeover, taking five months to develop the Model A. The changeover cost $250 million, and within two weeks of its introduction the Model A had received 400,000 orders. But production lags proved costly to Ford, and it ended that production year with only 15.4 percent of the market and a net loss of $74 million. A surge in production in 1929 enabled Ford to outstrip Chevrolet and take about 44 percent of the market, but then the depression hit, which crushed the industry and caused a huge decline in Model A sales. Barely four years after its introduction, the Model A began to encounter buyer resistance, and it was discontinued after 1931. Ford was now a follower of automotive trends, rather than a leader. In 1932 he introduced a V-8 engine, but sales lagged, with losses totalling $25 million. This was his last automotive innovation, and by 1936 Ford Motor had settled into third place among U.S. auto manufacturers.

After 1932 Henry Ford spent more and more time on the development of "Greenfield Village," a historical museum and village in Dearborn on which he spent $30 million, and less time on the auto company. By the early 1930s he had come to depend heavily on Harry H. Bennett, an ex-boxer, who was director of personnel and plant security. Ford had had a poor record of labor-management relations throughout the 1920s and 30s, and during the depression the firm's wages lagged behind those of its competitors. After 1937 Ford was also the only holdout to the United Auto Workers among the major auto plants, causing much labor violence at his plants. Ford finally gave in to the union in 1941 when 70 percent of the workers voted for the union. After Henry Ford suffered a stroke in 1938, Bennett took over more and more power from him, and was responsible for many of the company's worst excesses during this period.

The principal wartime accomplishment of his company was the huge factory at Willow Run, near Ypsilanti, Michigan, for producing the B-24

Liberator Bomber. Upon the death of his son, Edsel, in 1943, Henry Ford again assumed the presidency of the firm, but Bennett wielded most of the power, and planned to take full control of the company when Henry died. He was thwarted in these plans by Henry Ford II, the eldest grandson, who had joined the company in 1943. Young Ford obtained the resignation of his grandfather in 1945 and removed Harry Bennett from the firm.

Henry Ford was an Episcopalian and married Clara Bryant in 1888. His only child was Edsel Bryant Ford (1893–1943), and together they set up the Ford Foundation in 1936 as a small family foundation to preserve family control of Ford Motor Company. Ninety-five percent of the Ford Company stock went into the foundation with the balance going to the family heirs, which saved a federal estate tax of some $321 million. Edsel Ford became secretary of Ford Motor Company in 1915, upon the resignation of James Couzens. Several years later he also became treasurer. From 1915 onward, Edsel Ford took a leading role in all aspects of the motor company, helping to introduce the Fordson Tractor, and watching over sales, advertising, and foreign operations. In 1918 he was elected president of the company, but was merely a figurehead for his father, who held the real power. He married Eleanor Lowther Clay, niece of Joseph L. Hudson,* the Detroit department store owner. They had four sons: Henry Ford II; Benson Ford (b. 1919); Joseph Ford (b. 1923); and William Clay Ford (b. 1925).

Henry Ford II was born in Dearborn, Michigan, and educated at Detroit University School and Hotchkiss School. In 1936 he entered Yale as an engineering student, but later switched to sociology. He spent four years there, but never graduated. He served in the U.S. Navy during World War II, and in 1943 was released from the Navy to return to Ford Motor Company. In 1944 he was made a vice-president and replaced his grandfather as president in 1945. Henry II remained president of the firm until 1960, when he became chairman and chief executive officer, a post he held until 1980.

After wresting control of the company from Harry Bennett in 1945, Henry II began the massive recovery of the firm, which was losing money at the rate of $9.5 million a month. He saved the company in 1945 by surrounding himself with men ideally suited for their roles in the enterprise: John R. Davis; Charles R. ("Tex") Thornton*; Ernest R. Breech; Robert S. McNamara*; Arjay Miller; and Lee Iacocca*. When he took over the company there was no accounts system, and there had never been an audit in the firm's history. In 1937 the company was making a profit of only $5 a car, compared to $50 for Chevrolet and $39 for Plymouth. After his takeover, he fired more than 1,000 executives, including many of Bennett's cohorts. He sold the Brazilian rubber plantations, which had cost the firm more than $20 million, plus the soybean farms, mineral and timber tracts, and many of its other properties.

His most important acquisition in 1946 was Ernest R. Breech, president of Bendix Corporation (a General Motors subsidiary), who had tripled production in two years there. Breech brought new blood into the company, and they reorganized and decentralized Ford in a pattern similar to that at General Motors. An audit system was established, and automation was begun at the Ford plants, which saved the company millions. Henry Ford II also attempted to improve the firm's terrible record in labor relations, and in 1946 the company signed an agreement with the U.A.W. for an 18¢ per hour raise, getting a union guarantee against illegal strikes, which had been plaguing the plant in the postwar period. Another contract in 1948 gave a 15 percent wage hike, and in 1947 the employees were allowed to smoke in the plant for the first time. In 1949 a contract with the union set up the industry's first pension plan, providing $1.00 per month to each Ford worker with more than thirty years on the job.

In 1947 Breech and Henry II decided to bring out an all-new car in 1949, the first major postwar innovation in the industry. The model sold 806,766 units and Ford had its biggest year since 1929. In 1950 it had net profits of $265 million. In 1953 Ford moved past Chrysler into second place in sales in the industry. In 1954 a new model with an overhead valve V-8 engine sold 1.4 million units, putting Ford just 17,000 behind Chevrolet. Between 1945 and 1955 the company spent one billion dollars on expansion, and in 1956 the firm went public for the first time. The $690 million stock sale was the largest in the history of Wall Street. Ford Motor had finally become a mature, well-structured enterprise, and its recovery was legendary in American industry.

In the years after the mid-1950s Ford Motor Company was one of the most innovative in the industry, introducing the Falcon, the Fairlane, the Mustang, and the Maverick. They also went into racing in a major way, with a multimillion dollar program that was the most extensive in the industry. But Henry Ford II proved to be as autocratic and difficult as his grandfather, and the company has one of the highest executive turnover rates in American industry. Its sales level also seemed to peak at some 25 to 30 percent of the market, and Ford has not beaten Chevrolet since 1959. The Lincoln-Mercury Division sells just about 5 percent of the market, and Ford has dumped more than $350 million into Philco Corporation, including the $94 million purchase price in 1961.

The Falcon, which was developed by Robert McNamara, was the first of the Big Three's compact cars. It came out in 1959 and sold 417,107 units, an all-time first year record. Then, in 1964, Lee Iacocca redesigned the Falcon and brought out the Mustang to appeal to younger drivers. The Mustang sold 417,811 units in its first year, and introduced the small, peppy sports-like car to America. Then, in 1969, came the Maverick, designed to compete against foreign competition. It sold 150,000 in six months. A major failure of the company during Henry II's tenure was the Edsel, an attempt to crack the medium-priced market. Introduced with vast market research and great fanfare in 1957, it sold just 110,247 units in three years before it was dropped, costing the company $250 million. By 1969 Ford Motor Company was America's third largest corporation, with total assets of $9 billion, 435,000 employees, operations in more than 33 foreign countries, and annual gross sales of $14 billion.

Henry Ford II was raised a Methodist, but converted to Roman Catholicism when he married his first wife, Anne McDonnell of New York, in 1940. They were divorced, and when he married his second wife, Maria Christina Vettore Austin in 1965, he was excommunicated from the Catholic Church. He married for the third time in 1980. He has three children: Charlotte, Anne, and Edsel Ford II.

Benson Ford became a vice-president of Ford Motor Company in the mid-1940s, continuing to serve in that position into the 1970s. William Clay Ford was also a vice-president of Ford Motor Company after 1956, and became president and owner of the Detroit Lions professional football club. (**A.** *DAB*, Supplement 3; *NCAB*, E:10; 38:1; G:199; *Current Biography*, December, 1944; May, 1947; 1946; *New York Times*, October 19, 1969; *Who's Who in America, 1978-79*; H. H. Bennett, *We Never Called Him Henry*, 1951; Roger Burlingame, *Henry Ford*, 1957; John Cate Dahlinger, *The Secret Life of Henry Ford*, 1978; Booter Herndon, *Ford*, 1969; David L. Lewis, *The Public Image of Henry Ford*, 1976; Allan Nevins and F. E. Hill, *Ford: The Times, the Man and the Company*, 1954; K. Sward, *The Legend of Henry Ford*, 1942; Reymold M. Wik, *Henry Ford and Grass Roots America*, 1972. **B.** Alfred D. Chandler Jr., *Giant Enterprise*, 1964; Allan Nevins and F. E. Hill, *Ford, Expansion and Challenge*, 1957, and *Ford: Decline and Rebirth*, 1963; John B. Rae, *American Automobile Manufacturers*, 1959; Charles E. Sorenson, *My Forty Years With Ford*, 1956.)

FORD, JOHN BATISTE (November 17, 1811–May 1, 1903) and **Edward Ford** (January 21, 1843–June 24, 1920). Glass manufacturers, Pittsburgh Plate Glass Company and Edward Ford Plate Glass Company. **John B. Ford** was born in Danville, Kentucky, son of pioneer parents, Jonathan Ford and Margaret Batiste. He received a scanty education at home and became an apprentice to John Jackson, a saddler. He soon left that position, traveling to New Albany, Indiana, and then to Greenville, Indiana, where he learned the saddlery trade. Later, he bought his master's shop, to which he added a grain, flour, and commission business. After a time he sold the saddle business and opened a general store in Greenville. Prospering in this endeavor, he began the manufacture of kitchen cabinets and feed cutting boxes for farmers. Just prior to the Civil War, he set up a foundry and rolling mill, with railroad and commercial iron as his products.

Ford was attracted to the prospects of steamboat building, and during the Civil War he and his two sons built and sold river boats and operated a line of thirty-eight steamboats and flatboats, which they captained. The fleet served both the North and the South in a purely commercial way during the war, being always in danger of destruction from one side or the other, but it was financially very successful. At about this time Ford sold his iron business for $150,000 and embarked upon the manufacture of plate glass. Sometime before this he had become interested in the plate glass industry of Belgium and England. Writing to the *Scientific American*, he raised the question of the possibility of making plate glass in America. The answer given to him on all sides was discouraging. The cost of labor in the United States was said to be too high and raw materials too hard to secure.

Despite this, Ford obtained numerous glass formulae, engaged the services of expert workmen, and imported European machinery. With his sons, he worked for ten years in a factory situated in New Albany, Indiana, just across from Louisville, Kentucky. The depression following the Civil War and the Panic of 1873 deprived John Ford of most of his fortune, and he was forced to finance the undertaking with $30,000 obtained from the sale of a glass tube to New York interests. This tube was a rough glass sewer pipe which made the detection of stoppage easier. In addition, he raised $20,000 as an agent for the sale of General Fremont's western holdings.

At the age of 73 John Ford moved to Creighton, near Pittsburgh, Pennsylvania, where he established the Ford Glass Company. The venture was successful from the very beginning, and the company soon opened a number of plants. Ford City in Pennsylvania became "glass city," and Ford made a second great fortune in the industry. Later, when he entered one of the earliest great industrial combinations, he and his sons held the majority of the stock of the Pittsburgh Plate Glass Company, of which the Ford Company was the largest unit. In this combination he was associated with John Pitcairn,* of the Pennsylvania Railroad, who acted as president. In 1893 the Fords disagreed with Pitcairn on a question of policy and decided to sell their holdings. His son, Edward, then established a large plant in Ohio, and the elder Ford also developed a large firm in Wyandotte, Michigan, called the Michigan Alkali Company, which was the first American firm to manufacture soda ash, baking soda, and other important by-products. He also aided in bringing into utilization the gas deposits of the great Pittsburgh district and conducted a successful pipeline company himself.

John Ford was a Methodist, and built and equipped churches in Greenville, Ford City, and Wyandotte. He married Mary Bower in 1831 and they had two sons and a daughter. The younger son, Emory Low Ford (1846-1900) was born in Greenville and was educated there and at Merchants College in Pittsburgh. He was associated with his father and brother in steamboats and the glass business, serving as secretary and treasurer of Pittsburgh Plate Glass until 1894, when he retired. His grandson, Emory M. Ford (1906-1971) became chairman of the board of the Wyandotte Chemical Corp.

Edward Ford was born in Greenville, Indiana, and was educated in the public schools of New Albany, Indiana, and at Bryant and Stratton Business College in Indianapolis. At eighteen he became a clerk with his father's steamboat company, and for ten years navigated boats on the Ohio and Mississippi rivers. In 1868 he became associated with his father and brother in the manufacture of glass; the firm was first known as the Star Glass Company, and later as John B. Ford and Sons. In 1880 they organized the Pittsburgh Plate Glass Company in Pittsburgh, to build a factory in Creighton, Pennsylvania. Three years later a second plant was erected at Tarentum, Pennsylvania. In 1888 they constructed what was then the largest plate glass factory in the world at Ford City in Armstrong County, Pennsylvania. He retired from PPG after fifteen years of service as president and general manager.

He then undertook the active management of the Michigan Alkali Company in Wyandotte, of which he was also president. In 1898 he established in a suburb of Toledo, Ohio, the Edward Ford Plate Glass Company, and erected the largest plate glass factory in the world. The production of the plant in the first year was over one million square feet of polished plate glass. This industry became the nucleus of the town of Rossford, Ohio, which at the time of his death had a population of 4,000, and also had the largest beet sugar mill in the U.S., the largest feed mill in the country, and several other manufacturing establishments. At the time of his death, Edward Ford Plate Glass comprised fifteen large buildings, covering 75 acres and employing 1,500.

Edward Ford was a Presbyterian and later a Christian Scientist. A member of the Republican party, he served on the city council of New Albany from 1870 to 1872. He was twice married: to Evelyn C. Penn of New Orleans, Louisiana, in 1864, who died in 1870; and to Carrie J. Ross of Zanesville, Ohio, in 1872. He had three daughters and two sons. Of his sons, George Ross Ford became president of Ford Plate Glass Company, and John Batiste Ford II (1866–1941) became president of Michigan Alkali Company, and of Huron Portland Cement Company and Huron Transportation Company. (**A.** *DAB; NCAB*, 13:505; 18:312; 45:166; *New York Times*, March 2, 1903; June 26, 1920; *Who Was Who*, vol. H. **B.** Warren C. Scoville, *Revolution in Glassmaking*, 1948.)

FORGAN, JAMES BERWICK (April 11, 1852–October 28, 1924). Banker, First National Bank of Chicago and Chicago Clearing House Commission. Born at St. Andrews, Scotland, son of Robert Forgan and Elizabeth Berwick. His father was a manufacturer of golf clubs and golf balls. James Forgan was educated at Forres Academy and apprenticed to a lawyer in St. Andrews. Within a year, however, he took up an apprenticeship as a clerk in the branch of the Royal Bank of Scotland at St. Andrews. He was subsequently sent to Canada as an employee of the Bank of British North America, arriving in Montreal in 1873. After a time he was transferred to a

Halifax, Nova Scotia bank, where he remained for over a year. He then spent a year and a half with an insurance company before returning to banking with the local branch of the Bank of Nova Scotia in 1875. He was made inspector of branch banks, and in 1885 became agent in charge of the branch at Minneapolis, Minnesota. In 1888 he was named cashier of Northwestern National Bank in that city.

At about this time Forgan became an American citizen and made contact with Lyman Gage,* the president of the First National Bank of Chicago and later Secretary of the Treasury under McKinley. Through Gage, Forgan in 1892 became vice-president of the Chicago bank, remaining with it until his death over thirty years later. By 1900 he was principal stockholder and president of the concern. Through a series of mergers with smaller Chicago banks, and by radical changes in the internal organization of the bank, he made the First National one of the most powerful financial institutions in the Middle West.

His most important contribution to banking, however, lay in his activities with the Chicago Clearing House Commission, with which he was associated for twenty-five years. He was largely responsible for the establishment of the system in 1906, which provided bank examinations for member banks. He also took a lively interest in currency reform, and was vice-chairman of the currency committee of the American Bankers Association. He served six years as a director of the Federal Reserve Bank at Chicago, and was member of the executive committee and president of the Federal Advisory Council of the Reserve System during a like period. During the fifteen years of his administration, the assets of First National grew from $50 million to $250 million.

His brother, David Robinson Forgan (b. 1862), became vice-president of First National of Chicago in 1900. In 1907 he reorganized the National City Bank of Chicago, resigned from First National, and became head of the new organization. This bank also was to become a major force in the financial world. David's son, James Russell Forgan (1892–1974), was with National City Bank for a time and then opened his own stock brokerage firm in Chicago.

James B. Forgan was a Presbyterian and a Republican and married Mary Ellen Murray, daughter of a Halifax, Nova Scotia, merchant in the early 1870s. They had three sons and a daughter. (*DAB; NCAB*, 18:176; *New York Times*, October 29, 1924; *Who Was Who*, vol. 1.)

FORTEN, JAMES (1766–1842) Black sail maker and abolitionist. Born in Philadelphia, Pennsylvania, son of a free black father. His great-grandfather had been brought from Africa as a slave, and his grandfather had been born a slave, but became a free man later in his life. James was educated in the Quaker school of the abolitionist Anthony Benezet, but quit to take a job in 1775 when his father died. He worked in a grocery store to support his mother, and at fifteen enlisted in the Revolutionary army as a powder boy on a privateer. He was captured by the British and faced enslavement in the West Indies, but was spared because the British captain's son had taken a liking to him. Then the father, Captain Beasley, offered to educate and rear him in England with his son, but Forten refused to desert his own country. Beasley then sent him to the prison ship, *Jersey*, anchored off Long Island. Thousands died on the disease-ridden ship, but Forten survived seven months' imprisonment. He then returned home to his mother, and after that spent a year in England. Upon his return to Philadelphia, he apprenticed himself to a white sail maker in the city, Robert Bridges.

Forten proved so able at his craft that several years later, in 1786, Bridges made the twenty-year-old black youth foreman of the sail loft. When Bridges retired in 1798, Forten took control of the business. He prospered, employing as many as forty men, white and black, and amassed a fortune of $100,000 by 1832. A major reason for Forten's success was his invention of a device to handle sails.

Despite his wealth and status in the community, Forten nonetheless found himself frequently insulted and humiliated because of his color. He thus became a leading abolitionist. In 1800 he circulated petitions protesting fugitive slave legislation. Standing firmly in favor of racial equality, he strongly opposed colonization arguments and chaired protest meetings against the American Colonization Society for many years. He was a leader in the Negro Convention Movement of 1830 and after. Forten supported William Lloyd Garrison, enlisted black subscribers for his *Liberator*, and served on the board of managers of Garrison's American Anti-Slavery Society. He contributed more money to the abolition cause than anyone except Arthur and Lewis Tappan.* His son-in-law, Robert Purvis, was a leading black abolitionist, and his granddaughter, Charlotte L. Forten, also became a leader for black rights. (*DAB*.)

FOX, WILLIAM (January 1, 1879–May 8, 1952). Motion picture executive, Fox Film Corporation and Loew's Incorporated. Born in Tulchva, Hungary, son of Jewish parents, Michael Fox and Anna Fried. His parents brought him to the United States as an infant and settled in New York City, where he was educated in the public schools. After working for a few years in the garment industry, Fox started his motion picture career in 1904 when he bought a nickleodeon theater in Brooklyn. Within four years he had a chain of over a dozen neighborhood nickleodeons, located in the densely populated tenement districts. In 1908 the city of New York, at the urging of the police department, began a crack-down on nickleodeon operations, resulting in the revocation of 600 nickleodeon licenses in the city. Fox led a group of the theater owners in obtaining an injunction to allow the theaters to remain open, but new laws within a few months raised the licensing fees, placed nickleodeons under police jurisdiction, and controlled children's attendance.

For many small nickleodeon owners in New York these new regulations were a disaster, and they soon went out of business. Fox, in a manner characteristic of his later career, turned the new laws to his own advantage. Recognizing that the new statutes mandated a larger-scale and more expensive manner of operation, Fox began taking over vaudeville houses in New York City, with one-half of the program devoted to movies. With this move Fox accomplished two objectives. First, he made vaudeville accessible to the working classes for the first time, and, second, by his use of the larger and more comfortable theaters he was able to attract the vaudeville-going middle class to the movies for the first time. As a consequence, vaudeville acts, which had trouble filling their theaters, were now playing to packed houses, and the middle classes now became an integral component of the movie-going public for the first time.

Fox's next step was to expand into film distribution, organizing the Greater New York Film Rental Company. This activity would, in 1912, bring him into conflict with Thomas A. Edison* and associates who had organized the General Film Company in 1910 to absorb all licensed film exchanges in the United States. Edison's company, known as "The Trust," was determined to establish a monopoly over the production, distribution, and exhibition of films; by 1912 had bought out 57 of the 58 exchanges they had licensed to handle their films, with only Fox holding out. When Fox refused to sell out to them, his license was revoked by the Trust. In a reversal of the usual procedure in these operations, Fox took General Film to court, winning the right to keep his license, becoming the only distributor to successfully resist takeover.

After winning his court battle, Fox decided to move into the production end of the industry, making his own pictures to guarantee a steady supply of products for distribution and exhibition. With this move Fox pioneered in the vertical integration of the movie industry, combining production, distribution, and exhibition under single or affiliated ownership. This soon became the standard arrangement in the industry, until it was disrupted by a Justice Department antitrust case a generation later. In 1915 Fox started the Fox Film Corporation, with his first production, *Carmen*, starring Theda Bara. In 1919 he acquired a studio on Tenth Avenue in New York City, producing dozens of pictures there; but at the same time he also began producing films in Hollywood, California, a suburb of Los Angeles. Before long he transferred all his production facilities to Hollywood. Along with Adolph Zukor,* Fox was largely responsible for making Hollywood the movie capital of the world, both in physical and symbolic terms.

After World War I Fox made his greatest impression on the movie industry, producing such films as *What Price Glory?* (1927); *Evangeline* (1929); *Cleopatra* (1934); *Les Miserables* (1935); and *Tale of Two Cities* (1935). In 1925 Fox spent $60,000 to acquire a 90 percent interest in the western hemisphere rights to Tri-Engon, which included important fly-wheel patents for talking pictures. He was thus the only one of the major film producers to demonstrate an interest in the new process, which was further enhanced a year later when he purchased MovieTone, a sound film process. Although it was the upstart Warner brothers* who brought out the first successful "talkie" with the *Jazz Singer* in 1927, Fox followed close on their heels with sound production. For several years Warner Brothers and Fox were the only two studios involved in sound production, and they engaged in vigorous competition to expand their empires. Both firms acquired hundreds of movie theaters, and both made a bid to acquire the exhibitor-owned production company, First National, with Warner emerging victorious.

Fox's next step was to put in motion a plan to purchase a controlling interest in Loew's Incorporated following the death of Marcus Loew.* Besides controlling a large chain of theaters, Loew's subsidiary on the production side was Metro-Goldwyn-Mayer, the acquisition of which would give Fox control of two of Hollywood's largest studios. Fox planned to merge MGM, under the leadership of Louis B. Mayer,* into his own production company. To accomplish his objectives, Fox had to convince Nicholas Schenck,* president of Loew's, to assemble a sufficient block of available shares to give Fox control, at the same time keeping the deal secret from MGM executives. Schenck's price for delivery of Loew's stock was $10 million, a full 25 percent over and above what Fox was willing to pay for the shares. Nevertheless Fox went ahead with the deal, getting his creditors to advance him more than $50 million, plus additional millions for his purchase of Gaumont British Picture Corporation, the largest production, distribution, and exhibition company in Great Britain. At this point Fox's massive entertainment empire began to unravel.

The total value of Fox's properties on the eve of the Great Depression was estimated at some $300 million and included the Fox Film Corporation, Loew's Incorporated, and Gaumont Pictures in Britain. In the summer of 1929 Fox was injured in an auto accident and a few months later the stock market crash took its toll on his heavily mortgaged financial empire. Within a year he was forced to sell his personal holdings in the United States and abroad for about $18 million, and a few years later he declared bankruptcy. Finally, in 1941, he pleaded guilty to and served a short prison sentence on a charge of attempting to bribe a judge during his bankruptcy proceedings. Meanwhile, Fox Film Corporation suffered heavy losses under its new ownership, barely escaping receivership, and in 1935 merged with the up and coming Twentieth Century Film Corporation.

Fox blamed much of his troubles during this period on his Wall Street banker, Halsey, Stuart and Company, which he accused of conspiring with AT & T to gain control of his assets, loot them, and abandon them, with the connivance of numerous attorneys, financiers, government officials, and many of his own trusted executives. To a certain extent, however, Fox was equally culpable. Much of his energy during the late 1920s and early 30s was spent in political machinations with the antitrust division of the Justice Department in order to obtain a favorable ruling on his acquisition of Loew's. In the end he failed, as the Justice Department secured a negative ruling on the merger from the courts. One of the reasons that Fox was the first movie tycoon to suffer at the hands of the federal government was that he had incurred the enmity of Louis B. Mayer of MGM. Mayer was one of the most powerful factors in California Republican politics, and even Fox's personal appeals to President Hoover* were unsuccessful in getting the Justice Department to accommodate him. In 1944 Fox tried to stage an unsuccessful comeback in the film industry.

Jewish and a Republican, Fox married Eva Leo in 1900, and they had two daughters. (**A.** *DAB*, Supplement 5; *Biographical Encyclopedia of American Jews*; *New York Times*, May 5, 1939; May 9, 1952; *Who Was Who*, vol. 3; Upton Sinclair, *Upton Sinclair Presents William Fox*, 1933. **B.** Philip French, *Movie Moguls*, 1969; Bernard B. Hampton, *A History of the Movies*, 1931; Kenneth Macgowen, *Behind the Screen*, 1965; Robert Sklar, *Movie Made America*, 1975.)

FRENCH FAMILY: George Henry French (February 23, 1825–October 12, 1888); **Nathaniel French** (September 7, 1854–February 14, 1920); **George Watson French** (October 26, 1858–   ). Metal wheel manufacturers, Bettandorf Metal Wheel Company and French and Hecht. **George H. French** was born in Andover, Massachusetts, son of Capt. George French and Mary Richardson. His family had come to Massachusetts in 1635. He was educated at Phillips Academy in Andover and at Lowell, Massachusetts, high school. His business career began in 1840 when he entered the hide and leather business in Boston. Although he was successful, he was forced to sell his interests and seek a change of climate for reasons of health. He moved to Davenport, Iowa, where he entered the lumber business, first with James Cannon and later with John L. Davies. The firm of French and Davies furnished most of the lumber for the barracks and other bids at Camp McClelland and to the prisons on Rock Island.

In 1875 French became president of the Eagle Manufacturing Company, makers of agricultural implements, which he ran until his death. He also organized and was president of the First National Bank of Davenport and was active in obtaining the great governmental arsenal on Rock Island. He was also prominent in western railroad development, serving as president of the Davenport and St. Paul Railroad, and was one of the promoters of the Hennepin Canal.

A Republican and a Unitarian, he served as president of the Davenport School Board, as mayor of the city from 1861 to 1863, and on the governor's staff during the balance of the Civil War. He married Frances Wood

Morton, daughter of Marcus Morton, governor of Massachusetts, in 1848. They had six children, including Nathaniel and George W. French.

Nathaniel French was born in Andover, Massachusetts, and graduated from Griswold College in Davenport in 1873. He subsequently spent two years at Heidelberg and the Sorbonne. Returning to the United States, he received his law degree from Harvard in 1876. In that same year he began in practice with Col. Robert G. Ingersoll in Peoria, Illinois. Returning to Davenport in 1879, he organized the firm of Thompson and French with John W. Thompson. In 1882 he was appointed city attorney, and the following year was elected judge of the circuit court until 1885, when he resumed private practice, specializing in patent law.

After the death of his father in 1888, he discontinued his law practice and joined his brother, George W., in conducting Eagle Manufacturing Company. This company, under his direction, made the first issue of industrial pre-ferred stock in the United States, and continued the manufacture of agricul-tural implements until 1897, when the business was sold and the plant moved to Kansas City. Meanwhile, in 1888, he and his brother had become associated with William Peter Bettandorf in the organization of the Bettandorf Metal Wheel Company. Several years later they purchased Bettandorf's interest, gaining control of the company. In 1909 the firm was merged into French and Hecht, which became the recognized leader of Davenport's industrial scene and the largest manufacturer of metal wheels in the world. They also established a large branch plant at Springfield, Ohio.

From 1915 to 1917 Nathaniel aided in the reorganization of the Chicago, Rock Island and Pacific Railroad, and was involved in the Iola Portland Cement Company, which was later absorbed by the International Cement Company. He had an interest in the Sylvan Steel Company, which merged with Republic Iron and Steel, and had many other financial and industrial undertakings. Originally a Democrat, he later became an independent in politics. A member of the Episcopal Church, he married Marion M. Eldridge of Binghamton, New York, in 1883. They had two children.

George W. French was educated at Griswold Academy in Davenport and at Phillips Academy in Andover. He entered business with Eagle Manufac-turing Company, succeeding his father as president in 1888. He remained with the firm until it was sold in 1897. He had also earlier become involved with the Bettandorf Metal Wheel Company, which became French and Hecht in 1909, and was incorporated under that same name in 1927. George W. French was elected president of the new corporation. He was also chairman of the board of the Republic Iron and Steel Company for a time and director of the Chicago, Rock Island and Pacific Railroad.

A Republican and an Episcopalian, he married Clara V. Decker of Davenport in 1886. She died in 1908 and three years later he married Anna E. Decker, her sister. He had one son. (*NCAB*, 21:368; C:451.)

FRICK, HENRY CLAY (December 19, 1849–December 2, 1919). Coke operator and steel manufacturer, H. C. Frick Coke Company and Carnegie Steel Company. Born in West Overton, Westmoreland County, Pennsylvania, son of John W. Frick and Elizabeth Overholt, of Swiss and Mennonite backgrounds. Young Frick grew up on his father's hard-scrabble farm and attended district schools during the winter, achieving only a sporadic education. He soon grew to have only disdain for his unsuccessful father, while admiring his grandfather, Abraham Overholt, who had made a fortune distilling Old Overholt whiskey. After working for a time in an uncle's store in Mt. Pleasant, Pennsylvania, and for a store in Pittsburgh, Frick obtained a position as a bookkeeper in his grandfather's distillery.

While still working in the distillery, Frick, along with several associates, began building and operating coke ovens in the Connellsville coke district in 1870. Recognizing the ascendency of steel production in the Pittsburgh area, he knew steel depended upon coke and planned to supply as much of it as he could to the industry. To organize the H. C. Frick Coke Company in 1871 Frick called on Judge Thomas Mellon, of the Pittsburgh banking family, to provide funds for the venture. Mellon had known Frick's grandfather quite well, and in the end was convinced to risk $10,000 on the venture. Frick's initial expansion and success seemed suddenly stalled by the panic and depression of 1873, which hit the Connellsville district very hard. Frick saw this as a golden opportunity rather than as a disaster and convinced Mellon to advance him more money, thereby buying more coal lands at bargain prices. When prosperity returned, coke prices rose steadily, and both he and Mellon made a fortune. By 1880 Frick had 1,000 coke ovens and 3,000 acres of land and was worth more than one million dollars.

In the meantime, Andrew Carnegie,* Frick's largest coke customer, had quietly been acquiring stock in H. C. Frick Coke Company. In 1881, while Frick was honeymooning in New York City, Carnegie met with him and announced that they were now partners. Although this was the first Frick had heard of the arrangement, he rapidly agreed to it, and in 1881 the Frick Coke Company was reorganized with a capital stock of $2 million. By 1883 Carnegie owned a majority of the shares, but Frick continued as president. Although friction developed between the two men in 1887 over Frick's hard-handed treatment of labor problems in the coal fields, in contrast to Carnegie's more conciliatory approach, Carnegie was nonetheless impressed with Frick's executive ability. When Frick resigned as president over this disagreement, Carnegie invited him to return to the office and allowed him a free hand in labor-management relations in the coke fields. Carnegie was to have even greater responsibilities in mind for him.

The Carnegie steel firm underwent rapid expansion during the 1880s, but by the latter part of the decade showed the need for a forceful executive. With the death of Tom Carnegie in 1886, nominal leadership of the firm had passed to Henry Phipps,* but he had shown himself incapable of handling the responsibilities. Carnegie also wanted to install a new organizational structure to maximize the advantages of horizontal and vertical integration. Carnegie wanted an executive officer between him and the operational managers, someone already attuned to his goals and methods, who could effectively coordinate all efforts in the rapidly expanding Carnegie properties. Accordingly, in 1887 Frick was invited to acquire a 2 percent interest in Carnegie Brothers and Company, and in 1889 took up an 11 percent interest and was named chairman of the firm. The steel firm was then reorganized, with the reorganization including the building of connecting railroads, the improvement of operating methods, the dismissal of some of Carnegie's early partners, and the advancement of capable young men such as Charles M. Schwab* and Thomas Morrison. Under Frick's stewardship the profits of Carnegie Steel rose rapidly, from $2 million in 1888 to $3.5 million in 1889, and to $5.4 million in 1890.

Frick's first achievement as Carnegie chairman was the acquisition of Duquesne Steel Company. Duquesne Steel at that time was the most modern steel works in the world, and its acquisition allowed Carnegie Steel to emerge at the forefront of scientific technology. The Duquesne firm had been suffering from labor problems, however, and in 1890 Frick offered the owners $1 million in bonds for the company, which they accepted. Before the bonds matured in five years, they had earned the principal and interest five times over. Once Duquesne was absorbed, Frick began to streamline the entire company. In 1892 Carnegie Steel Company, Limited took over all assets of Carnegie Brothers and of Carnegie Phipps. The new firm had a nominal capital of $25 million (although its real worth far exceeded that figure), and owned three complete steel mills, plus Keystone Bridge, Union Iron, Lucy Furnaces, and other supportive operations. Frick also had plans for more extensive consolidation and vertical integration, but before he could put these into effect, the Homestead strike broke out.

Over the years prior to 1892, the Carnegie mills had experienced few labor problems. Carnegie had concentrated on keeping his mills running full at all times, and had not adopted the militantly anti-union stance of other steel employers. Although Carnegie had constantly pressured Captain William R. Jones* to cut wages, the latter had persuaded him that high wages made happy and productive workers. By 1892 Jones was dead from a mill accident and Carnegie now put full confidence in Frick to handle contract negotiations with the Amalgamated Association, while Carnegie himself sailed off to Scotland. Both men, however, wanted the union out of the mill, and Carnegie was well aware of Frick's stern anti-labor methods. Frick then took the offensive against the union. He built a large wooden stockade around the plant, complete with watch towers and rifle slits, referred to by the workers as "Fort Frick." Next he ordered 300 Pinkerton guards to take up positions in the plant. When they attempted to enter the plant at night, the guards were met with a hail of fire in a battle that lasted all day. With the defeat of the Pinkertons, Frick persuaded the governor to send in 8,000 national guard troops to occupy the plant. Frick's unyielding stance was ultimately successful, but Frick himself was shot and stabbed by Alexander Berkman, an anarchist who had no connection with the union, and nearly died from his wounds.

At first Carnegie was elated with Frick's victory over the union, but as public opinion turned against the firm, his attitude toward Frick privately turned cool. Although Frick was to significantly expand Carnegie Steel's operations in several areas over the next couple of years, relations between the two men were increasingly strained. In 1894 Frick submitted his resignation to Carnegie over a minor disagreement, and Carnegie accepted it. Frick meanwhile was appointed honorary chairman of Carnegie Steel and continued as head of the coke company, but his 11 percent interest in the steel firm was reduced to 6 percent. During the 1890s Frick induced Carnegie Steel to cooperate with Henry W. Oliver* in purchasing ore properties in the Lake Superior region. Carnegie himself opposed this as "pioneering," but Frick held firm and the mines proved to be exceedingly valuable.

With relations between Carnegie and Frick becoming more bitter with each passing year, the latter and Henry Phipps began to look for a syndicate to buy out Carnegie's interest. In 1899 they handled the negotiations between Carnegie and the Moore brothers* for the purchase, refusing to reveal the name of the purchasers to Carnegie. When he found out that it was the Moore brothers, who represented everything he despised in business, he was delighted when the option to purchase the steel firm fell through and Frick and Phipps were forced to pay a portion of the $1.7 million out of their own pockets. Frick and Phipps next looked for another buyer, and Frick resigned all association with the company after a dispute over a coke contract in 1900. In the negotiations leading to the formation of U.S. Steel in 1900, Frick served as an intermediary between J. P. Morgan* and John D. Rockefeller* in acquiring the latter's iron ore lands for the new steel consolidation. He later became a director of U.S. Steel, served on the board of the Pennsylvania Railroad, and recommended the reorganization of the Equitable Life Assurance Company in 1905. Increasingly, however, his main interest was the acquisition of Pittsburgh real estate, and he became the largest realty holder in the city.

Having developed one of the largest fortunes of his time (his holdings in Carnegie Steel alone were sold to U.S. Steel for some $60 million), Frick set up several philanthropic ventures during his later years. The most significant of these was the donation of his home in New York City, along with an endowment of $15 million, to establish the Frick Art Museum. He also gave liberal donations to Princeton University and donated Frick Park to Pittsburgh, along with an endowment of $2 million. An Episcopalian and a Republican, Frick married Adelaide Howard Childs, daughter of a prominent Pittsburgh merchant, in 1881. (**A.** *DAB; NCAB*, 23:31; *New York Times*, December 6, 1919; *Who Was Who*, vol. 1; George Harvey, *Henry Clay Frick: The Man*, 1928. **B.** Herbert Casson, *The Romance of Steel*, 1907; Burton J. Hendrick, *Life of Andrew Carnegie*, 2 vols., 1932; Harold C. Livesay, *Andrew Carnegie*, 1975; Joseph F. Wall, *Andrew Carnegie*, 1970.)

FRITZ, JOHN (August 21, 1822–February 13, 1913). Steel manufacturer and inventor, Bethlehem Iron Company. Born in Londonderry Township, Chester County, Pennsylvania, son of George Fritz and Mary Meharg. His father, a small farmer, had been born in Germany and came to the United States in 1802. His mother was of Scotch-Irish heritage. In later years his father became a millwright and a machinist, in addition to his farming, and his three sons were attracted to similar work. John Fritz attended school between intervals of helping on the farm until age sixteen. He then went to Parkesburg, Pennsylvania, as an apprentice in a blacksmithing and country machine works.

In 1844 he obtained a job as a mechanic at the Norristown Iron works of Moore and Hoover, where he was put in charge of all machinery. After five years there, he accepted a position in a new mill at Safe Harbor, Pennsylvania, owned by Reeves, Abbott and Company, taking a drastic cut in pay in order to learn about blast furnace practice and the manufacture of rails. In 1851, during an illness, he made a trip to Lake Superior and saw the iron ore deposits of the Marquette district. He tried to convince capitalists in Philadelphia to invest in these lands, but was unsuccessful, since they felt it was too distant from eastern centers. In 1852 he superintended the building of the Kunzie blast furnace on the Schuylkill River near Philadelphia, a plant which used the new anthracite fuel instead of charcoal. A year later he and his brother, George, along with others, built a foundry and machine shop in Catasauqua, Pennsylvania, to furnish supplies for the blast furnaces and rolling mills.

A major turning point in John Fritz's career came in 1854 when he became superintendent of the Cambria Iron Works in Johnstown, Pennsylvania. The Cambria works were at that time in very poor condition, both financially and mechanically, but over the next six years Fritz converted them into one of the most technically advanced in the industry. The works had been founded in 1851, and among Fritz's innovations were the three-high mill, lifting plates, "live" or driven rollers, and the use of heavy cast guide rails. From the Cambria Works these innovations spread to other mills, with Benjamin F. Jones* of Jones and Laughlin calling "Cambria . . . the cradle in which the great improvements in rolling mill practice were rocked." Yet he was a cautious innovator, never making an innovation until he was wholly convinced in his own mind that it would not fail. He was, in fact, so cautious that for more than five years after the Pennsylvania Steel

Company had begun making Bessemer steel he delayed adoption of the process at his subsequent position at Bethlehem Iron. Even after that he had strong doubts concerning the financial success of the process in the long run. His employers at both plants, however, were even more conservative than he, and he succeeded in bringing about his innovations only with repeated bluffs, threats, and stratagems.

In 1860 Fritz took the position of chief engineer and general superintendent for the Bethlehem Iron Company. At the Bethlehem Works, Fritz introduced many blast-furnace and rolling-mill changes and pioneered in the use of British hydraulic presses in place of steel hammers. Bethlehem shared the lead in experimenting with alloys in America, and at the turn of the century introduced high-speed tool steel. Fritz also brought in open hearth furnaces, the Thomas Basic Process, the Whitworth forging press, and automatic devices of many kinds. In 1892, at seventy, Fritz retired from active business. In 1897 he was asked by the federal government to make plans and estimates for a proposed government armor plate mill works.

In 1902 he was the first recipient of the John Fritz Gold Medal, established by members drawn from the American Society of Mechanical Engineers and other organizations in celebration of his eightieth birthday. Earlier, he had received the Bessemer Gold Medal of the Iron and Steel Institute of Great Britain, and in 1910 received the Elliott Cresson Medal of the Franklin Institute. In 1894 he served as president of the American Society of Mining Engineers, and was president of the American Society of Mechanical Engineers in 1895–1896. He married Ellen Maxwell in 1851. (**A.** *DAB; NCAB*, 13:74; *New York Times*, February 14, 1913; *Who Was Who*, vol. 1; John W. Jordan, ed, *Encyclopedia of Pennsylvania Biography*, vol. 3; *Iron Age*, October 30, 1902; February 20, 1913; American Society of Mechanical Engineers, *Transactions*, vol. 35; Thomas C. Martin, "John Fritz, Iron Master," *The Penn-Germania*, vol. 14, 1913; John Fritz, *The Autobiography of John Fritz*, 1912. **B.** W. Paul Strassmann, *Risk and Technological Innovation*, 1959; James M. Swank, *Cambria County Pioneers*, 1910, and *History of the Manufacture of Iron in All Ages*, 1892.)

FROHMAN, CHARLES (June 17, 1860–May 7, 1915). Theatrical agent and producer, Theatrical Syndicate and Empire Stock Company. Born in Sandusky, Ohio, son of Henry Frohman and Barbara Straun and brother of Daniel Frohman (1851–1940). His father was a native of Germany who had immigrated to America at fourteen, becoming a peddler in New York City, then a cigar manufacturer in Sandusky. In 1864 the family returned to New York City, where Charles was educated and worked in his father's cigar store in the heart of the Rialto, then New York's theater district. Into his father's shop came some of the most famous actors of the time and this had a strong influence on the young man. He first appeared on stage when he was nine years of age as an extra, and later became a ticket seller at a theater in Brooklyn owned by his brother Gustave. During the daytime he worked in the offices of the *Daily Graphic*, after which he served an apprenticeship with another brother, Daniel, who owned the Madison Square Theater troupes. In 1883 Charles became an independent producer in his own right, taking the famous Wallach Theater Company on tour. Subsequently he opened a booking office in New York City, laying the foundations for what later became the powerful Theatrical Syndicate.

Charles Frohman's first great success as an independent producer was the production of *Shenandoah* in 1889 at the Star Theater in New York. The play had been a failure in Boston, but Frohman had faith in it and made several changes, and it succeeded in New York. In 1892 he engaged John Drew, who became the nucleus of the Empire Stock Company, which soon developed into the greatest of all American theatrical star factories. Out of it emerged such distinguished figures as Maude Adams, William Faversham, Arnold Daly, Ethel Barrymore, Margaret Anglin, Arthur Byron, Ida Conquest, Edna Wallace, W. J. Ferguson, and Elsie DeWolf, among others. The stock company's greatest initial success came in 1893 with the production of *The Girl I Left Behind Me*, which established a theatrical tradition.

After that point Charles Frohman rapidly became the most dominant individual in the theatrical industry. He became a star-maker and play arbiter who was often called the "Napoleon of Drama." He especially developed a close relationship with Sir James M. Barrie, and introduced the Scottish author to the American public with his play, *The Little Minister*, in 1897. The outstanding event of their collaboration was the production of *Peter Pan*. Frohman was also instrumental, in association with Abraham Erlanger* and Marc Klaw,* in the development of the modern-day booking system in the American theater. In 1896 they organized the Theatrical Syndicate to set up a centralized booking system for theaters throughout the United States. In 1915 Charles Frohman was one of the passengers on the *Lusitania*, which sent him to his death when it was torpedoed by a German submarine. He was Jewish and never married.

Daniel Frohman also became a major factor in the theatrical and motion picture world. In 1879 he had organized the Madison Square Theater troupes, which traveled the towns and cities of America playing current New York theater attractions. He later became an independent producer at the Lyceum Theater in New York, achieving great success over the years. In 1912 he became managing director of Famous Player Film Company, placed a number of former stage stars under contract, and produced several successful films. (*DAB; NCAB*, 11:440, 441; *New York Times*, May 8, 9, 1915; December 27, 1940; I. F. Marcossen and David Frohman, *Charles Frohman — Manager and Man*, 1916.)

FRYE, JACK (March 18, 1904–February 3, 1959). Airline executive, Trans-

World Airlines. Born in Sweetwater, Oklahoma, son of William Henry Frye. His mother died when he was eight years old, and he spent much of his time after that with his father and grandparents on a 15,000 acre family ranch near Wheeler, Texas. He began his aviation career at age fourteen, when he ran errands for several stranded airmen who were forced down near his home. He was educated in public schools, but left high school before graduation, spending a year in the Army engineering corps. In 1923 he went to California where he worked as a soda jerk in Los Angeles. He also began taking flying lessons at $20 per hour, paying for them from his soda fountain savings. Soon he was soloing, and before long he began taking passengers up with him.

He and his flying instructor purchased an old World War I airplane, put it into working order, and formed a flying school and air taxi service known as the Burdett Flying School. By 1926 he had become president of the Aero Corporation of California, which operated a flying school as well as a service and maintenance base. He remained president of this until 1930. In 1927 the company launched a regular service between Los Angeles and Tucson, Arizona, and a year later the route was extended to El Paso, Texas, using Fokker single engine planes. By 1929 they were using three engine Fokker F-10's. He subsequently formed Standard Air Lines, as a subsidiary of Aero Corporation, to provide service between Los Angeles and Phoenix, Arizona, using one plane. He was president of this until 1930, when it merged with Western Air Express, and he was named vice-president of operations of the new company. Later in the same year, Western merged with Transcontinental Air Transport-Madduz, to become Transcontinental and Western Air Incorporated (T.W.A.).

The new firm immediately inaugurated the first coast-to-coast service to carry passengers entirely by air. The flight took thirty-six hours, with a stopover in Kansas City. In 1931 it acquired Northrup mail planes and took the lead in flying mail while continuing its passenger service. Later that same year the company drew up specifications for a faster, larger, and more comfortable plane, which Donald Douglas* agreed to build for the company, calling it the DC-1; it was the first Douglas plane designed exclusively for passenger service. From this developed the DC-2, which TWA was the first to fly. By the spring of 1934, TWA had 31 DC-2's in service, and had reduced the cross-country flying time to sixteen hours.

Jack Frye took over as president of TWA in 1934. In that same year the government cancelled all mail contracts with private companies and began using the army air force to fly domestic mail. But when ten air force pilots died carrying the mail that year, the government reoffered contracts to the commercial lines on a bid basis. In 1935 TWA began to experiment with high-altitude flying to overcome one of the major dangers of scheduled flights—pilots had trouble clearing cloud formations which might obscure mountain peaks. By 1940, TWA had a fleet of 33 passenger four engine

Boeing Stratocruisers built to cruise at high altitude, which were equipped with "pressurized" cabins.

In 1941, Frye, with Howard Hughes,* began work on plans for the Lockheed Constellation, a triple rudder transport which was very fast and could carry fifty-seven passengers and crew. With pressurized cabins, it was capable of cruising at 30,000 feet for 4,000 miles at speeds of over 300 miles per hour. In 1944 he and Hughes flew one of the Constellations from Burbank, California, to Washington, D.C., a distance of 2,663 miles, in six hours and fifty-eight minutes, establishing a new record. In 1945 Frye began to push for trans-Atlantic air flights for TWA, which had previously been held only by Pan-American and American Export Airlines. In July of that year the Civil Aeronautics Board authorized TWA to initiate flights to Europe. This started a rate war for the European business among the three major American carriers. Frye served as president of TWA until 1947. Then he was president of General Aniline and Film Corporation from 1947 to 1955, and president and chairman of the board of The Frye Corporation from 1955 to 1959.

He married Nevada Smith in 1930, and they had one daughter. In 1941 he married Helen Warren Vanderbilt, ex-wife of Cornelius Vanderbilt Jr.* (**A.** *Current Biography*, 1945, 1959; *Who Was Who*, vol. 3; *New York Times*, February 4, 1959. **B.** Charles Kelly Jr., *The Sky's the Limit: A History of the Airlines*, 1963.)

FULLER, ALFRED CARL (January 13, 1885–December, 1973). Brush and household goods manufacturer, Fuller Brush Company. Born in Wellsford, Nova Scotia, Canada, son of Leander Joseph Fuller and Phoebe Jane Collins. His ancestors had come from England on the *Mayflower*, settling in the Connecticut River Valley. Then, in 1761, his great-grandfather moved to Nova Scotia to accept a 100 acre crown grant, which his father eventually inherited. Alfred Fuller was educated in the public schools of Nova Scotia until 1903, when his family moved to Somerset, Massachusetts. Upon arrival, Fuller entered the employ of the Boston Elevated Railroad Company, and after two years joined the Somerville Brush Company. After learning the details of the brush business, he organized his own company, the Capital Brush Company, in 1906.

The Capital Brush Company was organized in Hartford, Connecticut, and set up in a shed Fuller rented for $11 per month, where he worked with one assistant. By 1910 he had twenty-five men selling for him and six factory workers. At that point the name of the firm was changed to the Fuller Brush Company. He recruited salesmen while on selling trips through New England, New York, and Pennsylvania by advertising in local newspapers. In 1911, after he placed a small advertisement in a national magazine, he was deluged with replies. Within three months he had added about 100 salesmen throughout the United States. In 1913 the firm was incorporated under the same name, with Fuller as president, treasurer, and director. The firm was capitalized at $50,000, of which $30,000 was "good will."

The Fuller firm specialized in a new kind of brush for household uses, made on what is termed the twisted wire method of construction, and developed in a diversity of shapes and sizes to be used for many purposes for which brushes had not previously been manufactured. Sales in 1910 were $40,000, and by 1924 reached $12 million. By 1930 the company employed about 1,200 people in its factories and offices, and had about 3,600 salesmen operating from 200 branch offices, who sold brushes directly to the consumer. The firm operated throughout the United States, Canada, and the West Indies, retaining its head offices in Hartford. Fuller salesmen were called "dealers" to make clear their status as independent businessmen. They purchased the brushes wholesale from Fuller Brush and then sold them retail to the consumer, with an average profit of 30 percent. By 1948 the firm had gross sales of $30 million, and only $50,000 was spent on advertising.

With the outbreak of World War II, the firm decreased its output of civilian brushes to make brushes for cleaning guns, and Fuller served as a member of the Committee of Purchases in the Procurement Division of the War Department. He was also a member of the Connecticut State War Council from 1942 to 1946. In 1943 his son, Alfred Howard Fuller (1913–1959) took over as president of the company, with Alfred moving up to chairman of the board. During this time the company began manufacturing brush-making machines and brought out a line of industrial brushes.

In 1948 women "Fullerettes" appeared when the company added "Debutant Cosmetics" to its line. Similar to Avon Cosmetics, these were to be sold door-to-door by the women. By this time his dealers made 50 million calls yearly, and the company manufactured 90 percent of the brushes used in American-made vacuum cleaners. Each Fuller dealer was given an extensive territory of about 2,000 homes, and in 1948 had an average profit of about $70 per week. The company has a very high turnover in dealers, and Fuller must recruit about 5,000 new men a year. Those who remain with the firm may advance to field manager, in which position they receive a 20 percent commission on all sales in their area, and to district supervisor, in which they receives a salary plus a bonus. Factory employees in Hartford have membership in the Fuller Club and the use of Fuller Park.

A Republican and a Christian Scientist, Alfred Fuller married Evelyn Winifred Ells of Nova Scotia in 1908. They had two sons. In 1932 he married Mary Primrose Pelton. (*NCAB*, A:351; *Current Biography*, 1950; *Who Was Who*, vols. 3 and 6.)

G

GAGE, LYMAN JUDSON (June 28, 1836–January 26, 1927). Banker and public official, First National Bank of Chicago and Secretary of the Treasury. Born in Deruyter, Madison County, New York, son of Eli A. Gage and Mary Judson. His parents were both natives of New York State, and his ancestors came to America from England in 1650. He was educated in the common schools of Madison County, and after his parents moved to Rome, New York, in 1848, he continued his education at Rome Academy. At age fourteen his schooling came to an end, and he began working for the Rome and Watertown Railroad. When he was seventeen he entered the Oneida Central Bank of Rome as an office boy and junior clerk. Two years later, in 1855, he left Rome for Chicago, where he secured employment as a clerk in a lumber yard and planing mill. Three years later he was made a bookkeeper for the Merchant's Savings, Loan and Trust Company. In 1861 he was made cashier of the firm.

Seven years later, in 1868, Gage accepted a similar position with the First National Bank of Chicago. During the 1870s he was one of the organizers and acted as treasurer of the "Honest Money League of the Northwest," which inaugurated a vigorous campaign against irredeemable paper money. His writings were widely circulated and he made a reputation as a sound, conservative businessman. In 1882 the First National was reorganized, and he was elected vice-president and executive officer of the new corporation. A year later he was elected president of the American Bankers Association, and was twice reelected. The Haymarket Riots of 1886 convinced him of the necessity of reconciling the conflicting views of capital and labor, and with others he organized a series of conferences which conducted an open forum on current questions concerning capital and labor. Although they were able to arrive at no clear solutions, they did awaken public discussion, and his conferences led directly to the organization of the Civic Federation of Chicago, which was formally organized in 1894, as a consequence of the Pullman Strike. The conferences also gained Gage the sympathy of the working class, which he held throughout his career. In 1891 he was elected president of the First National Bank, a position he held until he entered public life.

Gage was the prime mover in the organization of the Chicago Clearing House Association in 1870; was chairman of its first clearing house committee; served as its president for several years; and was a member of its executive committee for many years. He was also a founder and first president of the Bankers Club of Chicago. In 1890–1891 he served as president of the Chicago board of directors of the World's Columbian Exposition, which brought him national prominence.

Gage had originally been a Republican, but he supported Grover Cleveland for president in 1884, and upon Cleveland's election in 1892 was offered the post of Secretary of the Treasury. He declined, but served as a vigorous opponent of "free silver" and supported Cleveland wholeheartedly on the currency question. During the Panic of 1893 he proposed that the government issue $200 million in bonds for subscription in treasury notes which were then to be withdrawn from circulation. During the campaign of 1896 he was a staunch defender of the gold standard, and accepted the treasury post when it was offered by McKinley in that year. At the opening session of Congress in 1897 he submitted a complete plan to place the United States on a gold basis, and in support of his efforts, the business interests of the nation sent delegates to a national monetary conference at Indianapolis, Indiana, in 1898. This became the basis of the law of 1900. He also recommended a federated system of banks, but was not successful in the venture. His management of national finances during the Spanish-American War added greatly to his financial reputation. In 1902 he resigned as secretary, and from 1902 to 1906 was president of the United States Trust Company of New York. In the latter year he retired from active business and moved to California.

Gage was a Methodist and was married three times: to Sarah Etheridge of Hastings, Nebraska, who died in 1874; to Mrs. Cornelia (Washburne) Gage, his brother's widow, who died in 1901; and in 1909 to Mrs. Frances Ada Ballou of San Diego, California. He had two children, Fannie and Eli A. Gage. (*DAB; NCAB*, 26:444; *Memoirs of Lyman Gage*, 1937.)

GANNETT, FRANK ERNEST (September 15, 1876–December 3, 1957). Newspaper chain publisher, Gannett Company, Incorporated. Born in Bristol, New York, son of Joseph Charles Gannett, a farmer, and Maria Brooks. His ancestors had come to America in 1638, and Frank Gannett was educated in local schools and graduated from Cornell University in 1898. While at Cornell he was on the editorial staff of the *Cornell Sun* and manager of the *Cornell Magazine*. He also worked as Cornell correspondent of the Ithaca *Journal* and other newspapers. During vacations he worked on the Syracuse *Herald*. In 1899 he became secretary to Jacob Shurman, president of Cornell, accompanying him on the first Philippine Commission after the Spanish-American War. He returned to the United States after nearly a year and edited the *Cornell News* for a time. Later he joined the Ithaca *Daily News* as city editor, and subsequently as managing editor and business manager. In 1905–1906 Gannett served as editor of the Pittsburgh (Pennsylvania) *Index*.

In 1906 Frank Gannett purchased his first newspaper, the Elmira *Gazette*, and within a short time had merged it with three other upstate New York papers to form the Gannett Company. This was the beginning of a communications empire which, by the time of his death, would encompass more than thirty newspapers and a string of radio and television stations. During the early years all of these papers were located in medium-sized cities in New York State. After acquiring papers in Ithaca and Elmira, in 1918 Gannett consolidated the *Union and Register* and *Evening Times* of Rochester into the Rochester *Times-Union*, which became the flagship paper in his newspaper empire. During the 1920s and 30s he purchased papers in Newburgh, Plainfield, Beacon, Olean, Ogdensburg, and Albany, New York, along with the Hartford (Connecticut) *Times* and the Brooklyn *Eagle*, which he later sold.

The Gannett Company has been described as the chain that buys "small Mom and Pop dailies in one-newspaper towns," and as a chain of "small monopolies." As these titles indicate, Gannett's policy was to acquire daily newspapers in small, one-newspaper towns and cities. Even though as late as the 1970s the average circulation of Gannett newspapers was only 40,000, the total circulation of its 82 dailies was over 3.6 million. Although these papers shared a generally Republican tone with their founder, Frank Gannett's policy was to give his editors full control of editorial policy, and the newspapers were urged to continue their local traditions and to preserve their identity by remaining free of outside influence. Gannett personally edited only the Rochester *Times-Union*. One rule he did insist on with all his papers was that they could accept no advertisements for intoxicants. He arranged for the continuation of these properties by the organization in 1935 of the Frank E. Gannett Newspaper Foundation, Incorporated, which was enjoined to continue publication of the papers, and became controlling owners of all the stock of Gannett Company, Incorporated. The surplus earnings of the company were alloted to charitable, educational, and philanthropic purposes.

Although the papers in the Gannett chain have been accused of being editorially bland, and of being the only big chain without a single prestigious newspaper, commentators also recognize that Gannett's formula has been exceptionally profitable. These one-newspaper towns and cities are good markets for lucrative advertising and expandable circulation, and a former employee has commented that the goal at Gannett is to make money, not change the world. By the late 1970s it was the nation's largest newspaper chain, in terms of number of newspapers. In 1978 Gannett annexed the Arizona-based Combined Communications Company, which greatly expanded its broadcasting empire, as well as bringing it into billboards, with the second largest outdoor advertising business in the country. Until the purchase of the Oakland *Tribune* and Cincinnati *Enquirer* in 1979, Gannett's largest papers were the *Times-Union* and *Democrat and Chronicle* in Rochester, with a combined circulation of 140,000. The smallest, and most remote, was the *Pacific Dateline*, a Guam paper with a circulation of 2,000.

Frank Gannett was one of the principal organizers of the New York State Publishers Association in 1919, serving as its president for seven years. In 1922 he established the Empire State School of Printing in Ithaca, the only school maintained by a state organization of newspapers for the training of printers. He was also president of the New York Associated Dailies in 1916-1917, and of the New York Press Association in 1917-1918. He was a Republican and a Unitarian and married Caroline Werner of Rochester, New York, in 1920. They had two children. (**A.** *NCAB*, 48:609. **B.** Milton Moscowitz, et al., *Everybody's Business*, 1980; Kenneth Norman Stewart and John William Tebbel, *Makers of Modern Journalism*, 1962.)

GARFIELD, JAMES RUDOLPH (October 17, 1865-March 24, 1950). Public official, commissioner, Bureau of Corporations. Born in Hiram, Ohio, son of James A. Garfield, twentieth president of the United States, and Lucretia Rudolph. During his youth, young Garfield split his time between living in Washington, D.C., where his father was then a United States Congressman, and his home in Hiram, and then Mentor, Ohio. He attended various private and public schools, and after his father was assassinated in 1881 enrolled in Williams College in Massachusetts. After graduation he entered Columbia Law School, while at the same time working for the law firm of Bangs and Stetson in New York City. After graduation in 1888 he returned to Ohio, passed the bar exam, and opened a law office with his brother Henry in Cleveland. They concentrated on estate and corporate law, with special interests in railroads.

A Republican, Garfield early joined a reform wing of the party which pushed for political and administrative improvements in government but supported the existing economic order. He was twice elected to the Ohio State Senate, where he was a strong supporter of Marcus A. Hanna* for appointment to the United States Senate. Garfield twice sought the Republican nomination in his Congressional district, but was unsuccessful. In 1902 he was appointed to the United States Civil Service Commission by Theodore Roosevelt. This was the beginning of a long association with Roosevelt and his policies. In 1903, upon passage of the Bureau of Corporations Bill, Roosevelt appointed Garfield first Commissioner of Corporations and director of the new bureau.

Both Roosevelt and Garfield shared the view that the proper way to deal with the "trust" problem was through legislation and regulation, not trust-busting. Garfield himself had powerful friends among businessmen, and had close ties with his old Williams classmate, Francis Lynde Stetson,* a Morgan lawyer. He was also friendly with important Standard Oil lawyers. Garfield's main task during his first year was to define the legal functions of the Bureau in the field of corporate regulation, as well as those of the national government. By 1904 Garfield had decided that the function of the

Bureau of Corporations "is not to enforce the antitrust laws," or even to gather information indicating the need for their enforcement. Information gathered by the Bureau would be released only at the discretion of the president, and its information could not be used by other departments for purposes of possible legislation. Garfield's main interest was in gaining the cooperation of business, not in arousing their antagonism. This stand was welcomed by most businessmen, as was Garfield's support for the federal licensing of corporations.

In 1904 Garfield turned his attention to Standard Oil Company, meeting with company executives, including Henry H. Rogers,* John D. Archbold,* and Samuel C. T. Dodd,* to decide the best manner to investigate allegations of Standard rebating and monopoly in Kansas and the Midwest. Standard agreed to cooperate with the bureau, but quickly reneged on its agreement. Relations between the bureau and Standard Oil became increasingly strained during 1905, and Garfield reluctantly became highly critical of the firm, beginning to classify it as a "bad trust" in Roosevelt's terminology. He also passed an investigation of the meat packing industry on to the courts in the same year. With the support of major elements in the insurance industry, Garfield appealed to Congress to consider whether the Bureau of Corporations had the power to regulate insurance. Powerful New York insurance companies had supported federal regulation of insurance for some thirty years, and were greatly encouraged by Garfield's move in this direction. Opposition, however, was led by Senator Morgan Bulkeley,* president of Aetna Life Insurance of Hartford, Connecticut, who feared that their New York competitors would dominate a federal bureau. They were successful in thwarting the passage of federal legislation.

One of Garfield's most significant actions as commissioner came in 1905, when he arranged a personal conference between Elbert H. Gary* and President Roosevelt at which arrangements were made for the informal cooperation of the corporation and government. The bureau began an investigation of the steel firm, which dragged on until 1911, but U.S. Steel continued to supply the statistical information requested, and its relationship with the government remained amicable. Garfield also participated in the agreement in 1907 whereby the Tennessee Coal and Iron Company was acquired by U.S. Steel, on the basis of a "gentleman's agreement" between the steel company, President Roosevelt, and the Bureau of Corporations. The Senate decided to investigate the transactions in 1909, but the bureau refused to deliver confidential information to the Senate committee, forcing the Senate to rule that it could not pass judgement on the transaction, due to lack of information. Garfield's last action as commissioner came in 1907, after Congress had passed a resolution ordering an investigation of International Harvester. He met with Harvester officials Cyrus McCormick* and Charles Deering,* and Morgan partners George Perkins* and Elbert Gary. After the meeting International Harvester announced it would give full support to the bureau's investigation, and Garfield praised their coop-erative stance. The study was not completed until 1913, and largely stalled more aggressive court action on the part of the Justice Department.

During Garfield's tenure as commissioner he was often criticized for not being zealous enough in his investigations of industry. These charges were particularly made of his investigations of U.S. Steel, which was defined as a "good trust" and protected by a gentleman's agreement. Many critics felt that Garfield's stand was far too lenient. His initially cordial handling of Standard Oil was also criticized, but the penetrating information he was able to secure from the firm ultimately made possible the successful Supreme Court case of 1911, which ordered the giant oil firm broken up into several constituent units. In 1907 Roosevelt appointed Garfield Secre-tary of the Interior, where he pushed for an aggressive program of scientific land management of the federal domain. He established national parks, reclaimed arid lands, withdrew coal, oil, gas, and phosphate lands from private sale, and took steps to prevent the monopolization of water and electric power. During his two years in office he worked closely with the head of the Forestry Bureau, Gifford Pinchot.

Unlike his actions as Commissioner of the Bureau of Corporations, his policies as Secretary of the Interior provoked a great deal of antagonism from business interests, especially those in the West. Garfield's successor as Secretary of Interior, Richard A. Ballinger, brought Garfield and Pinchot's withdrawal of water power sites as ranger stations to President Taft's attention, asserting the land should be returned to the public domain. This caused the dismissal of Pinchot, provoking the famous Pinchot-Ballinger controversy which resulted in the formation of the Progressive League, composed of young, anti-Taft supporters of Roosevelt. Garfield joined the National Progressive Republican League in 1911, but refused to support Senator Robert M. LaFollette. In 1912 he supported Roosevelt for presi-dent on the Bull Moose ticket, and two years later was Progressive Party candidate for lieutenant governor of Ohio, but was unsuccessful. He there-upon rejoined the regular Republican party, leading a harmony movement within it.

Garfield's interest in politics subsided after World War I and he devoted himself to his private law practice. Serving as counsel for an American land and cattle company which owned seven million acres of land in northern Mexico, he headed negotiations with the Mexican government when they tried to expropriate the land. (**A.** *DAB*, Supplement 4; *NCAB*, 42:35; *New York Times*, March 25, 1950; *Who Was Who*, vol. 2. **B.** Samuel P. Hays, *Conservation and the Gospel of Efficiency*, 1959; Gabriel Kolko, *The Triumph of Conservatism*, 1963; George E. Mowry, *The Era of Theodore Roosevelt and the Birth of Modern America*, 1958; James Weinstein, *The Corporate Ideal in the Liberal State*, 1968; Robert H. Wiebe, *Businessmen and Reform*, 1962.)

THE GARRETT FAMILY: Robert Garrett (May 2, 1783–February 4, 1857); **John Work Garrett** (July 31, 1820–September 26, 1884); **Robert Garrett II** (April 9, 1847–July 29, 1896); **Thomas Harrison Garrett** (February 11, 1849–June 7, 1888); **Robert Garrett III** (June 24, 1875–April 25, 1961); **John Work Garrett II** (May 19, 1872–June 26, 1942). Merchants, bankers, and railroad executives, Robert Garrett and Sons and Baltimore and Ohio Railroad.

Robert Garrett was born in Lisburn, County Down, Ireland, of Scotch-Irish ancestry. When he was seven years old his family immigrated to America. His father died soon afterward, and his mother bought a farm in Cumberland County, Pennsylvania. In 1798 they moved to another farm in Washington County, and at age sixteen Robert had his first venture in business. Accompanying an older brother on a trading expedition among the Indians, they were forced by cold weather to spend the winter in an Indian hut near the Ohio River. This experience gave him a lasting interest in the development of the West which was to form the basis of his later business ventures. Shortly after 1800 he went to Baltimore, Maryland, where he served as a clerk in a produce and commission house for four years. He subsequently formed the partnership of Wallace and Garrett, which afforded him further experience in the western trade. In 1812 the partnership was dissolved and he moved to Middletown, Pennsylvania, but he returned to Baltimore about 1820.

Upon his return to Baltimore, Garrett opened a business house which soon took the name of Robert Garrett and Sons. Before long the firm became an important factor in the wholesale grocery, produce, forwarding, and commission business of the city. He very early appreciated the strategic position Baltimore held as a seaport with connections to the frontier and he resolved to capture western trade by developing superior transportation facilities for the farmers of the West. He improved upon the slow method of shipping produce by pack horses over the Alleghenies by establishing fast wagon trains which ran night and day over turnpikes and plank roads, prior to connecting up with the Pennsylvania Canal. When the project of the Baltimore and Ohio Railroad began to be discussed, he strongly supported it and invested heavily in its stock.

To further meet the demands of the frontier trade, he established direct connections with Latin America, and at the same time sought an outlet for American products in Europe. In order to better finance its expanding business operations, and to meet the credit demands of its customers, the house established its own banking operations and became the American correspondent for such firms as George Peabody* (a former Baltimorian and a friend) and Company of London and other foreign houses. It soon became one of the leading banking houses of the city and its financial operations gradually overshadowed the commission and shipping business.

Garrett also took an active part in the development of many local business interests, serving as director of the Baltimore Water Company, the Gas Company, and the Shot Tower Company. He helped organize the Western Bank in 1836, serving as a director until his death. In 1847 he helped found the Eutaw Savings Bank and served as a director of it all his life, and was a director of the Savings Bank of Baltimore. To help make Baltimore attractive to the western trade, he purchased the Eutaw House, in order to provide pleasant accommodations in the city. Five years later he purchased the Wheatfield Inn, which he replaced with a new hotel. He also built the *Monumental City*, the largest steamship constructed to that time in Baltimore, to link the trade of that city with the trade of San Francisco.

In 1817 he married Elizabeth Stouffer, daughter of Henry Stouffer, a prominent Baltimore merchant. They had two sons, John Work and Henry S. Garrett.

John Work Garrett was born in Baltimore and was educated for two years at Lafayette College in Pennsylvania. At age nineteen he became associated with his father and older brother, Henry, in the family's commission house. He spent seventeen years as a partner in the firm, gaining valuable experience in its diverse operations. During the sharp recession of 1857, when the Baltimore and Ohio Railroad, of which he was a stockholder, experienced serious difficulties, he was called upon to prepare a report to financiers to raise capital. The report was so well received by Johns Hopkins,* the largest individual stockholder, that he was elected president of the road in 1858.

Upon assuming the presidency, he at once inaugurated new policies, in which economy was stressed, and despite the general financial crisis his first annual report showed a net gain in earnings. The second year results were even more remarkable. He then pressed for a reorganization of the board, which partially freed it from political control. When the Civil War broke out, Garrett firmly allied himself with the Union cause, and he used his railroad as an early warning system for attack on Washington, D.C. In this manner he saved the road from being seized by the government, but the Baltimore and Ohio became a main object of Southern attacks. Only Garrett's great skill and energy kept it from being abandoned. In 1863 the first military rail transport in history, the transfer of 20,000 men from the Potomac to Chattanooga, was a monumental triumph for Garrett. Profits also rose to very high figures in the latter years of the war.

With the return of peace, Garrett first repaired the war damages, and followed closely the expansionist moves of Jay Gould* at the Erie and J. Edgar Thomson* at the Pennsylvania. Becoming a strong advocate of alliances, he built a feeder into Pittsburgh and in 1866 leased the Ohio Central in order to connect Wheeling with Columbus. Early in 1869, as Gould began to negotiate with the Ohio roads, Garrett moved quickly to purchase full control of a line running north to Lake Erie at Sandusky. The B & O also substantially increased it holdings in the Cincinnati and Marietta (connecting Wheeling to Cincinnati), but then Garrett stopped, troubled by the high costs of expansion. The road was still largely financed by the Garrett family banking firm and they were reticent about further expansion. Nevertheless, in 1874, the board agreed that Garrett should build a 263-mile line connecting Chicago with the Sandusky road. In 1878 he obtained full control of the Ohio and Mississippi Railroad, when that road went into receivership, which gave the B & O connections with St. Louis, Louisville, and Chicago, and with roads west of Chicago at Peoria. In the 1880s the Baltimore and Ohio built its own road into Philadelphia, but continued to rely on the Reading and New York Central railroads to carry its traffic into New York.

Garrett also moved the Baltimore and Ohio into nonrailroad properties during this time. To restore Baltimore as a seaport huge wharves were built at Locust Point to accommodate ocean liners of the North German Lloyd, with which the company had entered into an alliance, and a system of elevators was erected. The road purchased coal properties and in 1872 built and operated a steel rolling mill. Garrett also made the road into a self-contained unit, by building its own sleeping and dining cars, setting up large hotels in the Alleghenies, creating its own express company, and fostering its own separate telegraph company. In 1880 Garrett was at the height of his success, ruling the board and the politicians with an iron hand; but this had not been obtained without a ruinous rate war with the other trunk lines, which lasted until they began to form pools. When these were formed, the roads had to combat charges of discrimination against local shippers. The most desperate problem came in 1877 when, after the railroad had cut wages to reduce expenses, the line was hit with the great railroad strikes of that year. All of this finally took a toll on Garrett's health and he resigned. On the eve of the Civil War the Baltimore and Ohio had 514 miles of track, with gross earnings of $4 million; at the end of his presidency, its track mileage had been increased to 1,711.

John W. Garrett married Rachel Ann Harrison, daughter of Thomas Harrison, a Baltimore merchant. They had two sons, Robert Garrett II and Thomas Harrison Garrett. **Robert Garrett II** was born in Baltimore and educated at Dahl School in that city and at Friend's School in Providence, Rhode Island. At sixteen he ran away from home and joined Robert E. Lee's forces in Virginia, despite the fact that his father was a firm Union supporter. His father convinced him to return home, however, and he entered Princeton, graduating in 1867. He then entered the family's banking house, of which his father was head. Since the latter found all of his time was consumed with the affairs of the Baltimore and Ohio, he put full management of the banking house in the hands of his two sons. They developed it into one of the strongest banking houses in the South.

In 1871 Robert Garrett II succeeded Robert E. Lee as president of the Valley Railroad in Virginia, and during the four years of his presidency extended it to Staunton, Virginia, making it a branch of the Baltimore and Ohio system. In 1879 he was elected third vice-president of the latter road, and upon the death of his father was elected president, serving until he retired in 1887. His administration covered the period of the road's greatest expansion. During this time its lines were extended to Philadelphia, and the Staten Island Rapid Transit System was acquired. The extension of the line into Philadelphia was a very real accomplishment which was made at the cost of $14 million and carried out in the face of the frantic opposition of the Pennsylvania Railroad. Garrett had first tried to purchase the Philadelphia, Wilmington and Baltimore Railroad, but failing that, his alternative was to build his own expensive line into Philadelphia.

His greatest achievement, however, was the extension of the Baltimore and Ohio telegraph system, which soon acquired a formidable business, becoming a major rival to Western Union. While he was out of the country, and in spite of his strong opposition, the system was sold to Western Union in 1886, and at the same time the line's express company and sleeping and parlor car departments were disposed of. Garrett also had many other financial connections. With John Mackay* and James Gordon Bennett* he was concerned in the establishment of the Commercial Cable, and was one of the organizers of the American Union Telegraph Company, which was also sold to Western Union. He was president of the Baltimore Drydock Company, and director of Consolidation Coal Company of Maryland, the National Mechanics Bank, and the Merchants and Miners Transportation Company. In 1872 he married Mary Sloan Frick, daughter of Frederick Frick, a leading Baltimore lawyer. They had no children.

While Robert Garrett II was running the Baltimore and Ohio, his brother, **Thomas H. Garrett**, was running the family banking business. He had been born in Baltimore and graduated from Princeton in 1868. He then entered the banking house, which he managed until his death in 1888. He was also a director of the Baltimore and Ohio and took an active part in the management of its affairs. In 1870 he married Alice Whiridge, and they had three sons, including Robert Garrett III and John W. Garrett II.

Robert Garrett III was born in Baltimore and educated by private tutors and at a lycée in France. He graduated from Princeton in 1897. After doing postgraduate work at John Hopkins in history and economics until 1909, he became a general partner in the investment banking firm of Robert Garrett and Sons. He continued as such until 1947, serving thereafter as a limited partner until his retirement in 1957. In addition, he was a director of the Baltimore and Ohio; Provident Savings Bank, Safe Deposit and Trust Company; Maryland Trust Company; Davison Chemical Company; and the Roland Park Company. He was also a major benefactor to the Baltimore community, serving as president of the Public Athletic League and as head of Baltimore Parks and Recreation until he retired in 1950. He helped found the Playgrounds Association of America in 1910 and brought the

Boy Scouts into Baltimore in the same year. In addition, he founded the
Baltimore Federation of Churches in 1918 and served as its president from
1926 to 1929. He was a Presbyterian and a Republican, and a trustee of
Princeton from 1905 to 1946.

Robert Garrett III married Katharine Barker Johnson of Baltimore in
1907. They had ten children. His brother, **John Work Garrett II**, was born
in Baltimore and served as a partner in the family banking house of Robert
Garrett and Sons from 1896 to 1934. During this time he also served the
United States State Department as a foreign service officer. He was a
Republican and married Alice Warden in 1908. (**A.** *DAB; NCAB*, 18:3, 4. **B.**
Edward Hungerford, *The Story of the Baltimore and Ohio Railroad*, 1928;
Robert L. Thomson, *Wiring A Continent: The History of the Telegraph
Industry in the United States*, 1947.)

GARY, ELBERT HENRY (October 8, 1846–August 15, 1927). Lawyer
and steel company executive, United States Steel Company. Born near
Wheaton, Illinois, son of Erastus Gary and Susan Vallette. His father was a
native of Connecticut who had migrated to DuPage County, Illinois, in the
1830s, becoming a prosperous farmer and influential citizen there. Elbert
Gary worked on his father's farm as a youth and was educated at the
Illinois Institute, a Methodist college which his father had helped found.
After serving a short stint in the Union army during the Civil War, he
taught school for a time. At the suggestion of his uncle, Henry Vallette,
Gary began reading law in 1865 at the firm of Vallette and Cody in
Naperville. The following year he entered Union College of Law in Chicago,
graduating in 1868 at the head of his class. After serving three years as
clerk of the superior court, he joined his uncle's law firm. His brother also
joined the firm, and as Gary, Cody and Gary it built up a wide practice.
Gary began representing several important railroads and industrial firms as
counsel during this time, often sitting on their boards of directors. In 1898,
upon the urging of J. P. Morgan,* he gave up the practice of law to accept
the presidency of the Federal Steel Company, moving to New York City.

Gary's interest in the steel industry had developed gradually, starting
first when he became a director at Illinois Steel Company in the early
1890s and then through his work in helping to organize the American
Steel and Wire Company and Federal Steel in 1898. It was while he was
engaged with the organization of the latter firm, which had been financed
by Morgan, that he impressed the financier with his work. After taking
over as head of Federal Steel, Morgan turned over to Gary the major
burden in the development of United States Steel. After the giant steel
firm was organized in 1901, Gary dominated its policies almost completely from that time until his death over a quarter of a century later.
He acted as chairman of the executive committee until that group was
dissolved in 1903, then he served as chairman of the board until 1927.

After 1907 he was also chairman of the finance committee.

During his years as head of U.S. Steel, Gary was primarily concerned with three major areas—relations with the federal government, relations with the rest of the steel industry, and relations with unions and labor—leaving the actual management of the firm to various top executives. In the area of government relations, he very early established contact with James R. Garfield,* the newly appointed Commissioner of the Bureau of Corporations in the Theodore Roosevelt administration. When the House of Representatives ordered an investigation of U.S. Steel in 1905, turning the matter over to the Bureau of Corporations, Gary met with Garfield and Roosevelt later that year, establishing a verbal understanding. He began providing the government with the desired information on the steel company's activities, giving Garfield full access to the firm's books in exchange for the promise that the government would use publicity to punish the company only if it found something wrong. This memorandum of understanding did much to clarify U.S. Steel's relations with the government, and also did a great deal to establish the general policy of the Roosevelt administration toward the large new corporate giants. The next step along this line came in 1907 when Gary and Henry Clay Frick,* in consultation with Morgan, approached Roosevelt about the prospect of U.S. Steel acquiring Tennessee Coal and Iron Company in Birmingham, Alabama, claiming an important Wall Street firm (Moore* and Schley) stood in danger of imminent collapse if they did not. Roosevelt backed the take-over, promising that he would not prosecute U.S. Steel. In 1909 the Senate commenced an investigation of the takeover, but the Bureau of Corporations refused to transmit confidential U.S. Steel Company material to the committee, and the investigation was dropped for lack of information. In 1911, however, the Democrats in the House launched a new investigation of the transaction. The investigation was soon picked up by the Taft administration, causing a decided rift between him and ex-president Roosevelt and his followers. The whole affair was not finally resolved until 1919, when the Supreme Court finally gave response to the long-standing trust suit and gave the steel corporation a clean bill of health, terming it a "good trust."

In developing relations with the rest of the steel industry, Gary created policies which also impinged on government action and policies. In order to establish the principle of "price leadership" in the industry, Gary began holding the "Gary Dinners," at which steel executives informally discussed pricing and other policies. The first of these was held on November 21, 1907, at the Waldorf Astoria, attended by 49 steel industry leaders. Gary not only invited the steel men, he also notified steel trade journals, the Department of Justice, the Department of Commerce, and the newspapers. He was anxious to avoid the impression that he was creating illegal price-fixing agreements or that there was anything secretive in his actions. He insisted that the meeting was not an effort to fix prices but was instead an effort to maintain them by "gentlemen's agreements." At the same time he took steps to prevent government prosecution of his voluntary agreements. By 1908, however, the Gary meetings had proved a failure, as smaller steel companies began cutting prices, followed by price cuts by major steel firms to meet the competition. This inaugurated a period of intense price competition in the steel industry which lasted until World War I, when Gary helped to establish, under the auspices of the American Iron and Steel Institute, a working coordination over prices. This was Gary's famous "umbrella concept" where he avoided cut-throat competition through putting a price umbrella over the weaker firms in the industry that did not force these firms out of business.

Gary's final area of major concern was with labor. He had long advocated relatively high wages in his plants, and had worked to make the mills safer and to ameliorate working conditions. On the other hand, he insisted on long hours, favoring the twelve hour day, and was adamant in his insistence on the open, nonunion shop. In 1919, however, the great steel firm was rocked by a violent and highly publicized strike calling for recognition of the union. Under Gary's general direction U.S. Steel responded to the strike with the use of harassment and outright violence. The strike lasted three and one-half months, but in January, 1920, it was called off by the union. The steel firm had won an apparent victory, but public opinion turned decidedly against the company, tarnishing Gary's carefully nurtured benign image. Even President Harding, in 1923, expressed his keen disappointment to Gary over his actions. The following week the industry pledged to eliminate the twelve hour day as soon as the labor supply permitted, and within a few months the eight hour day was largely in effect. Collective bargaining in the steel industry, however, was to await fulfillment until the 1930s.

Although Gary had little direct responsibility for the day-to-day operations of his steel mills, he nonetheless was largely responsible for setting policy. In this respect he must share much of the blame for U.S. Steel's poor performance during his tenure. In large measure U.S. Steel was "born old." Although it controlled about 65 percent of the U.S. steel industry, it was not designed to be a sleek, efficient producer. The steel firm started life with watered stock, a group of obsolete mills, and an almost unmanageable mixture of divisions and subdivisions. Slow and conservative, it was vulnerable to more efficient rivals and was reluctant to abandon obsolete and poorly located Pittsburgh mills. By 1920 U.S. Steel's share of steel output had slipped from 61.1 percent in 1901 to only 39.9 percent. The rise of the auto industry made the situation even worse. Instead of moving mills closer to Detroit, it instituted the "Pittsburgh Plus" price system under which all steel was priced as if it had been made in Pittsburgh, and won another "gentleman's agreement" from the industry not to locate in Detroit. Newer Ohio firms, however, better located and better able to produce the sheet steel needed by the auto industry, took away much of this business during the 1920s.

Gary was a Methodist and a Republican who was twice married. In 1869 he married Julia Graves of Aurora, Illinois. She died in 1902, and three years later he married Emma Townsend of New York City. (**A.** *DAB; NCAB*, 14:69; *New York Times*, August 16, 1927; *Who Was Who*, vol. 1; Ida Tarbell, *Life of Elbert Gary*, 1925. **B.** Frederick Lewis Allen, *The Lords of Creation*, 1935; David Brody, *Steelworkers in America*, 1960, and *Labor in Crisis: The Steel Strike of 1919*, 1965; Charles A. Bulick, *Trusts and Corporation Problems*, 1929; Gabriel Kolko, *The Triumph of Conservatism*, 1963; Milton Moskowitz et al., *Everybody's Business*, 1980; Gertrude Schroder, *The Growth of Major American Steel Companies*, 1953.)

GATES, JOHN WARNE (May 8, 1855–August 9, 1911). Financier and speculator, American Steel and Wire Company; Illinois Steel Company; Republic Iron and Steel Company; and Tennessee Coal and Iron Company. Born in West Chicago, Illinois, son of Asel Avery Gates and Mary Warne. His father was a farmer, and his family was originally from Massachusetts, whence they moved to Ohio and then to Illinois. Gates was educated in the village academy and at North-Western College at Naperville, Illinois, where he took a six month commercial course. At nineteen he purchased a one-half interest in the village hardware store, after having spent two years in the grain business. A short time later he moved to St. Louis, Missouri, where he opened a hardware firm.

In 1878 Gates entered into a partnership with Isaac L. Ellwood to manufacture barbed wire, with Gates serving as salesman of the company. At this point the manufacture of barbed wire for fencing was just beginning to gain some importance because of the opening of wide tracts of western lands, whose needs could not be met by rail fencing. It was this observation which made Gates seek out Ellwood to form the partnership. Finding that the Texas ranchers to whom he tried to sell the wire were skeptical of its usefulness, he rented a tract at San Antonio, built a corral with the wire, and issued a challenge to the ranchers to allow their best Texas steers to test its endurance. The test was highly successful and orders began to pour into the company. With this success, Gates began a series of consolidations in 1880 that by 1898 resulted in the formation of the American Steel and Wire Company of New Jersey, a $90 million corporation.

First he found a partner with some capital in St. Louis and set up a manufacturing plant there. This caused some legal complications with Ellwood, but Gates exhausted his opponent by ingeniously moving the plant from one side of the river to the other to thwart the service of injunctions. They finally reached an agreement and Gates turned his full attention to consolidation. Each successive consolidation saw him buy up the stock of the previous one at more than par value and then issue its own stock at considerably more than the appraised values of the constituent properties. Even after this "watering," his firm's stock rose in value on the exchanges.

Gates' greatest talents lay in promotion, and his greatest achievement was the organization of American Steel and Wire, which made him the leader of the wire industry in America. He was much less interested in the technical and managerial aspects of his particular enterprises, so that he often lost interest in the companies after using his boundless energy to put together the new organizations and secure capital for the new consolidations. In 1894 Gates succeeded Jay C. Morse as president of Illinois Steel Company, and he converted the firm into a moneymaking venture. It was also Gates who foresaw before anyone else the possibilities of a huge steel combination by acquiring the Carnegie interests. In 1899 Gates broached the idea of a "billion dollar corporation" to Henry Clay Frick,* Elbert H. Gary* and William H. Moore.* But he was too much of a plunger for J. P. Morgan,* so he did not participate in the final formation of the giant steel firm.

Gates was one of the organizers of the Republic Iron and Steel Company of Youngstown, Ohio, and in 1906 was part of a syndicate which took over the Tennessee Coal and Iron Company. The latter organization was hit by the Panic of 1907 and taken over by U.S. Steel. He was known as "Bet-A-Million Gates" to the general public. Although his general reputation was as a plunger, he actually relied heavily on the advice of expert technicians such as William R. Walker, and developed an elaborate network for gathering information. But when he did decide to act, he did so with utmost daring. His taste for gambling and speculation, however, had early drawn him into wide-ranging stock market activities. In 1896 he managed a speculative operation in Chicago Gas, and in 1897 he was reputed to have cleared $12 million in Wall Street in connection with his wire interests. It was chiefly as a marauder that he was known and feared on the stock exchange. At one time his fortune was wiped out in a venture on the Chicago Grain Exchange, but he kept quiet about it to maintain his credit and managed in a short time to retrieve his losses.

His greatest financial disaster came with the Louisville and Nashville Railroad. J. P. Morgan needed the road in connection with a consolidation he was managing, but Gates secretly gained control of it and then resold it to Morgan at a very high price. Morgan, who had long detested Gates, pretended to be amused, extended Gates a great deal of credit, and then manipulated a drop in the securities. Morgan then dictated his terms to Gates, forcing him to forsake the stock exchange for good. Gates accepted the terms. He then went to Port Arthur, Texas, where he organized the Texas Company and invested in the Spindletop Oil Field. This was to prove his shrewdest investment of all, and as the oil industry grew, Gates' massive fortune grew along with it. He also owned a large portion of real estate in Port Arthur and controlled its industries. He showed as much zeal for this small town operation as he did for his large-scale enterprises.

He married Dellora Baker of St. Charles, Illinois, in 1876. He had one son, Charles G. Gates, who set up the stock brokerage firm of C. G. Gates and Company, one of the largest speculative houses on Wall Street. (**A.** *DAB; NCAB*, 18:102; 14:67; *New York Times*, August 9, 1911; *Iron Age*, August 10, 1911; March 23, 1899; Robert Irving Warshow, *Bet-A-Million Gates*, 1932. **B.** Frederick L. Allen, *The Lords of Creation*, 1935.)

GENEEN, HAROLD SYDNEY (January 22, 1910–   ). Communications company executive and conglomerate organizer, International Telephone and Telegraph. Born in Bournemouth, England, son of S. Alexander Geneen and Aida De Cruciani. His father was a Russian-born concert manager who moved to the United States when Harold was just one year old. His parents later separated. Geneen was educated in boarding schools and summer camps and graduated from Suffield (Connecticut) Academy at age sixteen. He then studied accounting evenings at New York University while working as a page on the New York Stock Exchange. In 1934 he graduated from N.Y.U. and joined the Manhattan accounting firm of Lybrand, Ross Brothers and Montgomery. After eight years with that firm, he worked as chief accountant at the American Car Company (1942–1946), as comptroller of Bell and Howell (1946–1950), and as vice-president of Jones and Laughlin Steel from 1950 to 1956.

Geneen left Jones and Laughlin in the latter year to become executive vice-president of the ailing Raytheon Manufacturing Company, headquartered in Waltham, Massachusetts. He was mandated by the company president, Charles Francis Adams, to "make some money," so he imposed strict cost controls, acquired more working capital, and persuaded banks to open new lines of credit for the firm. He insisted that Raytheon pay its bills within the time limit to receive the standard discount, while dunning its own customers for debts outstanding. It was at Raytheon that Geneen developed the basic system for which he became well known in management circles. The company was divided into twelve autonomous divisions, with the head of each division responsible in detail for all aspects of production and under constant scrutiny by top management. Essential to his management system were internal controls, monthly management reviews, constant pressures, and samplings to measure progress.

Although Geneen increased Raytheon's earnings by 400 percent, he was not given absolute authority at the company, so in 1959 he abruptly resigned to accept the presidency of International Telephone and Telegraph, a stagnating monopoly with sales of $765 million from its loosely organized worldwide communications system. Under Geneen's aggressive management, ITT diversified, acquiring shares of companies ranging from the Sheraton Hotel Chain to the Hartford Insurance Company, growing into one of the largest multinational conglomerates in the world, with revenues exceeding $8.5 billion.

ITT had been founded by Sosthenes Behn,* who had incorporated it in 1920 for the purpose of controlling several small Caribbean telephone companies he had acquired, with the long-range goal of building an international telephone network to rival and complement the American system. Behn remained in control of ITT until 1956, the year before his death. A subcommittee then ran it for three years until Geneen took over. When he assumed control, the net earnings of ITT were only 3.8 percent of sales and Geneen made it clear that he would clean up every aspect of the organization. He ended the traditional autonomy of the ITT units and instituted a system of strict accountability which still prevails. The comptrollers of all subsidiaries report directly to the corporation's overall comptroller, and all unit heads are required to draw up careful five year plans and to participate in marathon monthly meetings held in New York and Brussels, Belgium, ITT's European headquarters.

During the 1960s, especially after Latin American countries began nationalizing telephone companies owned by ITT, Geneen made many new acquisitions, mostly in the United States, without regard to what they produced, as long as they were likely to add to the corporation's earnings. In 1961 he bought up the remaining stock in American Cable and Radio (ITT was already the major stockholder), and subsequently acquired the Gilfillon Corporation, a radar technology firm; General Controls, a manufacturer of thermostatic equipment; Bell and Gosset, a pump manufacturer; the Aetna Finance Company (which merged with the Great International Life Insurance Company); Howard W. Sams and Company, the major stockholder in Bobbs-Merrill Publishing house; Levitt and Sons, builders of the "Levittown" housing developments; the Hamilton Management Company, a mutual fund firm; the Cannon Electric Company; and the Sheraton Corporation. An attempt to acquire the American Broadcasting Company was thwarted by the Department of Justice.

ITT's biggest acquisition came in 1970 when it purchased Hartford Fire Insurance Company, a massive source of constant funds. The Justice Department filed an antitrust suit against this action, but an out-of-court settlement in 1971 allowed ITT to retain the insurance company, while divesting itself of several other firms, including Avis Rent-A-Car and the Canteen Corporation, a large but ailing food vending firm. A year later, several ITT scandals began clouding its public image when a memo from Dita Beard, ITT's Washington lobbyist, revealed connections of the Hartford "deal" with an ITT pledge of $400,000 for the 1972 Republican National Convention. Later allegations emerged which charged that ITT had conspired with the CIA to sabotage the election of Salvador Allende of Chile, who had promised to nationalize ITT's Chilean Telephone Company. Geneen admitted the basic truth of the Allende accusation, but denied the Hartford/Republican Convention charge. These events nevertheless led to the downfall of attorneys general John Mitchell and Richard Kleindienst.

By the 1970s, ITT was growing at an annual rate of 10 percent per year, and managed 250 companies in some sixty countries, including: the British Insurance Group; Excess Holdings; the Continental Baking Company; Graho, which wholesales and retails foods in European supermarkets; Standard Electric Lorenz of West Germany, a mammoth manufacturer of a broad range of telecommunications and other electronic equipment; World Communications, Incorporated; Bell Telephone Manufacturing Company; and the Pennsylvania Glass Sand Corp.

Geneen has been married twice. His first marriage ended in divorce in 1946, and in 1949 he married June Elizabeth Hjelm. He has no children. He is an Episcopalian and a Republican. (**A.** *Current Biography*, February, 1954; *Who's Who in America, 1978-79.* **B.** Anthony Sampson, *The Sovereign State of ITT*, 1973.)

GERBER, (DANIEL) FRANK SR. (January 12, 1873–October 7, 1952) and **Daniel (Frank) Gerber Jr.** (May 6, 1898–March 16, 1974). Baby food manufacturers, Gerber Products Company. **Frank Gerber** was born in Detroit, Michigan, the son of Joseph Daniel Gerber and Agnes Mayer. His father owned a tannery. Frank graduated from Fremont high school in 1887 and spent one year at the Valparaiso Normal School. Then, at age sixteen, he entered his father's tannery. Within five years he became a partner in the firm, and managed it until it was closed in 1905. Earlier, in 1901, he had helped found the Fremont Canning Company, which began with a modest capital of $10,000 to provide a market for local farmers by canning their peas, and later, beans and small fruits. This small-town cannery was the basis for the later baby food industry.

Although the early years of the company were difficult, Frank Gerber put it on a firm financial footing, and when the economy recovered after 1908, there was a great growth in profits. He expanded the plant in 1914-1915, to enable it to engage in year-round production. When his father died in 1917, he succeeded him as president, with sales that year exceeding one million dollars. Fremont was hit by a postwar slump in 1919-1920, but steady growth ensued in the later 1920s. The major change in the firm's direction was to come in 1928, primarily at the instigation of Frank Gerber's son, Daniel.

Daniel Gerber was born in Fremont, Michigan, and educated at St. John's Military Academy in Delafield, Wisconsin, from 1913 to 1916. He served in the army during World War I, after which he spent a year at the Babson Institute of Business Administration (1919-1920). In 1920 he joined the family firm. By 1926 he had become assistant general manager of the company. A year later, he began urging his father to begin the production of strained baby foods at the cannery. Although this was not a new idea, most babies were still given solely a liquid diet until they were one year old.

So, if they were to begin manufacturing baby foods, they would be bucking long-held traditions of baby care, and had no idea of what their potential market might be.

Frank Gerber ordered thorough tests of the market possibilities and of the products themselves. Experimental batches were tested on Daniel's daughter, Sally, and other babies, with great success. Fianlly, for three months in 1928 the company launched a large-scale advertising campaign in *Good Housekeeping, Children* (later *Parents*) *Magazine*, the *Journal of the American Medical Association*, and others. Their task entailed not just advertising a product, but also convincing parents to adopt new feeding concepts for their children.

Existing baby foods were sold through pharmacies on prescription, with prices at about 35 cents a can. The Gerbers proposed to sell theirs at 15 cents a can through the grocery stores, thus reaching a much larger market. To identify the product, and to reassure mothers, the "Gerber Baby" symbol was adopted, which soon became famous throughout the world. Under a coupon offer, the firm gained the names and addresses of the customers and their local grocery outlets. Gerber's brokers could then persuade reluctant wholesalers to stock their product. Within sixty days, "Gerber Strained Foods" had gained spotty national distribution. In the first year their gross sales were $345,000, which was much greater than had been expected. Despite the onset of the Great Depression, Gerber expanded its baby food output and added new lines during the 1930s.

The firm employed scientists in special laboratories, helped farmers improve their crops, published child care pamphlets, and issued classroom guides for home economics and nutrition classes. In 1938 the Gerbers began dealing directly with the wholesaler through their own company outlets. By 1941 baby foods exceeded adult foods in the Gerber line and the firm changed its name to the Gerber Products Company. Two years later it dropped all adult foods. By this time local farm output could not sustain Gerber's needs, so plants were opened in Oakland, California; Rochester, New York; and Niagara, Ontario. When Frank Gerber died in 1952, Daniel became senior member of the firm.

In 1956 Gerber Products Company was listed on the New York Stock Exchange for the first time, and during the 1960s expanded into many foreign countries. Non-baby food products were added to the firm's line, including plastic panties, lotions, vaporizers, and toys. In 1962 the company began making its own metal cans, and in 1969 it survived an intensive Senate investigation into its use of salt and monosodium glutamate in baby foods. By 1973 Gerber sales were $278 billion, and it had become the world's largest supplier of baby foods. Its growth had been achieved partially through expansion and partially through acquisition. In 1943 it acquired Elmhurst Packers, Incorporated in Oakland, California. In 1947, through a joint arrangement with Armour and Company, the company added to its line strained and junior meats, which were processed at its own plant in Fremont. In 1949 it joined forces with Ogelvie Flour Mills, Ltd., forming Gerber-Ogelvie Baby Foods Ltd., later to be Gerber Products of Canada, Ltd., with Daniel Gerber as president.

In 1950 Gerber purchased a canning plant at Rochester, New York, and in 1952 added teething biscuits to its line. In 1955 the Gerber Plastics Company was acquired for the manufacture of toys for babies, and in 1959 a subsidiary in Mexico was opened. A year later it purchased Knoll and Company, a manufacturer of waterproof pants and bibs for babies. In 1965 it began to market an extensive line of Gerber Babyware, including shirts, socks, crib sheets, and so forth. In 1962 Gerber entered into an agreement with Corn Products Company, a leading American producer with operations in 24 foreign countries. The latter company began producing Gerber baby foods in Europe, and by 1963 twenty strained varieties were distributed in France and West Germany. From 1945 to 1964 the number of employees of the firm increased from 2,000 to 5,500, and sales increased from $16.4 million to $178.3 million.

Both Frank and Daniel Gerber were Christian Scientists and Republicans. Frank married Dora Pauline Platt of Fremont, Michigan, in 1896. Daniel married Dorothy Marion Scott in 1923. They had five children. (*DAB*, Supplement 1; *NCAB*, 41:392; K:603; *New York Times*, October 8, 1952; March 18, 1974.)

GERSTLE, LEWIS (December 17, 1824–November 19, 1902). Pioneer merchant and shipper in Alaska, Alaska Commercial Company. Born in Bavaria of Jewish stock, he came to America in 1847. He first lived in Louisville, Kentucky, where he worked as a peddler. Two years later he went to New Orleans, and in 1850 moved to California. When he arrived there he opened a fruit stand, but soon entered the gold mines in El Dorado County as a day laborer. While working there he met Louis Sloss,* another Bavarian immigrant, and they formed a business partnership and friendship which was to last for fifty years. Leaving the mines, they first opened a wholesale grocery business in Sacramento, then moved to San Francisco to become mining stock brokers. Their firm (Louis Sloss and Company) also became the most extensive buyer of wood and manufacturer of sole leather on the Pacific Coast.

After the purchase of Alaska in 1867, Gerstle's firm and others acquired the rights and privileges of the Russian-American Company. Three of the firms were amalgamated to form the Alaska Commercial Company, in which Gerstle was very active and prominent. In 1867 the firm acquired from the United States the exclusive rights for twenty years of seal fishing on the islands of St. Paul and St. George. In return for this monopoly, the company paid the government a yearly rental and a royalty on each seal captured. The company supplied the whole world with seal skins, and its payment to the government was sufficient to cover the entire cost of the purchase of Alaska–$7 million. As part of its agreement, the company established trading posts, schools, and churches in various parts of Alaska and in many other ways contributed to the development of the young area.

Under Gerstle's leadership the firm established a line of ocean steamers between San Francisco and Alaska, and put into operation more than a score of large river boats on the Yukon, with steamers sailing between Nome and Dawson. For many years until his death, Gerstle was president of the company and made a very large fortune from its activities. In addition, he was one of the promoters of the Union Iron Works in San Francisco, the San Joaquin Valley Railroad, the Pioneer Woolen Mills, and many other manufacturing ventures. In the later 1880s he cooperated with Senator Warner Miller in the establishment of a company to build the proposed Nicaragua Canal. He was also director of the Nevada National Bank, the Union Trust Company, and the California-Hawaii Sugar Company, and held an extensive amount of real estate in San Francisco.

Lewis Gerstle was Jewish, and married Hannah Greenebaum of Philadelphia in 1858. She was the sister of his partner's wife, and was also a native of Bavaria. They had seven children. (*DAB*; *NCAB*, 13:245.)

GETTY, JEAN PAUL (December 15, 1892–June 6, 1976). Oil producer, Getty Oil Company. Born in Minneapolis, Minnesota, son of George Franklin Getty and Sarah McPherson Risker. His ancestors came from Ireland to Maryland in 1790. His father was a lawyer, public official, and oil producer. Jean Paul was educated in public schools and at the University of California. He did graduate work in economics at Oxford University in England in 1913. His father had gone into the oil business in Oklahoma in 1903, and two years later moved to California, where Paul was reared.

At age twenty-one, Paul Getty arrived in Tulsa, Oklahoma, ready to work and determined to earn a million dollars in two years. Tulsa was the site of his father's Minnehoma Oil Company, and Getty began to buy oil leases in the so-called red beds area of Oklahoma. The considered opinion was that it was impossible for there to be any oil in the area, so Getty paid very little for the leases. They turned out to be exceedingly valuable oil lands. By buying and selling oil leases, with his father's backing, he had made his first million by 1916, only one year behind his own ambitious schedule. He then returned to Los Angeles, where he lived the life of a playboy for two years.

In 1919 he reentered the business world in association with his father in the buying and selling of oil leases and in the drilling of wildcat wells. Most of these ventures were successful, so that during the 1920s Getty accumulated a fortune of about three million dollars, including a one-third interest in a company which was to evolve into the Getty Oil Company. His father, however, had been shocked by Paul's rather profligate personal life, and especially by his several marriages during this time, so when he died in 1930 he left him only $500,000 out of a $10 million fortune. Most of his fortune went to Getty's mother.

When the depression hit, Getty picked up the Pacific Western Oil Corporation, a holding company with large oil reserves and a heavy cash balance. He also negotiated with his mother to gain a controlling interest in his father's company, the George F. Getty Company of Los Angeles. Then, in a series of maneuvers, he obtained control by 1953 of the Mission Corporation and its holdings in Tidewater Oil (then called Tidewater Associated Oil Company) and Skelly Oil Company. These companies, with their reserves, refineries, and retail business, eventually became part of a pyramid of corporations at the top of which stood the Getty Oil Company, which was more than 80 percent owned by Getty.

In a complicated rearrangement of his properties in 1967, Getty merged the Tidewater Oil Company and the Missouri Oil Company into the Getty Oil Company. The surviving company had assets of more than $3 billion, a figure that multiplied many times over when oil prices skyrocketed in the 1970s. The profits of the concern averaged about 10 percent of assets. He had had to battle Standard Oil for the control of both Tidewater and Skelly. During this same time he also began to acquire a large number of other properties. In 1938 he purchased the Hotel Pierre in New York City for $2,350,000 and twenty years later sold most of the suites to the residents, while retaining, through a subsidiary company, the service rooms, bars, restaurants, and reception rooms. He also built the twenty-two story Getty Building at 600 Madison Avenue in the 1950s, which he owned through Getty Oil. He also owned a skyscraper in Los Angeles, an office building in Tulsa, and the Pierre Marques Hotel near Acapulco, Mexico. During World War II, Spartan Aircraft, a Skelly subsidiary, manufactured trainers and airplane parts under Getty's personal supervision. After the war it was turned profitably to the production of mobile homes.

His most daring venture, however, came in 1949, when he obtained a sixty year concession in Saudi Arabia's half of the neutral barren tract lying between Saudi Arabia and Kuwait. He paid King Saud $9.5 million in cash for the concession and agreed to pay one million dollars a year for its duration, whether oil was struck or not. The gamble paid off lavishly for Getty. After an investment of $30 million, Getty found oil in enormous quantities in 1953, and the production of the field was in excess of 16 million barrels of oil per year. This made Getty a billionaire. He also owned a tanker fleet and an interest in the Minnehoma Insurance Company, the Minnehoma Financial Corporation, and the Spartan Cafeteria Company, all of Tulsa.

Getty was married five times. In 1923 he married Jeannette Dumont; in 1925, Allene Ashby; Adolphine Helmle in 1928; Ann Rork, a film starlet, in 1932; and Louise Dudley Lynch, a debutante and cabaret singer, in 1939. He had four sons, all of whom had stormy relationships with their father.

(**A.** *NCAB*, G:121; *New York Times*, February 6, 1974; June 7, 1976; *Who Was Who*, vol. 6. **B.** Anthony Sampson, *The Seven Sisters*, 1975; J. Paul Getty, *As I See It*, 1976.)

GIANNINI, AMADEO PETER (May 6, 1870–June 3, 1949) and **Attilio Henry Giannini** (March 2, 1874–February 7, 1943). Bankers, financiers, and motion picture studio executives, Bank of America, Transamerica Corporation, United Artists Studio Corporation.

A. P. Giannini was born in San Jose, California, son of Luigi Giannini and Virginia DeMartini, Italian immigrants who had settled in the Santa Clara Valley in 1869. His father had originally been a hotelkeeper, but moved his family to Alviso, California, where he engaged in farming. In 1877 he was killed by a disgruntled workman on his farm. His widow later married Lorenzo Scatena, a self-employed teacher, who moved the family to San Francisco in 1882. Scatena worked for a time for a produce firm until he opened his own produce business. Young Giannini was educated in the public schools of Alviso and San Francisco and at Heald's Business College. He then became an entry clerk in his stepfather's produce commission firm, L. Scatena and Company. By the time he was nineteen he was a partner in the company, proving himself to be a brilliant merchant. During the next dozen years he helped build the firm into one of California's leading commission houses. That, coupled with the fact that he married the daughter of a wealthy San Francisco businessman, allowed him to retire at thirty-one to build his dream home in San Mateo.

When his father-in-law died, Giannini inherited a seat on the board of a small savings bank in North Beach, in the center of San Francisco's Italian community. Frequent battles with the conservative directors of this firm caused him in 1904 to set up his own lending institution, the Bank of Italy. It was designed to cater to small businesses and average depositors, and offered a full range of banking services. Alone among San Francisco's banks it encouraged small loans, amounting to as little as $25. Giannini was also unorthodox in the solicitation of deposits, walking the streets of North Beach looking for prospective depositors. He instituted popular, eye-catching advertisements. Thus was laid the foundation of a financial institution that gradually extended a network of branches throughout California and overseas, becoming the world's largest bank before his death.

In 1908 Giannini heard Lyman J. Gage,* a prominent Chicago banker and Secretary of the Treasury, extol the benefits of branch banking. A year later California enacted a law which provided the legal basis upon which he started his vast banking empire. The first Bank of Italy branch was opened in San Jose in 1909. He bought a small bank there and converted it into a branch, which he continued until 1917. Then he began using corporate affiliates and holding companies to facilitate acquisitions. By the end of 1918, with twenty-four branches in California, and total resources of more than $93 million, Bank of Italy had become the first statewide banking system in the United States. This aroused the strong opposition of other California bankers, who delayed, but did not stop him. In 1921 the Federal Reserve Board ruled that no bank belonging to the federal reserve system could open new branches. Giannini skirted the federal order by buying the Bank of America of Los Angeles, which had 21 branches. The federal reserve soon relaxed its restrictions and branches of both the Bank of Italy and the Bank of America began opening throughout the state.

Giannini had built the popularity of his bank by stressing banking services for the many rather than the few. One of his first innovations in banking was the introduction of home loans repayable in monthly installments to bring home ownership within the reach of more people. He also made loans on small collateral. He was never a large stockholder of the institution he created. He served as its president from 1914 to 1924 and sponsored wide public ownership of the institution, encouraging his employees to become shareholders through a program of profit sharing. In 1919, when it had become the largest bank in California, he organized the Bancitaly Corporation, an investment trust, holding stock in American and European banks. Through this organization he entered the New York banking field in the same year with the purchase of the East River National Bank. From time to time he purchased other New York banks, and in 1928 got control of Bank of America, one of New York's oldest banking institutions. Shortly thereafter, the Bancitaly-controlled banks in New York were consolidated to form the Bank of America National Association of New York.

In 1928 Giannini organized the Transamerica Corporation as a holding company to succeed Bancitaly, and he served as its president until 1931, when he retired. He appointed a Wall Street investment banker, Elisha Walker, to head Transamerica, but as soon as Giannini left on a European vacation, Walker repudiated his policies and began dismantling his empire. Giannini had underestimated the loyalty Walker owed to New York's older financial elite and the degree to which Wall Street resented the intrusion of an upstart of Italian origin. On returning to California Giannini led a popular crusade to recapture his banking empire, gathering proxies from small investors all over the state at meetings in which he denounced the "Wall Street racketeers." He won the battle, but the depression soon forced him to foreclose on the farms and businesses of many of the "little people" who had supported him. Giannini and his bank (by now called Bank of America) were saved largely by his friendship with Franklin Roosevelt. When it came time to finance the massive dam-building projects of the West during the early years of the New Deal, Bank of America got the bid. In 1945 Giannini stepped down as chairman of Bank of America, retaining the special title of founder and chairman.

By 1939 Bank of America's assets were $6 billion, but it had been criticized during the 1930s for acting in collusion through its affiliate,

California Lands Incorporated, in helping large landowners to exploit migratory labor and in frustrating unionization attempts among these workers. By this time, Bank of America had 493 branches in California. At his death Giannini was chairman of the board of the Transamerica Corporation; honorary chairman of the Banca d'America e d'Italia; and director of National City Bank and City Bank Farmers Trust Company, both of New York; Fireman's Fund Insurance Company, and Fireman's Fund Indemnity Company, both of San Francisco; and the First National Bank of Portland, Oregon. He gave $1.5 million for the establishment of a school of agricultural economics at the University of California, and in 1945 created the Bank of America–Giannini Foundation.

He was Roman Catholic and an independent in politics. He married Clarinda Agnes Cuneo, and they had six children, three of whom died young. His son, Lawrence Mario Giannini (1894–1952), joined the Bank of Italy as a clerk in 1918. In 1932 he was named senior vice-president, and in 1936 was appointed president, a post he maintained until his death. He was especially responsible for the development of the bank's international banking facilities. Meanwhile, in 1924 he became vice-president of Transamerica Corporation, and its president in 1930. He served in the latter position only until 1932, although he remained a member of the advisory council. When his father died in 1949 young Mario took over Bank of America. He expanded the bank's operations overseas during the three years of his control, and these policies were continued by his successors. By 1970 Bank of America had become a prime international lender, following closely in the footsteps of its eastern rival, Citibank. By 1979 it was America's largest bank, both in terms of total deposits and total loans.

A. H. Giannini, brother of A. P. Giannini, graduated from St. Ignatius College in San Francisco and got a degree in medicine from the University of California in 1896. He then began his medical practice in San Francisco and served in the Spanish-American War. He abandoned his medical practice in 1909, having been elected a vice-president of the Bank of Italy in the previous year. In 1919 he moved to New York City as president of the East River National Bank, and in 1928 he became president of the board of the Bank of American National Association of New York and vice-president of Transamerica Corporation until 1931. He then returned to California to assume the chairmanship of the general executive committee of the Bank of America National Trust and Savings Association, with headquarters in Los Angeles.

During this time, A. H. Giannini became intimately involved in the motion picture industry, serving as president and chairman of the board of the United Artists Studio Corporation until 1938. After that time he continued in the movie industry as a trustee of Universal Pictures and as a director of Columbia Pictures Corporation; Selznick International Pictures Incorporated; Lesser-Lubitsch and Company; and Fox West Coast Theaters,

Incorporated until his death. He was the outstanding pioneer in the financing of motion picture productions. He early foresaw the possibilities of the
industry as a sound financial investment and probably did more than any
other individual in the banking field to develop it and establish it on a
sound business footing.

A. H. Giannini's first large loan was to Charlie Chaplin, to whom he gave
$500,000 to finance "The Kid" in 1920. He was much criticized in banking
circles for this investment, but when the picture netted the producer
several million dollars, they began to change their attitudes. He also financed "Snow White and the Seven Dwarfs" with Walt Disney,* "Gone
With The Wind," and all of Samuel Goldwyn's pictures. He retired from
banking in 1936.

A Roman Catholic, he married Leontine Denker of Los Angeles in 1905.
They had one son, Bernard. (**A.** *DAB*, Supplement 4; *NCAB*, A:108; 38:37;
31:462; 41:304; *Current Biography*, March, 1947; July, 1949; *Who Was
Who*, vol. 2; J. Dana, *A. P. Giannini: Giant of the West*. **B.** Marquis James
and Bessie R. James, *The Story of Bank of America*, 1954; Matthew
Josephson, *The Money Lords*, 1972; Milton Moscowitz, et al., *Everybody's
Business*, 1980.)

GIBSON, TRUMAN KELLA (August 5, 1882–August 27, 1972). Black
insurance executive, Supreme Life Insurance Company of America. Born
in Macon, Georgia, he received degrees from Atlanta University and
Harvard. Early in his career he organized the Fireside Mutual Insurance
Company of Ohio, and then the Supreme Life and Casualty Company of
Ohio. In the 1920s he joined Supreme Life Insurance Company, becoming
chairman of the board in 1929. In 1943 he became head of the company
and ushered in a period of growth and financial stability until 1950. After
1950 the record was less favorable and the rate of growth slowed sharply,
due to shortcomings in the sales force. He remained as honorary chairman
of the concern until his death.

Just after Gibson became chairman of the board, the depression hit the
newly merged company very hard. The very survival of the company was at
stake, as the black insurance market of the North virtually disappeared and
two of the largest Negro insurance companies failed. Supreme Life was in a
very vulnerable position, since it held a high percentage of ordinary life
insurance and its surplus at the end of 1929 was only $20,463, with its
mortgage investments experiencing a rapid shrinking of their value in the
black ghettoes. Gibson reduced operating expenses at the company, cut
the par value of its stock, tried to increase its insurance sales, and disposed
of some of the real estate it had acquired through foreclosures. These
measures did not fully compensate for the drain of cash on the firm, and
the company's policy holders received first consideration. The assets of the
firm fell from $1,830,000 in 1930 to $1,570,000 in 1934, and investment

income virtually disappeared. But the company survived, and from 1938 on it became increasingly profitable.

The rapid recovery was largely based upon its expansion of the use of industrial insurance, by which policy holders paid relatively high insurance rates in very small weekly installments, collected by thousands of part-time insurance agents in the struggling black ghettoes. During these years, the industrial insurance in force had increased from $9 million in 1929 to $53.8 million in 1943. Supreme Life concentrated its entire sales effort on industrial insurance, using a "mass production" technique, whereby agents wrote out policies for as many persons as they could get to furnish the necessary information, without requiring a cash payment. The application was then processed and a policy issued, and then the agent would try to place it, stressing the very small weekly premium cost of the coverage to the customer.

These mass production techniques allowed the firm to use inexperienced and untrained agents when no funds were available to raise agents' salaries. The policy continued after 1940, which greatly raised operating expenses. They issued thirteen policies for every one in force and had a very high lapse rate, so virtually all of the expense for issuing these policies was borne by the company and those policy holders who kept their insurance in force. The worst effects of the system were on the sales force, whose agents learned almost nothing about the sales approaches necessary to sell life insurance as a long-term commitment, or about selling large policies. The agents were not well paid and there was a high degree of turnover, as many of their better agents were lost to other firms.

Thus, in 1953 Gibson instituted a number of changes which were designed to improve the flow of information and centralize control of the company. In 1955 a modern profit and expense control system was adopted, covering all phases of active information on the current state of any department. Several promising junior executives were promoted, and a new president, Earl B. Dickerson, was installed.

Gibson married Alberta Dickinson and had three children. (**A.** *Who Was Who*, vol. 5. **B.** Robert C. Puth, "Supreme Life: The History of a Negro Life Insurance Company, 1919–1962," *Business History Review*, 1969.)

GIFFORD, WALTER SHERMAN (January 10, 1885–May 7, 1966). Communications industry executive, American Telephone and Telegraph Company. Born in Salem, Massachusetts, son of Nathan Poole Gifford and Harriet Maria Spinney. He was educated at Salem high school and graduated from Harvard in 1905. A year before his graduation, he took his first position as a clerk at Western Electric Company in Chicago, Illinois. The following year he was transferred to the New York office of Western Electric as an assistant secretary and assistant treasurer of the company. While at Western Electric, Theodore N. Vail,* the president of the parent company, American Telephone and Telegraph, was impressed with the graphic charts Gifford made up to supply information. So he offered him the post of chief statistician with the parent company in Boston in 1908. Three years later he was transferred to the New York office of that company.

In 1916, the U.S. Naval Consulting Board decided to make an industrial preparedness survey and Gifford was chosen to direct it. Under his supervision the manufacturing resources and possibilities of more than 27,000 industrial establishments were inventoried and classified. At the end of that year he was chosen a director of the Council of National Defense and charged with coordinating the nation's industries and resources for the national security and welfare. Gifford was the chief executive officer of this board. After the declaration of war in 1917, he was put in active charge of the mobilization and creation of state and local councils of defense and a system of committees and subcommittees through which the cooperation of industry with the government was obtained. Several of these subcommittees developed into powerful and active war agencies, including the War Industries Board, the Aircraft Production Board, and the War Labor Policies Board. Between December 1916 and March 1917 the Council of National Defense laid out many wartime policies; it devised a system of purchasing war supplies, planned for press censorship, designed a system of food control with Herbert Hoover* as its director, and developed a daylight-savings plan. The council also insisted on universal military service and that there be exemptions for skilled labor. Despite the broad overall powers mandated to the council, it had little real authority and control over purchasing and the establishment of priorities; these functions remained under the Secretary of War, Newton D. Baker, a firm opponent of centralization. By the end of 1917 the Council was primarily "a jerry-built array of 150 committees ... associated helter-skelter with various army bureaus." Ultimately greater power would be vested in the War Industries Board, while in 1918 Gifford himself left the council to serve as U.S. representative in the organization of the Inter-Allied Munitions Council, serving for four months as its secretary.

At the end of his government service in 1918, he returned to the Bell System, where he was appointed comptroller of A.T.& T. A year later he was elected vice-president of the company in charge of accounts and finances. He became a director in 1922 and executive vice-president in 1923. Two years later he was elected president, an office he held until 1948 when he became chairman of the board, an office created for him. He retired in 1949 and was named honorary chairman. During his term as president, the company was marked by tremendous growth in its capital structure and in the telephone service it rendered. Operating revenue was increased from $657 million to $2.25 billion, and investment in plant equipment increased from $2.25 billion to $7.5 billion. The wire mileage grew from 39.5 million to 113 million, and the number of Bell telephones in use went from 11,250,000 to 28,500,000.

In 1927 Gifford inaugurated the company's overseas service, which opened for public use radio telephone channels between the United States and England. By 1948, 72 foreign countries were linked by wire and radio with Bell lines, and 57,420,000 telephones, or 96 percent of all instruments in the world, could be reached by any user of the Bell System services. With the onset of the depression, Gifford was again called upon by the government to render service. In 1931–1932 he served as chairman of the President's Organization on Unemployment Relief, and from 1933 to 1935 he was a member of the business advisory council of the U.S. Department of Commerce. With the outbreak of war in Europe in 1939, he was named a member of the War Resources Board, and from 1941 to 1947 he was chairman of the industry advisory committee of the Board of War Communications. In 1950 he was appointed U.S. Ambassador to England.

All of his contact with the government during this period, however, was not pleasant. In 1934 the federal government began a major "Telephone investigation" into the "world's biggest monopoly," under the auspices of the newly created Federal Communications Commission. The investigation cost the government two million dollars and A.T.& T. one and one-half million. The report criticized the company's methods of figuring depreciation, and asserted that telephone rates could be reduced without interfering with the standard of service; that the company had evaded state regulations; and that it was treated as a unit for purposes of profit and as a group of separate companies or entities for the purposes of regulation. Ten years later, in 1944, organized labor made an attempt to gain direct representation on the company's board of directors, but the attempt failed and the union's demands for revisions of the pension system were also defeated.

Gifford was a Republican and married Florence Pitman of Brooklyn, New York, in 1916. She died in 1937, and in 1944 he married Augustine (Lloyd) Perry of New York City. He had two sons, Walter Sherman Jr., who died while serving as a naval officer during World War II, and Richard Pitman Gifford. (**A.** *NCAB*, H:28; *Current Biography*, January, 1945; June, 1966; *New York Times*, May 8, 1966; *Who Was Who*, vol. 4. **B.** John Brooks, *Telephone: The First Hundred Years*, 1976; Horace Coan, *American Telephone and Telegraph*, 1939; N. R. Danielian, *AT & T: The Story of an Industrial Conquest*, 1939; James Weinstein, *The Corporate Ideal in the Liberal State*, 1968.)

GILBRETH, FRANK BUNKER (July 7, 1868–June 24, 1925) and **Lillian Moller Gilbreth** (May 24, 1878–January 2, 1972). Industrial efficiency experts, Gilbreth Incorporated. **Frank Gilbreth** was born in Fairfield, Maine, son of John Hiram Gilbreth and Martha Bunker. His Scotch-Irish ancestors had come to America in 1760. Frank Gilbreth was educated in the schools of

Andover and Boston, Massachusetts, graduating from high school in the latter city in 1885. Although he was accepted at Massachusetts Institute of Technology, he decided instead to enter the employ of a Boston construction engineering firm, completing his technical education in night school. He started in the firm as a bricklayer's apprentice, advancing steadily in the firm's service until he became general superintendent. In 1895 he opened his own contracting business in Boston, erecting mills, factories, power plants, dams, and canals. Branch offices were established in New York City, San Francisco, and London. During this period he invented an improved scaffold for bricklayers; a method of waterproofing cellars; concrete mixers, conveyers, and other labor-saving devices; and improvements in construction methods.

Increasingly, however, Gilbreth's interests were centered in the area of worker efficiency and the broader field of industrial management. As a young construction worker Gilbreth noticed that most workers' methods were based on tradition rather than a study of the most appropriate techniques. When he established his own construction company he began to consider ways of improving these methods, particularly those used in bricklaying. By providing bricklayers with better equipment and reorganizing their methods, Gilbreth was able to significantly increase their output. His success in changing a job that had defied change for centuries greatly impressed Frederick Winslow Taylor,* the "father" of scientific management. Gilbreth's bricklaying work became one of Taylor's favorite examples of "scientific management in action." Gilbreth and Taylor first met in 1907, soon becoming close associates. Gilbreth was the only "outsider" who was nearly fully accepted within the Taylor "circle," most members of which had been trained by Taylor himself. Gilbreth himself became a confirmed Taylorite, promising in 1908 to devote the rest of his life to "installing the Taylor system."

Over the next few years, however, the two men became increasingly estranged, partially due to Gilbreth's problems in implementing the Taylor system at several work-sites, and partially because of Gilbreth's developing interest in the field of time and motion studies. The latter involved a significant innovation in the field of scientific management and made Gilbreth a competitor of Taylor himself within the movement. By 1911 Gilbreth was using a camera to conduct his studies in "micromotion," and at the same time discontinued his contracting business to establish the firm of Frank B. Gilbreth, Incorporated, consulting engineers. In his micromotion studies he coupled his motion picture technique with a timing device capable of indicating movements to the thousandth of a minute. These films were then combined with instruction cards to teach workmen new methods. Gilbreth was so excited about this technique that he decided to devote the rest of his life to "standardizing performance of labor." Taylor, however, was less than enthusiastic, feeling conventional time and motion study was good enough for his purposes. Gilbreth offered Taylor "ownership" of the micromotion method and established a "Frederick Winslow Taylor Hall" in Providence where he gave weekly lectures on Taylorism. Taylor remained unmoved by these gestures, coldly rejecting Gilbreth's offer of the micromotion method and offering him little encouragement in his other activities. Their final break came in 1914, when Gilbreth ran into difficulties in applying the Taylor concepts at the Herrmann, Aukam Company of South River, New Jersey. Taylor accepted the company's various accusations against Gilbreth and advised the firm to drop him. In the following years Frank Gilbreth, in association with his wife Lillian, went his own separate way, avoiding the Taylor Society (which Frank Gilbreth had been instrumental in founding), and concentrating his efforts on motion study. Soon the Gilbreth system of management differed substantially from the Taylor system.

The most important way in which the Gilbreth system began to differ from the Taylor system was in its broader view of the "human factor" within scientific management. Frank Gilbreth's interest in motion study had led him to study the internal as well as external causes of worker motivation in his search for the "best way" to perform a job. He sought to identify the causes of worker fatigue in the worker's mental disposition as well as in the physical working conditions. In this transition away from traditional Taylorism, Gilbreth was particularly aided by his wife, **Lillian Moller Gilbreth**. Lillian Gilbreth was born in Oakland, California, daughter of William Moller and Annie Dilger. She graduated in psychology from the University of California in 1900 and married Frank Gilbreth in 1904. She had intended to become a practicing psychologist, but during the early years of her married life found she was devoting most of her energies to the raising of their twelve children (which was forever immortalized in the book and movie entitled *Cheaper By the Dozen*).

Lillian Gilbreth, however, fully appreciated the applicability of the industrial psychology of Hugo Munsterberg and Walter Dill Scott to the problems of scientific management. It was through her, and only indirectly through her husband, that the tools of industrial psychology became the tools of scientific management. Together, the Gilbreths after 1914 attacked the "scientific pretensions" of Taylor's system and its authoritarianism, seeking to remedy its shortcomings through the use of the new social sciences. With their emphasis on the welfare and training of the worker, they began to bridge the gap between scientific management and worker psychology, bringing the scientific management movement into closer contact with corporate liberal personnel management. As Lyndall Unwick has stated, "the emphasis placed by Lillian Gilbreth on 'the human element' and the 'psychology of management' reflected the beginnings of a shift of attention from the physical aspects of the job to the worker himself."

Lillian Gilbreth's transition from mother and housewife to industrial psychologist was neither easy nor rapid. During the years when she was home with her children she first began to apply her husband's ideas of efficiency and scientific management to the kitchen, developing her home into a model of industrial efficiency. Through her writings and lectures over the years she was to put thousands of American kitchens on an efficiency basis. Her most influential works in this area were *The Home-maker and Her Job* (1927) and *Living With Our Children* (1928). Prior to this, however, she had begun to formally and informally assist her husband in developing and applying ideas of scientific management and industrial psychology to the workplace. In 1912 she wrote *Psychology of Manage-ment*, and in the following years co-authored a series of books with her husband: *Applied Motion Study* (1917); *Fatigue Study* and *Motion Study for the Handicapped* (both in 1919); and *Time Study* (1920). When Frank Gilbreth died in 1925 Lillian went to Europe to read his papers at confer-ences and took his place on various committees. Finally coming out from under his shadow, she became president of Gilbreth, Incorporated and joined A. A. Potter and the Department of Industrial Management at Purdue University, where she lectured until 1948. During the 1930s she served on the President's Emergency Committee for Unemployment and the President's Organization for Unemployment Relief.

In 1948 Lillian Gilbreth was selected "Woman of the Year" in the United States, and a year later became known to millions of Americans as "mother" in *Cheaper By the Dozen*, a best-seller and motion picture written by two of her children. This was followed by a sequel, *Belles on Their Toes*, in 1950. She had gained her doctorate in industrial psychology from Brown University in 1915. (**A.** *NCAB*, 26:401; *Current Biography*, May, 1940; September, 1951; February, 1972; *Who Was Who*, vols. 5 and 6; Edna Vost, *Frank and Lillian Gilbreth: Partners for Life*, 1949; *New York Times*, June 15, 1924. **B.** Samuel Haber, *Efficiency and Uplift*, 1962; Milton Nadworny, *Scientific Management and the Unions*, 1955; Daniel Nelson, *Managers and Workers*, 1975; David F. Noble, *America By Design*, 1977; Lyndall Unwick, "Management's Debt to Engineers," *Advanced Management*, 1952.)

GILLESPIE, FRANK L. (d. May 1, 1925). Black Insurance executive, Liberty Life Insurance Company. Born in Arkansas and educated at Boston Conservatory, Howard University, and Harvard Law School. Gillespie held a wide variety of jobs in his early years, including private secretary to a Chicago financier, and working for the telephone company and for a black real estate dealer. In 1916 he became the first black superintendent employed by a white-owned insurance company—Royal Life Insurance Company. Royal Life was a training ground for a large number of black insurance executives during this time. Later, Gillespie worked for the Public Life Insurance Company of Illinois, another white-owned insurance company which sold industrial insurance to blacks. This experience gave him widespread experience with both black and white businesses and with civic and religious leaders in Chicago and Detroit.

Drawing upon this background and experience, in 1919 Gillespie founded the Liberty Life Insurance Company and began selling stock in the company. The stock sales were carried out by salesmen who contacted black communities all over the Midwest and South. His widespread connections were valuable during this period. The usual shareholders were physicians, dentists, lawyers, ministers, bankers, and businessmen. Most purchased only a few shares each, but George F. Liebrandt, president of the Lincoln State Bank, purchased 200 shares and provided the crucial financial support needed to complete the stock sales.

Liberty Life began operations in 1921 with offices at 35th and Grand Boulevard (now Martin Luther Boulevard) in Chicago. Gillespie was elected president, and two men just graduated from college and law school, W. Ellis Stewart and Earl B. Dickerson, became secretary and legal counsel. At this time the company's prospects looked quite good. Although the Negro market in Chicago was still quite small, with only 109,000 blacks living there in 1920, it was growing rapidly. Thus, Liberty Life became the first black insurance company organized in the North, although there were six others in the South at that time. As it developed, it became the third largest black insurance firm in the United States, and by 1965 had assets of over $33 million, with $208 million worth of insurance in force. Virtually all of its business was transacted in large northern cities.

The biggest single advantage the firm enjoyed was that white insurance companies often either refused black applications for insurance, or sold them only a limited range of plans. This policy had been adopted by most white firms since the 1880s, when it had become apparent that the black mortality rate was significantly higher than that for whites at all ages. This refusal of service was a major factor in the development of the black life insurance companies. Liberty Life initially sold only ordinary insurance, unlike other black firms, which were concentrating on industrial insurance with its small weekly premiums, high policy rates, and expensive administrative costs. The ordinary life market had the advantage also of being almost totally free from competition from white insurance firms, who also concentrated on industrial insurance for blacks.

Gillespie tried to obtain as many experienced agents as he could and to give them the greatest amount of training. Few experienced men were available and training of new men was very expensive, so it became necessary to employ a large number of part-time agents, often ministers or post-office employees. Nevertheless, advances to agents were a heavy financial burden to Liberty Life during its first seven years. While sales rose steadily every year through 1925, sales expenses and policy lapses were high. Thus there was little income afforded for investments and its initial surplus dwindled rapidly. This forced the company to issue additional stock. By the end of 1925, Liberty Life had $8,280,000 of insurance in force and only $495,000 in admitted assets.

During Gillespie's presidency, he had been the driving force behind the company, its best salesman, and its best contact with both the black and white business community. His death in 1925 was, therefore, a staggering blow to the firm, especially to its sales program.

Liberty Life's investments in the 1920s were heavily concentrated in real estate. The home office building was purchased for $250,000 in 1924 and black residential mortgages were also purchased. Part of the reason for the investment in black mortgages was altruistic, since blacks had great difficulty in obtaining mortgage funds elsewhere; but it was also an aid to insurance sales, and the investment yielded higher returns than others open to the company. The real estate loans were virtually its only earning assets during the 1920s.

In 1929 Liberty Life merged with the Supreme Life and Casualty Company of Columbus, Ohio, and the Northeastern Insurance Company of Newark, New Jersey. The size of the company was nearly doubled and its major characteristics were substantially changed. Supreme Life and Casualty had substantial holdings of industrial life insurance, with an agency force trained in these operations. Northeastern Life had an excellent investment portfolio and experienced management. But both had suffered small operating losses in 1928. The new combination was able to survive the disastrous depression of the thirties, largely because of the combination of strengths represented by the three constituent companies. (Robert C. Puth, "Supreme Life: The History of a Negro Life Insurance Company, 1919–1962," *Business History Review*, 1969; W. O. Bryan Jr., *Negro Life Insurance Companies*, 1948.)

GILLETTE, KING CAMP (January 5, 1855–July 9, 1932). Inventor, safety razor manufacturer, and social planner, Gillette Safety Razor Company and World Corporation. Born in Fond du Lac, Wisconsin, son of George Wolcott Gillette and Fanny Lemina Camp, author of the *White House Cook Book*. King Gillette was educated in the schools of Chicago until age sixteen, but the destruction of his father's possessions in the Chicago Fire of 1871 forced him to go out on his own. After working for hardware concerns in Chicago and New York, he was a traveling salesman for a similar firm in Kansas City. He then represented a bottle stopper manufacturing company. Like his father and brothers, he was always tinkering with inventions; his goal was the discovery of things which could be used and then thrown away, forcing the customer to keep coming back for more.

When faced with the necessity of honing an old-fashioned razor, he thought of using instead a thin blade of steel sharpened at both ends, clamped between plates, and held together by a handle. Although experts scoffed at the idea, since it would be impossible to sharpen the blades,

Gillette continued his experiments. They were so successful that in 1901 the Gillette Safety Razor Company was organized, of which he was president. The sales in 1903 consisted of 51 razors and 168 blades. By the end of the next year, the number had risen to 90,000 razors and 12,400,000 blades. Through ingenious advertising and merchandising, the business steadily expanded until eight plants in various parts of the world were established to manufacture the product. King Gillette retired from active business in 1913, although he remained president of the company until 1931. During the last ten years of his life he lived in and around Los Angeles, California, where he engaged in real estate operations.

Increasingly his interests after 1913 shifted to the realm of social theories, and he wrote a number of books detailing his ideas. He believed that the competitive system wasted 85-90 percent of human productive efforts, and fostered the greed which caused industrial and international strife. He sought to substitute cooperation for competition and proposed a gigantic trust which would acquire existing production facilities. To this end he incorporated the "World Corporation" in Arizona in 1910 and offered Theodore Roosevelt one million dollars to act as its president for four years. Roosevelt declined the offer. Gillette envisioned an engineer's utopia in which maximum production was to be insured by concentrating population and production near Niagara Falls with its potential power sources. Compensation was to be based on the labor performed, and agricultural services were to be rendered by battalions of labor moving from field to field. Domestic drudgery for the housewife was to be minimized by housing the population in mammoth apartment buildings with great central kitchens.

He married Alanta Ella Gaines of Willoughby, Ohio, in 1890 and they had one son, King G. Gillette. (*DAB,* Supplement 1; *NCAB,* 10:522.)

GIMBEL, ISAAC (April 24, 1856-April 11, 1931) and **Bernard Feustman Gimbel** (April 10, 1885-September 29, 1966). Merchants, Gimbel Brothers Department Stores. **Isaac Gimbel** was born in Vincennes, Indiana, son of Adam Gimbel and Fridolyn Kahnweiler. His father was a native of Bavaria who immigrated to New Orleans in 1835 and moved to Vincennes in 1842, where he established a general store called "The Palace of Trade" from which the large Gimbel Department store chain developed. Adam Gimbel moved to Philadelphia in 1865, leaving the Vincennes store in charge of his eldest son, Jacob Gimbel. Isaac, the second son, began his career at age thirteen, working for his brother Jacob.

In 1882 branch stores were opened at Danville, Illinois, and Washington, Indiana, and in 1887 they established a department store in Milwaukee, Wisconsin, under the name of Gimbel Brothers. The store was a success from the outset, and within a few years more of the brothers joined the business. Soon, seven of Adam Gimbel's sons (Jacob, Isaac, Charles,

Daniel, Ellis A., Louis S., Benedict, and an adopted son, Nathan Hamburger) constituted the firm of Gimbel Brothers. The success of the Milwaukee venture led the brothers to purchase the business of Granville B. Harris in Philadelphia in 1894. They converted it into a second Gimbel Department Store, and it became one of the leading houses of the city. In that year Adam Gimbel died, and Isaac—not the oldest, but the smartest brother— became president. By 1909 the Philadelphia store was such a success that Isaac decided to build a store in New York City. To take charge of this undertaking he chose his oldest son, Bernard, whom he made vice-president at twenty-four. The store was opened in 1910.

In 1922 the three units in Milwaukee, Philadelphia, and New York were incorporated into one organization, Gimbel Brothers, Incorporated, with Isaac Gimbel as president. Five years later he was succeeded in that position by his son Bernard, while he became chairman of the board. During the years of his presidency, Isaac traveled all over the world in search of merchandising ideas and was an authority on department store layouts and retail techniques. In 1925 a sixteen-story building opposite the original New York store was purchased. Three more floors were added to the structure, giving Gimbel Brothers twenty-seven acres of floor space devoted to the sale of a wide variety of merchandise. By 1930 net sales of the seven Gimbel Department stores were $123 million, with 20,000 employees. It had become the largest department store organization in the world.

Isaac was Jewish and a Democrat and married Rachel Feustmann, daughter of a Philadelphia merchant. They had two sons, Bernard F. and Frederick A. Gimbel. **Bernard Gimbel** was born in Vincennes, Indiana, and was educated at public schools in Milwaukee and at William Penn Charter School in Philadelphia. He graduated from the University of Pennsylvania in 1907. In the same year he joined Gimbel Brothers Department Stores, working on the receiving platform in the Philadelphia store. After two years in which he advanced through positions of greater responsibility in various departments, he was named a vice-president in 1909. He went to New York City with his father in 1910 to supervise the planning, construction, and equipping of the new ten-story Gimbel Brothers Department Store there, which he helped enlarge a few years later. The store was an immediate success.

Bernard Gimbel was instrumental in converting the family firm into a public stock corporation in 1922, and he personally negotiated the purchase of a competitor, Saks and Company, in 1922–1923. Gimbel Brothers continued to operate the Saks stores on Fifth Avenue and 34th Street under the old name. In 1925 Bernard was also primarily responsible for the purchase of the Kaufman and Baer Department Store in Pittsburgh. He was elected president of the company in 1925. He held that position until 1953, when he became chairman of the board, which he remained until his death. He also served as chief executive officer of the company until 1961 and as chairman of the subsidiary, Saks and Company.

During his association with the company, annual sales grew from $15 million to $500 million. During World War II the company reaped enormous profits on scarce consumer goods, which Bernard had earlier purchased at low prices. Gimbel's began a new branch program in 1954, opening stores in the suburbs of Milwaukee, Philadelphia, and New York City. By 1965 its retail network consisted of 53 stores throughout the country, which included 22 Gimbel Department Stores, 27 Saks Fifth Avenue Stores, and four Saks-34th Street Stores.

Bernard Gimbel was also a director of Coca-Cola and Burlington Mills, and chairman of the board of Madison Square Garden Corporation in New York City. He served nine terms as president and chairman of the New York Convention and Visitors Bureau, and was chairman of the organizing committee for the New York World's Fair of 1964–1965. He also founded the Gimbel Marketing Center at Wharton School of Finance at the University of Pennsylvania. Jewish and a Democrat, he married Alva Bernheimer of New York City in 1912. They had five children. His eldest son, Bruce A. Gimbel (b. 1913), was born in New York City and graduated from Yale in 1935. He joined Gimbel Brothers, becoming vice-president of sales in 1946, president in 1953, and chairman of the board and chief executive officer in 1973. Another of Bernard's sons, Peter R. Gimbel (b. 1928), became a prominent film and television producer. (**A.** *NCAB,* 23:133; 53:201; *Current Biography,* 1950, 1966; *Who's Who in America,* 1978–79. **B.** Leon Harris, *Merchant Princes,* 1979.)

GINTER, LEWIS (April 4, 1824–October 2, 1897). Cigarette manufacturer, Allen and Ginter. Born in New York City, son of John and Elizabeth Ginter. His family had settled in Manhattan in the eighteenth century, and his father was a grocer. Lewis Ginter was self-educated and went to Richmond, Virginia, in 1842 looking for work. There he started his own house furnishings business. The firm prospered and by the early 1850s had become an importer of fancy goods as well as a dry goods wholesaler trading extensively with village and country merchants. After a time he formed a partnership with John F. Alvey in the firm of Ginter and Alvey, specializing in silk, linen, and white goods. Ginter made annual trips to Europe to buy goods, and by 1860 the firm was earning annual profits of $40,000.

Shortly after the Civil War broke out, Ginter closed down his business to join the Confederate army as quartermaster, with the rank of major in Virginia. He served until 1865, when he returned to New York City and became associated with a brokerage firm which failed on "Black Friday" in 1869. This adversity turned Ginter's attention to the tobacco business. His desire to return to Richmond encouraged him to form a partnership with

John F. Allen in that city in 1872. They began to manufacture smoking and chewing tobacco and cigars in a small way, and Ginter traveled extensively to place their goods on the market.

To survive and grow in a highly competitive market, Ginter caught the eye of the consumer by handsome lithographed labels and attractive packaging designs. Most important, however, was the firm's decision in 1875 to venture into the manufacture of cigarettes, which were then a foreign product as yet untried with Virginia tobacco. Ginter introduced "Richmond Gems," paper-rolled cigarettes made from the Virginia leaf, which enjoyed a rapidly increasing popularity. In the early 1880s the firm became Allen and Ginter, and erected the Gem Tobacco Works in Richmond in 1881. Ginter used painted advertisements to sell his product years before this mode of advertising was widespread. His brands, Richmond Gem cigarettes, Opera Puffs, and Virginia Brights, became well-known among smokers whose taste had been cultivated by Allen and Ginter. They also sold pipe tobaccos, called Old Rip and Richmond Gem Curly Cut.

The first factory began operations with twenty unskilled girls doing the work. By 1888, a new plant employed over 1,000 women and girls, and cigarette production had increased from 100,000 a month to 2,000,000 a day. The activity of the firm's selling agents extended throughout the United States and into leading foreign markets. Meanwhile, the competition in advertising costs among the principal cigarette manufacturers— Allen and Ginter, W. Duke and Sons, Kinney Tobacco Company, W. S. Kimball and Company, and Goodwin and Company—was growing so bitter that they were forced to combine under the aegis of James B. Duke* for their own advantage. In 1890, after several unsuccessful attempts, Ginter succeeded in negotiating the sale of all the businesses to the American Tobacco Company, organized for that purpose. It was capitalized at $25 million and incorporated in New Jersey. Allen and Ginter acquired stock amounts of $7,500,000 in the new corporation, of which Ginter was a director until shortly before his death. He also built the Jefferson Hotel in Richmond in 1895 at a cost of $1,350,000.

Ginter joined the Episcopal Church a few years before his death. He never married. (**A.** *DAB; NCAB,* 18:309. **B.** American Tobacco Company, *Sold American,* 1954; H. Kroll, *Riders in the Night,* 1965; P. Glenn Porter, "The Origins of the American Tobacco Company," *Business History Review,* 1969; Richard Tennant, *The American Cigarette Industry,* 1950; Nannie Tilley, *The Bright Leaf Tobacco Industry,* 1948. See also James B. Duke, *q.v.*)

GIRARD, STEPHEN (May 20, 1750–December 26, 1831). Banker and merchant, Bank of Stephen Girard and Second Bank of the United States. Born in Bordeaux, France, son of Pierre Girard and Odette Lafargue. His father was in the Royal Navy and then Burgess of the City and a captain of the port. His mother died when he was twelve. Stephen Girard had a scanty education, and at age fourteen went to sea as a cabin boy. After six voyages, chiefly to Santo Domingo, he was licensed in 1773 to act as captain, master, or pilot, despite the fact that he was not yet twenty-five years of age and had not served the usual two years in the navy. In 1774 he made his first independent voyage as an officer of a ship sailing from Bordeaux to Port-au-Prince. The venture was unsuccessful and he found himself in debt. Putting together what money he could, he sailed for New York with a consignment of sugar and coffee. Because of this experience he avoided doing business on credit for the rest of his life and never returned to his native city.

In New York City he entered the employ of the shipping firm of Thomas Randall and Son, making several voyages, first as a mate and then as a captain. Apparently he also traded on a small scale on his own account, and gradually he acquired enough capital to become master and half-owner of the vessel *La Jeune Babe*. As a result of a rough voyage in 1776, he put into Philadelphia. Within a month after his arrival the Revolutionary War broke out. He took no great interest in the controversy, but the risks to shipping during these years forced him to abandon it temporarily for merchandising. After the departure of the British from the city, Girard took an oath of allegiance to the Commonwealth of Pennsylvania, becoming a free citizen of that state. He established himself on North Water Street, and again turned his attention towards foreign commerce. Like other merchants, he financed the activities of privateers with a fair degree of success, and with his brother Jean as residential agent, he developed a profitable trade with Santo Domingo. Both brothers were adept at evading the law. If sugar and coffee shipments were proscribed, the cargo became lumber. It was not uncommon to mix poor grades of flour into a higher grade, which was not detected until the bread was being baked. Later, Girard turned his attention to Europe and Asia as well. Although some of his ventures were complete losses, by dint of his unusual business acumen and foresight, coupled with industry and persistence, along with a penchant for hard dealing, Girard developed a large fortune from trade. At one time or another he was the owner of eighteen vessels, although six was the largest number he held at any one time. His ships were named after the great philosophers of France.

During this time Girard also became interested in real estate, insurance, and banking. He was a strong supporter of the First Bank of the United States, and served on a committee of five in 1810 to draw a memorial to Congress to renew its charter. When Congress refused and the bank was forced to close its doors, Girard bought the building and other assets, and started the "Bank of Stephen Girard" as a private venture with an initial capital of $1.2 million. In the banking business he rapidly built up a remarkable system of credit, not only in the United States, but also abroad.

Business relations were maintained with many small banks and with the federal treasury. He also greatly expanded his relations with the Baring Brothers of London. As a result, during the War of 1812 he was able to float a government loan which had been foundering.

After the war, he was appointed by the Treasury Department as one of five commissioners to receive subscriptions for the new Second Bank of the United States, and was elected president of the commission. Since no buyers were found for $3 million of new stock, Girard himself purchased the entire amount. This made possible the organization of the Second Bank of the U.S. in 1816, in Girard's banking house. He was then made one of five directors of the bank appointed by President Madison. He soon became dissatisfied with the management of the bank, gradually selling his stock and again turning his attention to private banking.

Girard also served the city of Philadelphia in various capacities. He was superintendent of the fever hospital during the yellow fever epidemic in 1793, and in his will gave $140,000 to relatives and various charities; $300,000 to the Commonwealth of Pennsylvania; $500,000 to the City of Philadelphia; and the residue of cash and real estate, amounting to over $6 million, in trust to the city for the education of poor white orphan boys. This became Girard College. (**A.** *DAB; NCAB,* 7:11; *Who Was Who,* vol. H; Kenneth L. Brown, "Stephen Girard and the Second Bank of the United States," *Journal of Economic History,* 1942; C. A. Herrick, *Stephen Girard,* 1943; J. B. McMaster, *Life and Times of Stephen Girard,* 2 volumes, 1918; H. E. Wilders, *Lonely Midas: The Story of Stephen Girard,* 1943. **B.** Ralph C. H. Catterall, *Second Bank of the United States,* 1903; Bray Hammond, *Banks and Politics in America,* 1957; John R. Holdsworth, *The First Bank of the United States,* 1910.)

GIRDLER, TOM MERCER (May 19, 1877–February 4, 1965). Steel manufacturer, Republic Steel Corporation. Born in Clark County, Indiana. His father, Lewis Girdler, was superintendent of an Indiana cement mill, one of several owned by his sister and her husband. Tom grew up on the farm needed to grow the fodder for the horses and mules used in the mill operations. When he was fourteen the family moved to the nearby town of Jeffersonville, Indiana, and he attended the Manual Training High School in Louisville, Kentucky, just across the river. He received a thorough mechanical training there which made him a great asset to his father. While still in school he devised an engine to do what it formerly had taken six mules to do, and a short time later built a locomotive from an old vertical boiler twin engine. His wealthy aunt sent him to Lehigh University in 1877 to become a mechanical engineer. At Lehigh he was an outstanding student, graduating second in his class in 1901. He then went to the Buffalo Forge Company, spending two months in the home plant before being sent to England to assist in the London branch. After a year abroad he was homesick, and when he received an offer from the Oliver Iron and Steel Company in Pittsburgh, owned by the uncle of a college friend, he accepted. This was his first contact with the steel business.

After three years at Oliver Iron and Steel, two spent as superintendent of the nut factory, Girdler left Pittsburgh for a better position with the Colorado Fuel and Iron Company in Pueblo, Colorado. There he took a job in the rail rolling mill, where he learned much about steelmaking. In 1907 he left Colorado to become superintendent of the rolling mills of Atlanta (now Atlantic) Steel Company. Within a year he was superintendent of the entire plant, but was unhappy in his locale. Then, in 1914, he was hired by Pittsburgh's Jones and Laughlin Steel Corporation and put to work in their Aliquippa, Pennsylvania, plant. Within a short time he became assistant general superintendent, with the responsibility for running the steel town around the plant. His labor policies at Aliquippa were such that the town was known to the industry as "the perfect company town," and to critics as "the Siberia of the industry." In any event, Girdler himself described his role as that of a "benevolent dictator."

In 1929, after fifteen years with Jones and Laughlin, Girdler left to join Cyrus Eaton* in forming the Republic Steel Corporation in Cleveland, Ohio. The origins were very shaky, with the stock market on the verge of collapse and banks very reticent to extend credit. It was only through Girdler's ceaseless efforts and unusual skill at management that the business was kept alive. In the first few years there were heavy losses, but in 1935, for the first time, it finished the year with a small profit. Republic had taken its place as one of the "Big Three" in the industry, along with U.S. Steel and Bethlehem Steel. His management of Republic was generally recognized as a "one man show," as he revamped plants and brought new companies under Republic's roof.

At the same time, however, Girdler also earned the undying enmity of labor by his hard-fisted tactics. He was militantly antiunion, and said in 1934, "We are not going to deal with the Amalgamated or any other professional union, even if we have to shut down." Republic employed spies, discredited and attacked union leaders, incited violence, and coerced employees into signing petitions opposing outside or independent unions. Although the CIO in 1937 claimed a majority of Republic's employees, Girdler refused to follow U.S. Steel's lead in recognizing the union. He stated that his "employee representation plan," a company union, was the form of unionism which the majority of the employees in his plant preferred. One of the most violent struggles between Republic Steel and the union took place near the company's South Chicago plant on Memorial Day, 1937. In this confrontation, in which tear gas, crude weapons, and pitched battles were featured, there were ten deaths and many injuries among the demonstrators as well as some injuries among the police.

After four years, in which eight men were killed near steel plants, the

Republic Corporation, the National Labor Relations Board, and the CIO signed a stipulation settling all charges of Wagner Act violations. Then, in 1942, when a count of union cards held by employees showed that a majority wanted CIO representation, the union and Republic signed a contract. Nearly 42,000 workers were brought under the agreement in various plants of the company, and tens of thousands of dollars in back wages were paid.

In 1937 Girdler joined the board of Cord Corporation, later known as Vultee Aircraft Division of Aviation Manufacturing Company. Under his management, there were great advances made in airplane design and manufacture, and Vultee expanded significantly. In 1941 he tried to arrange a merger with Consolidated Aircraft Corporation, but was unsuccessful. Finally, at the end of 1941, Vultee bought Consolidated, producers of long-range flying boats and four engine bombers. Girdler arrived in San Diego, California, in 1942 to take charge of Consolidated, changing careers at age 65. He became chairman of the board and chief executive officer of both Consolidated and Vultee, with interests extending from coast to coast. The two companies' assets at the end of 1941 stood at $600 million. His plants turned out the PBY flying boats and the B-24 Liberator bomber and had fantastic production records, with profits in 1943 of over $19 million. He was also a director of Goodyear Tire and Rubber, the Petroleum Corporation of America, Union Trust of Cleveland, Union National Bank of Pittsburgh, and Chase National Bank of New York.

Girdler married Mary E. Hayes from his home town. She died in 1917, and his second wife was Lillian Compton of Laurel, Maryland. In 1942 he married Helen R. Brenna. He had four children, including Jane B. Girdler, who married Alfred C. Dick of Chicago. (*NCAB*, A:117; *Current Biography*, April, 1944; March, 1965; *New York Times*, February 5, 1965; *Who Was Who*, vol. 4; Thomas Girdler, *Bootstraps*, 1943.)

GLEASON, KATE (November 25, 1865–January 9, 1933). Business executive, Gleason Company; and real estate developer. Born in Rochester, New York, daughter of William Gleason and Ellen McDermott. Her parents were Irish immigrants and her father was a former mechanic's apprentice who opened a small toolmaking shop in Rochester in the late 1860s. He was sympathetic with the ideals of woman's emancipation and was determined that his sons and daughters would be equally educated to the marvels of mechanical engineering. At eleven Kate persuaded her father to let her help out in the machine shop, and during her high school years she worked as a bookkeeper in the firm. Her mother, a staunch supporter of Susan B. Anthony, also encouraged Kate's career ambitions. Kate was educated in Rochester's parochial schools and a public high school, graduating in 1884. She then enrolled in Cornell University as a special student, taking mainly nontechnical courses. Financial difficulties forced her to leave after her first year, but she reentered in 1888, leaving again at the end of the academic year. This ended her formal education.

She returned to Rochester, where she worked for her father, whose business was in the midst of a gradual but profound change. In 1874 William Gleason had designed a machine for automatic planing of beveled gears, which had previously been cut or cast individually with unavoidable imprecision and irregularities. Gleason's new machine permitted mass production of uniform assemblies with standardized replaceable parts. This enabled the firm to discontinue the manufacture of conventional machine tools in the late 1890s. Demand increased greatly with the rise of the automobile industry, and the Gleason company soon dominated the market for gear cutting machinery. Although Kate Gleason was elected to the American Society of Mechanical Engineers in 1914 in recognition of her accomplishments in gear design, in actuality she possessed little technical ability and never claimed to have made any significant contribution to the design and development of Gleason machines.

Kate Gleason's main talent was for business promotion. As secretary and treasurer of the company from 1890 to 1913, she served as its chief sales representative, traveling widely in the United States and Europe. It was as the invaluable middle link between her father's inventive genius and the business world that Kate helped to build her family's small machine tool factory into the leading American producer of gear cutting machinery. She resigned from the company in 1913, partly due to family disagreements, to begin her independent business career. As her first independent venture, she served as bankruptcy receiver for a small machine tool factory in East Rochester, and rapidly nursed it back to health. From 1917 to 1919 she also served as president of the First National Bank of East Rochester.

It was at this time that she began to perceive the untapped opportunities in suburban residential and industrial development, and during the next four years helped to launch eight new businesses in the East Rochester area. The largest of these involved the construction of 100 low-cost, six room, poured-concrete houses. Using standardized designs and mainly unskilled labor, she sought with some success to apply to the construction of suburban homes the techniques of mass production she had encountered in her father's business and later in the auto industry. Her other projects in East Rochester included the construction of various recreational facilities.

Continuing to experiment with low-cost standardized residential housing during the 1920s, Gleason purchased a large block of land in the Sea Island region of Beaufort, South Carolina, and began construction of a resort complex, intended originally as a writer's colony. Several of the units were completed before her death and others were added under the supervision of her younger sister, Eleanor Gleason. In the late 1920s, after an extended tour of California where she studied adobe buildings, she drafted plans for the multiple construction of poured-concrete suburban homes in Sausalito, across from San Francisco. Although several units were completed, the project was abandoned when the state of California demanded portions of the original tract for a public works facility. She left an estate of $1,400,000, half of it going to the Kate Gleason Fund for educational and charitable purposes. One hundred thousand dollars of the money went to the City of Rochester to finance a local history alcove at the public library. (*DAB*, Supplement 1; *NAW*; *New York Times*, January 10, 1933; *Who Was Who*, vol. 1; Caroline Bird, *Enterprising Women*, 1976.)

GODDARD, SARAH UPDIKE (c. 1700–January 5, 1770) and **Mary Katherine Goddard** (June 16, 1738–August 12, 1816). Colonial Printers and Publishers, *Providence Gazette, Pennsylvania Chronicle*, and *Maryland Journal*. **Sarah Goddard** was born in Cocumscussuc, Rhode Island, daughter of Lodowick Updike and Abigail Newton. Her paternal grandfather emigrated from Germany to Long Island in 1635, and her father in 1664 moved from New Amsterdam to Kingston, Rhode Island, where he anglicized his surname to Updike and became a substantial landowner, also holding several public offices. Sarah was educated by a tutor and in 1735 married Dr. Giles Goddard of Groton, Connecticut. Both were Anglicans and they had four children, but only two reached adulthood, William and Mary Katherine. Sarah taught the children herself.

When Giles Goddard died in 1757, leaving an estate of 780 pounds, she gave 300 of it to her son, William, who in 1762 founded Providence's first printing shop. Sarah and Mary Katherine Goddard worked in the shop with William, but their newspaper, the *Providence Gazette*, was not a success and they ceased publication in 1765. They continued to run the printing office, however, and to publish *West's Almanack* and various pamphlets under the name of "S. and W. Goddard." In 1766 the *Providence Gazette* was revived under "Sarah Goddard and Company," and Sarah Goddard became Providence's second printer. She continued to print the weekly newspaper and run a bookstore until 1768, when she sold out to a partner, John Carter, for 500 pounds. She then joined her son William in Philadelphia, where he was printing the *Pennsylvania Chronicle*. Her financial assistance aided him in his struggle with his silent partners, Joseph Galloway and Thomas Wharton,* though she remained largely in the background in this venture, only occasionally supervising the shop.

Mary Katherine Goddard was born at Groton, near New London, Connecticut. She was educated at home by her mother. In 1762 she and her mother joined her brother William in Providence, Rhode Island, where he established a printing shop and where Kate and her mother began their career as printers. Kate assisted her mother in running the printing shop and in publishing the weekly *Providence Gazette* from 1765 to 1768. In the latter year they joined William in Philadelphia and during most of the last year of the existence of the *Pennsylvania Chronicle* Mary Katherine managed the shop.

In 1773 William, an ardent supporter of the colonial cause against Britain, started a new printing business in Baltimore, Maryland, and began publishing Baltimore's first newspaper, the *Maryland Journal*. In 1774 they closed the Philadelphia shop and Mary Katherine moved to Baltimore to take over the new plant and newspaper there, while William concerned himself with setting up an intercontinental postal system. In 1775 the first issue appeared officially recognizing what had been true for some time — "Published by M. K. Goddard." During the Revolutionary War she was Baltimore's official printer, usually its only one. From her press in 1777 came the first printed copy of the Declaration of Independence to include the names of the signers. Even after her brother returned at the end of 1776, she continued to publish in her own name and she remained an efficient manager for several years.

In 1784 a bitter quarrel split the Goddards, and William took over the Baltimore press from his sister. The two were never reunited and Mary Katherine never worked again as a printer. In 1775 she had become postmaster of Baltimore and she continued in that position until 1789, when she was relieved against her will. Two hundred Baltimore business-men endorsed a petition to keep her as postmaster. She then operated a bookstore in Baltimore until 1809 or 1810. (*NAW; DAB.*)

GOLDENSON, LEONARD HARRY (December 7, 1905-   ). Motion picture and television executive, Paramount Pictures, Incorporated; Paramount Theaters; American Broadcasting-Paramount Theaters, Incorporated. Born in Scottdale, Pennsylvania, son of Lee Goldenson, a merchant, and Esther Broude. He was educated in the local public schools and graduated from Harvard University in 1927. Three years later he received a degree from Harvard Law School, and was admitted to the Pennsylvania bar. After working for a brief time as a law clerk he was associated with a New York City law firm from 1931 to 1933. In the latter year he joined Paramount Pictures, Incorporated, working out of the Boston office, where he was given the responsibility for reorganizing the firm's New England theaters. In 1938 he was placed in charge of theater operations for the entire country, numbering some 1,700 theaters, with head offices in New York City. He was elected a director of the company in 1944, serving in that capacity until 1950.

In 1944 the Justice Department had taken Paramount and seven other principal producer-distributor organizations to court, claiming that the only way to prevent the monopolistic abuse of power in the motion picture business was to break up the vertical integration of the industry — to divorce the major studios from ownership of theaters. In 1949, in the *United States v. Paramount Pictures, Incorporated, et al.*, the Supreme Court ruled in favor of the government, forcing Paramount to divest itself of its theater interests. Goldenson was named president of the newly formed United

Paramount Theaters, Incorporated, and on his recommendation in 1953 it was merged with the American Broadcasting Company to form American Broadcasting–Paramount Theaters, Incorporated. He was chosen president of the newly organized company and over the next several years became known as the man who "wed television to the movies."

Goldenson's first major decision was to lend Walt Disney* $4.5 million to complete Disneyland, in return for a Disney show. This was the first time a movie company had produced a show for television, but in 1955 Goldenson convinced Warner Brothers to follow Disney's example, producing such series as "Maverick," "Lawman," and "Colt 45." In 1957 Goldenson purged ABC-TV of its president, Robert Kintner, and eight other top television executives, taking charge of the television division himself. He subsequently signed Frank Sinatra to a television contract, scheduled new programs like "Lawrence Welk" and "Wyatt Earp," and hired Mike Wallace from the Dumont network to conduct a weekly interview show. He also signed Pat Boone and Guy Mitchell to perform on variety shows. His most drastic step, however, was the decision to have ABC-Paramount produce feature-length films for television, while at the same time beginning to liquidate most of its theaters. ABC finally sold the last of its theaters in 1978.

All of these moves helped bring respectability to ABC-TV, which had been languishing in third place, far behind CBS and NBC when Goldenson took over. Until the mid-1970s, however, the entertainment and news divisions were rarely able to challenge the other two networks for supremacy. ABC's top division remained the sports department, which included its "Wide World of Sports," "Monday Night Football," and coverage of the Olympics. The entertainment division, and ABC as a whole, were finally able to reach the top in 1976, a year after Goldenson hired Fred Silverman to run the network. Through the development of shows like "Laverne and Shirley," "Bionic Woman," and "Love Boat," ABC achieved supremacy in prime-time ratings, and also captured most of the daytime ratings by expanding its soap operas to one hour and featuring controversial subjects such as feminism and abortion. In recent years the news department was put under the direction of Roone Arledge, producer of "Wide World of Sports," showing dramatic improvement in the ratings. By 1979 sales had reached two billion dollars, with profits of $159 million.

The ABC division of the company includes a national radio and television network, five company owned television stations, and fourteen radio stations. It also has interests in television stations in foreign countries. In 1955 Goldenson established a phonograph record subsidiary, ABC-Paramount Records, Incorporated, which became a major factor in the record industry. In the publishing field it acquired the Prairie Farmer Group, comprised of three of the leading and oldest farm publications in the Midwest. ABC also owns and operates three recreational parks in Florida: Weeki Wachee Spring, Silver Springs, and Wild Waters.

Goldenson is Jewish, and married Isabel Weinstein of New York City in 1939. They have three daughters. (**A.** *NCAB*, J:77; *Current Biography*, 1957; *Who's Who in America, 1978-79*. **B.** Erik Barnouw, *The Image Empire*, 1970; Les Brown, *Television: The Business Behind the Box*, 1974; Milton Moscowitz et al., *Everybody's Business*, 1980.)

GOODHUE, JONATHAN (June 21, 1783-1848). New York City merchant, Goodhue and Company. Born in Salem, Massachusetts, son of Benjamin Goodhue. His ancestors had come to Massachusetts in 1636 and his father was a leading politician during the Revolutionary period, serving at the Massachusetts Constitutional Convention (1779-1780), the state house of representatives (1780-1782), the Massachusetts Senate (1786-1788), and the United States House of Representatives (1789-1796). In 1796 he was elected to the U.S. Senate, serving until 1800. A staunch Federalist, he strongly supported Jay's Treaty. Jonathon Goodhue was educated at grammar school in Salem, and at fifteen entered the counting house of Henry John Norris, a wealthy merchant engaged in commerce with Europe and the East Indies. He remained there for several years, acquiring a knowledge of general business, and in 1803 was sent out by his employers as supercargo, making his first voyage to Aden, Arabia, where he remained for six months. He then sailed to the Cape of Good Hope and the Isle of France. He made another voyage at the end of 1805, going to Calcutta, India.

In 1807 Goodhue moved to New York City and started in business for himself. Aided by the patronage of Norris, by Joseph Peabody,* one of the most eminent merchants of Salem, and by William Gray of Boston, he was able to gain the business friendship of some of the leading merchants of New York. He suffered a lull in his business during the War of 1812, but afterward his firm soon extended its relations through all the commercial parts of Europe, the East Indies, Mexico, and South America. Goodhue and Co. were the confidential correspondents of Baring Brothers and Company of London and William Ropes and Company of St. Petersburg, Russia, among other houses of distinction. His firm continued to exist for many years after his death and was always one of the most highly respected mercantile houses in the country. He was a Federalist and a Christian of no denomination. (*DAB*; *NCAB*, 1:500; 5:200; *Who Was Who*, vol. H.)

GOODNIGHT, CHARLES (March 5, 1836-December 12, 1929). Texas cattleman. Born in Macoupin County, Illinois, son of Charles Goodnight and Charlotte Collier. His great-grandfather had emigrated from Germany to Virginia and then to Kentucky, where his father was born. They later migrated to Illinois. When young Charles was still a child his father died and his mother remarried. In 1846 the family moved to Texas, settling upon the Milam County frontier. Here Charles was thrown into contact with border Indians. He entered the cattle business in 1856, and a year later moved to Palo Pinto County, on the northwest Texas frontier. There he joined companies of independent rangers, or minute men, as a scout and guide against the Indians. With the outbreak of the Civil War he joined the frontier regiment of Texas Rangers, participating in many Indian fights and becoming a noted guide.

In 1886 he opened the first Texas cattle ranch in southern New Mexico on the Pecos River. Two years later he established another ranch on the Apishapa, in Colorado, and in 1870 located a permanent range on the Arkansas, four miles above Pueblo. Meanwhile, with Oliver Loving, he laid out the Goodnight Cattle Trail from Belknap, Texas, to Fort Sumner, New Mexico, in 1866 and blazed an extension into Wyoming known as the Goodnight-Loving Trail. In 1875 he laid out a new Goodnight Trail from Alamogordo Creek, New Mexico, to Granada, Colorado. In that same year he suffered financial reverses and at the same time his ranges had become overstocked. This prompted him to trail back to Texas; with a herd of 1,600 cattle he crossed 300 miles of wilderness, and in 1876 settled in the Palo Duro Canyon in the Texas Panhandle, 250 miles from a railroad. In the next year he blazed his last cattle trail from his JA Ranch in the Panhandle to Dodge City, Kansas.

It was also in 1877 that he formed a partnership with John George Adair of Ireland and began development of the great JA Ranch, which soon embraced nearly one million acres of land and almost 100,000 head of cattle. On that range Goodnight took a herd of longhorn cattle, brought in shorthorn and Hereford stock for breeding, and in eleven years developed one of America's finest beef herds. In the late 1870s he roped three buffalo calves from which he raised a large herd, thereby preserving the buffalo on the southern plains. He also crossed the buffalo with Polled Angus cattle and produced the first herd of cattalo, a new breed of stock. Because of his extensive experiments as a breeder, he was sometimes referred to as the "Burbank of the Range."

Goodnight also actively fought outlaws for some forty years and made friends with the Comanche, Kiowa, and Pueblo tribes. In 1880 he organized the first Panhandle stockman's association to fight lawlessness. During the 1880s the organization paid the salaries of many of the local officials, employed its own counsel, prosecuted cattle thieves and outlaws, and suppressed attempts at vigilante methods. It also introduced pure-bred cattle, systematized range work, and policed the trails, practically revolutionizing the Panhandle cattle business. Goodnight dominated its policies and battles throughout its existence. He joined with other cattlemen in establishing the first frontier schools, and later, at the town of Goodnight, founded one of the pioneer educational institutions of West Texas, the Goodnight College, which in 1917 became a public high school.

He married Mary Ann Dyer in 1871 and she died in 1926. A year later he married Corinne Goodnight (no relation), who was from Butte, Montana. His only child did not live to adulthood. (**A.** *DAB; Who Was Who*, vol. 4; Daniel B. Boorstin, *The Americans: The Democratic Experience*, 1973; J. Evarts Haley, *Charles Goodnight, Cowman and Plainsman*, 1949. **B.** Robert G. Athearn, *High Country Empire*, 1960; James Brisbin, *The Beef Bonanza*, 1885; Edward Everett Dale, *Cow Country*, 1942; C. L. Douglas, *Cattle Kings of Texas*, 1939.)

GOODRICH, BENJAMIN FRANKLIN (November 4, 1841–August 3, 1888). Rubber manufacturer, B. F. Goodrich Company. Born in Ripley, New York, son of Anson Goodrich and Susan Dinsmore. His ancestors had come to New England in 1643, and he was educated in academies in the nearby towns of Westfield and Fredonia, and also at Austinburg, Ohio. On completing his education at age seventeen he began the study of medicine with John Spencer, a physician in Westfield. A year later he enrolled in the Cleveland Medical College (later the medical department of Western Reserve College), where he graduated in 1861. That same year he enlisted in the 9th New York Cavalry as a private, serving until 1862 when he became a contract surgeon with the Army of the Potomac. After serving a few months he entered the University of Pennsylvania to take a course in surgery. In 1863 he was commissioned as assistant surgeon of the 9th New York Cavalry, serving until 1864. He then established himself as a practicing physician in Jamestown, New York, but about a year later gave it up to go into the real estate business in New York City with a lawyer friend.

In 1867, through one of his real estate transactions, Goodrich assumed ownership of the Hudson River Rubber Company at Hastings-on-the-Hudson, New York, which had been engaged in the manufacture of rubber goods under a licensed agreement with Charles Goodyear. Neither Goodrich nor his partner, J. P. Morris, knew anything about rubber, but in the hope of securing some financial benefit from their acquisition, they bought out the other stockholders with $5,000 of Morris' money. They next organized a new company, with Goodrich becoming president and taking complete control of the new business. During 1867–1868 he operated the plant and tried to sell its product, learning as he went along. In the process he became a staunch believer in the future of rubber. Competition was very keen, however, and he was handicapped by outmoded equipment. The factory could not produce a satisfactory product and the two partners were soon forced to abandon it.

Goodrich, nevertheless, had not lost his interest in rubber and he soon prevailed upon Morris to buy another small rubber factory at Melrose, New York. This venture, even with the $10,000 invested by Morris, was also unsuccessful. By 1869 the two partners were losing money rapidly. In looking for a suitable location for their plant, further away from their principal New England competitors, Goodrich came upon an advertisement by the Board of Trade of Akron, Ohio, inviting the establishment of manufactories in that town. A visit to the city convinced Goodrich to transfer his rubber business to that place, and he got the Akron Board of Trade to advance him money with which to move his equipment from Melrose and to erect a new factory. In December, 1870, a new firm, Goodrich, Tew and Company, was formed, consisting of Goodrich, Harvey W. Tew, and David Mewland Marvin (his brothers-in-law), Robert Newland (an uncle of Mrs. Goodrich), and Henry S. Sanderson. A two-story building was completed in the spring of the next year and the first manufactured products were sold about a month later. These consisted largely of fire hose, billiard cushions, and belting. During the first ten years of it existence, Goodrich found it extremely difficult to keep the company afloat, due to the lack of working capital and the lack of confidence of local people in his undertaking, which prevented him from acquiring either an adequate supply of raw materials or a proper workforce. The company was reorganized in 1874 as Goodrich and Company, with new members added to the firm, but with only marginal success.

In 1879 it seemed that the final collapse of the company was inevitable, but Goodrich would not give up on it. He next approached George W. Crouse to finance the venture and was successful in gaining his support. For the first time the company had adequate financial backing. The B. F. Goodrich Company was thereupon reorganized yet again in 1880, with Goodrich as president, and from that time forward success matched his every effort. In 1881 he took over the duties of manager in addition to those of president, but the strain on him was too great, and he died seven years later, at the age of 46.

In this inauspicious manner B. F. Goodrich helped make Akron the center of the rubber industry in the United States. The first rubber firm to locate there, it was followed in 1898 by Goodyear Rubber and in 1900 by Firestone Tire and Rubber. Later, General Tire also located there. From the very first B. F. Goodrich has been the most innovative of the tire and rubber companies. While Benjamin Goodrich was in charge of the firm in 1884 he substituted hydraulic presses in the vulcanizing process for the old hand methods, and in later years Goodrich made the first cotton-covered fire hose, the first pneumatic automobile tire, and the first commercial tubeless tire. Yet, despite being the oldest and the most technologically advanced of the Big Four rubber companies, it has remained the smallest. Unlike the industry leader, Goodyear, Goodrich never set up extensive distribution and selling systems to market its products, nor until recently did it invest much money in advertising. To partially offset this, Goodrich had emphasized its industrial and chemical divisions, becoming the nation's leader in the manufacture of polyvinyl chloride. With over 42,000 employees, Goodrich had sales of $3 billion in 1979.

B. F. Goodrich was a Democrat and a member of the Congregational Church. He served on the City Council of Akron in 1880–1881. In 1869 he married Mary Marvin of Jamestown, New York, and they had two sons and a daughter. His youngest son, David Marvin Goodrich (1876–1950) was involved for a time with his older brother, Charles C. Goodrich, in the promotion of mining properties in the Southwest and Mexico. David Goodrich also became a director of B. F. Goodrich in 1910, was appointed chairman of the board in 1927, and during the 1930s directed the firm's research on synthetic rubber. This resulted in 1938 in the establishment of the Hycon Chemical Company, a Goodrich affiliate, of which he was president. By the time of Pearl Harbor, when the Japanese cut the United States off from the Far East plantations that supplied 97 percent of the nation's rubber, Hycon had a 100,000 ton a year capacity. Goodrich then built and ran many of the government-owned plants supplying rubber for the war effort. David Goodrich was a Republican and an Episcopalian. (**A.** *DAB; NCAB*, 28:180; 39:33; *Who Was Who*, vol. H. **B.** Milton Moscowitz et al., *Everybody's Business*, 1980; Howard and Ralph Wolf, *Rubber: A Story in Greed*, 1936.)

GORDY, BERRY JR. (1929–   ). Black recording and motion picture executive, Motown Record Corporation. Born in the black ghetto of Detroit, Michigan. His father was a plastering contractor and his mother was an insurance agent. He was educated in the public schools of his native city, dropping out of school in his junior year to become a prize fighter. After just three fights he was inducted into the army in 1951. During his two years in the service he saved his money, and upon his discharge in 1953 purchased an inventory of jazz records and opened a record store in Detroit. Gordy soon found that white middle class audiences were no longer interested in jazz, preferring instead a new music known as rock and roll. This field of music had previously been known as "race music" in the record catalogs, but with the emergence of Bill Haley, Elvis Presley, and Fats Domino it was gaining great popularity with white audiences.

After the record shop went bankrupt in 1955 Gordy worked as a plasterer with his father and as a chrome trimmer at Ford Motor Company. He relieved the monotony of the assembly line by making up songs in his head. Some of his compositions were recorded by local singers and groups he met in nightclubs. Dissatisfied with the way some of his songs were handled, he began producing his own recordings in a rental studio with hired musicians and singers. His first brush with success came when Jackie Wilson achieved stardom with Decca Records performing Gordy's songs, "Reet Petite," "Lonely Teardrops," and "That's Why." With $700 borrowed from his family in 1959, he founded Motown Records in a bungalow on Detroit's Grand Boulevard. The company was to become the most successful black enterprise in the United States, with sales in the early 1970s of $50 million, and with 32 artists under contract. The company came to encompass music publishing, talent management, and its own orchestra and accompanists, along with its recording activities.

The first Motown issue was "Bad Girl." Recorded by Smokey Robinson and the Miracles in 1959, it was distributed by Chess Records nationally. Managing to hit 93rd on the record charts for two weeks, it rapidly slid into oblivion. Motown's first gold record was "Shop Around" by Smokey Robinson and the Miracles in 1960, issued nationally on the Tamla label. This was followed by an impressive series of hits by the Marvelettes; Stevie Wonder; Marvin Gaye; Martha Reeves and the Vandellas; the Temptations; the Four Tops; and Tammie Terrell. By far the most popular proponents of the Motown sound in the 1960s, however, were Diana Ross and the Supremes. They became the most successful all-female singing trio in the world, with record sales totaling more than $12 million, second only to the Beatles. In the early 1970s the Jackson Five became the most lucrative property in the Motown stable, but the most respected artists, winning an impressive number of Grammy Awards, were Gladys Knight and the Pips. Both groups eventually left Motown.

Gordy moved his headquarters to Los Angeles in 1972, when he also began producing motion pictures. His first film was *Lady Sings the Blues*, starring Diana Ross, in 1972. It won five Academy Award nominations and grossed more than $8.5 million. In 1975 Gordy produced *The Bingo Long Traveling All Stars and Motor Kings* and *Mahogany*. Gordy is married and has two sons and a daughter. (*Current Biography*, July, 1975; *Who's Who in America*, 1978–79; L. Robinson, *Black Millionaire*, 1973.)

GOSSETT, BENJAMIN BROWN (August 18, 1884–November 13, 1951). Textile manufacturer and association executive, Cotton Textile Institute and Gossett Textiles. Born in Williamston, South Carolina, son of James Pleasant Gossett and Sallie Acker Brown. The Gossett family had emigrated from England to Pennsylvania in 1760. His father was a leader in the development of the southern textile industry and a prominent civic leader in South Carolina. Benjamin Gossett was educated at Clemson College in Clemson, South Carolina, from 1899 to 1901, and two years later was appointed to the U.S. Naval Academy at Annapolis, Maryland, being commissioned a second lieutenant in the U.S. Marines in 1905. After serving two years in the marines, he joined his father in his cotton manufacturing firm, being named secretary, vice-president, and assistant treasurer of the Williamston Mills in 1908. He continued in these positions until 1938, serving also as vice-president of its many affiliated companies: the Gossett Mills; Chadwick-Hoskins Company; Cohannet Mills; Martinsville (Virginia) Mills; Southern Worsted Company; Calhoun Mills; Textron; Textron Southern; Riverside Manufacturing Company; Judson Mills; and Dan River Mills. He was also assistant treasurer of the Brogan (later Appleton) Mills in Anderson, South Carolina, from 1909 to 1920; president and treasurer of Riverside Manufacturing and Taxaway Mills, both in Anderson, from 1913 to 1925; president of the Panola Mills in Greenwood in 1920–1921, and of Cohannet Mills (later Franklin Process Spinning Mills) from 1921 to 1923.

In 1928 Williamston Mills, Riverside Manufacturing Company, Gossett Dyeing and Finishing Company, and Pendleton Cotton Mills were merged to form the Gossett Mills, a South Carolina corporation with headquarters in Anderson. Gossett was elected vice-president and treasurer of the new combination. In 1936, upon the death of his father, he became president and treasurer. During the next ten years he developed it into a complex of seven plants with 103,000 spindles and 2,500 looms. In 1946 he sold the Gossett textile interests to Textron of Providence, Rhode Island, for about $13 million, through its affiliate, Textron Southern. Gossett served for a brief time as director of Textron and as chairman of the board of Textron Southern.

But Gossett's major contribution to the textile industry was in his role as one of the founders of the Cotton Textile Institute, which was organized in the mid-1920s during an industry-wide depression. It was a new form of trade association in the industry, being national in scope, with an emphasis on stabilization, cooperation, and control. Gossett and his father belonged to the group of uninhibited southerners who took the initiative from the New England textile leaders and created a "policy shaping organization." Benjamin Gossett served on the board of directors and was its vice-president from 1931 to 1933. He also served as president of the Cotton Manufacturers Association until that group merged with the Cotton Textile Institute.

Gossett was president of the Bank of Calhoun Falls, South Carolina, from 1912 to 1928; vice-president of Citizen's Bank of Anderson, South Carolina, from 1914 to 1921; and a director and vice-president of American Trust Company of Charlotte. He was also a director of a large number of other corporations at one time or another. During World War I he served as federal fuel administrator for South Carolina and was chairman of the State Board of Conservation and Development from 1927 to 1930. During the Second World War he became an industry member for the regional organization of the National Labor Board and chairman of the industrial salvage division of the War Production Board for North Carolina. He was a Methodist and a Democrat, and married Katharine Coleman Clayton of Annapolis, Maryland. They had two sons and one daughter. (**A.** *DAB*, Supplement 5; *NCAB*, 49:15; *New York Times*, November 14, 1951; *Who Was Who*, vol. 3. **B.** Louis Galambos, *Competition and Cooperation*, 1966.)

GOULD, JAY (May 27, 1836–December 2, 1892) and **George Jay Gould** (February 6, 1864–May 16, 1923). Financiers and railway developers, Erie Railroad; Union Pacific Railroad; Missouri Pacific Railroad; Texas and

Pacific Railroad; St. Louis and Western Railroad; Western Union Telegraph; Denver and Rio Grande Railroad; Western Pacific Railroad.

Jay Gould was born in Roxbury, New York, son of John Burn Gould and Mary Moore. His ancestors had come from England to Connecticut in 1647 and his father was a poor hill farmer. Jay Gould received a meager amount of education in a local academy and worked for a blacksmith and later as a clerk in a country store. He also learned the rudiments of surveying during this period. He put this talent to use from 1854 to 1857, preparing county maps of New York, and in 1856 published a couple of books on local history. By age twenty-one he had managed to save $5,000. In that year, with Zodach Pratt, a New York politician, he opened a large tannery in northern Pennsylvania. Shortly afterward he persuaded the New York leather merchant, C. M. Leupp, to help him to gain full control of it. He subsequently began engaging in speculations which his enemies declared were responsible for Leupp's suicide in 1857. Gould abandoned the tannery, and after a short time as a leather merchant in New York City (1859-1860), he began speculating in small railways. A profitable deal in bonds of the Ruttledge and Washington was followed by his management of the Rensselaer and Saratoga and his investments in other lines.

Gould first acquired notoriety in 1868 when he joined Daniel Drew* and Jim Fisk* to prevent Cornelius Vanderbilt* from taking over the Erie Railroad. In the wild battle that ensued with Vanderbilt, Gould supplied the strategic imagination; defying a court order, they broke Vanderbilt's attempt to corner the stock by flooding the market with 50,000 shares of newly printed Erie stock. The trio were forced to flee to New Jersey, and then went to Albany, where they secured passage of a bill legalizing the issuance of Erie stock and forbidding a union of the Erie and Vanderbilt's New York Central. Lavish bribes to legislators were used to secure this legislation. After the battle, Drew and Fisk sold out, with Gould becoming the road's largest stockholder and its president. There is some confusion concerning Gould's next moves. On the one hand, the Erie had been a pitifully weak road before his takeover and needed desperately to create alliances with western railways if it was to build up its traffic. On the other hand, the pattern of his whole career was one of stock watering to sell his stocks at a higher profit, rather than careful building and growth.

Whatever the incentive, Gould in 1868 first leased the poorly managed Atlantic and Western Railroad and then began his campaign to gain control of the Pennsylvania Railroad's western allies. He first tried to gain control of the Indiana Central, which would have connected the Atlantic and Great Western with St. Louis. He was unsuccessful in this maneuver, so he turned his sights on both the Cleveland and Pittsburgh and the Pittsburgh, Ft. Wayne and Chicago, but again was thwarted by vice-president Thomas A. Scott,* of the Pennsylvania. Gould next attempted to obtain lines running along the southern shores of Lake Erie. First, he renewed an

agreement with the Michigan Southern to obtain access to Chicago, and
before long had merged that line with others into the Lake Shore and
Michigan Southern. At the same time he began to buy stock in the Toledo,
Wabash and Western, connecting Toledo and St. Louis. At this point
Gould's continuing speculations with Fisk got him into trouble.

Gould and Fisk, in concert with Peter Sweeney and William Marcy
Tweed of Tammany Hall, carried out a daring raid on the nation's gold
market in 1869. Gould thought he could lay his hands on enough cash to
corner all loose gold in the open market, but in order for the plan to be
successful, he had to ensure that the Treasury Department would not
release any of its own large stocks of the metal. He approached President
Grant's brother-in-law, A. R. Corbin, and offered to purchase one and
one-half million dollars worth of gold in his name—without any payment
on Corbin's part. He next purchased gold in the name of General Daniel
Butterfield, Assistant Secretary of the Treasury. By September Gould had
bought forty million dollars worth of gold when he learned that Grant had
disavowed any connection with Corbin. Gould began to quietly unload his
gold, and on September 24th Grant ordered the government to start selling
gold. This brought on the disastrous panic known as "Black Friday" on
Wall Street, ruining many speculators. The result was an avalanche of
popular anger. With Fisk's death soon afterward, and the overthrow of the
Tweed Ring, Gould was soon forced out of the Erie, finally losing control
in 1872. For all his ambitions, Gould had failed to put together a railroad
system out of the Erie.

Gould was hardly finished with his speculations and railroad building.
On being forced out of the Erie he had a fortune of $25 million and was in a
position to undertake ambitious ventures. He turned his eye to the West,
and began buying large blocks of Union Pacific Railroad stock. The depression of 1873 had weakened the railroad's financial position and its stock
was selling at a very low price. By early 1874 Gould had control of the road.
His first job was to reorganize the Union Pacific's finances and management.
While doing this he began to improve the road's eastern connections,
purchasing stock in two of the three roads which made up the Iowa Pool:
the Northwestern and the Rock Island. Then, in 1877, he attempted to
work out with them and with the Burlington an agreement which included
joint ownership of the Burlington and Missouri in Nebraska. He was not
successful. So, again, Gould began a system of western connections of his
own. By 1881 he controlled the Kansas Pacific; the Missouri Pacific; the
Missouri, Kansas and Texas; the Wabash; the Lackawanna; the Central of
New Jersey; and the New York and New England; and had regained control
of the Erie. By this point it was the largest railroad empire in the nation. He
owned 15,854 miles of roads, or 15 percent of the nation's mileage.

Gould's control proved to be short-lived. He made no attempt to
coordinate, integrate, or efficiently manage the activities of his various

properties. Some of his roads did not actually connect with others, so freight shipments were hampered. It was mostly a speculative enterprise, and the empire began to collapse rapidly. By 1882 he had pulled out of the Union Pacific, using the proceeds to build up his new network south and west of St. Louis. Then the recession in 1884 forced him to dispose of most of his eastern lines. From that point onwards, he concentrated on building a regional system in the Southwest. By 1890 the Gould system in that area included the Missouri Pacific, the smaller Texas and Pacific, the St. Louis Southwestern, and the International and Great Northern. All told, it made up about one-half of the mileage in the Southwest.

During this time Gould also made investments and speculations in other areas. His most dramatic venture outside of railroads came when he acquired control of Western Union Telegraph. He was able to do this by using the telegraph subsidiaries of the railroads under his control. After gaining control of the Union Pacific, he cancelled that road's contract with Western Union, and began to expand the railroad's subsidiary, the Atlantic and Pacific Telegraph Company, paralleling Western Union's lines. He enlarged the system further by gaining control of the International Ocean Telegraph Company, with cable lines to Latin America. By 1878 Western Union was forced to buy the Atlantic and Pacific at Gould's price. Gould had offered Vanderbilt (the largest shareholder in Western Union) a controlling share in Michigan Central if Vanderbilt persuaded the Western Union board to purchase Atlantic and Pacific. Then, during the next year, Gould formed the American Union Telegraph Company and gave it the contracts for the telegraph subsidiaries of his roads in the Southwest. When Gould announced plans for building a new transatlantic cable, the price of Western Union stock plummeted and Gould began to buy. Soon he was its largest stockholder and he convinced Western Union to purchase American Union at an inflated price. He then became the controlling member of Western Union's board.

After gaining control of the telegraph firm, Gould moved to strengthen it. He first purchased Baltimore and Ohio's telegraph subsidiary in 1886, and at the same time reached an agreement with Postal Telegraph which permitted the two companies to have mutual use of each other's equipment. Gould, however, took no part in the management decisions of the company, leaving that to the professional managers. He also owned the New York *World* from 1879 to 1883 and had become nearly full owner of New York City's elevated railroads by 1886.

Gould married Helen Day Miller of New York City in 1863. They had six children, including **George Jay Gould**. George Gould was born in New York City and educated in private schools of the city. He then entered the business world and was trained by his father to handle the Gould fortune. Upon his father's death in 1892, George was given almost complete control of the estate.

The main properties George Gould had under his control were Western Union Telegraph; Manhattan Elevated Railroads; the Missouri Pacific; the Texas and Pacific; the International and Great Northern; and the Wabash. George felt that the four western roads should be retained and made secure, and in the process of consolidating these lines he began a policy of expansion that envisioned a fully transcontinental railroad, which his father had earlier attempted. He began first to expand his roads to a new terminus on the East Coast, buying up local lines and constructing an entirely new line from Toledo to Baltimore by way of Pittsburgh (at Carnegie's* urging). The entrance to Pittsburgh was one of the most expensive construction jobs ever completed to that time, costing $380,000 a mile for 60 miles. The project was bitterly opposed by the Pennsylvania Railroad, which went to the extreme of destroying Western Union poles and wires on its right of way.

George Gould found it necessary to devote much of his funds and energies to his western lines, which had long suffered from the lack of a proper outlet to the Pacific. By 1900 the situation had become even worse than it had been before. Gould had antagonized E. H. Harriman* in a fight for control of the Colorado Fuel and Iron Company, and the latter's Union Pacific discriminated against the Missouri Pacific. Gould's response was to purchase the Denver and Rio Grande, which gave him a through line as far as the end of the Union Pacific at Salt Lake City. Harriman responded by buying the Southern Pacific and was therefore able to divert traffic from Gould's roads both in the North and the South. Gould's only recourse was to charter the Western Pacific and start building his own line to San Francisco, which was completed in 1911. By this time his resources had become overextended, and he had been affected adversely by the financial panic of 1907 and the opening of the Panama Canal. The opposition, headed by Harriman and Kuhn and Loeb, took away road after road from his control, so that he had lost control of most by 1912. The last one, the Denver and Rio Grande, went in 1918.

George Gould then retired from active business, but was hounded constantly by law suits of all kinds, including a family suit over his management of the Gould estate. The most expensive piece of private litigation to that time, it was in the courts from 1916 to 1927. He married Edith M. Kingdon, an actress, in 1886. They had seven children and she died in 1921. Prior to this, however, he had met Guinevere Jeanne Sinclair, an actress, who became his mistress. They had three children between 1915 and 1922, and in the latter year they were married. (**A.** *DAB; NCAB*, 7:218; 13:522; *New York Times*, December 3, 1892; *Who Was Who*, vol. H; J. Grodinsky, *Jay Gould: His Business Career*, 1957; E. P. Hoyt, *The Goulds*, 1969; Richard O'Conner, *Gould's Millions*, 1962. **B.** Robert G. Athearn, *Rebel of the Rockies*, 1962; Alfred D. Chandler Jr., *The Visible Hand*, 1977; John P. Davis, *The Union Pacific Railroad*, 1894; Elisha P. Douglass, *The Coming* of Age of American Business, 1971; Wesley S. Griswold, A Work of Giants, 1962; Julius Grodinsky, Transcontinental Railroad Strategy, 1962; Edward Hungerford, Men of Erie, 1946; James McCague, Moguls and Iron Men, 1964; Robert Riegel, Story of the Western Railroads, 1926; Mira Wilkins, The Emergence of Multinational Enterprise, 1970.)

GRACE, EUGENE GIFFORD (August 27, 1876–July 25, 1960). Steel manufacturer, Bethlehem Steel Corporation. Born in Goshen, New Jersey, son of John Wesley Grace and Rebecca G. Morris. His ancestors had come to Philadelphia in the early eighteenth century and his father was a ship's captain for many years before becoming a country storekeeper. Eugene Grace was educated at Pennington (New Jersey) Seminary and graduated from Lehigh University with a degree in electrical engineering in 1899. He then entered the employ of Bethlehem Steel Company as an electric crane operator. Within six months he was transferred to the open hearth department, and in 1902 became superintendent of yards and transportation. One of his duties in this position was to systematize the handling of material in the yards. His skill at this brought him to the attention of Charles M. Schwab,* president of the Bethlehem Steel Corporation. In 1905 he was appointed general manager of the Juragua Iron Company in Santiago, Cuba, a subsidiary which supplied most of the iron ore used by Bethlehem Steel. He reorganized its operations and in 1906 was named assistant to the general superintendent of the Bethlehem Steel Company, in charge of the construction of the new Saucon plant in South Bethlehem. Later that same year he was advanced to general superintendent. In 1908 he was named general manager and a member of the board of directors of Bethlehem Steel; he became vice-president and general manager in 1911, and president in 1913. In 1916 he succeeded Schwab as president of the parent company, while continuing as president of Bethlehem Steel Company. In 1917 he was named president of the newly formed Bethlehem Shipbuilding Corporation, a position he retained until 1925. He remained president of both Bethlehem Steel Corporation and Bethlehem Steel Company until the end of 1945, when he became chairman of the board of the latter and chairman of the board and chief executive officer of the former. He held these positions until he retired in 1957, becoming honorary chairman of both.

When he entered Bethlehem Steel Company in 1899 it was a relatively small producer of ordnance items, rails, and other miscellaneous steel products. But when it was taken over by Schwab in 1903, he began to convert it into a giant competitor of U.S. Steel. The company grew particularly rapidly during World War I. It produced 1,108,000 net tons in 1915 and 3,339,800 tons by 1919. During this same period its employees increased in number from 22,064 to 93,964; at its peak it had over 100,000. It was the largest supplier to the Allied powers during the early years of the war, with $180 million worth of contracts from Great Britain and $75 million from Russia. When the United States entered the conflict, the War Department placed huge orders with Bethlehem, and the Navy ordered fleets of destroyers and submarines, while the U.S. Shipping Board ordered many merchant vessels. Throughout the conflict, Grace personally supervised the shipbuilding effort. Then, with the conclusion of the conflict, it fell to Grace to handle the massive conversion of the ordinance department to peacetime production. He was also put in charge of a program of acquisitions to further strengthen the enterprise for peacetime competition. During the years from 1916 to 1928, Bethlehem Steel purchased United Engineering Works (Alameda, California), Baltimore Sheet and Tin Plate, and American Iron and Steel Manufacturing Company in 1916; Lackawanna Iron and Steel Company and Lehigh Coke Company in 1917; Cornwall Railroad Company, Cornwall Iron Company, and Elkins Coal and Coke Company (with 46,000 acres of coal lands in West Virginia) in 1919; Jamison Coal and Coke Company (with 7,000 acres of coal lands in West Virginia) in 1920; the shipbuilding and ship repair plants of Baltimore Dry Dock Company of Boston, Massachusetts, in 1923; the Lackawanna Steel Company in 1922; Midvale Steel and Ordnance and Cambria Steel Companies in 1923; and Atlantic Works in Boston in 1928. By 1929 the corporation operated nine major steel plants, with a total annual capacity of 7,795,200 net tons of pig iron and ferromanganese and 8,960,000 net tons of steel ingots and castings.

Bethlehem Steel was hit especially hard by the depression of the 1930s, since much of its production was in the form of heavy steel products such as rails and structural steel. Grace responded by building a new sheet and strip mill at Lackawanna, New York, and by enlarging Bethlehem Steel's tinplate facilities at Sparrow's Point, Maryland. This enabled the firm to substantially increase sales to the automobile industry. It also took steps to compete effectively in other steel markets. The result of this was that by 1935 the firm was again showing a profit. Large number of additional acquisitions were made during the 1930s, including: Pacific Coast Steel Company; Southern California Iron and Steel; Danville (Pennsylvania) Structural Steel Company; McClintic-Marshall Construction Company; Eastern Steel Company; Levering and Garrigues Company; Hay Foundry and Iron Works; Hedden Iron Construction Company; Lakman Steel Company; Seneca Iron and Steel Company; Williamsport Wire Rope Company; and United Shipyards, Incorporated. In 1942 Bethlehem took over Cambria Iron Company; in 1943, Atlas Steel Barrel Corporation; in 1944, American Well and Prospecting Company and Pacific Coast Forge Company; in 1945, Petroleum Equipment Company and Buffalo Tank Company; and in 1948 the J. H. Weaver Company.

With the outbreak of World War II, Bethlehem Steel under Grace's guidance again took a leading role in mobilizing the country's steel industry for war production. From 1939 to 1945 it produced about one-third of the armor plate and gun forgings required for the U.S. Navy and great amounts of other war materials. Bethlehem also undertook and completed the largest and most diverse shipbuilding and ship repair program ever attempted by a single privately owned industrial corporation, building 1,127 ships and converting or repairing some 37,000 other vessels. The number of employees reached a high of 289,232 in 1943, and stood at 202,905 at the end of the war. Grace also played a role in developing the federal government's Controlled Materials Plan for the allocation of scarce commodities during the war.

After the war, Grace was again in charge of the firm's massive reconversion efforts, followed by a long-range program for modernization and improvement. These efforts added more than 7,600,000 tons to its rated annual capacity for steelmaking, so that by 1953 Bethlehem Steel had a capacity of 17,600,000 net tons of raw steel ingots and castings. When the Korean Conflict broke out in 1950, Bethlehem operated at slightly over 100 percent of rated capacity. By 1957 the rated capacity was over 20,000,000 net tons. By the time of his retirement, Bethlehem Steel was the second largest steel producer in the world, and the world's largest shipbuilding concern. Grace instituted a number of advanced employee welfare plans, well before the general acceptance of these plans in the steel industry. He set up a contributory pension plan, paid vacations, benefit payments to sick and injured workers, an employee stock purchase plan, and accident prevention campaigns. He also established a Share the Work plan for employees during the depression, and was one of the first to issue annual corporate reports to employees as well as stockholders. He helped set up company unions in the plants in 1918–1919, and Grace personally met with these committees each year.

A winner of the Bessemer Gold Medal of the British Iron and Steel Institute, he was a Presbyterian and married Marion Brown of Bethlehem, Pennsylvania, in 1902. They had one daughter and two sons. (**A.** *NCAB*, 50:1; *Current Biography*, April, 1941; October, 1960; *New York Times*, July 26, 1960; *Who Was Who*, vol. 4. **B.** Robert Hessen, *Steel Titan: The Life of Charles M. Schwab*, 1975; Gertrude G. Schroeder, *The Growth of Major Steel Companies*, 1953; Melvin Urofsky, *Big Steel and the Wilson Administration*, 1969.)

GRACE, WILLIAM RUSSELL (May 10, 1832–March 21, 1904) and **J(oseph) Peter Grace** (May 25, 1913–   ). Financiers, shipping, mineral and chemical company executives; Peruvian Corporation, Ltd., William R. Grace Company, Grace Chemical Company. **William R. Grace** was born in Queenstown, Ireland, son of James Grace and Mary Russell. They were a prominent family in the area, but William ran away to sea at a fairly early age and roamed the world for about two years. At the end of that time his father bought him an interest in a Liverpool firm of ship chandlers. It wasn't long, however, before he became bored with that and he went to Callao, Peru, where his father helped place him with a different firm. His brother, Michael P. Grace, joined him, and the firm evolved from Bryce and Company, through Bryce, Grace and Company, to Grace Brothers and Company. Their influence and affluence in Peru increased steadily, but shortly before 1860 William had to leave Peru because of ill health. Michael remained behind to manage the family business there.

William Grace drifted around Ireland and other countries, but in 1865 settled in New York City, where he organized W. R. Grace and Company, originally designed to serve as the New York correspondent for Grace Brothers and Company of Peru. When Peru built up its railroad system, the Grace concerns secured contracts for providing practically all the supplies. William Grace also became confidential advisor to the Peruvian government, and between 1875 and 1879 handled the business of arming and equipping the Peruvian army. It was also largely through his efforts that the Peruvian navy was developed. W. R. Grace and Company furnished the country with most of its arms and secured additional ships for it during its war with Chile in 1879, which left Peru with an unstable government and a debt of some $25 million. The country's bondholders, especially in England, grew restive with the situation and this provided Grace with the opportunity for his master stroke. By the Grace-Donoughmore Contract of 1890, he practically secured a mortgage on the nation, taking over the national debt and receiving extraordinary concessions in return. The Peruvian Corporation, Ltd., formed to manage the concessions, was nominally directed by Lord Donoughmore, but Grace was the power behind all of its moves. In return for securing two bond issues, the company received outright the valuable silver mines of Cerro de Pasco, the entire output of the guano deposits, and five million acres of land containing valuable oil and mineral deposits, as well as the lease of two railroads for sixty-six years and the right to build and hold in perpetuity another road.

In exploiting these concessions, the company did much to develop the nation's resources, but Grace did not limit his attention to Peru. In 1895 the Grace Companies united under a Virginia charter as William R. Grace and Company, opened offices in practically every country in Latin America, and established importing, exporting and banking offices with worldwide contacts. Extending into Chile, it developed nitrate properties; cotton and sugar mills; and traction, light, and power companies. In addition, Grace also began to be involved in shipping, organizing the New York and Pacific Steamship Company in 1891 and, later, the Grace Steamship Company. He came to own and manage a large number of vessels and controlled a large portion of the trade between South America and the United States. He was also president of the Export Lumber Company and director of several New York banks and insurance companies. He was known by his critics as the "Pirate of Peru."

William Grace also became involved in politics in New York City during the 1880s. He was strongly opposed to Tammany Hall and conducted a campaign against them, becoming the first Roman Catholic mayor of New York City in 1880. During his administration he attacked patronage, police scandals, and organized vice. He was elected for a second time in 1884 as an independent. In 1897 he founded the Grace Institute to give girls and women a practical education in stenography, dressmaking, and the domestic arts. He married Lillian Gilchrist, daughter of a shipbuilder of Thomaston, Maine, in 1859. They had ten children. Of his sons, Joseph Peter Grace (1872–1950) was head of W. R. Grace and Company for many years, and William R. Grace Jr. (1878–1943) was a director.

J. Peter Grace was born in Manhasset, New York, son of Joseph Peter Grace and Janet MacDonald, and grandson of William R. Grace. He graduated from Yale in 1936, thereupon becoming a clerk for W. R. Grace and Company. He became assistant secretary in 1940, secretary in 1942, director in 1943, and vice-president in 1945. Later that same year he was elevated to the presidency of the company. During his presidency W. R. Grace and Company established itself as a major manufacturer and processor of chemicals in the United States. The Grace Chemical Company was formed in 1952 for the production and marketing of anhydrous ammonia and urea, which were produced in Memphis, Tennessee. A year later it purchased the Davison Chemical Corporation, which included plants operated by Naco Fertilizer Corporation and Thurston Chemical Company. In 1954 Dewey and Almy Chemical Company was merged with W. R. Grace, and in 1955 the polymer chemical division was formed to manufacture Grex high density polyethylene. In 1958 a new Washington Research Center was established to carry out long-range basic research, and in 1957 he established International Metalloids Incorporated, with its office and plant in Puerto Rico. In 1959 he bought Hatco Chemical Company in New Jersey.

J. Peter Grace also did a great deal to expand the shipping activities of the company. His activities were centered on the Grace Line, and a fleet replacement program was undertaken. The firm operates a regularly scheduled service between the United States and Atlantic ports and the west coast of South America and the Caribbean. By 1958 it was operating 33 vessels, including several famous Caribbean cruise ships. In 1947 he formed the Gulf and South American Steamship Company, which operates regularly scheduled service from U.S. gulf ports to the west coast of South America. Earlier, in 1928, W. R. Grace and Company had merged with Pan American Airways, Incorporated to form Pan American Grace Airways. Grace was closely involved with this in the years after World War II, when it became one of the world's major airways. Also, in 1952, he purchased stock in Roster and Kleiser Company, the second largest outdoor advertising concern in the United States, with 32,000 structures in 450 communities. They also own the Grace National Bank in New York City, chartered as a national bank in 1924, which had deposits of nearly $200 million in 1958.

J. Peter Grace's achievement had been to transform a company, long known as "the old lady of Hanover Square," into a diversified industrial complex. At the time he took it over it was a transportation, trading, and agricultural giant that dominated the economy of South America's west coast. In 1950 Latin American operations brought in 60 percent of Grace's sales; in 1962 they accounted for only 19 percent; and by 1977, zero. Shipping provided 28 percent of sales in 1950; 13 percent in 1962, and zero in 1977. Chemicals moved in the other direction, from 6 percent in 1950 to 55 percent in 1977. The other elements of Grace's $5 billion in sales in 1977 had nothing to do with the company's original businesses. The firm's assets increased from $34 million in 1945 to $222 million in 1958. In 1978 it was the fifth largest chemical producer in the United States, with fertilizers being its most important chemical product. The other big part of Grace's sales comes from a variety of consumer businesses. It owns 257 restaurants, ranging from "theme" dinner houses to fast-food stands and coffee shops. It also owns 69 Herman's sporting goods stores, six Sheplers western wear outlets, and several chains of do-it-yourself home centers, in addition to one of the nation's largest book wholesalers, Baker and Taylor, and four automotive parts companies.

J. Peter Grace exercises nearly complete personal control over the massive industrial empire he has created. He drives his employees as hard as he drives himself, and he makes his managers turn out reams of reports crammed with figures on the firm's operations. He demands a huge "spreadsheet" on every major project; sometimes with thousands of columns. He is also a director of a large number of corporations, including Kennecott Copper, Brascan, Ltd., Citicorp, First National Bank of New York, Ingersoll-Rand, Stone and Webber, and Deering-Milliken. W. R. Grace had long been a closely held family corporation, but was listed on the New York Stock Exchange for the first time in 1953. The Grace family presently owns about 5 percent of the stock, with 28 percent held by a West German group. J. Peter Grace is a Roman Catholic and married Margaret Fennelley of New York City in 1941. They have eight children. (**A.** *DAB; NCAB*, 36:303; L;66; *Current Biography*, 1960; *Who's Who in America, 1978–79.* **B.** John G. B. Hutchins, *The American Maritime Industries and Public Policy*, 1941; Charles Kelly Jr., *The Sky's The Limit: History of Airlines*, 1963; Milton Moscowitz et al., *Everybody's Business*, 1980.)

GRANT, JOHN THOMAS (December 13, 1813–January 18, 1887). Georgia planter and railroad developer. Born in Greene County, Georgia, son of David Grant and Lucy Critchfield. His family had come to Georgia from Virginia after the Revolutionary War. When John Grant was a boy, the family moved to Athens, Georgia, so that he could be educated at the University of Georgia, from which he graduated in 1833. In 1844 he moved to Walton County, where he acquired a huge tract of land and developed one of the greatest plantations in antebellum Georgia. He owned more than 2,000 acres and held more than 100 slaves.

Grant had even greater significance for the development of Georgia in his role as a major developer of railroads in the state. He very early foresaw the future of railroads and threw himself with great energy into the new industry, executing building contracts for railroads in Georgia, Alabama, Tennessee, Mississippi, Louisiana, and Texas. As a pioneer in that field in the South, he became immensely wealthy and powerful, meriting an important place in the economic history of the region. The Civil War, however, wiped out his investments, and during the war he became an aide to his close friend, General Howell Cobb. At the end of the war, he and his son, William D. Grant, who had been a captain in the Confederate Army, moved to Atlanta, where they became prominent among the businessmen of that city. John Grant resumed the building of railroads and became one of the largest holders of real estate in the city.

He was a Presbyterian and a Democrat and served one term in the State Senate of Georgia in 1856. He married Martha Cobb Jackson, grandaughter of Governor James Jackson of Georgia in 1834. (**A.** *DAB*; *NCAB*, 1:502; *Who Was Who*, vol. H. **B.** Milton S. Heath, *Constructive Liberalism*, 1954; Ulrich B. Phillips, *A History of Transportation in the Eastern Cotton Belt to 1860*, 1908.)

GRANT, WILLIAM THOMAS (June 27, 1876–August 6, 1972). Department store chain founder, W. T. Grant Company. Born in Stevensville, Pennsylvania, son of William T. Grant and Amanda Louise Bird. He was from an old New England family who had come to America in the 1620s, and his father was a flour miller and tea store owner. When he was quite young, his family returned to Massachusetts, where he was raised, attending school at Malden, Massachusetts. He left school before graduating to become an errand boy for a lawyer in Boston. Later he ran still more errands for a wholesale shoe house in that city and worked in a warehouse for a whetstone manufacturer. At nineteen he entered retailing as a $6 a week clerk in a Boston shoe store, which was followed by other jobs in the area as a department store buyer and department store manager. He also worked for a brief time as a prize fight promoter.

In 1906 he got an idea that he thought would make his name a household word throughout the country. As a buyer for the bargain counter at Almy, Bigelow and Washburn, in Salem, Massachusetts, he had noticed that the fastest selling merchandise was priced at 25¢. It dawned on him that 25¢ was a "magic price." With the backing of three partners, whom he bought out nine years later, he opened his first store of about 5,000 square feet in

Lynn, Massachusetts. Occupying the ground floor of the YMCA, Grant's carried items selling for up to 25¢, with twenty-one departments selling such fast moving merchandise as notions, toiletries, jewelry, and knit underwear. The opening day was very successful, with receipts of $1,500 in cash. In the first year the store earned $10,000 on gross sales of $19,000, despite generally poor business conditions. All of this was done on a total initial investment of $8,000, $1,000 of which came from Grant's life savings, and the balance from the three partners. Grant worked 15 to 18 hours a day, handling all the buying and merchandising functions. He maintained a 25¢ limit on goods at a time when department store goods began at 50¢ and Kresge and Woolworth sold at 5¢ and 10¢. Taking advantage of this gap in the market, he built his store into a profitable national enterprise. By 1972 the chain had 1,176 units, registered sales of $1.2 billion, and had 60,000 employees, placing it among the largest retailing companies in the United States.

In 1908 W. T. Grant opened a second store in Waterbury, Connecticut, and the first W. T. Grant store was opened in New York City in 1913 at 6th Avenue and 18th Street, which was then one of the busiest shopping sections in the city. There was a fire at the store soon after its opening, which ended the firm's participation in Manhattan retailing, although it did maintain its national headquarters at 1441 Broadway. By the end of World War I, when he had 30 stores, the 25¢ limit on merchandise was raised to one dollar. By 1940 a no-price-limit policy was adopted and the company's stores, which soon extended over 44 states, sold even large-ticket items such as refrigerators, televisions, and so forth.

W. T. Grant Company went public in 1928 and by 1972 there were over 19,000 stockholders. He established the Grant Foundation in 1936 to assist in the emotional development of children and youth, and this foundation continued to control about one-quarter of the stock. W. T. Grant was president of the company until 1924 and then chairman of the board until 1966. He retired in that year, remaining honorary chairman of the board until his death, although he was no longer involved in the active management. Three years after his death, in 1975, W. T. Grant company went bankrupt—the biggest bankruptcy in retailing history. The company, which had so successfully found a retailing niche during the early twentieth century, was unable to do so in the 1960s. Caught between the rapidly expanding Sears' and Penney's chains on one hand, and the new discount chains on the other, W. T. Grant seemed unable to decide on a retailing focus. William Grant married Lena Blanche Brownell in 1907, and after she died married Beth Bradshaw in 1930. He adopted three daughters. (**A.** *New York Times*, August 7, 1972; *Who Was Who*, vol. 5. **B.** Godfrey Lebhar, *Chain Stores in America, 1859–1959*, 1959.)

GRAY FAMILY, Winston-Salem, North Carolina: Bowman Gray (May 1,

1874–July 7, 1935); **James Alexander Gray Jr.** (August 21, 1889–October 29, 1952); **Bowman Gray Jr.** (January 15, 1907–April 11, 1969). Cigarette manufacturers, R. J. Reynolds Tobacco Company. Bowman and James A. Gray Jr. were both born in Winston-Salem, North Carolina, sons of James Alexander Gray and Aurelia Bowman. Their father was a native of North Carolina who graduated from Trinity College (later Duke University), served in the Confederate Army, and then entered Wachovia National Bank in 1879 and the Wachovia Loan and Trust Company in 1893. The two were consolidated in 1911 as Wachovia Bank and Trust Company, of which he was president until he died in 1913. He was also one of the organizers of the railroad from Winston-Salem to Roanoke, Virginia. He was a Methodist and a Democrat.

Bowman Gray was educated at local schools and the University of North Carolina at Chapel Hill, after which he became a clerk at his father's Wachovia National Bank. In 1895 he joined R. J. Reynolds Tobacco Company as a traveling salesman covering the state of Georgia. He was transferred to Baltimore, Maryland, in 1897 and was later promoted to the position of eastern sales manager. In 1912 he returned to Winston-Salem as vice-president and director of the company. Twelve years later he succeeded William Neal Reynolds* as president of the company, and in 1931 he also became chairman of the board. He continued in both positions until his death in 1935.

R. J. Reynolds Tobacco had been organized by Richard J. Reynolds* in Winston in 1874. By 1887 he was marketing 86 brands of chewing tobacco, and soon moved into cigarette manufacture as well. In the 1890s he sold his firm to James B. Duke* and the American Tobacco Company, but continued to be active in the business, using Duke's money to build new, well-equipped factories. When the Supreme Court broke up American Tobacco's monopoly in 1911, Reynolds regained his company. Shortly before World War I he came out with Camel cigarettes, and during the war created a generation of loyal Camel smokers by giving away free cigarettes to American soldiers in France. Camel thereby became the first national cigarette brand, and within ten years of their introduction nearly half of the nation's smokers were smoking them. His three sons, however, had little interest in the tobacco business, and his favorite nephew, Richard S. Reynolds,* left the firm to found Reynolds Metals. So the mantle of leadership passed to Bowman Gray and his family.

It was during Gray's years of leadership that Camel developed its famous advertising slogan: "I'd walk a mile for a Camel," and Reynolds became an early radio advertiser, sponsoring the Camel Pleasure Hour in the 1930s. It was Bowman Gray and his brother and son who fought American Tobacco's George Washington Hill* and adman Albert Lasker* in a twenty-year fight between Lucky Strike and Camel for supremacy in the American cigarette market. The two brands alternated in the number one spot during the

1930s and 40s. Bowman Gray made his biggest mistake at the beginning of the Great Depression in 1929. Assuming that people would continue to pay high prices for cigarettes despite the economic downturn, he raised prices. That opened the door for price-cutting smaller companies such as Philip Morris to gain market share. Bowman Gray was a Methodist and a Democrat and married Nathalie Lyons of Ashville, North Carolina, in 1902. They had two sons, Bowman Gray Jr. and Gordon Gray.

James A. Gray Jr. was educated in local schools and graduated from the University of North Carolina in 1908. He began as a clerk at the Wachovia National Bank, moving up to assistant treasurer from 1911 to 1915, treasurer from 1915 to 1918, vice-president in 1918–1919, and member of the board of directors after 1918. In 1920 he was also named vice-president of R. J. Reynolds Tobacco Company, serving in that position until 1934, when he was named president. He remained in the latter position until 1946, when he became chairman of the executive committee until 1949. From 1949 to 1952 he was chairman of the board. He was a Democrat and a Methodist and married Pauline L. Bahnson in 1918. They had six children.

Bowman Gray Jr. was born in Winston-Salem, son of Bowman Gray and Nathalie Lyons. He was educated in the public schools of his native city and at Woodbury Forest (Virginia) School. He graduated from the University of North Carolina in 1929. During his youth, his father was president of R. J. Reynolds Tobacco and he grew up surrounded by the tobacco business. He began working for the company at age eleven as a summer factory hand, and in 1930 joined the company full-time as a retail salesman. During the years that followed he advanced steadily through the executive ranks, becoming assistant sales manager in 1939, vice-president in 1949, sales manager in 1952, executive vice-president in 1955, and president of the company in 1957. He continued in that position until 1959, when he became chairman of the board and chief executive officer, a position he retained until 1967. He remained as chairman of the board until his death.

In 1954 Bowman Gray Jr. helped to develop Winston cigarettes, the company's first filter-type cigarettes, and two years later brought out Salems. By 1965 Winston had become the country's largest selling cigarette brand, replacing Camel, and Salem was not far behind. He also led the company into diversification and directed much plant expansion and modernization, including the development of Whitaker Park, the largest and most modern cigarette factory in the world. In addition, he acquired Hawaiian Punch, Chun King Chinese foods, and other products for the firm. In 1961–1962, under his leadership, Reynolds integrated all of its plants, one of the most extensive integration programs in southern industry. During his years in the presidency, the company's growth, as measured by several indicators, was outstanding. In 1957, it had sales of just over one billion dollars; by 1967 sales stood at nearly two billion. The number of employees was 12,188 in 1957 and 21,127 ten years later. Assets grew from $713 million to $1.2 billion during these years.

Bowman Gray Jr. was also the major spokesman for the entire cigarette industry during the time when it was under attack as a leading cause of cancer. He appeared at Congressional hearings to oppose government controls on cigarettes and advertising. Under his guidance, the industry established a multimillion dollar program to explore the health aspects of tobacco, including the funding of the Council for Tobacco Research, and an $18 million commitment to the American Medical Association's Educational and Research Foundation. He was also a member of the executive committee of Wachovia Bank and Trust Company, and chairman of the executive committee of the Tobacco Institute.

A Methodist and a Democrat, he married Elizabeth Palmer Christinna of Richmond, Virginia, in 1936. They had five children. His brother, Gordon Gray (b. 1909) was the president of Piedmont Publishing Company, which owned Winston-Salem's morning, evening, and Sunday newspapers, and also owned stations WSJS and WSJS-TV. He was president of this concern from 1937 onward. In addition, in 1949 he was named secretary of the army, serving until he resigned one year later. He then was named president of the University of North Carolina at Chapel Hill until 1955, when he became assistant secretary of defense. From 1958 to 1960 he was special assistant to the president for national security affairs. He also served as a director of R. J. Reynolds Tobacco. He was an Episcopalian. (**A.** *NCAB*, 31:117–118; 54:520; J:75. **B.** Milton Moscowitz, et al., *Everybody's Business*, 1980; Richard B. Tennant, *The American Cigarette Industry*, 1951; Nannie Tilley, *The Bright-Leaf Tobacco Industry*, 1948.)

GRAY, CARL RAYMOND (September 28, 1867–May 9, 1939). Railroad executive, Union Pacific Railroad, Western Association of Railway Executives, and Association of American Railroads. Born in Princeton, Arkansas, son of Oliver Crosby Gray and Virginia LaFayette Davis. His ancestors had arrived in Massachusetts in 1654, and both parents were natives of Maine who moved to Arkansas shortly before the Civil War. Oliver Gray was head of a military school there and then a colonel in the Confederate army. After the war he became professor of mathematics at the University of Arkansas at Fayetteville. From a very early age, Carl Gray was fascinated by trains, and his eagerness attracted the attention of the local station agent, who taught him telegraphy. After completing a preparatory course at the university, Carl went to work for the St. Louis and San Francisco Railroad in 1883. In one year he had become a station agent and telegraph operator at Rogers, Arkansas. Next he became agent and operator at Oswego, Kansas, until 1886. After serving as a clerk in the traffic department at Wichita, Kansas, for one year, from then until 1890 he was commercial agent at the same place. His next assignment saw him spend seven years as divisional freight agent, until he became division superintendent at Neodesha, Kansas in 1897.

During the succeeding twelve years, Gray advanced to superintendent of transportation, general manager, second vice-president, and in 1909 senior vice-president of the "Frisco" railroad system. He left that road in 1911 to become president of the Spokane, Portland and Seattle Railroad, jointly owned by the Great Northern and the Northern Pacific railroads. In the following year he was named president of the Great Northern. Then, from 1914 to 1919, he was head of the Western Maryland Railroad at Baltimore, Maryland. He was on leave from this post, however, from 1917 to 1919 to serve in the West as director of operations of the Federal Railroad Administration, which took over virtually all railroad properties in the country.

In 1920 he joined the Union Pacific, where he was to spend the rest of his business life, becoming vice-chairman of the board in 1937. Under his management the Union Pacific was one of the few railroads in the country to pay dividends on common stock during the depression and was one of the pioneers in the introduction of streamlined diesel-powered passenger trains. Even more important was the fact that he took a leading role in the period after 1920 in representing the railroads in matters of national railway policy. He was the person most responsible for the creation of the Western Association of Railway Executives in 1932, and for developing its unique plan for compromising their differences through the medium of a commission. He also played a major role in the organization in 1934 of the Association of American Railroads, a body which represented all the large American railroads in such common concerns as the handling of car service, statistical records, accounting procedures, operating rules, maintenance practices, and proposals for federal legislation.

In 1938 he was one of a "Committee of Six" to submit recommendations to Franklin Roosevelt on the general transportation situation, which led to the Transportation Act of 1940. While with the Frisco Railroad he had great success in promoting the advancement of profitable agriculture in the area served by the railroad. He established scholarships in agriculture in each of the states through which the railroad traversed. He was a Baptist and married Harriette Flora of Oswego, Kansas, in 1886. They had three sons, two of whom followed their father into railroading and one of whom became a surgeon at the Mayo Clinic. (**A.** *DAB*, Supplement 2; *NCAB*, 36:20; *New York Times*, May 10, 1939. **B.** Robert G. Athearn, *Union Pacific Country*, 1971; Earl Latham, *The Politics of Railroad Coordination, 1933-36*, 1939.)

GRAY, GEORGE ALEXANDER (September 28, 1851–February 18, 1912). Southern textile manufacturer. Born in Crab Orchard Township, Mecklenburg County, North Carolina, son of George Alexander Gray and Mary Wallace. His ancestors had come to North Carolina from Pennsylvania after the Revolutionary War, and his father was a farmer who later worked in cotton mills in the area. His father died suddenly in 1859, forcing his older brothers to go to work, but young George stayed home as his mother's pet and companion. When the Civil War broke out in 1861 George was forced to go to work in the factory, but the mill soon closed and the Grays moved to Caleb Lineberger's cotton mill in the "Pinhook" section on the South Fork of the Catawba River. George began work there as a sweeper boy at 10¢ a day. Shortly afterward, he had an accident in the factory, forcing the amputation of his arm. He attended school during his convalescence, and this one year constituted the whole of his formal education. He did show a mechanical aptitude, however, and devoted much time to the study of mechanics. As he was given more and more responsibility in the mill, he soon became assistant superintendent, taking on a broad range of duties.

When he was but nineteen years of age he was made superintendent of the Woodlawn Cotton Mill, and in 1878 was engaged by the Oates brothers to equip and operate the Charlotte Cotton Mills, the first plant in what later became a major textile center. He conducted this factory for four years and then was employed by Col. R. Y. McAden to start a mill at McAdenville. In 1888, having saved a little money, he went to Gastonia, North Carolina, then a tiny settlement at the junction of the Southern Railroad and a smaller road. With the assistance of Robert G. Love and James D. Moore, Gray organized the first mill in that district, the Gastonia Cotton Manufacturing Company. He was confident that Gastonia, with its cheap fuel, abundant labor, raw materials, and good transportation facilities, would someday be an important center of cotton manufacture.

In 1893, with George W. Ryan and Thomas Pegran, he built the Trenton Mill, and three years later, with John F. Love, erected the Avon Mill, capitalized at $200,000, to spin fine yarns and weave a fine grade of sheeting. He was president of this firm until 1910. In 1899 the Ozark Mill was organized with capital of $200,000 and Gray as president, and in 1900 the Loray Mills was started. Later, Firestone Textiles was organized with a capital of $1.5 million. In 1905 he organized and became president of the Gray Manufacturing Company (later, Bernside Mills, Incorporated), the first combed cotton mill in the South and one of the earliest electrically driven cotton mills in the entire world. It was also one of the first air conditioned buildings in the world. He also organized the Clara Manufacturing Company, the Holland Manufacturing Company, and the Flint Manufacturing Company, all in 1907. Only two mills built in Gastonia during his lifetime were developed without his assistance. He also introduced a night shift in the plant directed by him at McAdenville in 1884 and installed electric lights above the machines, probably the first example of such industrial illumination in America.

Gray helped organize the Wylie Mill at Chester, South Carolina; the

Scottdale at Atlanta, Georgia; and the Mandeville at Carrollton, Georgia. He was president of Gastonia Metal and Roofing Company, and director of the First National Bank of Gastonia, Piedmont and Northern Electric Railroad, and the Carolina and Northwestern Railroad. He was a Democrat and from 1900 to 1904 was a member of the board of aldermen of Gastonia, and during the same years served as city treasurer. He was a Methodist and married Jennie Withers of Dallas, North Carolina, in 1877. They had ten children. His son, Charles Dowd Gray (b. 1890) became president of Gray Cotton Company in 1914, serving until 1931. In 1921 he founded the Priscilla Spinning Company and was its president until 1927. In 1931 he became a salesman for Textiles, Incorporated, and was a director of the firm after 1933. In 1936 he organized Gray and Daniel, Incorporated, selling agents for textile firms, and served as its president. He also incorporated a number of mills in North Carolina on his own account during the World War I period. (**A.** *DAB*; *NCAB*, 37:92; K:158, **B.** Jack Blicksilver, *Cotton Manufacturing in the Southeast*, 1959; Broadus Mitchell, *The Rise of Cotton Mills in the South*, 1921.)

GRAY, WILLIAM (June 27, 1750–November 3, 1825). Merchant in Salem and Boston. Born in Lynn, Massachusetts, son of Abraham Gray and Lydia Calley. His father was a shoemaker who moved to Salem when William was a small boy. There young William was apprenticed to Samuel Gardner and later entered the counting house of Richard Derby.* At age twenty-eight Gray opened his own business. His ventures proved highly profitable and he bought a number of privateers during the Revolutionary War. He was one of the first New England merchants to enter the trade with Russia, India, and China; and from 1801 to 1807, when Salem's prosperity was at its peak, he annually employed about 300 seamen. Before 1815 he owned at least 113 vessels. When he moved to Boston in 1809, he was the owner of fifteen ships, seven barks, 13 brigs, and one schooner, and his fortune was estimated at some $3 million.

William Gray was also actively involved in politics. As a Federalist he served in a number of offices for that party, several years as a selectman, and as a delegate to the state convention to consider the Federal Constitution in 1788. He voted for ratification. In 1807 he was chosen a Federalist Senator from Essex County, and was reelected the following year. In 1808 he came out in favor of the Embargo, although it was vigorously opposed by other New England merchants. This resulted in his being socially ostracized in Salem, so he moved to Boston. In 1810 he ran for lieutenant governor as a Republican, with Eldridge Gerry as the gubernatorial candidate. They were elected by a small plurality. He was reelected in 1811, but declined the office. Gray supported the Madison administration during the War of 1812, and ran for office several times in succeeding years, but was always defeated. In 1816 he was elected president of the Boston branch of the Bank of the United States, serving for six years. He married Elizabeth Chipman of Marblehead, Massachusetts, in 1782 and they had ten children. (**A.** *DAB*; *NCAB*, 5:337; Edward Gray, *William Gray of Salem, Mass.*, 1914. **B.** Tyler Dennett, *Americans in East Asia*, 1941; Foster R. Dulles, *The Old China Trade*, 1930; James D. Phillips, *Salem and the Indies*, 1947.)

GREEN, ANNE CATHARINE HOFF (c. 1720–March 23, 1775). Colonial printer and publisher. Born in Holland and brought to Pennsylvania as a young child. In 1738 she married Jonas Green, a journeyman printer from Boston. He worked for Benjamin Franklin in Philadelphia, and in that same year moved to Annapolis, Maryland, where he soon became a printer for the province of Maryland. In 1745 he began publication of the weekly *Maryland Gazette*, one of the earliest colonial newspapers, and an early vigorous opponent of the Stamp Act. During this time, Anne Green spent most of her time raising her fourteen children, who were born between 1738 and 1760. Sometime after 1767 she began to take an active part in the business, for upon her husband's death in that year, she produced the *Acts and Votes and Proceedings* of the Assembly of 1767 on schedule, and the *Gazette* appeared without a break.

She first carried on the business with the help of her son, William, and in 1768 the *Gazette* appeared under the name of Anne Catharine Green and William Green. With the death of William in 1770, her son Frederick replaced him. Her husband's allowance as a public printer expired with his death, however, and for more than a year Mrs. Green operated without public appropriations. She performed her duties so well that the following year the Assembly appointed her to her husband's position at the same compensation. She also published a yearly almanac and printed a few political pamphlets and some satirical works. Her most ambitious undertaking, apart from her newspaper and public business, was Elie Vallette's *Deputy Commissary's Guide*, in 1774, a book of 133 pages detailing the procedures and forms to be used in probating wills and settling estates.

Until 1773 when William Goddard* began publication of the *Maryland Journal* and *Baltimore Advertiser*, the *Gazette* was the only Maryland newspaper, and its role in reporting the political events leading to the Revolution was an important one. Through her columns, John Dickinson's *Letters From a Pennsylvania Farmer* reached the public. By publicizing the Boston Tea Party and the other acts of 1774, the *Gazette* probably helped push the Revolutionary cause in the province. But Mrs. Green kept her columns open to both sides of the debate. After her death, her son Frederick took over the business. (**A.** *NAW*. **B.** Julia C. Spruill, *Women's Life and Work in the Southern Colonies*, 1938.)

GREEN, HENRIETTA (HETTY) HOWLAND ROBINSON (November 21, 1834–July 3, 1916). Financier and speculator, Westminster Company.

Born in New Bedford, Massachusetts, daughter of Edward Mott Robinson and Abby Slocum Howland, both wealthy Quakers. Her great wealth was to be inherited from the Howland family, who had become rich dealing in whaling and foreign trade with the venerable firm of Isaac Howland Jr. and Company. Her maternal grandfather, Gideon Howland Jr., took an active part in the family firm until 1847. When he died, he left an estate to his two daughters, one of whom was unmarried, and the other of whom was Hetty's mother. Her father had been born in Philadelphia, but was from an old Rhode Island Quaker family. About 1830 he entered the Howland firm, a few years later marrying Hetty's mother. He was largely responsible for the vigorous expansion of the firm during the golden days of the whaling industry, and was for nearly thirty years a leading figure in New Bedford. His firm owned more than 30 vessels, and he was also president of the Bedford Commercial Bank. With the outbreak of the Civil War he removed to New York City, where he became one of the owners of William T. Coleman and Company, proprietors of a line of California packets, at one time in control of over 70 vessels. He also added to his wealth by successful operations on Wall Street, leaving a fortune of over $5 million when he died in 1865.

Hetty Green was educated at Eliza Wing School, Sandwich, Massachusetts, and at the Boston school run by Rev. Charles Russell Lowell and his wife Ann Cabot (Jackson) Lowell. Very early in her life she became interested in business, reading the financial pages of the newspaper to her grandfather and often accompanying her father on his rounds. Her inherited fortune began on a small scale; she received $8,000 from her mother's estate in 1860 and a gift from her aunt of $20,000. In 1865 she received about $1 million outright from her father's estate and annual net earnings of more than $4 million in a trust fund. Then her Aunt Sylvia died, leaving one-half of her fortune to charity and with the rest establishing a trust fund whose income of $65,000 annually was to go to Hetty, with the principal to be distributed to living Howland heirs at Hetty's death.

In 1866 Hetty brought a law suit in which she claimed her aunt's entire estate, with her major piece of evidence being a will in Hetty's handwriting but with her aunt's signature. This became the celebrated "Howland Will Case," which dragged on in court for five years and brought Hetty much notoriety. In 1871 the case was ended in a draw, with Hetty getting $600,000. During this time, in 1867, she married Edward Henry Green, a native of Bellows Falls, Vermont, who had been a partner for many years in the Philippine trading firm of Russell and Sturgis. They took a protracted trip to England, where for several years Green pursued his interests as a director of three London banks, while Hetty speculated on the price of United States Greenbacks, considerably augmenting her already enormous fortune. For the most part, however, her time was devoted to the raising of their two children, Edward Henry (b. 1868) and Sylvia Ann Howland (b. 1871).

In 1874 they returned to the United States and settled in New York City. Now Hetty, aided by her father's old financial advisors and by officials at Chemical National Bank, began investing in government bonds and railroad stocks. She helped finance her husband's purchase of stock in the Louisville and Nashville Railroad, of which he was soon elected president; and she contributed a large portion of her available funds to purchases of real estate or mortgages in such rapidly growing cities as New York, Chicago, Kansas City, St. Louis, and San Francisco. At her death, it was estimated that she owned 8,000 parcels of real estate, of which those in Chicago alone were worth five or six million dollars. She was also a major source of loans for active speculators, and she was described as the "recognized" ready money lender on Wall Street. She was always able to liquidate her assets prior to financial panics and then have the money to lend in periods of financial stringency, especially in 1907. Year to year her wealth multiplied itself. In the meantime, her husband, a more daring speculator, went bankrupt in 1885, and Hetty refused to underwrite his debts. The two then separated and lived apart for several years.

Hetty sent her children to Catholic parochial schools, and after her son, Edward Henry Jr., graduated from Fordham, she sent him first to Chicago to manage her real estate holdings and then to Texas, where in 1892 he bought for his mother a section of the Texas and Midland Railroad. He then was elected president of the line and moved to Texas, where he devoted himself to its modernization and expansion. In her later years Hetty became a standard topic of conversation in New York, as she dressed in shabby clothing, carried odd bits of food with her, haggled with shopkeepers over petty purchases, and sometimes sought free treatment at charity clinics, living in a series of run-down boarding houses to avoid the taxes of a permanent residence in New York.

In 1910 she organized, with her son, the Westminster Company, which assured continued active management of her financial empire. She willed her estate, estimated at some $100 million, to her two children. (*DAB*; *NCAB*, 25:415; 15:128; *NAW*; *Who Was Who*, vol. 1; *New York Times*, July 4, 1916; Boyden Sparks and Samuel T. Moore, *Hetty Green*, 1930.)

GREEN, JOHN CLEVE (April 4, 1800–April 29, 1875). China merchant and railroad financier, Russell and Company, Michigan Central Railroad, and Bleeker Street Savings Bank. Born in Maidenhead (now Lawrenceville), New Jersey, son of Caleb Smith Green and Elizabeth Van Cleve. His ancestors had come to New Jersey in 1700. He was one of the members of the first class to enter what became the Lawrenceville School, and after further schooling in Brooklyn, entered the employ of N. L. and G. Griswold and Company, prominent New York merchants with an extensive foreign trade. He spent the years from 1823 to 1833 at sea as a supercargo of

Griswold's ships, frequently visiting South America and China. During this time he married Sarah Griswold, daughter of George Griswold Jr., one of the partners in the firm. In 1833, while in Canton, China, as an agent for the Griswold firm, he accepted an invitation to join the firm of Russell and Company, the most powerful American house in the China trade.

A year later he was named head of the firm, and when the East India Company's monopoly of the lucrative opium trade was ended, he added that line to their previous tea and textile business. In doing so, he grew rich along with the company. It was while he was in China that he formed a life-long association with John Murray* and Robert B. Forbes. In 1839, after Commissioner Lin at Canton launched an attack on the opium trade, he retired, and Robert Forbes succeeded him as president of the company. Green then became head of the Chamber of Commerce of Canton, signing an agreement to abstain from the opium trade. He soon returned to New York with an ample fortune, which he was to put to shrewd advantage in other transactions.

He continued for some time as consignee of Chinese tea cargoes and also became director of the Bank of Commerce and president of the Bleeker Street Savings Bank. In 1846, he was the largest financial backer of John Murray Forbes, who purchased and became president of the Michigan Central Railroad. He also supported Forbes' takeover of the Chicago, Burlington and Quincy System, serving as director of that road and the New Jersey Central until his death. He was worth some $30 million by his death. Since his children died young, he made substantial charitable contributions, giving Princeton $500,000, which saved the school from a critical financial situation. He also endowed three chairs in science and financed a school of civil engineering. He served as a trustee of Princeton Theological Seminary and endowed a chair of church history. The Lawrenceville School received even more from him, and became one of the leading prep schools in the nation as a result of his gifts. He was a Presbyterian. (**A.** *DAB*; *NCAB*, 11:336; *Who Was Who*, vol. H. **B.** Tyler Dennett, *Americans in East Asia*, 1941; Foster R. Dulles, *The Old China Trade*, 1930.)

GREEN, NORVIN (April 17, 1818–February 12, 1893). Telegraph company executive, Western Union Telegraph. Born in New Albany, Indiana, son of Joseph Green and Susan Ball, who were natives of Virginia. When he was in his early youth, his family moved to Breckinridge County, Kentucky, where he was educated at country schools and worked on his father's farm. When his father went bankrupt, he was forced to make a living for himself, opening a grocery store on a flatboat at sixteen. He then traveled up and down the Ohio and Mississippi rivers selling supplies to the lumbermen on the banks. Later, he secured employment as a woodcutter, by which he earned money for his medical education. He first studied with

Dr. Mason of Carrollton, Kentucky, and later entered the Medical College of the University of Louisville, from which he graduated in 1840. During the next dozen years he practiced medicine and pursued a political career, being elected to two terms in the Kentucky legislature, and serving as a Democratic presidential elector in 1852.

In 1853 Green launched his business career. In that year, two rival telegraph lines from Louisville to New Orleans—the People's, and the New Orleans and Ohio—were consolidated after a period of vigorous competition. Green, along with several others, then leased the consolidated lines for operation. After an unsuccessful period of operation, the Louisville-New Orleans lines were reorganized as the Southwestern Telegraph Company, with Green as president. Under his management, the Southwestern became prosperous; but he had even greater visions. He was one of the first to conceive the idea of a truly national consolidation of telegraph companies, and in 1857 he took the first steps towards realizing his ambition by initiating the consolidation of the six largest telegraph lines in the United States. This resulted in the formation of the North American Telegraph Company. In 1866 the process was completed through a merger with the Western Union Telegraph Company, embracing all the lines in the United States. Green served as vice-president of Western Union until 1878, when he became president. He then continued in that capacity until his death, fifteen years later.

Green was also president of the Louisville, Cincinnati and Lexington Railroad from 1870 to 1873, and served in the Kentucky House of Representatives in 1867. He married Martha English of Carrollton in 1840, and they had four sons and one daughter. (**A.** *DAB*; *NCAB*, 11:550. **B.** Elisha P. Douglas, *The Coming of Age of American Business*, 1971; Robert L. Thomson, *Wiring a Continent*, 1947.)

GREENE, WILLIAM CORRELL (1851–August 5, 1911). Mining entrepreneur, Greene Consolidated Copper Company; Cananea Mining Corporation. Born in Chappaqua, Westchester County, New York, of uncertain parentage. He spent several years as a government contractor in Kansas and then in Colorado before becoming a cowboy in 1877 on the frontier rim of Arizona. Here he had many adventures with Indians and cattle rustlers, but made little or no money. He next prospected for a time in the Bradshaw Mountains and when the boom came to Tombstone, Arizona, at the end of the decade, he went there to mine. When the boom petered out, he purchased a small ranch in the San Pedro Valley. In the 1890s, Greene became convinced that a tract of grazing land known as La Cananea in the State of Sonora, in Mexico, contained mineral deposits. He filed mining claims, and with the aid of some Arizona capitalists obtained possession of the land.

In 1899 he formed the Cobre Grande Copper Company and sold a block of 31,000 of its shares to J. H. Costello, a Pennsylvania capitalist, who was placed in charge of operations. Several months later, Greene ousted Costello by means of a Mexican court order and formed a new company, the Cananea Consolidated Copper Company, a Mexican corporation. He persuaded a group of capitalists headed by Thomas W. Lawson,* who at the time was head of Amalgamated Copper Company, to give him financial backing. Lawson was to honor drafts up to one million dollars for development of the property and was to receive in return an option on a controlling block of shares in the newly formed Greene Consolidated Copper Company, at one-third par. Greene later contended that after honoring drafts for $135,000, Lawson refused to honor any more and called in the outstanding notes. Greene narrowly escaped losing his property and he was greatly embittered against Lawson and the eastern bankers.

In 1900 Greene moved to New York, where he set up offices on Wall Street. He was able to convince investors such as John W. Gates,* Collis P. Huntington,* and others to sit on his boards of directors and was also able to appeal to the small investor for funds. His talent for writing prospectuses amounted to genius. For several years he prospered greatly, but in 1903 the Gates-Hawley interests made systematic attacks on Greene Consolidated stock. Greene was able to withstand the challenge and several months later copper ore estimated at $100 million was discovered on his properties. He immediately extended his corporate organization and in 1904 formed additional companies to capitalize on the Cananea bonanza—the Greene Gold-Silver Company and the Greene Consolidated Gold Company. He bought a large section of Sonora for cattle ranching; bought mines and holdings in the Sierra Madre; organized the Sierra Madre Land and Lumber Company; secured control of a railroad tapping the Sierra Madre holdings; and built one to the Cananea holdings. By this time his mines were producing copper to the value of $10 million a year.

At the height of his prosperity Greene was at the head of companies capitalized at $100 million, of which his personal holdings amounted to less than one-half. He was hit very hard by the "Lawson Panic" of 1904, since he had been speculating heavily in the securities of other companies. It was equally clear that he had become the target of several groups on Wall Street. He had carried over to New York the Wild West ways which he had found effective in Arizona, where he had once shot a man on the street for a suspected injury. This kind of behavior did not endear him to the gentlemen of Wall Street. His fall from power was very rapid. In 1906 he capitulated to Thomas F. Cole, John D. Ryan,* and the Amalgamated Copper interests, which had already acquired the Cananea Central Mine. The result was the formation of the Greene-Cananea Consolidated Copper Company, capitalized at $60 million. Greene was to remain head of the new company, but within three months of its formation he was divested of all formal power and, shortly after that, dropped from the board of directors.

The Panic of 1907 destroyed the balance of his fortune. He still retained, however, several large Mexican cattle ranches and spent the last years of his life managing them. He was married twice, the second time to Mary Proctor. (*DAB*; *New York Times*, August 6, 1911; *Who Was Who*, vol. 1.)

GREGG, WILLIAM (February 2, 1800–September 13, 1867). Southern cotton mill owner and promoter of southern industrial development. Born in Monongahela County, Virginia (now West Virginia), of Quaker parents. His ancestors had come to Pennsylvania with William Penn in 1682, with later generations moving to the frontier in Virginia and South Carolina. His mother died when he was four years old, and he was raised by a neighbor until he was ten. At that time he was taken in by an uncle, Jacob Gregg, who was a prosperous watchmaker and manufacturer of cotton spinning machinery at Alexandria, Virginia. Then, during the War of 1812, his uncle established a small cotton factory at Little River, Georgia. Young William worked in the mill until it was destroyed by the peace in 1815, which brought a flood of English goods to America. His uncle then apprenticed him with another watchmaker in Lexington, Kentucky, where he also learned silversmithing. In 1821 Gregg went to Petersburg, Virginia, to complete his training. Three years later he established himself in business in Columbia, South Carolina, where he accumulated a comfortable fortune during a span of ten years, before he was forced to retire from business because of ill health.

While in retirement in Edgefield, South Carolina, Gregg took an interest in a small and poorly managed mill, the Vaucluse Cotton Works. In 1843, in partnership with his brother-in-law James Jones, he acquired full possession of the mill. It was also during this time that he began to play a major public role in the development of South Carolina and the South. Gregg was convinced that exclusive devotion to staple agriculture was economically ill-advised and that the entire region needed to embark on manufacturing, especially in cotton. He was influenced in his ideas by Henry C. Carey of Philadelphia, who was preaching American economic development through diversification of occupations and a protective tariff. In 1844 Gregg visited the textile districts of the North and began writing a series of articles, *Essays on Domestic Industry*, published in the *Charleston Courier*. His views gained a very large audience throughout the South.

Following his own advice, Gregg undertook to establish a cotton mill in the interior of his state, supported by Charleston capitalists. In 1845 he asked the South Carolina legislature for a charter of incorporation, a practice that was looked upon with great disfavor in the South at that time. Gregg issued a pamphlet explaining why the charter should be granted, but the legislature agreed by a margin of only one vote. In 1846 Gregg began erecting the plant of the Graniteville Manufacturing Company in Edgefield, near Aiken, South Carolina. The mill had nearly 9,000 spindles and 300 looms, and Gregg directed all the engineering operations. He used native materials and labor, building a granite factory and some one hundred cottages for operatives. This was the first of what later was to be the typical southern cotton mill village. As soon as the plant was finished, country people poured in seeking employment and living quarters, and the mill soon had 300 operatives, with 900 inhabitants in the village. Only the first superintendent and a few overseers were imported from the North to run the mill. The company began actual operation in 1848 with $300,000 in capital and Gregg as president. It had severe difficulties during its early years, never paying dividends during this time; but eventually it justified Gregg's faith, becoming a highly profitable venture from 1850 to 1866.

In response to this success, other cotton mills sprang up in the South and Gregg acquired a wide reputation as a southern cotton manufacturer. His standard advice was that southern mills should concentrate in a narrow range of coarse cloths and endeavor to sell their product in a national and world market rather than trying to turn out a variety of goods to meet the demands of local consumption. He also advised the mills to sell their product directly, without operating through commission agencies. He came out in favor of a high protective tariff in 1858, an extraordinary step for a South Carolinian at that time, and sat in the state house of representatives from 1856 to 1857. He was defeated for state senate in 1858.

Gregg also took the lead in establishing welfare programs for workers in the cotton mill villages. He advocated the establishment of schools with compulsory attendance for children; libraries; and health, recreation, and housing programs for villagers. In his own village he was a benevolent despot, but his policies advanced opportunities for the social betterment of poor whites through industrial employment. In 1860 he signed the South Carolina Ordinance of Secession and during the Civil War managed to keep his plant in operation in spite of the impressments of labor by the Confederate and state governments. After the war he went North and to Europe to secure new equipment for refining the mill. He took ill, however, and died before these were completed. Gregg is generally recognized as the "father of southern cotton manufacture." He married Marina Jones of Edgefield, South Carolina in 1829. (**A.** *DAB*; *NCAB*, 12:40; *Who Was Who*, vol. 4. **B.** Jack Blicksilver, *Cotton Manufacturing in the Southeast: An Historical Analysis*, 1959; Broadus Mitchell, *William Gregg: Factory Master of the Old South*, 1928.)

GREGORY, THOMAS BARGER (October 15, 1860–July 11, 1951). Oil and gas producer, Union Heat and Light Company; Manufacturers Light and Heat Company; Lone Star Gas Company; Columbia Gas and Electric Company. Born in Philadelphia, Pennsylvania, son of William Sheed Gregory and Amanda W. Miller. When he was nine years old, his family moved to Venango County, Pennsylvania, the heart of the oil regions of the state. It was here also that a number of the country's first national gas companies began their operation. Gregory was educated in the public schools of Philadelphia and Foxburg, Pennsylvania, and later at Brooks Military Academy in Ohio. Gregory began his career in the petroleum industry at eighteen, by purchasing gas leases in Venango and Clarion counties. He later established an oil equipment business at Foxburg.

In 1886 Gregory founded the Union Heat and Light Company, which supplied natural gas to Foxburg and St. Petersburg, Pennsylvania. During the next seven years he mastered the administrative and financial details of the firm and expanded his operations into other counties. He also formed new companies to distribute natural gas into West Virginia. Then, in 1895, he formed a partnership with Harry J. Crawford that would last until Gregory's death in 1951, with no other basis than a verbal agreement. They developed oil and gas properties in all of the major fields of the United States and Mexico, and by 1932 held an interest in more than 2,000 oil and gas wells. In 1902 Gregory and Crawford joined with George W. Crawford,* a cousin of Harry, and Milo C. Treat, to form the Ohio Fuel Company (later Ohio Fuel Corporation), a public utility holding company with electrical power and natural gas affiliates in Ohio, Kentucky, and West Virginia. In the next year they reorganized the Manufacturers Light and Heat Company as a public utility holding company with affiliates in New York, Pennsylvania, and West Virginia. In 1907 Gregory and his partners purchased control of the Lone Star Gas Company, the first major natural gas transmission company in the Southwest.

In 1926 Gregory and the Crawfords organized the Columbia Gas and Electric Corporation, with assets of $263 million. They later merged the interests of this company and Manufacturers Light and Heat into the Ohio Fuel Corporation. Eventually, Columbia Gas controlled fifty-five affiliates that covered 257 cities in New York, Pennsylvania, Ohio, Indiana, Kentucky, and West Virginia. Gregory served as an officer or director for 32 of the affiliates. When Samuel Insull's* public utility empire began to collapse in 1927, Congress authorized the Federal Trade Commission to investigate the industry. Its final report questioned several practices of Columbia Gas and Electric, especially its connection with its affiliate, Panhandle Eastern Gas Pipeline Company. In 1935 Gregory's companies complied with the new Public Utilities Holding Act by internal reorganization.

Gregory married Adda Sophia Whitling in 1888 and they had two daughters. (*DAB*, Supplement 5; *New York Times*, July 12, 1951; *Who Was Who*, vol. 3.)

GRIGGS, EVERETT GALLUP (December 27, 1868–March 6, 1938). Lumberman and association official, St. Paul and Tacoma Lumber Company; Pacific Coast Lumber Manufacturers Association; National Lumber Manufacturers Association; Douglas Fir Export Company. Born in Chaska,

Minnesota, son of Chauncey Wright Griggs and Martha Ann Gallup. His grandparents had been early New England migrants to the Middle West, and his father was a banker and politician in Minnesota. In 1877 Chauncey Griggs moved to Tacoma, Washington, where he organized and became president of the St. Paul and Tacoma Lumber Company, which owned large mills and 80,000 acres of timber. Everett Griggs was educated at St. Paul's at Concord, New Hampshire, and graduated from Yale in 1890. He took additional courses at Sheffield Scientific School, and in 1892 entered the employ of his father's lumber company. Learning the business from the ground up, he started as a timekeeper, worked up to mill superintendent, and became president in 1908. He held that position until 1933, when he became chairman of the board. During these years, St. Paul and Tacoma was one of the largest lumber operations in the Pacific Northwest.

It was a highly expansive and competitive time for the Douglas fir industry, and Griggs was a strongly "industry minded" manufacturer, opposing the rampant individualism and competition of the time. He organized and was president from 1903 to 1913 of the Pacific Coast Lumber Manufacturers Association, the first attempt of the Northwest mills to work together for standard lumber grades, better freight rates, and wider markets. Later, he was an active leader in the West Coast Lumberman's Association, which absorbed the earlier group and became a champion of the mills in trade promotion, lumber tariffs, production and price statistics, and expanding relations with the federal government. For many years he also represented the Northwest in the National Lumber Manufacturers Association at Washington, D.C., of which he was president in 1911–1912. He was one of the organizers in 1916 and president from 1923 to 1935 of the Douglas Fir Export Company, organized under the Webb-Pomerene Act to stimulate foreign trade.

During World War I he was an officer in the Army Signal Corps and served on the staff of the spruce products division, devoting much of his time to organizing Northwest logging camps and sawmills for maximum war production. He also gave his strong support to the "Loyal Legion of Loggers and Lumbermen," a labor-management organization designed to combat the activities of the Industrial Workers of the World. Griggs was also an advocate of the policy of reforestation of cutover lands as a commercially profitable venture. He believed that the only way that the lumber industry could avoid public regulation was to police itself. In that regard he became an active member of the Western Forestry and Conservation Association, created in 1909 to examine the holdings of its members and advise them on their timber-cutting policies. In his own company he took active steps to educate employees and the community on the importance of reforestation to perpetuate employment. He dramatized this by effective publicity over the planting of new trees in logged-over lands. From these beginnings he ultimately developed the 170,000-acre St. Paul and

Tacoma Tree Farm. He married Grace Isobel Wallace in 1895. They had no children. (**A.** *DAB*, Supplement 2; *Who Was Who*, vol. 1. **B.** Samuel P. Hays, *Conservation and the Gospel of Efficiency*, 1959.)

GRINNELL, JOSEPH (November 7, 1788–February 7, 1885); **Henry Grinnell** (February 13, 1799–June 30, 1874); and **Moses Hicks Grinnell** (March 3, 1803–November 24, 1877). Merchants and shippers, Fish and Grinnell; Grinnell, Minturn and Company; and Wamsutta Mills. The three Grinnell brothers were born in New Bedford, Massachusetts, sons of Captain Cornelius Grinnell and Sylvia Howland. Their father was a prosperous merchant and shipmaster; he was descended from Huguenots who had fled France in 1572 and came to America in 1642. Their mother was descended from Henry Howland, who had come to Plymouth in 1624. All three boys were educated in New Bedford Academy.

Joseph Grinnell entered his father's office after finishing his schooling in the academy, where he obtained a good mercantile training. In 1810 he went to New York where, with his uncle, John H. Howland, he engaged in the shipping business under the name of Howland and Grinnell. They were successful until the outbreak of the War of 1812, when they suffered severe losses, and the firm was dissolved two years later. In 1815, with Preserved Fish, a relative, he established the firm of Fish and Grinnell, acting as New York agents for the New Bedford whale oil merchants. This new firm was very successful, becoming the most substantial mercantile house in the city after a few years. In 1825 Fish retired and Grinnell induced his two brothers to join him as partners in Fish, Grinnell and Company. Three years later ill health forced him to retire.

After traveling in Europe, Joseph Grinnell returned to New Bedford where he reentered the shipping business, and at the same time engaged in other local commercial and financial ventures. In 1832 he became president of the Marine Bank (later First National Bank), a position he held for 44 years. In 1841 he became associated with the Boston and Providence Railroad as a director, also serving as its president for five years. He took an interest in politics during these years, being elected to the Governor's Council of Massachusetts in 1838, 1839, and 1840. In 1843 he was elected as a representative to the United States Congress, serving from 1843 to 1851. During his tenure as a congressman, Grinnell became interested in promoting the industrial progress of New Bedford, feeling that the solid dependence upon the whaling industry put it in a precarious position. This motivated him in 1846 to enlist the support of leading townsmen to obtain a charter for a cotton factory. He became the first president of the Wamsutta Mills and was continuously engaged in superintending its operations. The mill brought a new era of prosperity to New Bedford. By the time of his death it was composed of six units, with a total of 200,000 spindles and 4,300 looms; it employed 2,400 and was capitalized at $3 million.

Henry Grinnell went to New York in 1818 after graduating from New Bedford Academy. There he became a clerk in the commission house of H. D. and E. B. Sewell, remaining for seven years. In 1825 he and his younger brother, Moses, joined Joseph in the firm of Fish, Grinnell and Company. When Joseph left the firm in 1829 his place was taken by Robert Minturn,* Henry's brother-in-law, and the firm became Grinnell, Minturn and Company. Under the new name the firm's operations expanded greatly, entering into the general shipping business and becoming one of the strongest mercantile houses in the city. For 21 years Henry was an active partner in the firm, retiring a very wealthy man in 1850. After enjoying his retirement for several years, he entered the insurance field in 1859 as United States manager of the Liverpool and London Insurance Company. He was also one of the founders and president in 1862–1863 of the American Geographic and Statistical Society.

Moses Hicks Grinnell entered his father's office after completing his education and in 1821 entered the employ of William R. Ratch and Company of New Bedford, importers who were also in the whaling business. He made several voyages as a supercargo for the firm. In 1824 he went to New York to enter Joseph's mercantile firm, assuming charge of new development for the company after 1829 as it entered the shipping business and moved away from the commission business. The firm became agent for a line of packet ships between London and New York and proceeded to build its own ships. He retired from the firm in 1861. He was also involved in the Phoenix Bank, Sun Mutual Insurance Company, and the Institute for the Savings of Merchant's Clerks, all of which he was at one time president. He was also president of the New York Chamber of Commerce from 1843 to 1848. In 1839 he was elected as a Whig to the U.S. Congress, serving one term. He later became a Republican and served as a presidential elector in 1856 for Fremont. In 1869 he was appointed collector of the port of New York by President Grant.

Joseph Grinnell was married to Sarah Russell of New Bedford in 1812. She died in 1862, and three years later he married Rebecca Chase Kinsman of Salem, Massachusetts. He had one adopted daughter. Henry Grinnell married Sarah Minturn in 1822. Moses H. Grinnell married Susan H. Russell of New Bedford in 1826 and Julia Irving of New York, a niece of Washington Irving, in 1836. (**A.** *DAB*; *NCAB*, 3:281; 1:499. **B.** Robert G. Albion, *The Rise of the Port of New York, 1815–1860*, 1939.)

GRISCOM, CLEMENT ACTON (March 15, 1841–November 10, 1912). Ocean shipping company executive, International Navigation Company, and International Mercantile Marine Company. Born in Philadelphia, Pennsylvania, son of Dr. John D. Griscom and Margaret Acton. His ancestors had settled in New Jersey in 1680 and his father was a prominent physician. Clement Griscom was educated in public and private schools, graduating from Friend's Academy in 1857. At nineteen he started in business as a clerk with the importing firm of Peter Wright and Sons of Philadelphia. Three years later he was admitted to partnership. He prevailed upon the firm to purchase its own sailing ships and later guided it in its transformation to steam vessels. In the meantime he had taken up the study of marine architecture, and through his efforts, Peter Wright and Sons became the agents of the American Steamship Company, operating between Philadelphia and Liverpool, which was controlled by the Pennsylvania Railroad. In the same year, the firm became agents for the International Navigation Company, of which Griscom was made vice-president and elected president in 1888.

The ships of International Navigation, generally known as the Red Star Line, operated under a Belgian charter. In 1884 the Inman Line was purchased from British owners. It was at this time that Griscom's interest in marine construction came to the fore, since he felt that vessels with new improvements were important to the prestige and success of the company. He developed a vessel with twin propellers, transverse bulkheads, and water tight compartments, which were all new elements in shipbuilding.

For many years Griscom had also planned on eventually bringing most of the large steamship companies in the transatlantic trade under one firm, but it was not until 1902, when he associated himself with J. P. Morgan,* that the International Mercantile Marine Company was formed and International Navigation was merged into it. This brought under one ownership five large transatlantic lines whose aggregate fleet comprised 136 vessels with a tonnage of over one million. He was president of this firm for two years and then chairman of the board until his death. Although International Mercantile Marine became the largest shipping enterprise in the world, it was never profitable. Griscom and Morgan made little attempt to centralize its administration, allowing the firm to remain a loose confederation of autonomous lines. Since it failed to benefit from any gains of administrative coordination, it rarely paid a dividend even on its preferred stock. After Griscom's death it was reorganized financially, and the war boom temporarily revived it. But during the 1920s it continued to limp along until the depression, finally ceasing to exist as an operating company in 1937. Thus, unlike railroads and other forms of transportation, no successful giant shipping concern appeared in the United States. Nor did American shipping enterprise ever play a significant part in worldwide shipping or on the American business scene generally.

Griscom did much lobbying before Congress in the interests of the American Merchant Marine. He was a director of the Pennsylvania Railroad for many years and of the Bank of North America, Fidelity Trust and Safe Deposit, Western Saving Fund Society, and Insurance Company of North America.

He married Frances Canby Biddle of Philadelphia in 1862. They had two daughters and three sons. Of these, Rodman Ellison Griscom (1870–1944) became manager of Western Saving Fund Society, and Ludlum Griscom became a prominent ornithologist. (**A.** *DAB*; *NCAB*, 4:186; *Who Was Who*, vols. 1 and 3. **B.** Alfred D. Chandler Jr., *The Visible Hand*, 1977; N. S. B. Gras and H. Larson, *Casebook in American Business History*, 1939; John G. B. Hutchins, *The American Maritime Industries and Public Policy*, 1941.)

GROSS, ROBERT ELLSWORTH (May 11, 1897–September 3, 1961). Aircraft manufacturer, Lockheed Aircraft Corporation. Born in Boston, Massachusetts, son of Robert H. Gross and Mabel Bell. His father was a financier with interests in western mining. Robert E. Gross grew up in West Newton, Massachusetts, and was educated in public and private schools. He graduated from Harvard in 1919. In 1918 he left Harvard to serve a year in the army as an officer. After graduation Gross took a position with Lee and Higginson, the Boston banking and investment firm, and during the next nine years traveled to Europe and all over the United States investigating companies in which the bank had interests. He also invested personally in coal mines in Colorado, and before he was thirty years old he had made his first million.

Gross' association with aviation began in 1927 when he left the investment firm to join Stearman Aircraft Company of Wichita, Kansas. A year later, with his brother, Courtland S. Gross, he formed and became president of the Viking Boat Company, manufacturers of "sport model" seaplanes in New Haven, Connecticut. The depression wiped out the market for seaplanes, along with most of Gross' fortune, and in 1930 he moved to California to help organize the Varney Speed Lines, which flew the fast new Orion planes manufactured by the Lockheed Aircraft Corporation. The latter firm had been founded in 1916 by Allan and Malcolm Loughhead, who sold out in 1929 to Detroit Aircraft Corporation. In 1932, when the latter company fell victim to the depression, the general manager of Lockheed, Carl B. Squier, persuaded Gross and his brother to form a syndicate for its purchase. It cost $40,000 for a plant in Burbank, California, that covered 59,600 square feet and employed only fifteen people. Gross was treasurer and chairman of the board, adding the presidency in 1934 and dropping the treasurer designation in 1939.

Gross decided to begin in the small transport field, and spent $139,400 developing the Electra, a ten passenger all-metal plane for small airlines. He sold forty of these in the next year and this put Lockheed in the black. He then tried a bigger plane, the Model 14, and it also sold. Howard Hughes* then dramatized the plane by using it to fly around the world in record time. Lockheed's status as a major aircraft manufacturer stems from the development of the P-38, the two-engined military pursuit plane known during World War II as the Lightning in the United States and the Hudson in Britain. By the spring of 1939, Lockheed had obtained from the RAF $90 million worth of orders, and in order to fill them, the Burbank plant had to expand to twelve acres.

Accounting for 6 percent of United States airplane production during the Second World War, Lockheed built more than 19,000 planes, including Venturas, Flying Fortresses, Hudsons, and Lightnings. In its peak year, 1943, it had 94,000 employees. With peacetime conversion, the company reduced the number of employees and operated at a loss in 1946 and 1947. Lockheed began to show a profit again in 1948 through sales of its four engine Constellation on the commercial market. In the meantime, in 1946, the F-80 Shooting Star, Lockheed's jet fighter-bomber, was introduced. This was followed by a whole series of military jet planes, including the radar equipped F-94, which reached full-scale production in 1951 for Korean War needs.

If World War II did much to make Lockheed a major aircraft firm, the Korean War was known as "a Lockheed War." The conflict generated a large demand for Shooting Star fighters and Constellation transports, and Lockheed became the biggest defense company in the United States. Gross also tried to break into the commercial airline business with the Electra plane, but it had a propensity to crash, so he concentrated on the military market. In 1953 the company announced that it had established a new missile division at Burbank, with sales in the first year of over seven million dollars. By the early 1960s Lockheed had sales of $900 million in aircraft alone, and its joint venture in the Polaris missile with General Dynamics netted the two firms $427 million.

Troubles began mounting for Lockheed during the last years of Gross' administration. Starfighters sold to Germany in 1959 killed 85 pilots in that country in 175 crashes during the next few years, and the German minister of defense vowed never to do business with the firm again. Lockheed also tried to reenter the passenger plane business in the early 1960s with the L-1011 TriStar. At the same time it began to run into heavy weather with its military contracts. Lockheed overran its budget on the C-5A cargo jet by $2 billion, and in 1969 posted a loss of $32 million. Lockheed then advised the Pentagon that unless it received a loan of $600 million it would have to stop work on four military projects. By a one-vote margin in 1971, the government authorized loan guarantees of up to $250 million to save Lockheed.

Robert Gross was elected president of the Institute of Aeronautical Sciences in 1955 and was a director of Menasco Manufacturing Company of Los Angeles, Penn Mutual Life Insurance, and Pacific Finance Company of California; and secretary of the First National Bank of Los Angeles. An Episcopalian, he married Mary Bradford Perkins in 1920. They had one daughter. His brother, Courtland Sherrington Gross (1904–   ), was born in Boston and was educated at St. George's School and Harvard. He first worked for Lee and Higginson from 1927 to 1929 and then became an owner of Viking Flying Boat Company from 1929 to 1932. He next served as eastern representative of Lockheed Aircraft from 1932 to 1940; vice-president, general manager, and director of Lockheed Aircraft in Burbank from 1943 to 1952; executive vice-president from 1952 to 1956; and president from 1956 to 1961. He was then chairman of the board and chairman of the executive committee from 1961 to 1967. Lockheed had over 70,000 employees in the year he relinquished its presidency. (**A.** *NCAB*, K:437; *Current Biography*, 1956, 1961; *Who Was Who*, vol. 4; *Who's Who in America*, 1978–79. **B.** David Boulton, *The Lockheed Papers*, 1978; Charles D. Bright, *The Jet Makers*, 1978; Milton Moscowitz et al., *Everybody's Business*, 1980; John B. Rae, *Climb to Greatness*, 1968; Anthony Sampson, *The Arms Bazaar*, 1977.)

GROSSINGER, JENNIE (June 16, 1892–November 20, 1972). Resort owner, Grossinger's. Born in Austria, daughter of Selig Grossinger and Malke Grumet. Her family immigrated to the United States in 1900, settling on New York City's Lower East Side. Her father worked in a clothing factory, and at thirteen Jennie went to work, continuing her education in night school. A few years later the family opened a small restaurant in which Mrs. Grossinger did all the cooking, Mr. Grossinger was the waiter, and Jennie was the cashier. In 1914 her father had a physical and emotional breakdown and the doctor recommended that he change his lifestyle and move out of the city. He bought a small ramshackle farm house in the Catskill Mountains, near Ferndale, New York, where he hoped to raise crops.

In 1912 Jennie married her cousin, Harry Grossinger. When her parents moved to the farm in 1914, Jennie went with them, while her husband stayed at his job in the city. When they discovered that the farm would not produce enough crops to allow their survival, the Grossingers decided to take in a few boarders as a temporary measure. In their first season in the business they had nine boarders who paid a total of $81. Harry Grossinger recruited guests in New York and also spent his weekends helping out on the farm. In the next year the family added a six-room wing to the seven-room home, which allowed them to provide for 20 guests. By 1916 the Grossinger family was solidly, if modestly, established in the hotel business and Jennie's husband gave up his job in New York to devote full time to the business. Her father took care of the farming, marketing, and meeting of guests at the railway station, her mother took care of the kitchen, and Jennie, who by now had a baby, looked after the bookkeeping and management of the business.

Early in 1919 Jennie arranged for the purchase of a nearby hotel building, and the family moved from the small farm house to what officially became "Grossinger's Hotel." In the same year they bought a lake and the surrounding sixty-three acres of woodlands, so that they were able to offer guests fishing and sports facilities. Within the next decade, business expanded steadily and it became Grossinger Hotel and Country Club. By 1929 its guest capacity was over 500, and the original hotel was the main house of a group of buildings. A public relations man, Milton Blackstone, was hired to advertise the hotel. It was he who originated the idea of offering a free honeymoon to couples who met at Grossingers. The hotel also became one of the most widely publicized and best known in America over the next several years. In large measure this was due to the large number of celebrities who rose to stardom from a start at Grossingers. The most famous of these was Milton Berle, and established stars like Eddie Cantor and George Jessel became regular guests. Others who got their start at Grossingers were Jerry Lewis, Sid Caeser, Sam Levinson, Morey Amsterdam, Red Buttons, Eddie Fisher, and opera star Robert Merrill.

The main building of Grossingers can accommodate 100 guests and its dining room seats 1,300. There are two kitchens, following the dietary regulations of the Jewish faith, one for meat dishes and the other for dairy products. There is a night club with two stages, and surrounding the main building are smaller cottages and a children's day camp. At the peak of the summer season the hotel can accommodate about 1,000 guests. Jennie and Harry Grossinger lived on the hotel grounds, and in later years their son, Paul (b. 1915), shared in management of the enterprise. Grossingers has its own post office, newspaper, airport, ski slope, olympic swimming pool, golf course, and riding academy, and offers some of the most lavish nightclub acts in America to its 50,000 guests per year. (**A.** *Current Biography*, 1956; *Who Was Who*, vol. 5; *Who's Who in America*, 1978–79. **B.** H. J. Taub, *Waldorf in the Catskills*, 1952.)

GUFFEY, JAMES MCCLURG (January 19, 1839–March 20, 1930). Oil producer, Guffey and Galey, J. M. Guffey Petroleum, and Gulf Refining Company. Born in Sewickley Township, Westmoreland County, Pennsylvania, son of Alexander Guffey and Jane Campbell. His father operated a salt works and was an early user of natural gas. James Guffey was educated at "Old Sulphur Springs" school and worked on his father's farm. Later he attended Iron City Commercial College, a pioneer commercial school in Pittsburgh. At eighteen he entered the office of the superintendent of the Louisville and Nashville Railroad at Louisville as a clerk. He was next employed by the Adams Express Company in Nashville, returning to Pennsylvania in 1872 to become a salesman of oil well machinery and supplies at St. Petersburg for Gibbs and Sterrett Company.

This work gave Guffey a broad acquaintance in the oil regions and taught him a great deal about oil itself. He soon began to lease land and drill for oil. In 1875 he went to the Bradford oil region, where the town of Guffey in McKlean County was later named for him. In 1880, together with John H. Galey, he organized the firm of Guffey and Galey, for twenty-five years one of the most vigorous independent firms in the oil industry. Guffey settled at Titusville, drilling the famous Matthews and Lucas gushers, the latter with a capacity of 80,000 barrels. He and Galey soon expanded all over Pennsylvania and West Virginia, becoming the largest oil producer in the former state. Guffey himself would become one of the largest, if not the largest, individual landowner, producer, and operator in the United States.

The firm's rich Kansas holdings, consisting of 243,000 acres under lease, were transferred to the Forest Oil Company, then a Standard Oil subsidiary. An additional one and one-half million acres in the same state were never developed. The Magnolia Petroleum Company purchased the Texas holdings of Guffey and Galey and became one of the largest producers in the region. The two partners organized another firm, the J. M. Guffey Petroleum Company, capitalized at $15 million, for the purpose of building the first pipelines and refinery in the South Texas region. This company later became a valuable part of the Gulf Refining Company. In 1900 the firm held a blanket lease on 186,000 acres of the Osage nation in the Indian Territory, which it later sold for $1,250,000 to T. N. Barnsdale. Among the famous pools associated with the names Guffey and Galey were the Spindletop in Texas, the Coalings in California, the Sand Fork and the Kyle in West Virginia, and the McDonald in Pennsylvania.

The allied fields of gas and coal also caught Guffey's interest. In 1883 he turned his attention to the newly discovered natural gas territory in the Pittsburgh district and opened up many new fields. He became vice-president of the Westmoreland and Cambria Natural Gas Company and of the Wheeling Natural Gas Company; and president of the Southwest Natural Gas Company, Bellevue Natural Gas Company, and the United Fuel Company, all pioneers in the industry. He also had gold and silver mining interests in Idaho; mining and real estate holdings in Colorado, Florida, and Nova Scotia; and coal lands in Pennsylvania and West Virginia. But he was hit very hard by the Panic of 1907 and died a relatively poor man.

James Guffey was a Democrat, and at age twenty-seven had served as city clerk in Pithole City. In 1878 he ran for Congress, but lost, and in 1897 was elected a member of the Democratic National Committee, holding this position until 1908. He was bitterly opposed to William Jennings Bryan's third campaign and also opposed Woodrow Wilson. He was a Presbyterian and married Nancy Elizabeth Cook in 1887. They had one daughter. Both his brothers were also involved in the oil and gas industry in Pennsylvania. Wesley S. Guffey (b. 1842) had large interests in oil, gas, and coal lands in western Pennsylvania and was a prominent municipal reformer in Pittsburgh. John Guffey had oil, gas, and coal properties in Pennsylvania, Ohio, and West Virginia. His son, Joseph F. Guffey (1870–1955), was general manager of the Philadelphia Company, which operated public utilities in Pittsburgh, until 1918. He then became president of Guffey-Gillespie Oil Company,

Atlantic Gulf Oil Company and Columbia Syndicate. He was closely involved in Democratic politics on the national level and was elected U.S. Senator in 1934, serving until 1947. He was an ardent New Deal supporter. While in the Senate he sponsored the Guffey-Snyder Bituminous Coal Act, which was adopted by Congress in 1935. The act was declared unconstitutional and he then drafted and secured passage of Vinson-Guffey Coal Act. He was a Presbyterian and never married. (**A.** *DAB*; *NCAB*, 14:243–44; 49:84; *New York Times*, March 21, 1930; *Who Was Who*, vol. 1. **B.** Richard O'Connor, *The Oil Barons*, 1971; Anthony Sampson, *The Seven Sisters*, 1975; Samuel W. Tait, *The Wildcatters*, 1946; Craig Thompson, *Since Spindletop*, 1951.)

GUGGENHEIM FAMILY: Meyer Guggenheim (February 1, 1828–March 15, 1905); **Daniel Guggenheim** (July 9, 1856–September 28, 1930); and **Harry F. Guggenheim** (August 23, 1890–January 22, 1971). Mining entrepreneurs and financiers, American Smelting and Refining Company, and *Newsday* Magazine.

Meyer Guggenheim was born in Langnau, Switzerland, son of Simon Guggenheim (1792–1869) and his first wife, Schaefeli Levinger, who died in 1836. Simon Guggenheim was a tailor, and Meyer Guggenheim received only a rudimentary education in his native village. By the time he was in his teens he was working as a peddler. In 1847 Simon Guggenheim decided to immigrate to the United States, bringing with him his children, including the nineteen-year-old Meyer, and Simon's prospective wife, Rachel Weil Mayer, and her children. On shipboard Meyer met and fell in love with her eldest daughter, Barbara Mayer. On arrival in America Simon would marry Rachel Mayer, and a few years later Meyer Guggenheim married her daughter. After settling in Philadelphia both Simon and Meyer Guggenheim became peddlers, which seemed the quickest and surest way to make money. Father and son peddled a bit of everything—shoestrings, lace, stove and furniture polish, ribbons, pins, spices, and needles. They were able to build up a solid trade among German-speaking coal miners' wives and their local suppliers, along with a few Pennsylvania farmers. Meyer became upset over the fact that he and his father made only two cents on each can of stove polish they sold, so he went to a German chemist in Bethlehem, who analyzed the formula of the polish he had been selling and instructed him how to make it. Meyer soon afterward discovered a way of making stove polish that would not leave a residue of black lead on a housewife's hands, and Simon gave up peddling to stay at home to manufacture the polish. They were soon making an eight cent profit on each can. Their next move was to begin selling coffee essence, an inexpensive product made from coffee and chicory.

When the Civil War broke out, Meyer—who was by then operating a grocery store and conducting his stove polish and coffee essence business—

began speculating successfully in clothing items and foodstuffs needed by the Army of the Potomac. He did so well in this venture that he was able to accumulate enough capital to become a major wholesale merchant of spices. By 1873 he was a successful spice merchant, and in that year branched into the manufacture of lye. He bought up certain patent rights, purchased a small factory, and soon was putting a new product on the market cheaply and in large quantities under the name of the American Concentrated Lye Company. Before long he sold the firm for $150,000 to the Pennsylvania Salt Company. With this capital he began buying shares in the Hannibal and St. Joseph Railroad, which Jay Gould* was beginning to integrate into a new railway system called the Missouri Pacific. Gould was impatient to gain full control of the line, and after much bargaining was able to buy Guggenheim's shares—for $300,000 more than he had paid for them. Guggenheim now had $450,000 in capital and the stage was set for his next business: importing laces and embroideries from Saxony and Switzerland.

One of his wife's uncles in Switzerland had established a small factory for embroidering by machine in the early 1870s, and he sent Meyer samples, suggesting that he import the product and sell it in the United States. Guggenheim entered into a partnership with Morris Pulaski in the firm of Guggenheim and Pulaski, importers of fine laces and embroideries. This business turned out to be another gold mine for Guggenheim. By this time his oldest sons, Isaac (1854-1922) and Daniel, were ready to join their father. Isaac was sent to work with an uncle in Philadelphia, while Daniel was sent to Switzerland to perfect his German and study the embroidery business. Within a few years Solomon (1861-1949) and Murry (1858-1939) were also sent to Switzerland. In time the boys returned, Morris Pulaski retired, and in 1877 the firm of M. Guggenheim's Sons was formed, giving each son an equal partnership in the business. Meyer insisted his boys "be as one," and five of his sons—Isaac, Daniel, Murry, Solomon, and Simon (1867-1941)—took his advice and stuck together, constantly conferring, discussing, and bickering, but always coming to a unanimous decision. Within a few years Daniel, although not the eldest, became acknowledged as the "head" of the five brothers. As one of them commented, "wherever Daniel sits is the head of the table."

By the late 1870s M. Guggenheim's Sons was firmly founded, with four sons in the business and three more about to join. The business thrived, as did the Guggenheims' other concerns (for Meyer was still an importer of spices, a dry goods merchant, and a stove polish manufacturer), and Meyer was a near millionaire. But the Guggenheims were only just beginning their extraordinary climb. Within a quarter of a century they would become one of the most integrated dynastic enterprises in the history of American business. In 1881 Meyer took a "flyer" in two lead and silver mines, the "A.Y." and the "Minnie" in Leadville, Colorado. The mines had been fair to middling producers, but had been very expensive to operate. Again, however, Meyer's "golden touch" was evident, for these mines would turn into a bonanza. A few months after purchasing the mines, the operators struck a rich vein of silver. Soon Meyer was earning $17,000 a month from the mines, and by 1887 they had produced nine million ounces of silver and 86,000 tons of lead. Within a year the mines were earning Meyer $750,000 a year, and before they were exhausted the Guggenheims would garner some $15 million from them. And this was just the beginning of the family's mining ventures, as they soon moved to create a worldwide empire of copper and silver and gold.

As soon as Meyer Guggenheim realized how profitable mining could be he began to visualize much broader horizons. He quickly realized that the Holden Smelter at Denver, to which he sent his ore to be refined, was eating up most of his profits from the mines. Accordingly he sent one of his younger sons, Benjamin (1865-1912), to investigate and negotiate. On his recommendation Meyer bought stock in the Denver smelter and together with Edward R. Holden formed a new company called the Philadelphia Smelting and Refining Company. Soon after, Meyer began building, at a cost of $500,000, a new smelter at Pueblo, Colorado. This was the first step toward the Guggenheims' control of the smelting industry of America. Since the older Guggenheim brothers were still busy running the lace and embroidery business, Meyer relied in the early years of his mining and smelting operations on his three youngest sons: Benjamin, William (1868-1941), and Simon. Soon, however, it became apparent that the lace and embroidery business had to be gradually phased out so that Meyer and all his seven sons could concentrate wholly on mining and smelting. This decision was made imperative by the fact that the Guggenheims' smelter was losing money, with losses running as high as $500,000 in six months. All seven brothers bent their efforts to assist their father in the crisis, and operations slowly began to change for the better.

In 1888 Meyer Guggenheim closed out the embroidery business and the family moved the base of their operations from Philadelphia to New York. It took only three years after the completion of the first smelter in Pueblo before the Guggenheims had built up a powerful machine capable of undertaking almost any mining enterprise. There was a strict division of labor among the brothers, with each following the lines indicated by their various talents. Isaac, the oldest and most conservative, acted as treasurer; Daniel, the most energetic and ambitious, became chief organizer and negotiator; Murry handled and sold the metals; Solomon became the popular "contact" man; Benjamin became an excellent operating superintendent; Simon devoted his attention to the purchase of ores and the maintenance of friendly relations with the miners; and William, who had a technical metallurgical education from the University of Pennsylvania, furnished what technical expertise the brothers had. In large measure, however, they followed the practice of hiring the best talent available, no matter what the cost, to make up for their own mediocrity in metallurgy and smelter management. This rule paid off handsomely, giving them a strong platform for their forte—corporate finance and metal marketing. While one family member usually inspected most propositions and the family made a team decision, expert advice was always sought and never dismissed for frivolous reasons.

With his sons increasingly taking over operation of the Guggenheim enterprises, Meyer began settling into retirement in the 1890s, allowing Daniel to become the family leader. **Daniel Guggenheim** was born in Philadelphia and educated there. In 1873 Meyer sent him to Switzerland to study business techniques and to help manage the embroidery factory owned by his father. He returned to the United States in 1884 to head the family's lace importing business and, with his brothers, helped liquidate that business a few years later to assist his father in the development of the silver and lead mining and smelting business. With the passage of the Sherman Silver Purchase Act in 1890, whereby the government agreed to buy four million ounces of silver each month, the Guggenheims received an unexpected new outlet for their product. The price of silver soon increased by nearly 40 percent and profits of the Pueblo smelter rose to $60,000 a month. Before long it became the most profitable smelter in the West. Daniel and his brothers were so encouraged by the operation that they decided to take another giant step into mining and smelting in Mexico.

Daniel and Murry made a rapid tour of Mexico and concluded that several mines should be leased or bought in the north, near Monterrey in Nuevo Leon, that a smelter should be built in Monterrey, and that several more mines should be leased or bought in the south in Jalisco, with a smelter built in Aguascalientes also. Daniel went down to obtain the concession, which would be the first of its kind, directly from the president of Mexico. Porfirio Diaz was in power at the time, and he and Daniel got along famously, with the Guggenheims gaining a highly favorable agreement from the government. Solomon Guggenheim was sent down to erect the first smelter in Monterrey for the Guggenheims' new company—the Compania de La Gran Fundicion Nacional Mexicana. William was later sent down to supervise the actual construction of the smelter. When the first smelter proved to be successful, Solomon was sent to Aguascalientes, where he purchased the famed Tepesala copper mines, the Guggenheims' first step into the copper field. William was again sent there to build a second Mexican smelter—this one for copper. By 1895 the Guggenheim smelters at Pueblo, Monterrey, and Aguascalientes were bringing in a net profit of over a million dollars a year, and the Guggenheim brothers had become the foremost industrial power in Mexico.

While the Guggenheims had been carving out their mining and smelting empire, other business interests had been carving out their mining and smelting empires as well. Toward the end of the century there came an inevitable clash between the Guggenheims and these "other" interests. In 1889 the Guggenheims had formed the Guggenheim Exploration Company, an independent corporation whose purpose was to search for potentially profitable mines throughout the world, purchase them, develop them, and then invite public participation in them. Daniel Guggenheim was made president of the new concern. At about the same time, Henry H. Rogers,* an associate of William Rockefeller,* and Adolph Lewisohn,* an important copper producer, had formed the United Metals Selling Company, a trust formed to dominate the sale of metals in America. The success of this operation led to the formation of a still larger trust, the American Smelting and Refining Company (later called ASARCO), consisting of 23 different smelting concerns designed to give Rockefeller interests control of all mineral resources in America. H. H. Rogers was the new company's mastermind, and William Rockefeller was its chief backer. They at first tried to absorb Guggenheims' interests in the new consolidation, and when the latter refused to sell, determined to ruin them. An intensive price competition ensued between the two firms in 1899–1900, but in the latter year workers at ASARCO struck for two months, giving the Guggenheims a distinct advantage. Daniel Guggenheim now pressed to take over ASARCO. There were months of courtroom battles and boardroom battles, but in the end the Guggenheims emerged in control of ASARCO, with Daniel as chairman of the board and president. Solomon was treasurer, and Isaac, Murry and Simon were members of the board. Benjamin and William had left the family enterprises earlier in the struggle.

Now in control of gigantic resources, Daniel was to expand them even further over the next few years, becoming one of the greatest industrial leaders of all time, and his policies were to mean economic life or death to entire nations. The company soon acquired large interests outside lead and silver, buying copper mines and gold fields in Chile, tin mines in Bolivia, and rubber plantations and diamond mines in the Congo and Angola. Daniel also directed the operations of such subsidiary firms as American Smelting Securities Company, Chile Copper Company, and Utah Copper Company, along with Guggenheim Exploration, until he retired in 1919. Daniel's policy was essentially a continuation of his father's, as the mining operations were more and more combined with smelting under centralized control. The mining survey was elevated to a crucial position in the sphere of operations, and no money was spared in hiring competent engineers to do the surveys. Once a site was selected, the Guggenheim method was to be exceedingly swift and bold, and huge sums were spent to overcome engineering obstacles. Even more important was the Guggenheims' policy of ruthlessly replacing old production methods in smelting with new technological processes. They aimed at mass production and often utilized ores of low grade content which previous methods had often found unprofitable.

Daniel Guggenheim was the driving force which made ASARCO the dominant firm in world nonferrous metal mining and smelting. ASARCO's characteristic mark was the large project, and it became involved in numerous copper enterprises ranging from the huge open pit copper mine at Bingham Canyon, Utah, a pioneering achievement, to the immense Chuquicasnata copper undertaking in Chile. The Guggenheim strategy, as devised by Daniel, was essentially three-fold: first, always go in for the big development when the business barometer is low; second, always use the cheap labor and raw materials of undeveloped countries to depress your own country's industries, to force its wages and prices down until they are so cheap you can afford to buy them up and integrate them into your own monopoly; third, there was no sense in attempting to compete in the metals industry unless you owned everything from mine mouth to finished product. You had to own the mine and processing plant, and also control the marketing of the metal. This triple strategy worked so well that it did not take the Guggenheims long to realize it could be used to control the mineral wealth of the entire world.

As Daniel moved the Guggenheims toward this goal, he began to team up with the rulers of high finance in the United States, especially J. P. Morgan.* In 1907 Daniel wanted to gain control of the immense copper deposits above Kennecott Creek in Alaska. Before long a deal was set, and the great "Alaska Syndicate" was formed, composed of the Guggenheims, J. P. Morgan, and Jacob Schiff.* The Guggenheims contributed a little over a third of the capital and all the administrative and engineering know-how. Morgan and Schiff and their associates put up the rest of the money. It was an enormous undertaking. A two hundred mile railroad had to be built through rough virgin country. Then a multimillion dollar breakwater had to be constructed in the bay at the terminus of the railroad; a steamship line had to be bought or formed to transport the copper to the Guggenheim smelter at Tacoma, Washington; and coal mines had to be found, bought, and developed to provide fuel. All of this was to be done in one of the bleakest wildernesses in the world. The end result was enormously successful, despite the great expense. Kennecott's copper soon became the cheapest in the world, and by the end of 1912 the mines had paid $3 million to the Syndicate. With the outbreak of World War I copper prices soared, and the Guggenheims extracted immense profits from the Alaskan mines.

This development also helped precipitate the Ballinger-Pinchot dispute of 1910–1911. In 1907 Richard A. Ballinger, then a commissioner of the General Land Office, approved the sale of extensive coal fields to the Guggenheim-Morgan syndicate. When Ballinger became Taft's Secretary of the Interior in 1909, he terminated an inquiry into these claims and discharged chief investigator Louis R. Glavis. Gifford Pinchot, head of the U.S. Forest Service, and other government officials loyal to Theodore Roosevelt publicly attacked Ballinger's conservation policies, including the

Guggenheim decision. This forced Ballinger to resign in 1911, but the Taft administration refused to invalidate any sales of government mineral deposits to the Guggenheim-Morgan syndicate.

Daniel Guggenheim and ASARCO also became embroiled in political controversy during the Mexican Revolution of 1910–1920 as owners of large mining and smelting operations in that country. During the revolution the Guggenheim mines were able to work only fitfully, and since many of the major holdings were in northwest Mexico, occupied by Pancho Villa's forces, a working arrangement was negotiated. Coal was supplied for Villa's locomotives in exchange for protection. When Villa suffered decisive military defeats in 1916, ASARCO switched its support to Venustiano Carranza.

Because of a heart condition, Daniel Guggenheim was forced to retire from ASARCO in 1919. He devoted the remaining ten years of his life to his many philanthropies. For some years he and his wife had been contributing sums of money to certain charities that were particularly close to his wife's heart. In 1924 they decided to institutionalize this by establishing the Daniel and Florence Guggenheim Foundation for "the promotion, through charitable and benevolent activities, of the well-being of man throughout the world." The first grants of the new foundation were mostly to organizations in which Florence was interested: free band concerts in Central Park, the American Woman's Association, and several Jewish organizations. By 1975 the foundation had made over 400 grants to 98 organizations in the United States and abroad, including hospitals and medical facilities in Chile, the Congo, and Israel. In 1926 Daniel created the Daniel Guggenheim Fund for the Promotion of Aeronautics. His son Harry had interested Daniel in aviation during World War I, and the foundation did much to put aviation in the United States on a firm footing. The Guggenheims also supported the work of Robert H. Goddard in missile research, at a time when nearly everyone else thought Goddard was an eccentric visionary.

Daniel Guggenheim married Florence Sloss in 1884 and they had two sons and a daughter. Only one of these sons, **Harry F. Guggenheim**, developed much of an interest or aptitude for business. Daniel's other son, as was true of the sons of the other Guggenheim brothers, did not evidence much of the remarkable business acumen that had characterized their fathers. They married well, but they didn't do very well, and their own children fared even more poorly. Harry Guggenheim was born in West End, New Jersey, educated in New York City, and spent one year at Sheffield Scientific School at Yale. He was then sent to Mexico for practical experience in mining and metallurgy. In 1910 he entered Cambridge University to study English, receiving his B.A. in 1913 and his M.A. in 1918. Afterward he began to work on the development of mining properties when he became a director of several of ASARCO's affiliates. From 1916 to 1923 he played a leading part in the operations of the South American interests of the Guggenheim brothers. After 1926 he left the mining business, becoming president of the Daniel Guggenheim Foundation for the Promotion of Aeronautics. In 1929 he became ambassador to Cuba, serving until 1933.

Harry Guggenheim's principal business success came in 1939 when he purchased *Newsday*, a daily Long Island newspaper, with his third wife, Alicia Patterson,* daughter of Joseph Medill Patterson,* publisher of the New York *Daily News*. Harry had originally bought the paper to give his young, energetic wife something to occupy her time, installing her as editor-in-chief of the paper. But Harry shrewdly retained 51 percent of the stock, letting her have 49 percent. During the first seven years the paper operated in the red, and Harry had to put $750,000 into it. Then, miraculously, it began to turn around. The mass exodus of New Yorkers to the suburbs, especially Long Island, after World War II was the cause. *Newsday* was to become the largest suburban daily newspaper in the United States, with a circulation of 450,000. It was later sold to the Times Mirror Company for an enormous profit. Prior to his marriage to Alicia Patterson, Harry had been married to Helen Rosenberg and Caroline Morton. He had a son and daughter by his first wife and a daughter by his second wife.

Over the generations the Guggenheims married into some of the most powerful and prestigious of the Jewish and Gentile families in America, along with several marriages to titled European nobility. Daniel's daughter, Gladys, married Roger W. Straus,* son of Oscar Straus,* head of Macy's. Murry's daughter, Lucille, married Fred A. Gimbel,* also of department store fame. Solomon Guggenheim married Irene Rothschild and Benjamin Guggenheim married Florette Seligman, descendents of prominent banking families. Rose Guggenheim married Albert Loeb and Cora Guggenheim married Louis F. Rothschild, heirs of great banking fortunes. (**A.** *DAB*; *DAB*, Supplements 3 and 4; *EAB*; *NCAB*, 12:54; 22:7; 33:198; 57:127; 39:74; C:47; *Current Biography*, 1956; *New York Times*, March 17, 1905; February 23, 1925; E. P. Hoyt, *The Guggenheims and the American Dream*, 1967; Harvey O'Connor, *The Guggenheims*, 1937; John J. Davis, *The Guggenheims*, 1979; Milton Lomask, *Seed Money, The Guggenheim Story*, 1964. **B.** Marvin D. Bernstein, *The Mexican Mining Industry, 1890–1950*, 1965; Reginald M. Cleveland, *America Flexes Wings: History of the Daniel Guggenheim Fund for the Promotion of Aeronautics*, 1942; Milton Lehman, *The Guggenheim Aeronautical Laboratory of the California Institute of Technology*, 1954; Isaac F. Marcossen, *Metal Magic, The Story of American Smelting and Refining Company*, 1949; T. A. Rickard, *A History of American Mining*, 1932.)